The Routledge Handbook of Destination Marketing

This book examines key contemporary marketing concepts, issues and challenges that affect destinations within a multidisciplinary global perspective. Uniquely combining both the theoretical and practical approaches, this handbook discusses cutting edge marketing questions such as innovation in destinations, sustainability, social media, peer-to-peer applications and web 3.0.

Drawing from the knowledge and expertise of 70 prominent scholars from over 20 countries around the world, *The Routledge Handbook of Destination Marketing* aims to create an international platform for balanced academic research with practical applications, in order to foster synergetic interaction between academia and industry. For these reasons, it will be a valuable resource for both researchers and practitioners in the field of destination marketing.

Dogan Gursoy is the Taco Bell Distinguished Professor in the School of Hospitality Business Management at Washington State University and the Editor-in-Chief of the *Journal of Hospitality Marketing & Management.* His research has been published broadly in refereed Tier I journals such as *Annals of Tourism Research, Journal of Travel Research, Tourism Management, International Journal of Hospitality Management*, and *Journal of Hospitality and Tourism Research.* He has also developed and designed the "Hotel Business Management Training Simulation" (www.hotelsimulation.com/), a virtual management training game where participants are divided into teams and assigned the task of running 500-room hotels in a competitive virtual marketplace.

Christina G. Chi is an associate professor at the School of Hospitality Business Management in the Carson College of Business, Washington State University. Her area of research includes tourism marketing, travellers' behaviours, and hospitality management. She is well published in top-tier tourism/hospitality journals such as *Annals of Tourism Research, Journal of Travel Research,* and *Tourism Management.* Dr. Chi serves on the editorial boards of several hospitality/tourism journals and reviews papers regularly for top tier hospitality/tourism journals.

The Routledge Handbook of Destination Marketing

Edited by Dogan Gursoy and Christina G. Chi

LONDON AND NEW YORK

First published 2018 by Routledge

2 Park Square, Milton Park, Abingdon, Oxon OX14 4RN
605 Third Avenue, New York, NY 10017

Routledge is an imprint of the Taylor & Francis Group, an informa business

First issued in paperback 2022

Publisher's Note

The publisher has gone to great lengths to ensure the quality of this reprint but points out that some imperfections in the original copies may be apparent.

British Library Cataloguing-in-Publication Data
A catalogue record for this book is available from the British Library

Library of Congress Cataloging-in-Publication Data
A catalog record for this book has been requested

ISBN: 978-1-138-11883-6 (hbk)
ISBN: 978-1-03-233913-9 (pbk)
DOI: 10.4324/9781315101163

Typeset in Bembo
by Apex CoVantage, LLC

Contents

Figures

Tables

Contributors

Introduction

Dogan Gursoy is the Taco Bell Distinguished Professor in the School of Hospitality Business Management at Washington State University and the Editor-in-Chief of the Journal of Hospitality Marketing & Management. His research has been published broadly in refereed Tier I journals such as *Annals of Tourism Research, Journal of Travel Research, Tourism Management, International Journal of Hospitality Management, Journal of Hospitality and Tourism Research.* He has also developed and designed the "Hotel Business Management Training Simulation" (www.hotelsimulation.com/), a virtual management training game where participants are divided into teams and assigned the task of running 500-room hotels in a competitive virtual marketplace.

Christina G. Chi is an associate professor at the School of Hospitality Business Management in the Carson College of Business, Washington State University. Her area of research includes tourism marketing, travellers' behaviours, and hospitality management. She is well published in top-tier tourism/hospitality journals such as *Annals of Tourism Research, Journal of Travel Research, and Tourism Management.* Dr. Chi serves on the editorial boards of several hospitality/tourism journals and reviews papers regularly for top tier hospitality/tourism journals.

Chapter 1 A critical review of destination marketing

Sevda Sahilli Birdir is an associate professor in the department of tourism management at Mersin University. She completed her Master of Science degree in 2001 and completed her PhD in 2009 in the field of production management and marketing. Her research interests include tourism marketing and hospitality innovation.

Ali Dalgic is a Research Assistant and PhD candidate in the department of tourism management at Mersin University. He completed his Master of Science degree in Management in December 2013. His research interests include event management, alternative tourism and special interest tourism.

Kemal Birdir is a full time Professor in the Department of Tourism Management at Mersin University. He completed his PhD thesis on Hospitality Human Resources Management in 1998. His research interests include tourism management and hospitality management.

Chapter 2 Destination marketing organisations: roles and challenges

Dr Vanessa G.B. Gowreesunkar completed her PhD in Tourism Destination Management and Marketing, a merit scholarship based on her outstanding academic achievement. She is a lecturer at the Faculty of Arts and Humanities of the Mauritius Institute of Education. She has publications in various international peer-refereed journals. Her research interest is not limited to tourism management and marketing. Dr Vanessa also serves as cluster secretary for the African Union ECOSOCC – Woman and Gender cluster.

Hugues Séraphin holds a PhD from the Université de Perpignan Via Domitia (France). He joined the University of Winchester (Business School) in 2012 and has been teaching for over 10 years. He is also a visiting lecturer at Normandy Business School (France), Sup de Co Larochelle (France), ESC Pau (France) and Université de Perpignan Via Domitia (France). Hugues has published in various international peer-refereed journals and has contributed in various book chapters.

Professor Alastair Morrison is a Distinguished Professor Emeritus specializing in tourism and hospitality marketing in the School of Hospitality and Tourism Management at Purdue University, West Lafayette, Indiana, USA, and the CEO of Belle Tourism International Consulting (BTI). He is the Past-President of the International Tourism Studies Association (ITSA). Prof. Morrison is a Visiting Professor at the University of Greenwich in London and the Editor of the International Journal of Tourism Cities (IJTC). He is the author of five leading books on tourism marketing and development, *Marketing and Managing Tourism Destinations*, 2nd edition (Routledge, 2018), *The Tourism System*, 8th edition, (Kendall/Hunt Publishing Company, 2018), *Global Marketing of China Tourism* (China Architectural and Building Press, 2012), *Hospitality and Travel Marketing*, 4th edition (Cengage Delmar Learning, 2010), and *Tourism: Bridges across Continents* (McGraw-Hill Australia, 1998).

Chapter 3 Destination marketing research

Drita Kruja is Professor of Services Marketing and Marketing Research at Management & Marketing Department, European University of Tirana, Albania. She is involved in a wide range of academic and scientific activities, which are mainly related to marketing and tourism problems.

Chapter 4 Marketing tourism experiences

Merve Aydogan Cifci is a Research Assistant in Tourism Management Department at Istanbul University. She is also a PhD student at Tourism Management Program at Istanbul University. Her research interests include co-creation and tourism technology.

Gurel Cetin is an Associate Professor of Tourism Management Department at Istanbul University. His research interests include tourism marketing and tourist behaviour.

Fusun Istanbullu Dincer is a Professor and the Chair in Tourism Management Department at Istanbul University. Her research interests include sustainable tourism, tourism marketing and tourist behaviour.

Chapter 5 Entrepreneurial marketing in tourism and hospitality: how marketing practices do not follow linear or cyclic processes

Frode Soelberg, PhD, is associate professor in marketing at Nord University Business School, Norway, and has a particular research interest in Entrepreneurial Marketing.

Frank Lindberg, PhD, is associate professor in marketing at Nord University Business School, Norway, and currently visiting scholar at School of Business Economics and Law, University of Gothenburg, Gothenburg, Sweden. He obtained his Ph.D from Copenhagen Business School, Denmark, and has published articles in journals and books within tourism and marketing. His research interests cover areas such as experiential marketing, tourism marketing, and consumer culture theory.

Øystein Jensen, PhD, is working as Professor in Tourism and Marketing at University of Stavanger, Faculty of Social Science, Norwegian School of Hotel Management, Stavanger, Norway, and as adjunct professor at Nord University Business School, Bodo, Norway.

Chapter 6 Destination marketing and destination image

Sevda Sahilli Birdir is an associate professor in the department of tourism management at Mersin University. She completed her Master of Science degree in 2001 and completed her PhD in 2009 in the field of production management and marketing. Her research interests include tourism marketing and hospitality innovation.

Ali Dalgic is a Research Assistant and PhD candidate in the department of tourism management at Mersin University. He completed his Master of Science degree in Management in December 2013. His research interests include event management, alternative tourism and special interest tourism.

Kemal Birdir is a full time Professor in the Department of Tourism Management at Mersin University, Turkey. He completed his PhD thesis on Hospitality Human Resources Management in 1998. His research interests include tourism management and hospitality management.

Chapter 7 Destination attachment: conceptual foundation, dimensionality, antecedents and outcomes

Girish Prayag, PhD, is an Associate Professor of Marketing at the University of Canterbury Business School in Christchurch, New Zealand. His areas of interest include place attachment, tourist emotions and organizational resilience. His work has appeared in leading international tourism and marketing journals such as *Journal of Travel Research*, *Tourism Management* and *Journal of Business Research.*

Chapter 8 Service quality and marketing

Ibrahim Yilmaz is an associate professor in the Faculty of Tourism, Nevsehir Hacı Bektas Veli University, Turkey. He currently works as Head of Tourism Guidance Department. His main areas of interest include service quality, tourism marketing, tourism education, and tourism-environment relationship.

Chapter 9 Crisis management and marketing

Dr Sam Sarpong is currently a Lecturer in Business and Management at the Faculty of Integrated Management Sciences, University of Mines and Technology, Ghana. Since obtaining his PhD from Cardiff University, he has taught at Cardiff University, University of London, Birkbeck College and Swansea Metropolitan University respectively.

Chapter 10 Marketing destinations to customers from diverse generations

Medet Yolal is Associate Professor in the Department of Tour Guiding in the Faculty of Tourism at Anadolu University, Turkey. He received his PhD in Tourism and Hotel Management at Anadolu University. His research interests mainly focus on tourism marketing, consumer behavior, event management, regional studies and tourism management.

Chapter 11 Marketing destinations to domestic travelers

Shailja Sharma is Assistant Professor of Tourism at Indian Institute of Tourism and Travel Management, Noida, UP, India. She obtained her PhD in Tourism in 2014. Her research interests include tour leadership, tour guiding, tourism marketing and destination management.

Rahul Pratap Singh Kaurav is Assistant Professor of Marketing and Tourism at the Prestige Institute of Management, Gwalior, MP, India. He obtained his PhD in Marketing and Tourism from Jiwaji University, Gwalior in 2014 and is the editor of several publishing journals. His research interests include tourism marketing, destination marketing and management, rural tourism management of service enterprises, and internal marketing practices for success of DMOs.

Chapter 12 Marketing destinations through events: research on satisfaction and loyalty in festivals

María-Pilar Llopis-Amorós (PhD) is lecturer of Marketing at the ESIC Business & Marketing School in Valencia (Spain). Her main teaching and research interests include branding and communications, and tourism marketing. The results of her research have been published in several journals and conference proceedings.

Irene Gil-Saura (PhD) is Professor of Marketing at the University of Valencia (Spain). Her main teaching and research interests include services marketing, retailing and tourism and hospitality. She has published articles in several international journals as *Tourism Management, International Journal of Hospitality Management, Service Industries Journal, International Journal of Contemporary Hospitality Management*, and *Annals of Tourism Research*, among others.

María-Eugenia Ruiz-Molina (PhD) is Associate Professor in the Marketing Department of University of Valencia. Her studies are published in several international journals, e.g. *International Journal of Hospitality Management, International Journal of Contemporary Hospitality Management, Journal of Hospitality, Leisure, Sport and Tourism Education*, etc. Her current research interests are tourism marketing, sustainability and ICT business solutions.

Martina G. Gallarza (PhD) is Associate Professor in the Marketing Department of the Universidad de Valéncia (Spain). She formerly taught at the Universidad Católica de Valencia, where she was Dean of the Business Faculty. Her research interests include consumer behaviour, non-profit marketing, and services marketing. Her particular research areas focus on perceived value related to satisfaction and loyalty. She has published articles in *Annals of Tourism Research, Tourism Management, Journal of Consumer Behaviour, Journal of Services Marketing, International Journal of Hospitality Management, International Journal of Culture, Tourism and Hospitality Research*, and *International Journal of Voluntary and Nonprofit Organizations*, among others.

Chapter 13 Senior tourism: an emerging and attractive market segment for destinations

Adela Balderas-Cejudo is a Research Fellow at the Oxford Institute of Population Ageing, University of Oxford; Professor at CámaraBilbao University Business School; and Assistant Professor at Basque Culinary Center-University of Mondragon, Spain. Dr. Balderas has a PhD in Business Administration. Her doctoral thesis is on Senior Tourism: determinants, motivations and behaviour of an evolving market segment. Dr. Balderas has a wealth of teaching experience at the undergraduate and graduate levels. She is currently serving as the Director of a Master degree at Basque Culinary Centre-University of Mondragon and as a consultant for several international hotel chains in the hospitality industry. Dr. Balderas is Visiting Professor and Lecturer at the University of Salamanca, Spain and the College of Economics of the University of Xiamen, China, and Lecturer at the University of Regensburg, Germany, University of Northumbria, UK and Ecole hôtelière de Lausanne, Switzerland.

Dr. George W. Leeson is Co-Director of the Oxford Institute of Population Ageing, University of Oxford. Dr. Leeson's first degree was in Mathematics, followed by a Masters in Applied Statistics, both from Oxford. His Doctoral work was in Demography. Dr. Leeson directs the Institute's research networks in Latin America (LARNA) and in Central and Eastern Europe (EAST) and also the Centre for Migration and Ageing Populations (MAP Centre). Dr. Leeson has directed the Danish Longitudinal Future Study, which elucidates the attitudes and aspirations of future generations of older people in Denmark, and he is Principal Investigator with Professor Sarah Harper on the Global Ageing Study, a survey of 44,000 men and women aged 40 to 80 in 24 countries.

Elena Urdaneta is Director of Cooperative Innovation at Euskampus, University of the Basque Country, Spain. Dr. Urdaneta has been director of Innovation and Research at the Basque Culinary Center-University of Mondragón. Elena has made a number of postdoctoral visits to centres abroad including the UCLA Faculty of Medicine (Los Angeles, California) and the Physiology Department at the University of California in Irvine (UCI). In the past, she combined her position as Contracted Lecturer as Doctor in Physiology at the Public University of Navarra with her role as Research Director at BCC, which promotes research projects in the field of the promotion of both nutrition and e-health. She is the principal researcher on numerous funded research projects on physiology, gerontology and nutrition and is the author or co-author of over twenty scientific research articles in international periodicals. In 2004 she was awarded the "Beca Ortiz de Landázuri" grant from the Health Department of the Government of Navarre. She is a member of the Spanish Society of Physiological Sciences, Spanish Society of Geriatrics and Gerontology, International Society for the Advancement of Alzheimer's Research and Treatment, and the American Physiological Society. She is currently supervising three doctoral theses and is a peer-reviewer of international books and articles on physiology. She worked at the Ingema Foundation on projects related to gerontology (2007–2012).

Chapter 14 Value-satisfaction-loyalty chain in tourism: a case study from the hotel sector

Martina G. Gallarza (PhD) lectures in the Marketing Department of the Universidad de Valéncia (Spain). Her research interests include consumer behaviour, non-profit marketing, and services marketing. Her particular research areas focus on perceived value related to satisfaction and loyalty.

Giacomo Del Chiappa (PhD) is Associate Professor of Marketing at the Department of Economics and Business, University of Sassari (Italy), and Associate Researcher at CRENoS. His research is related to destination governance and branding, consumer behaviour, and digital marketing.

Francisco Arteaga is Associate Professor of Statistics and Econometrics at the Universidad Católica de Valencia (Spain). His research focuses on statistical techniques for quality and productivity improvement, especially those related to multivariate statistical projection methods.

Chapter 15 Destination brand potency: a proposition framework

Gaunette Sinclair-Maragh is an Associate Professor in the School of Hospitality and Tourism Management at the University of Technology, Jamaica. She holds a PhD in Business Administration with a specialization in Hospitality and Tourism Management from the Washington State University in the USA. Her research interests include tourism planning and development, destination marketing, attraction management and event planning management.

Chapter 16 Communication strategies for building a strong destination brand

Maja Šerić is an assistant professor in the Department of Marketing at the University of Valencia in Spain. Her research area is focused on integrated marketing communications, brand equity, and tourism marketing. Her papers have been published in a number of tourism journals, such as: *Tourism Management, Current Issues in Tourism, International Journal of Tourism Research, Journal of Destination Marketing & Management, Journal of Vacation Marketing, Journal of Hospitality Marketing & Management, International Journal of Hospitality Management, International Journal of Contemporary Hospitality Management*, and others.

Maria Vernuccio is an associate professor in the Department of Management at Sapienza University of Rome in Italy. Her investigation is centered on integrated marketing communications, brand management, and consumer brand engagement. She published a number of papers in marketing and management journals such as: *European Management Journal, European Journal of Innovation Management, Journal of Brand Management, Journal of Product and Brand Management, Journal of Business Communication*, and others.

Chapter 17 Brand personality and destination marketing

Kostas Alexandris is an Associate Professor at Aristotle University of Thessaloniki, Greece and an Adjunct Faculty Member at Open University, Greece, teaching sport and tourism management.

His research interest is in the area of leisure, sport and tourism consumer behavior. He is the co-author of *Sport Consumer Behavior: Marketing Strategies* (2016, Routledge Publications, co-authored with Funk, D., & McDonald, H.).

Chapter 18 Gastronomy tourism as a marketing strategy for place branding

Dr. Albert Barreda is an assistant professor in the Department of Hospitality Leadership at Missouri State University. He completed his PhD degree in the Rosen College of Hospitality Management at the University of Central Florida. He earned his Master degree in Hospitality and Tourism Management in the Isenberg School of Management at the University of Massachusetts, Amherst, MA. His research focuses on revenue management, vacation ownership, strategic intuition, destination branding, social networks, hospitality bankruptcy, corporate finance, and information technology. Dr. Barreda's research has been presented in predominant industry and research conferences around the world including: Macau, China; Taipei, Taiwan; Portugal; Seoul, South Korea; London, United Kingdom; Hong Kong, and United States of America. He is the author of several refereed papers in leading academic journals including *Tourism Management, Computers in Human Behavior, Journal of Vacation Marketing, Journal of Relationship Marketing,* and others. He has also received several awards for his research contributions, and has consulting experience in the areas of hotel investments, and market research for hospitality and tourism organizations.

Chapter 19 Understanding the destination branding strategies for hospitality and tourism engagement in an intelligent rural community

Samuel Adeyinka-Ojo holds a PhD in Hospitality and Tourism from Taylor's University, Malaysia. Sam is the Head, Department of Marketing, Faculty of Business at Curtin University Malaysia. He teaches hospitality, marketing and tourism courses on the undergraduate programmes and project quality management at the postgraduate level. Samuel researches in tourism destination marketing and branding, hospitality marketing, guest behaviour, food festivals, visitor memorable experience, health tourism and sustainable practices in rural and ecotourism destinations.

Vikneswaran Nair obtained his PhD in Systems Engineering (Ecotourism Systems) from the Universiti Putra Malaysia. He is currently the Dean of Graduate Studies and Research at the University of The Bahamas in Nassau, The Bahamas, and also a visiting professor in sustainable tourism at Taylor's University, Subang Jaya, Malaysia. He is the Programme Leader for the Responsible Rural Tourism Network in Malaysia. A seasoned researcher and keynote speaker, Dr. Nair's exceptional research achievements have earned him many national and international awards including the Merit and Honorary Award and the Outstanding Young Malaysian Award respectively for Academic Leadership and Accomplishment in 2006 and 2009 by the Junior Chambers International.

Chapter 20 A critical review of tourists' behavior

Uğur Çalişkan is Assistant Professor in Muğla Sıtkı Koçman University, Faculty of Tourism, Department of Hospitality Management, Turkey. He obtained his PhD in Tourism Management from Dokuz Eylul University (İzmir/Turkey) in 2010. His research interests include tourist satisfaction, tourist behaviour, tourism planning, local residents' reactions towards tourism, entrepreneurship in tourism, tourism sociology.

Chapter 21 Destination decision making and selection process

Kurtulus Karamustafa is Professor of Tourism Management at the Faculty of Tourism, Erciyes University, Kayseri, Turkey. He obtained his PhD in Tourism Management from Strathclyde University, Glasgow, UK, in 1999. He made a number of publications in the areas of tourism marketing; more specifically his research interests include destination management, hotel operations and hospitality management, crisis and risk management.

Kenan Gullu is Associate Professor of Marketing at the Faculty of Tourism, Erciyes University, Kayseri, Turkey. He obtained his PhD in Marketing from Erciyes University, Kayseri, Turkey, in 2005 and published mainly on the following areas of marketing; retailing, internationalization and services marketing. His current research interests include service marketing.

Chapter 22 A critical review of consumer trends in tourism and destination marketing

Christine A. Vogt is professor in the School of Community Resources and Development at Arizona State University (ASU). She also directs the Center for Sustainable Tourism at ASU. She studies consumer behavior in travel and applies it to destination and hospitality marketing. She conducts survey research and evaluation and is widely published in tourism, leisure, recreation and parks, and natural resource journals.

Jada Lindblom, M.S., is a PhD student in the School of Community Resources and Development at Arizona State University and a research assistant at ASU's Center for Sustainable Tourism.

Chapter 23 Online travel information and searching behavior

Jie Kong is a lecturer in the School of computer science at Xi'an Shiyou University, China.

Gang Li is an Associate Professor in the School of Information Technology at Deakin University, Australia.

Chapter 24 Revisiting destination loyalty: an examination of its antecedents

Christina G. Chi is an associate professor at the School of Hospitality Business Management in the Carson College of Business, Washington State University. Her area of research includes tourism marketing, travelers' behaviors, and hospitality management. She is well published in top-tier tourism/hospitality journals such as *Annals of Tourism Research*, *Journal of Travel Research*, and *Tourism Management*. Dr. Chi serves on the editorial boards of several hospitality/tourism journals and reviews papers regularly for top tier hospitality/tourism journals.

Chapter 25 Role of tourist emotions and its impact on destination marketing

Dr. Soma Sinha Roy is Assistant Professor in the discipline of Marketing Management at J.D. Birla Institute (Department of Management). She obtained her Ph.D from Indian Institute of Technology, Kharagpur, India in 2015. Her research interests include customer delight, services marketing, consumer behavior and brand management. Besides teaching, she is interested in research and publications.

Chapter 26 Holiday or no holiday! How much power do children have over their parent by choosing traveling pattern and preferred travel destination? An explorative study in Medan, Indonesia

Christie Xu is a Research Assistant at the Research Department, BINUS University, Jakarta, Indonesia.

Christian Kahl is Vice-Rector for Research and International Development at Almaty Management University, Almaty, Kazakhstan, as well as Associate Professor for the Graduate School of Business at Almaty Management University. His research interests are in education management, teaching and learning, HRM, Gen Y, cultural management, cultural tourism and alternative tourism.

Chapter 27 Personal values, quality of the tourism experience and destination attributes: the case of Chinese tourists in Egypt

Omneya Mokhtar Yacout is professor of marketing, vice dean and the former managing director of the executive MBA program, Faculty of Commerce, Alexandria University, Egypt. She worked as a visiting professor at Vaxjo University, Sweden, and a visiting scholar at Georgia State University, USA. She has published a number of papers on subjects including experiential marketing, segmentation and targeting strategies in touristic markets, service quality, customer relationship management, Islamic marketing, ethical consumer behavior and consumption values. In 2008, she received the Best Paper Award from the Journal of Tourism Research published by the Egyptian Ministry of Tourism.

Lamiaa Hefny is an assistant professor of tourism in the Tourism Department, Pharos University, Egypt. Her most important research interests are tourist destination marketing, with emphasis on destination branding and tourist behavior. She has published articles in the *Journal of Vacation Marketing* and *International Journal of Customer Relationship Marketing and Management*.

Chapter 28 Corporate social responsibility and sustainability in tourism

Dr. Huong Ha is currently affiliated with Singapore University of Social Sciences. She has been affiliated with UON Singapore and University of Newcastle, Australia. Her previous positions include Dean, Director of Research and Development, Deputy Course Director, Chief Editor, Executive Director, and Business Development manager. She holds a PhD from Monash University (Australia) and a Master's degree from Lee Kuan Yew School of Public Policy, National University of Singapore. She was a recipient of a PhD scholarship (Monash University), Temasek scholarship (National University of Singapore), and a scholarship awarded by the United Nations University/International Leadership Academy, and many other scholarships, professional and academic awards, and research related grants. She has authored or co-edited the following books: (i) Ha, Huong (2014). *Change Management for Sustainability.* USA: Business Expert Press, (ii) Ha, Huong (2014). *Land and Disaster Management Strategies in Asia.* H. Ha (Ed.), Springer; and (iii) Ha, Huong & Dhakal, T. N. (2013). *Governance Approaches to Mitigation of and Adaptation to Climate Change in Asia.* H. Ha, & T. N. Dhakal (Eds), Basingstoke: Palgrave Macmillan; and Ha, Huong; Fernando, Lalitha and Mahmood, Amir (2015), *Strategic Disaster Risk Management in Asia,* Springer. She has about 75 published journal articles, book chapters, conference papers and articles in encyclopedias. She has been an invited member of (i) the international editorial boards of many international journals/book projects in Romania, the Philippines, Singapore, the USA and the UK; (ii) the scientific and/or technical committees of several international conferences in many countries; and (iii) international advisory board of many associations. She has also been a reviewer of many international journals and international conferences.

Dr. Hui Shan Loh is currently lecturer at Singapore University of Social Sciences (SUSS). She received a BSc (Maritime Studies), MSc (Logistics) and a Ph.D. degree in Maritime Studies from NTU in 2008, 2010 and 2015 respectively. Before joining SUSS, Hui Shan worked as Research Fellow at NTU, and Assistant Manager at The Maritime and Port Authority of Singapore.

Chapter 29 Consumers' environmental attitudes and tourism marketing

Dr. Hsiangting Shatina Chen currently serves as an Assistant Professor in the College of Human Environmental Sciences, Department of Nutrition and Hospitality Management at The University of Alabama. Her research focuses primarily on traveler behavior, consumer psychology, and sustainability (particularly in food waste prevention).

Chapter 30 A review of green experiential quality, green farm image, green equity, green experiential satisfaction and green behavioral intentions: the case of Green World Ecological Farm

Dr. Hung-Che Wu is an associate professor at the Business School in Nanfang College of Sun Yat-sen University, China. He obtained his MSc in tourism and hospitality management from the University of Wisconsin-Stout (USA) and PhD in hospitality and tourism marketing from Lincoln University (New Zealand). He has published over 40 peer-reviewed articles and his work has been published in *Tourism Management, Journal of Environmental Planning and Management, Journal of Hospitality Marketing & Management, International Journal of Economics and Financial Issues, Journal of Travel Research, Journal of Destination Marketing & Management, British Food Journal, Marketing Intelligence & Planning, Multimedia Tools and Applications, International Journal of Tourism & Hospitality Administration, Journal of Convention and Event Tourism, Tourism Planning and Development, Tourism Review International, Journal of the Knowledge Economy, Industrial Management & Data System, Journal of Organizational Change Management, Innovative Marketing, Tourism Analysis, Journal of Tourism, Hospitality & Culinary Arts, Journal of Quality Assurance in Hospitality & Tourism, Asia Pacific Journal of Marketing and Logistics, Event Management, Journal of Foodservice Business Research, Asia Pacific Journal of Tourism Research, International Journal of Tourism Research, International Journal of Tourism Sciences, International Journal of Contemporary Hospitality Management, Journal of Hospitality and Tourism Management, Journal of China Tourism Research, Tourism and Hospitality*

Research, and *Journal of Hospitality & Tourism Research*, among others. He is currently working as one of the editorial board members for the *Neuroscience Journal, Cogent Business & Management, Tourism Analysis, Journal of Hospitality Management and Tourism, International Journal of Business and Management, Journal of Tourism & Hospitality, International Business Research, Journal of Hospitality and Tourism Research, International Journal of Marketing Studies, Science Journal of Business and Management*, and *Business and Management Studies*. His research interests include hospitality and tourism management, service quality, customer satisfaction, consumer behavior and green branding.

Chapter 31 Innovations in destination marketing

Evrim Çeltek is Assistant Professor of Zile Dinçerler School of Tourism and Hotel Management, Gaziosmanpaşa University, Tokat/TURKEY. She obtained her MA in tourism business administration from Sakarya University (Turkey) and she obtained her PhD in tourism and hotel management from Anadolu University (Turkey). Her researches focused on tourism marketing, social media marketing, mobile marketing, e-commerce, mobile commerce, advergame and electronic customer relationship management.

İbrahim İlhan is Associate Professor of Tourism Faculty, Nevşehir Hacıbektaş Veli University, Nevşehir. He obtained his MA in tourism and hotel management from Schiller International University and he obtained his PhD in tourism and hotel management from Dokuz Eylül University (Turkey). His researches focused on gastronomy, managerial ethics in hospitality and tourism industry, and regional tourism planning.

Chapter 32 Innovation in product/service development and delivery

Osman Ahmed El-Said Osman is associate Professor of Hotel Management & Innovation at the Department of Hotel Management, Faculty of Tourism and Hotels, Alexandria University, Egypt. He obtained his PhD in Innovation Management in the Hospitality Industry from Alexandria University in 2011 and is the author of several articles in international Tourism & Hospitality journals. His research interests include Innovation Management Human Resources Management, Service Quality, Entrepreneurship, Corporate Social Responsibility and Marketing.

Chapter 33 The sharing economy and tourism destination marketing

Adam Pawlicz (PhD) is Associate Professor at Szczecin University, Poland and a visiting professor at Klaipeda University, Lithuania with 15 years of research experience in the hospitality and e-tourism area. He has coauthored over 100 publications, is a scientific editor of *European Journal of Service Management*, member of Advisory Board of Masters International Research and Development Center, member of scientific committee of various international journals such as *Academica Science Journal*, University of Tirgu Mureş, Romania and "Entrepreneurship" issued by SWU "Neofit Rilski", Bulgaria. His current research focuses on the impact of sharing economy and online travel agencies on hospitality market.

Chapter 34 Innovative approach to destination marketing

Marie Chan Sun has embarked on a PhD work at the Open University of Mauritius since July 2013 while being on the academic staff at the University of Mauritius where she is involved in public health and medical programmes.

Robin Nunkoo is Associate Professor in the Department of Management, University of Mauritius, Mauritius, Part-Time Lecturer at the Open University of Mauritius and the Head of the International Center for Sustainable Tourism and Hospitality.

Chapter 35 Impact of internet and technology on tourist behavior

Aviad A. Israeli is an Associate Professor for the B.S. in Hospitality Management and M.S. in Hospitality and Tourism Management degree programs at Kent State University (KSU). Dr. Israeli was ranked among the 100 most prolific researchers in hospitality and tourism research by the *Journal of Hospitality and Tourism Research*. He is a member of the *International Journal of Hospitality Management* editorial board. His current research projects focus on service failure, service recovery and their impact on consumers reading and writing of electronic Word of Mouth. In recent years, Dr. Israeli served as a consultant for the Israeli Ministry of Tourism. He has published over 40 peer-reviewed articles and his work has appeared in leading journals such as the *International Journal of Hospitality Management*, *Journal of Hospitality Marketing and Management*, *Journal of Service Management*, *Service Industries Journal*, *Tourism Management*, and *Tourism Economics*.

Swathi Ravichandran is an Associate Professor and Coordinator for the B.S. in Hospitality Management and M.S. in Hospitality and Tourism Management degree programs at Kent State University. In 2015, Dr. Ravichandran was recognized as a Meetings Trendsetter by *Meetings Focus*. In 2014, she received the *Distinguished Educator of the Year* award from Professional Convention Management Association (PCMA). She also received a commendation from the 131st General Assembly of Ohio, naming her one of "Ohio's finest educators." Her research focuses on hospitality human resources management and hospitality marketing and has been published in prestigious peer-reviewed journals such as *International Journal of Hospitality Management*, *International Journal of Contemporary Hospitality Management*, *Journal of Hospitality and Tourism Education*, *Journal of Hospitality Marketing and Management*, *Journal of Foodservice Business Research*, and *Journal of Human Resources in Hospitality and Tourism*. Dr. Ravichandran also regularly writes blog posts focusing on human resources and legal issues for *Restaurant Hospitality* titled Foodservice@Work in addition to contributing to *EasyIce.com* on similar topics.

Shweta Singh is a graduate student majoring in hospitality and tourism management at Kent State University. She holds a bachelor's degree in Mathematics and a post graduate diploma in travel management. Although she has multiple years of marketing and operations experience in various aspects of the tourism and hospitality industry, the most notable is her time working for Indian Railways' luxury tourist train, the *Maharaja Express*, voted the world's leading luxury train. At present, Shweta is exploring her research interests in the field of hospitality and tourism while assisting with a number of research projects as a graduate assistant at Kent State University. Shweta is currently serving as the vice president of the Kent State University chapter of Eta Sigma Delta and is a recognized blog contributor for the AroundCampus Group, a college media and marketing company. She also contributes regularly to industry blog posts published in *Restaurant Hospitality* and *EasyIce.com*.

Chapter 36 Consumer empowerment in the hospitality industry

Jeynakshi Ladsawut is Lecturer in the department of Management at Charles Telfair Institute, Moka, Mauritius. Her research is focused on Tourism and Hospitality Marketing, with major interest in trust in social media, tourist satisfaction and tourist loyalty, consumer behavior and marketing activities.

Dr. Robin Nunkoo is Associate Professor, Department of Management, Head, International Center for Sustainable Tourism and Hospitality at the University of Mauritius, Reduit, Mauritius. His research is on political science, trust, citizens' political support, voting behavior, sustainable tourism and tourist behavior.

Chapter 37 Evolving destination and business relationships in online distribution channels: disintermediation and re-intermediation

Marios Sotiriadis is Visiting Professor at University of South Africa, South Africa and at University of Ningbo, China. Formerly he was Professor of Tourism Business Management Department, TEI of Crete, and Tutor of the Hellenic Open University, Greece. He received his PhD in Tourism Management from the University of Nice Sophia-Antipolis, Nice, France. He is the author of nine books and monographs, three distance learning manuals and three e-learning materials on aspects of tourism marketing and management. He has undertaken a variety of research and consultancy projects (e.g. feasibility studies, business plans, marketing researches and plans, human resources projects) for both public and private organisations of the tourism and travel industry. His research and writing interests include tourism destination and businesses marketing and management. His articles have been published by international journals and presented at conferences.

Chapter 38 How to successfully handle online hotel reviews: practical recommendations

Prof. Dr. Beykan Çizel is a dean of Akdeniz University, Tourism Faculty in Antalya, Turkey. His research interests span both tourist behavior and tourism management. He has focused on tourist behavior with the lens of social psychology.

Edina Ajanovic is a lecturer at Tourism Faculty and PhD candidate of Social Science Institute at Akdeniz University in Antalya, Turkey. Her main research interest is in online tourist behaviour examined from social psychological perspective including topics such as attitude structure, attitude change and persuasive communication in online travel communities. Other areas of interests are use of ICTs in tourism education and tourism destination governance.

Chapter 39 Destination marketing: approaches to improve productivity in an era of technology disruption

Yinghua Huang is an assistant professor at Department of Hospitality, Tourism, and Event Management, San José State University. She received her PhD in Hotel and Restaurant Administration from Oklahoma State University. Her research interests include destination marketing, place attachment, service management and research methods.

Introduction

Dogan Gursoy

Destination marketing refers to all marketing efforts directed towards the increase of number of tourists and revenues in a destination (Nunkoo, Gursoy and Ramkissoon, 2013). Over the past several decades, destination marketing has witnessed a tremendous growth in the amount of information and knowledge generated by both academics and practitioners (Gursoy, Uysal, Sirakaya-Turk, Ekinci and Baloglu, 2014). The main reason for this tremendous growth is that as the number of destination offerings has been increasing rapidly over the years, researchers and practitioners have been trying to better understand visitors' decision making processes and the factors that may influence those processes (Romero, 2017) because understanding the reasons and motivations of travellers for purchasing and consuming one of the many travel experiences offered by a number of destinations can enable destination marketing managers to develop effective marketing strategies to attract those customers to their destinations (Ladeira, Santini, Araujo and Sampaio, 2016). This understanding is even likely to become more critical as some destinations fiercely fight to protect their market share while others strive for larger tourism market share and income, especially those destinations which rely heavily on tourism earnings for their economies (Gursoy, Saayman and Sotiriadis, 2015).

As the destination marketing practices experience maturity and scientific sophistication, it is important that we as researchers and practitioners fully understand the breadth and depth of existing knowledge that can help us explain, understand, monitor, and predict concepts and constructs related to destination marketing (Tresidder, 2015). Furthermore, considering the fact that destinations offer very complex "multi-faceted" and "hybrid" experiential products that encompass both physical goods and services to their visitors and aim to create compelling consumer experiences within a very competitive marketplace, the planning, design and management of destination marketing activities is a focal challenge for destinations in a globalized and highly competitive environment. Creation of compelling customer experiences requires close collaboration among various private and public entities in a destination because tourism experience takes place in phases and visitors use services from more than one existing organization (Yoon and Lee, 2017). The hybrid nature of travel experiences suggests that experiential travel and tourism products are "deconstructed" products because they bring together a number of services from a number of individual businesses. Because of its fragmented nature, destinations face a number of marketing issues and challenges that are pertinent to all businesses within a destination (Xu and Gursoy, 2015). These key marketing issues and challenges can prove critical for the success of any destination regardless of its product offerings, location, size and target markets (Jiang, Ramkissoon and Mavondo, 2016). Ignoring these key marketing issues and challenges can have detrimental effects.

The Routledge Handbook of Destination Marketing carefully examines marketing issues and challenges that are raised in the contemporary destination marketing literature and faced by destinations in their everyday operations. Defining key marketing concepts and issues, and exploring the type of impacts they may have on the success of destinations can enable us to set the stage for a better understanding of the supply and demand issues destinations are facing today. Furthermore, examining the current key trends and issues such as sustainability and innovation, and then focusing on future trends within destinations can provide critical insights for successful development and implementation of destination marketing strategies and activities. *The Routledge Handbook of Destination Marketing* attempts to examine key marketing issues and challenges faced by destinations by carefully investigating destination marketing practices and academic literature in order to develop/propose strategies to address those key marketing issues and challenges.

Our vision for this handbook is to create an international platform for balanced academic destination marketing research with practical applications for marketing managers of destinations, in order to foster synergetic interaction between academia and industry. More than 70 prominent scholars have contributed to this handbook. The collection of topics presented in this handbook represents an unprecedented scholarly attempt to cover a large number of both conceptual and practical topics not regularly found in standard destination marketing texts. Contributors to this handbook have provided an in-depth coverage of each conceptual and practical topic so that each chapter can serve as a trusted source of reference that can provide essential knowledge and references on the respective topic for academics and practitioners. It is our strong belief that the topics included in this handbook will appeal to both researchers and practitioners. It is our sincere hope that those chapters will contribute to the knowledge and theory of destination marketing as distinct, multifaceted fields approached through the administrative disciplines, the liberal arts, and the social sciences. Furthermore, this handbook provides an outlet for innovative studies that can make a significant contribution to the understanding, practice, and education of destination marketing. We strongly believe that each chapter included in this handbook will make a significant contribution to the dissemination of knowledge while serving as a unique forum for both industry and academia

The Routledge Handbook of Destination Marketing addresses cutting edge marketing issues such as innovation in destinations, sustainability, social media, peer-to-peer applications, web 3.0 and experience marketing. A unique feature of this handbook is that it combines both the theoretical and practical approaches in debating some of the most important marketing issues faced by destinations. Because of the nature of destination offerings which often makes it inseparable from other industries such as hospitality, events, sports and even retail, this handbook examines key contemporary marketing concepts, issues and challenges that affect destinations within a multidisciplinary global perspective. This handbook is international in its nature as it attempts to examine marketing issues, challenges and trends from around the world drawing from the knowledge and expertise of experts from around the world. By compiling and presenting critical research topics that capture a variety of concepts and constructs used in destination marketing field, *The Routledge Handbook of Destination Marketing* aims to be a go to resource for credible destination marketing knowledge. We know that this handbook will help the researchers and practitioners in our field to refer and locate destination marketing knowledge with minimal effort.

This handbook has the following specific objectives: (i) identify, define and analyse the application of main destination marketing concepts, issues, and challenges; (ii) provide a comprehensive review of the development of destination marketing over the years; (iii) explore the adoption and implementation of various destination marketing approaches in various contexts and geographical locations; (vi) to examine current key marketing trends, issues and challenges that affect destinations; (v) address cutting edge marketing issues such as innovation in destination marketing and management, sustainability, social media, peer-to-peer applications, web 3.0; and (vi) identify future trends & issues within a multidisciplinary global perspective. The handbook also provides marketing implications and recommendations for destinations to enable them to successfully create and manage marketing strategies and actions.

The handbook book includes 40 chapters originating from leading destination marketing scholars in the field. The book is divided into seven themes; each theme exploring marketing issues that are critical for destinations.

Part I provides an overview of destination marketing and provides definitions of various marketing concepts, the role of destination marketing organizations and the role of research in destination marketing. Part I also provides a critical review of factors such as destination image and destination attachment, that are likely to play critical roles in destination marketing. Part II focuses on marketing destinations to specific segments of visitors. Marketing issues and challenges posed by various segments and marketing strategies that are appropriate for each segment are discussed in this chapter. Part III examines destination branding and the factors that are likely to influence destination branding such as communication strategies, brand personality, and branding strategies. Part IV examines issues related to consumer behaviour in destination marketing. Part IV includes chapters on a critical review of tourist behaviour, destination decision making and selection process, a critical review of consumer trends in in destination marketing, travellers information search behaviour, pricing, destination loyalty, role of emotions in destination marketing and case studies. Part V focuses on sustainability and environmental issues that may affect destination marketing. Part VI covers destination marketing issues related to innovation while part seven focuses on the impact of internet and technology on destination marketing.

We, as editors of the Handbook, acknowledge the fact that we may have left out some critical topics and/or concepts. For the sake of simplicity and functionality we have focused on the topics that are most critical for destination marketing researchers and practitioners. Thus, the list of topics included in this handbook is not complete and nor exhaustive in its coverage of destination marketing topics. For this, we apologize. Our goal is to simply provide a list of most critical destination marketing topics in one place in order to create a credible source of information that today's and future destination researchers and practitioners could use as a point of departure for their research initiatives and business endeavours.

Contributors to this handbook have spent countless hours to provide in-depth coverage of each conceptual and practical topic so that each chapter can serve as a trusted source of reference that can provide essential knowledge and references on the respective topic for academics and practitioners. We would like to express our sincere gratitude and thanks to all the contributors who graciously volunteered their time and effort to put this amazing handbook together.

We also would like to thank our colleagues and the researchers who have created both the theoretical and practical knowledge on the topics included in this handbook; you have given us reasons to initiate a project like this one. You are a true inspiration and source of this Handbook's birth, hoping that you would find this handbook useful. We, as the editors, extend our sincere thanks to the publisher Routledge and their highly skilled staff members for making this project a reality.

References

Gursoy, D., Uysal, M., Sirakaya-Turk, E., Ekinci, Y. and Baloglu, S., 2014. *Handbook of scales in tourism and hospitality research.* CABi.

Gursoy, D., Saayman, M. and Sotiriadis, M.D. eds., 2015. *Collaboration in tourism businesses and destinations: A handbook.* Emerald Group Publishing.

Jiang, Y., Ramkissoon, H. and Mavondo, F., 2016. Destination marketing and visitor experiences: The development of a conceptual framework. *Journal of Hospitality Marketing & Management, 25*(6), pp. 653–675.

Ladeira, W.J., Santini, F.D.O., Araujo, C.F. and Sampaio, C.H., 2016. A meta-analysis of the antecedents and consequences of satisfaction in tourism and hospitality. *Journal of Hospitality Marketing & Management, 25*(8), pp. 975–1009.

Nunkoo, R., Gursoy, D. and Ramkissoon, H., 2013. Developments in hospitality marketing and management: Social network analysis and research themes. *Journal of Hospitality Marketing & Management, 22*(3), pp. 269–288.

Romero, J., 2017. Customer Engagement Behaviors in Hospitality: Customer-Based Antecedents. *Journal of Hospitality Marketing & Management, 26*(6), pp. 565–584.

Tresidder, R., 2015. Experiences marketing: A cultural philosophy for contemporary hospitality marketing studies. *Journal of Hospitality Marketing & Management, 24*(7), pp. 708–726.

Yoon, S.J. and Lee, H.J., 2017. Does Customer Experience Management Pay Off? Evidence from Local versus Global Hotel Brands in South Korea. *Journal of Hospitality Marketing & Management, 26*(6), pp. 585–605.

Xu, X. and Gursoy, D., 2015. A conceptual framework of sustainable hospitality supply chain management. *Journal of Hospitality Marketing & Management, 24*(3), pp. 229–259.

Part I

Destination marketing

1

A critical review of destination marketing

Sevda Sahilli Birdir, Ali Dalgic and Kemal Birdir

Introduction

As competition has been intensified among the destinations for every single traveler around the globe for the last 20 years, destination marketing has become a hot topic to study and discuss among the practitioners and academia. According to Morrison (2013a), the number of destination marketing related webpages accessed by the Google search engine rose from 4 in 1970–1979 to 4,310 between years 2000–2009 and to 3,260 between years 2010–2012 (in only three years!). And this interest on the topic is not a surprise at all. Today, there are more than 3,000 destinations around the globe that are providing some sort of tourism products and services and they are continuously seeking new tools and methods to attract more tourists to their destinations. Considering that creating new jobs for the people in almost every country in the world is getting tougher and tougher, the fight for more tourists to create more job opportunities seems to be continuously rising for all the tourism centers in the coming decades. Of course, one of the most powerful tools that destinations can utilize to attract more tourist to their home is marketing and its related instruments. Via presenting the resources and creating interest and especially boxing the destinations to differentiate them from their rival lands, marketing is able to benefit destinations in many different ways. During the last two decades, hundreds of academic studies have been trying to present the destination marketing tools and the best practices to help destinations better market themselves.

Destination management organizations and destination marketing

In their compelling work, "Destination marketing organizations and destination marketing: a narrative analysis of the literature," Pike and Page (2014) claim that destination marketing is "a pillar of the future growth and sustainability of tourism destinations in an increasingly globalized and competitive market for tourists". Destination marketing is one of the most important roles of Destination Management Organizations (DMOs). DMOs are the bodies that "have the overall responsibility for the coordination and integration of the destination mix elements, and for destination marketing" (Morrison, 2013a: 2). DMOs have various leadership roles to help the destinations grow and keep them competitive. According to Morrison, (2013b), DMOs' key leadership activities might be summed up under the following topics:

1 Setting the tourism agenda: A DMO should set the agenda for tourism and coordinate all tourism stakeholder efforts toward achieving the agenda. Of course, the DMO does not and should not do the agenda-setting on its own. It needs to do this with the active involvement and input from tourism stakeholders within the destination. Setting the agenda really means defining a long-term vision for tourism and engaging the tourism sector in long-range planning. The visionary role of the DMO is one of the key requirements for its leadership.
2 Guiding and coordinating tourism sector stakeholders: The DMO needs to guide and coordinate the efforts of tourism sector stakeholders. This is a difficult task given the diversity of stakeholders and their opinions and viewpoints on tourism. The coaching role of the DMO is to bring all of the team together to focus on a shared set of goals and objectives.
3 Championing tourism: Tourism is generally not well understood and under-appreciated as an economic sector. It is often afforded the role of a second-class citizen when compared to manufacturing, agriculture, and even mining. It does not always get the respect it deserves. The championing role of the DMO is to continuously communicate and confirm the positive contributions to their destinations.
4 Educating about tourism: By conducting research and keeping up to date about tourism, the DMO is a source of data, information and facts for tourism sector stakeholders and community residents. DMO management and staff should continuously participate in training and professional development, since tourism is a dynamic and fast-changing economic sector. The scholar/teacher role of the DMO makes everybody in the destination better understand tourism and the trends in the sector and its markets.
5 Leading tourism marketing: The DMO is the body entrusted with marketing the destination as a whole. It needs to set the directions for tourism sector stakeholders to follow and provide partnering opportunities to achieve marketing goals and objectives. The DMO should develop the destination positioning and branding approaches that provide a promotional platform for all involved in tourism. The promoter role of DMOs increases awareness and brings in more visitors to the destination.
6 Serving visitors: The DMO serves visitors in many different ways, especially in providing information about tourism in the destination. It must assist in taking steps to assure the safety and security of visitors, and their ease of movement within the destination. The visitor servant role of the DMO enhances the satisfaction of people who come to the destination on business or for leisure.
7 Maintaining tourism quality standards: The DMO must participate in the setting and monitoring of tourism quality standards. It must ensure that quality standards match with the positioning and branding of the destination. The quality controller role of the DMO enhances the experiences of visitors in the destination and makes them want to return.
8 Stewarding resources: The DMO must advocate a sustainable approach to tourism development. The DMO must also be a careful steward of the funds and other resources with which it is provided. The steward role of the DMO means that resources are used prudently and that natural and cultural resources are preserved for future destinations.

Hence, since marketing and promotion activities are very expensive activities, destination marketing efforts must be well structured, strategically planned and perfectly executed to benefit the destination most. That's why DMOs must follow a strict approach to use the destination resources effectively and on point. Some of the important questions to ask, for example, are: a) which markets to target? b) what slogans and messages to convey? and c) which products and/or resources to be promoted and advertised? Some of the critical components of a successful destination marketing plan generally carry the following features (Morrison, 2013a):

1 Destination vision: Every DMO's destination marketing efforts should be driven by a set of explicitly articulated marketing goals. These goals should be established to achieve the destination vision, which is identified through a planning process known as visioning where the outcome is the definition of a "super long-term goal" for the destination.

   A more formal description of the destination vision statement is that it represents a concise, desired "word picture" of the destination at some point in the future. It is a verbal image of the destination that local people aspire for it to become. The vision provides a clear focus on what the destination will strive to be. This sets the overall direction for the tourism marketing and development of the destination in the upcoming years. The destination vision should be articulated in a vision statement. The destination visioning process should be completed in three stages: (1) envisioning an image of the desired future destination state, which (2) when effectively communicated to those responsible (3) serves to empower these people so they can enact the vision.
2 DMO vision: The destination vision statement creates a pathway for future marketing action. However, the prime responsibility and accountability for achieving the destination vision is given to the officially recognized DMO. The next step is for the DMO to define its own vision for the future that will set it on the right course to achieving the destination vision in cooperation with its internal and external stakeholders.
3 Destination marketing goals: The destination marketing goals are like stepping-stones on the DMO's path to realizing the destination and DMO visions. They are longer-term (three to five years) measurable results that the DMO wants to achieve for its destination marketing. It is best if the destination marketing goals are target-market and time-specific, and state an intended result in a quantified format, but not all marketing goals exactly fit these criteria.
4 Destination marketing objectives: Destination marketing objectives are short-term (usually within one year) measurable results that the DMO wants to achieve. These objectives must be based on the marketing goals and be interim steps toward achieving these goals. As with the goals, marketing objectives should, if possible, be target-market and time-specific, and indicate a quantified result. It should be realized here that many DMOs have marketing objectives, but have not derived these through a visioning process and goal-setting. Marketing objectives are often set as part of the annual process of developing a marketing plan. While marketing objectives are essential foundations for a marketing plan, they are more effective when derived from a long-term visioning process and goal setting.
5 DMO mission: The DMO mission, articulated in its mission statement, describes its reason for being. It is a broad statement about the organization's business and scope, services and products, markets served and overall philosophy. The mission statement is not a goal or objective, but rather it is a clear description of what the DMO does and who it serves. DMO mission statements are sometimes confused with vision statements and goals, but these are three quite different concepts. In fact, the DMO's mission statement should be derived from the destination and DMO vision statements, and be consistent with the destination marketing goals.

Naturally, a successful destination marketing plan must be systemized and articulated to follow a systematic approach (Garcia, Gomez & Molina, 2012; Pawascar & Goel, 2014). According to Rita (2000), critical success factors of a Destination Marketing System (DMS) are:

1 A comprehensive product database of attractions, accommodation, and other travel information, with explicit data quality control and cost-effective data maintenance procedures
2 Statistics gathered to inform the overall tourism impact
3 An official destination web site with full accommodation and tourism supplier data, automated availability update as well as online booking and reservation
4 Monitoring and evaluation procedures in place for systems and assessing impact
5 A link between the DMS and any Global Distribution Systems (GDS), uni or bi-directional.

As the professional link between tourists, suppliers, travel intermediaries and tourist boards, a DMS should provide (Rita, 2000):

1 Consolidation, evaluation and organization of accurate detailed information on destinations, services and package tours
2 Definition of standardized and general selection criteria
3 Input and maintenance of main data via a service center
4 Standardization of presentation in various distribution interfaces
5 Integration of various services in one area
6 Individual organization of offers in alignment with the requirements of various target groups and markets
7 A reservation capability for accommodations and other facilities in the destination.

Of course, while the above destination marketing approach carries the traditional marketing approach, today's destinations tend to lean on more technology-lead efforts to market their destinations (Burgess, Parish, & Alcock, 2011; Wang & Fesenmaier, 2003). Rita (2000) posits that a successful web marketing effort needs three main components: web site design, promoting the web site and assessing the web site marketing effectiveness. After a comprehensive meta-analysis

Table 1.1 Success factors for destination marketing

Information quality	Variety, scope, currency, conciseness, accuracy of information, authority, reliability, uniqueness of information
Ease of use	Usability, accessibility, navigability, logical structure
Responsiveness	Accessibility of service representatives, e-mail service, reply to online reservations
Security/privacy	Protecting information during transmission and subsequent storage, security for online purchases/reservations, privacy/confidentiality statement
Visual appearance	Attract attention, convey image, aesthetics
Trust	Brand recognition, consistency, intentions, credibility
Interactivity	Interactive features such as virtual tours, interactive communication (FAQs, guest books, chat)
Personalization	Personalized or individualized attention, customization of offerings and of information
Fulfillment	Order process, accuracy of service promises, billing accuracy, online booking process and confirmation, on-time delivery

of the literature, Park and Gretzel (2007) propose that the success factors for destination marketing as shown in Table 1.1.

Another emerging web-based marketing instrument is a powerful tool called travel blogs. Pan, MacLaurin and Crotts (2007), through analyzing travel blogs, revealed the major strengths of Charleston, South Carolina to be: historic charm, Southern hospitality, beaches, and water activities. The weaknesses were found to be: weather, infrastructure and fast-service restaurants. According to researchers, "travel blogs are an inexpensive means to gather rich, authentic, and unsolicited customer feedback" (Pan, MacLaurin & Crotts, 2007: 35).

A new invention named Virtual Reality Imagery (VRI) was also examined for its possible destination marketing persuasiveness (Tussyadiah, Wand & Jia, 2016). After experiments and interviews with 23 participants who used Google Cardboard VR viewer, the researchers "identified factors that support and distract users from being fully immersed in the virtual environment, including moment of truth, representation, social experience, and continuity" (Tussyadiah, Wand & Jia, 2016: 1).

Destination marketing research

While there were only four studies on destination marketing during years 1970–1979, there were more than 4,000 between years 2000–2009 and over 3,000 in the following three years (2010–2012). Destination management literature showed a similar growth at the same period also and raised from one study between 1970–1979, 217 studies between 1990–1999 to 2,540 studies between years 2010–2012.

The reason for this tremendous interest on the subject is of course competition for every tourist dollar traveling the globe (Wang, 2008; Chang, Chen & Hsu, 2012; Chen & Phou, 2013). More important than that, tourism is also a huge employment generator, probably what each and every country around the world fights for. An examination of this exhaustive body of knowledge shows clearly that this interest is an ongoing activity which will probably continue to grow our understanding of destination management, marketing and competition all together. Pike and Page (2014) reported in their very comprehensive destination marketing literature analysis that there are 41 destination marketing related texts, 11 destination marketing related academic conferences, a selection of destination marketing-related reports from UNWTO and 11 journal special issues on the subject and related fields.

To understand the research themes regarding destination marketing, a detailed analysis of the key subjects in the destination marketing literature has been exercised. The major literature published between the years 1996–2016, containing 168 articles published in some of the major tourism publications was examined (see Table 1.2).

The analysis shows that the most studied destination marketing related theme is "internet/ web usage." Out of 168 examined studies, 24 of them were found to be on this subject. While Lee and Gretzel (2012) studies persuasive destination web sites, Romanazzi, Petruzzellis and Lannuzzi's (2011) study is on the effect of a destination website on tourist choice. Some of the other studies focusing on web-based destination marketing included such subjects as website contents analysis (Govers & Go, 2004), effectiveness of destination marketing organizations' websites (Li & Wang, 2010), assessing the critical factors for the management and implementation of web-based destination marketing systems (Wang, 2008) and enhancing destination image through travel website information (Jeong, Holland, Jun & Gibson, 2012).

The second most studied destination marketing related theme is found to be "branding." Out of the 16 identified branding studies, some of the important and contributing studies of the concept might be listed as Garcia, Gomez and Molina (2012) "A destination-branding model: An empirical analysis based on stakeholders" study, Ekinci (2003) "From destination image to

Table 1.2 Destination marketing related research themes 1996–2016

Destination marketing related themes	*Frequency*	*Percentages (%)*
Internet/Websites	24	14.29
Branding	16	9.52
Destination personality	15	8.93
Destination competitiveness	13	7.73
Destination marketing organizations	11	6.55
Image	10	5.95
TV shows/movie tourism	10	5.95
Destination promotion	10	5.95
Local cuisine/gastronomy tourism	9	5.36
Destination marketing collaboration	8	4.76
Sports events	7	4.17
Positioning	6	3.57
Brand image	5	2.98
Recommendation/Intention to revisit	4	2.38
Social media	4	2.38
Meeting/conference	4	2.38
Rural tourism	3	1.79
Cultural heritage/cultural tourism	3	1.79
Destination marketing information system	2	1.19
Logo/brochure	2	1.19
Brand value	2	1.19
Total	168	100.3

destination branding: An emerging area of research," and Blain, Levy and Ritchie (2005) "Destination branding: Insights and practices from destination management organizations."

Another 15 studies were found to be on "destination identity" among the more important being: Hosany, Ekinci and Uysal (2006) "Destination image and destination personality: An application of branding theories to tourism places," Baloglu, Henthorne and Sahin (2014) "Destination image and brand personality of Jamaica: A model of tourist behavior," and Matzler, Strobl, Stokburger-Sauer, Bobovnicky and Bauer's (2016) "Brand personality and culture: The role of cultural differences on the impact of brand personality perceptions on tourists' visit intentions."

Destination competitiveness and Destination Management Organization were the fourth and fifth most studied Destination Marketing Related subjects with 13 and 11 articles respectively. Image, TV shows/Movie tourism and Destination promotion were the following themes with 10 articles in each subject area. The other notable subjects studied related to destination marketing were found to be local cuisine/gastronomy tourism (nine studies), destination marketing collaboration (eight studies), sports events (seven studies) and positioning (six studies).

Conclusion and recommendation

As implied by Morrison (2013a),

> Destinations management and destination marketing have become 'mainstream' topics in the tourism research literature since the year 2000. Today these two concepts are also integral to

professional practice in tourism destinations; they now represent the platform for achieving excellence in tourism destinations.

This interest is also evident in the number and quality of the studies conducted on the topic, especially during the last two decades. As discussed earlier, only 357 destination marketing studies were published between the years 1990 and 1999, while more than 3,000 destination marketing studies have been published between 2010 and 2012.

Considering the serious competition among destination all over the world, this interest is quite understandable. However, an analysis of the literature shows that most of the studies on the subject are still very theoretical and not focusing much on the needs of the practical site of the concept/field. As indicated by Pike and Schultz (2009: 327),

> Of the 5,000 plus tourism academic contributors referred to by McKercher, how many have disseminated their findings to practitioners by way of a presentation or report? How many have attended a recent tourism industry conference? What incentive is there to do either? Why are there so few conferences at tracking a good representation of academics and practitioners? What other means of engagement are used by academics to situate and ground the research problem from the perspective of those people who experience it in the field? If we are not bridging the divide and engaging with industry, how do we know our research is relevant and our recommendations are being implemented or whether they work? Or is publishing in academic journals the end game, in the hope that somehow the findings will make their way to the frontline?

At their comprehensive review of the destination marketing literature, rather than making predictions about the future of research in this field, Pike and Page (2014) focus on existing gaps and propose the following topics for the short to medium terms;

1 To what extent is the DMO is responsible for the competitiveness of the destination?
2 How can we quantify the success of DMO promotional activities over the long-term?
3 To what extent is the success of individual businesses reliant on destination competitiveness?
4 To what extent is the academic literature impacting on current best practices of DMOs?

Apparently, destination marketing will continue to be a hot research topic among the tourism academia in the coming years. While the current literature has reached a certain maturity academically, call for more industry and practice focused research seems to be more prevalent in the field. Studies focusing more on the industry and practice, and helping the practitioners to better understand not only the consequences but also the solutions and possible impacts of various marketing efforts on the destination might receive more attention from the academia also.

References

Baloglu, S., Henthorne, T. L., & Sahin, S. (2014) "Destination Image and Brand Personality of Jamaica: A Model of Tourist Behavior," *Journal of Travel & Tourism Marketing*, 31(8), 1057–1070.

Blain, C., Levy, S. E., & Ritchie, J. B. (2005) "Destination Branding: Insights and Practices From Destination Management Organizations," *Journal of Travel Research*, 43(4), 328–338.

Burgess, L., Parish, B., & Alcock, C. (2011) "To What Extent Are Regional Tourism Organisations (Rtos) in Australia Leveraging The Benefits of Web Technology for Destination Marketing and Ecommerce?" *Electronic Commerce Research*, 11(3), 341–355.

Chang, K. C., Chen, M. C., & Hsu, C. L. (2012) "Identifying Critical Brand Contact Elements of a Tourist Destination: Applications of Kano's Model and the Importance–Satisfaction Model," *International Journal of Tourism Research*, 14(3), 205–221.

Chen, C. F., & Phou, S. (2013) "A Closer Look at Destination: Image, Personality, Relationship and Loyalty," *Tourism Management*, 36, 269–278.

Ekinci, Y. (2003) "From Destination Image to Destination Branding: An Emerging Area of Research," *E-review of Tourism Research*, 1(2), 1–4.

Garcia, J. A., Gómez, M., & Molina, A. (2012) "A Destination-Branding Model: An Empirical Analysis Based on Stakeholders," *Tourism Management*, 33(3), 646–661.

Govers, R., & Go, F. M. (2004) "Projected Destination Image Online: Website Content Analysis of Pictures and Text," *Information Technology & Tourism*, 7(2), 73–89.

Hosany, S., Ekinci, Y., & Uysal, M. (2006) "Destination Image and Destination Personality: An Application of Branding Theories to Tourism Places," *Journal of Business Research*, 59(5), 638–642.

Jeong, C., Holland, S., Jun, S. H., & Gibson, H. (2012) "Enhancing Destination Image Through Travel Website Information," *International Journal of Tourism Research*, 14(1), 16–27.

Lee, W., & Gretzel, U. (2012) "Designing Persuasive Destination Websites: A Mental Imagery Processing Perspective," *Tourism Management*, 33(5), 1270–1280.

Li, X., & Wang, Y. (2010) "Evaluating The Effectiveness of Destination Marketing Organisations' Websites: Evidence From China," *International Journal of Tourism Research*, 12(5), 536–549.

Matzler, K., Strobl, A., Stokburger-Sauer, N., Bobovnicky, A., & Bauer, F. (2016) "Brand Personality and Culture: The Role Of Cultural Differences on The Impact Of Brand Personality Perceptions on Tourists' Visit Intentions," *Tourism Management*, 52, 507–520.

Morrison, A. (2013a) "Destination Management and Destination Marketing: The Platform For Excellence in Tourism Destinations," *Tourism Tribune*, v. 28(1): 6–9.

Morrison, A. (2013b). *Marketing and Managing Tourism Destinations*. Routledge, London.

Pan, B., MacLaurin, T., & Crotts, J. C. (2007) "Travel Blogs and The Implications For Destination Marketing," *Journal of Travel Research*, 46(1), 35–45.

Park, Y. A., & Gretzel, U. (2007) "Success Factors For Destination Marketing Web Sites: A Qualitative Meta-Analysis," *Journal of Travel Research*, 46(1), 46–63.

Pawaskar, P., & Goel, M. (2014) "A Conceptual Model: Multisensory Marketing and Destination Branding," *Procedia Economics and Finance*, 11, 255–267.

Pike, S., & Page, S. J. (2014) "Destination Marketing Organizations and Destination Marketing: A Narrative Analysis of The Literature," *Tourism Management*, v. 41: 202–227.

Pike, S. & Schultz, D. E. (2009) "Tourism Research – How Is It Relevant?" *Tourism Recreation Research*, 34(3): 326–328.

Romanazzi, S., Petruzzellis, L., & Lannuzzi, E. (2011). "Click & experience. Just virtually there. The Effect of a Destination Website on Tourist Choice: Evidence from Italy," *Journal of Hospitality Marketing & Management*, 20(7), 791–813.

Rita, P. (2000) "Web Marketing Tourism Destinations," ECIS 2000 Proceedings. Paper 120. Available online at: http://aisel.aisnet.org/ecis2000/120

Tussyadiah, L., Wang, D., & Chenge (Helen) Jia (2016), "Exploring the Persuasive Power of Virtual Reality Imagery for Destination Marketing," *Tourism Travel and Research Association: Advancing Tourism Research Globally*. Paper 25. Available online at: http://scholarworks.umass.edu/ttra/2016/Academic_Papers_Oral/2

Wang, Y., & Fesenmaier, D. R. (2003) "Assessing The Determinants of The Success of Web-Based Marketing Strategies by Destination Marketing Organisations in The United States," Information and communication technologies in tourism 2003: Proceedings of the International Conference in Helsinki, Finland, 306–315.

Wang, Y. (2008) "Web-Based Destination Marketing Systems: Assessing The Critical Factors For Management and Implementation," *International Journal of Tourism Research*, 10(1), 55–70.

Further reading

Baker, M. J., & Cameron, E. (2008) "Critical Success Factors in Destination Marketing", *Tourism and Hospitality Research*, 8(2), 79–97.

Buhalis, D. (2000) "Marketing the competitive destination of the future," *Tourism Management*, 21(1), 97–116.

Della Corte, V., Piras, A., & Zamparelli, G. (2010) "Brand and Image: The Strategic Factors in Destination Marketing," *International Journal of Leisure and Tourism Marketing*, 1(4), 358–377.
Kladou, S., & Kehagias, J. (2014) "Assessing Destination Brand Equity: An Integrated Approach," *Journal of Destination Marketing & Management*, 3(1), 2–10.
Mykletun, R. J., Crotts, J. C., & Mykletun, A. (2001) "Positioning an Island Destination in The Peripheral Area of The Baltics: A Flexible Approach to Market Segmentation," *Tourism Management*, 22(5), 493–500.
Niininen, O., Szivas, E., & Riley, M. (2004) "Destination Loyalty and Repeat Behaviour: An Application of Optimum Stimulation Measurement," *International Journal of Tourism Research*, 6(6), 439–447.
von Friedrichs Grängsjö, Y., & Gummesson, E. (2006) "Hotel Networks and Social Capital in Destination Marketing," *International Journal of Service Industry Management*, 17(1), 58–75.
Wang, Y., & Fesenmaier, D. R. (2007) "Collaborative Destination Marketing: A Case Study of Elkhart County, Indiana," *Tourism Management*, 28(3), 863–875.
Wang, Y., & Krakover, S. (2008) "Destination marketing: competition, cooperation or coopetition?", *International Journal of Contemporary Hospitality Management*, 20(2), 126–141.

2

Destination marketing organizations

Roles and challenges

Vanessa G.B. Gowreesunkar, Hugues Séraphin and Alastair Morrison

Introduction

Tourism is probably one of the most difficult products to market, involving many stakeholders over which a destination marketer has little or no control. The experience is co-produced by the tourist, private companies and public service providers as well as a common pool of resources, and the product only exists when the tourist activates that particular network of services. Since the tourism product covers the whole destination, it poses a number of challenges to marketing managers who have no control over the path the tourist takes through a destination (Ritchie and Crouch, 2003). Because tourism is the choice of the tourist, it is often difficult for destination marketers to predict the purchase behavior of tourists and hence devise appropriate strategies that fit into the marketing realities of a given destination. Thus, for the marketing of destinations to be effective, the tourism product needs to be understood from both demand and supply side (Figure 2.1). According to the United Nations World Tourism Organization (2011), destination marketing has emerged as a central pillar of the future growth and sustainability of tourism destinations and Destination Marketing Organizations (DMOs) are the main vehicle to drive these ideologies and principles. Likewise, Morrison (2012) argues that destination marketing is one of the most important roles of the DMO and this should not be planned haphazardly, but requires a systematic, step-by-step approach. As such, there is a growing interest worldwide in the topics of destination marketing as more places are vying for a share of global tourism (Morrison, 2013).This is also evidenced by the number of professional organizations that have emerged in the global fronts in order to assist destinations in their marketing objectives; for instance, the Destination Marketing Association International in Washington DC, European Cities Marketing in France, the Pacific Asia Travel Association in Bangkok *inter alia*. DMO is therefore the organizational instrument that coordinates marketing activities taking into account the realities of destinations from both demand and supply sides (Figure 2.1).

Literature reveals that the structures, functions and roles of DMOs can vary widely, as does the level and type of support provided by industry and government (Morrison, 2013). DMOs may be established with direct or indirect government support and their activities may include, for instance, destination branding and marketing, industry collaboration and capacity building, and in some cases, investment attraction and product development (Wang and Pizam, 2011). Studies

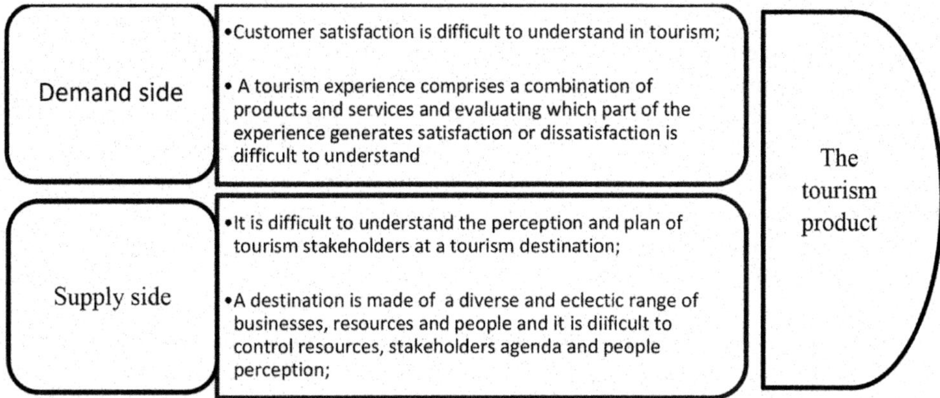

Figure 2.1 Realities of demand and supply side of a tourism destination
Source: Authors

show that various terminologies are utilized to describe the DMO (Ashworth, 1991) and these include National Tourism Organizations (NTO), Local Tourism Organizations (LTO) or Regional Tourism Organizations (RTO) and they operate under the ambit of the public sector or the private sector or simply by both public-private sectors.These entities are usually multifunctional in nature and they fulfill the role of DMO at a tourism destination. For example, tourism destinations like Morroco, Serbia and India have NTOs that assume the role of the destination marketing organization in order to promote the destination. In places like New Zealand, Ontario and Queensland, the RTO fulfills this role. In Finland, Estonia, Poland and Latvia the marketing function is assumed by the LTOs. A high level of subjectivity is therefore involved due to the difference in size, geographical location and resources (Scott *et al*, 2008). While the origins and functions of DMOs vary from context to context, they all tend to share a common task, that of marketing.

Why tourism destinations need a DMO

According to Fyall et al. (2009), one of the primary frustrations for many destination marketers is their inability to control elements of the destination product. A destination is made of a diverse range of businesses, resources and stakeholders and the latter often operate with vested interest and without any common vision directed towards the prosperity of the destination community. In the absence of an authority leading the marketing activities, tourism businesses often compete with each other within a same destination and, in the process, tourism heritage and resources are exploited by tourism operators. Moreover, marketing a destination individually in the international market using different marketing strategies may have negative consequences on the image of the destination. The success of individual tourism ventures and cooperatives will depend to some extent on the competitiveness of their destination (Pike, 2004) and the leadership of the amalgam of stakeholders associated with the tourism industries (Leiper, 2008). For instance, in the island of Mauritius, small tourism entrepreneurs operate their individual websites and present the tourism product differently. Research on small and micro businesses has indicated that not all stakeholders are necessarily interested in the viability of the destination, when their principal objective for operating a business is lifestyle (Thomas et al., 2011). As a result, tourism sites in Mauritius like Ilot Bernaches and Ilot Cerfs have lost their appeal due to the growing number of visitors caused by excessive marketing conducted by individual operators (Gowreesunkar, 2012). Likewise, Solomon Islands and Palau Islands (Philippines) have also suffered negative consequences due to uncontrolled marketing from private tour operators. Without a DMO, tourism operators market and sell public resources to tourists for short term benefit whereas the negative impacts on the destination are felt in the long run. Ritchie and Crouch (2000) cited the example of Russia which is a destination well-endowed with natural resources but underperforms due to poor marketing strategies in comparison to destinations such as Singapore and Las Vegas, which, with limited space and resources have developed successful tourism strategies. The justification to market destinations by DMO is anchored in the following beliefs:

- the variety of stakeholders involved in the development and production of tourism products;
- the complexity of the relationships of local stakeholders conflicting stakeholders' interests makes controlling and marketing destinations as a whole extremely challenging and DMOs are an effective mechanism through which these relationships can be organized and managed;
- the destination experience is essentially comprised of regions, resources which often do not belong to individuals;
- the rational use of zero-priced public goods, such as landscapes, mountains, and the sea for the benefit of all stakeholders and at the same time preserving the resources for future generations;
- a large number of nations, states and cities are now funding a DMO as the main vehicle to compete and attract visitors to their distinctive place or visitor space.

In most cases, destinations have a rich history and legacy development which needs to be taken into consideration when developing tourism marketing strategies. Hence, under the leadership of a DMO, marketing is used as a mechanism to achieve strategic objectives of destination regions and is guided by the policies for regional development. DMOs do not limit their role as a tool for attracting more visitors to a region, as has been the case for most destinations. Instead, they coordinate the overall marketing activities of the destination in such a way that the image and interests of the destination and its people are safeguarded. The DMO is therefore that organizational instrument used to lead destination marketing or to coordinate and manage industry interests in a destination (Morrison, 2013; Ritchie & Crouch, 2003).

Definitions of DMO

From a single definition like 'selling of cities' (Gartrell, 1988) to a multi-functional definition like 'strategic, operational and organizational decision taker' (Franch and Martini, 2002), DMOs have been described from various point of views. The first definition of a DMO was proposed by Wahab et al. (1976: 24) as follows:

> The management process through which the National Tourist Organisations and/or tourist enterprises identify their selected tourists, actual and potential, communicate with them to ascertain and influence their wishes, needs, motivations, likes and dislikes, on local, regional, national and international levels, and to formulate and adapt their tourist products accordingly in view of achieving optimal tourist satisfaction thereby fulfilling their objectives.

In their study on DMOs, Pike and Page (2014) concur with the above and they argue that it is a realistic definition in that DMOs are limited in what they can undertake as logistical issues are often managed by local authorities (e.g. car parking, street cleaning, waste removal, control of crowds and visitors by the police during special events), a point also shared by Page and Hall (2003).

According to Gretzel et al. (2006), DMOs are non-profit entities aimed at generating tourist visitation for a given area. They are generally responsible for developing a unique image of the area, coordinating most private and public tourism industry constituencies, providing information to visitors, and leading the overall tourism industry at a destination. This definition takes into account the marketing aspect and image building of the destination and is concerned with private and public coordination.

For Pike and Page (2014), customer satisfaction is central in destination marketing and based on this philosophy, they adapt Wahab et al. (1976)'s definition that 'destination marketing is the management process through which the National Tourist Organizations and/or tourist enterprises identify their selected tourists, actual and potential, communicate with them to ascertain and influence their wishes, needs, motivations, likes and dislikes, on local, regional, national and international levels, and to formulate and adapt their tourist products accordingly in view of achieving optimal tourist satisfaction thereby fulfilling their objectives'.

From the practitioner's perspective, the Tourism Management Institute describes a DMO as an entity which is involved in informing or attracting visitors to and in geographical locations and for planning, developing, marketing, training and administering tourism services for the economic, social and environmental benefit of the recipient business and residential communities.

This definition takes into account the management and marketing roles of a DMO (Gowreesunkar, 2012).

The UNWTO (2008) combines both practitioners' and theorists' standpoints and proposes that a DMO is a national government department, a 'non-profit' association for tourism, a 'non-profit' public-private partnership, a profit-driven commercial company or simply an agency accountable to the regional state or local government which is responsible for the management and/or marketing of destinations. This implies that the DMO might be a public or private entity and it not only manages, but also markets the destination.

Historical development of DMOs

Historically, DMOs have always been viewed as destination marketing organizations (Dore and Crouch, 2003). The main objectives were to share information and facilitate the travelling. The work of Pike and Page (2014) on 'DMO – a narrative analysis of research' shows that the existence of DMOs dates back to the seventies. This is evidenced by the first journal article by Matejka (1973) and the first destination marketing publication by Wahab et al. (1976). However, an earlier study of Pike (2008) shows that DMOs were probably existent since the emergence of the 'Grand Tour' in the sixteenth century. The 'Grand Tourists' were primarily interested in visiting cities that were considered as major centres of culture of that time – Paris, Rome, Venice, Florence and Naples. DMOs were thus born out of the need to share information and facilitate the trip of the potential travelers. As such, the first destination travel guides were printed in France in the sixteenth century according to Läesser (2000) and, in a way, the travel guides were distributed by the authority which served as a DMO. The author further reveals that Switzerland was the first country to have a RTO in 1864 while in England the Blackpool Municipal Corporation enacted the role of a DMO in 1879. A further study by Ford and Peeper (2008) indicates that the first convention and visitors bureau was established in the USA at Detroit in 1896 and then, in 1901 the first world's first national tourism office (NTO) was established in New Zealand (McClure, 2004), and in 1903 the first state tourism office (STO) was launched in Hawaii (Choy, 1993). The number of DMOs grew considerably during the post-war period and they established their core marketing role in the 1960s and 1970s alongside the rise of the package holiday, introduction of jet aircraft and the rise of the holiday brochure (Laws, 1995) and the 1980s and 1990s saw the creation of many new DMOs as the value of a coordinated approach to destination marketing was recognised. It is not known how many DMOs now exist globally, although it has been estimated by McKercher there are now well in excess of 10,000 (Pike, 2008) and Morrison (2012) concludes that DMO have become 'mainstream' from 2000 onwards.

Roles of DMOs at a tourism destination

Traditionally, the role of the DMO was underpinned by an industrial policy paradigm (Dredge et al., 2016) and was mainly about competitiveness, productivity and industry performance (Dredge, 2016; Haxton, 2015). Thus, the DMO sought to promote the destination by connecting the supply and demand sides of tourism in order to maximize the use of destination resources (Pike, 2008).On the demand side, they focused their activities on image and reputation building, product bundling and sales and distribution management. On the supply side, they were involved in various functions like information services, coordination among the tourist stakeholders, infrastructure operation or support as well as destination planning functions. They were thus serving visitors and fulfilling destination marketing functions (Table 2.1). In fact,

Table 2.1 General roles of DMOs

Key Role	*Elaborations*	*Source*
External marketing	Promotion, branding, positioning, e-marketing	Dredge, 2015 Haxton, 2015 Morrison, 2013
Internal marketing and information dissemination	Communication and knowledge sharing within the destination and externally	Spotts, 1997 Gowreesunkar, 2012 Grönroos, 1994
Economic development	Promotion of employment and regional development and investment; business opportunities; revenue generation	Pike and Page, 2014 Pechlaner et al, 2007
Market research	Destination analysis, market research and product development	Kotler et al, 2006 Mill and Morrison, 2012
Destination management	Destination structuring, coordination and integration of the destination mix, capacity building, resource management	Pike and Page, 2014 Ritchie et al, 2005 Kaurav et al, 2015
Relationship building and networking with stakeholders	To promote public– private linkage and external partnerships, and local community; affiliation with international tourism organisations	Morrison, 2013 Ritchie and Crouch, 2003 Pearce, 1997

Source: Authors

various destinations establish DMOs mainly to market tourism rather than to manage their tourism resources (Gowreesunkar, 2012). This observation is also supported by Butler et al. (2010) – the DMO is simply a term for marketing agencies, and rarely if ever, manages anything beyond promotion, let alone an actual destination so that overall development is rarely examined until a crisis occurs. For example, the Cyprus Tourism Organization and Malta Tourism Organization are engaged solely in marketing activities and do not engage in the management of their tourism destinations. Likewise, in Mauritius, various companies are registered as a destination management organization, but their roles are limited to marketing only. Similarly, in Indonesia, DMOs mostly conduct activities that would enhance the image of the destination and sustain its success in the global market.

New roles of DMOs

In the twenty-first century, the new roles of the DMOs are mostly driven by technology (Figure 2.2). Due to various impacts caused by external forces on tourism destinations, DMOs are having to assume new roles out of survival reflex. For example, international issues such as global warming, changing international relations (Brexit), Gulf war and terrorist attacks in popular

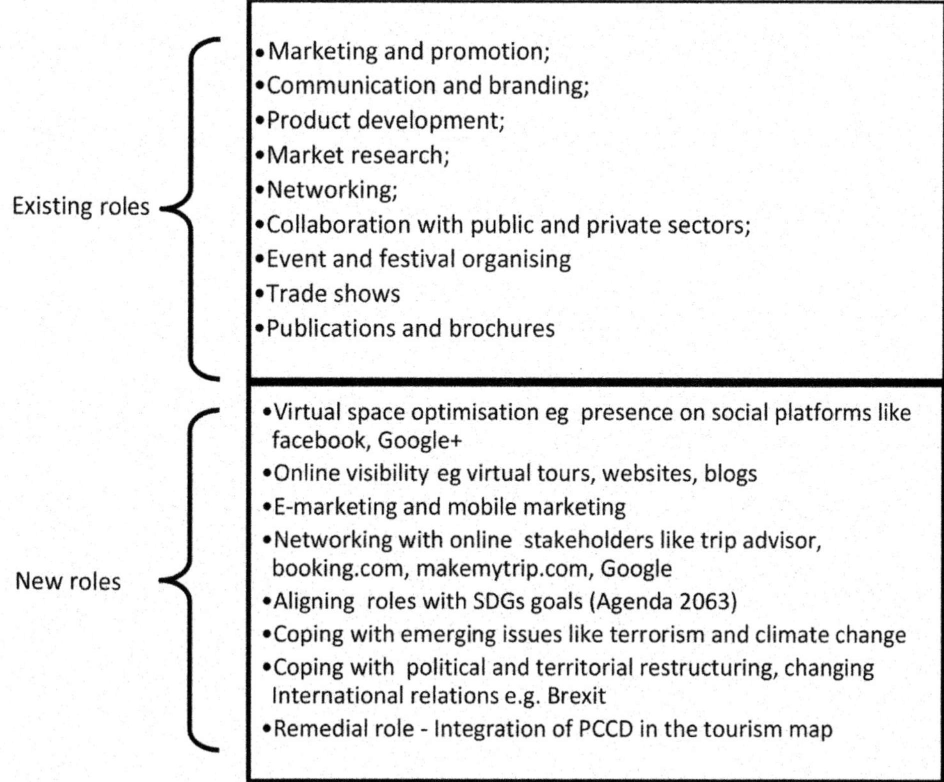

Figure 2.2 Existing and new roles of DMOs
Source: Authors

tourism destinations like Egypt and France have urged DMOs to review their roles as destination marketers. For instance, DMOs have to strengthen their virtual presence, as comments are posted instantly on social media like Facebook and Trip Advisor, and these are supported by pictures taken by tourists. To defend against these unsafe images, DMOs are assuming new roles in Post Conflict, Post Colonial and Post Disaster Destinations (PCCD) like Kurdistan, Haiti, Uzbekistan and Syria. For instance, after the proclamation of Damascus and Aleppo as world heritage sites and the re-capture of the ancient city of Palmyra, DMOs are making effort to correct the unsafe image of Syria and attract tourists to the country. DMO can therefore have a remedial role for declining destinations. To support this view, a study conducted by Séraphin et al. (2016) shows that a re-branding exercise conducted by the Haitian DMO helped in re-launching Haiti, as a PCCD destination. Haiti was perceived as an insecure destination. Therefore, as a first step, the Haitian DMO took a decision of re-branding Haiti tourism through the adoption of a new logo.

Dwyer et al. (2004) suggest that the 'challenge for tourism stakeholders in both private and public sectors is to combine both existing and new roles in order to achieve and maintain competitive advantage'. With new developments at destinations, the adoption of public-private organizational models, with a vast and diverse number of stakeholders within their governing bodies, has pushed DMOs to take on more 'sophisticated' roles including management, planning and/or strategy (Serra et al., 2016). The bottom-line will not be just profitability and marketability, but also the sustainability of the destination and of its people (Gowreesunkar, 2012)

DMO: a marketing or management entity?

Whether a DMO is a marketing or management entity is still an unresolved debate within the literature (Ritchie and Crouch, 2003). This is also explained by Pike and Page (2014) who put forward that the literature relating to destination management is diverse and frequently overlaps with fields like destination governance and marketing. A study conducted by Dredge et al. (2016) shows that, in practice and in theory, DMOs have evolved significantly over the last four decades. The acronym 'DMO' stands for either 'Destination Marketing Organization' or 'Destination Management Organization' depending on the focus of the organization's activities. What they have in common is that both of them are a type of policy tool used to stimulate tourism growth, where the emphasis on marketing or management is simply a reflection of the dominant political discourse about whether tourism should be solely market-driven, or driven by a mixed marketing /management approach. Regardless, since the last few decades, the tourism industry worldwide has been facing daunting challenges (climate change, depletion of resources, sophistication of customers, international relationship issues, *inter alia*) and to cope with such an unpredictable and turbulent environment, DMO is no longer focusing just on marketing strategies but also on management issues. In this respect, tourism destination marketing is now widely recognized as an essential component in the management of destinations (Blumberg, 2005). This point is also echoed in the definition of the UNWTO (2008) – DMO is the organization responsible for the management and/or marketing of destinations and generally falling into one of the following categories:

- National Tourism Authorities, responsible for management and marketing of tourism at a national level;
- regional, provincial or state DMOs, responsible for the management and marketing of tourism in a geographic region defined for that purpose, sometimes but not always an administrative or local government region such a county, state or province; and

- local DMOs responsible for the management and marketing of tourism based on a smaller geographic area or city/town

(UNWTO, 2008)

To further support the above, Ritchie and Crouch (2000) argue that DMO should not be restricted to a tool for attracting more visitors to a region, rather it should operate as a mechanism to facilitate the achievement of tourism policy coordinated with the regional development strategic plan. Likewise, Kaspar (1995) advocates that management and marketing for tourism destinations need to work hand-in-hand, as DMOs are responsible for the overall destination and hence, they have to undertake multiple tasks that are directed towards the sustainable development of the destination and guest satisfaction. The multiple management and marketing tasks undertaken by DMOs are:

- internal and external marketing;
- host community relationship building;
- guidance and support in the marketing of small tourism enterprises;
- planning, research and development;
- destination promotion and branding;
- information and advice on the destination;
- events development and management;
- sustainable tourism practices;
- co-ordination and networking with stakeholders;
- affiliation with relevant professional bodies for training and capacity building;
- compliance with global exigencies like the Sustainable Development Goal 8, 12 and 14

(UNWTO, 2016)

In contrast with the views advanced by Ritchie and Crouch (2000) and Kasper (2005) that DMOs should undertake both management and marketing tasks, Page and Hall (2003) observe that, from a management perspective, DMOs are limited in what they can undertake and achieve in terms of practical and logistical issues managed by local authorities (e.g. car parking, street cleaning, waste removal, control of crowds and visitor during special events). In this respect, Fyall (2011: 345) puts forward that 'unless all elements are owned by the same body, then the ability to control and influence the direction, quality and development of the destination pose very real challenges'. For example, while Canada's national, provincial and regional DMOs have evolved beyond a traditional promotion orientation, the nation's tourism industry lacks destination management as 'an integrated approach to destination management involving the country's multiple stakeholders has yet to be developed' (Vallee, 2005: 229). Thus, the unresolved debate on the role of DMO by Ritchie and Crouch (2003) is somehow justified given that the term Destination Management Organization is unhelpful in adding clarity to the discussion of the DMO's role because it confuses the perceived need for management with the largely marketing function it actually undertakes. Certainly, DMOs will continue to undertake both marketing and management functions, but the degree of involvement in both will depend on the characteristic of the destination. In recent years, tourism marketing has gone through strategic changes with the advances in new technologies, the pursuit of a relationship approach with customers and suppliers, as well as the importance of sustainability issues in marketing. Looking to the future, Morgan et al. (2011) propose that DMOs need to re-orientate their activities, embrace social responsibility, stewardship and sustainability, and argue that DMOs must build new alternative coalitions between civil society, government and business to confront future challenges.

Assessing the performance of DMOs

According to the Destination Marketing Association International (DMAI), the performance of a DMO is based on its ability to:

- increase the economic benefits of tourism and meetings to their respective destinations;
- inspire travelers to visit their destination;
- influence travel throughout their communities to increase spending and enhance the visitor experience;
- attract conventions, meetings and events to their destination.

However, assessing the performance of DMOs is complex in that their task is concerned with the whole destination. Because the destination is an amalgam of tourist products, services and public goods consumed under the same brand name, the tourism destination becomes the unit of analysis (Croes, Shani and Walls, 2010). As such, it is difficult to understand which specific component or combinations of components of the tourism destination are performing effectively and hence, are generating satisfaction to tourism stakeholders (including the tourists). To this effect, Bornhost et al. (2009) argue that it is difficult to establish a model to quantify the performance of DMOs. Regardless, Kaurav et al. (2015) put forward a series of variables to evaluate the performance of a DMO. Based on their interpretations, it may be argued that the performance of a DMO depends on the performance of the various components forming part of the tourism destination and these might be summarized as follows:

- customer satisfaction;
- marketing communication and branding;
- quality of relationship with tourism stakeholders;
- profitability of tourism businesses;
- benefit of local community;
- destination management and sustainability issues.

Customer satisfaction

According to Kotler et al. (2006), marketing is the art of attracting and keeping customers. This suggests that customer satisfaction and loyalty are influenced by the performance of the marketers. Likewise, the success of marketing at a tourism destination will also depend on the performance of the destination marketer if success is interpreted by the level of tourist satisfaction and their loyalty towards the destination. Tourism businesses depend on the demand of tourists and the latter is the result of positive feedback and successful tourism experience offered separately or jointly by various service providers. However, customer satisfaction is complex to understand in tourism, as several attributes contribute to tourist satisfaction namely destination services, recreational facilities, cultural tours, hotel services, restaurant services and host culture, destination's natural environment, local culture and climate among others affect tourist satisfaction (Yuksel et al., 2010). Tourists normally do not evaluate each component of the offering in the same way as products and services have different features and the feeling of satisfaction cannot be weighted using the same assumptions. For instance, food and massage do not give the same type of satisfaction. Due to subjective perceptions, tourists are unable to assess the characteristics of product offerings consistently and they often add their own interpretations (Johnston and Heineke, 1998). For instance, a tourist will not evaluate the heritage attribute of a destination if it was not part of the trip. Satisfaction should therefore be measured separately from the elements of tourism offers. Hence, the measurement of customer satisfaction is based on general destination attributes, and the calculated score of satisfaction will be limited on the choice of tourists.

Marketing communication and branding

Marketing communication at a destination is based on the ability of the DMO to convey the brand image, and to assist visitors through the provision of pre-visit information, and additional information (Bornhost et al., 2009). The DMO's marketing communication not only refers to external communication, but also internal communication. According to Kaurav et al. (2015), internal communication is a powerful enabler where loosely connected independent stakeholders need to come together to recreate an intangible experience for tourists visiting the destination. The DMO's task is also related to the monitoring of the marketing communications that attempt to communicate the brand position and image of the destination in the market. The purpose is to succinctly convey the brand identity and be noticed by the target consumers in a meaningful and memorable way. It is also worth noting that branding and marketing have changed profoundly due to digital media and co-creation processes (Dredge, 2016) and their effectiveness will depend on the DMO's ability to relate to its market virtually. Tourists of the present era live in a wired world and they are sophisticated, savvy and above all, have permanent online presence through social networks. As such, information on products and services of several destinations, perceptions of a holiday destination, comparisons of different facilities, best deals and level of service are constantly fed online. As a result, the performance of the DMO will be based on its ability to keep pace with this trend, and utilize the integrated marketing communications method combining online and traditional promotions to inform and persuade tourists to come to the destination.

Quality of relationship with stakeholders

The performance of a destination may also be evaluated by the quality of relationships the DMO entertains with internal and external tourism stakeholders. According to Cooper and Hall (2007), a tourism destination comprises a diverse range of stakeholders nurturing compatible and conflicting interests. As such, Weaver and Opermann (2000) proposes that one of the main forces driving the tourism development is the support of its stakeholders. For instance, DMOs build alliances and partnership with public and private sectors for product development and marketing goals. Some of the partnerships are established within the destination (travel trade, transportation, entertainment *inter alia*) while others are with external parties like the United Nations World Tourism Organization (UNWTO), the World Travel and Tourism Council (WTTC), the Destination Marketing Association International (DMAI) among others. Jamal and Jamrozy (2006) argue that destinations are complex in that where there are multiple stakeholders with varying degrees of influence over decision-making, and no single stakeholder can fully control development and planning. They pursue that key stakeholders are not always located at the destination and places may have to deal with impacts locally that stem from actions and pressures exerted elsewhere in a local-global tourism system. As a result, creating shared value involves connecting company success with social progress (Serra et al., 2016). To this effect, Bornhost et al. (2009) propose that coordination of the constituent elements of the tourism sector is important to achieve a single voice for tourism. The success of the DMO depends extensively on tourism stakeholders' willingness to align their marketing goals with that of the DMOs in the vision of attracting tourists and sustaining tourism businesses while protecting the interest of the destination and its people.

Profitability of tourism businesses

Admittedly, the profitability of tourism businesses is dictated by a range of factors – namely market conditions, government policy, incentives to run tourism businesses among others. In the context of a tourism destination, the DMO's role in supporting and retaining tourism businesses are key to the overall success of the destination. The study of Gowreesunkar et al. (2015) on social entrepreneurship suggests that tourism has always been a fertile field for entrepreneurship, as tourists are more interested to buy from small and micro entrepreneurs to experience authenticity. Hence, the role of DMO as facilitator to encourage tourism businesses will also be considered a unit of analysis while assessing the performance of a DMO. The study of Kaurav et al. (2015) shows that incentive for investment in tourism related businesses like hotels, restaurants, tour operation, cultural centres and for strategic alliances are important determinants in tourism success. For instance, the richness of a tourism destination is considerably evaluated by the variety of tourism offers and facilities available at the destination and it is the task of the DMO to manage and monitor these.

Destination management and sustainability issues

According to Gowreesunkar (2012), destinations require a coordinated and focused type of management in order to ensure that their tourism capital is wisely and sustainably utilized. The study of Kaurav et al. (2015) reveals that destination management calls for collaboration of many organizations and their interests in working towards a common goal. Destination management implies the leadership and coordination of activities under a coherent strategy by bringing together resources and expertise and infusing them with a degree of independence and objectivity to lead the way forward. Cooper (2011) argues that DMOs should provide the tools to produce sustainable and competitive tourism at a destination going one step beyond destination marketing to take a more holistic and integrative approach to managing the destination. Managing a destination effectively will also include the coping capacity to deal with exogenous factors like terrorism, climate change, changing international relation. For instance, the British DMO effectiveness might be evaluated by its capability to sustain its tourism businesses after Brexit (Britain's exit from European Union). Thus, the principal question facing the DMO is the extent to which it can contribute to the sustainability of the destination with respect to the triple bottom-line, that is, the economy, the society and the environment.

Benefit to the locals

Tourism promoters utilize the local environment to operate their tourism businesses, and most of the time, the monetary and non-monetary benefits are not shared with local people. Benefit to the locals may be interpreted in the form of job opportunities, poverty reduction, revenue generation, quality of life, cultural exchange and infrastructure development. The DMO is therefore performing if it succeeds in meeting these objectives. In most destinations, locals are dependent on tourism for their livelihood and whether they perceive tourism to be beneficial according to their expectations need to be assessed by the DMO. Dupont (2004) proposes that the link between tourism development and poverty is going only one way, that is, to say that the reduction of poverty leads to the development of tourism and not the other way round. Therefore the performance of a DMO may also be evaluated by its capability of reducing poverty while encouraging small businesses and hence, the creation of economic wealth. How tourism development induces other forms of development that bring satisfaction to locals is also to be considered; to exemplify, whether parks and recreational facilities are extended to locals; whether cultural exchange between the local and the tourist such as organization of music, dance festivals, or handicraft are taking place. The DMO's task is therefore to facilitate these exchanges and extend the benefits to locals while drawing tourists to the destination. Additionally, the benefit to locals may also be interpreted in terms of the intra-generational and inter-generational equity as proposed by Kaurav et al. (2015). The former refers to the fair distribution of benefits and costs (economic, environmental and socio-cultural) among people of different income level of the same generation whereas the latter look is into fair distribution among people transcending several generations.

DMOs in the twenty-first century environment: scopes and challenges

The twenty-first century is framed with new realities and the existence of DMOs has been questioned in the study of Dredge et al. (2016). According to the authors, DMO performance will be judged by their ability to also re-align their roles to the broader context of emerging social paradigms. A few decades ago, travel trade and tourism companies controlled nearly every part of the tourism purchasing process. They advised potential tourists on the best holiday and provided information and planned the booking. Due to a lack of information, the potential tourists simply followed along. For instance, prior to the smart phone revolution, local knowledge about a town was restricted to guide books and memories, both of which required curation by a central source, that is, the DMO. Today, the marketplace is focused on direct relationships controlled by the tip of customer's fingers. From information and translation to flight tracking and touring, smart phones are equipped with applications. Destinations offer digital versions of listings and information. The transition from a product-focus to a consumer-focus has been rapid, expanding word-of-mouth from small and insignificant to viral and potentially harmful. The challenge with this new consumer economy is the focus on the relationship between the consumer and the product. It is no longer indirect, but rather an intimate bond, perpetuated by brands and accepted when useful by the consumer. The wired world resulting from internationalization and globalization, poses new challenges to the DMO. Additionally, natural disasters, terrorism and climate change have transformed a number for destinations into the PCCD category. A further challenge of the DMO is its ability to integrate the PCCD destinations into the tourism map. According to a study conducted by Gretzel et al. (2006), the following challenges mark the future of destination marketing:

1 confronting with new level of competition such as fight for market share with other destinations and competing for increasingly limited funding with other sectors
2 adapting to technological change;
3 managing of expectations and exigencies of demanding customers such as leadership role of DMOs in local communities;
4 communicating more effectively based on changes in consumer behavior;
5 need for community relations plan;
6 recognizing creative partnering through partnerships beyond geographical boundaries and/or jurisdictions;

7 more complex DMO responsibilities including destination management and the need to change bureau structures;
8 finding new measure of success by increasing accountability, finding the right benchmarks and benchmarking partners.

Coupled with the above, a destination represents an amalgam of a diverse and eclectic range of businesses and people, who might have a vested interest in the prosperity of their destination community; although research indicates that not all stakeholders are necessarily interested in the viability of the destination, when their principal objective for operating a business is lifestyle (Thomas et al., 2011). In this process, the challenge of the DMO remains to align all individual promoters' visions along collective lines and branding can still be the reason for DMOs to exist. DMOs' new roles also comprise the alignment of their vision with that of Agenda 2063 and collaborate with governments, private sectors, international institutions, UN agencies and international tourism organizations to achieve the SDG 8, 12 and 14 as proclaimed by the UNWTO (2016).

Case Study

Mauritius is a small tropical island in the Indian Ocean and it occupies an area of 720 square miles (Figure 2.3). The island is equipped with all necessary natural and cultural ingredients to successfully run a tourism industry. These include, among others, beautiful coral beaches, warm blue lagoons, cultural richness, tropical climate, safety and security and economic stability.

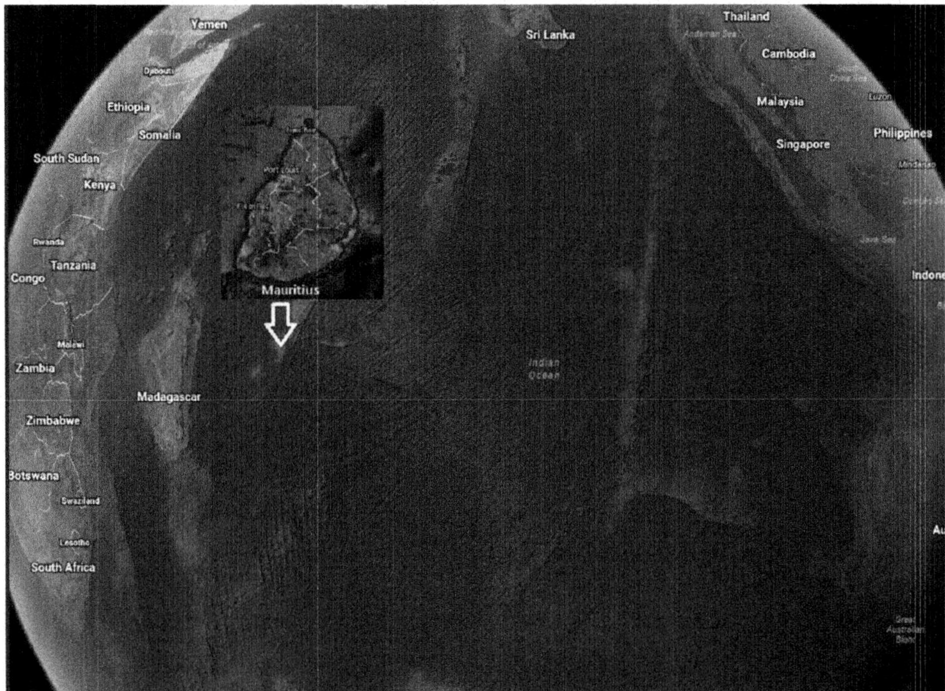

Figure 2.3 Location of Mauritius Island
Source: Google Earth, 2017

Based on well-calculated marketing strategies (the development of wedding and honeymoon packages, the opening of the sky, diversification of its tourism and beach activities), Mauritius has been able to position itself as one of the preferred sea, sun and sand destination in the Indian Ocean (Gowreesunkar and Sotiriades, 2015; Prayag and Ryan, 2011). Similar to other islands, Mauritius is made of a diverse range of businesses, resources and stakeholders and the latter often operate with vested interest and without any common vision directed towards the prosperity of the destination community. For instance, research on Mauritian tourism (see Gowreesunkar 2012; Gowreesunkar and Rycha, 2014; Gowreesunkar and Sotiriades, 2015) indicates that not all stakeholders are interested in the viability of the destination when their principal objective for operating a tourism business is money. While it is well established that DMOs have the overall responsibility for the coordination and integration of the destination mix elements, and for destination marketing (Mill and Morrison, 2012), Mauritius has still not created a DMO. The management and marketing of the tourism industry are dispensed jointly by the private and public sectors. From the private sector, the travel trade market their product individually or as a group; for instance, Beachcomber Group, Summertimes, Connection, White Sand Tours, Rogers, Medine and CIEL group. Small operators like Cap Soleil, Sand Holidays, Catamaran Cruise Limited, Manisa Hotel, and Craft Boutiques also market their products individually. From the public sector, the tourism industry is served by the following authorities operating under the aegis of the Ministry of Tourism and External Communications:

- The Beach Authority
- The Tourism Authority
- The Mauritius Tourism Promotion Authority
- The Tourism Police
- The National Coast Guard

Figure 2.4 shows various overlapping of duties and duplications of activities, which in turn, impacts on the cost, as additional amounts of resources and public funds are deployed to run these organizations. For instance, the Tourism Authority is responsible for inspections and monitoring of tourism activities, issue of license, safety and security of tourism activities while these tasks are also being looked into by Beach Authorities, National Coast Guard and Tourism Police. Moreover, marketing of beach activities is conducted by both the MTPA and the Beach Authorities, a further duplication of duties. Additionally, a tourism entrepreneur selling shells on the beach is accountable to two different authorities, namely the Beach Authority and the Tourism Authority, while both authorities operate under the same ministry. As a result, the main weakness of the Mauritian tourism industry is that the tourism objectives set by the Ministry of Tourism are delivered by too many entities. Regulators duplicate the work of their partners in a disjointed and fragmented fashion. Due to a lack of shared vision, several instances of mismanagement of resources have been reported. For instance, the case study of bottlenose dolphin-watching tourism at Tamarin Bay, Mauritius is perhaps one of many cases of bad marketing and mismanagement (Parsons and Scarpati, 2016). In another study conducted by Gowreesunkar and Sotiriades (2015), islets like Ilot Bernaches, Ilot Benitiers and Ile D'Ambre were found to be marketed by different individual tourism operators and resources were exploited to satisfy the demand of tourists. In the quest to maximize tourism business and profit, individual operators often overlook the sustainability aspect. Destination management activities which are not the responsibility of destination marketers are under the jurisdiction of government departments and ministries in Mauritius, a point also advanced by Morrison (2012) in his study on Chinese DMOs. In the absence of a DMO, tourism heritage and resources are ambitiously exploited by

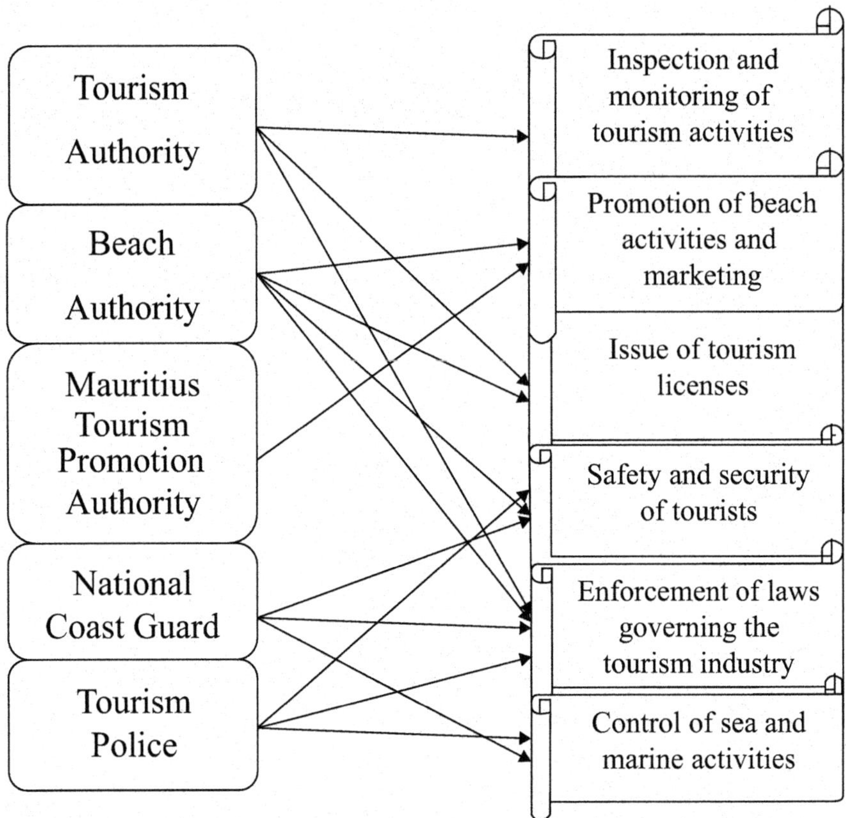

Figure 2.4 Duplication of roles by tourism regulators in Mauritius
Source: Authors

tourism operators. Without a common approach there is no shared vision, as individual operators are more interested in profit maximization (even if it is short term), whereas sustainability of tourism resources for future generations is not a priority. This goes in line with an earlier observation of Carlsen (1999) stating that uncontrolled tourism in island cases is more fatal than in a big continent. Without a common vision, a destination with wide range of stakeholders has a high potential for cooperation but also some potential to threaten the ability to achieve its objectives (Sheehan and Ritchie, 2005). The task of the DMO therefore lies in reinforcing collaboration between diverse stakeholders (Paskeleva-Shapira, 2001) in order to establish cooperative relationships, especially in matters of resource utilization and tourism development, as no single agency can control and deliver a rich combination of tourism product and service portfolio at a destination (Krakover and Wang, 2008).

At a stage where globalization, internationalization and technology have invaded the tourism market, Mauritius cannot afford to operate in the same way as it did at its developmental stage. Crouch and Ritchie (2000) state that a destination that has a tourism vision, shares the vision among all the stakeholders, has management which develops an appropriate marketing strategy and a government which supports tourism industry with an efficient tourism policy, may be more competitive than one that has never asked what role tourism is to play in its economy. The study of Gowreesunkar (2012) on destination management in Mauritius recommended the establishment of a DMO for the island so that private tourism operators do not limit their business objectives to profitability, but rather extend it to the sustainability of the destination and its people. In fact, as early as in 1963, the UN Conference on Travel and Tourism (Rome) recommended the creation of DMOs for islands. The crucial roles of DMOs in the development of a sustainable tourism industry have been recognized in various case studies. In Italy, the Ministry of Tourism and Entertainment re-organized its tourism industry by creating a DMO in 1959. In so doing, the state gave administrative autonomy and public law status to the DMO to manage its tourism industry (Bhatia, 2006) and the advantages enjoyed by Italian tourism managed by a DMO ranged from tourism business to tourism resource sustainability. The Japanese National Tourism Organization was created in 1979 for better coordination of tourism stakeholders, alignment of individual goals to collective goals and protection of the destination resources and appeal. Likewise, with the creation of the Russian DMO in 1994, the tourism industry enjoyed competitive advantages like research, publicity overseas, tourism policy and planning, effective marketing, infrastructure and product development. These case studies may serve as lessons to Mauritius to conclude that the establishment of a DMO can positively impact on the marketability, profitability and hence the sustainability of the destination.

Conclusion

The twenty-first century continues to unfold in a climate of insecurity and uncertainty and in a way, new developments in technology and society are expected to continuously redefine what the future of tourism will or can be (Dredge et al., 2016). Throughout the chapter, it has been established that the profitability and marketability and hence sustainability of tourism destinations will increasingly depend on the roles and functions assumed by the DMO. The chapter also offered a rich insight into emerging realities faced by DMOs in the twenty-first century and these were not limited to conflicting interests, diverse tourism stakeholders, fight for market share and tourism resources, changing international relationship, globalization and technology, unpredictable and knowledgeable tourists, climate change and sustainability issues, online feedback systems, exigency for the implementation of Agenda 2063 and the Sustainable Development Goals, and terrorism and integration of PCCD destinations in the tourism map. As a result, it was agreed that an integrated approach was required in the marketing of tourism destinations and DMOs are the organizations that could fulfill marketing activities within the broader context of a destination. The case study on Mauritius shed light on the realities and vulnerabilities of small islands and thus proposed that one of the critical success factors for an effectively managed and competitive destination lies in the quality of role played by DMOs at the destination. The case study showed that the tourism industry was regulated by various authorities and this resulted in duplication of duties and conflicting roles. It was also observed that due to a lack of shared vision, the tourism industry suffered from lack of control and mismanagement of resources. Based on the findings, it was proposed that the establishment of a DMO could bring a new dimension to the tourism industry. Drawing from successful case studies, it was apparent that the establishment of a DMO should not be restricted to a tool for attracting visitors in Mauritius, but rather it should operate as a mechanism to facilitate the achievement of tourism policy, thereby adopting a concern for the total impact of tourism development with an overall objective of sustainable development.

With regards to the future of DMOs, Dredge (2016) argues that DMOs are on a path to redundancy. The internet, in its various forms, is gradually taking the place of organizations. For instance, flight booking which was once done by airlines, is now operated online. Advice on choice of holidays which was done by tour operators and intermediaries has been replaced by online traders (Trip Advisor, Booking.com), booking of hotels which was done by holiday package dealers, is now directly available on hotel websites, safety and security advice once issued by Government to potential travelers is available on destination websites. Feedback on destinations, price deals, and almost all information can be retrieved online. While appreciating the points of view of these prominent authors, it would seem that tourism destinations will continue to need DMO for the effective marketing and management of their resources. Just like virtual companies would still need human resource to run their organizations, DMOs will remain significant components of tourism systems as these are the entities that have the prerogative to oversee that destinations are conforming to sustainability principles and are aligning their marketing objectives within the broader context of the globe.

References

Ashworth, G. J. (1991). Products, places and promotion: Destination images in the analysis of the tourism industry. In M. T. Sinclair and M. J. Stabler (Eds.), *The tourism industry. An international analysis.* Wallingford, Oxfordshire: CABI.

Bhatia, A. K. (2006). *The business of tourism: concepts and strategies.* New Delhi: Sterling Publishers.

Blumberg, K. (2005), Tourism destination marketing – A tool for destination management? A case study from Nelson/Tasman Region, New Zealand. *Asia Pacific Journal of Tourism Research*, 10(1), pp. 45–57.

Bornhost, T., Ritchie, B. and Sheehan, L. (2009). Determinants of tourism success for DMOs and destinations: An empirical examination of stakeholders' perspectives. *Tourism Management*, pp. 1–18.

Butler, R., Williams, A. and Weidenfeld, A. (2010). Knowledge transfer and innovation among attractions. *Annals of Tourism Research*, 37(3), 604–626.

Carlsen, J. (1999). A system approach to island tourism destination management. *System Research and Behavioral Science*, 16(4), 321–327.

Choy, D. J. L. (1993) Alternative roles of national tourism organizations. *Tourism Management*, 14(5), pp. 357–365.

Cooper C. (2011). *Essentials of Tourism*. London: Pearson.

Cooper, C. and Hall, C. (2007). Contemporary Tourism Marketing. *Contemporary Tourism*. Oxford: Butterworth-Heinemann.

Crouch, G. and Ritchie, J. R. (2000). The Competitiveness Destination: A Sustainability Perspective. *Tourism Management,* 2(1), pp. 1–7.

Dore, L. and Crouch, G. I. (2003). Promoting destinations: An exploratory study of publicity programmes used by national tourism organisations. *Journal of Vacation Marketing*, 9(2), pp. 137–151.

Dredge, D. (2016) Are DMOs on a path to redundancy? *Tourism Recreation and Research*, in press.

Dredge, D., Hall, M. and Munar, A (2016). *Tourism Recreation and Research*, in press.

Dupont, L. (2004). Cointégration et causalité entre développement touristique, croissance économique et réduction de la pauvreté : Cas de Haïti. *Revue Caribéennes*, available online at: http://etudescaribeennes.revues.org

Dwyer, L., Mellor, R., Livaic, Z., Edwards, D. and Kim, C. (2004). Attributes of destination competitiveness: a factor analysis. *Tourism Analysis*, 9(1), pp. 91–101.

Franch, M. and Martini, U. (2002). Destinations and destination management in the Alps: A proposal for a classification scheme in the light of some ongoing experiences. Paper presented at meeting 'Territoires et marchés 2ème colloque de recherche en tourisme de l'Association française des IUP Tourisme, Hôtellerie et Loisirs', Université de Savoie, Site de Chambery (F), 12–14 September.

Ford, R.C. and Peeper, W.C. (2008). *Managing Destination Marketing Organizations.* Orlando: Forper Publications.

Fyall, A. (2011). Destination management: Challenges and opportunities. In Wang, Y. and Pizam, A. (Eds). 2011. *Destination Marketing and Management – Theories and Applications.* Wallingford, Oxfordshire: CABI, pp. 340–358.

Fyall, A., Kozak, M., Andreu, L., Gnoth, J. and Lebe, S. S. (2009). *Marketing Innovations for Sustainable Destinations.* Oxford: Good fellow Publishers.

Gartrell, R.B. (1988). *Destination Marketing for Convention and Visitor Bureaus.* Dubuque, Iowa: Kendall/Hunt Publishing.

Gowreesunkar, V. (2012). The role of internal marketing in island destination management: Mauritius as a case study. Doctoral Thesis, University of Technology, Mauritius.

Gowreesunkar, V. and Ramnauth, T. (2013). Ilot Bernache (Mauritius) as a tourism recreation islet: Impacts, challenges and implications. *International conference on climate change: Impacts and responses*, Common Ground, Mauritius, 18–19 July.

Gowreesunkar, V. and Rycha I. (2015). A Study on the Impacts of Dolphin Watching as a Tourism Activity: Western Mauritius as a Case Study. *International Journal of Trade, Economic and Finance*, 6(1), pp. 67–72.

Gowreesunkar, V. and Sotiriades, M. (2015). Entertainment of leisure tourists in island destinations: Evidence from the Island of Mauritius. *African Journal of Hospitality, Tourism and Leisure,* 4(2223), pp. 1–19.

Gowreesunkar, V. G., Van der Sterren, J., and Séraphin, H. (2015). Social Entrepreneurship as a tool for promoting Global Citizenship in Island Tourism Destination Management. *ARA Journal*, *5*(1), pp. 7–23.

Gretzel, U., Fesenmaier, D. Formica, S. and O' Leary, J. (2006). Searching for the Future: challenges faced by Destination Marketing Organizations. *Journal of Travel Research*, 45, pp. 116–126.

Grönroos, C. (1994). From Marketing Mix to Relationship Marketing: Towards a Paradigm Shift in Marketing. *Management Decision*, 32(2), pp. 4–20.

Haxton, P. (2015). *A review of effective policies for tourism growth.* OECD Tourism Papers 1/2015. Paris: OECD.

Jamal, T. and Jamrozy, U. (2006) Collaborative Networks and Partnerships for Integrated Destination Management. In Buhalis, D. and C. Costa (Eds) *Tourism Management Dynamics: Trends, Management and Tools.* Oxford: Elsevier Butterworth Heinemann, pp. 164–172.

Johnston, R. and Heineke, J. (1998). Exploring the relationship between perception and performance: priorities for action. *The Service Industries Journal*, 18(1), pp.101–112.

Kaspar, C. (1995). Management im tourismus. Eine Grundlage für das Management von Tourismusnternehmungen und – organisationen. vollständig überarbeitete und ergänzte Auflage), vol. 13. Bern, Switzerland: Verlag Paul Haupt.

Kaurav, R., Baber, R., Chowdhray, N. and Kapadia, S. (2015). Destination performance: importance of redefining DMOs. *Asia-Pacific Journal of Innovation in Hospitality and Tourism*, 4(1), pp. 125–142.

Kotler, P., Bowen, J. and Makens, J. (2006). *Marketing for Hospitality and Tourism.* Australia: Pearson Education Ltd., pp. 355–383.

Krakover, S. and Wang, Y. (2008). Destination Marketing: Competition, Cooperation or Coopetition? *International Journal of Contemporary Hospitality Management*, 20(2), pp. 126–141.

Läesser, C. (2000). Implementing destination-structures: Experiences with Swiss cases. In Manete, M. and Cerato, M. (Eds). *From Destination to Destination Marketing and Management.* Venice: CISET, pp. 111–126.

Laws, E. (1995). *Tourist Destination Management. Issues, Analysis and Policies.* London: Routledge.

Leiper, N. (2008). 'Why' the tourism industry is misleading as a generic expression: The case for plural variation 'tourism industries'. *Tourism Management* 29(2), pp, 237–251.

Matejka, J. K. (1973). Critical factors in vacation area selection. *Arkansas Business and Economic Review*, 6, pp. 17–19.

McClure, M. (2004). *The Wonder Country: Making New Zealand Tourism.* Auckland, N.Z: Auckland University Press.

Mill, R. and Morrison, A. (2012). *The Tourism System: An Introductory Text.* Dubuque: Kendall.

Morgan, N., Pritchard, A. and Pride, R. (2011). *Destination Brands: Managing Place Reputation*, 3rd ed. Abingdon, England: Butterworth-Heinemann Elsevier.

Morrison, A. (2013). Destination management and destination marketing: the platform for excellence in tourism destinations. *Tourism Tribune*, 28(1), pp. 6–9.

Morrison, A.M. (2012). *Global Marketing of China Tourism.* Beijing: China Architectural and Building Press.

Page, S. J. and Hall, C. M. (2003). *Managing Urban Tourism.* Harlow: Pearson Education.

Parsons, E. and Scarpati, C. (2016). Recent advances in whale watching research: 2014–2015. *Tourism in Marine Environment*, 11(4), pp. 251–262.

Paskeleva-Shapira, K. (2001). Promoting Partnership for Effective Governance of Sustainable Urban Tourism. *Paper presented at the INTA International Seminar* 'Tourism in the City – Opportunity for Regeneration and Development', Turin.

Pearce, D.G. (1997). Competitive destination analysis in Southeast Asia. *Journal of Travel Research,* 35(4), pp. 16–24.

Pechlaner, H., Raich, F. and Zehrer, A. (2007). The Alps: Challenges and potentials of a brand management. *Tourism Analysis*, 12(5/6), pp. 359–370.

Pike, S. (2004). *Destination Marketing Organisations.* Oxford: Elsevier.

Pike, S. (2008). *Destination Marketing. An Integrated Communication Approach.* Abingdon: Butterworth-Heinemann.

Pike, S. and Page, S. (2014). Destination marketing organizations and destination marketing: a narrative analysis of the literature. *Tourism Management*, 41, pp. 1–26.
Prayag, G and Ryan, C (2011). The relationship between the 'push' and 'pull' factors of a tourist destination: the role of nationality – an analytical qualitative research approach. *Current Issues in Tourism*, 14(2), pp. 121–143.
Presenza, A., Ritchie, J. R. B. and Sheehan, L. (2005). Towards a Model of the Roles and Activities of Destination Management Organisations. Available online at: http://hotel.unlv.edu.
Ritchie, J. R. B. and Crouch, G. I. (2000). The Competitive Destination: A Sustainable Perspective. *Tourism Management*, 21, pp. 1–7.
Ritchie, J. R. B. and Crouch, G. I. (2003). *The competitive destination: a sustainable tourism perspective.* Wallingford, UK: CABI.
Ritchie, J. R. B, Sheehan, L. and Presenza, A. (2005). Towards a Model of the Roles and Activities of Destination Management Organisations. Available online at: http://hotel.unlv.edu.
Scott, N., Cooper, C. and Baggio, R. (2008). Destination networks: four Australian cases. *Annals of Tourism Research*, 35(1), pp. 169–188.
Séraphin, H., Ambaye M., Gowreesunkar, V. and Bonnardel V. (2016). A marketing research tool for destination marketing organisations' logo design. *Journal of Business Research*, Elsevier Publications – in press.
Serra, J., Font X. and Ivanova, M. (2016). Creating shared value in destination management organization: The case of Barcelona. *Journal of Destination Marketing and Management*, in press.
Sheehan, L. and Ritchie, J. R. B. (2005), Destination stakeholders: exploring identity and salience, *Annals of Tourism Research*, 32(1), pp. 711–734.
Spotts, D. M. (1997). Regional analysis of tourism resources for marketing purposes. *Journal of Travel Research,* Winter, pp. 3–15.
Thomas, R., Shaw, G. and Page, S. J. (2011). Understanding small firms in tourism: a perspective on research trend and challenges. *Tourism Management*, 32(5), pp. 963–976.
UNWTO (2008). *UNWTO Tourism Highlights 2013.* Madrid: United Nations World Tourism Organization.
UNWTO (2016). *Sustainable Development of Tourism.* Madrid: United Nations World Tourism Organization.
Vallee, P. (2005). Destination management in Canada. In Harrill, R. (Ed.) *Fundamentals of Destination Management and Marketing.* Washington: IACVB, pp. 229–244.
Wahab, S., Crampon., L. J. and Rothfield, L. M. (1976). *Tourism Marketing.* London: Tourism International Press.
Wang, Y. and Pizam, A. (2011). *Destination Marketing and Management. Theories and Applications.* Wallingford: CABI.
Weaver, D. and Opermann M. (2000). *Tourism Management.* Brisbane: Wiley.
Yuksel, A., Yuksel, F. and Bilim, Y. (2010). Destination attachment: Effects of customer satisfaction and cognitive, affective and conative loyalty. *Tourism Management*, 31, pp. 274–284.

Further reading

Buhalis, D. (2000). Marketing the competitive destination of the future. *Tourism Management,* 21(1), pp. 97–116.
Cooper, C., Fletcher, J., Gilbert, D. and Wanhill, S. (1998). *Tourism Principles and Practice.* Essex, England: Pearson Education Ltd.
Croes, R., Shani, A. and Walls, A. (2010). The value of destination loyalty: Myth or reality. *Journal of Hospitality Marketing and Management,* 19(2), pp. 115–136.
Leiper, N. (1995) *Tourism Management.* Melbourne: RMIT.

3

Destination marketing research

Drita Kruja

Introduction

The tourism destination provides a geographically bounded locality, whether at a national, regional or local level, in which economic and social interactions take place and which embraces the idea of 'community' (Tinsley and Lynch, 2007: 16).

The major goal of destination marketing research is to understand the nature of the interaction between visitors and tourism providers at the destination, which naturally represents both the demand and supply sides of tourism. In today's highly competitive leisure travel market, the need for accurate, timely and relevant information is essential for both emerging and established destinations to stay competitive and also increase their share of the leisure travel market.

Marketing research helps the Destination Marketing Organizations (DMOs) to make better informed and less risky marketing and management decisions. Accordingly, the information obtained through marketing research must be objective, impartial, translatable, current and relevant.

This chapter explores the destination marketing research process and the six steps that are involved in conducting research, and discusses the nature of marketing research, emphasizing its role of providing information for marketing decision making.

Importance of destination marketing research

Marketing research is the systematic and objective identification, collection, analysis, dissemination, and use of information for the purpose of improving decision making related to the identification and solution of problems and opportunities in marketing (Malhotra, 2015: 28).

Clearly, any destination marketer with a market orientation conducts research to gain insight into their visitor market. Research results greatly contribute to creating long-term marketing plans; help set organizational goals and policies; can help communicate the DMOs role in contributing to the local economy in terms of visitor spending, tax revenues, and jobs supported.

The research function calls for (1) the design and development of research programs that track, analyze, and explain key trends and market conditions; (2) direct performance reporting programs to provide accurate assessment of program effectiveness; (3) the management of a communications program; and (4) the DMOs to act as a liaison with government officials and tourism industry principals in developing cooperative marketing programs.

Destination marketing research in practice

The most common activities in which destination marketing researchers engage are:

Visitor volume measurements, market share measurements, and visitor profiles. One way to identify a destination's customer base is by conducting a study that deals with the questions: To whom should we sell our destination? How do we find them? What do we tell them about the destination so they will come? The more information it can gather about its visitors, the more likely the DMO and its stakeholders will be able to successfully produce tourism products of interest and communicate them in compelling ways.

Key attributes of visitors include: where they live, spending, mode of transportation, demographics (age, gender, marital status, level of education, occupation, household income or individual income), ethnicity, social class, family life stage, type of tourist (leisure/business, domestic/international), leisure activities, type of accommodation selected, size of travel group, length of stay, purpose of trip, time of visit, source of information used.

Destination brand image studies can help a DMO to understand how a destination is perceived by visitors, how consumers feel about it (Tasci and Gartner, 2007).

Key attributes that can be studied are: the effect of visitation, segmentation, image differences between different groups, the effect of distance from the destination, intermediaries, induced images, top of mind awareness/decision sets, culture, temporal image change, positive/negative images, the effect of familiarity with the destination, less developed destinations, event impact, value, image formation, experience, stereotypes, budget travelers, intent to visit and DMO's policy. (Martín-Santana, Beerli-Palacio and Nazzareno, 2017: 14).

A *visitor impact study* is the most important research a DMO can undertake because it is a direct measure of the organization's operational effectiveness in generating revenue for its members and local community.

Forecasting is an attempt to estimate the most likely level of visitor volume and demand based on economic, market, and social conditions and circumstances.

Tourism barometers can help track trends on a weekly, monthly, or yearly basis. They can include airport arrivals, hotel occupancy, ticket sales at local attractions, or information inquiries.

The marketing and communications performance assessment looks at: number of programs, reach, frequency, impressions, co-op activity, in-kind services, online activity, media public relations, press releases, media interviews, newsletters, and events staged.

The advertising and promotions performance assessment measures the number of inquiries or fulfillments, Web site activity, bookings, and direct sales.

Destination marketing research process

In undertaking research, there is a sequence of steps called the research process, which can have followed when designing the research process. If they are correct, the research stands a good chance of being both useful and appropriate and if they bypassed or wrong, the research will almost surely be wasteful and irrelevant.

According to Malhotra 2015: 31 the marketing research process consists of six steps:

Step 1: Problem/opportunity identification and formulation
Step 2: Development of an approach to the problem

Step 3: Research design formulation
Step 4: Fieldwork or data collection
Step 5: Data preparation and analysis
Step 6: Report preparation and presentation

Step 1: Problem/opportunity identification and formulation

The first step of the research process is to define the problem/opportunity being addressed. This is crucial to ensure that any information collected is relevant.

Proper definition of a problem provides guidance and direction for the entire research process. Problem definition begins with discussions with the key decision maker(s).

In some cases, this is related to a gap in researcher knowledge or destination problems, concerns and opportunities.

We can usually observe that many tourists visit the destination, but we often know very little about their motivations for doing so, why they visit particular sites or what factors influenced their decision to travel. These are important questions from a social science point of view (finding out more about human behaviour) as well as from an economic perspective (how can we manage and market cultural facilities more effectively to increase tourist satisfaction, repeat visitation and spending?) (Richards and Munsters, 2010: 16).

Step 2: Developing an approach to the problem

As well formulating an aim, specific research questions (objectives) should be stipulated at the outset (Seaton and Bennett, 2000: 90).

The research objectives describe the purpose of the research and give direction to a researcher regarding what needs to be accomplished.

An *analytical model* is a set of variables and their interrelationships designed to represent, in whole or in part, some real system or process. *Graphical models* are visual and pictorial and are used to isolate variables and to suggest directions of relationships but are not designed to provide numerical results (Malhotra, 2015: 70).

Research questions (RQs) are refined statements of the specific components of the problem (Malhotra, 2015: 71).

A hypothesis (H) is an unproven statement or proposition about a factor or phenomenon that is of interest to the researcher (Malhotra, 2015: 71). Often, a hypothesis is a possible answer to the research question.

The establishment of hypothesis is the foundation of conducting research and is a valuable step in the problem solving process (Goeldner and Ritchie, 2012: 502)

The information needs is a list of the specific information that must be found to meet the research objectives. By focusing on each component of the problem and the analytical framework and models, research questions, and hypotheses, the researcher can determine what information should be obtained.

Step 3: Formulating a research design

A research design is a framework or blueprint for conducting the marketing research project. It details the procedures necessary for obtaining the information needed to structure or solve marketing research problems (Malhotra, 2015: 84).

Based on the problem definition, the researcher selects one or more of the basic research designs; these are exploratory, descriptive, and causal research.

When the researcher has little or no knowledge about the phenomenon to be investigated, exploratory research approach is the most appropriate research methodology to discover ideas and insights, and isolate key variables and relationships for further examination. Basic methods of exploratory research are: Secondary data analysis and Qualitative research.

Determine the sources of data

Primary data, secondary data or both can be used in research. Primary data are the new data gathered specifically for the project at hand. Secondary data are available data, already gathered for some other purpose.

One of the biggest mistakes made in marketing research is to collect primary data before exhausting what can learned from the information available in secondary sources.

The wide range of secondary data sources of interest to DMOs include:

- Central and local government statistics (census data used by marketers as part of geodemographic and lifestyle market segmentation).
- International organization reports such as by the WTTC, WTO, IATA, ICAO, UN, OECD, Eurostat.
- Commercial sources reports, such as Euromonitor, Travel and Tourism intelligence (TTI), Marketing Intelligence (MINTEL). For example, Euromonitor is specialized in international consumer market analysis, and part of their portfolio includes travel and tourism. It produces emerging market, market direction and international market intelligence reports.
- The academic literature (books, scientific journals, periodicals, master and PhD thesis).
- Internal records of DMOs.
- Trade associations, such as hotels, travel agents, tour operators and airlines, hold information on their members and the market.
- The news media.
- Internet.
- Syndicated marketing research services (*Syndicated services* are companies that collect and sell common pools of data of known commercial value designed to serve a number of clients Malhotra 2015: 97)

Qualitative research

Qualitative research is an unstructured, exploratory research methodology based on small samples that provides insights and understanding of the problem setting (Malhotra 2015:61).

Focus groups are the most popular form of qualitative research in destination marketing and management. Issues are explored from the perspective of various stakeholder groups, particularly residents, providers and managers (Echtner and Ritchie, 1993; Haukeland, Daugstad and Vistad, 2011; Mackay and Fesenmaier, 1997; Mackenzie, 2012; Pearce and Schänzel, 2013; Perdue, 2000; Salk, Schneider and McAvoy, 2010; Singal and Uysal, 2009). It involves interviewing eight to 12 people in an informal setting and uses open ended questions. It led by a trained moderator, who wants to get group interaction, to stimulate critical thinking and get immediate reactions. A typical session lasts from 90 minutes to two hours. The group is taped (either audio or video) so researcher can later analyze the discussion, looking for common themes.

In destination marketing and management research can be undertaken with online focus groups (four to six participants), because they remove geographical constraints and decrease costs.

Depth interviews are another method of obtaining qualitative data. The interviews are lengthy, freewheeling discussions between a researcher and an individual. Depth interviews are effective in situations that involve detailed probing of respondents, discussion of sensitive topics, or where strong social norms exist. They are unstructured or semi structured. They are used by some researchers in/or not in combination with quantitative research (Gartner and Ruzzier, 2011; Hanlan and Kelly, 2005; Hankinson, 2004, 2009; Hem and Iversen, 2004; Klenosky, Gengler and Mulvey, 1999; Komppula, 2014; Kruja and Hasaj, 2010; Kruja and Gjyrezi, 2011; McKercher, Wong and Lau, 2006; Tinsley and Lynch, 2001.)

Delphi Technique may be characterized as "a method for structuring a group communication process so that the process is effective in allowing a group of individuals to deal with a complex problem" (Linstone and Turoff, 1975: 3).

The Delphi technique was developed by Rand Corporation.

> A small group of experts must respond independently in a designated time-frame to a problem scenario. After each round, the information is consolidated and edited. Unlike focus groups, the respondents do not converse with the other study participants, but they are given feedback from the other respondents after each set of questions.
>
> *(Kaynak, Bloom and Leibold, 1994: 19)*

The Delphi technique is one qualitative technique which had been used with substantial success in predicting tourism demand and potential, where convergence of expert opinion is the underlying criterion to produce more precise projections. The Delphi technique is suitable to use when dealing with uncertainties in an area of imperfect knowledge.

Lin, Liu and Song, 2015, based on 46 studies, reviewed the application of the Delphi technique in tourism forecasting within top tourism and hospitality as well as management and forecasting research publications over the past four decades. The application of the Delphi forecasting technique has generally been categorized into three broad categories: event forecasting, forecasting tourism demand, and forecasting future trends/market conditions, but the third has been identified as the most popular application (Lin, Liu and Song, 2015: 1126). Specifically, they concluded that Delphi has been widely applied in projecting potential market trends or conditions, predicting the likelihood or the time of the occurrence of specified events and their impact on tourism, and forecasting tourism demand (e.g. Hawkins, Shafer, and Rovelstad, 1980; Kaynak and Macaulay, 1984; Kaynak, Bloom, and Leibold, 1994; Kaynak and Marandu, 2006, 2011; Kaynak and Pathak, 2006; Kaynak and Cavlek, 2007; Katsura and Sheldon, 2008; Kibedi, 1981; Pan et al., 1995; Seely, Iglarsh, and Edgell, 1980; Tideswell, Mules, and Faulkner, 2001).

There is a limited use of statistical techniques (e.g. mean, median, interquartile, standard deviation and statistical tests) in exploring and analyzing the results of Delphi techniques. As a result, this technique can be conducted in combination with one or more of the quantitative methods.

The basic interview can be supplemented in a number of ways:

Repertory grid analysis was developed almost 80 years ago. Repertory grid is a method of investigating an individual's world view that allows them to express their opinions in their own terms. Its application in destination research has been discussed by several authors (e.g. Embacher and Buttle, 1989; Hankinson, 2004, 2005; Timmermans, Heuden and Westerveld, 1982; Pike, 2003, 2007; Walmsley and Jenkins, 1993).

Q methodology was invented by the psychologist William Stephenson in the 1930s, and most applications of Q methodology have been within psychology (Stephenson, 1953).

Q methodology represents an attempt "to analyze subjectivity, in all its forms, in a structured and interpretable form" (Barry and Proops, 1999: 339). Q-method may open up possibilities for contemporary tourism researchers, to enhance the nature and richness of the methodological alternatives for developing tourism knowledge (Stergiou and Airey, 2011: 319).

The first attraction of Q-methodology to tourism researchers is its emphasis on the subjective, lived experiences of individuals (Stergiou and Airey 2011:317). It used from some authors in destination research (e.g. Davis, 2003; Dewar, Li and Davis, 2007; Fairweather and Swaffield, 2001, 2003; Hugé et al., 2016; Stringer, 1984).

The projective techniques are an unstructured, indirect form of questioning that encourages respondents to project their underlying motivations, beliefs, attitudes or feelings regarding the issues of concern (Malhotra, 2015: 132).

According to Hussey and Duncombe

> the projective techniques can be used to overcome communication barriers among the respondents, such as lack of awareness of repressed motivations; inability to express themselves; unwillingness to disclose certain feelings; irrationality, and subjects trying to say the right things to please the interviewer.
>
> *(1999: 23)*

Hussey and Duncombe, 1999; Prayag, 2007; Usakli and Baloglu, 2011; Wagner and Peters, 2009; and Wassler and Hung, 2015 used projective techniques in their destination research.

Wassler and Hung (2015) employ three projective techniques in their research to personify brand-as-person and brand-as-user for two tourist destinations, namely:

- *word association* (the respondents are usually asked to cite the images or thoughts that first come to their minds),
- *sentence completion* (respondents are given incomplete sentences and asked to complete them), and
- *brand personification* (brand personification is a technique that directly assigns human traits to a brand. In this case, the respondents are encouraged to create mentally a human metaphor for a specific target).

(Wassler and Hung, 2015: 846)

Projective techniques can be used in conjunction with focus groups and depth interviews to obtain responses that subjects would be unwilling or unable to give if they knew the purpose of the study.

Descriptive research

If a problem is precisely and unambiguously formulated, descriptive and causal research is needed. Descriptive research is used when we study how often something occurs or what, if any, relationship exists between two variables. The researcher might seek to learn whether men or women more often select vacation destinations. Methods of descriptive research are: surveys; panels; and observational and other data.

The observational method relies upon the direct observation of physical phenomena in the gathering of data (Goeldner and Ritchie, 2012: 511).

Facts and figures may be obtained by human and mechanical devices. Observation provides an opportunity to collect data about behavior as it actually occurs, but does not tell you why the subjects are doing it. Observation cannot delve into motives, attitudes, or opinions. Observation methods can be used but are rarely reported in the destination marketing literature.

Descriptive research designs generally employ surveys to learn the beliefs and thoughts, behavior, intentions, attitudes, awareness, motivations, and demographic and lifestyle characteristics of people being studied and is usually based on a questionnaire. The advantage of a survey is that information comes directly from the people you are interested in. Survey research is the most common method of collecting quantitative data, which is relatively easy to collect and lends itself easily to statistical analysis.

The survey method through questionnaire can be conducted by the telephone (traditional telephone, computer-assisted telephone interviewing-CATI); by mail (mail/fax interview, mail panel); in person (mall intercept, in home, computer-assisted personal interviewing-CAPI) or electronic (email, internet).

Telephone surveys generally have the advantages of being cheap, the physical appearance of the interviewer does not matter and potential sample size is huge (since most people have access to a telephone) (Finn, Walton and Elliott-White, 2000: 93). The primary advantage of this survey is the speed and low cost. Computer-assisted telephone interviewing (CATI) using random dialing is growing at a rapid pace. A limitation of telephone surveys is that the interview must be short.

The mail questionnaire is useful when extensive questioning is necessary the respondent can complete the questionnaire at their convenience; when large geographical areas must be covered and when it would be difficult to reach respondents (Goeldner and Ritchie, 2012).

Mail surveys provide no direct contact between the researcher and the respondent. This often results in a lack of motivation to respond, but sometimes the respondents may be more willing to fill in sensitive information, such as personal or family characteristics, because they can remain anonymous. They may be more likely to give truthful and honest responses. The questions must be simple and easy to follow, since no interviewer is there to help and the likelihood of misunderstandings and incomplete answers is increased. A major problem with mail surveys is the compilation of an appropriate and accurate mailing list.

Personal interviews are more flexible than telephone or mail interviews. Interviewers can probe more deeply if an answer is incomplete or unclear. Researchers need to be careful that having an interviewer involved doesn't affect the respondent's answer. Often the techniques can be combined. In destination marketing research, the tourists or visitors may be interviewed face to face on arrival about their expectations and at the end of the interview, handed a self-completion questionnaire to be completed at the end of their visit to ascertain experiences and levels of satisfaction and returned by post.

Electronic interviews are Web and mobile questionnaires delivered via a Web Link. This normally uses email or a web page to display the hyperlink (Web link) to the questionnaire and is dependent on having a list of addresses.

Designing the research instrument: questionnaire

The value of a survey questionnaire rests with its design (Seaton and Bennett, 2000: 97).

Deciding on the method of data collection that is right for the research being planned is not easy. The researcher must take into consideration the objectives of the research; must translate the marketing problem into a set of research questions that identify exactly what information is required; determine the appropriate target respondents; decide what data collection methods will be used to survey the respondents; identify any existing constraints (for example, time and budget), and the characteristics of the subject population.

Key attractions of questionnaires to destination researchers include:

- a standardized instrument can be used by multiple interviewers
- ease of administration of large samples
- relatively low cost, particularly using internet-based applications
- large geographic flexibility
- availability of data analysis techniques
- the ability to generalize results to the wider population of interest.

(Pike, 2008: 143)

Tour operators could give out questionnaires to holidaymakers on the flight home; airlines too adopt this approach capitalizing on having a captive audience whose views on the product/ service is at the forefront of their minds, and visitor surveys have applied in the same rationale (Seaton and Bennett, 2000: 65).

Questions wording is important as questions should be written with the potential respondent in mind. Vocabulary, reading level and simple words all must be considered.

Basic principles of the "art" of asking questions are:

1 Be clear and precise
2 Response choices should not overlap and should be exhaustive
3 Use natural and familiar language
4 Do not use words or phrases that show bias
5 Avoid double-barreled questions
6 State explicit alternatives
7 Questions should meet criteria of validity and reliability

The two principal *question formats* are: open and closed questions.

Open question – The respondent is free to write the answer on blank lines below the question. For example:

Please state below the main reason for your visit to this destination.

____

Closed question – the respondent chooses one or more alternatives of answers represented in questionnaire. The alternatives must be defined clearly and meaningfully to the respondents. Sometimes, you can add alternatives: Other (please specify) . . ., don't know, not sure, etc.

What is the major reason for your visit to this destination? Please check one category only.

1 Recreation
2 Business
3 Sightseeing
4 Visit relatives and friends
5 Health
6 Other (please specify) . . .

Question scaling is used to measure the attitudes or opinions of respondents. Semantic differentials and Likert scales are the most commonly used techniques in these surveys.

The Likert scale is most popular for easier construction and administration. Likert scale requires respondents to indicate the level of agreement or disagreement with a statement/s concerning a particular object. A typical five-level Likert item, is:

> To what extent do you agree or disagree that the destination X is very attractive?
>
> 1 Strongly disagree
> 2 Disagree
> 3 Neither agree nor disagree
> 4 Agree
> 5 Strongly agree

Semantic differentials scale combines verbal and diagrammatic techniques by inserting opposing adjectives at either end of the scale such as "bad–good", "strong–weak", "hot–cold" and so on (Finn, Walton and Elliott-White, 2000: 96).

The normal *questionnaire layout* is to begin with the easier questions and move to the more difficult or complicated questions. The sensitive and personal questions are normally placed at the end of a questionnaire.

All questionnaires should be pilot tested (*pretested*) prior to their delivery to assess the validity and likely reliability of the questions (Saunders, Lewis and Thornhill, 2016: 482).

Causal research

Causal research help to understand which variables are the causes (independent variables) and which variables are the effects (dependent variables) of a phenomenon and to determine the nature of the relationship between the causal variables and the effect to be predicted (Malhotra 2015). The experiment is the main method of causal research.

> While this research approach provides the greatest degree of certainty for marketers, the complex and expensive nature of experimental designs has meant that it is the least common in the tourism marketing literature. Causal relationships are extremely difficult to prove because of the difficulty in isolating and controlling the wide range of extraneous variables in the real world, which could also impact on the dependent variable at the time of the experiment.
>
> *(Pike 2008: 144)*

This method in destination research was used by some authors: Gopie and MacLeod, 2009; Kim and Richardson, 2003; Lee and Lockshin, 2012; Michaels, 1993; Morley, 1994; Woodside, 1990, etc.

For example, it is possible for resort areas to run advertising experiments or pricing experiments or to develop simulation models to aid in decision making (Goeldner and Ritchie 2012: 512).

Sampling process and sample size

After deciding on the research approach and instruments, the marketing researcher must design a sampling plan.

The marketing researcher must define the target population. It is usually impossible for marketing managers to collect all information about everyone in a population. Typically, they study only a sample – a representative part of population. Once the sampling unit is determined, a sampling frame must be developed so that everyone in the target population has an equal or known chance of being sampled.

Sample size is influenced by the availability of resources, financial support and time available to select the sample and to collect, input and analyze the data (Saunders, Lewis and Thornhill, 2016: 305).

Qualitative research (it does not aim to draw statistical inference) generally uses nonrandom sampling techniques, and quantitative research (it aims to draw statistical inference) uses random sampling techniques.

A probability sample is selected in such way that every member of the population has an equal chance of being included.

Probability sampling techniques include simple random sampling, systematic sampling, stratified sampling, cluster sampling, sequential sampling and double sampling (Malhotra, 2015: 361).

Non-probability sampling techniques include convenience sampling, judgmental sampling, quota, and snowball sampling (Malhotra 2015: 361).

Step 4: Doing field work/collecting data

Data collection involves field work, contact with respondents. If attention is not paid to ensuring that field work is carried out carefully, the planning that went into the marketing research process to this point has been wasted. Furthermore, if conclusions are drawn based on data that is not reliable due to poor field work, the marketing decision maker may be in a worse position than if no research had been done at all.

Step 5: Preparing and analyzing data

To turn collected data in information, the researcher must prepare and analyze the data. Processing involves editing, coding, and data entry.

Data analysis involves applying non-statistical and statistical techniques to summarize the collected data. Its purpose is to transform the data into meaningful information that will help the marketing manager solve the problem defined at the beginning of the marketing research process.

Thematic analysis, grounded theory method and content analysis are most used approaches to analyze the qualitative data from destination researchers (e.g. Hede, 2005; Martin and Woodside, 2008; Prayag and Ryan, 2011; Ryan and Cave, 2005).

According to Pike (2002) the most popular quantitative data analysis techniques were: factor analysis, t-tests, perceptual mapping, analysis of means, cluster analysis, conjoint analysis, importance-performance analysis, and mapping techniques.

Step 6: Preparing and presenting the report

Finally, the researcher puts the information generated by the analysis into a report. The report should begin with a concise summary of what the research was designed to do, what the results were, and what these results mean in terms of making marketing decisions. The report should be as clear and understandable as possible. The technical details (such as detailed statistical information, sampling, questionnaire forms) should be left to the appendices of the report. Besides a written report, the marketer may request one or more oral reports.

Marketing research and social media

Today, social media has emerged as an important domain for marketing research. Social communities open new avenues for understanding, explaining, influencing and predicting the behaviors of destination visitors/tourists. One of the key developments, both in technology and behavior, relates to user-generated media (UGM). Social media has changed the rules and everyone can use them for free. This ability to create and share content, this UGM, is a key part of the social media revolution.

Key aspects of social media and marketing research include: online research communities/ MROCs; community-enabled in-house panels; participatory blogs; blog and buzz mining; E-ethnography; and social networks and beyond (Poynter, 2010: 394).

Most forms of quantitative research have started to use online data collection, especially via the services of online access panels. Even though, it is still easier to list those areas where online is not a suitable medium as many qualitative researchers choose not to use online equivalents, preferring to stick to face-to-face methodologies.

In contrast to online, social media's history is much newer and far fewer types of project are currently considered suitable. The sorts of projects that tend to use the social media medium include: ethnographic approaches; co-creational research; and ideation and alternative/ additional customer feedback (Poynter, 2010: 399).

Conclusions

Destination marketing research provides the information base for effective decision making by DMOs and their stakeholders. Objective, impartial, translatable, current and relevant information helps managers to develop products, policies, plans, to operate, and control more efficiently and decreases risk in the decision making process. Useful destination marketing research depends on identification and formulation of an accurate and clear problem; research design; carefully data collection, analysis and interpretation; and reliable written report with appropriate recommendations for action.

References

Barry, J. and Proops, J. (1999) Seeking sustainability discourses with Q methodology. *Ecological economics, 28*(3), pp. 337–345.

Davis, C.H. (2003) Traveler perceptions of a destination as a source of new product concepts: Q-method study of summer visitors to the Bay of Fundy. In *Proceedings of the Tourism and Travel Research Association-Canada Annual Conference.*

Dewar, K., Li, W.M. and Davis, C.H. (2007) Photographic images, culture, and perception in tourism advertising: AQ methodology study of Canadian and Chinese university students. *Journal of Travel & Tourism Marketing, 22*(2), pp. 35–44.

Echtner, C.M. and Ritchie, J.B. (1993) The measurement of destination image: An empirical assessment. *Journal of Travel Research, 31*(4), pp. 3–13.

Embacher, J. and Buttle, F. (1989) A repertory grid analysis of Austria's image as a summer vacation destination. *Journal of Travel Research, 27*(3), pp. 3–7.

Fairweather, J.R. and Swaffield, S.R. (2001) Visitor experiences of Kaikoura, New Zealand: an interpretative study using photographs of landscapes and Q method. *Tourism Management, 22*(3), pp. 219–228.

Finn, M., Walton, M. and Elliott-White, M. (2000) *Tourism and leisure research methods: Data collection, analysis, and interpretation.* London: Pearson Education.

Gartner, W.C. and Ruzzier, M.K. (2011) Tourism destination brand equity dimensions: Renewal versus repeat market. *Journal of Travel Research, 50*(5), pp. 471–481.

Goeldner, C.R. and Ritchie, J.B. (2012) *Tourism: principles, practices, philosophies* (No. Ed. 12). New Jersey: John Wiley and Sons, Inc.

Gopie, N. and MacLeod, C.M. (2009) Destination memory: Stop me if I've told you this before. *Psychological Science, 20*(12), pp. 1492–1499.

Hankinson, G. (2004) Repertory grid analysis: An application to the measurement of destination images. *International Journal of Nonprofit and Voluntary Sector Marketing, 9*(2), pp. 145–153.

Hankinson, G. (2005) Destination brand images: a business tourism perspective. *Journal of Services Marketing, 19*(1), pp. 24–32.

Hankinson, G. (2009) Managing destination brands: establishing a theoretical foundation. *Journal of Marketing Management, 25*(1–2), pp. 97–115.

Hanlan, J. and Kelly, S. (2005) Image formation, information sources and an iconic Australian tourist destination. *Journal of Vacation Marketing, 11*(2), pp. 163–177.

Haukeland, J.V., Daugstad, K. and Vistad, O.I. (2011) Harmony or conflict? A focus group study on traditional use and tourism development in and around Rondane and Jotunheimen National Parks in Norway. *Scandinavian Journal of Hospitality and Tourism, 11*(sup1), pp. 13–37.

Hawkins, D. E., Shafer, E. L. and Rovelstad, J. M. (eds), *Tourism Planning and Development Issues.* Washington, DC: George Washington University, pp. 381–92.

Hede, A.M. (2005) Sports-events, tourism and destination marketing strategies: an Australian case study of Athens 2004 and its media telecast. *Journal of Sport Tourism, 10*(03), pp. 187–200.

Hem, L.E. and Iversen, N.M. (2004) How to develop a destination brand logo: A qualitative and quantitative approach. *Scandinavian Journal of Hospitality and Tourism, 4*(2), pp. 83–106.

Hugé, J., Velde, K.V., Benitez-Capistros, F., Japay, J.H., Satyanarayana, B., Ishak, M.N., Quispe-Zuniga, M., Lokman, B.H.M., Sulong, I., Koedam, N. and Dahdouh-Guebas, F. (2016) Mapping discourses using Q methodology in Matang Mangrove Forest, Malaysia. *Journal of Environmental Management, 183*, pp. 988–997.

Hussey, M. and Duncombe, N. (1999) Projecting the right image: using projective techniques to measure brand image. *Qualitative Market Research: An International Journal, 2*(1), pp. 22–30.

Katsura, T. and Sheldon, P. (2008) Forecasting mobile technology use in Japanese tourism. *Information Technology & Tourism, 10*(3), pp. 201–214.

Kaynak, E. and Cavlek, N. (2007) Measurement of tourism market potential of Croatia by use of Delphi qualitative research technique. *Journal of East-West Business, 12*(4), pp. 105–123.

Kaynak, E. and Macaulay, J.A. (1984) The Delphi technique in the measurement of tourism market potential: the case of Nova Scotia. *Tourism Management, 5*(2), pp. 87–101.

Kaynak, E. and Marandu, E.E. (2006) Tourism market potential analysis in Botswana: a Delphi study. *Journal of Travel Research, 45*(2), pp. 227–237.

Kaynak, E. and Marandu, E.E. (2011) Variations in tourism market potential in an emerging economy: Theoretical perspectives and analytical insights. *Journal of Quality Assurance in Hospitality & Tourism, 12*(1), pp. 1–27.

Kaynak, E. and Pathak, R.D. (2006) Tourism Market Potential of Small Resource-Based Economies: The Case of Fiji Islands. *Research Yearbook.*

Kaynak, E., Bloom, J. and Leibold, M. (1994) Using the Delphi technique to predict future tourism potential. *Marketing Intelligence & Planning, 12*(7), pp. 18–29.

Kibedi, G. (1981) Future trends in international tourism. *The Tourist Review, 36*(1), pp. 3–6.

Kim, H. and Richardson, S.L. (2003) Motion picture impacts on destination images. *Annals of tourism research, 30*(1), pp. 216–237.

Klenosky, D.B., Gengler, C.E. and Mulvey, M.S. (1999) Understanding the factors influencing ski destination choice: A means-end analytic approach. *Consumer behavior in travel and tourism, 25*(4), pp. 59–80.

Komppula, R. (2014) The role of individual entrepreneurs in the development of competitiveness for a rural tourism destination – A case study. *Tourism Management, 40*, pp. 361–371.

Kruja, D. and Hasaj, A. (2010) Comparisons of stakeholders' perception towards the sustainable tourism development and its impacts in Shkodra Region (Albania). *Turizam vol. 14 (1).*

Kruja, D. and Gjyrezi, A. (2011) The special interest tourism development and the small regions. *Turizam, 15*, pp. 77–88.

Lee, R. and Lockshin, L. (2012) Reverse country-of-origin effects of product perceptions on destination image. *Journal of Travel Research, 51*(4), pp. 502–511.

Lin, V.S., Liu, A. and Song, H. (2015) Modeling and forecasting Chinese outbound tourism: An econometric approach. *Journal of Travel & Tourism Marketing, 32*(1–2), pp. 34–49.

Linstone, H.A. and Turoff, M. eds. (1975) *The Delphi method: Techniques and applications* (Vol. 29). Reading, MA: Addison-Wesley.

MacKay, K.J. and Fesenmaier, D.R. (1997) Pictorial element of destination in image formation. *Annals of tourism research, 24*(3), pp. 537–565.

Mackenzie, C.A. (2012) Accruing benefit or loss from a protected area: Location matters. *Ecological Economics, 76*, pp. 119–129.

Malhotra, N.K. (2015) *Essentials of Marketing Research: a hands-on orientation.* London: Pearson Education.

Martin, D. and Woodside, A.G. (2008) Grounded theory of international tourism behavior. *Journal of Travel & Tourism Marketing, 24*(4), pp. 245–258.

Martín-Santana, J.D., Beerli-Palacio, A. and Nazzareno, P.A. (2017) Antecedents and consequences of destination image gap. *Annals of Tourism Research, 62*, pp.13–25.

McKercher, B., Wong, C. and Lau, G. (2006) How tourists consume a destination. *Journal of Business Research, 59*(5), pp. 647–652.

Michaels, C.F. (1993) Destination compatibility, affordances, and coding rules: A reply to Proctor, Van Zandt, Lu, and Weeks. *Journal of Experimental Psychology: Human Perception and performance, 19*, pp. 1121–1127.

Morley, C.L. (1994) Experimental destination choice analysis. *Annals of tourism research, 21*(4), pp. 780–791.

Pan, S.Q., Vega, M., Vella, A.J., Archer, B.H. and Parlett, G.R. (1996) A mini-Delphi approach: An improvement on single round techniques. *Progress in tourism and hospitality research, 2*(1), pp. 27–39.

Pearce, D.G. and Schänzel, H.A. (2013) Destination management: The tourists' perspective. *Journal of Destination Marketing & Management, 2*(3), pp. 137–145.

Perdue, R.R. (2000) Destination images and consumer confidence in destination attribute ratings. *Tourism Analysis, 5*(2–3), pp. 77–81.

Pike, S. (2002) Destination image analysis – a review of 142 papers from 1973 to 2000. *Tourism management, 23*(5), pp. 541–549.

Pike, S. (2003) The use of repertory grid analysis to elicit salient short-break holiday destination attributes in New Zealand. *Journal of Travel Research, 41*(3), pp. 315–319.

Pike, S. (2007) Repertory grid analysis in group settings to elicit salient destination image attributes. *Current Issues in Tourism, 10*(4), pp. 378–392.

Pike, S. (2008) *Destination marketing: An integrated marketing communication approach.* Oxford: Elsevier Butterworth-Heinemann.

Poynter, R. (2010) *The handbook of online and social media research: Tools and techniques for market researchers.* UK: John Wiley & Sons.

Prayag, G. (2007) Exploring the relationship between destination image and brand personality of a tourist destination: An application of projective techniques. *Journal of Travel and Tourism Research, 2* (Fall 2007), pp. 111–130.

Prayag, G. and Ryan, C. (2011) The relationship between the 'push'and 'pull' factors of a tourist destination: The role of nationality–an analytical qualitative research approach. *Current Issues in Tourism, 14*(2), pp. 121–143.

Richards, G. and Munsters, W. eds. (2010) *Cultural tourism research methods.* Preston, UK: Cabi.

Ryan, C. and Cave, J. (2005) Structuring destination image: A qualitative approach. *Journal of travel research, 44*(2), pp. 143–150.

Salk, R., Schneider, I.E. and McAvoy, L.H. (2010) Perspectives of sacred sites on Lake Superior: The case of Apostle Islands. *Tourism in Marine Environments, 6*(2–1), pp. 89–99.

Saunders, M., Lewis, P. and Thornhill, A. (2016). *Research methods for business students.* London: Pearson Education.

Seaton, A.V. and Bennett, M.M. (2000) *Marketing of tourism products: Concepts, issues and cases.* London: International Thomson Business Press.

Seely, R.L., Iglars, H. and Edgell, D. (1980) Utilizing the Delphi technique at international conferences: a method for forecasting international tourism conditions. *Travel Research Journal*, (1), pp. 30–36.

Singal, M. and Uysal, M. (2009) Resource commitment in destination management: The case of Abingdon, Virginia. *Turizam: znanstveno-stručni časopis, 57*(3), pp. 329–344.

Stephenson, W. (1953) *The study of behavior; Q-technique and its methodology.* Chicago: University of Chicago Press.

Stergiou, D. and Airey, D. (2011) Q-methodology and tourism research. *Current Issues in Tourism, 14*(4), pp. 311–322.

Stringer, P. (1984) Studies in the socio-environmental psychology of tourism. *Annals of Tourism Research, 11*(1), pp. 147–166.

Tasci, A.D. and Gartner, W.C. (2007) Destination image and its functional relationships. *Journal of Travel Research, 45*(4), pp. 413–425.

Tideswell, C., Mules, T. and Faulkner, B. (2001) An integrative approach to tourism forecasting: A glance in the rearview mirror. *Journal of Travel Research, 40*(2), pp. 162–171.

Timmermans, H., Heuden, R. and Westerveld, H. (1982) The identification of factors influencing destination choice: an application of the repertory grid methodology. *Transportation, 11*(2), pp. 189–203.

Tinsley, R. and Lynch, P. (2001) Small tourism business networks and destination development. *International Journal of Hospitality Management, 20*(4), pp. 367–378.

Tinsley, R. and Lynch, P.A. (2007) Small business networking and tourism destination development: A comparative perspective. *The International Journal of Entrepreneurship and Innovation, 8*(1), pp. 15–27.

Usakli, A. and Baloglu, S. (2011) Brand personality of tourist destinations: An application of self-congruity theory. *Tourism Management, 32*(1), pp. 114–127.

Wagner, O. and Peters, M. (2009) Can association methods reveal the effects of internal branding on tourism destination stakeholders? *Journal of Place Management and Development, 2*(1), pp. 52–69.

Walmsley, D.J. and Jenkins, J.M. (1993) Appraisive images of tourist areas: application of personal constructs. *The Australian Geographer, 24*(2), pp. 1–13.

Wassler, P. and Hung, K. (2015) Brand-as-Person versus Brand-as-User: An Anthropomorphic Issue in Tourism-related Self-Congruity Studies. *Asia Pacific Journal of Tourism Research, 20*(8), pp. 839–859.

Woodside, A.G. (1990) Measuring advertising effectiveness in destination marketing strategies. *Journal of Travel Research, 29*(2), pp. 3–8.

4

Marketing tourism experiences

Merve Aydogan Cifci, Gurel Cetin and Fusun Istanbullu Dincer

Introduction

The markets and theories trying to explain consumer behaviour are evolving rapidly. New approaches emerge to explain changing economies and consumers' behaviours. One of the contemporary models trying to conceptualize and understand organizational success and to create value for the customer in the post-modern world is framed by Pine and Gilmore (1998) as the *Experience Economy*. According to them, markets have been evolving from functional to experiential offerings and there are four phases of economic value offered by firms. These are commodities, goods, services and finally experiences. They claim markets have been progressing from commodities to experiences.

Memorable, enjoyable, novel and engaging consumption experiences are becoming critical in creating loyal customers that spread positive word of mouth. Hence, customer experiences are used to explain the evolution in consumer behaviour from functional (e.g. rational) to hedonistic (e.g. emotional) behaviours. Traditional competitive advantages are also shifting from product features and service characteristics to experiences offered by organizations. Tourism is an experience intensive service and experiences are the main outcomes from a trip. Despite there is a wide consensus on the importance of guest experiences, its adoption to marketing strategies has been a difficult task for practitioners and planners in tourism destinations.

Traditional marketing theories are insufficient in explaining changing tourist behaviours. Hence creating, pricing, communicating and distributing experiences are still fuzzy concepts in tourism destination marketing. This section of the book is an initial step to adopt the concept of customer experiences to tourism destinations' marketing strategies. By comparing components of experiential marketing with traditional marketing, the study provides implications on production, pricing, promotion and distribution of tourist experiences.

Tourism experience

Although experience is not a new concept, there are various approaches in different disciplines to this phenomenon. For instance, from a philosophical perspective experience is defined as "a personal trial which generally transforms the individual" (Caru and Cova, 2003). For a destination marketing book however, experience would not be understood as a notion that describes one's daily cognitive routine (Uriely, 2005), but as an economic phenomenon. Experience is not studied in leisure contexts before the 1970s (Csikszentmihalyi, 1975). As the understanding of leisure, hospitality and tourism evolved gradually after the 1970s, the epistemology of experience in a tourism context also changed and expanded. Tourism experience can be defined as a combination of goods and services, which engage tourists on a personal level and provide memorable feelings that are likely to be shared with others (Gao et al. 2012). Larsen (2007) also defined tourist experience as "a past personal travel-related event strong enough to have entered long-term memory".

Another approach to experience typology in tourism considers the intensity of experience. Quan and Wang (2004) imply that there are two types of experience: the peak and the supporting experiences. The peak experience is differentiated from supporting experience based on its novelty and one's personal background. For instance, for a nature-based tourist the scenery from the pulpit rock in Norway might be the peak experience, and accommodation facilities or the restaurants that he/she used while getting to Ryfylke might create the supporting experiences.

For a better understanding of the tourist experience from the perspective of destination marketing, a network of experiential factors in an organization or a destination might also be examined. The elements of such a network system would consist of locals, physical environment, other tourists, local entrepreneurs as well as hotels, travel agencies, guides, attractions, events and governmental agencies (Binkhorst and Dekker 2009). All of these elements might play a role in shaping the tourist experience. Thus, tourist experience is explained from different perspectives and closely relates to consumer behaviour and marketing in tourism literature.

Experiential marketing in tourism

Experience economy as a new phenomenon also requires a shift in the traditional understanding of marketing (Park, Ha and Park, 2017). Tourism is considered among experience intensive services and primary examples for the experience economy (Quan and Wang, 2004). Therefore, experiential marketing is particularly important for destinations' overall success in a tourism context. Tsiotsou and Ratten (2010) also discuss that experiential marketing has recently become the cornerstone of marketing strategies particularly in tourism.

Verma and Jain (2015) argue that experiential marketing has become influential for two reasons. First, there is a process of mass commoditization of products and services in the tourism industry and second the consumer profile is shifting from rational to emotional decision makers. Similarly, Pine and Gilmore (1998) explain the evolution of experiential marketing based on: diffusion and improvements in technology, increasing competitive intensity, the progress of economic value from commodities to experiences, and rising affluence. Because the tourism market is competitive and unstable, experiential marketing strategies become essential to differentiate tourism products among others (Yoon and Lee, 2017).

Experience, in the context of tourism as an economic activity, is related to tourists' higher-order needs (excitement, enjoyment, novelty, prestige), socialization and learning (Prebensen et al. 2014). On the other hand, marketing tourism experiences is concerned with identification of these needs, converting them into wants and exceeding expectations by providing a delightful service. Because the needs are highly dependent on time, place, customer involvement and other environmental variables, they are almost infinite in variety and amount (Goldsmith and Tsiotsou, 2012) and usually unknown even to the consumer himself. Thus tourism organizations should consider identifying hidden needs and exceeding new expectations rather than merely meeting and satisfying existing desires.

Table 4.1 Traditional marketing versus experiential marketing

	Traditional marketing	*Experiental marketing*
Focus	Functional features and benefits	Customer experiences and emotions
Products	Narrowly defined	Consumption is a holistic experience
Customers	As rational decision makers	As emotional animals
Methods	Analytical and quantitative	Eclectic and qualitative

Source: Adapted from Frochot and Batat (2013)

A tourist experience is a mental perception of physical environment (e.g. decoration, scenery, background music) and social interactions (e.g. professionalism, courtesy, attitude) (Cetin and Walls, 2016). Hence, tourist experience is considered as very personal (Volo 2009). Thus, it is unlikely to have a single objective evaluation for experiences (Scott et al., 2009). Tourists have individual and unique experiences and standardization and production of an experience become difficult. Since tourism experiences are subjective and unstable (Volo, 2009), marketing experiences should be adapted to certain circumstances.

Traditional marketing strategies generally focus on service excellence and customer satisfaction rather than creating extraordinary memories. Experiential marketing on the other hand focuses on customer experiences versus features, characteristics and benefits of products. In experiential marketing, the product is holistic, versus narrowly defined. Experiential marketing treats customers as emotional decisions makers rather than rational buyers. Marketing research methods are also eclectic versus analytical and qualitative rather than numeric (see Table 4.1) (Frochot and Batat 2013). For instance, while traditional marketing emphasizes benefits (e.g. cleanliness and price of a hotel room) to convince potential clients, experiential marketing position the brands on feelings created in the facilities.

Unlike traditional tourism marketing activities, the main objective of experiential tourism and hospitality marketing is to transform daily events and perceptions into unique and memorable experiences. Sidali et al. (2015) suggest various managerial guidelines to provide memorable experiences. These are; (1) provision of a theme to contextualize the experience and staging it by means of a story, (2) harmonization of impressions, (3) avoidance of negative cues, and (4) creation of material and sensory memorabilia to reinforce recollections. Therefore, experiential marketing activities for tourism are related to providing novel products and services different from the competition that are integrated and engage travelers in an emotionally personal way. For a better understanding of experiential marketing, experience and marketing strategies can also be discussed in the context of marketing mix (4Ps: Product, Price, Promotion and Place). The marketing mix and its adoption in experiential marketing are explained in the following sections.

Experiential products and services

Product and product related decisions are among most important factors affecting the long-term effectiveness of marketing strategies. Because experiences usually appear during the consumption process, products and services are the main sources of experiences in tourism industry. Smith (1994) discusses tourism product and processes as inseparable and the production utilizes intermediate inputs such as facilities and services to generate final outputs as experiences. In other words, guest experiences are usually produced at the augmented product level rather than the basic product or service. The core product in a hotel is a clean and safe bed; however, it is the surrounding services and destination features, offering different potential positive experiences, which convince travellers to pay higher rates.

Another challenge in sustaining experiences is when they are standardized and homogenized they lose their essence and become ordinary and impersonal. As soon as the supporting services become standard, they might no longer create the desired outcome. Hence, customization and innovation becomes important to create extraordinary experiences and drive customer value in the long run. For example, *Burning Man* is an event held annually attracting thousands of experience seeker travellers to Black Rock Desert in Nevada. One of the success factors of this event is that it is organized with different themes every year so as not to become ordinary. Novel ideas, new technological adoption, tourism trends, creative co-creation are continuously needed for attracting and sustaining visitors.

Another continuous source of extraordinary guest experiences is service staff. Professional, friendly and motivated staff might also create the desired experiences. Cetin and Walls (2016) found social interactions with staff as more important than physical attributes in creating tourist experiences. Unlike physical components of an experience, social interactions are harder to imitate as well. The importance of staff in tourism cannot be stressed enough and is already covered in *internal marketing* and *service profit chain* literature elsewhere.

Experiences are also considered to extend the product life cycle for an organization (Cetin, 2012). By the time a destination reaches stagnation, its product and services should be updated to offer different experiences. If the evolution of experiences is found to be successful by the customers, the tourism product life cycle rejuvenates. In order to continue their success, tourism destinations need to reinvent what tourists might expect and desire in a way that creates new memorable experiences differentiating the destinations from previous experiences and competitors (Tung and Ritchie, 2011).

Creativity and innovation are essential to generate unique tourism experiences. Experiences are creative offerings because they are unexpected, they have various meanings for tourists and they are co-created by various tourism networks. Co-creation of experiences adds value to both tourists and organizations by contributing to the uniqueness and authenticity of the products and services at the destination. Without a creative component, differentiation is not possible, and the product becomes ordinary without an experiential element. Hence integrating arts, culture, and festivals to destination experience becomes significant (Karayilan and Cetin, 2016).

A major challenge in creating experiential products and services is the ability to customize and keep these offerings novel on a mass scale. When standardized, experiences might lose their authenticity and become ordinary. Mass customization is one way to solve this problem for large organizations and destinations that host millions of guests every year. Using technology in personalizing the services is one way to customize services on a mass scale. Offering location based services, utilizing RFID technology, using artificial intelligence to suggest activities for travellers are various tools to be used in customizing travellers' experiences.

Experiential value and price

Price is another major component in tourism destination marketing considering the perishable and intangible nature of services. Compared to the traditional value that is believed to be acquired after the exchange, experiential value is derived during the consumption. Even though creating experiences during the service encounter costs much time, finance and energy, tourism marketers still consent to these costs because of the positive impact experiences create on customers' recommendation and loyalty behaviours (Binkhorst and Dekker, 2009). The fact that experiences are memorable and worthy of being shared with others results in repeat purchases and referrals. Besides these advantages, customers are also willing to pay more for the additional experiential value.

The customization of experiences for customers is another way to reduce price sensitivity. Tourists might have different needs based on their personal (e.g. demographic) and tripographic (e.g. trip motivation) profiles. Rather than standard products, marketers would offer different combinations of experiences so that customers would choose among different offerings and pay a price premium (Adhikari et al., 2013) for different experiences (e.g. business lounge). Pricing of an intangible and subjective experience requires a thorough analysis of both market characteristics and product value. Customer evaluations about utility of products and services vary whether it is just a single service available elsewhere or a bundle of unique experiences. This price subjectivity can also be used as a revenue management tool and a driver of unplanned consumption which provides additional revenue for tourism organizations.

Experiences are also believed to create a unique value hard to be imitated by competition. Hence, price sensitivity of customers seeking experiences is also lower than for standard services. For example, entrance fees to the nightclubs or a supplement for the live music can be considered as a fee paid for the experience inside the facility. Because of the experiential offering, customers are willing to pay more for the same liquor they would consume outside cheaper. Tourists also use their past experiences to determine their reference prices. If a destination fails to exceed past experiences for a higher price, the rate might as well be considered unfair which would result in customer churn. In order to make correct price positioning, the tourism organizations should take previous prices and customer profiles into consideration in addition to customer's willingness to pay. Thus, experiential offerings must be priced based on target customers rather than based on costs or competition.

As stressed before, in the tourism context experiences are co-created by customers. Thus, customer engagement is another pre-requisite. Hence, destination marketers need to think continuously about how to involve customers in their service production and delivery. Ikea's success is very dependent on the creative component in their products. Customers build their own furniture using the manuals included in the package. Besides involving customers and creating an intellectual experience, this engagement even helps Ikea to reduce its transportation and inventory costs. The co-creation process of experiences causes both positive and negative impacts on costs and revenue. Benihana is one of the restaurants that assists customers to customize their own food by discussing it with the chef while he/she is cooking at the front of the table. Hence special equipment, additional staff and training might also be required for some of the experiential tourism products. Yet as long as these additional services create valuable positive experiences for customers as happened for Benihana, guests would be willing to pay for the difference.

Price is also used as a clue by the customers about the quality of experiences offered by tourism service providers. Because of the intangible nature of these services and asymmetric information in the market, the rating of a facility is used to reduce the uncertainty and risk attained to tourism purchases. Thus, price is associated with the quality of experiences and creates some expectations. This is why the tourism industry is able to charge very different prices for the same basic product (e.g. safe and clean bed) (Cetin and Istanbullu Dincer, 2014). However, with recent developments in tourism distribution systems and emergence of powerful online travel agencies (OTAs) this perception is also shifting and tourism product pricing is being depressed by the commodification created in online channels (Cetin et al., 2016). This issue will be tackled further in the distribution (Place) section.

Experiential communication and promotion

Another element of the marketing mix is promotion. When an organization advertises using visual clues, the consumers see, recognize and combine the messages with past experiences and make a decision. A tourist does not just see, hear, touch, smell or taste while travelling. Rather, he/she is physically, emotionally and intellectually involved and uses his/her whole body and mind to feel and understand usually an unfamiliar surrounding (Laursen, 2008). People are more receptive to experiential clues during their trips than their daily life in their regular surroundings. Thus, tourism marketing communications should focus on authentic experiential clues rather than ordinary messages. For example, Bombay (one of the destinations providing medical services for eye surgeries) has been promoted for medical tourism by using an attractive message; "open your new eyes on the beach at Juha" (Connell, 2006).

Promotion of tourism experiences should appeal to all five senses (sight, sound, smell, taste and texture). Hence, destination managers and marketers must design multi-sensory experiential products to add value to ordinary tourism services (Agapito et al., 2013) and communicate them using sensory clues. Barnes et al. (2014) also found that visitor behaviours are primarily driven by sensory experiences and he suggests that tourism marketers should focus on drawing attention to the five senses. To promote multi-sensory experiential products, destination management organizations should also use multi-sensory channels that create emotional, intellectual and spiritual feelings and make customers desire the illustrated experiences. Images, videos, testimonies, metaphors and themes are also useful.

Guerrilla marketing is one of the contemporary ways of marketing experiences. Different from traditional promotional methods, these tactics are considered unconventional, cheaper and more effective. Guerrilla marketing activities tend to be communicated in public spaces such as streets and recognized as creative, surprising, personal and memorable. A café might use a large hot coffee pot on the street, to attract customers into the facility or a beach destination would use real sand in design of their booth in a travel fair for a more effective experiential communication with its target. In the promotion context, Tresidder (2015) proposes that marketing language should also consist of a very particular set of words, images and contextual structures that presents organization's experiential promises such as escape, authenticity, luxury and hedonism.

Another aspect of experiential marketing communications is creation of slogans. Slogans are used to create a desire to experience the tourism product in potential tourists' minds. Laursen (2008) discusses the case of New York City's slogan, which is *Mirror yourself in Manhattan. What happens in Vegas stays in Vegas* is another example that suggests the type of experience offered in the destination. Ritz Carlton's *We are ladies and gentlemen serving ladies and gentlemen* also suggests clues about the quality of the service and treatment of guests. Since slogans try to introduce experiences offered in a destination or an organization, they have to be consistent, memorable, welcoming, and attractive. Experiences differentiate from services by motivating tourists more at an emotional rather than cognitive level. Experiential messages do not use price as their main USP (Unique Selling Proposition).

Using a theme or a story in promotional material can also make a tourism product memorable and meaningful (Mossberg 2007). Appealing stories may be used to communicate to customers' emotional needs and improve their desire to purchase. For instance, Sternberg (1997), investigates Niagara Falls based on two elements which are *staging* (desirable motif) and *thematising* (integrating motif to other concepts; terror, history, authenticity, romance etc.). He argues experiences should be marketed by myths, histories and fantasies appealing the customer's imaginative associations. For example, Sweden may be marketed to people who want to experience places made up of ice. The Ice Hotel can be promoted by offering the theme of an arctic experience with arts on ice. Framing the experience with this theme, Ice Hotel is able to charge 500 Euros for an overnight in rooms five degrees below zero.

Before designing promotional messages, marketers should identify the features of their products and services, the experience they desire to create, their target markets and their characteristics thoroughly. Failure to do so might result in a *Paris Syndrome* which is a set of physical and psychological symptoms that are experienced by tourists and travellers who visit Paris for the first time and realize that the city is not quite as they imagined, contrary to what is communicated in the media (Frochot and Batat, 2013). This syndrome indicates that there needs to be a match between the features of the tourism product, customer characteristics and motivation, and design and communication of promotional messages. The fact that positive experiences create a desire to be shared with others through word of mouth also makes communication of experiences easier and more effective for destinations. Encouraging and facilitating customer-to-customer (C2C) interaction through direct e-mails, social media and blogs are also important strategies.

Experiential distribution and place

Place, also referred to as distribution channels, plays an important role in tourism particularly during the pre-purchase experiences of guests. One of the features of tourism services is that their production and consumption are inseparable, meaning that tourists need to come to the destination to consume tourism services. This has implications on distribution channels in tourism. Besides the direct channels offered by tourism organizations such as call centers, brand.com (e.g. hotel's web site) and other direct communication mediums, there are also various intermediaries such as travel agencies and tour operators usually located accessible to the customers at the origin. Particularly because of the inseparability of tourism services, destinations used to be dependent on these intermediaries.

Yet, distribution of tourism services has evolved during the past few decades. With the wide adoption of internet, traditional travel agencies lost most of their power in the distribution and brand.com became an important medium. Hotels had an opportunity to reach and communicate with the end customer directly in a cost-effective way. However, the evolution of e-commerce has also created large online travel agencies (OTAs) which have started to dominate the markets and destinations, which have now become dependent on these OTAs. These *e-mediaries* are well developed through online channels and provide various benefits for organizations such as the *billboard effect* (Anderson, 2009). Yet, because few large players dominate the OTA market, these metamediaries also pose some threats for tourism destinations and the experiences they offer (Cetin et al., 2016).

Traditional offline travel trade organizations usually know their suppliers, clientele and what their preferences are. However, OTAs serve millions and their relations with customers are based on transactions, datasets and algorithms. Gretzel and Fesenmaier (2002) also argue that existing online distribution systems providing functional information, fail to communicate in a holistic, experiential and conversational way needed for tourism services. One of the negative effects of these OTAs is the commodification. Hundreds of hotels are listed in every destination and OTAs' listings are usually designed based on benefits offered to OTAs rather than to the guests. Pine and Gilmore (1999) also state commodification as a real threat for sustaining experiences. Participants in tourism distribution systems try to avoid the commodification of experiences (Kracht and Wang 2010). Because of standard OTA templates, it is also very complicated for suppliers to differentiate their product based on experiential offerings at different OTAs. Price based competition rather than value based pricing on OTAs is another factor affecting the intensity of commodification.

Another disadvantage of online distribution is that because these OTAs are accessible through the internet to everyone, the ability to target different customers with different characteristics is also reduced. Cetin and Walls (2016) discuss other customers and interaction among them as an important part of the experience. An incompatible and heterogeneous customer base would affect guest experiences negatively (Verhoef et al., 2009). When present on large OTAs, hotels also lose their ability to fence undesirable markets, and customers segment themselves rather than marketers (King, 2002). For example, a hotel that targets families with children might have to confirm reservations of a soccer fun club made through OTAs.

Thus, tourism services should be very selective in their distribution. Rather than being listed in every possible channel, hotels and other services should concentrate on channels operating without the rate parity rule and valuing the individual characteristics of a differentiated product portfolio (Cetin et al., 2016). Hence rather than an intensive distribution that uses many middlemen, tourism services should choose to have a selective list of channel members that are compatible and controllable. The success of Apple is also attributed to their selective distribution strategy (Pine and Gilmore, 1999). Rather than being in every department store, Apple sells its products in specialized Apple stores only. With their special design and trained staff, these middlemen are able to offer a consistent Apple experience. DMOs should also facilitate a collective stand against these meta-mediaries (e.g. commission rates).

An experiential offering however would also reach to its customers through social media. One of the characteristics of unique experiences is that they create a desire to be shared with others (Cetin and Bilgihan, 2016). Cetin et al. (2016) also discuss reputation as the next stage of tourism distribution after reintermediation through OTAs. As long as positive experiences are created, the services will be promoted by existing customers to a large number of potential customers through social media and the dependency on OTAs as intermediaries will be reduced. Thus, organizations need to focus on creating great experiences to their customers and the rest would be handled by C2C interaction through positive word of mouth on third party social media channels and blogs.

Conclusions

This section of the book explores the experiential marketing approach to destination marketing within the context of the marketing mix (4Ps). First, the experience concept is defined, tourist experiences are discussed and experiential marketing is explained and compared with traditional marketing. Various suggestions and examples are also provided concerning product, price, promotion and distribution strategies for the tourism industry and destinations. DMOs and individual stakeholders might use these suggestions and strategies in order to create, communicate, evaluate and distribute their experiential offerings to their target customers.

A tourist experience is a combination of services and products consumed and activities attended during the trip. Positive experiences are usually created by meaningful, novel and extraordinary services and perceptions that are remembered by tourists. Experiential marketing thus would be defined as all the activities targeted to create memorable positive experiences, adding value to the trip that communicates with tourists via multi-sensory tools and reaches them in a selective way. Offering new, authentic, and novel products and services, theming the experience in a harmonious way, involving tourists into production and letting them co-create their own experiences, pricing based on value offered rather than based on costs or competition, communicating through novel mediums and using tools that target various senses, selecting the correct distribution channels that are able to represent the holistic experience the destination offers are other strategies that might be adopted by destinations and the tourism industry.

Table 4.2 Traditional tourism marketing and experiential tourism marketing compared

4Ps	*Traditional tourism marketing*	*Experiential tourism marketing*
Product	Goods, services	Memories, feelings
Price	Cost, competition	Customers
Promotion	Visuals and text	Multi-sensory
Place	Every possible channel	Selective channels only

Table 4.2 is a summary of the distinctions between traditional and experiential tourism marketing. Experiential tourism marketing focuses on the augmented product rather than the basic and expected goods and services. The main aim is to create positive feelings and events that are novel enough to be stored in long-term memory using physical facilities and service processes. Because of the subjective nature of experiences, the production should also be flexible and customizable to individual needs. Co-creation, innovation and tourist involvement are other concepts that relate to production of positive experiences. Because novelty is an important component of tourist experiences, using authentic clues that represent the locality in design of the experiencescape might also be suggested.

Since these extraordinary experiences are not available elsewhere, tourism organizations in the destination are advised to price their services based on the experiential value rather than costs and competition. The marketing communications should also be designed consistent with distinctive experiences destinations desire to create. These messages should appeal to all five senses and include emotional, spiritual and intellectual references. Using multi-sensory tools and media, organizations might offer clues about the experiences. The marketing communications should also be consistent and refer to a theme or a story. Finally, the evolving distribution channels have been very important in tourism services. Yet, there are challenges with commodification created by large OTAs. These online distribution systems also prevent an effective segmentation strategy. A consistent purchasing experience is only possible with a selective distribution system that would reflect the overall experience that the destination and tourism organizations offer.

The factors that might affect positive experiences are extensive and multi-dimensional. Although organizations cannot grant experiences without the involvement and participation of their customers, they can construct the environment to facilitate customer experiences to emerge. This chapter explored the experiential marketing in destinations by comparing it with traditional marketing. Implications for marketing experiences in the tourism industry are also discussed for each of the individual components of the marketing mix. Because experiences and marketing are closely related, future empirical studies on experiential marketing in tourism would shed more light on creation, communication, pricing and distribution strategies for tourism destinations in the experience economy.

References

Adhikari, A., Amiya, B., & Raj, S.P. (2013) "Pricing of experience products under consumer heterogeneity," *International Journal of Hospitality Management*, 33, 6–18.

Agapito, D., Mendes, J., & Valle, P. (2013) "Exploring the conceptualization of the sensory dimension of tourist experiences," *Journal of Destination Marketing & Management*, 2, 62–73.

Anderson, C.K. (2009) "The Billboard effect: Online travel agent impact on non-OTA reservation volume," *Cornell Hospitality Reports*, 9, (16), 5–6.

Barnes, S.J., Mattsson J., & Sorensen, F. (2014) "Destination brand experience and visitor behavior: Testing a scale in the tourism context," *Annals of Tourism Research*, 48, 121–139.

Binkhorst, E. & Dekker, T.D. (2009) "Agenda for co-creation tourism experience research," *Journal of Hospitality Marketing & Management*, 18 (2–3), 311–327.

Caru, A., & Cova, B. (2003). "Revisiting consumption experience: A more humble but complete view of the Concept,". *Marketing Theory*, 3 (2), 267–286.

Cetin, G. (2012) "The Impact of Customer Experience on Loyalty and Recommendation in Hospitality," (Unpublished Doctoral Dissertation), Istanbul University, İstanbul, Turkey.

Cetin, G. & Bilgihan, A. (2016) "Components of cultural tourists' experiences in destinations," *Current Issues in Tourism*, 19 (2), 137–154.

Cetin, G. & Istanbullu Dincer, F. (2014) "Influence of customer experience on loyalty and word-of-mouth in hospitality operations," *Anatolia*, 25 (2), 181–194.

Cetin, G. & Walls, A. (2016) "Understanding the customer experiences from the perspective of guests and hotel managers: Empirical findings from luxury hotels in Istanbul, Turkey," *Journal of Hospitality Marketing & Management*, 1–30.

Cetin, G., Aydogan Cifci, M., Istanbullu Dincer, F. & Fuchs, M. (2016) "Coping with reinter mediation: The case of SMHEs," *Journal of Information Technology and Tourism*, 1–18.

Connell, John, (2006), "Medical Tourism: Sea, Sun, Sand and . . . Surgery," *Tourism Management*, 27, 1093–1100.

Csikszentmihalyi, M. (1975) *Beyond Boredom and Anxiety: The Experience of Play in Work and Games,* San Francisco: Jossey-Bass Publishers.

Frochot, I. & Batat, W. (2013) *Marketing and Designing the Tourist Experience*, Oxford: Goodfellow Publishers.

Gao, L., Scott, N., Ding, P. & Cooper, C. (2012) "Tourist experience development: Designed attributes, perceived experiences and customer value," in Tsiotsou, R.H. & Goldsmith, R.E. (eds), *Strategic Marketing in Tourism Services*, Bingley: Emerald Group Publishing, 215–230.

Goldsmith, R.E & Tsiotsou, R.H. (2012) "Introduction to experiential marketing," in Tsiotsou, R.H. & Goldsmith, R.E. (eds), *Strategic Marketing in Tourism Services*, Bingley: Emerald Group Publishing, 207–214.

Gretzel, U. & Fesenmaier, D.R. (2002) "Building narrative logic into tourism information systems," *IEEE Intelligent Systems*, 17 (6), 59–61.

Karayilan, E., & Cetin, G. (2016). "Tourism destinations: Design of experiences," in Sotiriadis, M. & Gursoy, D. (ed.), *The Handbook of Managing and Marketing Tourism Experiences*, Bingley: Emerald Group Publishing, 65–83.

King, J. (2002) "Destination marketing organizations: Connecting the experience rather than promoting the place," *Journal of Vacation Marketing*, 8 (2), 105–108.

Kracht, J. & Wang, Y. (2010) "Examining the tourism distribution channel: Evolution and transformation," *International Journal of Contemporary Hospitality Management*, 22 (5) 736–757.

Larsen, S. (2007) "Aspects of a psychology of the tourist experience," *Scandinavian Journal of Hospitality & Tourism*, 7 (1), 7–18.

Laursen, B. (2008) "What makes Rome: ROME? A curious traveller's multisensory analysis of aspects of complex Roman experiences," in Sundbo, J. & Darmer, P. (eds) *Creating Experiences in the Experience Economy*, Cheltenham: Edward Elgar Publishing, 60–82.

Mossberg, L. (2007). "A marketing approach to tourist experience," *Scandinavian Journal of Hospitality and Tourism*, 7, 59–74.

Park, K., Ha, J. and Park, J.Y., 2017. An Experimental Investigation on the Determinants of Online Hotel Booking Intention. *Journal of Hospitality Marketing & Management*, 26(6), 627–643.

Pine, B. J., & Gilmore, J.H. (1998) "Welcome to the experience economy," *Harvard Business Review*, 76, 97–105.

Pine, B.H. & Gilmore, J.H. (1999) *The Experience Economy: Work is Theater and Every Business a Stage*, Boston: Harvard Business School Press.

Prebensen, N.K., Chen, J.S. & Uysal, M. (2014) "Co-creation of tourist experience: Scope, definition and structure," in Prebensen, N.K., Chen, J.S. & Uysal, M. (eds) *Creating Experience Value in Tourism*, Oxfordshire: Cab International Publishing, 1–10.

Quan, S. & Wang, N. (2004) "Towards a structural model of the tourist experience: An illustration from food experiences in tourism," *Tourism Management*, 25, 297–305.

Rihova, I., Buhalis, D., Moital, M. & Gouthro, M.B. (2015) "Conceptualising customer-to-customer value co-creation in tourism," *International Journal of Tourism Research*, 17, 356–363.

Scott, N., Laws, E. & Boksberger, P. (2009) "The marketing of hospitality and leisure experiences," *Journal of Hospitality Marketing & Management*, 18 (2–3), 99–110.

Sidali, K.L., Kastenholz, E. & Bianchi, R. (2015) "Food tourism, niche markets and products in rural tourism: combining the intimacy model and the experience economy as a rural development strategy," *Journal of Sustainable Tourism*, 23 (8–9), 1179–1197.

Smith, S.L.J. (1994) "The tourism product," *Annals of Tourism Research*, 21 (3), 582–595.

Sternberg, E. (1997) "Iconography of the tourism experience," *Annals of Tourism Research*, 24 (4), 951–969.

Tresidder, R. (2015) "Experiences marketing: A cultural philosophy for contemporary hospitality marketing studies," *Journal of Hospitality Marketing & Management*, 24 (7), 708–726.

Tsiotsou, R., & Ratten, V. (2010) "Future research directions in tourism marketing," *Marketing Intelligence & Planning*, 28 (4), 533–544.

Tung, V. W.S., & Ritchie, J. (2011) "Exploring the essence of memorable tourism experiences," *Annals of Tourism Research*, 38 (4), 1367–1386.

Uriely, N. (2005) "The tourist experience: Conceptual development," *Annals of Tourism Research*, 32 (1), 199–216.

Verhoef, P.C., Lemon, K.N., Parasuraman, A., Roggeveen, A., Tsiros, M., & Schlesinger, L.A. (2009) "Customer experience creation: Determinants, dynamics and management strategies," *Journal of Retailing*, 85, 31–41.

Verma, Y. & Jain, V. (2015) "How experiential Marketing is used in Indian Luxury Hotels?" *Romanian Journal of Marketing*, 1, 2–11.

Volo, S. (2009) "Conceptualizing experience: A tourist based approach," *Journal of Hospitality Marketing & Management*, 18 (2–3), 111–126.

Yoon, S.J. and Lee, H.J., 2017. Does Customer Experience Management Pay Off? Evidence from Local versus Global Hotel Brands in South Korea. *Journal of Hospitality Marketing & Management*, 26(6), 585–605.

Further reading

Bitner, M.J. (1992) "Servicescapes: The impact of physical surroundings on customers and employees," *J Marketing*, 56, 57–71. (Design of physical environment and service processes)

Csikszentmihalyi, M. (1991) *Flow*. New York: HarperCollins. (Peak experience)

Gilmore, J.H., & Pine, B. J. (2002) "Differentiating hospitality operations via experiences: Why selling services is not enough," *Cornell Hotel and Restaurant Administration Quarterly*, 43 (3), 87–96. (Importance of themes in Hospitality)

Holbrook, M.B & Hirschman, E.C. (1982), "The experiential aspects of consumption: Consumer fantasies, feelings and fun," *Journal of Consumer Research*, 9, 132–140. (Earlier experience concept in consumption)

Otto, J.E & Ritchie, J.R.B. (1996) "The service experience in tourism," *Tourism Management*, 17 (3), 165–174. (Earlier experiential perspective to tourism)

Schmitt, B. (2003) *Customer Experience Management: A Revolutionary Approach to Connecting with your Customer*, New Jersey: John Wiley and Sons, Inc. (Experiential marketing)

5

Entrepreneurial marketing in tourism and hospitality

How marketing practices do not follow linear or cyclic processes

Frode Soelberg, Frank Lindberg and Øystein Jensen

Introduction

Marketing remains a central issue within tourism and hospitality research. As a complex phenomenon tourism has been approached from a wide spectrum of disciplines (Darbellay and Stock 2012) and tourism marketing related problems have frequently been addressed by researchers from various disciplinary backgrounds, for example tourism geography (Lew and Duval 2010; Buhalis 2000). However, it can be asked whether the dominant perspectives within tourism marketing research have the sufficient range to keep up with the challenges of contemporary tourism (Li and Petrick 2008; Hall 2008). It can be questioned to what extent marketing frameworks applied by researchers from non-marketing related disciplines generally are sufficiently up-dated compared to recent developments within marketing research, such as within marketing strategy (Hall 2005, 2008; Buhalis and Costa 2006), and the marketing-entrepreneurship interface (Hills et al. 2008).

A main challenge for tourism marketing is to deal with the complexity and fragmented structure of the industry, fluctuations in demand and the dependency of local firms to the geographical area where they are located with regard to resources, product offerings and their roles as hosts for tourists and other travelers. We draw on key tenets of entrepreneurial marketing for the study of applied marketing for entrepreneurs in the contexts of tourism and hospitality (Siu and Kirby 1998; Chaston 2000; Grant and Perren 2002; Bjerke and Hultmann 2002; Hills et al. 2008). This stream of research suggests that new ventures are challenged with an array of problems particular to them. These are associated with limited experience, modest size, and their uncertain and turbulent markets (Gruber 2004). Notably, these challenges are prone to be present in many industries including tourism and hospitality (Bhidé 2000).

Recent developments within entrepreneurial marketing question the relevance of traditional marketing management in new or very young ventures (Gruber 2004; Fletcher and Watson 2007; Jones and Holt 2008). The purpose of this chapter is therefore to study marketing practices of new tourism and hospitality firms. However, the question; "How is marketing performed in new ventures?" has been raised by several researchers, but few studies have so far addressed how marketing models and theories are used and practised in businesses (Mason et al. 2015).

We are thus interested in how dominant models and theories related to the marketing management school (Shaw and Jones 2005) are applied in practice. We reject the notion of marketing in new businesses as unprofessional, unsophisticated, or DIY (Do-It-Yourself) marketing (Carson, 1985), and instead argue for increased understanding of the circumstances in which models and theories are put to work in entrepreneurial marketing within tourism and hospitality. There is a need to investigate how the entrepreneurs use the models, how their networks of relevant stakeholders influence such use, and how the models are represented and translated due to changed conditions of the venture.

Theory

Marketing management school

The traditional model of marketing is rooted in the "social exchange paradigm" (Bagozzi 1975), and the mainstream interpretation of this paradigm is inspired by the concept of rationality. Thus, the marketing management school of thought "follows the positivist sequence of analysis, planning, control" (Baker 2016: 13). This theory of marketing is therefore perceived as rational or analytical, and it focuses on how organizations *should* market their products and services. Fundamentally, the analysis and planning of marketing mix elements such as distribution, pricing, product planning, selling and advertising still dominates the marketing field (Shaw and Jones 2005). The rationale behind this focus is the idea that effectiveness of the marketing mix effects business sales and the market share of an industry. Thus, the planning of segmentation, products, prices, distribution and communications becomes the primary objective for managers who aim at satisfying the needs and wants of customers.

There has been increasing acceptance of the idea that a market driven strategy (e.g., Kohli and Jaworski 1990; Webster 1994) may have important limitations, both in entrepreneurial and other contexts, as it plays down the relevance of innovation (Mohr and Sarin 2009). Recent perspectives have criticized the exchange focus of the marketing management school. Especially relevant for tourism and hospitality are relationship marketing (Grönroos, 2004; 2006), service-dominant logic (SDL) (Vargo and Lusch, 2004; 2008) and experiential marketing (Prahalad and Ramaswamy, 2004; Mossberg, 2007) that argue for a change from goods logic towards service or experiential logic of marketing. In the heart of the new developments lies the acknowledgement of the (intangible) nature of value co-creation which take place as processes among several relational partners (e.g., customers, producers) that contribute with different kind of resources. Thus, the transaction based marketing model is questioned in tourism and hospitality research (Li and Petrick 2005), and the manner in which marketing is performed in entrepreneurial marketing can be understood in terms of relationships and processes.

Entrepreneurial marketing in practice

Entrepreneurship and marketing are separate streams of academic interest, but there is an overlap between the two fields that has been labeled entrepreneurial marketing (Hills and LaForge 1992). A wide range of subjects is of interest to entrepreneurial marketing scholars (Hills et al. 2008) such as marketing tactics, market entry strategies, and innovation, but presumably inspired by Shane and Venkataraman's (2000) seminal definition of entrepreneurship, there are two major topics in entrepreneurial marketing: opportunity recognition, and opportunity exploitation.

Within research on opportunity recognition, two classical streams of research dominate. These take the advantage of the seminal writings of Schumpeter (1983); the concept of entrepreneurship as disruptive innovation and Kirzner (1973); defining entrepreneurship as the discovery of business opportunities. The common thread in classical writings is the notion of the latency of business opportunities. Latency holds that business opportunities are preexisting and await discovery by the alert entrepreneur. However, Kirznerian thought implies the acknowledgement of a market process that involves entrepreneurial creativity, industrial partners, customers, and competitors, and a dialectic perspective is thus implied. Accordingly, business opportunities are created in a process, involving several actors. It would therefore be incorrect to put Kirzner into the latency frame of thinking. The major sources of inspiration to entrepreneurial marketing therefore have different ontological viewpoints, but pass on to the latency of business opportunities. Thus, research findings are often in contrast to its philosophical underpinnings (Chabaud and Ngijol 2004), resulting in an emerging awareness in the entrepreneurial marketing literature that new perspectives are in demand (Bruyat and Julien 2000; Sarason et al. 2006; Fletcher and Watson 2007; Hansen et al. 2011). The emerging perspective is inspired by the market process view, suggesting that entrepreneurs, opportunities and contexts are idiosyncratic; i.e. that entrepreneurial marketing activities are lived experiences of situated entrepreneurs that are always involved in dialogues within contexts and time.

The research stream on opportunity exploitation is leaning towards marketing theory, and is typically focusing on strategy and tactics. Two schools of thought can be identified in entrepreneurial contexts (Fjelldal-Soelberg 2010); a normative school aiming for a more innovative way of doing marketing and a descriptive school aiming for interpreting marketing practices. Thus, the first school is heavily influenced by marketing management and suggests how marketing strategy and tactics may become more creative, and/or innovative, and less bureaucratic. The Schumpeterian notion of entrepreneurship takes the high ground in the normative school of thought. The second school is interpretative as it takes a marketing in practice approach. The much broader Kirznerian (2008) view inspires radical, modified and copied business opportunities as involved in entrepreneurial marketing practice.

Applying a marketing in practice view on entrepreneurial marketing implies that any marketing activity is a lived experience of a situated entrepreneur. The dialectic perspective differs from rationalism (objective world view) on one hand, and constructivism (subjective world view) on the other, by claiming that reality is a product of dialogue (intersubjective world view). A practice theory "looks at how meaning are produced and reproduced in an evolving dialectic between everyday life and wider cultural forces" (Saren 2016: 47). As actors are dynamic, entrepreneurs are not isolated or static beings. They are always involved in dialogues ("interactions-with") within contexts and time. Furthermore, these dynamic characteristics define the experiences and the construction of meaning. The marketing challenges involved in developing prosperous businesses, and how entrepreneurs handle these, are the focal point of this perspective.

Marketing practices in hospitality and tourism

Tourism and hospitality entrepreneurs frequently demonstrate limitations in systematic planning and business skills (Getz and Carlsen 2000; Hjalager 2010; Komppula 2013; Richie and Crouch 2003). As the close consumer-producer interaction within many local businesses tends to influence product innovations (Hjalager 2010; Eide and Mossberg 2013) it can be assumed that close consumer–producer relationships have an impact on the way the firms are marketing themselves. Local tourism companies are generally quite dependent on the assets and the attractiveness of the place or destination where they are located. From a holistic perspective they offer single elements of a wider destination product that consist of several complementary product elements and they are, moreover, influenced by the image or brand of that destination (Buhalis 2000). The emphasis on non-economic factors (such as history, culture and social capital) and local learning for territorial industry development (Aasheim, 2001) should be of particular relevance for the development of tourism destinations where a great proportion of the attraction resources and their particular characters initially are of a non-economic nature (Buhalis 2000; Krippendorf 1980). The destination as source of a "place identity" also embraces the identity of the local entrepreneur who needs to cope with this in the cooperation with other community stakeholders in the business performance (Hallak et al. 2012). The competitiveness of local business actors will thus be influenced by the competitiveness of the destination as a whole (Crouch, 2011) as well as by joint efforts of competence development and deployment of local resources (Denicolai et al. 2010). Despite such interdependence between local entrepreneurs and other stakeholders on both local and global levels, local tourism entrepreneurs frequently do not seem to see the consequences of their actions in the bigger picture (Richie and Crouch 2003) and this would also have an impact of their marketing performance. One reason for this could be a resistance towards too much rational planning as that could take away some of the joy of working as "lifestyle entrepreneurs" (Getz and Nilsson 2005) where achieving lifestyle goals is significant compared to making profits (Getz and Petersen 2005; Hallak et al. 2012).

Method

A hermeneutical framework was applied for the study of entrepreneurial marketing practices (Alvesson and Sköldberg 2009; Thompson 1997). To interpret and understand the use of marketing throughout the course of the start-up period, the researchers have focused on the experiences of the entrepreneur through a circular interplay between his/her practice (micro) and relational partners and the context of the venture (meso) and the conditions for business start-up in Norway (macro). By attaining an interpretive focus onto these three levels we tried to overcome the weakness of subjectivist approaches in entrepreneurial marketing.

We aimed at studying processes the entrepreneurs undergo, such as how they learn and cope (Wenger 1998) dealing with marketing models and theories during planning processes prior to start-up and during the initial phases of the start-up. It was important to follow the social practices to which the entrepreneur belonged, and how they zoomed in and out of various use situations involving multiple actors and stakeholders.

The empirical investigations are primarily based on in-depth interviews with nine Norwegian entrepreneurs who were preoccupied with startup of tourism and hospitality ventures. The entrepreneurs, five women and four men, did not have any prior experience in starting businesses. A dialectical approach developed insights in collaboration with actors in the actual context, and a four-step data collection was performed; 1) exploratory phase (including identification and recruitment of entrepreneurs), 2) in-depth interviews, 3) document analyses (business plans, marketing plans, tactical deliberations), 4) follow up interviews (including entrepreneurs' review of transcripts). The data collection lasted more than 12 months, and its findings originate from "thick descriptions" (Ponterotto 2006) of the tourism and hospitality ventures. The data were analyzed through part/whole spiral logic of (pre)understanding–interpretation–understanding, with the aim of meaning condensation (Kvale and Brinkmann 2009).

Findings

The entrepreneurs in the sample have all participated in business start-up training organized by Innovation Norway, a governmental funded agency that supports innovation and development of Norwegian companies. It was, therefore, not surprising that all of them had a written business/

marketing plan. This points towards a formal marketing process in new hospitality ventures, as all of the reviewed business plans contained market information, analyses and tactical dispositions. Thus, taken at face value the new ventures are performing a formalized strategic process. However, when exploring the marketing process in practice a different picture emerges. The overall impression is that the entrepreneurs struggle with applying the marketing plan as intended.

> [planning] is very useful, but it's so hard to follow through. You see, I have all these ideas on marketing tactics – but the financial situation is dragging me down. So, my plans [aren't very realistic]
>
> *(Entrepreneur no 2)*

Apparently, the financial situation is critical, but it may also be the case that the entrepreneur is underestimating the difficulties and overestimating the potential in the process of planning (Karlsson 2005). This may explain why many entrepreneurs engage in opportunistic adaptation – described by Bhidé (2000) as having a detailed written plan and not sticking to it in real life. However, the marketing process in the new ventures seems to be continuous, but importantly, it changes in style when start-up training is over.

> [I] do think it through, and staying focused was a valuable lesson learned in start-up training, but I'm not spending time on writing a business plan: It's time consuming and I have better ways to spend precious time.
>
> *(Entrepreneur no 8)*

We find that start-up training triggers formal marketing planning, and that some of the ideas herein – i.e. the importance of having a strategic focus – remain essential as the process changes into strategic thinking. Notably, intuitive entrepreneurial strategy (Bengtsson and Skärvad 2001) was not found in the sample. But, we found several instances of applying rules of thumb like "having satisfied customers is the best way to promote the business" – and the heuristics (Busenitz and Barney 1997) of entrepreneurial decision-making were thereby highlighted. A mix of heuristics, market analysis and other market planning activities appears simultaneously in several cases, also reported by Vaghely and Julien (2010). Our findings show that entrepreneurs engage in formal marketing planning due to external pressure – in this case during start-up training, which they experience as a challenge due to the highly unsecure and complex circumstances. To understand the tense situation, one has to appreciate the desperate financial position most new ventures and their entrepreneurs have to deal with. This causes several creative ways to fund the business – also called bootstrapping (Bhidé 1992). One of these funding strategies is to apply for support from governmental agencies, which demand marketing plans as part of the application. Certain institutional pressure from salient stakeholders thereby causes the practice of both informal heuristics *and* analytic marketing planning in these firms.

The entrepreneurs express that they find themselves in a contradictory situation. On one hand the governmental agencies require formal marketing plan as a precondition for financial support. On the other hand, the entrepreneurs do not regard such plans as feasible in practice because formal planning requires resources such as skills, time and money which they do not have (despite start-up training). Thus, the entrepreneurs keep the planning regime at an arm's length.

> I'm an entrepreneur; I'm neither good at administrating nor planning.
>
> *(Entrepreneur no 3)*

The entrepreneurs are situated in a role conflict because they do not want to enter the role as "market planner". They express a distance toward the role and are actually denying the self that is implied in the role since the "term role distance was introduced to refer to actions which effectively convey some disdainful detachment of the performer from a role he is performing" (Goffman 1972: 98). The entrepreneur therefore tries to twist and turn their situated role to achieve control of the definition of the situation. When this manoeuver is not possible, then we have a role conflict that leads to role distance.

> [the marketing plan] wasn't realistic, it was just a piece of paper that I needed to secure the funds. I knew it had to look good and I worked with determination to achieve my goal – so I worked on the budget, the strategy and tactics, but it was pure fantasy. I haven't looked at the plan since then.
>
> *(Entrepreneur no 5)*

To transcend the situation they fake the market planner role. Thus, entrepreneurs adapt to the governmental initiated regime both by honest internalization (i.e., doing their best), and by a more cunning opportunism: In order to qualify for support a *pro forma* plan is written without the intention to follow through.

The entrepreneurs have difficulties in pinpointing the origin and the action that enable them to "find" or recognize an opportunity. In general, they do not point at any frustrating periods or situations when they have problems generating business opportunities. However, the challenge involves transforming an idea into viable business.

> Our [initial] idea? I'm not sure if I remember what it was – you know, we've been going back and forth on this and never really agreed on what this business is about. It's been a long journey, and some of the things we've done are conscious decisions, but mostly they're not – hey, let's be honest, most things in life are coincidental.
>
> *(Entrepreneur no 1)*

The entrepreneurs give accounts of opportunity recognition that implies that business opportunities do not appear in form of an epiphany. Even though prior research argues that opportunity recognition often occurs as a rational process (Schwartz and Teach 2000), our informants point at practices in which rationality seems to be an inadequate concept and phenomenon. The entrepreneurs instead account of long-term crafted opportunities.

> What happened was that things started to change, it was more like the snowball rolling down a hill. Ideas and refinements just kept on coming in an endless stream, and the business has moved far away from the original idea.
>
> *(Entrepreneur no 6)*

We find that entrepreneurs are embedded in interactive marketplace processes in which they engage in relationships with customers, other entrepreneurs and businesses, and relevant industrial networks. Our findings show that the contact with customers is generating an opportunity crafting process which is gaining in momentum as the entrepreneur applies interactive marketing towards salient customers. Thus, we do not find support for the argument that business opportunities are latent in the marketplace (Schwartz and Teach 2000). Our results suggest instead a shift in perspective and support an emerging view on business opportunities as crafted in an interactive marketing process.

> I've been travelling around, meeting people, customers, potential partners – small businesses, big businesses – working really hard to gain a foothold, and the more I'm out there, the better my ideas become.
>
> *(Entrepreneur no 9)*

The findings challenge the "latency-of-opportunities" view, and implies that traditional marketing planning, even though strongly advocated by the marketing management literature (e.g., Kotler 2000), may have limited value to entrepreneurs when crafting business opportunities in a tourism and hospitality context.

Prior research show that entrepreneurs have a tendency of acting before planning (Bhidé 2000; Deacon and Spilsbury 2004), and that this preference for acting throws the entrepreneur into market relations.

> It all happened very quickly. All of a sudden, customers were calling and I had to set up ways to register bookings and preferences as I was speaking to them.
>
> *(Entrepreneur no 4)*

Throughout the initial processes of start-up, the customer relationships resume a character of opportunity testing that the entrepreneur then acts upon and generates strategic and tactical adjustments. In tourism and hospitality contexts, we find that the entrepreneur faces several opportunities and chooses to perform testing through acts of interactive marketing towards primarily customers and other central stakeholders. Notably, the first customers emerge through interactive marketing – a finding very common in research on new ventures (Stokes 2000; Mankelow and Merrilees 2001; Roukalainen 2008). The rather urgent financial situation that characterizes new ventures makes it impossible to ignore the importance of generating sales. However, the entrepreneurs point at another reason why the first customer and the first sale plays an important role; it contributes to opportunity crafting. Even though the new venture appears to be set up somewhat hastily, it is attracting initial stakeholder relations that spur a creative and adaptive process that has profound effect on opportunity recognition and exploitation. The findings indicate that opportunity recognition and opportunity exploitation are inseparable events. The findings challenge the latency of opportunities perspective, and the adequacy of a traditional linear and cyclic approach to marketing in tourism and hospitality.

Discussion and conclusion

Few empirical studies have so far addressed how marketing theories are used and "performed" in marketing practice (Mason et al. 2015). The purpose of this chapter has been to apply an entrepreneurial marketing perspective for exploring the practices or performativity of marketing in new tourism and hospitality firms. Instead of being preoccupied with the application of central tenets of the marketing management school (Shaw and Jones 2005), e.g. how *well* entrepreneurs apply marketing mix elements to achieve a successful startup, we have been interested in the consequences of activities, practices, doing and sayings during their startup. Through a longitudinal investigation we have been able to reveal some of their marketing efforts through the lens of opportunity recognition and exploitation (Shane and Venkataraman 2000).

Our results support prior research that claims that entrepreneurs within the tourism and hospitality industry possess limited business skills (Komppula 2013). However, in a Norwegian context the government is aware of such shortcoming and offers entrepreneurs start-up seminars so that they may become intelligible actors in the marketplace. At the heart of such seminars is the planning of strategic marketing which is close to a copy of the normative marketing plan model which can be found in most basic marketing textbooks. One may expect then that the performance of tourism and hospitality entrepreneurs would follow this prescriptive model of the marketing management school when establishing their firms. Instead, our results show that entrepreneurs are entangled into pragmatic use of theories and models in dialectic and dynamic processes together with stakeholders. Such pragmatic use is colored by the context (i.e. culture and industry) of the firm and the situation (i.e. time and place) of the entrepreneurs. Unexpectedly, the consequence of adjusting to the marketing plan model resulted in role conflicts (on a personal level) in early stages of the start-up process which had consequences for the pragmatic use of marketing tools in later phases.

The pragmatic use of theories and models is expected to ease the start-up process, the producer-customer interaction and customer satisfaction. Prior research has theorized expectations of improved competitive advantage and profitability (Mason et al. 2015), but tourism and hospitality ventures depend on close contact with customers and other local stakeholders (e.g., Destination Marketing Organizations) where they are located. Consequently, the (innovative) design of products depends on intangible resources where the customers play an important role as co-creating partner (Eide and Mossberg 2013) in addition to the image and brand of the destination (Buhalis 2000). Other marketing decisions, such as prizing, depend on informal relationships found in the personal networks of the entrepreneur in addition to the results of the early producer-customer interactions. In line with prior research (Getz and Carlsen 2000; Hallak et al. 2012) our results show that lifestyle goals are important for entrepreneurs in tourism and hospitality contexts which may explain why expected profits are not the only important outcome of pragmatic use of marketing theories and models.

In the process of adapting a pragmatic use of marketing, opportunity recognition and exploitation are interdependent and overlapping (idiosyncratic events). Our findings show that the entrepreneurs "throw" themselves into the practices of marketing, in which they continuously struggle with the demands and challenges of various stakeholders in the making of the new venture. Although they face stakeholders (e.g., government, banks) that demand the use of cyclic and linear approaches in their marketing practices, they refuse to adjust to a rational-analytic marketing planner role. This situation creates role conflicts (cf. Goffman 1972) because they do not have the skills and they do not feel comfortable in the role as a "marketing planner". However, if they do not perform the role they will not be able to get funding from the government and banks to start their business. The solution to this dilemma is to "fake" the role as a "market planner" and construct a nice looking, but fake, marketing plan so that stakeholders are convinced that the marketing strategy is feasible. The outcome of this process was that the entrepreneurs became aware of the rigid rationality of the cyclic marketing management plan, and this resulted in the rejection of such a performance of marketing. While the application of marketing theories may nurture business performance (Morgan 2001), central stakeholders (e.g., government agency) do not question whether models and theories actually work. Instead, the "model use" demonstrated here is an example of its malfunction in non-felicitous circumstances (Mason et al. 2015).

This study demonstrates that the predominant marketing practices within the context investigated (tourism and hospitality ventures in Norway) are not in line with the linear and/or cyclic conceptualization of the marketing management school. Instead, marketing in such ventures is, characterized by a non-cyclical process which implies a step away from traditional conceptualizations.

The findings contribute to new insights into opportunity recognition, marketing strategy, and marketing tactics of new entrepreneurial firms. Thus, further research on marketing performativity in tourism and hospitality start-ups is in demand.

References

Aasheim, B. (2001). "Localiced Learning, Innovation and Regional Clusters". In Å. Mariussen *Cluster Policies – Cluster Development.* Stockholm: Nordregio report 2001:2.

Alvesson, M., and Sköldberg, K. (2009). *Reflexive Methodology. New Vistas for Qualitative Research,* 2nd edn. London: SAGE Publications Ltd.

Bagozzi, R. P. (1975). "Marketing as Exchange," *Journal of Marketing*, October, pp 32–39.

Baker, M. (2016). "Marketing: Philosophy or function?" in Baker, M. J., and Saren, M. (eds) *Marketing Theory*, SAGE.

Bengtsson, L., and Skärvad, P-H. (2001). *Företagsstrategiska perspektiv*, Studentlitteratur.

Bhidé, A. (1992). "Bootstrap finance: The art of start-ups," *Harvard Business Review*, 70, 109–117.

Bhidé, A. (2000). *The origin and evolution of new businesses*, Oxford University Press.

Bjerke, B., and Hultman, C. M. (2002). *Entrepreneurial Marketing: The Growth of Small Firms in the New Economic Era*, Cheltenham: Edward Elgar.

Bruyat, C., and Julien, P-A. (2000). "Defining the field of research in entrepreneurship," *Journal of Business Venturing*, 16, 165–180.

Buhalis, D. (2000). "Marketing in the competitive destination of the future," *Tourism Management*, 21, 97–116.

Buhalis, D., and Costa, C. (2006). *Tourism Management Dynamics: Trends, Management and Tools*, London: Butterworth Heinemann.

Busenitz, L. W., and Barney, J. B. (1997). "Differences between entrepreneurs and managers in large organizations: Biases and heuristics in strategic decision-making," *Journal of Business Venturing*, 12, 9–30.

Carson, D. (1985). "The evolution of marketing in small firms," *European Journal of Marketing*, 5(19), 8–16.

Chabaud, D., and Ngijol, J. (2004). "The recognition of market opportunities by entrepreneurs: Towards a constructivist perspective," UIC-symposium on marketing and entrepreneurship, Conference proceedings, UIC.

Chaston, I. (2000). *Entrepreneurial Marketing: Competing by challenging convention*, London: MacMillan Business.

Coviello, N. E., Brodie, R. J., and Munro, H. J. (2000). "An investigation of marketing practice by firm size," *Journal of Business Venturing* 15, 523–545.

Crouch, G. I. (2010). "Destination competitiveness: An analysis of determinant attributes," *Journal of Travel Research* 50(1), 27–45.

Darbellay, F., and M. Stock (2012). "Tourism as complex interdisciplinary research object," *Annals of Tourism Research*, 39(1), 441–458.

Deacon, J. H., and Spilsbury, H. (2004). "Planning for marketing at the interface: Multiple views from Wales," Proceedings of the UIC-conference on Entrepreneurship and Marketing, UIC.

Denicolai, S., Cioccarelli, G., and Zucchella, A. (2010). "Resource-based local development and networked core-competencies for tourism excellence," *Tourism management*, 31(2), 260–266.

Eide, D., and Mossberg, L. (2013). "Towards More Intertwined Innovation Types: Innovation through Experience Design Focusing on Customer Interactions," in Sundbo J., and Sørensen, F. (eds.) *Handbook on the Experience Economy*, Cheltenham, UK: Edward Elgar, 248–69.

Fjelldal-Soelberg, F. (2010). *Entreprenøriell markedsføring: En studie av Entreprenørskap og markedsføring som overlappende fenomen (Entrepreneurial Marketing: The Marketing-Entrepreneurship Interface)*, Bodø Graduate School of Business, Ph.D. serie 23.

Fletcher, D. E., and T. J. Watson (2007). "Entrepreneurship, Management Learning and negotiated Narratives: Making it Otherwise for Us – Otherwise for Them," *Management Learning*, 38(1), 9–26.

Getz, D., and Carlsen, J. (2000). "Characteristics and goals of family and owner-operated businesses in the rural tourism and hospitality sectors," *Tourism management*, 21(6), 547–560.

Getz, D., and Nilsson, P. A. (2004). "Responses of family businesses to extreme seasonality in demand: the case of Bornholm, Denmark," *Tourism management,* 25(1), 17–30.

Getz, D., and Petersen, T. (2005). "Growth and profit-oriented entrepreneurship among family business owners in the tourism and hospitality industry," *International Journal of Hospitality Management*, 24(2), 219–242.

Goffman, E. (1972). *Encounters: Two Studies in Sociology of Interaction*, Harmondsworth, UK: Penguin Books.

Grant, P., and L. Perren (2002). "Small business and entrepreneurial research," *International Small Business Journal*, 20(2), 185–211.

Grönroos, C. (2004). "The relationship marketing process: communication, interaction, dialogue, value," *Journal of Business & Industrial Marketing*, 19(2), 99–113.

Gruber, M. (2004). "Marketing in New Ventures: Theory and Empirical Evidence," *Schmalenbach Business Review*, 56(April), 164–199.

Hall, C. M. (2005). *Tourism: Rethink the Social Science of Mobility*, Ontario: Pearson.

Hall, C. M. (2008). *Tourism Planning. Policies, Processes and Relationships*, Harlow, UK: Pearson Education Limited.

Hallak, R., Brown, G., and Lindsay, N. J. (2012). "The Place Identity–Performance relationship among tourism entrepreneurs: A structural equation modelling analysis," *Tourism Management*, 33(1), 143–154.

Hansen, D., Shrader, R., and Mollnor, J. (2011). "Defragmenting Definitions of Entrepreneurial Opportunity," *Journal of Small Business Management*, 49(11), 283–304.

Hills, G. E., Hultman, C. M., and Miles, M. P. (2008). "The evolution and development of entrepreneurial marketing," *Journal of Small Business Management*, 46(1), 99–112.

Hills, G. E, and LaForge, R. W. (1992). "Research at the Marketing Interface to Advance Entrepreneurship Theory," *Entrepreneurship Theory and Practice*, Spring, 33–59.

Hjalager, A.-M. (2010). "A review of innovation research in tourism," *Tourism Management*, 31(1), 1–12.

Jones, O., and Holt, R. (2008). "The creation and evolution of new business ventures: an activity perspective," *Journal of Small Business and Enterprise Development*, 15(1), 51–73.

Karlsson, T. (2005). *Business plans in new ventures: An institutional perspective*, JIBS Dissertation Series, no 030.

Kirzner, I. M. (1973). *Competition and Entrepreneurship*, University of Chicago Press.

Kirzner, I. M. (2008). *The alert and creative entrepreneur: A clarification*, IFN Working paper no. 760, New York University.

Kohli, A. K., and Jaworski, B. J. (1990). "Market orientation: the construct, research propositions, and managerial implications," *Journal of Marketing*, 54(2), 1–18.

Komppula, R. (2014). "The role of individual entrepreneurs in the development of competitiveness for a rural tourism destination–A case study," *Tourism Management*, 40: 361–371.

Kotler, P. (2000). *Marketing Management*, 11 ed. Englewood Cliffs, NJ: Prentice Hall.

Krippendorf, J. (1980). *Marketing im Fremdenverkehr*, Bern: Peter Lang A.G.

Kvale, S., and Brinkmann, S. (2009). *Interviews: Learning the craft of qualitative research interviewing*, 2nd ed. Los Angeles, CA: Sage.

Lew, A. A., and Duval, D. T. (2008). "Geography and tourism marketing: topical and disciplinary perspectives," *Journal of Travel & Tourism Marketing*, 25(3–4), 229–232.

Li, X. R., and Petrick, J. F. (2008). "Tourism Marketing in an Era of Paradigm Shift," *Journal of Travel Research*, 46: 235–244.

Mankelow, G., and Merrilees, B. (2001). "Towards a model of entrepreneurial marketing for rural women: A case study approach," *Journal of Developmental Entrepreneurship*, Norfolk, Dec.

Mason, K., Kjellberg, H., and Hagberg, J. (2015). "Exploring the performativity of marketing: theories, practices and devices," *Journal of Marketing Management*, 31(1–2), 1–15.

Mohr, J. J., and Sarin, S. (2009). "Drucker's insight on market orientation and innovation: implications for emerging areas in high-technology marketing," *Journal of the Academy of Marketing Science*, 37, 85–96.

Morgan, M. S. (2001). "Models, stories and the economic world," *Journal of Economic Methodology*, 8, 361–384.

Mossberg, L. (2007). "A marketing approach to the tourist experience," *Scandinavian Journal of Hospitality and Tourism*, 7(1), 59–74.

Ponterotto, J. G. (2006). "Brief Note on the Origins, Evolution, and Meaning of the Qualitative Research Concept Thick Description," *The Qualitative Report*, 11(3), 538–549.

Prahalad, C. K., and Ramaswamy, V. (2004). "Co-creation experiences: The next practice in value creation," *Journal of Interactive Marketing*, 18(3), 5–14.

Ritchie, J. B., and Crouch, G. I. (2003). *The competitive destination: A sustainable tourism perspective*. Wallingford: CABI.

Ruokolainen, J. (2008). "Constructing the first customer reference to support the growth of a start-up software technology company," *European Journal of Innovation Management*, 11(2), 282–305.
Sarason, Y., Dean, T., and Dillard, J. F. (2006). "Entrepreneurship as the nexus of individual and opportunity: A structuration view," *Journal of Business Venturing*, 21(3), 286–305.
Saren, M. (2016). "Marketing Theory," in Baker, M. J., and Saren, M. (eds). *Marketing Theory*, SAGE.
Schumpeter, J. A. (1983). *The theory of economic development*, Transaction Publishers.
Schwarz, R. G., and Teach, R. D. (2000). "A Model of Opportunity Recognition and Exploitation: An Empirical Study of Incubator Firms," *Journal of Research in Marketing & Entrepreneurship*, 2(2), 93–107.
Shane, S., and Venkataraman, S. (2000). "The promise of entrepreneurship as a field of research," *Academy of Management Review*, 25(1), 217–226.
Shaw, E. H., and Jones, B. (2005). "A history of schools of marketing thought," *Marketing Theory*, 5(3), 239–281.
Siu, W., and D. A. Kirby (1998). "Approaches to small firm marketing: A critique", *European Journal of Marketing*, 32 (1/2), 40–60.
Stokes, D. (2000). "Entrepreneurial marketing: a conceptualisation from qualitative research," *Qualitative Market Research: An International Journal*, 3(1), 47–54.
Thompson, C. J. (1997). "Interpreting Consumers: A hermeneutical framework for deriving marketing insights from the texts of consumption stories," *Journal of Marketing Research*, 34(4), 438–455.
Vaghely, I. P., and Julien, P-A. (2010). "Are opportunities recognized or constructed? An information perspective on entrepreneurial opportunity identification," *Journal of Business Venturing*, 25(1), 73–86.
Vargo, S. L., and Lusch, R. F. (2004). "Evolving a new dominant logic for marketing," *Journal of Marketing*, 68(1), 1–17.
Vargo, S. L., and Lusch, R. F. (2008). "Service-dominant logic: Continuing the evolution," *Journal of the Academy of Marketing Science*, 36(1), 1–10.
Webster, F. E. (1994). *Market-Driven management: Using the new marketing concept to create a customer oriented company,* Wiley.
Wenger, E. (1998). *Communities of practice: Learning, Meaning, and Identity*, Cambridge: Cambridge University Press.

Further reading

Bhave, M. P. (1994). "A Process Model of Entrepreneurial Venture Creation," *Journal of Business Venturing*, 9(3), 223–243.
Bhidé, A. (2000). *The origin and evolution of new businesses*, Oxford University Press.
Bjerke, Bjørn, and Hultman, Claes M. (2002). *Entrepreneurial Marketing: The Growth of Small Firms in the New Economic Era*, Edward Elgar.
Castrogiovanni, G. J. (1996). "Pre-start-up planning and the survival of new small businesses: Theoretical linkages," *Journal of Management*, 22(6), 801–822.
Cohen, E. (1979). "A Phenomenology of Tourist Experiences," *Sociology*, 13(2), 179–201.
Goulding, C. (2005). "Grounded theory, ethnography and phenomenology: A comparative analysis of three qualitative strategies for marketing research," *European Journal of Marketing*, 39(3/4), 294–308.
Grönroos, C. (2006). "Adopting a service logic for marketing," *Marketing Theory*, 6(3), 317–333.
Honig, B., and Karlsson, T. (2004). "Institutional forces and the written business plan," *Journal of Management*, 30(1), 29–48.
Jernsand, E. M., Kraff, H., and Mossberg, L. (2015). "Tourism Experience Innovation Through Design," *Scandinavian Journal of Hospitality and Tourism*, 15(sup1), 98–119.
Mason, K., Kjellberg, H., and Hagberg, J. (2015). "Exploring the performativity of marketing: theories, practices and devices," *Journal of Marketing Management*, 31(1–2), 1–15.
Pernecky, T., and Jamal, T. (2010). "(Hermeneutic) Phenomenology in tourism studies," *Annals of Tourism Research*, 37(4), 1055–1075.
Ritchie, J. R. B., and Hudson, S. (2009). "Understanding and meeting the challenges of consumer/tourist experience research," *International Journal of Tourism Research*, 11(2), 111–126.
Ronstad, R. (1988). "The Corridor Principle," *Journal of Business Venturing*, 3(1), 31–41.
Ryan, C. (2000). "Tourist experiences, phenomenographic analysis, post-postivism and neural network software," *The International Journal of Tourism Research*, 2(March/April), 119–131.
Szarycz, G. S. (2009). "Some issues in tourism research phenomenology: a commentary," *Current Issues in Tourism*, 12(1), 47–58.

6

Destination marketing and destination image

Sevda Sahilli Birdir, Ali Dalgic and Kemal Birdir

Destination and destination marketing

As an amalgam of touristic products and unique experiences (Buhalis, 2000: 97), destinations are the places that have actual or perceived geographical boundaries (Kotler, Bowen & Makens, 2010: 504). Generally, the destination is widely accepted as a mixture of both "tangible" and "intangible" assets (Howie, 2003; McCabe, 2010; Morrison, 2013). Physical elements are the tangible assets of a destination which involve attractions, amenities, and buildings (Holloway, Humphreys & Davidson, 2009: 184). Psychological assets are the intangible features of the destination that could include, hospitality, tolerance, and local atmosphere (Holloway, Humphreys & Davidson, 2009: 184). Based on this complex characteristic of the destination, scholars believe that success of a destination in the high competitive market such as tourism is positively related to attention paid to both elements – in other words, the integration of physical and psychological elements in the destination marketing activities (Holloway, Humphreys & Davidson, 2009: 184). In order to help destinations to achieve this goal, researchers have developed different frameworks/typologies. For instance, Buhalis (2000: 98) provided a typology called 6As which involves the six major elements that make a destination successful in terms of tourism;

- Attractions (man-made, natural, artificial, purpose built etc.)
- Accessibility (transportation vehicles, terminals, transportation systems etc.)
- Amenities (accommodation and refreshments facilities etc.)
- Available packages (packages prepared in destination)
- Activities (all activities existing in destination)
- Ancillary services (banks, telecommunication, hospital etc.)

Morrison (2013: 20–21), on the other hand, developed a framework with 10 features (10As), namely;

- Awareness: This attribute is related with information about tourist's destination. As the information about a destination is increased, this attribute is affected positively.
- Attractiveness: It is an attribute formed as a result of integration of attractiveness in a destination with geographical features.

- Availability: Making easy reservations to destination, sufficient number of channels for search and reservation.
- Access: Attribute that includes convenience in reaching a destination and returning from there, and situations such as easy transportation to the surrounding of a destination.
- Appearance: This attribute is the impression given to tourist by a destination. It is formed when tourist reaches a destination and during his/her stay.
- Activities: All activities existing for tourists in a destination.
- Assurance: Security and safety for tourists in a destination.
- Appreciation: The attribute related with welcome and hospitality in a destination.
- Action: Existence of a long-term touristic and marketing plan for a destination.
- Accountability: Attribute related with the evaluation of destination performance.

As can be understood from the above frameworks/typologies, destination is a multi-facing phenomenon. Along with this character, by increasing the travelers' expectations of the destination and cutthroat competition between destinations, destination marketing is getting more and more complicated and challenging. Fyall, Garrod and Tosun (2006: 76–83) summarized the key challenges of destination marketing into 15 factors (15 C Framework), as follow;

- Complexity: Complexity of destination product is increased with each passing day. Complexity is reinforced with the fact that the destination has forces and stakeholders inside and outside.
- Control: As the number of elements included in destination is increased, the fact of control becomes more complicated. Control of physical and psychological elements included in destinations is more complicated with each passing day.
- Change: Change is one of the most important things to pay attention to in terms of destination management and marketing. Macro environment such as demographic changes, technological changes, political changes, economic changes as well as suppliers, buyers and competitors in the micro environment should be taken into consideration.
- Crisis: Facts such as war, terrorist attacks, ecological disaster, epidemics, political problems, economical problems complicate the destination marketing.
- Complacency: Complacency in destination marketing is inhibited due to continual change and fear of crisis.
- Customers: Dimensions of customer must be taken into consideration in destination marketing. The perceptions, expectations, and desires of those who participate individually in tourism are more complicated than mass tourist.
- Culture: In destination marketing, cultural dimension is important both in terms of demand and supply. It is necessary to know the cultures of potential customer groups in the market and to make products and make promotions in this context.
- Competition: Today many destinations are in sight in the "tourism supermarket". The destinations around the world, which want to increase their incomes from ever-increasing tourism activities, are in cutthroat competition.
- Commodification: With the increase of competition, the destinations of many parts of the world began to resemble each other over time. The main reason of this is the "commercialization" policy. Some categories, especially in the Mediterranean basin, Southeast Asia and the Caribbean are good examples. Due to affinity and commercialization, a policy of price reduction is applied in destination marketing every year.
- Creativity: Creativity is important both in the destination products and in the marketing activities. "Branding" in destination products can be given as examples of creativity.

- Communication: Brochures, leaflets, promotional materials, and promotional activities are created for destination marketing to reach purchasers. In addition to this effort spent to reach the buyer, it is important in organizations that operate in the destination to respond to the buyer's questions and requests. It can be said that the reason for this is so that the communication between the destination and the receiver can be achieved completely.
- Channels: There is a need for a variety of channels for the promotion and marketing of destination products.
- Cyberspace: The internet has become one of the important channels for the promotion and marketing of the global world destinations.
- Consolidation: Mergers and acquisitions have become important in order to become a stronger tourism destination.
- Collaboration: The ability to be effective and successful in destination marketing depends on the cooperation of stakeholders in the destination.

Building upon what has been said, it can be concluded that destination marketing is a complicated process considering the success factors and the problems that may be encountered (Jiang, Ramkissoon, Mavondo & Feng, 2017). In addition, the fact that there are many alternatives similar to and different from each other for the buyers makes this process even more complicated (Wang, 2011: 1).

Destination marketing organization

The Destination Marketing Organization (DMO) can be defined as "any organization at any level, which is responsible for the marketing of an identifiable destination" (Pike, 2007: 14). Middleton, Fyall, Morgan and Ranchhod (2009: 344–345) have indicated the following duties for DMOs:

- Communicating with industry partners, conducting research and identifying promotional priorities.
- Managing destination image and the branding process.
- Affecting and liaising with private sector partners to achieve goals and objectives.
- Coordinating the promotion of the destination that is not provided by the private sector (e.g. establishment of tourist information centers and management of destination websites)
- Providing investment and marketing support to create new products and improve existing products.
- Developing marketing campaigns for hundreds of small businesses that cannot participate in marketing activities.
- Providing leadership on destination information resources.

In addition to this general categorization of DMO's duties, Morrison (2013: 28) suggested that studying of duties based on geographical factors can be more helpful. Consequently, by dividing DMOs into two groups (national and regional) provided the following responsibilities for DMOs:

- Tourism legislation and regulations: To introduce and enforce tourism laws and regulations. These laws and regulations concern businesses operating in the tourism sector, such as accommodation businesses, restaurants, tour guiding, travel agencies and tour operators.
- Tourism policy making: Preparing tourism policies in countries.

- Tourism planning and strategies: Coordinating the process of developing plans and strategies on the level of country.
- Tourism development: Encouraging different types of tourism via financial and technical aids.
- Tourism research: Conducting tourism research on the national level.
- Destination marketing: Applying the strategies and plans of local and international marketing.
- Education and training programs: Organizing education and training programs to increase the number of tourism professionals in the country.
- Quality improvement and assurance: Forming strategies and programs to increase the quality of tourism.
- Sustainable tourism: To promote sustainable tourism practices throughout the country and to engage in sustainable tourism activities.

Additionally, he believes that a single authority cannot effectively carry out destination marketing in one country. Considering the size of the countries, complexities of destinations and intensity of competition among destinations and countries, this argument makes a strong statement in itself. It is possible to examine DMOs operating in one country in four different categories, namely; 1) Country, 2) State, province and territory, 3) Region, and 4) County and city (Morrison, 2013: 24–25). At the regional and national levels Morrison offers the following responsibilities for DMOs:

Responsibilities of the national tourism organization

The DMO operating at the country level is called National Tourism Organization (NTO). The National Tourism Organization can be described as an organization that is fully responsible for the marketing of a country as a tourism destination (Pike, 2007: 14). NTO primarily focus on policies, such as mission, strategy, and marketing plans. Besides, it decides the necessary budget for the destination marketing. In accordance with the established budget found during promotion activities directly (advertising, public relations, web site, destination marketin systems) or indirectly (trade shows, joint campaigns, reservation systems, foreign representative offices) tries to reach potential customers (Middleton, Fyall, Morgan & Ranchhod, 2009: 347). In a broader context, NTO is responsible for the following functions (Kotler, Bowen & Makens, 2010: 529–530):

- Flow of research data: NTO coordinates tourism research for the area. It gathers and shares the information such as types of visitors, their stay durations, type of accommodation and expenses. This information is important for tracking trends and developments, and for setting a marketing strategy. At the same time, collected information is shared with hospitality and travel businesses.
- Representation in markets: In large markets, the NTO usually has offices. It can carry out marketing surveillance activities through advertisements and can provide additional information about the country. NTO offices operating in major markets answer and provide information to incoming inquiries.
- Organization of workshops and trade shows: NTO is interacting with distribution channel members such as travel agents and wholesalers. They can organize workshops, and participate in trade shows by purchasing stands.
- Familiarization trips: NTO conducts familiarization trips to key members of distribution channels and travel writers.
- Participation in joint marketing schemes: Some NTOs may provide advertising support to their members in order to increase their share in some markets. For example, the British Tourist Authority has provided advertising support for British Airways in the United States.

- Support for new or small business: NTOs can support new products and small businesses that may be important for tourism. For example, rural tourism and regional festivals are often supported by NTOs.
- Customer assistance and protection: NTOs assist customers by providing information about products in the destination. For example, some countries provide detailed schemes of accommodation businesses. Sometimes, NTOs help to design accommodation brochures and menus based on the targeted market segment.
- General education: NTOs provide conferences and courses to inform national travel and tourism sectors and meet the need to understand foreign markets.

Based on the mentioned functions, it is possible to classify NTOs into four categories (Kotler, Bowen & Makens, 2010: 530):

- Economics: To optimize the contribution of tourism and recreation to economic welfare, full employment and regional economic development.
- Consumer: To make opportunities and benefits of travel and recreation universal for local people and visitors, to contribute to personal improvement and education of local people and to encourage their appreciation of the geography, history and ethnic diversity of the region.
- Environmental and natural resources: To preserve historical and cultural structures in the destination, to work to transfer cultural heritage to future generations, to protect energy resources, environmental values and natural resources by carrying out compatible tourism policies.
- Government operations: Having a role in promoting all government-related activities that support tourism and recreation to the highest possible level, supporting the needs of public and private sector organizations operating in sectors related to tourism and recreation, leading everyone who has role in protecting tourism, recreation and cultural heritage.

Responsibilities of state, province and territory organizations

An organization responsible for destination marketing in countries that have Federal political system (e.g. the USA) or territory (e.g. in Australia) can be given as an example for such organizations (Wang, 2011: 6). These organizations are included in NTOs and they are in cooperation and in contact with NTOs. For example, Queensland in Australia has established Tourism Queensland, and this organization has developed a ten year strategic plan for the region in which it acted. New York State's STO has developed the campaign "I Love New York". Businesses in the tourism sector can promote their works by cooperating with STOs (Kotler, Bowen & Maken, 2010: 531).

Responsibilities of the regional destination marketing organization

Regional Destination Marketing Organizations can be stated as the ones responsible for the destination marketing of a particular region. Convention and visitor bureau (CVB) in the USA and regional tourism boards (RTB) in the UK are examples of such organizations (Wang, 2011: 7). Such organizations under the State, Province and Territory Organizations are generally more common in medium-sized countries. For example, New Zealand and Italy have regional destination marketing organizations. There are 30 regional tourism organizations in New Zealand (Morrison, 2013: 30).

Responsibilities of county and city destination marketing organizations

Such destination marketing organizations can also be called as local tourism offices. At local levels, these organizations, usually operating in counties, are cooperating with local tourism businesses (Wang, 2011: 7; Morrison, 2013: 32).

Destination marketing promotion mix

The combination of tools such as promotion mix named as marketing communication mix occurs by the combination of advertising, sales promotion, personal selling, public relations-publicity, direct marketing, and interactive marketing (Kotler, Bowen & Makens, 2010: 358; Kotler & Keller, 2012: 500). These tools, which can be used in the marketing of any product or service, are also frequently used in destination marketing. DMOs in the destinations are trying to reach more potential customers by using promotion mix tools (Pike, 2007: 141). According to the ETC / UNWTO report (2010), 24% of the DMOs' budgets were found to be spent on advertising, 16% to attend fairs, 11% on brochures and mailings, and 6% on internet and e-marketing. Kotler and Keller (2012) described the widely used communication platforms as follows:

- Advertising: Print and broadcast ads, brochures and booklets, posters and leaflets, billboards, display signs.
- Sales promotion: Fairs and trade shows, exhibits, demonstrations, coupons.
- Events and experiences: Sports, entertainment, festivals, arts, street activities.
- Public relations and publicity: Press kits, seminars, annual reports, publications.
- Direct and interactive marketing: Catalogs, mailings, e-mail, fax, blogs, web sites.
- Word of mouth marketing: Person to person, blogs.
- Personal selling: Sales presentations, fairs and trade shows.

The majority of the instruments involved in the marketing-promotional mix are also important in the destination branding and destination positioning processes. In addition to these, they are also important elements in the destination image activities (Pike, 2007).

Destination image

Image is a marketing concept with vital importance in the tourism industry (Kişioğlu, 2013). Avcıkurt (2005), described destination image as "the expression of objective information, impressions, prejudices, dreams and emotional thoughts about a specific place". According to Kotler (1994) destination image provides "clear results of beliefs, ideas, emotions, anticipations and impressions that one has about the destination". Image will influence tourists when they want to choose a destination, make an assessment of the trip, and in their future intentions towards a destination (Chia & Qu, 2008). Kişioğlu (2013) pointed to image surveys carried out in the tourism field which reflect different views: the relationship between destination selection and image, the process of image formation, the change in image and the image measurement. The image formation for the destination is the most important phase before tourists travel to a given destination, and it is important to know how the image is formed before it affects behavior.

Destination image is a very popular and frequently researched subject (Hosany, Ekinci & Uysal, 2006; Ayaz, Batı & Gökmen, 2015). According to Hosany, Ekinci and Uysal (2006), studies on destination image started in the early 1970s. Today a Google scholar search on destination image turns out more than 2 million results. According to Tasci (2003) destination image involves three important steps, including pre-trip (such as trip planning, decision making, destination choice and travel time), during (such as spent time in the destinastion, entertainment and pleasure), and post-trip (recommend the destination to others with word-of-mouth, intention to revisit and loyalty to the destination) behavior of tourists.

Destination image has a key role in destination selection (Watkins, Hassanien & Dale, 2006; Kıycı, 2010). It is very important for destination marketing to examine the elements that can be effective in the selection of a holiday destination for the undecided tourist and to show how these elements are formed (Baloğlu & Bringberg, 1997). Destination image is a picture in the minds of tourists, which helps one country become a center of attraction for tourists and at the same time encourages tourists to spend more (Kıycı, 2010). According to Gallarza, Saura and García, (2002) anthropology, sociology, geography, semiotics and marketing disciplines all have an impact in understanding human behavior. That's why a destination's image affects a tourist's perception and behavior, and destination choice. Destination image can impact the tourists' visit intentions in future and their willingness to suggest the destination to others (Banyai, 2009). Destinations constantly conduct studies on destination image to get market share and to protect or increase their share of the international tourism market. Destination image is classified differently in various studies such as organic image, persuasive image, complex image, final image, neutral image, overloaded image and solid image (Kıycı, 2010).

Components of the destination image

Before travel to a specific destination is planned, the formation of an image of the destination is the most important stage and it is necessary to understand how the image is formed before it affects selection behavior. For example, various studies show that age and education level mostly affect the image within the socio-demographic characteristics. At the same time, easy transportation, price/quality adaptation, climate, event presentation and diversity are found to be common features of successful destinations (Öter & Özdoğan, 2005).

Tourists have an image of a destination as a result of information obtained from different sources. The destination image includes a process that ends with an organic image and induced images. Organic image takes shape from friends' and relatives' opinions and past experiences while induced image is shaped as a result of professional promotions (Gunn, 1972). Additionally, Fakeye and Crompton (1991) emphasized that image formation has three stages: organic, induced, and complex images. While "organic image . . . is based on past travel experiences, induced image . . . is based on the marketing influences, and complex image . . . is based on tourists' actual visit to the destination" (Lin, 2011: 24). In addition, it's argued that pre-actual visitations cause organic and induced image formation, whereas post-actual visitation to the destination causes complex image (Fakeye & Crompton, 1991; Lin, 2011).

The image is not made up of a single factor that affects the traveling behavior of people, but is rather a combination of many factors. There are many theoretical and conceptually based studies on the formation of the destination image (Kıycı, 2010). Buhalis (2003) collected the necessary characteristics of tourism destinations under the 6A framework. These destination characteristics are; attractions (natural formations or constructed structures), accessibility (transportation systems and structures), amenities (accommodation, catering and shopping facilities), available packages, activities and ancillary services (banks, communication tools).

According to (Kıycı, 2010), the common points of those who research destination images are the role of perceptual, cognitive and effective evaluations in image formation. Many investigators agree that destination image has two components which are known cognitive and affective components (Tasci, 2003).The cognitive component can be evaluated as beliefs and knowledge about the physical attributes of a destination. On the other hand, the affective component indicates feelings towards the attributes and the surrounding environments of a destination (Baloğlu & McClearly, 1999). Cognitive assessments include tourists' knowledge and beliefs about the destination. Emotional evaluations include what tourists feel about the destination (Baloğlu & McCleary, 1999; Tasci, 2003). According to Banyai (2009), combination of perceptual/cognitive evaluations and affective evaluations forms the global image of destination. Studies suggest that both cognitive and affective components are likely to affect tourists' attitudes and behaviors towards a destination (Tasci, 2003).

Gartner (1993, 1996) mentioned that destination image has three related components: cognitive, affective, and conative. The cognitive factor includes the estimation process to tourism destination choice. The affective factor is the tourists' beliefs, ideas and the behavior of the destination to visit; and the conative factor is the action component which relates to the final selection of a target destination. Gartner also maintains that these components are hierarchically interrelated. Baloglu and McCleary (1999) also say that cognitive and affective components are interrelated. According to these researchers, the affective component is a function of the cognitive component and depends on it.

The general framework of destination image is shaped by: (a) personal factors (psychological, such as consumers' values, motivations, and personality); (b) social factors (such as consumers' age, marital status); and (c) stimulant factors (information sources, tourists' previous experience and distribution channels) (Baloglu & McCleary, 1999; Ayaz, Batı & Gökmen, 2015). According to Beerli and Josefa (2004) and Chen (2001), the dimensions that determine the image of the destination are natural resources, the atmosphere of the destination, general infrastructure, tourist infrastructure, natural environment, social environment, culture, history and art, political and economic factors, touristic and leisure time, and leisure activities. Factors influencing the formation of the destination image include travel brochures, posters about the destination, family, friend circles, travel agencies, newspapers, magazines, books, television, and cinema (Echtner & Ritchie, 2003). In addition, experiences in the destination, psychological characteristics, motivation, social and economic characteristics, level of education and tourism marketing have a separate prescription (Lopes, 2011; Kişioğlu, 2013).

Destination image formation models

Although the initial work on destination image lasted 30 years, it still maintains its popularity (Pike, 2002). Destination image has important roles in tourist behaviors, such as to affect the destination choice decision-making process and to affect tourists' behavior intentions in the future (Bigne, Sanchez & Sanchez, 2001; Chen & Tsai, 2007; Lee, Lee & Lee, 2005). According to Baloglu and McCleary (1999), there are two approaches to the destination image formation process which are known static and dynamic.The static formation is the study of the link with image and tourist attitude such as satisfaction and destination option. On the other hand, the dynamic formation is stressing the importance of destination image all around (Gallarza, Saura & García, 2002).

Gunn model

According to Gunn (1989), tourist destination image formation is a process comprising seven components. First of all, a tourist begins to create a mental image of the vacation experience. Then, developing the first image in his/her mind he/she searches for more information.

The third component includes deciding to go to the destination and fourth component is actually visiting the destination. Then, a tourist shares the destination experience with others on returning from the destination. The last component is refreshing the image of the destination after a living experience.

Baloglu and McCleary model

Baloglu and McCleary (1999) argued that destination image has three dimensions: affective, cognitive and conative. Both affect and cognition are mental responses to environment stimuli, which are interrelated and form a dynamic and interactive system; the cognitive and the affective dimensions significantly influence the conative image of a destination. According to Baloglu and McCleary (1999), the cognitive image and affective image directly affect the overall image, and the overall image can be positive or negative.

Echtner and Ritchie model

Echtner and Ritchie (2003) developed a destination image model with three axes to determine the position of a destination image in the conceptual framework: functional/psychological, common/unique and holistic/attribute-based. In brief, the image of the destination is composed of an interpretation of a core group of properties that generally evaluate and compare all destinations (Echtner & Ritchie, 2003). Functional features can be seen in almost all the destinations which compose most of the general tourism features such as climate, nightlife, landscape and prices. On the psychological and common axes, the perception of situations such as hospitality, security, fame and restraint can be the major attributes to count in since these attributes vary from person to person. The characteristics of the locality specific to the destination are considered rare/unique. On the other hand, according to each tourist, each rare/unique attribute has a psychological qualification because it will be perceived differently by different tourists. The holistic/attribute dimension deals with the mental thoughts of individuals. Tourists develop attitudes as a result of their experience with destinations in their holidays.

Beerli and Martin model

The model of the destination image formation developed by Beerli and Martin (2004) is based on the assumption that there may be different reasons for attitudes towards the destination between the first-time visiting tourists and repeat visiting tourists. In this model, the most important factors affecting the formation of destination image are information sources and personal factors. In the Beerli and Martin (2004) model, cognitive image is influenced by information sources and affective image is influenced by personal factors. The general image consists of cognitive and emotional imagery.

Conclusion

Destinations should have various elements such as attractions, accessibility, amenities, available packages, activities, ancillary services in order to be successful in terms of tourism (Buhalis, 2000: 98). Contemporary tourists can search for these elements as well as different elements in destinations (Morrison, 2013). These factors, which are found in the destinations, constitute the image in terms of the customers and potential customers.The positive image of the destination is important for the visits of customers and potential customers to the destination (Kotler, 1994;

Watkins, Hassanien & Dale, 2006; Chia & Qu, 2008). Destination Marketing Organizations (DMOs) have important tasks in order to increase the positive image both at the regional and national level. A DMO should help in coordinating all marketing activities of a destination including budgeting, rasing funds and articulating a proper marketing strategy. Among them, probably formation of the destination image and keeping this image current and desired is one of the most important tasks of such an organization. Of course, fierce competition, constant changes in tourists' wants and needs, trends and demographic changes are all very important challenges for every destination to deal with in today's higly dynamic tourism industry. Therefore, marketing and image efforts of destinations must also benefit from all sorts of developments in information technology. At the present time, effective usage of social media seems to be a key element for competition and success in what can be easily called "information era". What you hear and see in the internet seems to be the "real thing" today, and successful destinations of current times appear to be the champions of the social media and information media.

References

Avcıkurt, C. (2005).*Turizmde Tanıtma ve Satış Geliştirme.* İstanbul: Değişim Yayınları.

Ayaz, N., Batı, T. & Gökmen, F. (2015).Safranbolu'yu Ziyaret Eden Yabancı Turistlerin Destinasyon İmajı Algıları. *Karabük Üniversitesi Sosyal Bilimler Enstitüsü Dergisi,* Özel Sayı: 1, 54–69.

Baloglu, Ş. & McClearly, K.W. (1999).A Model of Destination Image Formation. *Ann Tour Res.* 26(4): 868–97.

Baloğlu, Ş. & Brinberg, D. (1997).Affective Image of Tourism Destinations. *Journal of Travel Research,* 35(4): 11–15.

Banyai, M. (2009). The Image of Tourism Destinations: A Case of Dracula Tourism. Master of Arts. The University of Waterloo. Recreation and Leisure Studies – Tourism Policy and Planning. Waterloo, Ontario, Canada.

Beerli, A. & Josefa, D.M. (2004). Tourists' Characteristics and The Perceived Image of Tourist Destinations: A Quantitative Analysis – A Case Study of Lanzarote, Spain. *Tourism Management,* 25: 623–636.

Beerli, A. & Martin, J. D. (2004). Factors influencing destination image. *Annals of Tourism Research,* 31(3): 657–681.

Bigne, J., Sanchez, M. & Sanchez, J. (2001). Tourism Image, Evaluation Variables and After Purchase Behavior: Inter-Relationships. *Tourism Management,* 22(6): 607–616.

Buhalis, D. (2000). Marketing The Competitive Destination of The Future. *Tourism Management,* 21(1): 97–116.

Buhalis, D. (2003). *eTourism: Information Technology for Strategic Management,* 1st edition. London: Prentice Hall.

Chen, C. & Tsai, D.C. (2007). How Destination Image and Evaluative Factors Affect Behavioral Intentions?. *Tourism Management,* 28: 1115–1122.

Chen, J.S. (2001). A Case Study of Korean Outbound Travelers' Destination Images by Using Correspondence Analysis. *Tourism Management,* 22: 345–350.

Chia, C.G. & Qu, H. (2008). Examining The Structural Relationships of Destination Image, Tourist Satisfaction and Destination Loyalty: An Integrated Approach. *Tourism Management,* 29: 624–636.

Echtner, C.M. & Ritchie J.R.B. (1993). The Measurement of Destination Image: An Empirical Assessment. *Journal of Travel Research,* 31: 3–13.

Echtner, C.M. & Ritchie, J.R.B. (2003). The Meaning and Measurement of Destination Image. *The Journal of Tourism Studies,* 14(1): 37–48.

ETC/UNWTO (2010). Budgets Of National Tourism Organisations: 2008–2009. [http://www.etc-corporate.org/reports/budgets-of-national-tourism-organisations]. Access date: 26 April 2017.

Fakeye, P. & Crompton, J. (1991). Image Differences Between Prospective, First-Time, and Repeat Visitors to the Lower Rio Grande Valley. *Journal of Travel Research,* 30 (2): 10–16.

Fyall, A., Garrod, B. & Tosun, C. (2006). *Destination Marketing: A Framework for Future Research.* In Progress in Tourism Marketing (Ed. Kozak, M. and Andreu, L.), 75–86.

Gallarza, M.G., Saura, I.G. & García, H.C. (2002). Destination Image: Towards A Conceptual Framework. *Annals of Tourism Research,* 29(1), 56–78.

Gartner, W.C. (1993). Image Formation Process. *Journal of Travel and Tourism Marketing* 2(2/3), 191–215.
Gartner, W.C. (1996). *Tourism Development: Principles, Policies, and Policies.* New York: Van Nostram Reinhold.
Gunn, C.A. (1989). *Vacationscape: Designing tourist regions.* Second edition, New York: Van Nostrand Reinhold Publishers.
Gunn, C.A. (1972). *Vacationscape: Designing tourist regions.* Washington DC: Taylor & Francis/University of Texas.
Holloway, J., Humphreys, C. & Davidson, R. (2009). *The Business of Tourism,* 5th edition. Harlow, England: Financial Times.
Hosany, S., Ekinci, Y. & Uysal, M. (2006). Destination image and destination personality: An application of branding theories to tourism places. *Journal of Business Research,* 59(5): 638–642.
Howie, F. (2003). *Managing The Tourist Destination.* Cengage Learning EMEA, Thomson, London.
Jiang, Y., Ramkissoon, H., Mavondo, F.T. and Feng, S., (2017). Authenticity: The Link Between Destination Image and Place Attachment. *Journal of Hospitality Marketing & Management,* 26(2): 105–124.
Kişioğlu, E. (2013). Yerel Etkinliklerin Destinasyon İmajı Açısından Değerlendirilmesi: Tekirdağ Kent Merkezindeki Paydaşlar Üzerinde Bir Araştırma. Yüksek Lisans Tezi. Düzce Üniversitesi, Sosyal Bilimler Enstitisü, Turizm ve Otel İşletmeciliği ABD. Düzce.
Kıycı, Ş. (2010). Bir İmaj Çeşidi Olarak Destinasyon İmajı ve Turizmde Destinasyon İmajının Ölçülmesi (Amasra Örneği). Yüksek Lisans Tezi. Zonguldak Karaelmas Üniversitesi. İşletme ABD. Zonguldak.
Kotler, P. (1994). *Marketing Management. Analysis, Planning, Implementation, and Control.* New Jersey: Prentice-Hall.
Kotler, P. & Keller, K.L. (2012). *Marketing Management.* Pearson Education, New Jersey.
Kotler, P., Bowen, J. & Makens, J. (2010). *Marketing for Hospitality and Tourism.* Fifth Edition. Pearson Education, New Jersey.
Lee, C., Lee, Y. & Lee, B. (2005). Korea's Destination Image Formed by the 2002 World Cup. *Annals of Tourism Research,* 32(4): 839–858.
Lin, J.L. (2011). An Investigation of the Relationships Among Destination Image, Place Attachment, and Visitation Intention of Heritage Tourists. Doctor of Philosophy. The faculty of The Graduate School at Middle Tennessee State University. Murfreesboro, TN.
Lopes, S.D.F. (2011). Destination Image: Origins, Developments and Implications. *PASOS. Revista de Turismo y Patrimonio Cultural.* Vol: 9 (2): 305–315.
McCabe, S. (2010). *Marketing Communications in Tourism and Hospitality.* Routledge, Oxford: Butterworth Heinemann.
Middleton, V.T., Fyall, A., Morgan, M. & Ranchhod, A. (2009). *Marketing in Travel and Tourism.* Routledge.
Morrison, A.M. (2013). *Marketing and Managing Tourism Destinations.* Routledge, Oxford: Butterworth Heinemann.
Öter, Z. & Özdoğan, O. N. (2005). Kültür Amaçlı Seyahat Eden Turistlerde Destinasyon İmajı: Selçuk-Efes Örneği. *Anatolia: Turizm Arastirmalari Dergisi,* 16(2).
Pike, S. (2002). Destination Image Analysis: A Review of 142 Papers from 1973 to 2000. *Tourism Management,* 23(5): 541–549.
Pike, S. (2004). *Destination Marketing Organisations.* Elsevier, Oxford, UK.
Pike, S. (2007). *Destination Marketing Organisations.* Routledge.
Tasci, A.D.A. (2003). Determinants of Destination Image. Doctor of Philosophy, Doctor Dissertation, Michigan State University, Department of Park, Recreation and Tourism Resources, United States.
Watkins, S., Hassanien, A. & Dale, C. (2006). Exploring the image of the black country as a tourist destination. *Place Branding,* 2(4): 321–333.
Wang, Y. (2011). Destination Marketing and Management: Scope, Definition and Structures. In *Destination Marketing and Management: Theories and Applications* (Ed. Wang, Y. and Pizam, A.), 1–21. CAB International: Oxfordshire.

Further Reading

Crompton, J.L. (1979). An Assessment of the Image of Mexico as a Vacation Destination and the Influence of Geographical Location Upon That Image. *Journal of Travel Research,* 17(1): 18–23.
Öter, Z. & Osman, N.Ö. (2005). Kültür Amaçlı Seyahat Eden Turistlerde Destinasyon İmajı: Selçuk-Efes Örneği. *Anatolia: Turizm Araştırmaları Dergisi,* Cilt 16 (2): 127–138.
Watkins, S., Ahmed, H. & Crispin D. (2006). Exploring The Image ofthe Black Country as a Tourist Destination. *Palgrave Journals,* 2(4): 321–333.

7

Destination attachment

Conceptual foundation, dimensionality, antecedents and outcomes

Girish Prayag

Introduction

This chapter critically evaluates the current state of research on the concept of place attachment as applied to tourism destinations. The chapter identifies issues of conceptualization, operationalization, and also offers areas of further research that would enhance our theoretical understandings of the concept in the tourism field. Several definitions of place attachment exist. In fact, there is no single accepted definition or theory of place attachment (Guilani & Feldman, 1993; Lewicka, 2011; Scannell & Gifford, 2010) but most authors recognize an emotional or affective component (Morgan, 2010) and a functional or cognitive component (Stedman, 2003). In the tourism field, the terms place (Gross & Brown, 2008; Hosany et al., 2017; Prayag & Ryan, 2012) and destination attachment (Yuksel et al., 2010; Veasna et al., 2013) are used interchangeably to describe the functional and emotional attachment that tourists form with destinations.

Researchers have borrowed extensively from fields such as geography, environmental psychology, consumer psychology, recreation and leisure, and marketing to inform the application of place attachment in the tourism field. Existing models of place attachment in the broader literature are quite diverse and integrative, not only in the method adopted, but also in epistemology (Proshansky et al., 1983; Kaltenborn, 1997; Hidalgo & Hernandez, 2001; Lewicka, 2011). As a result, the nature and nuances of people's emotional relationships with places have been conceptualised in numerous ways and under various related terms (Manzo, 2003; Moore & Scott, 2003) such as "sense of place" (Tuan, 1980), "place attachment" (Low & Altman, 1992) and "place belonging" (Proshansky et al., 1983). Place attachment remains the most commonly used term in a tourism setting (Gross & Brown, 2008; Prayag & Ryan, 2012; Yuksel et al., 2010; Veasna et al., 2013). Researchers have studied both attachment of tourists (Hosany et al., 2017; Prayag & Ryan, 2012) and residents (Gu & Ryan, 2008; Lemelin et al., 2015) to places while the broader literature investigates mainly attachment of the latter. Nonetheless, there is agreement that attachment develops for places at different geographical scales such as urban versus rural areas (Anton & Lawrence, 2014) and neighbourhoods versus cities (Rioux et al., 2017). Specifically, tourism studies have looked at attachment to national parks (Kil et al., 2012; Ramkissoon et al., 2013), destinations (Chen & Phou, 2013; Prayag & Ryan, 2012; Yuksel et al., 2010), festivals and events (Davis, 2016; Lee et al., 2012) and heritage sites (Dragouni & Fouseki, 2017; Suntikul & Jachna,

2015). Also, the nature of the experience itself matters in the formation of attachment with studies examining attachment to various touristic activities such as white water rafting (Beckman et al., 2017) and local food (Tsai, 2016) among others. Next, the major theories underpinning the concept of place attachment are discussed.

Conceptual foundations of destination attachment

Place has at least three common meanings in social science: (a) location: the spatial distribution of social and economic activities; (b) locale: the setting for everyday routine social interaction provided in a place; and (c) sense of place: the identification with a place emotionally or symbolically (Williams, 1995). As such place attachment has been treated as a multifaceted concept that characterizes the bonding between individuals and their important places (Scannell & Gifford, 2010). Others have defined place attachment in purely emotional terms such as Morgan (2010) who describes the concept as "an affective bond to a particular geographical area and the meaning attributed to that bond" (p. 12). As pointed out earlier, several definitions coexist (Lewicka, 2011) and the same can be seen in the tourism literature about destination attachment. For example, Suntikul and Jachna (2016) define tourists' attachment to the historic centre of Macao as the personal connection that one feels with a particular place. In other studies (e.g., Stylos et al., 2017) no precise definition of place attachment is provided. A conceptual definition of destination attachment remains elusive so far but this is not surprising given the multiplicity of understandings and definitions that underpins the concept of a tourism "destination" as well as the complexity inherent to the concept of place attachment itself.

As suggested above, there is no place attachment theory per se but several studies have grounded their findings in attachment theory, arguing that the formation of destination attachment mirrors the mother-infant bond (e.g., Gross & Brown, 2008; Tsai, 2012; Yuksel et al., 2010). Attachment theory describes the innate human need to form affectionate bonds (Bowlby, 1969). It is an emotion-laden mother-infant bonding where "each party manifests intense pleasure in the other's company and especially in the other's expression of affection . . . whereas distance and expressions of rejection are appraised as disagreeable or painful" (Bowlby, 1969, p. 242). Attachment theory "is one of the most useful and generative frameworks for understanding both normative and individual differences aspects of the process of affect regulation" (Mikulincer et al., 2003, p. 77). It is an "empirically validated framework in which both positive and negative aspects of human behaviour and experience can be conceptualized" (Mikulincer & Shaver, 2005, p. 139). While much has been written on attachment in interpersonal relationship contexts (Baumeister & Leary, 1995; Bowlby, 1969), attachment to products and services in general is a recent occurrence. For example, in the marketing field emotional attachment has been described as a deep desire to preserve security felt in connection with a brand and to actively avoid separation, manifesting in emotionally rooted repurchasing and avoidance of switching (Grisaffe & Nguyen, 2011). It implies deep feelings of connection, affection and passion (Thomson et al., 2005).

More recently, the developmental theory of place attachment has been suggested by Morgan (2010) as a way to understand the emotional aspects of attachment. According to this theory, place attachment emerges from social interactions and evaluations of the physical environment that shapes place behaviour. In this process, emotion is a critical aspect of the relationship between the person and the environment, including social relationships formed. The developmental theory of place attachment attempts to bring together attachment theory and the existing diverse place theories to explain the psychological processes underpinning the development of place attachment. This is in contrast to attachment theory (Bowlby, 1969) that focuses mainly on adult–infant proximity and care-giving responses motivated by subjective emotional states. Attachment theory places low importance on the person's relationship with the physical environment. For tourist destinations in particular, attachment can be both to the physical environment (tourist attractions, scenery, activities) but also the social relationships formed through, for example, visiting friends and relatives. As suggested by Relph (1976), a place is essentially its people given that it is people who turn a "blank" space into a "meaningful" place against a backdrop of physical features of the environment. Within this idea, many place theorists have used terms such as sense of place (Stedman, 2003) and place bonding (Hammitt et al., 2006) to describe attachment to physical environments. So far, except for the study of Hosany et al. (2017) that uses the developmental theory of place attachment to explain the relationship between emotions, satisfaction, attachment and behavioral intentions, the theory remains sparsely applied in tourism. However, the study of Hosany et al. (2017) captures mainly the outcome of attachment rather than the process of how attachment develops for tourist destination.

Also, underlying these conceptualisations of place is the idea that a sense of place results from people attaching meaning to what otherwise would simply be "space" (Moore & Scott, 2003). What begins as undifferentiated 'space' evolves into 'place' as we come to know it better and endow it with value (Tuan, 1977). Therefore, we turn space into place by imbuing space with meanings acquired through personal experiences we have had with places. These meanings are pluralistic and particularistic to that place and evolve over time as a result of continuous visitation or related experiences based on the intensity and quality of experiences (Hammitt & Stewart, 1996). Hence, people's relationships to places are an ever-changing, dynamic phenomenon, and as such, they can be a conscious process in which people are active shapers of their lives (Manzo, 2003).

Dimensionality of destination attachment

There is no consensus on the best way to conceptualise and measure place attachment in tourism studies for several reasons. First, given that emotional relationships to places can encompass a broad range of physical settings and emotions, not necessarily intrinsic to the physical setting itself, but residing in human interpretation of the setting, which are constructed through experience with it (Manzo, 2003), tourism researchers have failed to show which dimensions are more or less important for destinations at different geographical scales (e.g., attachment to local area, city, urban, rural and country destinations). Second, from the perspective of people-environment interactions, attachment represents a positive connection or bond between a person and a location. Tourism researchers have consistently considered attachment in a positive way (Prayag & Ryan, 2012; Yuksel et al., 2010). For example, Cheng and Kuo (2015) define the term place bonding as a "positive emotion that individuals associate with a certain place" (p. 546). However, relationships to places need not always be positive. People can develop aversion to certain places (Relph, 1976). Being connected to a place may give some people a positive sense of belonging, but for others, it may feel oppressive and restrictive thereby creating negative feelings for the place (Relph, 1976). Researchers have called for a broader understanding of emotional relationships to places that incorporates not only positive but also negative and ambivalent feelings (Manzo, 2003). Of particular relevance to destination attachment are ambivalent feelings attached to a place given that tourists have the ability to downgrade the importance of negative experiences at the expense of positive experiences. Therefore, identifying how and which aspects of the tourist experience generate negative and ambivalent feelings would be necessary to progress the conceptualization of destination attachment. Third, Cheng and Kuo (2015) demonstrate that individuals can develop attachment to places that they have never visited, suggesting that physical presence may not be necessary to the formation of place attachment. So far, the existing research on destination attachment is based mainly on tourists having physically visited the destination and therefore the emotional and functional connections are strong and well-articulated in tourists' minds.

Perhaps the most challenging aspect of conceptualizing and measuring destination attachment is the fact that the relationship between place attachment and other constructs such as sense of place and place belonging remains to be clarified given that these concepts are poorly articulated and often cannot be differentiated by their definitions (Stedman, 2003). Some researchers argue that sense of place, place dependence and place identity are forms of place attachment (Low & Altman, 1992; Bricker & Kerstetter, 2000; Williams & Vaske, 2003). Others suggested that sense of place is broader than place attachment and that the latter is a sub-dimension of the former (Hay, 1998; Jorgensen & Stedman, 2001; Stedman, 2003). Still others argued that place attachment focuses on evaluation of places, while place identity is more concerned with the way in which places form identity (Moore, 2000). While recognising these conceptual disparities, tourism researchers have mainly articulated place attachment in the form of three sub dimensions, place identity, place dependence and social bonding (Gross & Brown, 2008; Lee et al., 2012; Prayag & Ryan, 2012; Ramkissoon et al., 2013).

Place identity often takes the form of place belongingness and is characterised by the "combination of attitudes, values, thoughts, beliefs, meanings, and behaviour tendencies reaching far beyond emotional attachment and belonging to particular places" (Proshansky et al., 1983, p. 61). It was originally conceptualised as a "cluster of positively and negatively valenced cognitions of physical settings" (p. 62) but its operationalization has focused on positive bonds. As such, place identity has been described as a component of self-identity that increases one's feelings of belonging to a place (Relph, 1976; Tuan, 1980) and the setting enables individuals to both express as well as affirm their identity (Kyle et al., 2004). Its essence lies in the beholder's mind and is expressed through emotions, choices, and spatial behaviour (Bricker & Kerstetter, 2002). The symbolic meanings may range from the very personal to the publicly shared that contribute to the formation of an emotional bond with particular landscapes because their use has come to symbolise the users' sense of identity (Williams & Vaske, 2003). As such place identity can increase one's sense of belonging to a tourist destination (Prayag & Ryan, 2012). According to this view, a favorite place is a kind of place schema of place related knowledge and beliefs, which ultimately represents the special character of the place and one's personal connections to it. In turn, these cognitions can become incorporated into one's self-concept (Scannell & Gifford, 2010). As such, individuals draw similarities between self and the place and incorporate cognitions about the physical environment (memories, thoughts, values, preferences, categorizations) into their self-definitions (Scannell & Gifford, 2010). Salient features of a place that make it unique (e.g. attractions, historical monuments, a cultural community) can be attached to one's self-concept (Scannell & Gifford, 2010).

Place dependence has been defined as "how well a setting serves goal achievement given an existing range of alternatives" (Jorgensen & Stedman, 2001, p. 234). Places satisfying several needs typically lead to a more embedded, extensive or deep place dependence compared to places where fewer needs are met (Stokols & Shumaker, 1981). Often referred as functional attachment (Stedman, 2003), place dependence has been linked to motivation for visiting a place (Williams et al., 1992). Place dependence reflects the degree of harmony between individuals and places and the ongoing relationship with a particular setting, making this dimension comparative based (Chen et al., 2014). Social bonding has been defined as how a place facilitates the development of interpersonal relationships (Scannell & Gifford, 2010). People develop communal bonds based on the interactions they have in a place (Hammitt et al., 2006). Several studies (Chen et al., 2014;

Ramkissoon et al., 2013; Xu, 2016) in the tourism literature have shown that destinations facilitate the development of social bonds.

Others have also argued that dimensions such as place affect (Ramkissoon et al., 2013), place memory and place expectations (Chen et al., 2014) are sub-dimensions of place attachment. The emotions and feelings of an individual toward a particular place can be termed as 'place affect' (Halpenny 2010). Yet, the marketing literature argues that cognition and emotions are antecedents of behaviour (Lazarus, 1991). Following this line of thought, what a tourist knows and feels about a place are antecedents to the formation of a bond with that place. Recently, Hosany et al. (2017) argued that positive and negative emotions are antecedents to place attachment. Hence, rather than being a sub-dimension of place attachment, it can be argued that place affect is an antecedent. Chen et al. (2014) propose two additional dimensions: place memory and place expectation. Place memory was defined as how strong are the memories of stories associated with a place. According to these authors, place memory is created over time, is dynamic, and independent from the length of stay of the visitor. While place memory fits well with the developmental theory of place attachment, whereby interactions with the place create stories that are stored in mind by the visitors over time, whether the concept is a dimension of place attachment is debatable. For any destination, the tourist can form such stories by interacting online with destination marketing material, which would imply that the concept is an antecedent to place attachment. Likewise, after visitation, the so called stories in the memory of the tourist would be an outcome rather than a dimension of place attachment. Place expectation was defined as how much the future experiences associated with a place are likely to occur (Chen et al., 2014). Here again, according to the conceptualization of these authors, place expectation should be an antecedent to place attachment rather than one of its dimension.

Antecedents and outcomes of destination attachment

As outlined in the section above, there is often confusion between dimensionality, antecedents and outcomes of place attachment. In tourism literature, several concepts have been treated as the antecedents of place attachment such as motivation (Kil et al., 2012). These authors showed that motives such as exploration of nature, escape from pressure, and physical fitness significantly predicted place attachment in the context of national parks. Others have established destination image (Chen & Phou, 2013; Prayag & Ryan, 2012), destination attractiveness (Hou et al., 2005), destination source credibility (Veasna et al., 2013), service quality (Su et al., 2011), destination personality and trust (Chen & Phou, 2013), tourists' emotions (Hosany et al., 2017), authenticity of a place (Ram et al., 2016) and personal involvement (Gross & Brown, 2008; Hou et al., 2005; Prayag & Ryan, 2012) as significant antecedents. However, place satisfaction remains controversial as some researchers have treated the concept as an antecedent (Chen & Phou, 2013; Su et al., 2011) while others as an outcome of place attachment (Prayag & Ryan, 2012; Ramkissoon et al., 2013; Veasna et al., 2013; Yuksel et al., 2010).

More recently, Hosany et al. (2017) argue that if place attachment is considered developmental in nature, then place satisfaction should be treated as an antecedent given that satisfaction occurs as a result of the comparison between expectations and performance. The tourist can upgrade and downgrade the role of the various experiences to form overall satisfaction with a place. Satisfaction is both cognitive and affective and as such contributes to the formation of attachment. Each subsequent visit creates a new level of satisfaction with place that can either strengthen or weaken place attachment. The outcomes of place attachment are numerous such as pro-environmental behaviour (Ramkissoon et al., 2013), positive word-of-mouth (Chen et al., 2014), loyalty (Chen & Phou, 2013; Yuksel et al., 2010), and positive revisit intentions (Prayag & Ryan, 2012).

Further developments

Having shaped the current theoretical debates surrounding the conceptualization and operationalization of the concept in the literature, this section outlines some of the areas where research is much needed to improve our understandings of the concept and its application in tourism. First, different spatial scales interact in the formation of destination attachment. Figure 7.1, adapted from the study of Scannell and Gifford (2010), highlights the need for tourism researchers to understand tourists' place attachment for local areas as well as for multiple destinations. For example, strong emotional or functional bonds can be developed with national parks in a country and these bonds can translate into attachment to the country destination and vice-versa. So far, the geo-spatial interactive elements have not been sufficiently researched to understand how destination attachment develops. Second, while conceptualizations outside the field of tourism suggest the use of a tripartite framework (people, processes and place) to understand place attachment (Scannell & Gifford, 2010), the existing research on destination attachment focuses mainly on place aspects, that is attachment to the natural and built environment and the social relationships in the place. Figure 7.1 proposes extending such understandings to specificities of tourism activities as well. It will be important in future studies to distinguish between destination attachment based on temporary features such as events and festivals and more permanent features such as built attractions and tourism activities. There are clearly interactions between the activities (micro scale elements) and the macro scale elements (e.g, city and country) in the development of attachment.

Third, much of the existing research on destination attachment is based on tourists having actually visited the place. Attachment due to visitation in the virtual world must be explored further as shown in Figure 7.1. Some researchers in the field of information systems have studied the barriers and intentions of users returning to virtual worlds (Goel et al., 2011), which can inform studies on destination attachment. Plunkett (2011) uses the virtual world of Second Life to examine place attachment. Fourth, the psychological processes underpinning the development of destination attachment remain under-researched. For example, not much is known about how tourists assign meaning and reconstruct place experience from memory in the formation of destination attachment. Other process related aspects include the interactions between affect, cognition, and other psychological constructs such as engagement. Fifth, within the people and place connection, the role of sensorial experiences and their impact on destination attachment have not been examined in sufficient depth. For example, embodiment theory with its two facets of sensation and cognition (Tsai, 2005) has only recently been applied to understand how geo-based technology impacts place experiences, including place attachment (Tussyadiah & Zach, 2012).

Sixth, the social processes underlying the formation of destination attachment are not well understood. The focus has been on social relationships based on guest–tourist interactions that develop into attachment. At the destination level, there are other social relationships such as those between tourists and their second homes that are based on stronger commitments and intimacies that need to be teased out for a deeper understanding of the emotional connections between tourists and place. Seventh, the focus on tourists' attachment to destinations has sidelined the attachment of other important groups such as migrants and residents. It is also not well understood how the presence or absence of other groups impacts the formation of attachment. For example, a crowded destination may attenuate attachment levels while a community that lacks

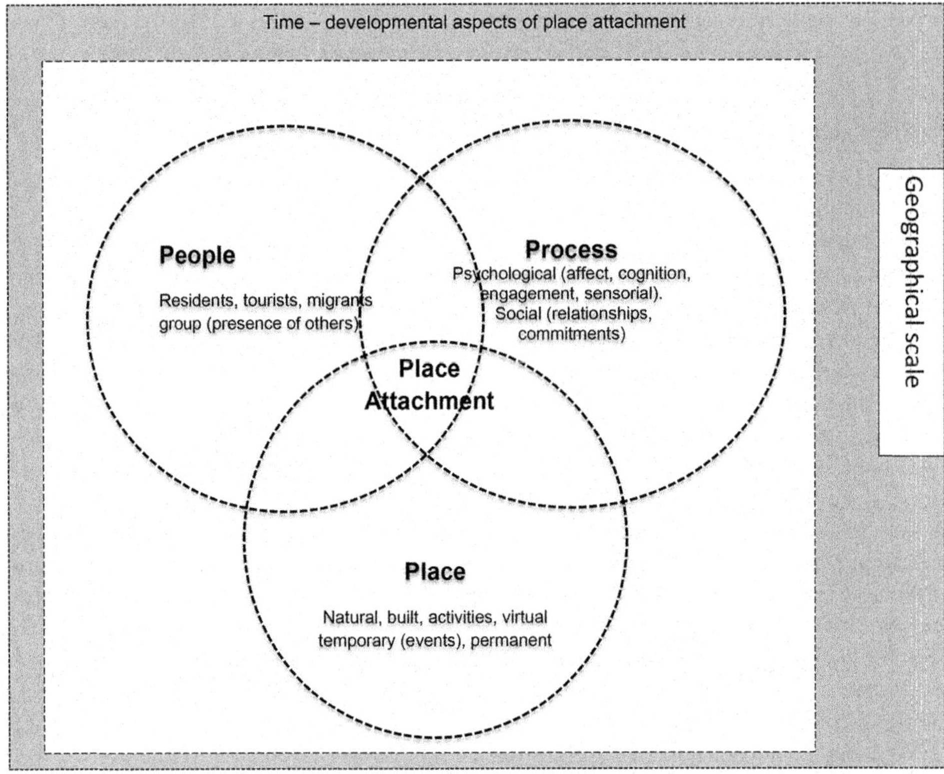

Figure 7.1 Further developments of destination attachment

amenities/facilities for tourists may generate attachment among tourists seeking escape from the modern world. Thus, destination attachment is a multi-faceted concept and requires studies on other groups and stakeholders to fully understand how it develops and impacts other constructs such as destination reputation and loyalty. Lastly, much of the existing research on place attachment in the tourism field is based on cross-sectional data. As such, there is limited understanding of how destination attachment develops overtime, the factors that strengthens or weakens that bond must be studied from a longitudinal perspective.

Conclusion

It is clear from the literature that destination attachment is an important concept in the tourism field. While there is no precise definition of the concept, researchers have borrowed extensively from other disciplines to inform the dimensionality of the concept, its antecedents and outcomes. The lack of a clear definition has led to researchers articulating different dimensions in the tourism field. Also, there is no consensus on some of the antecedents of place attachment. Place satisfaction has been treated as both an antecedent and as an outcome. As outlined in the chapter, there are several areas of further development to improve our understanding of the concept. Whether consensus will be achieved on the dimensions, antecedents and outcomes of destination attachment remains to be seen. In fact, the concept may end like other tourism concepts such as destination image which remains critical for destination marketing purposes but is atheoretical.

References

Anton, C. E., & Lawrence, C. (2014). Home is where the heart is: The effect of place of residence on place attachment and community participation. *Journal of Environmental Psychology, 40*, 451–461.

Baumeister, R. F., & Leary, M. R. (1995). The need to belong: desire for interpersonal attachments as a fundamental human motivation. *Psychological Bulletin, 117*(3), 497–529.

Beckman, E., Whaley, J. E., & Kim, Y. K. (2017). Motivations and Experiences of Whitewater Rafting Tourists on the Ocoee River, USA. *International Journal of Tourism Research, 19*(2), 257–267.

Bowlby, J. (1969). *Attachment and Loss: Vol. 1 Attachment.* New York, NY: Basic Books.

Bricker, K. S., & Kerstetter, D. L. (2000). Level of specialization and place attachment: An exploratory study of whitewater recreationists. *Leisure Sciences, 22*(4), 233–257.

Chen, N. C., Dwyer, L., & Firth, T. (2014). Conceptualization and Measurement of Dimensionality of Place Attachment. *Tourism Analysis, 19*(3), 323–338.

Cheng, C. K., & Kuo, H.Y. (2015). Bonding to a new place never visited: Exploring the relationship between landscape elements and place bonding. *Tourism Management, 46*, 546–560.

Chen, C. F., & Phou, S. (2013). A closer look at destination: Image, personality, relationship and loyalty. *Tourism Management, 36*, 269–278.

Davis, A. (2016). Experiential places or places of experience? Place identity and place attachment as mechanisms for creating festival environment. *Tourism Management, 55*, 49–61.

Dragouni, M., & Fouseki, K. (2017). Drivers of community participation in heritage tourism planning: an empirical investigation. *Journal of Heritage Tourism*, (in press), 1–20.

Giuliani, M. V., & Feldman, R. (1993). Place attachment in a developmental and cultural context. *Journal of Environmental Psychology, 13*, 267–267.

Goel, L., Johnson, N. A., Junglas, I., & Ives, B. (2011). From space to place: Predicting users' intentions to return to virtual worlds. *MIS Quarterly, 35*(3), 749–772.

Grisaffe, D. B., & Nguyen, H. P. (2011). Antecedents of emotional attachment to brands. *Journal of Business Research, 64*(10), 1052–1059.

Gross, M. J., & Brown, G. (2008). An empirical structure model of tourists and places: Progressing involvement and place attachment into tourism. *Tourism Management, 29*(6), 1141–1151.

Gu, H., & Ryan, C. (2008). Place attachment, identity and community impacts of tourism – the case of a Beijing hutong. *Tourism Management, 29*(4), 637–647.

Halpenny, E. A. (2010). Pro-Environmental behaviours and park visitors: The effect of place attachment. *Journal of Environmental Psychology, 30*(4), 409–421.

Hammitt, W. E., & Stewart, W. P. (1996, May). Sense of place: A call for construct clarity and management. In *Sixth International Symposium on Society & Resource Management, May*, 18–23.

Hammitt, W. E., Backlund, E. A., & Bixler, R. D. (2006). Place bonding for recreation places: Conceptual and empirical development. *Leisure studies, 25*(1), 17–41.

Hay, R. (1998). Sense of place in developmental context. *Journal of Environmental Psychology, 18*(1), 5–29.

Hidalgo, M. C., & Hernandez, B. (2001). Place attachment: Conceptual and empirical questions. *Journal of Environmental Psychology, 21*(3), 273–281.

Hosany, S., Prayag, G., Van Der Veen, R., Huang, S., & Deesilatham, S. (2017). Mediating effects of place attachment and satisfaction on the relationship between tourists' emotions and intention to recommend. *Journal of Travel Research*, doi. 0047287516678088.

Hou, J.S., Lin, C.H. & Morais, D.B. (2005) Antecedents of attachment to a cultural tourism destination: The case of Hakka and non-Hakka Taiwanese visitors to Pei-Pu, Taiwan. *Journal of Travel Research, 44*(2), 221–233.

Jorgensen, B. S., & Stedman, R. C. (2001). Sense of place as an attitude: Lakeshore owners attitudes toward their properties. *Journal of Environmental Psychology, 21*(3), 233–248.

Kaltenborn, B. P. (1997). Nature of place attachment: A study among recreation homeowners in Southern Norway. *Leisure Sciences, 19*(3), 175–189.

Kil, N., Holland, S. M., Stein, T. V., & Ko, Y. J. (2012). Place attachment as a mediator of the relationship between nature-based recreation benefits and future visit intentions. *Journal of Sustainable Tourism, 20*(4), 603–626.

Kyle, T. G., Mowen, A. J., & Tarrant, M. (2004). Linking place preferences with place meaning: an examination of the relationship between place motivation and place attachment. *Journal of Environmental Psychology, 24*, 439–454.

Lazarus, R. S. (1991). *Emotion and Adaptation.* New York, NY: Oxford University Press.

Lee, J., Kyle, G., & Scott, D. (2012). The mediating effect of place attachment on the relationship between festival satisfaction and loyalty to the festival hosting destination. *Journal of Travel Research, 51*(6), 754–767.

Lemelin, R. H., Koster, R., Bradford, L., Strickert, G., & Molinsky, L. (2015). People, Places, Protected Areas and Tourism: Place Attachment in Rossport, Ontario, Canada. *Scandinavian Journal of Hospitality and Tourism, 15*(1–2), 167–182.

Lewicka, M. (2011). Place attachment: How far have we come in the last 40 years? *Journal of Environmental Psychology, 31*(3), 207–230.

Low, S. M., & Altman, I. (1992). Place attachment. In *Place Attachment* (pp. 1–12). Springer US.

Manzo, L. C. (2003). Beyond house and haven: Toward a revisioning of emotional relationships with places. *Journal of Environmental Psychology, 23*(1), 47–61.

Moore, J. (2000). Placing home in context. *Journal of Environmental Psychology, 20*(3), 207–217.

Moore, R. L., & Scott, D. (2003). Place attachment and context: Comparing a park and a trail within. *Forest Science, 49*(6), 877–884.

Morgan, P. (2010). Towards a developmental theory of place attachment. *Journal of Environmental Psychology, 30*(1), 11–22.

Mikulincer, M., & Shaver, P. R. (2005). Attachment security, compassion, and altruism. *Current Directions in Psychological Science, 14*(1), 34–38.

Mikulincer, M., Shaver, P. R., & Pereg, D. (2003). Attachment theory and affect regulation: The dynamics, development, and cognitive consequences of attachment-related strategies. *Motivation and Emotion, 27*(2), 77–102.

Plunkett, D. (2011). On place attachments in virtual worlds. *World Leisure Journal, 53*(3), 168–178.

Prayag, G., & Ryan, C. (2012). Antecedents of tourists' loyalty to Mauritius: the role and influence of destination image, place attachment, personal involvement and satisfaction. *Journal of Travel Research, 51*(3), 342–356.

Proshansky, H. M., Fabian, A. K., & Kaminoff, R. (1983). Place identity: physical world socialisation of the self. *Journal of Environmental Psychology, 3*, 57–83.

Ram, Y., Björk, P., & Weidenfeld, A. (2016). Authenticity and place attachment of major visitor attractions. *Tourism Management, 52*, 110–122.

Ramkissoon, H., Smith, L. D. G., & Weiler, B. (2013). Testing the dimensionality of place attachment and its relationships with place satisfaction and pro-environmental behaviours: A structural equation modelling approach. *Tourism Management, 36*, 552–566.

Relph, E. (1976). *Place and Placelessness*. London: Pion.

Rioux, L., Scrima, F., & Werner, C. M. (2017). Space appropriation and place attachment: University students create places. *Journal of Environmental Psychology, 50*, 60–68.

Scannell, L., & Gifford, R. (2010). Defining place attachment: A tripartite organizing framework. *Journal of Environmental Psychology, 30*(1), 1–10.

Stedman, R. C. (2003). Is it really just a social construction?: The contribution of the physical environment to sense of place. *Society &Natural Resources, 16*(8), 671–685.

Stokols, D., & Shumaker, S. A. (1981). People in places: A transactional view of settings. *Cognition, Social Behavior, and the Environment*, 441–488.

Stylos, N., Bellou, V., Andronikidis, A., & Vassiliadis, C. A. (2017). Linking the dots among destination images, place attachment, and revisit intentions: A study among British and Russian tourists. *Tourism Management, 60*, 15–29.

Su, H. J., Cheng, K. F., & Huang, H. H. (2011). Empirical study of destination loyalty and its antecedent: the perspective of place attachment. *The Service Industries Journal, 31*(16), 2721–2739.

Suntikul, W., & Jachna, T. (2016). The co-creation/place attachment nexus. *Tourism Management, 52*, 276–286.

Thomson, M., MacInnis, D. J., & Park, W. C. (2005). The ties that bind: measuring the strength of consumers' attachment to brands. *Journal of Consumer Psychology, 15*(1), 77–91.

Tsai, C. T. S. (2016). Memorable tourist experiences and place attachment when consuming local food. *International Journal of Tourism Research*, 18(6), 536–548.

Tsai, S. P. (2005). Integrated marketing as management of holistic consumer experience. *Business Horizons, 48*(5), 431–441.

Tsai, S. P. (2012). Place attachment and tourism marketing: Investigating international tourists in Singapore. *International Journal of Tourism Research, 14*(2), 139–152.

Tuan, Y.F. (1977). *Space and Place: The Perspectives of Experience*. Minnesota: University of Minnesota Press.

Tuan, Y.F. (1980). Rootedness versus sense of place. *Landscape, 24*, 3–8.

Tussyadiah, I. P., & Zach, F. J. (2012). The role of geo-based technology in place experiences. *Annals of Tourism Research*, *39*(2), 780–800.
Veasna, S., Wu, W. Y., & Huang, C. H. (2013). The impact of destination source credibility on destination satisfaction: The mediating effects of destination attachment and destination image. *Tourism Management*, *36*, 511–526.
Yuksel, A., Yuksel, F., & Bilim, Y. (2010). Destination attachment: Effects on consumer satisfaction and cognitive, affective and conative loyalty. *Tourism Management*, *31*(2), 274–284.
Williams, D. R. (1995). Mapping place meanings for ecosystem management. A tech. report submitted to the Interior Columbia River Basin Ecosystem Management Project, USDA Forest Service, Washington.
Williams, D. R., & Vaske, J. J. (2003). The measurement of place attachment: Validity and generalizability of a psychometric approach. *Forest Science*, *49*(6), 830–840.
Williams, D. R., Patterson, M. E., Roggenbuck, J. W., & Watson, A. E. (1992). Beyond the commodity metaphor: Examining emotional and symbolic attachment to place. *Leisure Sciences*, *14*, 29–46.
Xu, Z. (2016). Sino-western Tourists' Place Attachment to a Traditional Chinese Urban Destination: A Tale from Hangzhou, China. *Asia Pacific Journal of Tourism Research*, *21*(6), 624–641.

8
Service quality and marketing

Ibrahim Yilmaz

Service definition and characteristics

Although service(s) have been described in several different ways, the conceptualizations are mainly focused on 'deeds, processes, and performances'. For instance, Vargo and Lusch (2004a: 326) defined services as "the application of specialized competences (skills and knowledge), through deeds, processes, and performances for the benefit of another entity or the entity itself." Yadav and Dabhade (2013: 77) noted that "services include all economic activities, output of them is intangible, production and consumption process is mainly the same, and they provide added value in forms that are intangible and it concerns of its first buyer."

Generally it is focused on four major distinguishing characteristics namely *intangibility, heterogeneity, inseparability, and perishability (IHIP)* between goods and services (Ghobadian, Speller, and Jones 1994: 45):

Intangibility means that it is difficult for the provider to describe the service and it is also difficult for the consumer to ascertain its likely virtues. Many services are not tangible and it is not possible to see, feel, taste, or smell before they are purchased.

Heterogeneity denotes that it is not easy for the provider to reproduce a service to the same standard. The heterogeneity of a service from one transaction to another, and from consumer to consumer, makes service quality difficult to control. Service organizations have to rely heavily on the skills of the employees to understand the need of the customer and to react in a timely and suitable manner.

The *inseparability* of production and consumption refers to the fact that services are usually produced at the same time as the consumption of them (fully or partially) takes place. This simultaneous production and consumption results in a highly visible activity that makes it very easy to identify service quality shortfalls. Also, presence of the customer in the delivery of the service and interaction with other customers may influence the service quality perceptions.

Perishability of services means that services can't be stored for later consumption. Thus, it is impossible to have a final quality control, and services should be provided accurately first time and every time.

Current debates on service characteristics

Service characteristics differ from goods based on the reasons summarized above which have a long academic background in service marketing literature. However, in recent years, important debates have been raised in this issue (Polyakova and Mirza 2015).

Some scholars made major contributions to the issue with successive studies. For instance, Vargo and Lusch (2004a) argue that "these characteristics don't differ from goods/imply appropriate normative strategies." They emphasized that "services enclose all products, and economic exchange is mainly about the provision of services." Vargo and Lusch (2004b) have also questioned the uniqueness of service characteristics particularly with advancements in technology.

Edvardsson, Gustafsson and Roos (2005) pointed out that the service characteristics should not be generalized to all services, but they can be used for some services when they are relevant. Gummesson (2007) has similar thoughts that IHIP characteristics don't separate services from goods. However, the characteristics can be applied very well among many other properties to characterize a value proposition and they may help to identify specific marketing situations.

Taking the current views into account, Jan (2012) tested the validity of basic assertion of services marketing theory that four specific characteristics make services uniquely different from goods. She concluded that "the theory has still the validity; however, the significance of each characteristic varies across services."

Vargo and Lusch (2008a; 2008b) carried the debates to a new dimension suggesting two perspectives for consideration: "goods-dominant (G-D)" and "service-dominant (S-D)" logic. According to goods-dominant logic services are an intangible type of goods. Production and distribution practices of goods should be modified to deal with the differences between tangible goods and services. Service-dominant logic considers service as the process of using one's resources for the benefit of and in conjunction with another party.

Gummesson (2007) noted that, service-dominant logic has more relevance and proposes service as the core concept and the term service has the same meaning with value. A provider has a value proposition, but value actualization takes place during the customer's usage and consumption process. Thus, these two parties are co-creators of value.

Grönroos and Voima (2013) analyzed value creation in services by defining value co-creation and value creation with a focus on the roles of the customer and the organization. They also analyzed co-creation as a function of the interaction between them. Grönroos and Gummerus (2014) also made a conceptual analysis of two approaches (service-logic and service-dominant logic) to understand service perspectives. Briefly, they conclude that "service-dominant logic and its generic view of value creation and value co-creation provide useful insights that broaden the notion of service."

Concept of service quality

Since service quality is an intangible term, it is not easy to conceptualize and describe it. However, there is a broad consensus that (perceived) service quality must be defined from the customer's view (Stauss and Weinlich 1997). Conceptualization revolves around the idea that it is the result of the comparison between customer perceptions and expectations about services. Thus, service quality is defined as "the degree and direction of discrepancy between consumers' perceptions and expectations" (Parasuraman, Zeithaml and Berry 1985). This conceptualization has been used in the studies of general service sector or particularly tourism industry. Thus, it is possible to say that, with some exceptions, this conceptualization is widely accepted in the literature.

Measurement of service quality

Within the framework of the considerations above, also the question of how perceived service quality should be measured from the customer's perspective by a reliable and valid measurement tool is very important. Thus, measuring service quality has become a main field of research in the literature so far.

The Service Quality (Gap) Model

Many models have been suggested for measuring service quality in service oriented organizations (Seth, Deshmukh and Vrat 2005). However, the Gap Model of Service Quality proposed by Parasuraman, Zeithaml and Berry (1985) has emerged as the most popular conceptual and operational model of service quality. The model draws attention to the gaps between customer's perceptions and expectations. According to the model, there are four gaps between perceived and expected service quality. These gaps are concerned with the service organization (or marketer) and can be controlled by that. The fifth gap is related to the customer utilizing the service itself and is a function of the previous four gaps. "This gap depends on size and direction of the four gaps associated with the delivery of service quality on the marketer's side" (Parasuraman, Zeithaml and Berry 1985: 44; Zeithaml, Berry and Parasuraman 1988: 46):

1 The gap between customer expectations and management perceptions of those expectations (marketing information gap)
2 The gap between management perceptions of customer expectations and the organization's service quality specifications (standards gap)
3 The gap between service quality specifications and actual service delivery (service performance gap)
4 The gap between actual service delivery and external communications to customer about the service (communication gap)
5 The gap between perceived and expected service quality (service quality gap)

Zeithaml, Berry and Parasuraman (1988) suggested the Extended Service Quality Model building on their initial model. They empirically identified a set of sub-factors potentially affecting the size and direction of the four gaps on the marketer's side of the model. In a way, they examined antecedents of service provider gaps which have positive (+) or negative (-) effects on these gaps (Parasuraman, Berry and Zeithaml 1991a: 341).

The Servqual Scale

Parasuraman, Zeithaml, and Berry (1988) developed a multiple item scale namely SERVQUAL to implement the Service Quality Gap Model in future service quality studies. According to the scale, quality of services can be measured by identifying gaps between customers' expectations of the service and their perceptions of the actual performance of the service providers. Perceived service quality is satisfactory if expectations are met or exceeded. The scale was initially built on ten dimensions (Parasuraman, Zeithaml and Berry 1985). Later, the dimensions were further reduced into five general dimensions; *tangibles, reliability, responsiveness, assurance, and empathy* (Parasuraman, Zeithaml and Berry 1988: 23).

Current thoughts about SERVQUAL

SERVQUAL has been widely used by both scholars and practitioners. Despite its growing popularity, the scale has been subjected to many criticisms on both theoretical and empirical grounds since it was developed (Buttle 1996:10).

Parasuraman and his colleagues have disputed some of the criticisms. However, they have considered some of them and made major modifications on these aspects of SERVQUAL scale (Parasuraman, Berry and Zeithaml 1991b; 1993; Parasuraman Zeithaml and Berry 1994a; 1994b). Although some scholars have continued to criticise the modified scales (some of them have also suggested partly or entirely different new scales), the review of the literature reveals that SERVQUAL scale is still a leading instrument to measure quality of services generally in service sector (or particularly in the hospitality and tourism industry).

Ladhari (2008) pointed out that despite the numerous criticisms of the scale, it continues to be the most useful instrument for measuring service quality. Ladhari (2009) also reviewed 20 years (1988–2008) of research on the SERVQUAL scale, identified and summarized widespread theoretical and empirical criticisms of the scale. Despite the criticisms, the study concludes that the SERVQUAL is a useful instrument for service quality research.

Khoshraftar and Rozan (2013) made a study focusing on the literature review of service quality research over a ten year (2003–2013) period. They emphasize that the SERVQUAL is considered as a useful and applicable instrument for the measurement of service quality.

Mauri, Minazzi, and Muccio (2013) conducted a literature review including studies from 1985 to 2013 on the Service Quality Gap Model. They summarized some theoretical and operational criticisms identified by scholars about the Model and the SERVQUAL scale. They conclude that the Gap model and the SERVQUAL scale are still the most useful tools for the measurement of service quality.

The service marketing triangle

All functions of the organization must work together to create effective service marketing (Vargo and Lusch 2004a). A strategic approach, *the service marketing triangle* shows the three key players (the organization, the customers, and the providers) that work together to deliver high service quality. These key players are labeled on the three points of the triangle. Between the points on the triangle, three types of marketing (*external marketing, internal marketing, and interactive or real time marketing)* must be successfully carried out (Hudson 2008; Zeithaml, Bitner and Gremler 2010; Yadav and Dabhane 2013).

> On the right side of the triangle are the *external marketing* efforts that the firm engages in to set up its customers' expectations and make promises to customers regarding what is to be delivered. Anything or anyone that communicates to the customer before service delivery can be viewed as part of this external marketing function. But external marketing is just the beginning for services marketers; promises made must be kept.
>
> *(Zeithaml, Bitner and Gremler 2010)*

The left side of the triangle indicates the critical role played by *internal marketing.* "The basic premise of internal marketing is that satisfied employees/well served internal customers will lead to satisfied customers/well served external customers" (Brown, Fisk and Bitner, 1994: 36). Organizations transmit the promises to customers with interactions between contact-employees and customers, and then effect customers' perception of the service's quality. Thus, the role of customer-contact employees is critical (Barnes and Morris 2000). Management engages in the activities (recruiting, training, motivating, rewarding etc.) to aid the providers in their skill to deliver on the service promise. If employees are able and willing to deliver on the promises made, the firm will be successful, and the service marketing triangle will remain standing (Zeithaml, Bitner and Gremler 2010).

On the bottom of the triangle is what has been called *interactive marketing*. This is where promises are kept or broken by the firm's employees or other intermediaries. If promises are kept, customers become satisfied. According to service marketing, employees are part time marketers, and their interactions with customers on the value co-creation platform entail interactive marketing. Thus, the human factor is more critical at this point (Grönroos and Gummerus 2014).

The service marketing mix

The main idea is that when it comes to service marketing, traditional 4Ps (product, price, promotion, and place) of marketing are not adequate for effective service marketing efforts. Three added Ps *people, physical evidence, and process* are also required (Hudson 2008; Zeithaml, Bitner and Gremler 2010; Lovelock, Vandermerwe, Lewis and Fernie 2011):

Because services are usually produced and consumed simultaneously, customers are generally present in the production process, interact directly with the contact-employees, and are actually part of this process. Since many services depend on the direct interaction between customers and contact-employees, the people element of the marketing mix is very important. The nature of these interactions strongly influences the customer's perceptions of service quality. Customers will often judge the quality of the service they receive largely on their assessment of the people providing the service. Successful service organizations devote significant effort to recruiting, training and motivating their employees, especially but not exclusively, those who are in direct contact with customers. Also, the contact-employees, the customer himself/herself, and other customers in the service environment each provide cues to the customer regarding the nature of the service itself.

Since services are intangible, customers look for any other visible cues (physical evidence) that help them understand the nature of services. Physical evidence pertains to the environment in which the service is delivered; all tangible components that facilitate performance or communication of the service also affect service marketing. All the tangible evidence of the service such as the appearance of buildings, landscape, interior furnishing, equipment, servicescape, signs, printed materials and other visible cues provide tangible evidence of an organization's service quality. Physical evidence needs to be managed carefully because customers often have little cue on which to judge the actual quality of an intangible offering, thus they will rely on any tangible components of the service offering.

As Parasuraman, Zeithaml and Berry (1985) noted, "service quality evaluations are not made solely on the outcome of a service; consumers also involve evaluations of the process of service delivery." The process (including the operating systems, procedures, mechanisms, and flow of activities by which the service is delivered) is an element of the service marketing mix. The process addresses how the service is delivered, which, in many cases, may be perceived by customers to be as important as the outcome of the service. Badly designed processes are likely to annoy customers when they experience slow, bureaucratic and ineffective service delivery. Similarly, poor processes make it difficult for customer-contact employees to do their jobs well, result in low productivity and increase the likelihood of service quality shortfalls.

Conclusion

In parallel with the increasing importance and share of the service industries in the world economy, service quality has become a more strategic tool for the success of service industries. It has received great interest in a wide range of service oriented organizations including tourism. The studies stress that service quality is a precondition for survival in current competitive marketing environment (Ghobadian, Speller and Jones 1994). Delivering high quality service is vital for the satisfaction of customers (Ladeira, Santini, Araujo and Sampaio, 2016; Shemwell, Yavas and Bilgin 1998). Also, high quality of services can improve the market share and profitability (Oh and Parks 1997).

Although the differences between goods and service products are not black and white by any means, it is not wrong to say that services are commonly distinguished from goods by four major characteristics. The distinguishing characteristics of services influence the perceptions of consumers while evaluating the quality of services. Despite the different ideas to date, there seems to be a broad consensus on the issue of "how best to evaluate/measure service quality from the consumer's perspective" in the relevant literature. In this sense, "service quality is viewed as the degree and direction of disperancy between consumers' perceptions and expectations" (Parasuraman, Zeithaml and Berry 1985).

The Gap Model of Service Quality determines two different types of gaps in service quality, the provider gap(s) and the customer gap. Customer gap depends on the size and direction of the provider gap(s) associated with the delivery of service quality on the marketer's side. Building on the Gap Model of Service Quality, Zeithaml, Berry and Parasuraman (1988) suggested the Extended Service Quality Model. They empirically identified organizational barriers to delivering high quality service in the model (Parasuraman, Berry and Zeithaml 1991). However, unlike the Service Quality Gap Model, the Extended Service Quality Model has not drawn enough interest in the literature. Perhaps, as Parasuraman, Berry and Zeithaml (1991a) drew attention to the fact, "one of the main reasons for this is that these types of studies require a quite complex research design and framework involving different service companies as well as customers, contact employees, and managers from each company."

To implement the Service Quality Gap Model in future studies, Parasuraman, Zeithaml and Berry (1988) developed a multiple item scale, namely the SERVQUAL. According to the SERVQUAL, "service quality can be measured by identifying gaps between customers' expectations of the service and their perceptions of the actual service performance." Despite all debates and thoughts, the Gap Model and the SERVQUAL scale has been widely used to measure service quality in general service sector or particularly in the hospitality and tourism industry.

Possible approaches to overcome the service quality shortfalls and the marketing challenges that arise due to the service characteristics are proposed. In this respect, the service marketing triangle suggested that as key players the company, the consumers and the providers must work together. The triangle also points out the importance of three types of marketing (external, internal, and interactive marketing) for success. At the same time, the service marketing mix includes three additional Ps, namely people, physical evidence, and process, apart from the traditional four Ps (product, price, place, and promotion) of marketing. These two approaches are vital to provide high quality services and for the success of service marketing efforts.

References

Barnes, B.R., & Morris, D.S. (2000) "Revising Quality Awareness through Internal Marketing: An Exploratory Study among French and English Medium-sized Enterprises," *Total Quality Management,* 11, 473–83.

Brown, S. W., Fisk, R. P., & Bitner, M. J. (1994) "The Development and Emergence of Services Marketing Thought," *International Journal of Service Industry Management,* 5, 21–48.

Buttle, F. (1996) "SERVQUAL: Review, Critique, Research Agenda," *European Journal of Marketing,* 30, 8–32.

Edvardsson, B., Gustafsson, A., & Roos, I. (2005) "Service Portraits in Service Research: A Critical Review," *International Journal of Service Industry Management,* 16, 107–21.

Ghobadian, A., Speller, S. & Jones, M. (1994) "Service Quality Concepts and Models," *International Journal of Quality & Reliability Management,* 11, 43–66.

Grönroos, C., & Voima, P. (2013) "Critical Service Logic: Making Sense of Value Creation and Co-creation," *Journal of the Academy of Marketing Science,* 41, 133–50.

Grönroos, C., & Gummerus, J. (2014) "The Service Revolution and its Marketing Implications: Service Logic vs Service Dominant Logic," *Managing Service Quality,* 24, 206–29.

Gummesson, E. (2007) "Exit Services Marketing-Enter Service Marketing," *Journal of Customer Behaviour,* 6, 113–41.

Hudson, S. (2008) *Tourism and Hospitality Marketing – A Global Perspective,* Los Angeles: Sage Publications Ltd.

Jan, A. (2012) "Services Marketing Theory Revisited: An Empirical Investigation into Financial Services Marketing," *IOSR Journal of Business and Management,* 4, 36–45.

Khoshraftar, A., & Rozan, M. (2013) "A Review of Ten Years of Research in Services Quality," *Journal of Information Systems Research and Innovation,* 1–9.

Ladeira, W. J., Santini, F. D. O., Araujo, C. F., & Sampaio, C. H., (2016). "A meta-analysis of the antecedents and consequences of satisfaction in tourism and hospitality." *Journal of Hospitality Marketing & Management,* 25(8), 975–1009.

Ladhari, R. (2008) "Alternative Measures of Service Quality: A Review," *Managing Service Quality,* 18, 65–86.

Ladhari, R. (2009) "A Review of Twenty Years of SERVQUAL Research," *International Journal of Quality and Service Sciences,* 1, 172–98.

Lovelock, C. H., Vandermerwe, S., Lewis, B., & Fernie, S. (2011) *Services Marketing,* Edinburgh: Edinburgh Business School.

Mauri, A. G., Minazzi, R., & Muccio, S. (2013) "A Review of Literature on the Gaps Model on Service Quality: A 3-Decades Period: 1985–2013," *International Business Research,* 6, 134–44.

Oh, H., & Parks, S. (1997). "Customer Satisfaction and Service Quality: A Critical Review of the Literature and Research Implications for the Hospitality Industry," *Hospitality Research Journal,* 20, 35–64.

Parasuraman, A., Berry, L. L. & Zeithaml, V. A. (1991a) "Perceived Service Quality as a Customer-Based Performance Measure: An Empirical Examination of Organizational Barriers Using an Extended Service Quality Model," *Human Resource Management,* 30, 335–64.

Parasuraman, A., Berry, L. L. & Zeithaml, V. A. (1991b) "Refinement and Reassessment of the SERVQUAL Scale," *Journal of Retailing,* 67, 420–51.

Parasuraman, A., Berry, L. L. & Zeithaml, V. A. (1993) "More on Improving Service Quality Measurement," *Journal of Retailing* 69, 140–47.

Parasuraman, A., Zeithaml, V. A., & Berry, L. (1985) "A Conceptual Model of Service Quality and its Implications for Future Research," *Journal of Marketing,* 49, 41–50.

Parasuraman, A., Zeithaml, V. A., & Berry, L. L. (1988) "SERVQUAL: A Multiple-item Scale for Measuring Consumer Perception of Service Quality," *Journal of Retailing,* 64, 12–40.

Parasuraman, A., Zeithaml, V. A., & Berry, L. L. (1994a) "Alternative Scales for Measuring Service Auality: A Comparative Assessment Based on Psychometric and Diagnostic Criteria," *Journal of Retailing,* 70, 201–30.

Parasuraman, A., Zeithaml, V. A., & Berry, L. L. (1994b) "Reassessment of Expectations as a Comparison Standard in Measuring Service Quality: Implications for Further Research," *Journal of Marketing,* 58, 111–24.

Polyakova, O., & Mirza, M. (2015) "Perceived Service Quality Models: Are They still Relevant?" *The Marketing Review,* 15, 59–82.

Seth, N., Deshmukh, S. G., & Vrat, P. (2005) "Service Quality Models: A Review," *International Journal of Quality & Reliability Management,* 22, 913–49.

Stauss, B., & Weinlich, B. (1997) "Process-Oriented Measurement of Service Quality: Applying the Sequential Incident Technique," *European Journal of Marketing,* 31, 33–55.

Shemwell, D. J., Yavas, U., & Bilgin, Z. (1998) "Customer Service Provider Relationships: An Empirical Test of a Model of Service Quality, Satisfaction and Relationship-oriented Outcomes," *International Journal of Service Industry Management,* 9, 155–68.

Vargo, S. L., & Lusch, R. F. (2004a) "Evolving to a New Dominant Logic for Marketing," *Journal of Marketing,* 68, 1–17.

Vargo, S. L., & Lusch, R.F. (2004b) "The Four Service Marketing Myths: Remnants of a Goods-Based, Manufacturing Model," *Journal of Service Research,* 6, 324–35.

Vargo, S. L., & Lusch, R. F. (2008a) "From Goods to Service(s): Divergences and Convergences of Logics," *Industrial Marketing Management,* 37, 254–59.

Vargo, S. L., & Lusch, R. F. (2008b) "Service Dominant Logic: Continuing the Evolution," *Journal of the Academy of Marketing Science,* 36, 1–10.

Yadav, R. K., & Dabhade, N. (2013) "Service Marketing Triangle and GAP Model in Hospitality Industry," *International Letters of Social and Humanistic Sciences,* 8, 77–85.

Zeithaml, V. A., Berry, L. L., & Parasuraman, A. (1988) "Communication and Control Processes in the Delivery of Service Quality," *Journal of Marketing,* 52, 35–48.

Zeithaml, V.A., Bitner, M.J. & Gremler, D.D. (2010) "Services Marketing Strategy," in R. A. Peterson, & R. A. Kerin (eds.) *Wiley International Encyclopedia of Marketing: Marketing Strategy,* Chichester: John Wiley & Sons, 208–218.

Further reading

Asubonteng, P., McCleary, K. J. & Swan, J. E. (1996) "SERVQUAL Revisited: A Critical Review of Service Quality," *The Journal of Services Marketing,* 10, 62–81. (A comprehensive review of SERVQUAL.)

Baron, S., Warnaby, G. & Hunter Jones, P. (2014) "Service(s) Marketing Research: Developments and Directions," *International Journal of Management Reviews,* 16, 150–71. (Development of researches in the service(s) marketing field from past to present.)

Caruana, A., Eving, M. T. &Ramaseshan, B. (2000) "Assessment of the Three-Column Format SERVQUAL: An Experimental Approach," *Journal of Business Research,* 49, 57–65. (Discussion on whether the three-column format SERVQUAL is suitable or not.)

Grönroos, C. (2011) "Value co-creation in service logic: a critical analysis," *Marketing Theory,* 11, 279–301. (A comprehensive analysis of value co-creation.)

Gursoy, D., Uysal, M., Sirakaya-Turk, E., Ekinci, Y. & Baloglu, S. (2015) *Handbook of Scales in Tourism and Hospitality Research,* Oxfordshire: CABI. (Performance evaluation and quality assessment scales in tourism and hospitality.)

Kayastha, S. (2011) "Defining Service and Non-Service Exchanges," *Service Science,* 3, 313–24. (A claim that suggests definitions to overcome the shortcomings of two most cited definitions of services.)

Lovelock, C., & Gummeson, E. (2004) "Whither Services Marketing? In Search of a New Paradigm and Fresh Perspectives," *Journal of Service Research,* 7, 20–41. (Suggestion of an alternative services marketing paradigm.)

Luk, S. T. K., & Layton, R. (2002) "Perception Gaps in Customer Expectations: Managers versus Service Providers and Customers," *The Service Industries Journal,* 22, 109–28. (Adding two additional gaps to the Service Quality Gap Model.)

Shahin, A., & Samea, M. (2010) "Developing the Models of Service Quality Gaps: A Critical Discussion," *Business Management and Strategy,* 1, 4–11. (Proposition of eight additional gaps to the Service Quality Gap Model.)

9

Crisis management and marketing

Sam Sarpong

Introduction

We live in a world characterised by risks and crisis. Potentially everyone and everything is at risk these days. We have lived through many of these crises and still harbour a lot. Crises can develop at any time and in any environment (Massey 2001). Day in and day out, we hear of or experience numerous cases that befall individuals, countries and organisations. These include recent terrorist attacks (France, Germany and Belgium, 2016; US, 11 September, 2001); the financial crisis in the European Union (2007/2008); product recalls (Toyota, 2015; Samsung's Galaxy Note 7, 2016); attempted coup in Turkey (2016); the 2010 Iceland volcanic eruption, the outbreak of foot and mouth disease in the UK (February 2001). The list seems endless (Elliott et al. 2005). Things happen so quickly around us that oftentimes we are unable to see them coming (Massey 2001).

The range of risks to which we are exposed and to which we expose others has also expanded as society has become more complex. Regardless of the country, the individual or industry, everybody or any entity has its own risks. A lot has happened in the last few years that provides a depiction of this world as one of fragility. The vulnerabilities of our interconnected and global economy are shared by all and sundry (Baubion 2013). Certainly, an Ebola outbreak in Africa or a Zika virus pandemic in South America has serious implications in the entire world because of its ability to spread across the globe. Such a situation was made manifest in 2010 when the Icelandic volcanic eruptions halted many international flights and created flight cancellations for major airlines in the world.

Currently, there is concern about France as a travel destination following recent terror attacks. France, Germany and Belgium, especially, have recently suffered a meltdown as a result of major disruptive incidents within their borders. The terror events have led to a downturn in travel which, in turn, has resulted in a crisis in the hospitality industry in that part of the world. Now, major airlines are warning of the impact from the "high level" of geopolitical and economic uncertainties as a consequence of the happenings in some parts of the world. Global leaders, meanwhile, have now become acutely aware in the wake of the recent financial and fiscal crises, that further systemic shocks could severely challenge economic recovery, social cohesion and even political stability.

What makes the whole situation startling is that, a crisis is an exceptional situation, the onset of which is uncertain. Even organizations whose exclusive task is to identify and plan to forestall such incidences or processes, cannot prepare adequately for every crisis. Since we are living in an era of crises, understanding and dealing with crises is today becoming especially, for business practitioners and researchers, a real challenge.

This chapter traces the development of the crisis process and its management. It also considers extant studies on crisis management and marketing services and examines how firms can react in order to protect their brands when confronted with a crisis. It explores the opportunities for reciprocal learning between the fields of crisis management and service marketing and offers stimulating situations on crises experienced by business organizations.

First, it offers an introduction to the subject matter. It then delves into the definition of crisis and its management. Subsequently, the chapter clarifies the different types of crisis, i.e. societal crises, which include natural disasters such as earthquakes, hurricanes, forest fires or even climate change, where individual organizations may be affected but only as part of broader community or national impact. It, however, positions organizational crisis as a basis for the chapter.

What is a crisis?

Crisis definitions and typologies

Just as it is difficult to construct one universal framework for managing crises, scholars also struggle to reach an agreement on how to define crisis as a phenomenon in itself (Smith 2005). Various disciplines have different ways of seeing a crisis, hence, different definitions have been offered as to what constitutes a crisis. Some are specific to organizations whilst others are expressed in general terms. A crisis, in more general terms, can be seen as a situation that suddenly happens and breaks the routine processes of a system. It involves an ill-structured situation (Turner 1976) and where resources are inadequate to cope with the situation (Webb 1994; Starbuck and Hedberg 1977). As Hermann (1963) explains, it is a major threat to system survival with little time to respond. In effect, crises are chaotic situations that might be experienced by people, states, governments or organizations (Isyar 2008).

Common to nearly all definitions of crisis is the element of surprise (Massey 2001). Crisis can also be seen as a situation which is not normal or stable. It can be explained as an incident that is, or is expected to lead to, an unstable and dangerous situation affecting an individual, group, community, or whole society. People may experience crisis as a result of many events. This can include the loss of a loved one, physical health issues, violence and trauma as well as organizational malfeasance. Crisis can be categorized in four different groups; namely (a) natural crisis, (b) civil conflicts, (c) epidemics, and (d) organisational/technology failures (Tse 2006; Cushnahan 2004).

In relating crisis to the firm, it can be said that a crisis is a situation that causes negative or undesirable outcomes for an organization. It is a non-routine, unexpected and sudden event that creates uncertainty and threatens the priority goals of the organization and also has the basis to cause financial losses and undermine a company's reputation (Coombs 2007; Dean 2004; Tsang 2000). Crisis occurs suddenly, demands quick reaction, interferes with organizational performance, creates uncertainty and stress, threatens the reputation and assets of the organization, escalates in intensity, causes outsiders to scrutinize the organization, and permanently alters the organization (Millar 2004). It also represents a fundamental threat to the stability of the system, a questioning of core assumptions and a risk to a company's goals (Waymer and Heath 2007).

The significance of a crisis is that it can destroy the reputation of a company which has been built up for years. It is, thus, a stressful event that causes significant interruptions within the business set-up. Its occurrence can be attributed to possible management failures (Prideaux et al. 2003). In crisis situations, the root cause of an event can, to some extent, be self-inflicted through inept management structures and practices or a failure to adapt to change, among others (Faulkner 2001).

In effect, a crisis creates uncertainty and threatens an organization's image, identity, and reputation. Therefore, organizations cannot simply ignore a crisis situation, in that it can happen in just about every industry or sector. It is, therefore, pertinent to understand what a crisis is, the course it may take, and the effects it ultimately has on an organization in order to halt its occurrence. In crisis management, the threat is the potential damage a crisis can inflict on an organization, its stakeholders, and an industry. A crisis can create three related threats: (a) public safety, (b) financial loss, and (c) reputation loss.

Some crises, such as industrial accidents and product harm, can result in injuries and even loss of lives. Crises can also create financial loss by disrupting operations, creating a loss of market share and purchase intentions, or creating the basis for lawsuits relating to the crisis. Consequently, a crisis reflects poorly on an organization and will damage a firm's reputation to some extent.

The effect of a crisis is based on numerous factors and varies with each occurrence. For instance, the effect of a plane crash can linger on for years as many passengers could proscribe the airline for fear of losing their lives in case they fly with it. In the aftermath of the Malaysia Airlines disaster in 2014, passenger bookings plummeted considerably causing the airline to re-strategize in order to win back its passengers. The airline therefore resorted to providing perks for passengers and cutting staff numbers. From this, it can be inferred too that a crisis holds the potential for profound changes in organizations. Although a crisis calls into question the survival of a system, it can also lead to either positive or negative organizational outcomes (Pauchant and Mitroff 1992; Marcus and Goodman 1991). Some scholars have even argued that the trauma inherent in crisis is developmental for a system, as it provides individuals within the system with opportunities for learning and change (Pauchant and Mitroff 1992). This is because a crisis creates a basis for organisations to look out for what went wrong and also to find solutions to the issues they are confronted with.

The crises on hand for organizations

Crises tend to bring deep uncertainties. As a consequence, no organization, regardless of its size or strength is immune from it. Crises can have profound negative effects on a firm's operations. It could even derail future growth, affect profitability, and even disrupt the organization's survival. Various incidents of late have created a new crisis landscape that presupposes the idea that the twenty-first century is likely to witness increasingly damaging and costly shocks. As Baubion (2013) notes, our society is becoming not only more complex and interconnected, but also increasingly vulnerable and exposed, as new or different threats emerge and spread more quickly through spill-over or multiplier effects.

According to de Sausmarez (2007), crises can be ranged in three time periods: potential, latent, and acute. Potential crises are threats that might occur in the future. Nevertheless, they have to be identified and considered so that they can be nipped in the bud. On the other hand, a latent crisis is one that is already in existence, but does not yet have a measurable negative influence. But once a perilous situation has turned into an acute crisis, its destructive effect can be clearly perceived and measured. Whilst some crises happen quickly and therefore do not present organizations the time to prepare for them, others develop at a slower pace and therefore, can be predicted. This allows for measures to be taken against them.

Crisis management

Having experienced a crisis, it is important to find a way of managing it. Crisis management entails the planning for, responding to and recovering from a crisis. In general, crisis management can be described as measures of all types which allow a business to cope with a suddenly occurring danger or risk situation in order to return as quickly as possible to normal business routine. In its most basic form, crisis management implies being prepared before the crisis strikes, effectively executing the crisis management plan during the crisis, and quickly recovering to normal after the crisis (Yu et al. 2005).

It can also be viewed as a strategic action designed to avoid or mitigate undesirable developments and to bring about a desirable resolution of the problems on hand (Burnett 1998). As Barton (2008) indicates, crisis management is an effective management tool to get to know what kind of threats there are to a business and it also helps to anticipate the threats for a quick remedy, and to control the damage to the business. In effect, crisis management is about being prepared to handle a misfortune, lessening the impact of the crisis and also pursuing a process of facilitating the management process during chaotic conditions.

Organizations that deal with a crisis in a timely and honest manner can minimize damage to their reputation and regain public trust (Seeger et al. 2001; Coombs 1999; Janis 1989). Managers must, however, recognize the necessity to develop the skills needed to handle any threat and challenge that would inevitably arise. They also need to be ready to handle such a crisis through careful and meticulous preparations.

In recent years, national and international events and the impact of pandemics, climate change and terror attacks have raised the importance of good crisis management. Whilst many organizations have existing crisis management plans in place and have matured in their overall crisis response capability, it is important, however, to further enhance this capability and to be better prepared to respond to new and unimagined risks. By having a crisis management plan in place, a company is better equipped to take actions that minimize potential liabilities and disruption to business.

Phases of crisis management

Crisis management can also be seen as a process designed to prevent or lessen the damage a crisis can inflict on an organization and its stakeholders. As a process, crisis management can be divided into three phases: (a) pre-crisis, (b) crisis response, and (c) post-crisis. The pre-crisis phase is concerned with prevention and preparation. The crisis response phase is when management must actually respond to a crisis. The post-crisis phase looks for ways to better prepare for the next crisis and fulfils commitments made during the crisis phase including follow-up information.

The pre-crisis phase aims to prevent crises through the process of identification, analysis and response to project risks. It also consists of estimating the probability of a particular crisis occurring, its expected frequency and its potential impact on operations. At the crisis stage, that is if and when crisis is triggered, efforts must be shifted to containing the crisis and minimizing its profound effects. In terms of that, it would be prudent to gather much information on the issue. After the assessment, it is important to communicate the situation to the public and other stakeholders. A quick, well-structured response allows for the framing of the crisis by preventing the spread of inaccurate information. It also gives a basis for the organization to show that it is in control of the situation on hand. Consequently, the organization can then be well-placed to describe corrective measures being put in place to stem the tide.

The post-crisis stage is when the risk is over. At this stage, the crisis is no longer the focal point of management's attention although it still requires some attention. The post-crisis phase tends to fulfil commitments made during the crisis phase. It also aims at repairing any reputational damage incurred during the crisis.

The need for a crisis management approach by an organization can be demonstrated by the fact that: a) factors such as disasters, accidents and mishaps have increased in the past years, and b) investment in crisis preparation may be justified by the significant costs to organizations in terms of financial losses, fatalities and missed market opportunities, and ultimately to damaged reputation (Elliott et al. 2005).

Corporate malfeasances and crisis

In business as in life, crises tend to be experienced in so many ways. Product-related crises alone range from outright failures, contaminations to unanticipated side effects. Major crises such as product recalls, plane and shipping disasters involving the tragic loss of lives are those which often engage the greatest public interest. In 1999, for instance, Coca Cola experienced a case of product contamination in Belgium. The case led to the company's biggest product recall to include the Netherlands, France and Luxemburg, resulting in the loss of US$60 million. It is this type of crisis that leads to the most visible and measurable erosion of public confidence.

There are severe consequences for the firm when products are withdrawn from the market. It can lead to poor sales, the loss of market share and high costs with the recall campaign, including logistic costs from the product withdrawal, communication campaigns and destruction costs of the product which is withdrawn. Aside from that, there is the possibility that the whole exercise could also lead to a reduction in the efficiency of the brand's investment in marketing as well as the company's reputation with stakeholders (Cleeren et al. 2013; Coombs 2007; Heerde et al. 2007).

Of late, many organizations have suffered huge crises as a result of the investigating of their activities by the media and civil society. Non-governmental organisations now mastermind increasingly sophisticated campaigns to bring to the fore much of the intransigence of business organizations. This vocal and energetic movement is growing in line with corporate unpopularity, tackling issues as diverse as food and health safety, pollution, animal welfare issues, trading standards, ageism, racism, nuclear disarmament, sexism in the workplace, pesticides and disclosure of information, among others. These effective consumer campaigns have contributed to a rise in popular sensitivity to a range of issues bordering on corporate governance, environmental and social issues.

Recent examples where major companies have fared badly include global labour standards (particularly in the realm of sweatshops), animal rights, socially responsible investment, product safety and corporate scandals. The recent collapse of some high profile institutions around the world has shown that no company can be too big to fail. A common trend that runs through these monumental failures has been poor corporate governance culture, exemplified in poor management, fraud and insider abuses by management and board members, poor asset and liability management, poor regulations and supervision among others. The celebrated Enron case in the US, the financial crisis in the South East Asian countries and a host of others, attest to the need for good governance in the public and the private sectors of the economy.

Again, we can make reference to the crisis in the subprime market in the US, and the associated liquidity squeeze in mid-2008, which had a major impact on financial institutions and banks in many countries. In the course of the turmoil, several banks failed in Europe and the US while others received government recapitalisation towards the end of 2008. At the end of 2009, Toyota also had to recall over 8 million vehicles worldwide to address issues of "unintended acceleration". It also suspended production of some of its most popular models and also testified before the US Congress in the light of the problems it faced. It was estimated that costs from its recall crisis topped US$5 billion and sales slid by 16 per cent.

Currently, Samsung is suffering considerably from the fall-out from its Galaxy Note 7 phones, which it finally abandoned after failing to resolve overheating problems which caused some of the phones to ignite.

Many organisations have indeed had difficult spells in the course of their activities. Very often when organisations undergo such difficulties, the only way out for them is to embark on a marketing drive in order to recover from their mishaps. Ultimately, this leads us to believe that marketing has a huge role to play in times of crisis.

The relation between crisis management and marketing

If indeed, marketing has a role to play in crisis management, then what exactly is the role of marketing in this? In order to answer this question, it would be pertinent for us to have an insight into marketing, in order for us to have some knowledge about the nature of this relationship between marketing and crisis management.

Marketing constitutes just one of the functions available to every business. It helps in determining and satisfying the needs of customers through products that have value and accessibility. Marketing, therefore, remains the pivotal function in any business. Along with a myriad of other functions, marketing contributes to the ability of a business to succeed. In many businesses, marketing may be deemed of highest importance. The very existence of business depends upon successful products and services, which in turn relies on successful marketing. For this reason, every business-minded person will have to learn and be guided by some basic principles of marketing. Marketing principles have even been effectively applied to several non-business institutions for years in fields such as politics, education, churches among others.

As businesses depend on the effectiveness of their marketing effort in order to advance their cause, marketing efforts can, therefore, be tailored towards situations where there is a crisis or disaster. This is so because marketing is recognized as an important part of crisis communication, especially during the long term recovery stage of a crisis or disaster. In cases where there have been service failures, it is important to mount a strong marketing response in order to stem the tide of public disgruntlement during crisis situations. If this is not done, the service provider-customer relationship that is always important in service encounters could be severed.

It is particularly important to realize that customer power is an ever-increasing phenomenon, particularly in relation to service failure. Dissatisfied customers have the tendency to withdraw patronage from a product or service if they perceive the organisation to be acting inappropriately or not living up to their expectations (Massey 2001; Coombs and Holladay 1996). For instance, following a series of air disasters in 2014, many people became disgruntled with Malaysia Airlines. Incidentally, the airline was unable to provide the appropriate response to the crisis situation, a development that has since led to the gradual demise of Malysia Airlines. Perhaps as a way of mitigating this effect, it would be pertinent to resort to Soñmez et al.'s (1999) postulation that marketers need to have a prepared crisis communication and marketing plan, as the cost of this will be far less than the costs associated with a downturn in customer confidence and patronage.

Quite significantly, any organization which appears to be floundering in its response, or which fails to quickly reassure its numerous internal and external stakeholders in a crisis situation, may suffer serious damage to its reputation, to its key relationships, and to its on-going business. Companies must therefore prepare to engage proactively with their stakeholders to ensure they respond swiftly and appropriately, and that they intend to do 'the right thing' when they are confronted with problems. As Rubel et al. (2011) note, all brands are liable to undergo a crisis. Marketing, thus, provides the leeway for a company to bounce back after a crisis.

It is critical for marketers to understand what is going on not just across their industry, but also in the broader environment in which they operate. One of the best ways to identify possible threats or vulnerabilities is to observe what is happening around them and to know how to confront the challenges that come up. If marketers look only at their insular world and not the cultural context it fits into, their communications would come off as insensitive. Crisis communication and marketing are important in the provision of information to key publics.

Tourism sector

In the tourism sector, for instance, marketing helps the tourism destinations to limit the impact of a crisis and also assists them to recover from incidents by safeguarding the destination image and reputation which is of immense value to the tourism industry. The development of crisis communication and marketing strategies by organisations is therefore a critical competency for tourism managers. Crisis management has become particularly important for those destinations which are heavily dependent on tourism as a source of income since they are the ones who suffer most when negative events occur. Tourism provides countries with income, foreign currency earnings and jobs, hence, when there is a negative publicity about particular destinations, it leads to dire consequences for the countries and communities affected.

In recent years, the tourism industry has experienced many crises. After some years of political turmoil and the downing of a holiday jet in 2015, tourism in Egypt has been left in a desperate state. Meanwhile, there was an exodus of tourists from Tunisia after an Islamist gunman killed 38 people in a single attack in 2015. As at now, tourism in Paris continues to feel the effects of the recent deadly tourist attack that left 130 people dead from shootings and suicide bombings. The deadly attacks in the French capital in November 2015 are believed to have cost French hoteliers an estimated €270 million (£210 million) in lost revenue and could continue to have an impact on hotel occupancy rates. The feeling of fear spread worldwide, with Japan Airlines saying it was extending the suspension of flights between Japan and Paris as demand remained slow following the atrocity.

But it needs to be noted that tourism crises do not always cause negative impacts on tourist destinations. It can also be considered as turning points along destination development. As Beirman (2003) notes, over a period of time, the scenes of past crises, such as wars, crimes, or natural disasters, can become tourist attractions in their own right. An example of this is that of Sobibor, the extermination camp set up by the Nazis, which today commands a lot of visitors. An effective management of a crisis and appropriate marketing efforts during and after crisis periods and ably supported by the media, can turn an unknown or infamous locality into a popular tourist destination.

To improve the image of a place, decision-makers have to decide on a suitable 'package' for marketing the place competitively. The complexity of the process requires that the packaging be under the guidance of strategic marketing professionals who could design a proper package that can lead to the reinvigoration of the place and also ensure its growth. It is important that tourism ensures it brings risk, security, and crisis management under control (Peters and Pikkemaat 2005).

Providing a common front for crisis management and marketing

What defines a crisis in business operations depends on a number of variables: the nature of the event; the importance of the issue to the stakeholders involved (Näsi 1995); the impact on other firms and industries; how many and how quickly individuals inside and/or outside of a particular firm need to be helped or informed; who and how many people need interpretation of the events, and how accessible those individuals are; how much interaction with the media is necessary; what the media choose to emphasize; who and how many people need emergency care; how much the organization needs to assert control and demonstrate that it is capable of responding; and how quickly the firm needs to respond (Shelton et al. 2003).

In times of crisis, communication with consumers is of special importance. Lost consumer interest, due to reduced discretionary income, can be re-acquired through promotion activities which are spearheaded by marketing overtures. By this means, organizations can also attract floating customers to their brands, since consumers tend to change their brand preferences more often during crises situations than at other times. As such, companies need to have the wherewithal to withstand the pressures associated with crisis situations. Advertising remains a strong pillar to build on. Ang (2001) makes a case for this when he stresses that during the Asian economic crisis, Singaporean businesses adapted much more because they were able to increase their promotion budget than US companies had done during the oil crisis. Also, offering higher quality products at the same price, or the same quality at a lower price, can have a positive effect on performance in times of crisis. But like any, product quality decisions should always be made in concert with pricing decisions.

A key challenge for any company involved in a crisis is to minimize negative or hostile media coverage which can undermine the confidence of customers, employees, investors, business partners and other stakeholders. Companies should also be quick to establish themselves as the best source of information about their organization and how it is responding to the crisis.

Crises can strike at any moment and with the pace of social media, a crisis can spiral out of control and damage a brand before the marketer can even map out his or her damage control plan. There is therefore the need to anticipate potential threats in order to ensure organization are well positioned to manage crisis situations. As is often the case, social media usage increases during crises as people tend to seek more information about issues from there (Choi and Lin 2009). For many of these users of social media, strength can also be drawn from the emotional support that is often provided on these platforms.

The exigencies in any crisis situation are influenced by the seriousness of the crisis and how the different audiences perceive the organization's responsibility for the crisis' occurrence (Benoit 1995). As an organization operating in today's society, it is quite common to have a detailed course of action ready to serve as a guide and to secure the ideal management of a potential crisis situation. Crisis management is indeed a vital factor for success in today's uncertain business environment. It is a useful tool in enabling organizations to develop proactive business decisions about long-term strategies since it gives them the ability to fight challenges to profitability and survival. Companies that are prepared for crises are better able to handle them more efficiently and successfully.

Incidentally, a crisis management plan does not necessarily provide a guarantee for controlling a crisis. To be successful during such a crisis, decision-makers and planners need to focus on promotional strategy, but in tandem with other strategies to ensure it pulls an organization from its doldrums. As Heath (1998) notes, crisis management is as much about dealing with human perceptions about the crisis as it is about physically resolving the crisis situation. The key issue in crisis management would therefore be to prepare in advance. Crisis management training; planned prevention and immediate response are all important interventions that can stem the tide of any crisis.

Conclusion

The chapter looked at crisis management and the role that marketing plays in it. It found that marketing indeed plays an enormous part in it especially in crisis communication and recovery.

It stressed the need for the development of strategies for managing crises and the integration of crisis management approaches into business strategy. It also noted that the capacity to coordinate crisis management is a fundamental element of good governance, as it tests organisational capacity to provide the appropriate responses at the right time in order to protect their stakeholders and businesses and also to mitigate the impact of crisis situations.

References

Ang, S.H. (2001) "Crisis marketing: a comparison across economic scenarios," *International Business Review*, 10(3): 263–284.

Barton, L. (2008) *Crisis leadership now: a real world guide to preparing for threats, disaster, sabotage*, New York: McGraw-Hill.

Baubion, C. (2013) *Strategic Crisis Management*, OECD Risk Management.

Beirman, D. (2003) *Restoring Tourism Destinations in Crises: A Strategic Marketing Approach*, Oxon: CABI.

Benoit, W. L. (1995) *Accounts, Excuses, and Apologies: A Theory of Image Restoration Strategies*, Albany, NY: State University of New York Press.

Burnett, J. J. (1998) "A strategic approach to managing crises," *Public Relations Review*, 24(4): 475–488.

Choi, Y. and Lin, Y.-H. (2009) "Consumer responses to Mattel product recalls posted on online bulletin boards: Exploring two types of emotion," *Journal of Public Relations Research*, 21(2): 198–207.

Cleeren, K., Heerde, H. Van and Dekimpe, M. G. (2013) "Rising from the ashes: how brands and categories can overcome product-harm crises," *Journal of Marketing*, 77: 58–77.

Coombs, W. T. and Holladay, S. J. (1996) "Communication and attributions in a crisis: an experiment study in crisis communication," *Journal of Public Relations Research*, 8(4): 279–295.

Coombs, W. T. (1999) *Ongoing crisis communication: Planning, managing and responding*, Thousand Oaks, CA: Sage.

Coombs, W. T. (2007) "Attribution theory as a guide for post-crisis communication research," *Public Relations Review*, 33(2): 135–139.

Cushnahan, G. (2004) "Crisis management in small-scale tourism," *Journal of Travel & Tourism Marketing*, 15(4): 323–338.

Dean, D. H. (2004) "Consumer reaction to negative publicity: effects of corporate reputation, response, and responsibility for a crisis event," *Journal of Business Communication*, 41(2): 192–211.

de Sausmarez, N. (2007) "Crisis management, tourism and sustainability: the role of indicators," *Journal of Sustainable Tourism*, 15(6): 700–714.

Elliott, D., Harris, K. and Baron, S. (2005) "Crisis management and services marketing," *Journal of Services Marketing*, 19(5): 336–345.

Faulkner, B. (2001) "Towards a framework for tourism disaster management," Tourism Management, 22: 135–147.

Heath, R. (1998) *Crisis Management for Managers and Executives*, London: Financial Times Management.

Heerde, H. Van, Helsen, K. and Dekimpe, M. G. (2007) "The Impact of a product-harm crisis on marketing effectiveness," *Marketing Science*, 26(2): 230–245.

Hermann, C. (1963) "Some consequences of crisis which limit the viability of organizations," *Administrative Science Quarterly*, 8: 61–82.

Isyar, O.G. (2008) "Definition and Management of International Crises," *Journal of International Affairs*, 13(4): 1–48.

Janis, I. L. (1989) *Crucial decisions: Leadership in policymaking and crisis management*, New York: Free Press.

Marcus, A. A. and Goodman, R. S. (1991) "Victims and shareholders: the dilemmas of presenting corporate policy during a crisis," *Academy of Management Journal,* 34(2): 281–305.
Massey, J. E. (2001) "Managing organizational legitimacy: communication strategies for organizations in crisis," *Journal of Business Communication*, 38(2): 153–182.
Millar, D. (2004) Exposing the errors: An examination of the nature of organizational crisis, in D. Millar and R. L. Heath (eds), *Responding to Crisis: A Rhetorical Approach to Crisis Communication*, Mahwah, NJ: Lawrence Erlbaum Associates, pp. 19–32.
Nasi, J. (1995) *Understanding Stakeholder Thinking,* Jyvaskyla, Finland: Gummerus Kirjapaino, Oy.
Pauchant, T. C. and Mitroff, I. I. (1992) *Transforming the crisis-prone organization: Preventing individual, organizational, and environmental tragedies*, San Francisco, CA: Jossey-Bass Publishers.
Peters, M. and Pikkemaat, B. (2005) *Innovation in hospitality and tourism.* London: Routledge.
Prideaux, B., Laws, E. and Faulkner, B. (2003) "Events in Indonesia: exploring the limits to formal tourism trends forecasting methods in complex crisis situations," *Tourism Management*, 24: 475–487.
Rubel, O., Naik, P. A. and Srinivasan, S. (2011) "Optimal advertising when envisioning a product-harm crisis," *Marketing Science*, 30(6): 1048–1065.
Seeger, M. W. and Ulmer, R. R. (2001) "Virtuous responses to organizational crisis: Aaron Feuerstein and Milt Cole," *Journal of Business Ethics*, 31(4): 369–376.
Shelton, C.K., Hall, R.F. and Darling, J.R. (2003) "When Cultures Collide: The Challenge of Global Integration," *European Business Review*: 312–323.
Smith, D. (2005) "Business (not) as usual: Crisis management, service recovery and the vulnerability of organizations," *Journal of Services Marketing*, 19(5): 309–320.
Soñmez, S., Apostolopoulos, Y. and Tarlow, P. (1999) "Tourism in crisis: Managing the effects on tourism," *Journal of Travel Research*, 38(1): 3.
Starbuck, W. and Hedberg, B. (1977) "Saving an organization from a stagnating environment," in H. Thorelli (ed.), *Strategy + Structure = Performance*, Bloomington, IN: Indiana University Press, pp. 249–258.
Stafford, G., Yu, L. and Armoo, A.K. (2002) "Crisis management and recovery: how Washington D.C. hotels responded to terrorism," *Cornell Hotel and Restaurant Administrations Quarterly*, 43(5): 27–40.
Tsang, A. S. (2000) "Military doctrine in crisis management: three beverage contamination cases," *Business Horizons*, 43(5): 65–73.
Tse, T.-S.-M. (2006) "Crisis Management in Tourism," in D. Buhalis and C. Costa (eds), *Tourism Management Dynamics: Trends, Management and Tools*, Oxford: Elsevier, pp. 28–38.
Turner, B. (1976) "The organizational and interorganizational development of disasters," *Administrative Science Quarterly*, 21: 378–397.
Waymer, D. and Heath, R. L. (2007) "Emergent agents: The forgotten publics in crisis communication and issues management research," *Journal of Applied Communication Research*, 35(1): 88–108.
Webb, E. (1994) "Trust and Crisis," in R. Kramer and T. Tyler (eds), *Trust in Organizations,* Newbury Park, CA: Sage.
Yu, L., Stafford, G. and Armoo, A. K. (2005) "A study of crisis management strategies of hotel managers in the Washington, D.C. Metro Area," *Journal of Travel and Tourism Marketing*, 19(2/3): 91–105.

Further reading

Elliott, D., Smith, D. and McGuiness, M. (2000) "Exploring the failure to learn: Crises and barriers to learning," *Review of Business*, 21(3): 17–24. (Learning from crises.)
Jaques, T. (2009) "Issue management as a post-crisis discipline: identifying and responding to issue impacts beyond the crisis," *Journal of Public Affairs*, 9(1): 35–44. (Dealing with issue management.)

Part II

Marketing destinations to specific segments

10

Marketing destinations to customers from diverse generations

Medet Yolal

Introduction

In tourism, markets can be segmented by several variables, such as geographic, demographic, psychographic and behavioral variables. Recently, one concept related to changes in tourist behavior that has been receiving much attention in the broader tourism literature is that of generational cohorts. In generational segmentation, it is assumed that the era in which a person is born and the experiences with which he/she grows up will affect his/her behavior, attitudes and values as a consumer in the marketplace (Fountain & Lamb, 2011). These values and subsequent behaviors are assumed to remain relatively stable throughout a generation's lifetime and set it apart from preceding and following generations. In line with this, McCrindle (2009) argues that it is important to remember that generational cohort members will differ based on dimensions such as culture, residence, gender, social class, level of affluence and personality. Thus, generational cohorts offer an additional form of market segmentation, which is considered to be richer than age segmentation alone and enables targeted marketing to these cohorts (Lancaster & Stillman, 2002; Pendergast, 2010). Based on this assumption, several studies have examined generational differences in decision making (Bakewell & Mitchell, 2003), consumption behaviors (Cleaver, Green & Muller, 2000; Li, Li & Hudson, 2013), motivations (Patterson & Pan, 2011; Elliot & Choi, 2011), online purchases (Beldona, Nusair & Demicco, 2009), working attitudes (Chi, Maier & Gursoy, 2013; Park & Gursoy, 2012), and online travel information searches (Beldona 2005). There is also growing interest in cohorts' travel consumption behaviors and attitudes.

Given the changing demographic patterns, especially in developed Western countries, understanding the differences among generations will help destination marketers and managers better tailor their products and services according to the differing needs of these generations. Determining the tourism behaviors of different generations is also important for predicting future generations' behaviors. Therefore, this chapter aims to shed light on the discussion about generations and their tourism consumption practices by summarizing the relevant literature. Accordingly, the generational theory is explained in consideration of tourism consumption. This is followed by an examination of the characteristics of different generations and their behaviors in the tourism market. Further, marketing destinations to customers from diverse generations is discussed. The chapter ends with theoretical and managerial implications according to the generational theory.

Generational theory

Scholars use the term 'generation' to refer to people born in the same general time span who share key historical or social life experiences (Kupperschmidt, 2000). A generation is considered to cover a span of approximately 20 years; however, specific age group classifications vary from author to author, depending on which major events are selected as having an influence on a particular generation (Treloar, Hall & Mitchell, 2004). For example, Strauss and Howe (1991) determined that there are seven generations currently living in the USA. However, the literature on generations mainly focuses on three generations: Baby Boomers, Generation X and Generation Y. More recently, studies on Generation Z (those born in 2000 and later) as a separate cohort have also appeared.

Generations and generational units are informally defined by social commentators, demographers, the press and media, popular culture, market researchers and members of the generation themselves (Pendergast, 2010; Moscardo & Beckendorff, 2010). Therefore, McCrindle and Beard (2007) criticize this form of grouping as being speculative rather than critical and analytical. However, Bonn, Furr and Hausman (2001) underline the fact that significant contributions to existing consumer behavior issues are possible through generational groupings compared to traditional demographic market research using age as an absolute value.

Generational theory suggests that each generation brings with it somewhat predictable traits, values and beliefs, along with skills, attributes, capacities, interests, expectations and preferred approaches, which are directly attributable to their generational location (Pendergast, 2010). This theory seeks to understand and characterize cohorts of people according to their membership in a generation, which is objectively assigned according to their year of birth. In this regard, it is generally assumed that different generations may, in fact, possess different psychographic characteristics based on society's changing lifestyle and behaviors (Bonn, Furr & Hausman, 2001).

A group that is born and raised during a particular historical period experiences similar environmental influences, and as a result of social change, each generation is born into and grows up during circumstances that are somewhat different from those experienced by the preceding generation (Salk & Salk, 1981). Therefore, a shared birth period and life stage cause lifestyle similarities within the same generation. The effects of these key life experiences tend to be relatively stable over the course of their lives (Smola & Sutton, 2002). Similarly, the era in which a consumer grows up creates a cultural bond with the millions of others who come of age during the same period (Solomon, 2006). For example, members of generations who come of age in years involving war or hard times tend to think and behave differently than those born and raised in peace and abundance. This generational personality is also likely to determine what individuals want from work, what kind of workplace environment they desire and how they plan to satisfy those wants and desires. Due to generational differences, these wants and desires tend to vary from generation to generation.

Generation theorists propose that as the macro-environment changes, there are concomitant and distinctive changes in patterns of consumer behavior (Strauss & Howe, 1991). In line with this, Glover (2010) argues that the exact delimitation of a generation is not that critical since the values, attitudes and beliefs that define each generation do not change abruptly from one year to the next. Instead, a transitional period occurs in which values of the older generation subside, and those of the younger generation emerge. Each cohort goes through life experiencing a unique social, political, technological, and economic environment. These shared experiences and similarities provide the basis for each cohort being targeted as a separate and increasingly profitable market segment (Pennington-Gray & Lane, 2001).

Characteristics of generations

Specific age group classifications vary from author to author, depending on which events are selected as having an influence on a particular generation. For example, Strauss and Howe (1991) determined that there are seven generations currently living in the United States. These generations are identified by the year in which individuals are born and their personalities. First, there is the "GI Generation" of individuals born between 1901 and 1924. The next generation is the "Silent Generation," which is followed by the "Baby Boomers." After the Boomers, the "Thirteenth Generation" or "Generation X" follows. The last and youngest generation is the "Millennial Generation" or "Generation Y". However, scholars have further introduced Generation Z as a group of individuals born in 2000 and later. This section will discuss the characteristics of Baby Boomers, Generation X, Generation Y and Generation Z.

Baby Boomers

The Baby Boomer age segment (people born between 1946 and 1964) consists of people whose parents established families following the end of World War II and during the 1950s when the peacetime economy was strong and stable (Solomon, 2006: 525). As such, Baby Boomers experienced peace, economic prosperity and a sense of optimism based on the technological advances that occurred while they were growing up (Glover & Prideaux, 2008). This progress in the economy and society also changed Baby Boomers' attitudes, perceptions and behaviors.

Boomers had opportunities to become more free spirited and broad-minded about political, cultural, racial, and gender-related taboos than any other generation before them. They are more accustomed to exotic cultures and tend to be more adventurous. It is, therefore, more likely that Boomer seniors will seek more active and self-fulfilling leisure activities and experiences in their late years. That is, they will begin to confront their mortality and realize that they only have a limited number of good years left, during which their physical and mental abilities will still allow them to comfortably enjoy certain types of travel and leisure activities (Lehto, Jang, Achana & O'Leary, 2008). They are likely to become heavy consumers of travel and hospitality related products.

Given the sheer size of this generation and its effects on the demand for consumer products and services, the tourism and hospitality industry cannot ignore the opportunities and challenges presented by this aging generation (Cleaver, Green and Muller 2000). Older consumers have fulfilled many of the financial obligations that constrain the income of younger consumers. Eighty percent of consumers past age 65 own their homes and no longer have child-rearing costs. Additionally, many seniors are now more inclined to spend money on themselves rather than skimp on spending for the sake of children and grandchildren (Solomon, 2006).

Generation X

People born between 1966 and 1976 were labeled "Generation X" following the best-selling 1991 novel of that name. They have also been called "slackers" or "baby busters" because of their supposed alienation and laziness (Solomon, 2006). Generation X was born into a rapidly changing social climate dominated by civil unrest and advances in science and technology that moved ordinary people into the computer age (Chi, Maier & Gursoy 2013: 43). This generation can also be considered the most educated and the first to be technologically savvy (Fitzpatrick, 2005). Education is crucial for this generation, and individuals expect immediate recognition through titles, praise, promotion and pay (Gursoy, Maier & Chi, 2008). Life outside of work is also important to this generation. They are ambitious about brands, and their brand loyalty is also high.

Since Generation X was born into two-income families, they are self-sufficient and confident in solving their own problems. Peltomäki (2015: 28) notes that they are in search of a tolerant and happy world. Therefore, this generation is also more sensitive to social problems, and they advocate traditional values.

Travel is a novelty for Generation X. They seek tours that allow them to encounter new cultures and different ethnicities. Generally, they are used to travelling to new destinations through packaged tours. Further, they love to experience ecological destinations and shopping, and they seek recreational activities during their travel (Li, Li & Hudson 2013: 161). They also love to spend time with their families, which makes them more sensitive to the risks associated with travelling.

Generation Y

Much of the recent generational research has focused on the emergence of the large and powerful consumer group of Generation Y, also known as the Echo-Boomers or Millennial Generation, and defined as those born between 1977 and 1994 (Benckendorf, Moscardo & Pendergast, 2010; Strauss & Howe, 2000). They have grown up in a world where massive amounts of information are a mouse click away. Generation Y has grown up during a period when marketing and technology have played a large part in their lives (Treloar, Hall & Mitchell 2004). Social networking sites such as Myspace and Facebook have become popular. In this regard, Weiler (2005) underlines that Generation Y has grown up in front of electronic screens: televisions, movies, video games, and computer monitors. However, Weiler (2005) suggests that due to screen exposure, individuals' critical thinking and other cognitive skills (as well as their physical well-being) are suffering because of the large proportion of time spent in sedentary pastimes, passively absorbing words and images rather than reading. Therefore, they are considered to be particularly skeptical of marketing messages and rely heavily on their support network of friends and family for opinions rather than marketers (Treloar, Hall & Mitchell 2004).

Another characteristic of the Generation Y cohort is its different decision-making style; individuals have a tendency to make rapid and somewhat emotive decisions with less consideration of the long-term or career consequences of their choices (Pearce & Coghlan, 2008). Further, Bakewell and Mitchell (2003) explain that individuals in Generation Y have been acculturated to materialism and consumerism more than other generations as a result of technological innovations. They are described as a sheltered and frequently rewarded generation with shortsightedness. Thus, Generation Y travelers are more likely to readily decide to volunteer, go abroad for an activity irrespective of immediate career consequences and expect to be well looked after and even praised while doing it.

A recent study by the World Youth Student and Educational Travel Confederation (WYSETC) of more than 8,500 Generation Y travelers, for example, revealed the following key features about these travelers (Richards, 2007): they travel more often; explore more destinations; spend more on travel; book more reservations over the Internet; are hungry for experiences; are hungry for information; are intrepid travelers; and get a lot out of their travels (Richards, 2007). In a study on the information-seeking behavior of individuals in Generation Y, it was found that they usually refer to the Internet first for personal, academic, or professional information (Weiler, 2005).

Generation Z

This generation is also called the "Crystal Children". Generation Z is defined as those born after 1994 (Williams & Page, 2011) or 1995 (Childs, 2015). Members of this cohort are dependent on technology, impatient, and imaginative, have the skills necessary to multitask and make decisions, and exhibit an instantaneous consumption profile. Since they have been born in an era of technology, they have grown up in an environment in which technology prevails. This generation has grown up in a world of intelligent technologies. They have a short-term focus, and they seek fast results in their tasks (Childs, 2015).

Individuals in Generation Z can quickly communicate their preferences to all their virtual friends. They are delighted to identify and share the most interesting findings in the world. Budac (2015) notes that this generation is used to solitary Internet browsing and online socializing, and they are not very good at teamwork. This generation can also be considered the most connected, educated and sophisticated generation ever. They communicate through a variety of online social networks, often talking with young people from other countries and cultures who have no significant influence on their decision-making process (Budac, 2015).

As expressed by Williams, Page, Petrosky and Hernandez (2010), individuals in this generation have experienced global terrorism, school violence, economic uncertainty, recession, and the financial crisis. This makes them vulnerable to external drivers. They have returned to values such as respect, trust, and restraint. Moreover, they are planned, structured, and self-controlled individuals.

Generation Z values authenticity in that realness is a core value of this generation. Their understanding of right and wrong may not be clear-cut though because they essentially have grown up in the midst of a moral meltdown. They are street-smart and have considerable marketing savvy (Labi, 2008). Currently, they are students and graduates, but Madden (2013) explains that they are also the employees and buyers of tomorrow with an unprecedented influence on purchasing decisions.

Marketing destinations from diverse generations

The literature on generational differences is rich, and many researchers have documented the generational differences among Baby Boomers, Generation Xers and Generation Yers (Gursoy, Chi & Karadag, 2013). These generations and the forthcoming Generation Z have differing attitudes and perceptions regarding tourism products. Moreover, the characteristics of older generations become more prominent as populations age. For example, the majority of Boomers will reach 75+ years old just after 2020. Therefore, the need to modify products and services to suit aging Baby Boomers becomes apparent. As such, destinations that target the older market segment need to take their customers' travel knowledge into account and ensure that the products targeted toward older consumers meet their expectations. In a similar vein, the aging of populations may also increase the number of individuals with mobility impairments. Nevertheless, an understanding of generational consumption preferences may be useful as a broad frame of reference when addressing a particular generation's needs and wants, especially when a long-term view is adopted.

The attitudes and lifestyles of Boomers have been shown to differ substantially from those of the current elderly generation with regard to leisure travel (Backman, Backman & Silverberg 1999; Uhlenberg & Miner 1996). Meanwhile, individual factors, such as family structure, employment, education, health status, travel experience and generational values, influence individual demand for tourism. In their study, Lehto, Jang, Achana and O'Leary (2008) report that different lifestyles and values exist in the proposed age cohorts and consequently lead to differences in behavioral outcomes among Baby Boomers. Similarly, in their study in Australia, Cleaver, Green and Muller (2000) identify distinct intergroup differences, which indicate a need to tailor the development and promotion of new tourism products to each segment of Boomers.

Lehto and associates (2008) also report that Baby Boomers seek more physical stimulation/excitement, adventure, and quality family time away from home. In this regard, the authors explain that the new generation of mature travelers, as represented by the older Boomers, could be viewed as being more similar to younger cohorts such as Generation X than the traditional mature traveler market, to which Boomers would be expected to be aspiring at this stage (Lehto et al., 2008). As the population ages and Baby Boomers begin to retire, it will not be surprising if this new generation of older travelers completely reshapes and redefines the vacation and activity landscape of the mature travel market sooner rather than later.

Boomers are a cohort that pays little attention to the dictates of their chronological age; more than half of them say that they feel younger than they are (Horneman, Carter, Wei & Ruys, 2002), and they are more active and physically fit than their predecessors. They take leisure trips more often than the previous generation because they have more time and higher disposable incomes, benefit from the advances in transport technology, and benefit from the development and increased accessibility of new destinations (Glover & Prideaux, 2008). The motivations for travel among this generation tend to be driven more by planned leisure trips for rest in association with friends and family.

Baby Boomers increasingly place travel as a higher priority in their retirement years mainly because they feel healthier, wealthier, better educated, and more independent, have an abundance of leisure time and fewer social and family obligations than younger people (Martin & Preston, 1994). Because many individuals have more time for leisure and are relatively free of family obligations, they generally prefer to take trips for longer periods of time, often travel in the off-season and have a greater concern for personal safety when travelling than younger age groups (Zimmer, Brayley & Searle, 1995). They have more time to travel, and travelling is among the first activities they do when retired, whether domestically or overseas (Muller & Cleaver, 2000). They are mostly willing participants and opt for self-fulfilling experiences that are physically challenging, more meaningful and authentic (Muller & Cleaver, 2000). Additionally, many Baby Boomers have the desire to feel young again or at least to relive some of the more pleasant experiences that characterized their youth (Patterson & Pegg, 2009). They also want to engage in exciting and adventurous activities in which their younger family members might also wish to participate with them. Therefore, destination marketers targeting this group should develop a better understanding of their needs. Since this group is ageing, destination facilities and tourism businesses should also be designed based on their changing needs.

Further, being informed about this market segment is critical to senior consumer marketers because senior consumers are heterogeneous and diverse in their needs and preferences as they experience various events throughout their lives (Mathur, Lee & Moschis, 2006). The literature suggests that older consumers across ages show disparate preferences when selecting tourism products and services (Cai, Hong & Morrison, 1995). This heterogeneity may be primarily attributed to individuals' health status, as well as the societal and economic environments in which they have lived. Jang and Ham (2009) suggest that the tourism industry must be attentive to the senior market because of the rapid increase in this market's size and potential buying power. To attract this lucrative market, destination marketers should earnestly consider how to accommodate the heterogeneous consumption patterns of senior travelers. Because of the greater heterogeneity and diversity of older populations, they often require a greater variety of choices in their travel experiences than previous generations of cohort groups (Patterson & Pegg, 2009). These can range from soft adventure travel that they organize themselves to booking travel on the Internet or to group package tours where everything is done for them by a travel agent, and they stay in luxury hotels.

Generation Xers are actually quite a diverse group of individuals who are enthusiastic about travelling. Similar to their parents, they are also interested in encountering new cultures and ethnicities. Li, Li and Hudson (2013) note that almost 45% of Generation Xers are married with children, and they mostly travel with their kids. Their primary motivation for travelling is to develop social bonds with people and tighten family relations (Elliot & Choi, 2011). Therefore, destinations targeting this larger group including their families should focus on their motivations and create services and products that cater to their needs of socialization and family togetherness. In this vein, it is also important to consider the specific needs of their children in the provision of tourism services.

This cohort of Generation Y grew up in generally stable economic conditions. Therefore, they are more consumption-oriented than previous generations and accustomed to abundance. Moreover, Generation Yers not only buy for themselves but also influence their family's purchasing decisions (Sullivan & Heitmeyer, 2008). As a result of increasing freedom to travel, a growing range of tourism opportunities and a greater choice of tourist destinations and activities, Generation Yers have been able to accumulate a distinctive set of tourism experiences in the past to which they will add new experiences in the future (Glover, 2010).

As consumer attitudes, behavior and skills are acquired via socialization agents such as family, peers, schools and the mass media (Moschis, 1987), the abundance of media choices such as television, the Internet, mobile phones, intelligent devices and magazines has led to a greater diversity of products and lifestyle choices for Generation Yers, and marketing to this cohort requires a different approach. According to Bakewell and Mitchell (2003), Generation Yers have been brought up in an era where shopping is not regarded as a simple act of purchasing. Therefore, they have developed a different shopping style compared to previous generations.

Researchers agree that Generation Yers are technologically savvy and more immersed in online purchase behaviors (Lester, Forman & Loyd, 2006). Macleod's (2008) survey found that individuals in Generation Y can be classified into three groups based on the patterns of their Internet usage: 26% are labelled "uninvolved functionalists" who only use the Internet for work purposes; 34% are labelled "viewers/readers" who are passive audiences of music, videos and photographs; and 26% are "enthusiastic contributors" to Internet content. Technological advances and experiences make Generation Yers confident at online shopping. With increasing competitiveness in online travel businesses, attracting and retaining existing customers online is a significant challenge (Boyer & Hult, 2005). It is critical that destinations develop strategies to commit Generation Y customers in long-term relationships. Consequently, the use of online technologies in a creative and innovative manner is a must for destination marketers. As such, tools offered by the technological advances, such as mobile phones, social networking sites, and blogs, require differing strategies to make destinations competitive in their markets.

Regarding the global youth market, Solomon (2006) notes that the market is massive, representing approximately US$100 billion in spending power. Much of this money goes toward 'feel-good' products such as cosmetics, posters, mobile devices and fast food. As the representatives of youth, Generation Z is completely different from its predecessors. Their loyalty and attachment to brands are low, which pose an important difficulty for marketers. Currently, they are teenagers or individuals in their 20s, but in forthcoming years, they will constitute the tourism market. As such, destination marketers should try to position themselves in the minds of Generation Z in earlier stages and find creative and innovative ways to gain these individuals' loyalty to their brands. Regarding the success of marketing efforts, Budac (2015) underlines the importance of adopting marketing tools based on new technologies and marketing channels such as text messages, mobile devices, and social networking portals. Therefore, Story and French (2004) note that multiple techniques and channels should be used to reach youth, beginning when they are toddlers, to foster brand-building and influence tourism product purchase behavior. In this vein, developing a presence in the online virtual environment with product information and purchase facilities has the potential to strengthen the marketing efforts of destinations.

Conclusion

The primary focus of this chapter is to describe the importance of generations and their characteristics in destination marketing. Being sensitive to the various generations and their characteristics and behaviors will help destination marketers become more conscious of and responsive to their customers' needs and wants.

The era in which a person grows up has the potential to determine the individual's attitudes and behaviors, which are shared by millions of others who come of age during the same period. It is generally accepted that each generation develops somewhat predictable traits, lifestyles, values, demographics and beliefs that influence their buying behaviors (Pendergast, 2010), which can be used by marketers to further segment their consumers, and destination marketing is not an exception to this. Since each generation has diverse lifestyles and purchasing behaviors, each requires different marketing approaches to address its needs. However, as Pennington-Gray and Lane (2000) warn, the use of chronological age as the sole determinant of differences in travel behavior could be misleading because people can also vary more among themselves. Therefore, in-group variations within each cohort should also be considered separately when marketing to these generations.

In summary, Baby Boomers seek more active, self-fulfilling, and adventurous experiences toward the end of their lives. Being relieved of most of their financial obligations, they are likely to become heavy users of travel and hospitality products. Generation Xers value family first, and socialization and family bonds are important to them. They seek a tolerant and happy world. Spending time with their families in ecological destinations, shopping and having fun are attractive to this group. Generation Yers have grown up in an era in which technological advances prevail. They are skeptical about marketing messages, and social networking is an important factor that affects their consumption behavior. Travelling often, trying new experiences and exploring new destinations are important to them. Generation Zers, as the youngest of the generations, have been born into an information age that is dominated by Internet technologies. They are heavily dependent on technology, and online communication with their network is more important than in-person contact. They appreciate the importance of values such as respect, trust, and restraint. Although they are experienced travelers with their parents, they represent an important market for destinations in forthcoming years. Therefore, destination marketers need to understand the characteristics of these generations deeply to better serve each cohort. Further, such an understanding may also help destinations cope with unused capacities and mitigate the side effects of seasonality.

References

Backman, K.F., Backman, S.J., & Silverberg, K.E. (1999). An investigation into the psychographics of senior nature-based travellers. *Tourism Recreation Research* 24(1): 13–22.

Bakewell, C., & Mitchell, V-W. (2003). Generation Y female consumer decision-making styles. *International Journal of Retail & Distribution Management*, 31(2): 95–106.

Beldona, S. (2005). Cohort analysis of online travel information search behavior: 1995–2000. *Journal of Travel Research*, 44: 135–142.

Beldona, S., Nusair, K., & Demicco, F. (2009). Online travel purchase behavior of generational cohorts: a longitudinal study. *Journal of Hospitality Marketing & Management*, 18(4): 406–420.

Benckendorf, P., Moscardo, G., & Pendergast, D. (Eds) (2010). *Tourism and generation Y.* CABI: Wallingford.

Bonn, M.A., Furr, H.L., & Hausman, A. (2001). Using internet technology to request travel information and purchase travel services: a comparison of X'ers, boomers and mature market segments visiting Florida. In J.A. Mazanec, G.I. Crouch, J.R. Brent Ritchie & A.G. Woodside (eds) *Consumer psychology of tourism, hospitality and leisure, Volume 2* (pp. 187–193). Oxon: CABI Publishing.

Boyer, K., & Hult, G. (2005). Customer behavior in an online ordering application: a decision scoring model. *Decision Sciences*, 36(4): 569–598.

Budac, A. (2015). Next generations of consumers-challenges and opportunities for brands. *Bulletin of Taras Shevchenko National University of Kyiv. Economics,* 6(171): 6–10.

Cai, L., Hong, G.S., & Morrison, A. (1995). Household expenditure patterns for tourism products and services. *Journal of Travel and Tourism Marketing*, 4(4): 115–140.

Chi, C.G., Maier, T.A., & Gursoy, D. (2013). Employees' perceptions of younger and older managers by generation and job category. *International Journal of Hospitality Management*, 34: 42–50.

Childs, C. (2015). Marketing to gen Z-Consumers unlike previous generations. Available online at: http://ehotelier.com/insights/2015/06/23/marketing-to-gen-z-consumers-unlike-previous-generations/ (accessed September 30, 2016).

Cleaver, M., Green, B.C., & Muller, T.E. (2000). Using consumer behavior research to understand the baby boomer tourist. *Journal of Hospitality & Tourism Research*, 24(2): 274–287.

Elliot, S., & Choi, H.S.C. (2011). Motivational considerations of the new generations of cruising. *Journal of Hospitality and Tourism Management*, 18: 41–47.

Fitzpatrick, M. (2005). *Building generation X loyalty*. Hospitality Upgrade, Fall 2005. Available online at: www.hospitalityupgrade.com/_files/file_articles/hufall05buildinggenxloyalty_fitzpatrick.pdf

Fountain, J., & Lamb, C. (2011). Generation Y as young wine consumers in New Zealand: how do they differ from Generation X? *International Journal of Wine Business Research*, 23(2): 107–124.

Glover, P. (2010). Generation Y's future tourism demand: some opportunities and challenges. In P. Beckendorff, G. Moscardo and D. Pendergast (eds.) *Tourism and Generation Y*, (pp. 155–163). Oxfordshire, UK: CAB International.

Glover, P., & Prideaux, B. (2008). Implications of population ageing for the development of tourism products and destinations. *Journal of Vacation Marketing*, 15(1): 25–37.

Gursoy, D., Chi, C.G-Q & Karadag, E. (2013). Generational differences in work values and attitudes among frontline and service contact employees. *International Journal of Hospitality Management,* 32: 40–48.

Gursoy, D., Maier T.A., & Chi, C.G. (2008). Generational differences: an examination of work values and generational gaps in the hospitality workforce. *International Journal of Hospitality Management*, 27: 448–458.

Horneman, L., Carter, R.W., Wei, S., & Ruys, H. (2002). Profiling the senior traveler: An Australian perspective. *Journal of Travel Research*, 41(1): 23–37.

Jang, S.C., & Ham, S. (2009). A double-hurdle analysis of travel expenditure: bay boomer seniors versus older seniors. *Tourism Management*, 30: 272–380.

Kupperschmidt, B.R. (2000). Multigeneration employees: strategies for effective management. *The Health Care Manager*, 19(1): 65.

Labi, S. (2008). Baby Bloomers: Our New Age. *Sunday Telegraph*, December 14, 50.

Lancaster, L.C., & Stillman, D. (2002). *When generations collide: Who they are. Why they clash. How to solve the generational puzzle at work.* New York, NY: Harper Business.

Lehto, X.Y., Jang, S.C., Achana, F.T., & O'Leary, J.T. (2008). Exploring tourism experience sought: a cohort comparison of Baby Boomers and the Silent Generation. *Journal of Vacation Marketing*, 14(3): 237–252.

Lester, D., Forman, A., & Loyd, D. (2006). Internet shopping and buying behavior of college students. *Services Marketing Quarterly*, 27(2): 123–138.

Li, X., Li, X.R., & Hudson, S. (2013). The application of generational theory to tourism consumer behavior: An American perspective. *Tourism Management*, 37: 147–164.

Macleod, A. (2008) *Generation Y: Unlocking the Talent of Young Managers.* Chartered Management Institute, London.

Madden, C. (2013) Generation-Z-Defined-Global-Visual-Digital. Available online at: http://clairemadden.com/wp-content/uploads/2013/07/Generation-Z-Defined-Global-Visual-Digital_McCrindle-Research-2013.pdf

Martin, L.G., & Preston, S, H. (1994). *Demography of aging.* Washington, DC: National Academy Press.

Mathur, A., Lee, E., & Moschis, G.P. (2006). Life-changing events and marketing opportunities. *Journal of Targeting, Measurement and Analysis for Marketing*, 14(2): 115–128.

McCrindle, M. (2009) Seriously cool: marketing, communicating and engaging with the diverse generations. Available online at: www.mccrindle.com.au

McCrindle, M., & Beard, M. (2007) In defence of Gen Y. Available online at: http://internationalaffairs.suite101. com/article.cfm/generation_y.pdf

Moscardo, G., & Beckendorff, P. (2010). Mythbusting: Generation Y and Travel. In P. Beckendorff, G. Moscardo and D. Pendergast (eds) *Tourism and Generation Y*, (pp. 16–26). Oxfordshire, UK: CAB International.

Moschis, G.P. (1987). *Consumer socialization: A life-cycle perspective.* Free Press.

Muller, T., & Cleaver, M. (2000). Targeting the CANZUS baby boomer explorer and adventure segments. *Journal of Vacation Marketing*, 6: 154–169.

Park, J., & Gursoy, D. (2012). Generation effects on work engagement among U.S. hotel employees. *International Journal of Hospitality Management*, 31: 1195–1202.

Patterson, I., & Pan, R. (2011). The motivations of Baby Boomers to participate in adventure tourism and the implications for adventure tourism. *Annals of Leisure Research*, 10(1): 26–53.

Patterson, I., & Pegg, S. (2009). Marketing the leisure experience to baby boomers and older tourists. *Journal of Hospitality Marketing & Management*, 18(2–3): 254–272.

Pearce, P.L., & Coghlan, A. (2008). The dynamics behind volunteer tourism. In K.D. Lyons and S. Wearing (eds). *Journeys of discovery in volunteer tourism: international case study perspectives* (pp. 130–143). Oxfordshire, UK: CAB International.

Peltomäki, S.M. (2015). *Crises in the Tourism industry and their effects on different generations.* (Unpublished Masters Thesis). Degree Programme in Tourism, HAAGA-HELIA University of Applied Sciences.

Pendergast, D. (2010). Getting to know the Y Generation. In P. Beckendorff, G. Moscardo and D. Pendergast (eds.) *Tourism and Generation Y* (pp. 1–15). Oxfordshire, UK: CAB International.

Pennington-Gray, L., & Lane, C.W. (2001). Profiling the Silent Generation: Preferences for Travel. *Journal of Hospitality & Leisure Marketing* 9(1/2): 73–95.

Richards, G. (2007) *New Horizons II: The Young Independent Traveller, 2007.* World Youth Student & Educational Travel Confederation, Madrid.

Salk, J., & Salk, J. (1981). *World population and human values: A new reality.* New York: Harper & Row.

Smola, K.W., & Sutton, C.D., 2002. Generational differences: revisiting generational work values for the new millennium. *Journal of Organizational Behavior*, 23: 363–382.

Solomon, M.R. (2006). *Consumer behavior: buying, having and being.* New Jersey: Prentice Hall.

Story, M., & French, S. (2004). Food advertising and marketing directed at children and adolescents in the US. *International Journal of Behavioral Nutrition and Physical Activity*, 1(3): 1–17.

Strauss, W., & Howe, N. (1991). *Generations: The history of America's future, 1584–2069.* New York: Quill.

Strauss, W., & Howe, N. (2000). *Millennials rising: the next great generation.* New York: Vintage.

Sullivan, P., & Heitmeyer, J. (2008). Looking at Gen Y shopping preferences and intentions: exploring the role of experience and apparel involvement. *International Journal of Consumer Studies*, 32(3): 285–295.

Treloar, P., Hall, C.M., & Mitchell, R. (2004). Wine tourism and the generation Y market: any possibilities? CAUTHE Conference, Brisbane, Queensland.

Uhlenberg, P., & Miner, S. (1996). Life Course and Aging: A Cohort Perspective. In R. Binstock and L. George (eds) *Handbook of Aging and The Social Science* (pp. 208–229). San Diego, CA: Academic Press.

Weiler, A. (2005). Information-seeking behavior in Generation Y students: motivation, critical thinking, and learning theory. *The Journal of Academic Librarianship*, 31(1): 46–53.

Williams, C.K., & Page, A.R. (2011). Marketing to the generations. *Journal of Behavioral Studies in Business*, 3: 3–11.

Williams, C.K., Page, R.A., Petrosky, A.R., & Hernandez, E.H. (2010). Multi-generational marketing: descriptions, characteristics, and attitudes. *Journal of Applied Business and Economics*, 11(2).

Zimmer, Z., Brayley, R.E., & Searle, M.S. (1995). Whether to go and where to go: identification of important influences on seniors' decisions to travel. *Journal of Travel Research*, 33(3): 3–10.

11

Marketing destinations to domestic travelers

Shailja Sharma and Rahul Pratap Singh Kaurav

Introduction

Domestic tourism is on the rise. Travel within one's own country has become the most practised form of tourism in the world. Many tourists prefer to spend their vacations within their own country and explore the length and breadth of their country rather than planning international travel. Domestic tourism has a share of its own benefits from a country's perspective. It leads to local generation of income within one's country. Besides, it has other sets of benefits for the travellers. Domestic tourism is more hassle free and easier to plan for the tourists as compared to international travel that involves lots of travel formalities and documentation besides dealing with language barriers. Also, domestic tourists are quite well-versed in the cultural context of the country. They know, in general, the laws, the customs, the local norms and the overall systems of a place when compared to travelling internationally where they have to take care of the cross cultural sensitivities.

Proximity to the domicile is another reason for increased domestic travel. This leads to increased travel during weekends especially long weekends where working professionals can manage to travel without taking any long holidays.

Due to low costs involved in domestic travel as compared to international travel, the social strata of people who are travelling is broader. Everyone travels, from rich to poor.

Also, due to the low cost involved in managing trips, the frequency of domestic visits is higher as compared to international travel. Even in terms of repeat visits, domestic tourism has more repeat visits as compared to international travel.

In the context of India, domestic tourism has become the backbone of tourism industry. The evolution of travel in India has been catalysed due to many reasons. Due to the increasing purchasing power of the middle-class and tourism becoming a part of everyone's lifestyle, variety of economical package offers, better accessibility, better sojourn facilities, options of more experiential and offbeat tourism products, domestic tourism has taken off in the country.

Lots of motivations contribute to this phenomenon of domestic travel. The way tourism products are being packaged and the way they are being marketed have contributed to the growth of domestic tourism in India. The young Indian traveller has shifting preferences for novelty products, road tripping and non traditional experiences. As suggested by the Trip

Barometer study by Trip Advisor, 'Overall, 82% of the Indian travellers plan to try something new in 2016, with the top choices being – Wildlife safari (35%), Cruise (33%) and Adventure travel (29%).' However, the major reason as to why domestic tourists travel is to visit their friends and relatives (VFR).

Further on the basis of interests and purpose of travel, the Indian domestic market may be further classified as backpackers, luxury seeking escapists, those looking for weekend getaway, adventure junkies, families and senior citizens, for example.

Need for a different marketing strategy for domestic tourists

Given the different kind of demographic and psychographic profile of domestic tourists, it is quite evident that the set of expectations of domestic travellers vary from that of international travellers as they are driven by a different set of push and pull factors as compared to international travellers. What may be appealing to domestic tourists may not be appealing to international tourists. Keeping in mind the difference in approach, destination marketers need to have different marketing communication strategies for these two sectors. The marketing mix that includes the product, price, place and promotion shall vary between domestic markets and international markets.

While aiming the marketing campaigns at domestic segments, the destination marketers must alter their marketing communication strategies according to the preferences of domestic markets so that it leads to increased footfall of tourists in that destination.

Concept of destination marketing

A destination is the heart of tourism industry. The whole tourism phenomenon takes place around a destination. A destination is an amalgamation of different tourism products put together.

Bornhost, Ritchie, and Sheehan (2009), described a tourist destination as 'a geographical region, political juridiction, or major attraction, which seeks to provide visitors with a range of satisfying to memorable visitation experiences.'

Destination marketing is a process aimed at communicating the attributes of a destination to the potential traveller who is likely to visit the destination in the near future. The idea of destination marketers is to influence the destination preference of potential travellers while creating a strong desire in the mind of the traveller to spend their next vacation in that destination. The underlying purpose of every destination marketer is to bring his travel destination into the final consideration decision set of the avid potential traveller.

Importance of destination marketing

In this era of stiff competition, where every destination is fighting for its share, marketing of destinations is a must to stay permanently in the mind of the discerning traveller. The tourist today has a myriad of destinations to choose from while planning his holiday. Therefore, only those destinations which are successful in marketing themselves aggressively in an innovative style are able to attract the footfall of tourists. Different destination marketers may be trying to achieve different objectives by marketing the destination. However, some of the common objectives of the destination marketers are as follows:

- To create awareness about the destination
- To increase the overall appeal of the destination
- To enhance the general public perception of the destination
- To create a desire and intention to book a holiday in the destination

- To encourage trial
- To increase visitation
- To increase the frequency of visits to the destination
- To increase the length of stay in the destination
- To tap new markets
- To create a strong destination image
- To communicate a suitable destination positioning
- To communicate destination differentiation by focusing on USP's
- To create a destination brand recall
- To rebrand the destination

Who markets the destinations?

In terms of tourism industry, the tourism marketers here are the DMOs. DMOs have been defined as 'formal entities in which a complex interaction of people, materials, and money is used for the creation and distribution of goods and services' (Inkson & Kolb, 1998). DMOs generally fall into one of the following categories:

National tourism authorities/administration (NTAs) or organisation (NTOs)

UNWTO (1979) introduced the term national tourism administration or authorities as 'the authorities in the central state administration, or other official organisation, in charge of tourism development at the national level'. The NTO is the National Tourism Organisation that is responsible for promoting countries as tourism brands. In the case of India, the NTO is the Ministry of Tourism, Government of India which has been promoting the renowned brand 'Incredible India' amongst the international markets.

RTOs are the Regional Tourism Organisations responsible for promoting tourism in particular regions or areas of that country.

Regional, provincial or state DMOs (RTOs)

The term region has a number of different meanings, ranging in geographic scope from a transnational area such as from South Asia to a local area. The term is used to represent 'concentrated tourism areas' (Prosser, Hunt, Braithwaite, & Rosemann, 2000), such as cities, towns, villages, coastal resort areas, islands and rural areas. A regional tourism organisation is defined as 'the organisation responsible for marketing a concentrated tourism area as a tourism destination' (Pike, 2008).

Taking India as an example, RTOs in India are known as the State Tourism Development Corporations, or STDCs. These STDCs promote tourism to domestic travellers in preference to international travellers. Their major business comes from domestic travellers. Therefore, most of their marketing campaigns are more focused on domestic travellers rather than international tourists.

We also have LTOs that are Local Tourism Organisations responsible for promoting their local areas or places to local community or domestic tourists.

Local, city or town administration/association/organisation (LTAs/LTOs)

Not all local tourism areas have a standalone RTO. Instead they may have an LTA/LTO, which is a term used to represent multiple meanings, a local tourism administration, a local tourism association, and local tourism organisation. The former may be the local government authority, while the latter is a form of cooperative association of tourism businesses. It may be available in any form, such as municipality, city/town development associations (C/TDA), community based association (CBA) and many other forms.

In India, the Jammu and Kashmir Tourism Development Corporation (JKTDC) has divided the state Jammu & Kashmir (J&K) into local regions designated as TDAs (Tourism Development Authority) which function under the aegis of concerned CEOs who are responsible for promoting these local areas of the state.

Considerations for destination marketing to domestic travellers

Destination marketers must take care of certain things while promoting their destinations to domestic segments. These are as follows:

1 The destination marketers must have separate marketing budgets for promoting marketing campaigns to domestic travellers. Understanding the different needs of domestic travellers from international tourists, various destination marketers across the world are allocating separate marketing budgets for promoting tourism in the countries.
2 Another important consideration while rolling out the marketing campaign for domestic segments is also that of timing. Domestic tourism is more perennial and throughout the year as compared to inbound tourism that is more seasonal in nature. Therefore, marketing campaigns must be also rolled out around the year rather than at particular times.
3 A focused, cost effective and customer driven approach is a must while designing marketing campaigns for domestic travellers.
4 Have a separate marketing mix for domestic travellers
5 Address the innate needs of domestic traveller

The starting point for any destination marketer here would be to understand the motivations and preferences of domestic travellers. Subsequently, on assessing their needs, destination marketers can tailor make the products and offer these to specific chunks of different segments within domestic markets with different marketing campaigns. Destination marketers need to very carefully craft out the marketing strategies focusing on domestic travellers backed by a strong and a well knit marketing plan. Destinations marketers must have a proactive marketing and communication strategy.

Tools for marketing destinations

There are multiple ways of reaching out to target markets. Due to the proliferation of internet, new tools are being aggressively used to tap the domestic markets. While marketing destinations to domestic travellers, we must ensure that the communication strategy syncs well with both traditional media and with the modern modes of media.

Placed below are some of the ways in which the destinations can be marketed to domestic travellers:

a) Advertising: Advertising is a non personal presentation of ideas by an identified sponsor. This is the most used method for marketing destinations to domestic travellers. While choosing to advertise through different modes of media, reach to markets and frequency of the advertisement are the two major considerations that must be borne in mind while choosing the kind of media. Various media maybe used for advertising as follows:

- Print media: One of the most used forms of promoting destinations is through print media. The various modes of print media used by destination marketers are as follows:
  - Newspapers: Packages of destinations may be advertised through national, regional or local newspapers.
  - Magazines: Various DMOs may promote themselves by placing their advertisement in travel magazines or giving write-ups in magazines.
  - Brochures: A well designed and glossy brochure with colourful pictures of destinations along with relevant literature on the destination in a concise way attracts the potential tourists to visit the destination.
  - Pamphlets: These are leaflets that may contain printed literature on destinations with a precise note of various places of interest.
  - Newsletters: Many companies publishin-house newsletters that contain latest updates about the organisation. DMOs can tap the segment of these employees working for the organisation by placing their advertisements in thesein-house newsletters who may like to plan a holiday.
  - Travel Guides: These are the most credible and most widely used piece of literature on destinations with information on important sightseeing points, modes of transportation, what to shop, from where to eat, what activities to try in the destinations etc. Lots of travellers especially free individual tourists or backpackers use these travel guides as a torch light to fortravelling to a new destination. One of the most famous travel guides amongst travellers that is widely used is the Lonely Planet that is a quintessence of information on destinations of the world.

b) Electronic media: The most popular and widely used form for promoting tourist destinations is placing advertisements in the broadcast media, including television and radio. Television is one of the most effective media as it combines both the audio-visual effects. In a country like India which is highly fragmented, radio is another commonly used means of communicating with the larger audiences who are dispersed in different parts of the country. The more the advertisement is shown on the television or heard on radio, the more potential travellers are able to identify with the destination, eventually seeking to choose to travel to that destination.

c) Outdoor media: The outdoor media is another extensively used media for promoting destinations. Various DMOs have huge marketing budgets for placing advertisements in outdoor media like billboards, hoardings, posters, kiosks, public places like bus stands, metros, mobile vans, garbage cans, petrol pumps and so on.

d) Internet advertising: Besides electronic and print media, internet advertising is one of the most widely used forms of advertising. Many DMOs place their digital advertisements using digital display banners, digital videos and pop ups or animations also called as interstitials that appear while surfing a website. The idea is to keep chasing the prospective traveller from every nook and corner and keep reminding him of the destination that he might choose to travel to in the future.

e) Advertising specialities: Besides placing advertising in print media or electronic media, many National Tourism Organisations or Regional Tourism Organisations use promotional material to promote their countries, states, areas or counties. The promotional material may include pens, pen stands, key chains, t-shirts, visiting card holders, electronic chargers or local souvenirs of the destination that acts as a silent salesperson in marketing the destinations to domestic travellers.

f) Sales promotion: Sales promotion refers to short term inducements given to customers to immediately increase the sales of the product/service. In the case of the tourism industry, DMOs use sales promotion techniques during off peak season when the momentum of tourists is slow. Sales promotion may be of two types i.e. consumer promotions and trade promotions. Consumer promotions are generally for the consumers, and may be discounts, coupons, offers, lucky draws, sweepstakes, freebies etc. Many DMOs give discounts in packages during off seasons to build up demand. Travel packages offered for Goa during summers are cheaper when the momentum of tourists is reducing as compared to packages offered from October to February when it is high season due to the favorable weather and festivals like Chrismas, New Year, Sunburn Festival and Goa Carnival. Similarly airlines and hotels pass deals to tourists with complimentary services or discounts to create demand during off peak season.

   In the case of trade promotions, incentive trips are offered to travel agents/tour operators by DMOs on giving large business of tourist bookings to them.

g) FAM trips: This is also one of the most popular methods of marketing destinations to travel agents/tour operators and media personnel who get sponsored trips from NTOs or RTOs. In return, when these local agents return back to their region, they try to promote that destination aggressively amongst the domestic travellers thereby giving business to the DMO. Also media personnel like travel writers and journalists give write-ups in print media or might broadcast a documentary or a travel show in that destination in order to promote it to the domestic segments of the country.

h) Organizing road shows: Roadshows are a primary tool used by destination marketers. When DMOs organise road shows in the tourist generating region, it might create a lot of buzz amidst the enthusiastic travellers as after watching the snapshots of destination, the travellers might be interested to visit that destination.

i) Organizing fairs/festivals/events: Branding a destination with a flagship event like a festival, a fair, a business event or a sport event is one of the most successful strategy destination marketers use for marketing their destinations to domestic travellers. These events are a major pull factor in attracting the domestic tourists to an attraction. Gradually the tourists associate that destination with a particular event. Tourists deliberately plan their vacations around these events to get the 'local feel' of the culture of that place. Some of the famous local events of India that pull a lot of domestic tourists to the destinations are:

   - Kumbh Mela – A pilgrimage fair that occurs once in 12 years in Indiaat Haridwar, Allahabad, Nashik and Ujjain that has the 'world's largest conglomeration of religious pigrims'
   - Rann of Kutch Festival of Gujarat
   - Tansen Music Festival of Gwalior
   - Goa Carnival
   - Ganesha Chaturthi of Maharashtra

j) Movies: Movies are a great way of attracting domestic travellers to a destination. When movies are shot in particular destinations, the destinations get popularised. Tourists want to travel those locations where the movie scenes have been shot or which have been visited by famous celebrities. In India, the movie 'Ye Jawani hai Diwani' starring the famous actors Ranbir Kapoor and Deepika Padukone had snippets shot in Kulu Manali positioning it as an 'Adventure destination' for adventure enthusiasts and Udaipur in Rajasthan as a 'Wedding destination'. As a result, many domestic tourists started travelling to Manali for adventure and Udaipur for organising their own wedding.

Various documentaries shot in destinations also give first hand information to the interested travellers about a destination. The various facets of the destination can be discovered by a discerning traveller while watching these documentaries.

k) Public relations: The process of maintaining good relationships with public (that includes customers, competitors, distributors, employees, stakeholders, local community and media) so as to create goodwill in the market and maintain the buzz in the eyes of public is called as public relations. Associating with noble causes like promoting sustainability, safe and honourable tourism, accessible tourism, responsible tourism, involving the local community in planning or promoting noble causes like 'Save Tigers' or taking the responsibility to clean monuments are some of the innovative ways in which the DMOs can maintain a buzz in the eyes of public and create a positive impression in the eyes of public.
l) Direct marketing: Direct marketing involves direct interaction of customer with marketer. In the case of the tourism industry, the following options are practised by destination marketers to promote their destinations to potential travellers using direct marketing:

    - Mobile marketing: This kind of marketing is also very successful where DMOs send direct messages to potential travellers about the latest packages that DMOs may be offering through SMS or Whatsapp. Kerala Tourism became the first tourism brand in the world to launch mobile ad campaign 'Your moment is waiting' that captures some scenic views of Kerala. Kerala Tourism won awards for the most innovative use of social media and mobile apps for the campaign.
    - Kiosk marketing: Kiosk marketing is a very effective medium for promoting destinations to domestic travellers. DMOs can place their kiosks at important sightseeing points of tourist-generating regions or at the local fairs and festivals of the destination where huge crowds conglomerate to witness an event. There, interested travellers can get first hand information about the destination's features and events that may take the form of pamphlets and brochures giving more details in black and white.

m) Apps: A travel application on smartphones is the latest medium of marketing by DMOs for marketing destinations. Many DMOs have applications that can be downloaded on mobiles and used while exploring these destinations. For example Kerala Tourism Development Corporation (KTDC) runs the mobile app, namely 'Expression', to present moods and expressions through various classical art forms of Kerala that are similar to smileys in smartphones. Sharing videos is also permitted on other media apps like Facebook Messenger and Whatsapp through this app.
n) Internet marketing: The Internet is one of the top sources used by vacation planners while choosing to travel to a destination. The travellers consider it to be the most credible source of information. The Internet has swayed the world with its fast evolving technology and the destination marketers have used this technology to their advantage for promoting destinations to domestic travellers. In this era of smart technology, every DMO has its presence on the internet through its website. They have all gone a step ahead by giving experiential marketing to the tourists. DMOs give a virtual tour to the potential traveller on their websites which creates a mental picture in the mind of traveller to visit that

destination. The beautiful videos posted on the websites and the pictures of the attractions create a positive image in the mind of traveller that may provoke him to visit that destination in the future.

o) Email: DMOs also keep sending emails to the travellers who may have travelled with them in the past or are likely to visit. Emails may include new packages being offered, new tourism products launched by the DMO or any special offers or discounts being given on booking with them.

p) Social networking sites: Social networking sites are the new rage in the internet world. Millions of travellers have their accounts on Facebook, twitter, youtube, flickr, Google+, Pinterest, Instagram which provides them a platform to connect to each other and share their travel experiences.

   Photographs of travellers posted on Facebook are a major motivator for potential travellers to travel to that destination. Even the videos posted by travellers on YouTube infuse an interest amongst avid travellers to choose to travel to that destination and try out similar kind of activities and get the same feelings after choosing to travel to these destinations.

q) Travel review sites: Travel review sites are the most reliable source of travel information for the potential tourists. These work on word of mouth publicity. Lots of tourists post their testimonials and share their experiences of places they have travelled. If the feedback about a destination is good, travellers might be interested to travel to that destination otherwise they may choose some other destination. Here DMOs can use these travel review websites to their advantage by asking the tourists who have already been to their destination to post their comments and feedback about the destination. These act as a catalyst for potential travellers as they consider it to be the most authentic first hand information from travellers whose opinion would be unbiased based on their personal experiences. Some of the famous review websites used by Indian travellers are

   - TripAdvisor.com
   - HolidayIQ.com
   - Expedia.com

r) Blogs: Holiday experiences of friends and relatives influence the travellers. Many travellers write their own blogs on the internet to share their travel experiences. Blogs are basically informal websites where travellers share their travel experiences. Blogs may reflect personal opinions of the traveller based on his service encounters in the destination with the local host community, the tourism service providers as well as the overall impression of the destination that he carries in his mind. Blogs can be a great influencing factor for travellers who might be juggling over which destination to visit.

Case study of tourism in Madha Pradesh

Madhya Pradesh is a state in central India bordered by neighbouring states of Gujarat, Rajasthan, Uttar Pradesh, Chhattisgarh and Maharashtra. It is also called the heart of Incredible !ndia as it enjoys a strategic location in central India. The state of Madhya Pradesh has been at the forefront of tourism. Madhya Pradesh Tourism Development Organisation (MPTDC) is a State tourism development corporation responsible for promoting tourism in the state.

MPTDC has a very aggressive publicity and promotional strategy. It has run many promotional campaigns in print media and electronic media. It has recently launched a new campaign

'MP mein dil hua bache sa' which means 'the heart becomes that of a child while visiting MP'. Besides it has aggressively participated in both domestic and international events to promote the state.

The state has been conferred with many accolades. The state was awarded five national tourism awards for excellent performance in tourism sector at National Tourism Award Function in 2016 in New Delhi, India. It included national award of best tourism state. The National Tourism Award 2016 was given for the year 2014–15 for creative initiatives taken by the tourism board to attract the domestic and international tourists. It became the best state for comprehensive development of tourism for giving complete and varied travel experiences to tourists. MPTDC was also awarded in the category of most tourism friendly website in India in International Travel Mart held in Pune in the year 2015. It was also awarded as the best tourism state in 2012.

Some of the famous destinations of MP are:

- Bhopal
- Magical Mandu – known for Jahaz Mahal that looks like ship
- Chanderi – famous for Chanderi sarees
- Orchha – a famous historical town known for cenotaphs of erstwhile rulers and temples
- Sanchi – a pilgrimage place known for its Sanchi Stupa
- Khajurao – famous for its temples and the Khajurao Dance Festial
- Omkareshwar-Maheshwar-Amarkantak – pilgrimage points for Hindus
- Kanha – famous for its national park, known for Bengal tigers
- Bandhavgarh National Park – famous for Bengal tigers and Bandhavgarh Fort
- Pachmarhi – a famous hillstation
- Jabalpur – famous for marble mountains
- Pench – famous for its National Park
- Burhanpur – a famous historical city
- Tawa-Madhai – known for lush green and blue waters

The marketing strategy of MP tourism is very clear. MPTDC has very categorically identified the segment it wants to cater to. Its major focus is on domestic travellers from India. The advertisements that are created are all in the official language of the country, Hindi, because it is focused on the domestic market of the country. Also, keeping in mind the different purposes of travel by the tourists, they are offering different products – wildlife, pilgrimage, nature etc. MP is the only state of India that has sales offices in the other parts of India. In fact, during the lean season the employees of the MPTDC focus on the school kids of nearby states and offer educational trips to MP.

Conclusions

This chapter provides insights into how domestic tourism is different from international tourism and how the marketing strategies of domestic segments vary from other markets. It started with the concept of destination maketing and the role of various destination marketers in promoting destinations. Besides this, it also covered the various objectives of marketing destinations to domestic travellers. The given chapter provided an in-depth overview of both the traditional and new ways that the destination marketers are using to woo the domestic segment in the intense competition that is hitting the DMOs. The chapter has been able to clearly identify the new emerging technologies which are being adopted by DMOs to market their destinations.

References

Bornhorst, T., Ritchie, J. B., & Sheehan, L. (2009). Determinants of tourism success for DMO and Destination: An empirical examinatin of stakeholders' perspectives. *Tourism Management*, 30(3), 1–18.
Inkson, K., & Kolb, D. (1998). *Management Destination.* Auckland: Addison Wesley Longman.
Kaurav, R. P. S. (2015). Assessing impact of internal marketing on business performance: Doctoral dissertation summary. *European Journal of Tourism Research*, 10, 136.
Pike, S. (2008). *Destination Marketing: An Integrated Marketing Communication Approach.* Burlington, USA: Butterworth-Heinemann.
Prosser, G., Hunt, S., Braithwaite, D., & Rosemann, I. (2000). *The Significance of Regional Tourism: A Preliminary Report.* Lismore: Centre for Regional Toursim Research.
UNWTO. (1979). *Tourist Images.* Madrid: UN World Tourism Organization.

12

Marketing destinations through events

Research on satisfaction and loyalty in festivals[1]

María-Pilar Llopis-Amorós, Irene Gil-Saura, María-Eugenia Ruiz-Molina and Martina G. Gallarza

This chapter addresses the role of festivals for destination marketing, by reviewing both positive and negative effects of events. After depicting the different stakeholders involved in managing events, the chapter focuses on explaining how festivals may involve behavioral outcomes of tourists as attendees of event host destinations.

In recent years, research into events has become a fundamental line in tourism literature. Events must be seen as an integral, significant part of developing destination tourism and its marketing strategies. Thus, destination and events are intrinsically linked since "develop, facilitate and promote events of all kinds . . . contribute to general place marketing (including contributions to fostering a better place in which to live, work and invest), and to animate specific attractions or areas" (Getz, 2008: 405).

Although there is a long tradition of events, scholars showed little interest until the late twentieth century (Jago and Shaw, 1998; Getz, 2008) when they burst onto the scene as a solid area for research due to the increase in planned events throughout the world. This area of study is rich and abundant in terms of the objects of study (i.e. types of events) and the subjects (i.e. the groups involved or stakeholders). The term "event" is used to describe a broad category of happenings ranging from World Trade Fairs to Olympic Games, football competitions, papal visits, Cultural Capitals, Festivals, international, national and regional carnivals and even local festivities. As regards the subjects, many different groups are involved in the holding of events (Jago, 1997); in addition to attendees, a variety of different parties help to organise the event, take part in it or live in the area where it is held.

This work reviews and describes this wealth of content to deepen our knowledge of the festival-attendees tandem, through a review of the literature on satisfaction and behavioural intentions of tourists towards the festival and thus towards the destination.

The chapter has the following outline. First, an introduction on events and destination management is offered, where the origins and scope of events for tourism destination management are presented and their role and external and internal relevance are explained. Second, the nature and type of events (objects) and their different stakeholders (subjects) are addressed, with special interest in festivals and attendees. Third, regarding this tandem, the chapter presents a review of 20 works on consumer behaviour in festivals, in terms of antecedents and consequences of satisfaction and behavioural intentions. A final concluding part presents managerial implications and a research agenda.

Events and destination management

Events: origins and scope for tourism destination management

Events have been celebrated since time immemorial. Originally, the main idea of an event was to provide a break for residents from their everyday lives, but in the modern world, residents organise themselves and plan events with broader objectives and stakeholders, with economic, social, tourism, commercial, media, environmental and urban planning effects.

The importance of events in developing tourism is crucial and not always recognised. Initially, event organisers sought to focus attention on a specific urban destination, through an important theme or with a special meaning at a given moment in time (Ritchie, 1984). Later on, in the 1980s, international interest was stimulated by the extraordinary growth in recent decades of events which have come to be regarded as an essential condition for our culture (Allen et al., 2011).

Event organisation is seen as an integral part of tourism development and as an additional element in the marketing mix strategies for holiday destinations. Thus, in the context of holiday destination planning, events are not only seen as tourist attractions for developing both domestic and international tourism (Hall, 1992; Jago, 1997; Sofield, 2003; Tassiopoulos, 2005; Hiller, 2006) but also as elements that can change the seasonal nature of tourism demand by extending the traditional holiday season (Hall, 1989; Getz, 1989, 1991, 2005; Sofield, 2003; Tassiopoulos, 2005).

They are also seen as part of a new wave of alternative tourism which minimises the negative impact, promotes better relations between guests and visitors (Getz, 1991), enhances social integration in communities (Ferdinand and Shaw, 2012) and helps the host destination to build its social capital (Zhang and Wu, 2008). Events are also intended to encourage permanent attractions in the host city, encourage visits and repeat visits to facilities and resorts, places of interest, markets and shopping centres, among others (Getz, 1991, 2005).

Role of events in destination management: external and internal relevance

From an external perspective, events undoubtedly promote economic development in the city/region/country where they are held (Ritchie and Beliveau, 1974; Ritchie, 1984; Getz, 1989, 1991, 2005; Hall, 1992; Jago, 1997; Aitken, 2002; Sofield, 2003; Hiller, 2006; Zhang and Wu, 2008; Allen et al., 2011; Ferdinand and Shaw, 2012). Events attract foreign investment (Hall, 1992; Aitken, 2002) and generate employment (Hall, 1992; Sofield, 2003). They also boost renewal in urban areas (Getz, 1991, 2005; Aitken, 2002; Hiller, 2006; Zhang and Wu, 2008) and the development of infrastructure in the area for the event (Ritchie, 1984; Getz, 1991, 2005; Jago, 1997; Aitken, 2002; Hiller, 2006; Zhang and Wu, 2008).

Events also have the ability to bring domestic and international attention to a destination (Ritchie, 1984) through global media (Mihalik and Simonetta, 1999). This media coverage helps to create and consolidate a destination's image (Getz, 1989, 1991, 2005; Hall, 1989, 1992; Jago, 1997; Mihalik and Simonetta, 1999; Sofield, 2003; Tassiopoulos, 2005; Zhang and Wu, 2008), and improves its short term positioning in international markets, helping to build, strengthen and maintain a unique destination brand (Aitken, 2002).

This coverage is not only beneficial from an external perspective, it also has internal benefits: Ritchie et al. (2007), for example, empirically confirm that the perceived image of the city of Canberra improved for residents after the broadcasting of a cultural event. Thus effectively, events have numerous internal benefits (i.e. for the host community and residents), such as trust (Roche, 1994), enthusiasm (Allen et al., 2011) and community pride at hosting the event (Hall, 1992; Mihalik and Simonetta, 1999; Sofield, 2003); modernisation of society (Roche, 2000), orientation of society towards globalisation and exchange, the transfer and dissemination of information, values and technologies (Roche, 2000) and legacy in terms of the equipment and infrastructures left behind by events after they have been held (Hiller, 2006).

For all the above reasons, rather than being promoted by individual or community initiatives as happened in the past, events today are in the hands of professionals. Thus, events management has become a specific area of professional practice and a field of applied study (Getz, 2000, 2005). Having thus far reviewed this initial aspect of practice, in the following section we examine the second aspect, its academic content as a field of study, describing the literature on the study object (definitions and types of destinations) and the subjects, stakeholders or agents involved.

Event tourism research: the nature of events and their different stakeholders

Definition and taxonomies of events

The topic of "events" as a research area started in the 1970s (see Table 12.1), when Ritchie and Beliveau (1974) from Laval University (Quebec, Canada) did a longitudinal study on the economic effect of the Quebec Winter Carnival. Later, the 1980s saw essential contributions such as Ritchie (1984) and Hall (1989) which enabled the research area to reach maturity in the 1990s (Jago and Shaw, 1998). During this evolution, there has been a major interest in classifying and framing conceptually what an event is, providing interesting taxonomies of events (e.g. Jago and Shaw, 1998; Getz, 1989; 1991; 2005). The types of events with major destination marketing effects are hallmark events, special events and festivals.

Hallmark events are defined by Ritchie (1984: 2) as: "one-time or recurring events of limited duration, developed primarily to enhance the awareness, appeal and profitability of a tourism destination in the short and long term". The aforementioned work from Ritchie and Beliveau

Table 12.1 Evolution of the study of events

Decade	*Study trends*
70s	Event as de-seasonaliser of tourism demand Macro focus: economic impact of holding the event
80s	Macro focus: economic impact of holding the event Identification of characteristics of events and definitions for categorising events
90s	Identification of the characteristics of events and definitions for categorising events Event management Micro focus: analysis of perception in different stakeholders (attendees, organisers, residents in the host city)
00s	Analysis of the terminology used in the study of events Development of models to support the event Social impacts: residents' attitudes. Gaps in event research New focus in the study of impacts: holistic approach (economic, social and environmental impact)
10s	Application of the *Triple Bottom Line* to the study of event impacts. Consolidation of event tourism study as the link between tourism and the study of events.

Source: Authors based on Getz (2008)

(1974) is considered the first study on hallmark events (Getz, 2008), as a possible strategy to fight against seasonality in tourism, thus the main function of this type of events is to be a positive influence on tourism in the host city or destination. Accordingly, the relationship between special events and host destination is crucial, and as Getz (1991) suggests the term "hallmark events" is used when a destination is well known because of a particular event, or when the event is so important that the destination assumes entirely the outcomes of the event.

The second main category of events are special events. Special events are a unique form of tourist attraction, and their particular attraction lies in the very uniqueness of each event which distinguishes them from permanent attractions. It is "a celebration or display of some theme to which the public is invited for a limited time only, annually or less frequently" (Getz, 1989: 125).

The third category of events are Festivals, which among the hallmark events, categorized by Ritchie (1984), are those which take place annually and last less than three weeks. Shortly afterwards, Getz proposes the following generic definition: "a festival is a public themed celebration" (1991: 54). These events are generally the result of the initiative of residents in a city or region to celebrate a special event, such as the Beer, or October Festival (Oktoberfest) in Munich (Germany) or they disseminate the traditions and customs of sixteenth and seventeenth century colonisers like the Carnival in Rio de Janeiro (Brazil).

From an academic perspective, festival management is a different sub-area within the study of events which has grown rapidly in universities around the world (Getz et al., 2010). Festivals are unique in the events industry and this exceptional nature is due to the large number of potential objectives they have to satisfy and the number of stakeholders involved in organising them, so they become a celebration related to the values that the community recognises as essential to its ideology, social identity, and historical continuity (Getz et al., 2010). In particular, Getz et al. (2010) establish three types of festivals according to ownership and control: (a) public, with costs and revenue largely assimilated by local authorities or other government bodies; (b) not-for-profit, where decisions are taken by a management board and committee and (c) private, where first, private investors risk their capital in the expectation of creating a festival that provides profits and second, they play a significant role in the festival through direct, more rigid control.

Finally, there are different themes on which festivals focus such as cinema, theatre, music, literature, food, dance, drink, advertising, etc. and within each festival there are different sub-themes, for example within music: classical, religious, Celtic, electronic, pop, rock, indie, jazz, etc.

Stakeholders in an event

As previously announced in our introduction, studying tourism events is rich and complex both because of the objects (i.e. number and types of events) and the subjects investigated (i.e. different stakeholders). These stakeholders have different interests to be met (Jago, 1997), not always coincident; according to Reid and Arcodia (2002) and Reid (2011), event stakeholders can be organized in hierarchical levels, distinguishing between secondary stakeholders (i.e. host community, emergency services, general business, media and tourism organizations) and primary stakeholders (i.e. employees, volunteers, sponsors, donors, suppliers, spectators, attendees and participants). Secondary stakeholders are less directly involved in the event, but are also crucial to the event. Primary stakeholders, without whom the event cannot take place, are responsible for bringing economic and social consequences for both the host community and event organizers. Among them, the distinctions between spectators, attendees and participants correspond to the level of contribution: low for spectators, medium for attendees, high for participants who are the people who attend an event and have a higher rate of involvement than just observing (Reid and Arcodia, 2002).

Event stakeholders' perception: the interest of attendees' behavioural outcomes in festivals

Varied stakeholders' perceptions in events

The tourism and events literature has paid uneven attention to analysis of the different stakeholders in an event. Most works on the perceptions of the different stakeholders have focused on the "event host community" and particularly, on the "residents" in the city hosting the event (e.g. Ritchie and Aitken, 1984; Mihalik and Simonetta, 1999; Fredline and Faulkner, 2000; Fredline et al., 2003; Wood, 2005; Ntloko and Swart, 2008; Zhou and Ap, 2009; Henderson et al., 2010) and on "spectators and/or attendees" at the event (e.g. Williams et al., 1995; Barker et al., 2003; Bowen and Daniels, 2005; Cherubini and Iasevoli, 2006; Gursoy et al., 2006; Lee et al., 2007; Lee et al., 2009; Mondéjar-Jiménez et al., 2010; Lee et al., 2011; Anderson et al., 2012; Anderson et al., 2013; Báez and Devesa, 2014; Kitterlin and Yoo, 2014; Wong et al., 2014; Hudson et al., 2015; Rivera et al., 2015), with less interest in "organisers" (e.g. Williams et al., 1995; Emery, 2002; Gursoy et al., 2004; Ntloko and Swart, 2008; Otto and Heath, 2009), "participants" (e.g. Cherubini and Iasevoli, 2006), "volunteers" (e.g. Gallarza et al., 2013), "sponsors" (e.g. Garry et al., 2008), "government" (e.g. Emery, 2002; Otto and Heath, 2009), "companies" (e.g. Wood, 2005), "tourist organisations and tourists" (Barker et al., 2003; Otto and Heath, 2009) and "employees" (e.g. Perez and García, 2007), and therefore all of them present future opportunities for research and integral understanding of the complex web of stakeholders in an event and their effects on destination management.

Behavioural experiences of attendees at festivals: customer satisfaction and behavioural intentions

Among the multiple stakeholders in an event, attendees are a main stakeholder, in the relationship between events and destinations: from the perspective of their behaviour as consumers, it is of interest to know who travels to events and why, why they attend an event while travelling, what they do and how much event tourists spend as well as analysing the value of events in promoting a positive image of the destination (Getz, 2008).

Studies on the festival and attendees' tandem vary widely. Regarding themes, there are studies on festivals in general (e.g. Gursoy et al., 2006), cultural multi-events (e.g. Bowen and Daniels, 2005; Cherubini and Iasevoli, 2006; Lee et al., 2007), music (e.g. Thrane, 2002; Mondéjar-Jiménez et al., 2010; Anderson et al., 2012; Anderson et al., 2013; Hudson et al., 2015; Rivera et al., 2015), cinema (e.g. Báez and Devesa, 2014), food and drink (e.g. Kitterlin and Yoo, 2014; Wong et al., 2014) and even specific products like ginseng (e.g. Lee et al., 2009) or mud (e.g. Lee et al., 2011).

Many behavioural variables have also been studied in this field (motivation, quality, value, perception, among others). As recent state of the art event research identified, through thematic analysis, that "papers have emphasized the importance of studies on evaluating satisfaction, service, and attendee decision-making processes" with "visitor behavior (e.g., motivation and antecedents of event visitor satisfaction or revisit intention)" being one of the most researched topics (Park and Park, 2017).

For the purposes of this chapter, as indicated in the introduction, because of the interest for destination management, we review works dedicated to "attendee satisfaction and behavioural intentions" in the sphere of festivals (see Table 12.2).

Table 12.2 Literature review of empirical studies on satisfaction and behavioural intentions of attendees in event tourism

Authors	*Type of event and destination*	*Objectives*	*Methodology*	*Constructs analysed*	*Data analysis*	*Results*
Lee, Petrick and Crompton (2007)	Cajun Catfish Festival in Conroe, Texas (USA)	Explore relationships between visitors' perceived service quality, perceived service value, satisfaction and behavioural intentions	7-Likert scale N = 234	Perceived service quality, perceived service value, satisfaction and behavioural intentions (loyalty and pay more)	Structural equations model (SEM)	For predicting visitors' intention to visit the festival, there is superiority of a structural model operationalising perceived service quality as a set of attributes better than an alternative model with quality measured as a visitor's judgment about a service's overall excellence. Perceived service value is the best predictor of behavioural intentions
Cole and Chancellor (2008)	Festival in a Midwest US city (USA)	Examine the impacts of a downtown festival's attributes (programmes, amenities and entertainment quality) on visitors' overall experience, their levels of satisfaction and intentions to return	Semantic differential (7) N = 177	Festival attributes • programmes, • amenities • entertainment • quality Overall experience Satisfaction Intention to return	SEM (Path analysis)	Entertainment quality had the strongest impact on visitors' overall experience satisfaction and intentions to return. All three attributes have effects (indirect) but just entertainment quality directly contributed to visitor satisfaction and re-visit intention

Liang, Illum and Cole (2008)	Fair Grove Heritage Reunion – Missouri USA)	Examine relationships between behavioural intentions, perceived benefits for a rural festival. Effects of origins and distance travelled	Focus groups (N = 34) 7-Likert Scale N = 413	Perceived benefits • history appreciation • socialisation • enjoyment Behavioural intentions	Exploratory Factor Analysis (EFA) Correlations ANOVA	Festival benefits (from more to less valued): enjoyment, socialisation and history appreciation Negative correlation between distance and revisit intention Socialisation benefit is higher for residents than for non-residents
Yuan and Jang (2008)	Vintage Indiana Wine and Food Festival – Indianapolis (EE.UU.)	Examines how festivals can promote wine products and wineries and influence customer behavioural intentions	7-Likert scale N = 501	Perceived festival quality Satisfaction with the wine festival Awareness of local wines and wineries Future Intentions to buy local wine products and to visit wineries	SEM	Festival quality positively influences satisfaction; and satisfaction exerts a positive and direct influence on awareness of local wines and wineries. Festival quality appears not to directly affect behavioural intentions, whereas satisfaction and awareness have positive and direct relationships with intentions
Esu and Arrey (2009)	Calabar Carnival Festival (Nigeria)	Examine relationships between festival characteristics and overall satisfaction	5-Likert scale N = 416	Festival attributes Overall satisfaction	Descriptive EFA Multiple Regression ANOVA	Positive impact of festival attributes festival (organization, promotion, facilities and residents kindness) on overall satisfaction

(*Continued*)

Table 12.2 (Continued)

Authors	*Type of event and destination*	*Objectives*	*Methodology*	*Constructs analysed*	*Data analysis*	*Results*
Lee, Lee and Yoon (2009)	Punggi Ginseng Festital (South Korea)	Capture the underlying quality dimensions (value antecedents) that distinguish between first-timers and repeaters and that cultivate festival loyalty	N = 443	Event quality dimensions • information service • program • souvenirs • food • convenient facilities • value • loyalty	SEM	Different quality dimensions as predictors of value: Program and convenient facilities are antecedents of value for repeaters, whereas food and souvenir, as well as program and convenient facilities are value antecedents for first-timers. Stronger value-loyalty relationship for repeat visitors than for first-time visitors.
Özdemir and Çulha (2009)	International Camel Wrestling Festival in Ephesus (Turkey)	Identify the details of event performance such as the programs of a festival and indoor/ outdoor facilities that influence the satisfaction and loyalty of festival visitors	5-Likert scale N = 132	Performance: • festival area • staff attributes • food • souvenirs • information • convenience Attendees Satisfaction/ Loyalty	EFA Multiple regression	Festival area has a direct positive effect on visitor satisfaction and loyalty, whereas other independent variables such as souvenirs, food, convenience and staff attributes of festival performance have indirect positive effects
Kim, Kim, Ruetzler and Taylor (2010a)	Annual Festival of Arts, Food and Music in Lafayette County – North Mississippi (USA)	To measure perceived value, satisfaction, and intention to revisit a small festival	7-Likert scale N = 424	Perceived value Satisfaction Intention to return	SEM	Attendees' satisfaction can be predicted by perceived value;Intention to revisit can be predicted by both perceived value and satisfaction

Kim, Suh and Eves (2010b)	Gwangju Kimchi Festival (South Korea)	Examine relationships between food-related personality traits, satisfaction and behavioral intentions.	7-Likert scale N = 335	Food neophobia, Food involvement Satisfaction, loyalty	SEM	Negative effect of food neophobia and positive effect of food involvement on satisfaction and revisits intention Positive satisfaction-loyalty link
Rigatti-Luchini and Mason (2010)	Five food and wine events concerning the promotion of asparagus. Friuli Venezia Giulia region (Italy)	Investigate the relations between the dimensions of experiential quality, perceived value (functional value and monetary price), satisfaction and behavioural intention	Exploratory study N = 368	Quality of the experience Perceived value • Functional value • Monetary price Satisfaction Behavioural intention	SEM	Both experiential quality and perceived value have direct and indirect impacts on visitors' future behavioural intentions
Yoon, Lee and Lee (2010)	Punggi Ginseng Festival. South Korea	Examine the relationships between quality, perceived value, satisfaction and loyalty of festival attendees	7-Likert scale N = 444	Quality of the festival • Information service • Program • Souvenir • Comida • Facilities Price Satisfaction Loyalty	SEM	All festival quality dimensions, except for the information service are positively related to the value of the festival, which in turn indirectly improves loyalty to the festival through attendee satisfaction

(*Continued*)

Table 12.2 (Continued)

Authors	*Type of event and destination*	*Objectives*	*Methodology*	*Constructs analysed*	*Data analysis*	*Results*
Lee, Lee and Choi (2011)	The Boryeong Mud Festival in Boryeong City (Korea)	Identify antecedents of emotional and functional values of attendance at the festival and the influence of these values on levels of satisfaction and behavioural intentions	Systematic sampling N = 442	Quality of the festival Emotional value Functional value Satisfaction Behavioural intentions	SEM	The festival programme predicts the functional and emotional value more strongly than other quality dimensions, with emotional value having greater affect. Stronger impact of emotional value (in comparison to functional value) on satisfaction. Emotional value promotes positive behavioural intentions
McDowall (2011)	Tenth Month Merit-Making Festival (TMMF) in Nakhon Si Thammarat (Thailand)	Investigate motivations for attending the event, assessment of products and services provided at the festival, satisfaction, WOM intention and repeat visit intention	5-Likert scale except "intention to return" as dichotomic N = 307	Reasons for attending Quality of products and services Satisfaction Return intention WOM	Descriptive EFA Multiple regression	Among the many motivations for attending the festival, respondents were most satisfied with arts and crafts, entertainment, ticket price, displays and exhibitions, and the festival's duration. The activity–culture factor was the best performer. And differences were found between likelihood of revisiting and recommending, in favour of the latter

Anil (2012)	Vize History and Culture Festival – Kirklareli (Turkey)	Identify factors related to the festival environment that determine attendee satisfaction and loyalty	5-Likert scale N = 352	Environment. • Staff • Food • Appropriate information • Convenience • Festival ground Satisfaction Loyalty	SEM	Identification of three dimensions related to environmental factors at the festival: food, festival ground and convenience. The dimension "food" is the most important for attendee satisfaction and in turn, has a considerable effect on loyalty.
Lee, Kyle and Scott (2012)	Three agricultural festivals in Texas (USA)	Examining the mediating effect of place attachment on the relationship between festival satisfaction and loyalty to the festival hosting destination	7-Likert scale N = 216	Satisfaction Attachment to the festival site Loyalty to the festival hosting destination	SEM	Visitors who are satisfied with the festival develop emotional attachment to the festival hosting destination and become loyal to that destination.
Kitterlin and Yoo (2014)	Food Network South Beach Wine & Food Festival (SOBE WFF) Florida (USA)	Examine the impact of factors in the festival environment on attendee motivation and loyalty behaviour, differentiated according to type of attendee	N = 244	Festival environment Hedonistic Loyalty Repeat intention	Descriptive EFA Multiple regression MANOVA	Significant impact of the festival on attendee motivation and loyalty. Type of attendees influences factors in the festival environment. However, only the factor of local residence was confirmed but did not support repeat visit

(*Continued*)

Table 12.2 (Continued)

Authors	*Type of event and destination*	*Objectives*	*Methodology*	*Constructs analysed*	*Data analysis*	*Results*
Wong, Wu and Cheng (2014)	12th Food Festival in Macao (China)	Examine interrelations between festival quality dimensions, emotion, image, loyalty and satisfaction with the festival. Moderating effect of festival image in the relations between festival quality and its dimensions	7-Likert scale (except emotions 5-Likert scale) N = 454	Quality of the festival Emotion Image Satisfaction Loyalty	SEM Hierarchical regression	Positive influence of quality of the interaction and the physical environment, quality results and programme quality in general on festival quality Moderating effect of festival image in relations between festival quality and its dimensions Emotion, festival quality and image positively influence satisfaction which in turn, together with quality, positively affects festival loyalty
Hudson et al. (2015)	Music festivals in USA	Examine social media interactions of music festival brands, consumer perceptions of brands and impact on desired marketing results.	N = 423	Social media Emotional attachment Brand relationship quality WOM	SEM	Influence of social communication media on emotional attachment to a festival. Direct effect of emotional attachment and relationship quality on WOM. Emotional attachment as mediator between social media and brand relationship quality

Rivera, Semrad and Croes (2015)	The Electric Music Festival in Aruba (Caribbean)	Analyse whether a music festival can be used as an experiential attraction to attract the Gen Y market segment to an island destination.	N = 288	Overall experience • Education • Leisure • Evasion • Atmosphere • Economic value Memorable experience Economic value Behavioural intentions	SEM	Including economic value in the overall experience improves Gen Y behavioural intentions in the context of the economics of the experience. The production of a music festival which creates a memorable experience at a small island destination provides a means of penetrating a new market willing to return and recommend the place as a holiday destination, even in the absence of the festival
Ilban et al. (2015)	Cultural festival in Burhaniye (Turkey)	Identify the relationship between the destination image perceived by domestic festival tourists and their perceived values and behavioural intentions	N = 405	Image Perceived values Behavioural intentions	CFA and SEM	Destination image positively affects value n and word-of-mouth communication. However, destination image had no effect on the intention to revisit. Perceived value positively affected likelihood of revisiting and suggesting the destination to others.

Source: Authors

Regarding the content of research on attendees' consumer behaviour at festivals, the literature has focussed on customer satisfaction and behavioural intentions. Regarding customer satisfaction, scholars have been interested in both antecedents and consequences of satisfaction, as Table 12.3 shows. Antecedents are perceived quality, perceived value, attendance motivations, festival attributes, cost and perceived value, place attachment, emotions and image. Assessment of the consequences of satisfaction has focused on varied forms of loyalty (behavioural as revisit and attitudinal as recommendation) occasionally operationalised as repeat/return intention and word-of-mouth communication intention.

Regarding behavioural intentions, the literature shows an interest in several constructs and their effects on different forms of loyalty as a final outcome: these are mostly classical variables like satisfaction (e.g. Thrane, 2002; Lee et al., 2007; Cole and Chancellor, 2009; Yuan and Jang, 2008; Kim, Shu et al., 2010; Rigatti-Luchini and Mason, 2010; Yoon et al., 2010; Lee et al., 2011; McDowall, 2011; Anil, 2012; Lee et al., 2012; Wong et al., 2014), perceived service quality (e.g. Thrane, 2002; Lee et al., 2007; Wong et al., 2014) and perceived value of the event (e.g. Lee et al., 2007 ; 2009; Rigatti-Luchini and Mason, 2010; Lee et al., 2011), as well as other more specific constructs and variables in the area of event studies like benefits of the festival (e.g. Liang et al., 2009), emotional attachment and brand relationship quality (e.g. Hudson et al., 2015) and the provision of a memorable experience (e.g. Rivera et al., 2015), distance travelled to attend the event (e.g. Liang et al., 2008), notoriety of event-related products and services (e.g. Yuan and Jang, 2008); and even utilitarian variables like the value of the perceived cost (e.g. Calabuig et al., 2012) and economic value (e.g. Rivera et al., 2015).

Table 12.3 Antecedents and consequences of satisfaction in event tourism

ANTECEDENTS	Perceived quality	Thrane (2002); Lee et al. (2007); Yuan and Jang (2008); Lee et al. (2009); Rigatti-Luchini and Mason (2010); Yoon et al. (2010); Lee et al. (2011); McDowall (2011); Calabuig et al. (2012); Wong et al. (2014)
	Perceived value	Lee et al. (2007); Lee et al. (2009); Rigatti-Luchini and Mason (2010); Yoon et al. (2010); Lee et al. (2011)
	Reasons for attending	Lee et al. (2004); McDowall (2011)
	Festival attributes/ environment	Cole and Chancellor (2009); Esu and Arrey (2009); Özdemir and Çulha (2009);Anil (2012)
	Festival benefits	Liang et al. (2008)
	Perceived value of the cost	Calabuig et al. (2012)
	Attachment to the place hosting the event	Lee et al. (2012)
	Emotion	Wong et al. (2014)
	Image	Wong et al. (2014)
CONSEQUENCES	Loyalty	Lee et al. (2009); Kim, Suh et al. (2010); Wong et al. (2010); Anil (2012); Lee et al. (2012); Wong et al. (2014)
	Behavioural intentions	Lee et al. (2007); Yuan and Jang (2008); Rigatti-Luchini and Mason (2010); Lee et al. (2011); Calabuig et al. (2012)
	Repeat/return intention	Thrane (2002); Cole and Chancellor (2009); Kim, Suh et al. (2010); McDowall (2011)
	Recommend /WOM intention	(2002); McDowall (2011)

Source: Authors

All these studies provide confirmation and/or variations on the classical patterns of relationships between behavioural constructs, in the form of the service quality-value-satisfaction-behavioural intentions chain, proven in many tourism settings (Gallarza et al., 2012). Similar patterns of effects also exist in research on consumer behaviour in festivals research, with particularities, reviewed below.

Several works have shown the general pattern of the service quality-value-satisfaction-behavioural intentions chain, with positive effects of satisfaction on behavioural intentions found in Anil (2012) for a cultural festival in Turkey, in Rigatti-Luchini and Mason (2010) for different wine festivals in Italy, in Wong et al. (2014) and Kim, Suh et al. (2010) for food festivals in Macao and South Korea respectively. Other works, however, have proven that revisit intention can be predicted simultaneously by both perceived value and satisfaction (Kim, Kim et al., 2010).

This chain of effects is sometimes completed with extra constructs, such as place attachment in Lee et al. (2012), who proved for three festivals in the US, that the link between satisfaction and loyalty to the festival hosting destination is mediated by place attachment. Also, Kim, Shu et al. (2010) introduced food-related personality traits in this chain of effects for the case of a food festival in Korea, with different positive and negative effects, but with direct effects of satisfaction on behavioural intentions towards the festival and the destination. And Yuan and Jang (2008) also found, for a wine festival, that awareness of local wines and wineries, alongside satisfaction, have positive and direct relationships with intentions to revisit the festival.

Alternatively, some works proved different sets of relationships, such as Lee et al. (2007), where revisit intention to the Cajun Catfish Festival in Conroe (Texas) is better predicted with service quality measured as a set of attributes than in an alternative model that measured quality by using a visitor's judgement about the overall excellence or superiority of a service. This work also found service value of the event as the best predictor of behavioural intentions, which is not the case of Kim, Kim et al. (2010) who also studied relationships between value, satisfaction and behavioural intentions in the case of a small festival, and found that satisfaction is the best predictor of festival revisit intentions. In other cases, results show some restrictions on this chain of effects. Cole and Chancellor (2008) show that quality of entertainment alone has effects on satisfaction and behavioural intentions towards the festival, placing more emphasis on this attribute than others. And similar results of a prominent service quality effect, such as festival area for the case in Özdemir and Çulha (2009), where this service quality attribute has a direct positive effect on visitor satisfaction and loyalty. Furthermore, a work by McDowall (2011) for a festival in Thailand, found differences in revisit intention and likelihood to recommend as attendees who were satisfied with the festival would encourage others to attend the festival, although they themselves might not attend again in the future. Regarding other effects such as origins of attendees (local, repeaters or non-repeaters), works also show interesting results for destination managers: in Liang et al. (2008) socialisation benefit was significantly higher among residents than non-residents, and Lee et al. (2009) found a stronger value-loyalty link for repeat visitors than for first-time visitors, assuming thus ways of attracting repeating tourists to the hosting destination.

Conclusions, managerial implications and research agenda

There is great dynamism and variety in the type of events held throughout the world, right down to the present day, and currently, due to the repercussions of organising and holding events, as there is strong competition to host them. Thus events are a systemic component in the economic, socio-cultural, tourism, political and strategic development of a territory and therefore key factors in the strategic development of destinations.

The object of interest in this chapter are festivals, as precise hallmark events (Ritchie, 1984), in the form of a cultural celebrations (Getz, 2008) and community entertainment (Arcodia and Robb, 2000), held annually and lasting under three weeks, conceived thus as a themed public celebration.

Festival management emerges as a sub-area in the study of events because of the exceptional nature of the event and the number of stakeholders involved in organising it (Getz, 2010) who may have differing expectations and conditions for success (Jago, 1997). Among the many stakeholders in festivals, the chapter focussed on attendees, defined by Reid and Arcodia (2002) as primary stakeholders in the event because their support is necessary for an event to exist given their high rate of participation.

The review of the literature on festival attendees shows a large variety of themes (cultural multievents, music, cinema, food and drink, products like ginseng and mud, etc.) and topics (e.g. reasons for attending, perceived quality, satisfaction, behavioural intentions, perceived value and loyalty). As regards the topics, festivals have been a field of application of consumer behaviour research regarding relationships between service quality, perceived value, customer satisfaction and behavioural intentions (e.g. Anil, 2012; Kim, Suh et al., 2010; Rigatti-Luchini and Mason, 2010; Wong et al., 2014). The quality-value-satisfaction-loyalty chain has predominantly been approved, with some peculiarities such as double effects of value and satisfaction on loyalty (e.g. Kim, Kim, et al., 2010) or both direct and indirect (via satisfaction) effects of festival service quality on loyalty (e.g. Özdemir and Çulha, 2009).

Differences have been noticed regarding behavioural and attitudinal loyalty: the likelihood of revisitation is not always the effect of higher perceived value and/or satisfaction because there is a novelty effect in festival attendees that affects perceptions of first time or repeat festival goers. Nevertheless, all these constructs (i.e. service quality, value and satisfaction) do contribute positively to attitudinal loyalty (positive WOM).

Attendees' experiences are rich and diverse; predictors for consumers' future behavioural intentions to attend festivals again are very varied. Festival attributes can be more functional such as (music or food) quality, information, location, facilities or more emotional and social such as socialisation, enjoyment, souvenirs, and staff relationship, all being relevant for understanding loyalty towards the festival, and therefore towards the host destination.

Thus, one of the key topics for event tourism managers and strategists is to design event experiences according to their target audiences and so they should be based on greater understanding of the experience of a planned event in all its dimensions (type of event, environment and management system). In addition, comparisons and different research focuses are required, such as evaluations of event attendees through qualitative studies to find out what they seek (expectations and motivations), the significance they attribute to their experiences (perceptions and emotions) and the influences on their attitudes and future behaviours. This information would enable festival organisers to identify and develop the attributes that determine, in the eyes of attendees, the authenticity and uniqueness of the experience in each edition of the festival, thus promoting intention to revisit the festival and thus the holiday destination.

We understand that academia may support festival organisers in taking informed decisions through further research on festival attendee behaviour, as well as in combination with research on other stakeholders as volunteers in Human Resources, or training in Education (Park and Park, 2017), that remain under-researched for the case of festivals. Table 12.4 proposes a (non-exhaustive) list of potential research questions as well as methodologies for further research in this setting.

Table 12.4 Proposed key questions and methodologies to further festival tourism studies with an approach focused on attendee behaviour

Key research questions/gaps in the theory for understanding event visitor experiences
• What are the antecedents of event tourism (e.g. motivation or benefit of events)? • What are the main determinants of customer satisfaction with events? • What are the antecedents of event visitor revisit intention? • How do people describe and explain why event tourism experiences are satisfactory, memorable and enriching? • How do they describe, explain and assign meaning to different experiences of event tourism (within each of these dimensions: conative (behavioural); affective (emotional); and cognitive)? • Describe and explain the formation of personal and social constructs in relation to event tourism experiences. • What is the attendee decision-making process? • What are the expenditure patterns of tourists regarding events? • How does the degree of involvement or commitment affect the event tourism experience? • Examine "excitation" and "flow" in different event scenarios. • How are "communities" formed in events? Can they be facilitated? • What is the role of other stakeholders in the event experience (e.g. employees, voluteers . . .) • What are the personal and social consequences of negative experiences of event tourism? • How were social representations of the events shaped? • How does the nature and scope of community participation operate in the success and result of event tourism? • Under what circumstances are events mercantilised and actually lost in comparison to the renewal of tradition and revitalisation of culture? • Who are the most profitable event tourists and how should they be attracted? • What is the value of a given event?
Research methodology
• Adopting multidisciplinary approaches • Mixed methods • Analysis of media content • Surveys • In-depth interviews • Market studies • Ethnography • Phenomenology (e.g. in-depth interviews at events) • Focus groups • Hermeneutics (text analysis, self-presented reports) • Experimental sampling (daily or sampling period with standard questions) • Direct, participative observation • Assessments

Source: Authors based on Getz (2008) and Park and Park (2017)

As Van Niekerk (2017) highlights, however, destination planners should be aware of the fact that festivals have their own life cycle trajectories that may exert an impact on the sustainability of the holiday destination. Since festivals are often used to reinvent destination value for tourists in a new and innovative way (Roxas and Chadee, 2013), festival organizers should understand attendees' expectations and perception in order to create unique and memorable experiences enticing festival attendees to recommend and revisit the holiday destination.

Note

1 Acknowledgments: The authors are very grateful for the support of the projects ECO2013–43353-R and ECO2016–76553-R of the Spanish Ministry of Education and Science.

References

Aitken, J. (2002). The Role of Events in the Promotion of Cities. *Events and Place Making*, 3–7.

Allen, J., O'Toole, W., Harris, R. & McDonnell, H. (2011). *Festival & Special Event Management.* Wiley and Sons. Australia. Tourism Series.

Andersson, T.D., Armbrecht, J. & Lundberg, E. (2012). Estimating Use and Non-use Values of a Music Festival. *Scandinavian Journal of Hospitality and Tourism, 12*(3), 215–231.

Andersson, T.D., Jutbring, H. & Lundberg, E. (2013). When a music festival goes veggie. *International Journal of Event and Festival Management, 4*(3), 224–235.

Anil, N.K. (2012). Festival visitors' satisfaction and loyalty: An example of small, local, and municipality organized festival. *Tourism, 60*(3), 255–271.

Arcodia, C. & Robb, A. (2000). A future for event management: A taxonomy of event management terms. *Events Beyond 2000: Setting the Agenda.* Proceedings of Conference on Event Evaluation, Research and Education. Australian Centre for Event Management. Sydney, 154–160.

Báez, A. & Devesa, M. (2014). Segmenting and profiling attendees of a film festival. *International Journal of Event and Festival Management, 5*(2), 96–115.

Barker, M., Page S.J. & Meyer, D. (2002). Evaluating the impact of the 2000 America's Cup on Auckland, New Zealand. *Event Management*, 7, 79–92.

Barker, M., Page S.J. & Meyer, D. (2003). Urban visitor perceptions of safety during a special event. *Journal of Travel Research. 41*, 355–361.

Bojanic, D.C. & Warnick, R.B. (2012). The Role of Purchase Decision Involvement in a Special Event. *Journal of Travel Research, 51*(November 2011), 357–366.

Bowen, H.E. & Daniels, M.J. (2005). Does the music matter? Motivations for attending a music festival. *Event Management, 9*(3), 155–164.

Calabuig Moreno, F., Crespo Hervàs, J. & Mundina Gómez, J. (2012). Efecto del coste percibido, la calidad de servicio y la satisfacción sobre las intenciones futuras del espectador. *Estudios de Economía Aplicada, 30*(2), 619–636.

Cherubini, S. & Iasevoli, G. (2006). Stakeholders Event Evaluation: Notte Bianca Case Study. Convegno "Le Tendenze del Marketing in Europa". Università Ca' Foscari. Venezia.

Cole, S.T. & Chancellor, H.C. (2009). Examining the festival attributes that impact visitor experience, satisfaction and re-visit intention. *Journal of Vacation Marketing, 15*(4), 323–333.

Crompton, J.L., McKay, S.L. & Society, J.H. (1997). Motives of visitors attending festival events. *Annals of Tourism Research, 24*(2), 425–439.

Emery, P.R. (2002). Bidding to host a major sports event. The local organising committee perspective. *The International Journal of Public Sector Management, 15*(4), 316–335.

Esu, B.B. & Arrey, V.M.-E. (2009). Tourists' satisfaction with cultural tourism festival: A case study of Calabar Carnival Festival, Nigeria. *International Journal of Business and Management, 4*(3), 116.

Ferdinand, N. & Shaw, S.J. (2012). Events in Our Changing World in N. Ferdinand & P. Kitchin (eds) *Events Management: An International Approach*, London. SAGE Publications Ltd., 5–22.

Fredline, E. & Faulkner, B. (2000). Host community reactions: A cluster analysis. *Annals of tourism research, 27*(3), 763–784.

Fredline, L. Jago, L. & Deery, M. (2003). The development of a generic scale to measure the social impacts of events. *Event Management, 8*, 23–37.

Gallarza, M.G., Arteaga, F. & Gil-Saura, I. (2013). The value of volunteering in special events: A longitudinal study. *Annals of Tourism Research, 40*, 105–131.

Gallarza, M.G. Gil, I. & Holbrook, M.B. (2012). Customer Value in Tourism Services; Meaning and Role for a Relationship Marketing Approach. In Tsiotsou, R. & Goldsmith, R.E. (Eds), *Strategic Marketing in Tourism Services Bingley*, England: Emerald Group Publishing, 147–162.
Garry, T., Broderick, A.J. & Lahiffe, K. (2008). Tribal motivation in sponsorship and its influence on sponsor relationship development and corporate identity. *Journal of Marketing Management, 24* (9–10), 959–977.
Getz, D. (1989). Special events: defining the product. *Tourism Management*, June, 125–137.
Getz, D. (1991). *Festivals, special events, and tourism.* New York: Van Nostrand Reinhold.
Getz, D. (2000). Developing a Research Agenda for the Event Management Field". *Events Beyond 2000:* Setting the Agenda. Proceedings of Conference on Event Evaluation, Research and Education. Sydney July 2000.
Getz, D. (2005). *Event Management & Event Tourism.* Cognizant Communication Corporation.
Getz, D. (2008). Event tourism: Definition, evolution, and research. *Tourism Management, 29*(3), 403–428.
Getz, D. (2010). The Nature and Scope of Festival Studies. *International Journal of Event Management Research, 5*(1), 1–47.
Getz, D., Andersson, T. & Carlsen, J. (2010). Festival management studies: Developing a framework and priorities for comparative and cross-cultural research. *International Journal of Event and Festival Management. 1.*
Gursoy, D., Spangenberg, E.R. & Rutherford, D.G. (2006). The hedonic and utilitarian dimensions of attendees' attitudes toward festivals. *Journal of Hospitality & Tourism Research, 30*(3), 279–294.
Gursoy, D; Kim, K. & Uysal, M. (2004). Perceived impacts of festivals and special events by organizers: an extension and validation. *Tourism Management, 25*, 171–181.
Hall, C.M. (1992). *Hallmark tourist events: impacts, management and planning.* Belhaven Press.
Hall, C.M. (1989). The definition and analysis of hallmark tourist events. *Geojournal, 19*(3), 263–268.
Henderson, J.C. Foo, K; Lim, H. & Yip, S. (2010). Sports events and tourism: the Singapore Formula One Grand Prix. *International Journal of Event and Festival Management, 1*(1), 60–73.
Hiller, H.H. (2006). Post-event outcomes and the post-modern turn: The Olympics and urban transformations. *European Sport Management Quarterly, 6*(4), 317–332.
Hudson, S., Roth, M.S., Madden, T.J. & Hudson, R. (2015). The effects of social media on emotions, brand relationship quality, and word of mouth: An empirical study of music festival attendees. *Tourism Management, 47*, 68–76.
Ilban, M.O., Kasli, M. & Bezirgan, M. (2015). Effects of destination image and total perceived value on tourists' behavioral intentions: An investigation of domestic festival tourists. *Tourism Analysis, 20*(5), 499–510.
Jago, L.K. (1997). *Special events and tourism behaviour: a conceptualisation and an empirical analysis from a values perspective* (Doctoral dissertation, Victoria University).
Jago, L.K. & Shaw, R.N. (1998). Special events: a conceptual and definitional framework. *Festival Management & Event Tourism, 5*, 21–32.
Kim, Y.G., Suh, B.W. & Eves, A. (2010). The relationships between food-related personality traits, satisfaction, and loyalty among visitors attending food events and festivals. *International Journal of Hospitality Management, 29*(2), 216–226.
Kim, Y.H., Kim, M., Ruetzler, T. & Taylor, J. (2010). An examination of festival attendees' behavior using SEM. *International Journal of Event and Festival Management, 1*(1), 86–95.
Kitterlin, M. & Yoo, M. (2014). Festival motivation and loyalty factors. *Tourism & Management Studies, 10*(1), 119–126.
Lee, J., Kyle, G. & Scott, D. (2012). The Mediating Effect of Place Attachment on the Relationship between Festival Satisfaction and Loyalty to the Festival Hosting Destination. *Journal of Travel Research, 51*(6), 754–767.
Lee, J., Lee, C. & Yoon, Y. (2009). Investigating Differences in Antecedents to Value Between First-Time and Repeat Festival-Goers. *Journal of Travel & Tourism Marketing, 26*(7), 688–702.
Lee, J.-S., Lee, C.-K. & Choi, Y. (2011). Examining the Role of Emotional and Functional Values in Festival Evaluation. *Journal of Travel Research, 50*(6), 685–696.
Lee, S.Y., Petrick, J.F. & Crompton, J. (2007). The roles of quality and intermediary constructs in determining festival attendees' behavioral intention. *Journal of Travel Research, 45*(4), 402–412.
Leenders, M.A. (2010). The relative importance of the brand of music festivals: A customer equity perspective. Journal of Strategic Marketing, *18*(4), 291–301.

Liang, Y., Illum, S.F. & Cole, S.T. (2008). Benefits Received and Behavioural Intentions of Festival Visitors in Relation to Distance Travelled and Their Origins. *Event Management, 4*(1), 12–23.

McDowall, S. (2011). The Festival in My Hometown: The Relationships Among Performance Quality, Satisfaction, and Behavioral Intentions. *International Journal of Hospitality & Tourism Administration, 12*, 269–288.

Mihalik, B.J. & Simonetta, L. (1999). A midterm assessment of the host population's perceptions of the 1996 Summer Olympics: Support, attendance, benefits, and liabilities. *Journal of Travel Research, 37*(3), 244–248.

Mondéjar-Jiménez, J.A., Cordente-Rodríguez, M., Gázquez-Abad, J.C., Pérez-Calderón, E. & Milanés-Montero, P. (2011). Visitor Profile of Cuenca Religious Music Week. *Journal of Business Case Studies (JBCS), 6*(7).

Ntloko, N.J. & Swart, K. (2008). Sport Tourism Impacts on the Host Community: A Case Study of Red Bull Big Wave Africa. *South African Journal for Research in Sport, Physical Education and recreation, 30*(2), 79–93.

Otto, I. & Heath, E.T. (2009). The Potential Contribution of the 2010 Soccer World Cup to climate Change: An Exploratory Study among Tourism Industry Stakeholders in the Tshwane Metropole of South Africa. *Journal of Sport & Tourism, 14*(2), 169–191.

Özdemir, G. & Çulha, O. (2009). Satisfaction and Loyalty of Festival Visitors. *Anatolia, 20*(2), 359–373.

Park, S.B. & Park, K. (2017). Thematic trends in event management research. *International Journal of Contemporary Hospitality Management, 29*(3), 848–861.

Pérez, I. & García, M.E. (2007). Voluntarios deportivos versus profesionales remunerados: dificultades y conflictos del desempeño de la acción voluntaria en la organización de acontecimientos deportivos". *RETOS. Nuevas tendencias en Educación Física, Deporte y Recreación, 11*, 5–10.

Pike, S. (2010). Destination Branding Case Study: Tracking Brand Equity for an Emerging Destination Between 2003 and 2007. *Journal of Hospitality & Tourism Research, 34*(1), 124–139.

Reid, S. & Arcodia, C. (2002). Understanding the Role of the Stakeholder in Event Management. *Events and Place Making*. Proceedings of International Event Research. Australian Centre for Event Management. Sydney, July, 479–515.

Reid, S. (2011). Event stakeholder management: developing sustainable rural event practices. *International Journal of Event and Festival Management, 2*(1), 20–36.

Rigatti-Luchini, S. & Mason, M.C. (2010). An Empirical Assessment of the Effects of Quality, Value and Customer Satisfaction on Consumer Behavioral Intentions in Food Events. *International Journal of Event Management Research, 5*(1), 46–61.

Ritchie, B.W., Sanders, D. & Mules, T. (2007). Televised Events: Shaping Destination Images and Perceptions of Capital Cities from the Couch. *International Journal of Event Management Research, 3*(2), 12–23.

Ritchie, J.B. (1984). Assessing the impact of hallmark events: conceptual and research issues. *Journal of travel research, 23*(1), 2–11.

Ritchie, J.R.B. & Aitken, C.E. (1984). Assessing the impacts of the 1988 Olympic Winter Games: the research program and initial results. *Journal of Travel Research, 22*, 17–25.

Ritchie, J.R.B. & Beliveau, D. (1974). Hallmark Events: An Evaluation of a Strategic Response to Seasonality in the Travel Market. *Journal of Travel Research, 13*, 14–20.

Rivera, M., Semrad, K. & Croes, R. (2015). The five E's in festival experience in the context of Gen Y: Evidence from a small island destination. *Revista Española de Investigación En Marketing ESIC, 19*(2), 95–106.

Roche, M. (1994). Mega-events and urban policy. *Annals of Tourism Research, 21*(1), 1–19.

Roche, M. (2000). *Mega-events and modernity: Olympics and expos in the growth of global culture*. London.

Roxas, B. & Chadee, D. (2013). Effects of formal institutions on the performance of the tourism sector in the Philippines: the mediating role of entrepreneurial orientation, *Tourism Management, 37*, 1–12.

Sofield, T.H. (2003). Sports tourism: From binary division to quadripartite construct. *Journal of Sport Tourism, 8*(3), 144–165.

Tassiopoulos, D (2005). *Event management: a professional and developmental approach* (2nd edn). Juta and Company Ltd.

Thrane, C. (2002). Jazz Festival Visitors and Their Expenditures: Linking Spending Patterns to Musical Interest. *Journal of Travel Research, 40*(3), 281–286.

Van Niekerk, M. (2017). Contemporary issues in events, festivals and destination management Guest Editorial. *International Journal of Contemporary Hospitality Management, 29*(3), 842–847.

Williams, P.W., Hainsworth, D. & Dossa, K.B. (1995). Community Development and Special Event Tourism: The Men's World Cup of Skiing at Whistler, British Columbia. *The Journal of Tourism Studies, 6*(2), 11–20.

Wong, J., Wu, H.C. & Cheng, C.C. (2014). An empirical analysis of synthesizing the effects of festival quality, emotion, festival image and festival satisfaction on festival loyalty: A case study of Macau Food Festival. *International Journal of Tourism Research, 17*(6), 521–536.

Wood, E.H. (2005). Measuring the economic and social impacts of local authority events. *The International Journal of Public Sector Management, 18*(1), 37–53.

Yoon, Y.S., Lee, J.S. & Lee, C.K. (2010). Measuring festival quality and value affecting visitors' satisfaction and loyalty using a structural approach. *International Journal of Hospitality Management, 29*(2), 335–342.

Yuan, J. & Jang, S. (2008). The Effects of Quality and Satisfaction on Awareness and Behavioral Intentions: Exploring the Role of a Wine Festival. *Journal of Travel Research, 46*(3), 279–288.

Zhang, J. & Wu, F. (2008). Mega-event marketing and urban growth coalitions: A case study of Nanjing Olympic New Town. *Town Planning Review*, 79(2–3), 209–226.

Zhou, Y. & Ap, J. (2009). Residents' Perceptions towards the Impacts of the Beijing 2008 Olympics Games. *Journal of Travel Research, 48*(1), 78–91.

13

Senior tourism

An emerging and attractive market segment for destinations

Adela Balderas-Cejudo, George W. Leeson and Elena Urdaneta

Introduction

The tourism industry faces enormous challenges emerging from external and internal changes. Constant technological progress and evolution, changes in the industry's markets and structures, economic slowdown, war and terrorist threats, climate changes and natural disasters, as well as disease-related problems have introduced states of crisis that affect destination marketing organizations in fundamental ways (Gretzel et al. 2006). Nevertheless, opportunities likewise emerge regarding the relevance of coping and reacting to these changes. As Prideaux and Cooper (2003) noted, destinations face a range of problems because of their complex and multifaceted nature when determining marketing arrangements, including the division of responsibilities between public and private sector agencies. Not only do destinations comprise a multitude of suppliers of tourism goods and services, but they also compete in a heterogeneous marketplace that has both domestic and international elements. Failure to anticipate the future and develop proactive and reactive strategies will create problems for the destinations and all the numerous stakeholders. Adaptation to technological changes, acknowledgment of new levels of competition, understanding and anticipation of changing global ageing patterns, collaborative relationships with the different stakeholders, involvement in planning and innovation and customer focus are not only needs but musts when considering new approaches to develop new visions and taking advantages of the opportunities that may arise. Having mentioned this, it is important to underline that, in terms of being organized in the market place, by getting all vested interests to work together, it is far more difficult for a tourism destination than other industry cooperatives (Pike 2015).

As a direct consequence of global ageing patterns and changes in older adult sociodemographic and travel patterns (Urdaneta 2016), senior travellers have become a significant proportion of annual total holiday spending (Sie et al. 2015). Tourism researchers have long been aware of the growing importance of senior travellers, usually taken to be those 55 or older, to the travel and tourism industry (Shoemaker 1989, 2000; Kotler et al. 1996; Reece 2004; Patterson 2006). This is partly due to an increase over the last decade in the number of senior travellers, coupled with the expectation of even greater growth in the future. Thus, in recent years, both practitioners and researchers have recognized the importance of seniors as a significant market segment of the tourism industry. Foreseeing senior travellers' needs, wants, and desires, understanding the diversity of travel preferences among the silver market segment, developing services appreciated by them, anticipating their expectations and a real customer-centred approach will not only provide knowledge to the tourism industry and the different stakeholders but a competitive advantage to those destinations which are able to adjust services, target this market segment with appropriate marketing strategies and to develop innovative services.

Senior travellers

Population ageing: some facts

The United Nations (2010) described population ageing as the most profound demographic change in history. In its introductory presentation made by the Population Division United Nations Expert Group Meeting on the Post-2015 Era: Implications for the Global Research Agenda on Population and Development, the following five key trends were highlighted and are important to emphasize:

1 Population ageing is one of the most important demographic trends of our time.
2 The cohort of older people is growing faster than any other age group.
3 Low and middle-income countries will experience the most rapid and dramatic demographic change in the proportion of their populations over the age of 60.
4 The older population itself is ageing.
5 Population ageing raises a number of issues, including the economic security of older people, the allocation of health and social care spending within a society, and the changing nature and direction of intergenerational support over the course of development.

Population ageing is a well-known phenomenon in most developed countries, where the proportion of older people has been steadily growing over the past century (Harper and Leeson 2008). The number of older persons – those aged 60 or over – has increased substantially in recent years in most countries and regions, and that growth is projected to accelerate in the coming decades. Between 2015 and 2030, the number of people in the world aged 60 or over is projected to grow by 56 per cent, from 901 million to 1.4 billion, and by 2050, the global population of older persons is projected to more than double its size from 2015, reaching nearly 2.1 billion (United Nations 2015).

These demographic shifts will be seen across all continents (United Nations 2000). Accordingly, many countries face demographic changes such as an ageing population, smaller household size, and increased mobility of people, all of which affects tourist demand (World Tourism Organization 2010).

These future population projections do not mean that becoming old restricts people's desire to travel or enjoy leisure; in fact, the opposite is occurring, together with behavioural shifts of active older adults, which will have a great impact on the tourism industry. Travel seems to be one of the most common and pleasant activities associated with retirement. Furthermore, the demand for leisure and tourism activities has grown steadily in our society, and these are now regarded as important aspects of life for enhancing psychological and physical well-being (Janke et al. 2006), and to assist in the achievement of a successful retirement (Silverstein and Parker 2002).

An important number of studies and researchers have confirmed that the senior market segment will be one of the largest in history and have a great impact on the tourism industry given its size and the increasing amount of disposable money that seniors will spend on consumer industries.

From the point of view of destination marketing, it is paramount for marketers, policy-makers and experts at destinations to understand those shifts – demographic and also behavioural- and to develop evidence-based marketing strategies so as to be able to comprehend their customers and to generate demand.

But, who are the "Seniors"?

A lack of consensus has been noted when it comes to a definition of "seniors", how they have been described and the different cut-off ages. When it comes to the "old" or "senior" population, the criteria for this population may vary depending on the literature.

Regarding naming, various terms have been used to refer to this group: "older market" (Carrigan and Szmigin 1998); "mature market" (Shoemaker 2000; Wang et al. 2007); "50-plus market" (Silvers 1997); "senior market" (Reece 2004); and "maturing market" (Whitford 1998).

Concerning age, various cut-off ages have been used (from 50 to 65 and older), and increasingly younger age groups have been considered in the research samples as seniors over time, whereas other research fields such as gerontology seem to have been more consistent, considering "retirement age of 65 years and older" (Patterson 2006: 13).

Several authors have also stated that the older population is typically treated as two or more age groups comprising 50 to 65 and post-retirement 65+, with the former being the most travelled age group (Dann 2007). In any event, the current perception of 'old' is not as it was perceived previously when it was related to a person's chronological age, and has now been found to be an unreliable predictor of consumer behaviour or a person's physical health (Ruys and Wei 2001). Some endeavours have suggested that there are substantial differences between the mind-set age and the actual birth certificate date or chronological age, which might be misleading when interpreting consumer decisions (Faranda and Schmidt 2000). The concepts of "felt age" or "subjective age" were first introduced by Barak and Schiffman (1981) in their Cognitive Theory of Ageing. The self-perceived age or "cognitive age" is generally lower than chronological age (Meiners and Seeberger 2010). Cognitive ageing is based on how people "feel they are", "think they look", "act" and "show their interests". Several researchers have concluded that many older adults today feel from seven to 15 years younger than their actual age (Meiners and Seeberger 2010; Patterson 2006) and is seen as a much more appropriate term that should be used in studies of older adult's behaviours and motivations. Thus, when it comes to analyzing and proposing strategies for more mature consumers, people are increasingly accepting that self-perceived age should replace chronological age (González et al. 2009). This age is a component of the self-image people have, and as a construct authors have named it "cognitive age" (Barak and Stern 1986; Moschis et al. 1993). Self-perceived age then may be more useful than chronological age when studying older adults as ageing does not always occur in the same way for all individuals (Jarvik 1975). Furthermore, homogeneity in individual lifestyles and conditions among people of the same age cannot be assumed. In fact, the number of years lived is often a poor indicator of a person's attitudes and behaviour (Sudbury-Riley et al. 2015).

Therefore, the issue of the use of cognitive age – whether subjective or self-perceived – to assess the buying behaviour of the older consumer as an alternative to chronological age arises (Barak and Schiffman1981; González et al. 2009; Patterson 2006). Yet, chronological age is still widely used in consumer research, despite self-perceived age being a potentially more important psychological influence on the way a person behaves in the market place (Barak and Gould 1985). As a result, there has been confusion that has derived from the multiplicity of definitions and descriptions offered by authors, marketers and researchers. However, in light of the discussion above, a hypothesis can be accepted that seniors cover an age spectrum from 50 to 80+, who are not at all homogeneous as self-perceived age may play a key role.

Researchers also point to the baby boomer generation as one that will introduce profound changes and transformations in the composition of markets in the coming decades. As the baby boomers enter the senior market, the potential for growth on a global scale is substantial. Baby boomers include people born between 1946 and 1966 (Butrica and Uccello 2005) when fertility rates increased dramatically after World War II. Baby boomers represent an important market segment or potential target market because of the sheer size of their generation. They are generally regarded as healthier, financially better off, more independent, better educated and with a greater desire for involvement in self-fulfilling outdoor adventure activities than previous cohorts of older people (Patterson 2006). They are becoming the fastest growing and the most powerful consumer segment in the Western World (Camden and McColl-Kennedy 1991) and as stated by Patterson and Pegg (2009: 255) "there is little doubt that baby boomers are increasingly placing travel as a higher priority in their retirement years".

The attractiveness of seniors and future seniors

What has made senior travellers so attractive? Many scholars state that this generation of seniors will become the most significant consumer group of the coming decades, as they are considered the richest generation in the world (Meiners and Seeberger 2010). Older people are not only growing rapidly in absolute numbers, but have also become substantially healthier. The length of healthy old-age appears to be increasing in a phenomenon referred to by demographers and health specialists as the 'compression of morbidity'. Part of this trend can be attributed to increases in the length of life, and part to shorter and later periods of illness. The net effect is an increase in the number of years lived at old age without major health problems (Bloom et al. 2010). Golik (1999: 65) stated that "one of the outcomes of this increase in life expectancy is that it will allow seniors to travel more, travel longer and travel later in life". As more and more people move into an advanced stage of their life, more people of this group will still want to travel (Möller et al. 2007). In 1999, over 593 million international travellers were aged 60 and over. This level of tourism activity accounted for approximately a third of the total amount spent on holidays in that year. By 2050, this figure is projected to grow to exceed two billion trips per annum (World Tourism Organization 2001). This increased propensity to travel will increase greatly in the future due to a more active generation of seniors. Understanding and acknowledging the attractiveness of senior travellers and their linkages between their current and future needs and wants is just a first yet crucial step towards a deeper knowledge of the silver market segment.

Seniors needs and wants

The empirical research into older consumers is sparse in comparison to younger samples, with older respondents frequently being ignored in studies of consumer behaviour (Sudbury-Riley et al. 2015). Yet, a body of evidence from cognitive psychology and cognitive and affective neuroscience supports the contention that older adults have different information processing strategies than their younger counterparts (Gutchess, 2010). Consequently, older consumers have different decision-making processes, all of which impact on their attitudes toward possessions, wants, expectations and even comprehension and interaction of marketing communications and brand choice (Lambert-Pandraud and Laurent, 2010). Many marketing theories and concepts have been designed predominantly for younger samples, and are not particularly conducive to attracting older segments (Sudbury-Riley et al. 2015). Gerontological and psychological studies have confirmed that older adults see themselves as younger than their chronological age (González et al. 2009). Woo et al. (2016) found in their study of measures of quality of life that engagement in leisure and tourism activities are very important aspects of later life for many individuals. Furthermore, following Patterson et al. (2017) and referring to baby boomers, they are having a significant impact on the type of holidays that they are taking, and although travelling to warmer climates is still popular, there has been increased spending on holiday experiences that specifically focus on such niche markets as adventure, education, and cultural tourism (World Tourism Organization, 2001). This is a generation that view themselves as a bridging generation between the old ways of their own parents and the fundamentally different views of the next generation. Consequently, new subcultures based on different lifestyles and purchasing and consumption ways emerge (Sudbury-Riley 2016).

Six special aspects that may have an immediate impact on the needs and wants of seniors and baby boomers and the type of holidays overtaken will be highlighted:

1 Health. Seniors will benefit from higher life expectancy, enjoy good health and physical condition for longer and a more active lifestyle.
2 Well-being awareness. Not only do seniors benefit from good health but they want - and strive - to maintain their good state of mental and physical health.
3 Time. They have more disposable time and fewer social and family obligations, which enables them to travel off peak season, more frequently and take longer vacations.
4 Money. Seniors are better off, spend more on leisure and there is a change in attitude towards lifetime savings.
5 Education. Seniors and particularly baby boomers are better educated and have a greater desire for self-fulfilment, novelty, escape and authentic experiences than previous retiree cohorts.
6 Technology. Following Patterson et al. (2017), the Internet has become popular among seniors and baby boomers, who are likewise now more confident regarding social network activities.

Such a shift in mind-set will have an immediate and notable impact on the type of holidays undertaken and the destinations that are chosen by older adults (Patterson and Pegg 2009). Responding to these issues, catering for the desires and wants of seniors and being able to offer services beyond their expectations will be an important challenge for destinations that may be able to offer what these vibrant and changing travellers are seeking.

Seniors: destination marketing, hospitality and the tourism industry

Tourism is a competitive and perishable economic product that shifts over time, depending on the changing needs and preferences of holiday travellers. Tourists are becoming increasingly demanding and selective about their holiday travel, which, in turn is leading to an increasingly competitive tourism market (European Travel Commission, 2006). These shifts in traveller behaviour, in turn, make predicting tourism demand quite challenging (Witt and Witt, 1995).

The senior segment is evolving and as a result, leisure travel is becoming very popular. Greater discretionary income, the changing age patterns of consumers and more free time are seen as essential factors for an increase in the travel demand of this segment. An important number of studies and researchers are aware and have confirmed that the senior market segment will be one of the largest in history and have a great impact to the tourism industry because of its size and the increasing amount of disposable money that seniors will spend on consumer industries. In spite of this, the travel industry has been criticized in the past for failing to recognize the diversity of travel preferences among the senior travel market (Javalgi et al., 1992). Part of this problem underlying this perception of the travel industry stems from an inaccurate and misunderstood stereotyped view of elderly people (Horneman et al. 2002; Moschis 1992). Stereotypes of senior travellers are that they are too old or frail to travel compared to many other demographic groups. Such a superficial assessment of the senior traveller has resulted in some efforts being made to cater for their needs, yet these are often based on false perceptions and stereotypes of the aged – stereotypes that assume conservatism and homogeneity (Horneman et al. 2002). Traditionally the tendency of tourism marketers and product developers has been to focus their attention on younger consumers ignoring those over the age of 50 and to treat senior consumers as one homogeneous segment. Nevertheless, more recent studies have clearly agreed that the senior market segment is heterogeneous. The resulting poorly developed and marketed products has led to a cycle of disinterest on the part of many older people towards many services and products. Research in the study of gerontographics has clearly indicated that older consumers are not "all alike" (Lehto et al. 2002). Senior travellers differ from younger travellers in many aspects, including their reasons for travel, or their destination choices (Reece, 2004). You and O'Leary (2000) found that senior travellers from different generation cohorts differed in terms of their travel propensity, destination activity participation and travel philosophy.

The politics, challenges and constraints inherent in marketing a tourism destination are very different to those faced by an individual tourism service business (Pike 2015) and definitely the complexity is due to a great extent to the variety of stakeholders and their different interests. As noted by Pike (2015), the success of individual tourism-related business is reliant on the competitiveness of the destination in which they are either located or to which they supply services. Concurring with Dwyer and Kim (2003: 369), any destination must ensure that its overall "appeal", and the tourist experience offered, must be superior to that of the alternative destinations open to potential visitors in order "to achieve competitive advantage for its tourism industry".

More experienced, demanding, technology-friendly and multichannel, this market segment will demand new and different products and services. New and memorable experiences and adventures, social interaction, cultural amenities, more sophisticated services, and search for discovery and knowledge will be some of the important aspects future seniors will request. Transactions will be the key and a real challenge that will provide greater comprehension not only of the senior market segment, but also of the new trends that emerge. Marketing will be decisive for destination managers to properly comprehend their insights and communicate with those seniors in the future. Recent research has indicated that marketing to chronological or a person's actual age rather than to his/her cognitive age may be a dangerous precedent. People generally age at different rates, and do not always look or act their age (Patterson and Pegg 2009). Sub-segments of senior tourists are likely to emerge in the future and due to this, it will be vital, at the level of competitive strategy, to choose market segments with the greatest potential and the most strategic positioning.

Destinations need to build trust, become intelligent and collaborative providers that are accessible for all and able to facilitate integration and interaction for their visitors. Furthermore, destinations should be able to generate greater knowledge and cooperation among their stakeholders in an attempt to improve the overall visitor experience and create not only an "age-friendly" destinations but "age-friendly" future.

Conclusions

At a time when there is increasing competition in the tourism and hospitality industries – between destinations worldwide (between established markets and from new markets), between destinations domestically, and between firms within a particular destination – further knowledge and the tireless pursuit of greater competition in destinations is crucial.

When the greater economic well-being of seniors is combined with their escalating numbers, more independent living, and better overall health, aging consumers definitely constitute a very attractive market for the travel and tourism industry (Faranda et al. 2000). It seems obvious that there is a clear need to grasp the potential of this market segment, its heterogeneity, travel patterns, culture and idiosyncrasies (Balderas et al. 2016). Concurring with Tung et al. (2011), it is vital for tourism practitioners to recognize that different travellers can experience a situation very differently even if equivalent services, events, and activities are provided. More so today than ever before, ageing has become a largely non-uniform process.

The greater the knowledge of these trends relating to tourism development in general, and the senior market segment in particular, the greater the capacity of all stakeholders to formulate strategies, contribute to new and innovative services and to achieve competitive advantage for their organizations and their regions. Understanding this reality, anticipating and responding to the forthcoming demographic changes and developing appropriate and proactive policies to address these shifts and challenges must be recognized as major issues. Therefore, understanding senior behaviour, preferences and trends is absolutely essential in order to offer innovative, efficient and appropriate services adapted to the requirements, expectations and needs of a heterogeneous, more sophisticated and expert customer.

Further research

There are further avenues for research into senior tourism. Following Tung et al. (2011), the senior travel market is one of the most challenging for scholars to understand due to its inherent complexities. The complexity and lack of comprehensive knowledge of the potential requirements and needs of the senior market suggest that building a more robust theoretical description of existing theory together with the identification of new drivers that can emerge from future generations of seniors and the need to analyze this market segment from an international dimension may help to expand knowledge of the trends underpinning tourism development, along with providing useful insights into the senior market segment. As noted by the European Travel Commission (2016), destinations acknowledge the need to remain competitive in a sector that is swiftly adapting to the diverse needs of travellers from both established and emerging markets.

References

Balderas-Cejudo, A., Rivera-Hernaez, O. and Patterson, I. (2016). "The Strategic Impact of Country of Origin on Senior Tourism Demand: The Need to Balance Global and Local Strategies". *Journal of Population Ageing*, 1–29.

Barak, B. and Gould, S. (1985). "Alternatives Age Measures: A Research Agenda". In Hirschman E. and Holbrook M. (eds) *Advances in Consumer Research*, Vol. 12 (pp. 53–58). Provo, UT: Association for Consumer Research.

Barak, B. and Schiffman, L. G. (1981). "Cognitive age: A nonchronological age variable". *NA-Advances in Consumer Research*, 8.

Barak, B. and Stern, B. (1986). "Subjective age correlates: A research note". *The Gerontologist*, 26(5), 571–578.

Bloom, D. E., Canning, D. and Fink, G. (2010). "Implications of population ageing for economic growth". *Oxford Review of Economic Policy*, 26(4), 583–612.

Butrica, B. A. and Uccello, C. E. (2005). "How Will Boomers Fare at Retirement?" Available online at: www.urban.org/sites/default/files/publication/52116/900892-How-Will-Boomers-Fare-at-Retirement-PDF
Camden, D. and McColl-Kennedy, J. (1991). "Travel patterns of the over 50's practical implications." In Camden, D. and McColl-Kennedy, J. (eds) *Papers on the over 50's in the 90's: Factors for successful marketing of products and services.* Netherlands: Esomar.
Carrigan, M. and Szmigin, I. (1998). "The usage and portrayal of older models in contemporary consumer advertising". *Journal of Marketing Practice: Applied Marketing Science*, 4(8), 231–248.
Dann, S. (2007). "Branded generations: baby boomers moving into the seniors market". *Journal of Product & Brand Management*, 16(6), 429–431.
Dwyer, L. and Kim, C. (2003). "Destination competitiveness: determinants and indicators". *Current issues in tourism*, 6(5), 369–414.
European Travel Commission Annual Report (2006). Available online at: http://etc-corporate.org/assets/pdf/reports/etc_report_2006_for_web-final.pdf
European Travel Commission Quarterly Report 2016 (2016). *Trends and Prospects.* Available online at: www.etc-corporate.org/reports/european-tourism-2016-trends-and-prospects-(q4–2016)
Faranda, W. T. and Schmidt, S. L. (2000). "Segmentation and the senior traveler: implications for today's and tomorrow's aging consume". *Journal of Travel & Tourism Marketing*, 8(2), 3–27.
Golik, B. (1999). "Not over the hill. Just enjoying the view". *Department of Human Services.* Adelaide.
González, A.M., Rodríguez, C., Miranda, M. R. and Cervantes, M. (2009). "Cognitive age as a criterion explaining senior tourists' motivations". *International Journal of Culture, Tourism and Hospitality Research*, 3(2), 148–164.
Gretzel, U., Fesenmaier, D. R., Formica, S. and O'Leary, J. T. (2006). "Searching for the future: Challenges faced by destination marketing organizations". *Journal of Travel Research*, 45(2), 116–126.
Gutchess, A. H. (2010). "Cognitive psychology and neuroscience of aging". *The Aging Consumer: Perspectives from Psychology and Economics*, 3–24.
Harper, S. and Leeson, G. (2008). "Introducing the journal of population ageing". *Journal of Population Ageing*, 1(1), 1–5.
Horneman, L., Carter, R. W., Wei, S. and Ruys, H. (2002). "Profiling the senior traveler: An Australian perspective". *Journal of Travel Research*, 41(1), 23–37.
Janke, M., Davey, A. and Kleiber, D. (2006). "Modeling change in older adults' leisure activities". *Leisure Sciences*, 28(3), 285–303.
Jarvik, L. F. (1975). "Thoughts on the psychobiology of aging". *American Psychologist*, 30(5), 576.
Javalgi, R. G., Thomas, E. G. and Rao, S. R. (1992). "Consumer behavior in the US pleasure travel marketplace: An analysis of senior and nonsenior travellers". *Journal of Travel Research*, 31(2), 14–19.
Kotler, B. and Bowen, J. and Makens, J. (1996). *Marketing for Hospitality and Tourism.* New York: Prentice Hall.
Lehto, X. Y., O'Leary, J. T. and Lee, G. (2002). "Mature international travelers: An examination of gender and benefits". *Journal of Hospitality & Leisure Marketing*, 9(1–2), 53–72.
Lambert-Pandraud, R. and Laurent, G. (2010). "Why do older consumers buy older brands? The role of attachment and declining innovativeness". *Journal of Marketing*, 74(5), 104–121.
Meiners, N. H. and Seeberger, B. (2010). "Marketing to senior citizens: Challenges and opportunities". *The Journal of Social, Political, and Economic Studies*, 35(3), 293–328.
Möller, C., Weiermair, K. and Wintersberger, E. (2007). "The changing travel behaviour of Austria's ageing population and its impact on tourism". *Tourism Review*, 62(3/4), 15–20.
Moschis, G. P. (1992). *Marketing to older consumers: A handbook of information for strategy development.* Greenwood Publishing Group.
Moschis, G. P., Mathur, A. and Smith, R. B. (1993). "Older consumers' orientations toward age-based marketing stimuli". *Journal of the Academy of Marketing Science*, 21(3), 195–205.
Patterson, I. and Pegg, S. (2009). "Marketing the leisure experience to baby boomers and older tourists". *Journal of Hospitality Marketing & Management*, 18(2–3), 254–272.
Patterson, I., Balderas-Cejudo, A. and Rivera-Hernáez, O. (2017). Changing trends in the baby boomer travel market: importance of memorable experiences. *Journal of Hospitality Marketing & Management*, 1–14.
Patterson, I. R. (2006). *Growing older: Tourism and leisure behaviour of older adults.* Wallingford: Cabi.
Pike, S. (2015). *Destination Marketing.* Oxon: Routledge.
Prideaux, B. and Cooper, C. (2003). "Marketing and destination growth: A symbiotic relationship or simple coincidence?" *Journal of Vacation Marketing*, 9(1), 35–51.
Reece, W. S. (2004). "Are senior leisure travelers different?" *Journal of Travel Research*, 43(1), 11–18.

Ruys, H. and Wei, S. (2001). "Senior tourism". In Douglas, N. and Derrett, R. (eds), *Special Interest Tourism*. Australia: John Wiley and Sons.

Shoemaker, S. (1989). "Segmentation of the senior pleasure travel market". *Journal of Travel Research*, 27(3), 14–21.

Shoemaker, S. (2000). "Segmenting the mature market: 10 years later". *Journal of Travel Research*, 39(1), 11–26.

Sie, Lintje, Ian Patterson and Shane Pegg. (2015). "Towards an understanding of older adult educational tourism through the development of a three-phase integrated framework". *Current Issues in Tourism*. DOI: 10.1080/13683500.2015.1021303

Silvers, C., (1997) "Smashing Old Stereotypes of 50-plus America". *Journal of Consumer Marketing*, 14 (4), 303–309.

Silverstein, M. and Parker, M. G. (2002). "Leisure activities and quality of life among the oldest old in Sweden". *Research on Aging*, 24(5), 528–547.

Sudbury-Riley, L. (2016). "The baby boomer market maven in the United Kingdom: an experienced diffuser of marketplace information". *Journal of Marketing Management*, 32(7–8), 716–749.

Sudbury-Riley, L., Kohlbacher, F. and Hofmeister, A. (2015). "Baby Boomers of different nations: Identifying horizontal international segments based on self-perceived age". *International Marketing Review*, 32(3/4), 245–278.

Tung, V., Tung, W. S. and Brent Ritchie, J. R. (2011). "Investigating the memorable experiences of the senior travel market: an examination of the reminiscence bump". *Journal of Travel & Tourism Marketing*, 28(3), 331–343.

UNWTO Tourism Highlights (2001). Available online at: www.eunwto.org/doi/book/10.18111/9789284406845

UWNTO Annual Report (2010). Available online at: www2.unwto.org/publication/unwto-annual-report-2010

United Nations (2010). *World population ageing 2009* (295). Department of Economic and Social Affairs, United Nations Publications.

United Nations, Department of Economic and Social Affairs, Population Division (2015). *World Population Ageing 2015*. ST/ESA/SER.A/390

Urdaneta, E. (2016). *SIforAGE: Social Innovation for healthy and active ageing for an economic growth*. Available online at: www.siforage.eu

Wang, K. C., Chen, J. S. and Chou, S. H. (2007). "Senior tourists' purchasing decisions in group package tour". *Anatolia*, 18(1), 23–42.

Whitford, M. (1998). "Seniors provide hoteliers with golden opportunities". *Hotel Motel Management*, 213, 41–43.

Witt, S. F. and C. A. Witt. (1995). "Forecasting Tourism Demand: A Review of Empirical Research". *International Journal of Forecasting*, 11, 447–447.

Woo, E., Kim, H. and Uysal, M. (2016). "A measure of quality of life in elderly tourists". *Applied Research in Quality of Life*, 11(1), 65–82.

You, X. and O'Leary, J. T. (2000). "Age and cohort effects: An examination of older Japanese travelers". *Journal of Travel & Tourism Marketing*, 9(1–2), 21–42.

Further reading

Harper, S. (2014). "Economic and social implications of aging societies". *Science*, 346(6209), 587–591. (Population ageing and implications.)

Vigolo, V. (2017). *Older Tourist Behavior and Marketing Tools*. Springer. (In-depth analysis of this tourist market.)

14

Value-satisfaction-loyalty chain in tourism

A case study from the hotel sector

Martina G. Gallarza, Giacomo Del Chiappa and Francisco Arteaga

Introduction

Perceived value is a key concept for marketing epistemology and marketing strategy (Holbrook 1999; Cronin et al. 2000; Day and Crask 2000). Indeed, understanding how consumers perceive value has interested scholars since the start of academic marketing research, and it has also caused struggles for practitioners and marketers, as offering distinctive value is the key for achieving competitive advantages. Hospitality settings have been, for a long time, a privileged field for studying value from both scholar and managerial perspectives. For scholars, there are three main reasons for this appropriateness (Gallarza et al. 2016). First, hospitality is multifaceted, and value is multidimensional. Second, hospitality products are predominantly experiential products, and the most complete approach to the concept of value is, as we will see later, the experiential approach. Third, hospitality settings are very appropriate for studying relationships between value, satisfaction and loyalty. As far as these relationships are concerned, it is worth noting that in the last two decades the development of the Internet, Information and Communication Technologies (ICTs) and peer-to-peer applications, as well as the changes that have been occurring in the economy and in the society as a whole, are dramatically changing the way customers perceive value when consuming products, services and experiences. Specifically, customers' value perception is changing, both in the content (the different dimensions of value: emotional, social, functional), and in the intensity (some are more relevant than others in the way they affect behaviors).

This chapter is relevant for both public and private organizations, as it aims to understand, also offering a case study, how consumers perceive and organize holistic value dimensions of the hospitality firm (how value creation happens in their minds) and how hospitality organizations (both private and public) should manage value outcomes in order to differentiate their offers. In this sense, this chapter aims to contribute to the value co-creation perspective by considering both the value creation processes (how different value dimensions interact in shaping perceived value) and value outcomes (e.g. satisfaction and loyalty).

In particular, the chapter's goal will be to explore the different value dimensions that tourists do experience in their hospitality consumption (functional, emotional, social and altruistic), with the aim of identifying the key value drivers on which tourism organizations (both public and private) should focus their attention to obtain higher levels of customer satisfaction and loyalty. This will be done by means of two approaches: theoretical and empirical. Theoretically, the chapter will review both the dimensionality of consumer value in the hospitality-related context (the intra-variable approach) and the relations between overall perceived value, satisfaction and loyalty (the inter-variable approach). This theoretical part will, first, show how, in spite of decades of research, there is not a unique value dimensionality that applies to hospitality experiences and, second, how the large amount of works on links between value, satisfaction and loyalty have provided a certain knowledge that allows considering the existence of a V-S-L chain of effects as it applies to hospitality (inter-variable). Furthermore, the chapter will include an empirical illustration of this reality as a case study that aims to test simultaneously the relations between experiential value dimensions (functional social, emotional and altruistic), overall perceived value and loyalty. This objective is undertaken by means of providing a Structural Equation Modelling (SEM) model tested with partial least squares (PLS) on a sample of 300 domestic tourists on the island of Sardinia (Italy), with the peculiarity of presenting a special interest on the experiential nature of value and a structure of relationships (double effects on value and loyalty) depicting the richness and complexity of perceptions held by consumers in a tourism experience.

Background information

The value concept in hospitality marketing: relevance and approaches

For any person interested in marketing – no matter if practitioner, academic or student – the notion of value has a key role, as it is at the very heart of what marketing is. The word "value" is contained in the last three definitions of marketing, offered by the American Marketing Association, in 2004, 2007 and 2013. As a result, a myriad of definitions of customer value have been proposed with no clear supremacy of one over the other (Bocksberger and Melsen 2011; Gallarza et al. 2011). The proposal by Zeithaml (1988: 14), defining perceived value as "the consumer overall assessment of the utility of a product based on the perceptions of what is received and what is given", has influenced a stream of studies focused on the "get-versus-give" trade-off (e.g., Martin-Ruiz et al. 2008). Nevertheless, this get-versus-give perspective is not necessarily the preferred way of conceptualizing value, especially when considering the need for a multidimensional approach (as tourism and hospitality settings need). In this sense, the conceptualization proposed by Holbrook (1999) has been considered "the most comprehensive approach to the value construct, because it captures more potential sources of value, than do other conceptualizations" (Sanchez-Fernández et al. 2009: 97). This conceptual framework on value originated in the seminal work by the same author and Elizabeth Hirschman in 1982. Specifically, Holbrook and Hirschman (1982) approached the first time consumption as "experiences" dealing with "fantasies, feelings, and fun". In contrast with the information-processing paradigm, where consumer behavior is only objective and rational, in this experiential paradigm, consumer behavior pursues the more-subjective, emotional and symbolic aspects of consumption, all of them fully applicable to hospitality consumption. Since then, experiential marketing has many times broken the restraints on the typical marketing tactics and connects more deeply with consumers (Goldsmith and Tsiotsou 2012).

Holbrook's proposal places the notion of value in a key position of any experiential behavior, assuming that consumer value, as a cognitive-affective assessment, is endemic to marketing theory and thus to consumer behavior understanding (Holbrook 1999). His definition of value is referred to as an axiology (that is, as a judgment of goodness/badness) and pursues thus a philosophical approach that conceives consumer value as "an interactive relativistic preference experience" (Holbrook 1999: 5), where, by experience, it is understood that value resides not in the product purchased or in the brand chosen but rather in the consumption experience derived therefore. This particular approach also offers a value typology that recognizes three distinctions or dimensions, enabling classification of the different types of value that can arise in the consumption experience: extrinsic versus intrinsic value, self-oriented versus other-oriented value and active versus reactive value. The combination of these three distinctions in a matrix gives rise to eight types of value: efficiency, excellence, play, aesthetics, status, esteem, ethics and spirituality. When omitting the active/reactive distinction, the typology comes to a four-fold categorization (Holbrook 1999): functional value, social value, emotional value and altruistic value.

According to current research (Gallarza and Gil-Saura 2006: 438), value can be studied by adopting two different perspectives: (a) an intra-variable approach that emphasizes the multidimensional nature of value and recognizes groups of dimensions through their cognitive, affective and social nature; and (b) an inter-variable approach that measures the relationships between perceived value and other variables, like service quality, customer satisfaction and customer loyalty. Each perspective will be presented and discussed in the next two sub-headings.

The intra-variable approach on value: a review of value dimensions and value typologies

As a combination of the general distinction of positive and negative values on one side and experiential values on the other, there can be many approaches to value dimensions that give rise to multi-dimensional value typologies (the so called intra-variable approach on value). Table 14.1 shows a review of value dimensionality in previous literature, both in theoretical and general literature on Marketing and Consumer Behavior and within empirical works on value dimensions in tourism and hospitality-related literature. Accordingly, and in relation to our first heading, three main approaches can be considered within the intra-variable perspective, namely: experiential, trade-off or mixed (experiential and trade-off) (Table 14.1).

In this sense, in advancing beyond the traditional confines of the get-versus-give trade-off, Holbrook's (1999) perspective has found empirical support in some service-dominant settings, such as students' trips (e.g., Gallarza and Gil-Saura 2006), restaurants (e.g., Sánchez-Fernández et al. 2009) and hotels (e.g., Gallarza et al. 2015), although not using all eight value types but just some of them.

These works and others, such as those from Table 14.1, offer experiential views concerning the multiple dimensions of value that have contributed to a comprehensive understanding of all facets of hospitality consumption. The contrast between, for instance, the get-versus-give approach and the many uses of this multidimensional holistic approach in consumer behavior literature indicates its richness and versatility (Table 14.1). In tourism-related literature, the experiential values encompass and interrelate all relevant facets of the tourism experience. In accordance with this, many works, alongside with the ones cited above that apply Holbrook's framework, have addressed the interest of this experiential approach to different hospitality settings, such as restaurants – e.g., luxury-hotel restaurants (e.g., Wu and Liang 2009), full-service restaurants (e.g., Jin et al. 2013) and eating out and fast food restaurants (e.g., Park 2004) – but also other sophisticated hospitality services, such as community-based homestay visits (e.g., Jamal et al. 2011), heritage settings (e.g., Laing et al. 2014), cultural theme parks (e.g., Yeh et al. 2012), online tourism shopping (e.g., Iniesta-Bonillo et al. 2012), attendance of international conventions (e.g., Lee and Min 2013) and tourism gift consumption (e.g., Clarke 2013).

Table 14.1 Approaches to value dimensions

Classical approaches to value dimensions in consumer behavior literature					
Approach	*Author(s) & context*	*Types of values*			
Experiential	Holbrook and Hirschman (1982)	Utilitarian Hedonic			
	Sheth, Newman and Gross (1991)	Functional Social Emotional Conditional			
	Holbrook (1999)	Self-oriented	Intrinsic	Active	Efficiency
				Reactive	Excellence
			Extrinsic	Active	Play
				Reactive	Aesthetics
		Other-oriented	Intrinsic	Active	Status
				Reactive	Esteem
			Extrinsic	Active	Ethics
				Reactive	Spirituality
Trade-off	Zeithaml (1988)	Costs Benefits			
Mixed approach	Sweeney and Soutar (2001)	Emotional Social Quality/performance Price/value for money			

Empirical studies on value dimensions in hospitality		
Approach	*Author(s) & context*	*Types of values*
Experiential	Babin and Kim (2001) STUDENTS' TRIPS	Planning Educational Safety Fun
	Yuan and Wu (2008) RESTAURANTS	Perception of the senses ("sense") Perception of feelings ("feel") Cognitive perception ("think") Emotional and functional service quality
	Sparks, Butcher and Bradley (2008) TIMESHARE	Relaxation, gift giving, status, quality, flexibility, fun, new experiences and financial worth.
	Sánchez-Fernández, Iniesta Bonillo and Holbrook (2009) VEGETARIAN RESTAURANTS	Efficiency Quality Social Value Play Aesthetics Altruistic Value

Empirical studies on value dimensions in hospitality

Approach	*Author(s) & context*	*Types of values*
	Kim and Perdue (2013) HOTELS	Cognitive attributes (price, service and food quality, national brand) Affective attributes (comfortable feeling and entertaining) Sensory attributes (room quality, overall atmosphere)
	Sánchez et al. (2006) TRAVEL AGENCY	Functional (from the agency: installations) Functional (from staff: professionalism) Functional (of package purchased: quality) Functional value price Emotional value Social value
Trade-off	Nasution and Mavondo (2008) HOTELS	Reputation for quality Value for money Prestige
	Martin-Ruiz et al. (2008) FAST FOOD RESTAURANTS	Service quality Perceived sacrifice (monetary and non-monetary) Service equity (image or brand equity) Confidence (trust, relational value) Emotional response Monetary price Behavioral price Reputation
	Gallarza and Gil-Saura (2006) STUDENTS' TRIPS	Efficiency Service Quality Social Value Play Aesthetics Time and effort spent
	Wu and Liang (2009) RESTAURANTS	(Restaurants) environmental factors Interaction with service employees Interaction with other customers Full price Time efficiency Excellent service Aesthetics Escapism

(*Continued*)

Table 14.1 (Continued)

Empirical studies on value dimensions in hospitality		
Approach	*Author(s) & context*	*Types of values*
	Eid and El-Gohary (2015) (MUSLIM) TOURISM	Quality Price Emotional Social Islamic physical attributes Islamic non-physical attributes Islamic physical attributes
	Pandža-Bajs (2015) DESTINATION	Quality of (touristic) services Monetary costs Non-monetary costs Reputation Emotional experience Destination appearance
	Prebensen, Vittersø and Dahal (2013) DESTINATIONS	Service quality Involvement Surrounding nature Other tourists Time spent Resources spent Money spent

The inter-variable perspective: the consensus on the Value-Satisfaction-Loyalty chain

Perceived value and loyalty are omnipresent constructs in consumer behavior literature (Cronin et al. 2000; Day and Crask 2000), and both have been deeply tackled in tourism-related literature over the last three decades (e.g., Babin and Kim 2001; Gallarza and Gil-Saura 2006; Jin et al. 2013; Pandža-Bajs 2015). Literature review shows a close, conceptual and methodological relationship existing between value and loyalty, as "the two coexist for a mutual goal of building a close relationship with customers" (Chu and Shiu 2009: 99). Indeed, contrary to what has happened in the intra-variable approach with no agreement on the number and name of value dimensions, for Marketing academic from last decade, a relatively broad consensus has evolved around the antecedent, mediating and consequent relationships among quality, value and satisfaction (Cronin et al. 2000; McDougall and Levesque 2000).

That said, it could be argued that the interest in value research is highly noticeable in tourism-related literature. In a joint vision of the two main perspectives on value research ("intra" and "inter-variable"), the majority of works have concentrated independently on either intra- (e.g., Petrick 2002; Nasution and Mavondo 2008) or inter-variable research (e.g., Chen and Chen 2010). However, several authors have undertaken empirical works, including both perspectives in the same study (e.g., Babin and Kim 2001; Gallarza and Gil-Saura 2006; Sánchez-Fernández et al. 2009; Gallarza et al. 2015).

Introduction to case study

For achieving our aim of addressing a value-based assessment of a hospitality setting, by means of an experiential approach, we choose to relate in a SEM model the four aforementioned experiential value dimensions (functional, social, emotional and altruistic values) with an overall value assessment and behavioral intentions, with this latter construct being considered as a measure of loyalty.

As in previous empirical works (e.g., Gallarza and Gil-Saura 2006; Sánchez-Fernández et al. 2009), dimensions of value are considered as exogenous variables of a structural model, being direct antecedents of perceived value. The hypotheses supporting this proposal are as follows:

H1: Functional value is positively related to perceived overall value.
H2: Social value is positively related to perceived overall value.
H3: Emotional value is positively related to perceived overall value.
H4: Altruistic value is positively related to perceived overall value.

With the aim of simultaneously testing double effects, experiential value dimensions have also been considered as predictors of loyalty behavior:

H5: Functional value is positively related to loyalty.
H6: Social value is positively related to loyalty.
H7: Emotional value is positively related to loyalty.
H8: Altruistic value is positively related to loyalty.

As a final relationship between the two endogenous constructs, we proposed a value-loyalty link that emerged as a trend from literature review in services (Gallarza et al. 2012).

H9: Perceived value directly and positively influences loyalty.

Methodology

A hospitality-based experience of a stay at a hotel is chosen for exploring relationships between dimensions of experiential value and overall value and loyalty. For the purpose of this case study, the island of Sardinia (Italy) was chosen as the specific setting for our empirical study. An ad-hoc questionnaire was developed, with items being sourced from existing literature (Table 14.2).

Specifically, for the purposes of this case study, functional value is understood as excellence (Holbrook 1999), and it is measured with the four first items from Cronin et al.'s (2000) service quality scale (four items). Social value corresponds to other oriented active value derived from a consumption experience (Holbrook 1999) and uses Sparks, Butcher and Bradley's (2008) status scale (three items). Emotional value relates to playfulness experiences (Holbrook 1999) and is assessed by an adaptation from Sparks et al.'s (2008) fun scale (three items). Altruistic Value is measured with an ad-hoc scale containing indicators of price transparency and management commitment to regulations. The overall value scale was taken from Cronin et al.' s (2000), with an extra item on the overall value perception (three items), and loyalty was measured with Zeithaml, Berry and Parasuraman's (1996) scale (first seven items).

Table 14.2 Items

Functional value (adapted from Cronin, Brady and Hult 2000)[a]
Generally, the employees provide service reliably, consistently and dependably.
Generally, the employees are willing and able to provide service in a timely manner.
Generally, the employees are competent (i.e., knowledgeable and skillful).
Generally, the employees are approachable and easy to contact.
Social value (adapted from Sparks, Butcher and Bradley 2008)[a]
Staying at this hotel increases my sense of self-esteem.
I get a great sense of achievement from staying at this hotel.
I get a sense of pride when staying at this hotel.
Emotional value (PLAY) (adapted from Sparks et al. 2008)[a]
The hotel offers many children's activities.
The hotel offers many family activities.
The activities that can be organized at the hotel are great fun.
Altruistic value (focus group with tourists and conversation with hotel managers)[a]
The hotel donates to good causes/social projects (NGOs or similar).
Prices in the hotel are transparent (services not included correctly announced . . .).
At this hotel, everything is run in a legal and proper way.
Perceived value (adapted from Gallarza and Gil-Saura 2006 and Cronin, Brady and Hulth 2000)[b]
Overall, the value of this tourist experience to me has been . . .
Compared to what I am used to, the overall ability of this tourist experience to satisfy my wants and needs has been . . .
Comparing the benefits I got and the sacrifices I made to have this tourist experience, I consider it as being . . .
Loyalty (adapted from Zeithaml, Berry and Parasuraman 1996)[a]
I will say positive things about the hotel to other people.
I will recommend this hotel to someone that seeks my advice.
I will encourage friends and relatives to stay at this hotel.
I will consider this hotel as my first choice if I came back to this destination on holiday.
I will be back to stay at this hotel in the next few years.
I will not be back at this hotel in the next few years.
If I should come back on holiday in this area, I will look for another hotel that offers me better prices.

[a] 5-point Likert Scale: 1 = strongly disagree, 5 = strongly agree; [b] 5-point Likert scale: 1= very poor, 5 = very good

All constructs were measured using a five-point Likert scale (1 = strongly disagree, 5 = strongly agree). The questionnaire included a final set of questions regarding the sample profile and the type of hotels researched (three-, four- or five-star hotels). Data were collected in September 2012 from Italians visiting Sardinia Island; potential respondents were approached in the boarding area at Olbia-Costa Smeralda airport at the time of their departure, thus allowing us to capture a finalized hospitality experience (N = 300).

Reasons for collecting data from Italians were twofold. First, to the best of our knowledge, no case study has been published so far with the aim of assessing how Italians assess their value experience with hotel services; this occurs despite the importance that the Italian tourism market represents for many countries worldwide, especially in Europe. According to Banca d'Italia (2013), in 2012, 59,197,000 Italians spent their holiday abroad (57.97% in EU countries, 31.11%

in extra-EU countries and 5% in the US), thus generating 256,367,000 overnight stays (53.9% in EU, 9.25% in extra-EU and 14.9% in the US) and 20,512 million Euros (50.39% in EU, 12.10% in extra-EU and 17.01% in the US). Further, the reason to focus on domestic tourists visiting the island is that in recent years Sardinia has experienced a steady decline in domestic demand (Global Travel Industry News 2012). Finally, from a theoretical perspective, it is relevant to understand the intricacies of domestic tourists' experiences and behavior. Indeed, as shown in prior studies, domestic tourists often differ from international tourists in terms of perceptions (Bonn et al. 2005; Tasci and Gartner 2007), attitudes, satisfaction levels (e.g., Yuksel 2004) and behaviors (e.g., Singh and Krakover 2015).

In 2011, 2.24 million tourists visited Sardinia, of which 60% were domestic tourists and 40% international tourists (CRENoS 2013). In 2013, according to statistics related to official accommodation facilities, 2.174 million tourists visited Sardinia, generating 10.681 million overnight stays. When compared to 2012, arrivals increase by 2.6%. Despite this, the number of overnight stays decreased by 1.5%. Further, the increase in incoming tourist flows is due to the international tourists arrivals (+14.9%); on the contrary, Italian arrivals decreased by 6% when compared to 2012. According to provisional data, in 2014, incoming tourist flows to Sardinia registered a further increase. Specifically, arrivals increased by 9% and overnight stays by 5.6%, with the number of Italian arrivals increasing more (+9.6%) than international ones (+8.3%) (CRENoS 2015).

Results and discussion

Scale depuration was conducted through Cronbach's alpha (ranging from 0.80 to 0.95), composed reliability (CR from 0.88 to 0.96) and the average variances extracted (AVEs ranging from 0.65 to 0.87). Along with the square roots of the average variance extracted (Table 14.3), all measures are correct, according to the threshold criteria (Fornell and Larcker 1981); thus, no items were deleted from the 10 scales.

Construct reliability and discriminant validity of the scales was thus proven. Convergent reliability was also proven. with the item-to-scale correlation matrix (not shown). Value dimensions show acceptable discriminant validity according to Sweeney and Soutar's (2001) first criterion: correlations among constructs significantly lower than one. They are also in line with other experiential approaches to hospitality settings (e.g., Wu and Liang 2009).

Furthermore, what is interesting to analyze is how these four value dimensions are interrelated (Holbrook 1999). The experiential values that are more related, one to each other, are functional and altruistic value (0.41) followed by social and functional values (0.35). The latter are considered in Holbrook's conceptual framework as extrinsic, which means that they share a

Table 14.3 Psychometric properties of the scales: construct reliability and discriminant validity

	Alpha	*CR*	*AVE*		*Funct*	*Soc*	*Emot*	*Altr*	*Value*	*Loy*
Functional	0.95	0.96	0.87	Functional	0.93					
Social	0.89	0.93	0.82	Social	0.36	0.91				
Emotional	0.80	0.88	0.71	Emotional	0.29	0.18	0.84			
Altruistic	0.84	0.91	0.77	Altruistic	0.40	0.26	0.17	0.88		
Value	0.91	0.94	0.85	Value	0.68	0.36	0.46	0.36	0.92	
Loyalty	0.91	0.93	0.65	Loyalty	0.52	0.40	0.44	0.45	0.78	0.81

utilitarian nature. The former, in spite of being more highly correlated, according to Holbrook (1999), do not share any of these discriminant criteria (ethics is other oriented and intrinsic, while functional is self-oriented and extrinsic). These findings, when contrasted with other studies on discriminant validity of experiential values (such as Jamal et al. (2011) which found higher correlations among value dimensions) show how complex value dimensionality can be, and how difficult it remains to find methodological and measurement procedures that merge with value conceptualizations (Gallarza et al. 2011: 182). The structure of the measurement model was tested with PLS (Figure 14.1); to estimate the confidence intervals for the path coefficients, we apply the Bootstrap method (Efrom and Tibshirani 1993) with 500 samples, each one with 300 individuals selected randomly, with replacements from the original sample.

The Bootstrap method has also been used for estimating R2 coefficient for the two endogenous constructs (value and loyalty). Seven of the eight path coefficients were significant (see Figure 14.1); no significant relationship was found between altruistic value/overall value (with p-value = 0.0163) and between functional value/loyalty (with p-value = 0.7125). We thus accept all hypotheses but H4 and H5.

Our case study reveals similarities and discrepancies with previous works on experiential value in tourism settings (e.g., Park 2004; Gallarza and Gil-Saura 2006; Wu and Liang 2009; Jamal et al. 2011; Jin et al. 2013). As a main result, with some expectation, the coexistence of experiential value dimensions in the same consumption experience is confirmed, alongside their cumulative effects on behavioral outcomes. The two effects that are rejected (altruistic on overall value and functional on loyalty) reveal interesting insights into the experience researched. According to our findings, altruistic value is the only experiential value dimension that is not considered as an antecedent of an overall value perception, although it does contribute to loyalty behavior (0.19). This could be explained by arguing that Italians do not value so much the fact that the hotel business is run according to ethical conduct, which could be explained by referring to the

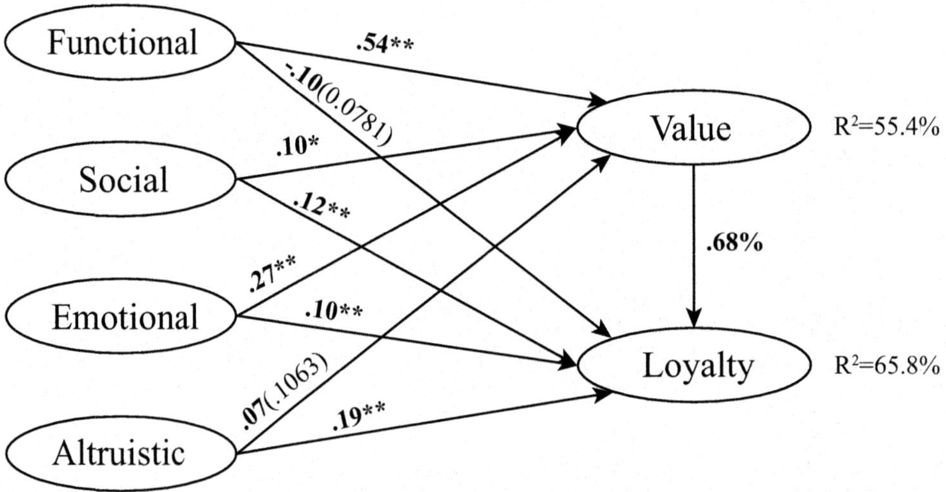

Figure 14.1 Conceptual model
* p-value < 0.05
** p-value < 0.01; p-value in parenthesis for the non-significant coefficients

quite-high level of individualism that characterizes this country. From an empirical standpoint, tourism customers' loyalty (positive word-of-mouth and likelihood to revisit the same hotel) does not depend on the functional value perceived by the tourist; said in other words, the functional aspects of consumption are considered as being a "basic or given factor". It relies more on the altruistic (0.19), social (0.12) and emotional (0.10) aspects derived from the experience. In return, functional value is, among the four experiential value dimensions, the stronger antecedent of overall perceived value (0.54), far above emotional (0.27) and social (0.10). The use of the same overall value scale in Gallarza and Gil-Saura's (2006) work revealed higher effects of hedonic dimensions (social and play) than utilitarian ones (efficiency and service quality), which shows, as stated in the introduction, the highly relativistic nature of value perceptions (changing across subjects and circumstances). Another result to further explore is the fact that some experiential value dimensions (namely social value and altruistic value) are stronger antecedents of loyalty than of overall value. Although the difference is very small (0.12 against 0.10 for social value and 0.19 against a non-significant path in altruistic), in the first case, it claims further analysis of the social aspects of loyalty in tourism.

Correlation between the two endogenous constructs is high (0.78), as it is also the link in the structural model (0.68), thus showing similarities with prior previous works in tourism settings measuring experiential values (e.g., Gallarza and Gil-Saura 2006). Taking into account that the link between overall perceived value and loyalty is the highest in the model (0.64), one major result when testing the double effects of experiential values on overall value and loyalty is that the direct influences of value experiential dimensions on loyalty, although existing, are rather weak (lower than 0.19); these effects are better explained when mediated through overall value perceptions.

Conclusion: managerial implications and limitations

This chapter aimed to investigate the extent to which different dimensions of the tourism experience cohabit in consumers' minds when making tourism choices and especially when valuing their experience (satisfaction and loyalty). Findings confirm the coexistence of experiential value dimensions in the consumption experience and their cumulative effects on behavioral outcomes. Specifically, social value and altruistic value were found to be stronger antecedents of loyalty than of overall value. Further, two effects were rejected, namely: altruistic on overall value and functional on loyalty. Broadly, findings revealed that the link between overall perceived value and loyalty is very strong (both in the simple correlation and in the path coefficient), thus being in line with previous studies in tourism settings.

Overall, this chapter is valuable for both researchers and hospitality managers. On the one hand, it adds to the growing body of knowledge, applying value and experiential approach in the context of tourism services, namely the hotel sector. On the other hand, it suggests that hotel marketers need to re-emphasize how guests feel about their experience of service delivery and should consider this knowledge when designing and planning their businesses so that they can better differentiate their offer from competitors, with the aim of increasing the perceived value of guests and their behavioral loyalty (intention to return and to recommend to others).

The case study is not free of limitations. First, it used a convenience sample of a relatively small size collected from a specific tourism destination, thus rendering findings not generalizable. Future empirical studies should focus on different tourism destinations and should consider the moderator effect that consumer-related characteristics (e.g., gender, age, trip motivation, etc.)

and service-related characteristics (e.g., type of accommodation, star category, etc.) could exert on the value-satisfaction-loyalty chain. This knowledge would surely further support managers in their attempt to tailor their products and services based on their target markets.

References

Babin, B. J. and Kim, K. 2001. "International students' travel behavior: a model of the travel-related consumer/dissatisfaction process." *Journal of Travel and Tourism Marketing, 10*(1), 93–106.

Banca d'Italia. (2013. September 29). "Turismo internazionale dell'Italia [Outbound tourism flows in Italy]". Available online at: www.bancaditalia.it/statistiche/rapp_estero/turismo-int

Boksberger, P. E. and Melsen, L. (2011) "Perceived value: a critical examination of definitions. concepts and measures for the service industry." *Journal of Services Marketing, 35*(3), 229–240.

Bonn, M. A., Joseph. S. M. and Dai, M. (2005). "International versus Domestic Visitors: An Examination of Destination Image Perceptions." *Journal of Travel Research, 43*(3), 294–301.

Chu, K.M. and Shiu, C. (2009). "The construction model of customer trust. perceived value and customer loyalty." *The Journal of American Academy of Business, 14*(2), 98–103.

Chen, C. F. and Chen, F. S. (2010). "Experience quality. perceived value. satisfaction and behavioral intentions for heritage tourists." *Tourism Management, 31*(1), 29–35.

Clarke, J. (2013). "Experiential aspects of tourism gift consumption." *Journal of Vacation Marketing, 19*(1), 75–87.

CRENoS (2013). "Economia della Sardegna." 20° rapporto. Cagliari. Italy: CUEC Editrice.

CRENoS (2015). "Economia della Sardegna" 22° rapporto 2014. CUEC. Cagliari.

Cronin, J. J., Brady. M.K. and Hult, G.T.M. (2000). "Assessing the effects of quality. value and customer satisfaction on consumer behavioural intentions in service environments." *Journal of Retailing, 76*(2), 193–218.

Day, E. and Crask. M. R. (2000). "Value assessment: the antecedent of customer satisfaction." *Journal of Consumer Satisfaction. Dissatisfaction and Complaining Behavior, 13*, 42–50.

Eid, R. and El-Gohary, H. (2013) "Muslim Tourist Perceived Value in the Hospitality and Tourism Industry." *Journal of Travel Research, 54*(6), 774–787.

Fornell, C. and Larcker, D. F. (1981). "Evaluating structural equation models with unobservable variables and measurement error." *Journal of Marketing Research, 28*(Feb), 39–50.

Gallarza, M. G., Arteaga. F., Del Chiappa, G. and Gil, I. (2015). "Value dimensions in consumers' experience: Combining the intra- and inter-variable approaches in the hospitality sector." *International Journal of Hospitality Management, 47*, 40–150.

Gallarza, M. G., Arteaga, F., Del Chiappa, G. and Gil, I. (2016). "Intrinsic value dimensions and the value-satisfaction-loyalty chain: a causal model for services." *Journal of Services Marketing, 30*(2), 165–185.

Gallarza, M. G. and Gil-Saura, I. (2006). "Value dimensions. perceived value. satisfaction and loyalty: an investigation of university students' travel behaviour." *Tourism Management, 27*(3), 437–452.

Gallarza, M. G., Gil-Saura, I. and Holbrook, M. B. (2011). "The value of value: Further excursions on the meaning and role of customer value." *Journal of Consumer Behaviour, 10*(4), 179–191.

Gallarza, M. G., Gil-Saura, I. and Holbrook, M.B. (2012). "Customer Value in Tourism Services; Meaning and Role for a Relationship Marketing Approach." In R. Tsiotsou and R.E. Goldsmith (eds). *Strategic Marketing in Tourism Services* (pp. 147–162). Bingley: Emerald.

Global Travel Industry News (2012). "Sardinia Island Is Not Just for the Wealthy." Available online at: www.eturbonews.com/31313/sardiniaisland- not-just-wealthy (accessed February 27. 2014).

Goldsmith, R. E. and Tsiotsou, R. H. (2012). "Introduction to experiential marketing." In R. Tsiotsou and R. E. Goldsmith (eds). *Strategic Marketing in Tourism Services* (pp. xxxii–xl). Bingley: Emerald.

Holbrook, M. B. (1999). *Consumer value. A framework for analysis and research.* Routledge: London.

Holbrook, M. B. and Hirschman, E. C. (1982). "The experiential aspects of consumption: consumer fantasies. feelings and fun." *Journal of Consumer Research, 9*(2). 132–140.

Iniesta-Bonillo, M. A., Sánchez-Fernández, R. and Cervera-Taulet, A. (2012). "Online Value Creation in Tourism Services: The Importance of Experience Valence and Personal Values." *The Service Industries Journal, 32*(15), 24–45.

Jamal, S. A., Othman, N. and Muhammad, N. M. N. (2011). "Tourist perceived value in a community-based homestay visit: An investigation into the functional and experiential aspect of value." *Journal of Vacation Marketing, 17*(1), 5–15.

Jin, N., Line, N. D. and Goh, B. (2013). "Experiential value. relationship quality. and customer loyalty in full-service restaurants: The moderating role of gender." *Journal of Hospitality Marketing and Management, 22*(7), 679–700.

Kim, D. and Perdue, R. R. (2013). "The effects of cognitive. affective. and sensory attributes on hotel choice." *International Journal of Hospitality Management, 35*, 246–257.

Laing, J., Wheeler, F., Reeves, K. and Frost, W. (2014). "Assessing the experiential value of heritage assets: A case study of a Chinese heritage precinct. Bendigo. Australia." *Tourism Management, 40*, 180–192.

Lee, J. and Min, C. (2013). "Examining the role of multidimensional value in convention attendee behaviour." *Journal of Hospitality and Tourism Research, 37*(3), 402–425.

Martin-Ruiz, D., Gremler, D. D., Washburn, J. H. and Cepeda-Carión, G. (2008). "Service value revisited: specifying a higher-order. formative measure." *Journal of Business Research, 61*(12), 1278–1291.

Nasution, H. N. and Mavondo, F. T. (2008). "Customer value in the hotel industry: what managers believe they deliver and what customers experience." *International Journal of Hospitality Management,* 27(1), 204–213.

Pandža-Bajs, I. (2015) "Tourist Perceived Value. Relationship to Satisfaction. and Behavioral Intentions: The Example of the Croatian Tourist Destination Dubrovnik." *Journal of Travel Research, 54*(1), 122–134.

Park, C. (2004). "Efficient or enjoyable? Consumer values of eating out and fast food restaurant consumption in Korea." *International Journal of Hospitality Management, 23*(1), 87–94.

Petrick, J. F. (2002). "Development of a multi-dimensional scale for measuring the perceived value of a service." *Journal of Leisure Research, 34*(2), 119–134.

Prebensen, N. K., Vittersø, J. and Dahl, T. I. (2013). "Value Co-Creation Significance of Tourist Resources." *Annals of Tourism Research, 42*, 240–261.

Sánchez, J., Callarisa, L., Rodriguez, R. M. and Moliner, M. A. (2006). "Perceived value of the purchase of a tourism product." *Tourism Management, 27*(3), 394–409.

Sánchez-Fernández, R., Iniesta-Bonillo, M. A. and Holbrook, M. B. (2009). "The conceptualisation and measurement of consumer value in services." *International Journal of Market Research, 51*(1), 93–113.

Sheth, J. N., Newman, B. I., Gross, B. L. (1991). "Why we buy what we buy: a theory of consumption values." *Journal of Business Research, 22*(2), 159–170.

Singh, S. and Krakover, S. (2015). "Tourist Experience at Home – Israeli Domestic Tourism." *Tourism Management, 46,* 59–61.

Sparks, B., Butcher, K. and Bradley, G. (2008). "Dimensions and correlates of consumer value: an application of the timeshare industry." *International Journal of Hospitality Management,* 27(1), 98–108.

Sweeney, J. and Soutar, G. (2001). "Consumer perceived value: the development of a multiple item scale." *Journal of Retailing*, 77, 203–207.

Tasci, A.D. A. and Gartner, W. C. (2007). "Destination Image and Its Functional Relationships." *Journal of Travel Research, 45*(4), 413–25.

Wu, C. H. and Liang, R. (2009). "Effect of experiential value on customer satisfaction with service encounters in luxury-hotel restaurants." *International Journal of Hospitality Management, 28*(4), 586–593.

Yeh, S., Chen, C. and Liu, Y. (2012). "Nostalgic emotion. experiential value. destination image. and place attachment of cultural tourists." *Advances in Hospitality and Leisure, 8,* 167–187.

Yuan, Y. H. and Wu, C. K. (2008). "Relationship among experiential marketing. experiential value. and customer satisfaction." *Journal of Hospitality and Tourism Research, 32*(3), 387–410.

Yuksel, A. (2004). "Shopping Experience Evaluation: A Case of Domestic and International Visitors." *Tourism Management, 25*(6), 751–759.

Zeithaml, V. A. (1988). "Consumer perceptions of price. quality. and value: a means-end model and synthesis of evidence." *Journal of Marketing, 52*(3), 2–22.

Zeithaml, V. A., Berry, L. L. and Parasuraman, A. (1996). "The behavioral consequences of service quality." *Journal of Marketing, 60*(2), 31–46.

Further reading

Al-Sabbahy, H, Ekinci, Y. Y. and Riley, M. (2004). "An investigation of perceived value dimensions: implications for hospitality research." *Journal of Travel Research, 42* (3), 226–234. (Perceived value consists of two dimensions – acquisition value and transaction value – and influences customer's choice behaviour but also their behavioral intentions.)

Bolton, R. and Drew, J. (1991). "A multistage model of customers' assessments of service quality and value." *Journal of Consumer Research, 17* (4), 375–384. (Model of how customers with prior experiences and expectations assess service performance levels, overall service quality, and service value.)

Cronin, J. J., Brady, M. K., Brand, R. R., Hightower, R. Jr. and Shemwell, D. J. (1997). "A crosssectional test of the effect and conceptualization of service value." *The Journal of Services Marketing, 11*(6), 375–391. (Service value as a central construct in consumer decision processes and determination of how best to conceptualize and measure service value.)

Efrom, B. and Tibshirani, R. (1993). *Introduction to the Bootstrap*. Chapman-Hall. New York.

Lee, C. K., Yoon, Y. S. and Lee, S. K. (2007). "Investigating the relationship among perceived value, satisfaction and recommendations: the case of the Korean DMZ." *Tourism Management, 28*(1), 204–214. (Tourist values concerning war-related tourism.)

McDougall, G. H. G. and Levesque, T. (2000). "Customer satisfaction with services: putting perceived value into the equation." *Journal of Services Marketing, 1*(5), 392–410.

Tam, J. L. M. (2000). "The effects of service quality, perceived value and customer satisfaction on behavioural intentions." *Journal of Hospitality and Leisure Marketing, 6*(4), 31–43. (The influence of service quality, perceived value and customer satisfaction on post-purchase behavior within the context of restaurant industry.)

Part III
Destination branding

15

Destination brand potency

A proposition framework

Gaunette Sinclair-Maragh

Introduction

Brands are frequently the primary points of distinguishing between competitive offerings and they are essential in a market environment where differentiation is imperative (Wood, 2000). A strong brand will inevitably result in more effective marketing and enable growth and expansion (Keller & Lehmann, 2006). While the concept of branding has been expansively used with products and services, tourism destination branding on the other hand is a fairly new phenomenon (Blain, Levy & Ritchie, 2005).

Branding a destination is important as it is very effective in differentiating it from others (Keller & Lehmann, 2006; Konecnik, 2004), especially since they tend to have similar features and offerings (Qu, Kim & Im, 2011). This has developed into an important topic among Destination Management Organizations (DMO) (Blain et al., 2005) but the literature remains sparse in this area. According to Pike (2005) the literature on destination branding had only been recent with the first academic conference held in 1996; the first journal article published in 1996 and the first book published in 2002. Another logical reason as noted by de Chenatony and Segal-Horn (2001) is that classical branding theory emerged only in the context of consumer products; hence, little emphasis has been given to studies on destination branding.

Notwithstanding the aforementioned arguments, given the level of importance of destination branding, it becomes imperative to conduct more studies in this area. An examination of extant literature shows that the construct destination brand has mostly been investigated in terms of governance (e.g. Beritelli, Bieger & Laesser, 2007; Bianchi, 2004; Bramwell, 2011), image (Baloglu & Mangaloglu, 2001; Baloglu & McCleary, 1999; Day, 2011; Konecnik 2004), destination choice (e.g. Hsu, Tsai & Wu, 2009; Lawson & Thyne, 2001; Lepp & Gibson, 2008) and brand equity (e.g. Hoeffler & Keller, 2002; Keller, 1993; Konecnik & Gartner, 2007). Despite these studies, Blain et al., (2005) note that the concept of destination branding remains narrowly defined and not well represented in the tourism literature.

This chapter proposes how three dimensions of brand, namely, brand features, brand identity and brand association can influence the potency of a destination brand in creating value for the destination and consequently competitive advantage. It is noted that these brand components can reduce the complex nature of destination brands (Hankinson, 2005), thereby suggesting that they are possibly measurable antecedents of destination brand.

Brand identity is considered for this study as opposed to brand image which has been given much more attention in the literature (e.g. Baloglu & McCleary, 1999; Coshall, 2000; Echtner & Ritchie 1993; Gallarza, Saura & Garcia, 2002; Hankinson, 2005; Hosany, Ekinci & Uysal, 2006; Qu et al., 2011) because specific to a destination, identity is created by the destination while image is what is perceived by the consumer (Kapferer, 1997). Hence, for the purpose of this review, brand identity will be used since the focus is on the destination as the supply-side and not the consumer as the demand-side.

Noteworthy is that the chapter focuses on branding within the context of a destination and should not be confused with nation branding of which tourism is only one component as indicated by Anholt (2002). The chapter will also assess the potential moderating effects of variables such as political factors, communication strategies, nation branding and the role of mega-events. Comprehensively, this analysis will provide an understanding of the role of brand, brand attributes and the various brand strategies to the value of a tourism destination and its competitive outcome. It is intended to improve the existing body of knowledge in destination branding and advance knowledge regarding such an important area.

Theoretical framework for understanding destination brand

Product brand versus destination brand

The American Marketing Association (1960) delineated brand as: "A name, term, sign, symbol, or design, or a combination of them, intended to identify the goods or services of one seller or group of sellers and to differentiate them from those of competitors" (Wood, 2000, p. 664). This definition is criticized by Wood (2000) as being too product-oriented as it focuses mainly on tangible features.

Bennett (1988) defines brand as: "A name, term, design, symbol or any other feature that identifies one seller's good or service as distinct from those of other sellers" (p. 664). Wood (2000), however, believes that although this definition relates to differentiation, its emphasis is on the corporate perspective. The definition by Ambler (1992) is believed to be more consumer-oriented: "The promise of the bundles of attributes that someone buys and provide satisfaction. . . . The attributes that make up a brand may be real or illusory, rational or emotional, tangible or invisible" (Wood, 2000, p. 664).

The commonality among these aforementioned definitions is that they are associated with branding from a firm's perspective. Branding within the context of destination tends to be more consumer-oriented. For example, Ritchie and Ritchie (1998) defined the concept of destination brand as:

> a name, symbol, logo, word mark or other graphic that both identifies and differentiates the destination; furthermore it conveys the promise of a memorable travel experience that is uniquely associated with the destination; it also serves to consolidate and reinforce the recollection of pleasurable memories of the destination experience.
>
> *(p. 103).*

This definition was modified by Blain et al. (2005) who in assessing the insights and practices of destination branding from a DMO perspective add "to *reduce consumer search costs and perceived risk*".

They believe that such a definition will generate a destination image which will positively influence consumers' destination choice.

There are other conceptualizations of destination branding referred to in the literature, for instance 'place branding' (e.g. Baker, 2007; Morgan, Pritchard & Pride, 2002; Hankinson, 2005) the use of which has extended across several other disciplines such as geography, political economy, strategic management, strategic marketing and tourism marketing (Hankinson, 2005). Branding is likewise explained in terms of "brand network", where the destination brand acts as a communicator and symbolizes ownership through trademark and logo; as a perceptual entity through its appeal to the senses and emotions of consumers; as a value enhancer where it leads to brand equity; and as relationships established with consumers (Hankinson, 2004).

It is believed that the conceptualization of destination brand is an issue (Blain, et al. 2005). It is more complex and difficult to conceptualize than doing so for goods and services because of the multidimensional nature of destinations (Pike, 2005). Hankinson (2005) supports this claim by indicating that place product is more complex than consumer products. This makes it more challenging for destination marketers, since it comprises several individual services and facilities for the visitor to experience. These include facilities for culture and heritage, sports, entertainment and shopping, thereby, allowing the same destination product to be used at the same time by different segments of visitors.

Importance of destination brand

Among the marketing strategies, branding is probably the most powerful weapon that can be used to mitigate the increased parity, competition and substitutability of destination products (Morgan & Pritchard, 2002). Accordingly, brand is a unique blend of functional and non-functional characteristics which are important in reducing substitutability. Destination branding is seen as a means of "creating the unique destination proposition" but in order for it to be successful, Morgan et al., (2002) indicate that it requires the implementation of a highly targeted, consumer-research based, multi-agency 'mood-branding' initiative.

Anholt (2002) posits brand as a way of defining the destination's offering. This differentiation strategy is very useful as destinations have similar offerings and they are all aiming to be identified as the ultimate place for visitor experience through the sun, sand and sea; cuisine and/or culture. Therefore, proper definition of a destination's offering is helpful to the confused and busy consumers who are trying to make travel decisions. In support, Qu et al., (2011) emphasize that a destination has to be unique and differential to enable its selection as the final decision by the consumer. Pike (2005) likewise emphasizes the importance for destinations to develop an effective brand as the name of a place is simply not sufficient for marketing purposes. A destination brand that is effective will assure visitors of quality experiences and will be a unique selling scheme for the destination (Blain et al., 2005).

Destination branding dimensions

Destination branding extends beyond the use of logo and taglines (Knapp & Sherwin, 2005). It includes other elements that are imperative to its development and execution (Day, 2011). These include other dimensions of brand features, brand identity and brand association. The features of a brand include its name, symbol and logo (Keller and Lehmann, 2006) which facilitate identification and awareness (Keller, 1993). Brand identity communicates the meaning of the brand (Kapferer, 1992; de Chernatony and Dall'Olmo Riley, 1998) and brand association

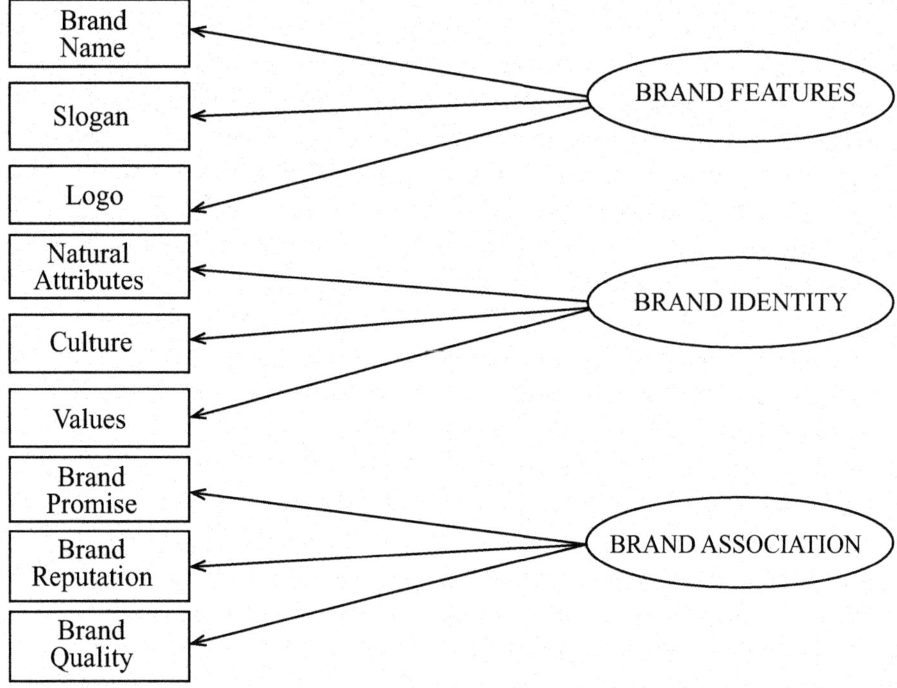

Figure 15.1 Proposed dimensions of destination brand features, brand identity and brand association

includes those elements that are remembered by consumers that help in developing the brand identity (Louro and Cunha, 2001). Figure 15.1 shows these brand elements as proposed measurable dimensions of destination brand features, identity and association.

Proposition framework

Figure 15.2 illustrates the proposed relationship between the destination branding elements (brand features, brand identity and brand association) and their influence on the potency of the destination brand; the outcome of which is the creation of value and subsequently competitive advantage for the destination. The proposed model also shows the relationship among the destination branding elements as well as the potential moderating effects of other variables; namely, political issues, communication strategies, nation branding and mega-events. The explanations are as follows:

Destination brand features

A destination's brand name and logo (Hankinson, 2005; Keller and Lehmann, 2006) as well as its slogan (Pike, 2005) are important features of a brand. These differentiate the brand from the competitors' (Keller and Lehmann, 2006; Kerr, 2006) and associate it with quality and intangible values (Keller and Lehmann, 2006). Brand name is perceived as the first reference for the destination and tends to be fixed by the actual geographical location (Hem & Iverson, 2004). The logo is considered the central feature of the brand that is representative of the destination and is therefore, a key component of branding (Hankinson, 2004). It stimulates awareness, communicates the attributes desired by visitors and serves as the connecting link to the marketer (Blain et al., 2005). The story of the brand is visualized through the slogan (Konecnik Ruzzier, 2011).

Based on the aforementioned discourse it seems plausible that brand features can determine the potency of destination brand and they are able to differentiate the destination from another. As indicated by Figure 15.2, the following is being proposed:

P_1: Brand features will positively and significantly influence the potency of a destination brand.

Destination brand identity

The way a destination is represented can inspire people not only to visit but also to revisit (Coshall, 2000; Tapachai & Waryszak, 2000). Therefore, brand identity is important in motivating persons to visit the destination. Brand identity is actually the foundation for creating a successful brand and its components are used to produce or maintain the brand (Aakar & Joachimsthaler, 2000).

Konecnik Ruzzier (2011) proposes a brand's mission, vision, values, personality, benefits and distinguishing attributes as examples of brand identity elements. Specifically, Morgan, Pritchard and Pigott (2002) point out that brand values are critical to the creation of a durable destination brand. These values can result in suitable brand personality which can ultimately communicate the brand message. The San Antonio Convention Visitors Bureau (SACVB) in the United States of America (USA) used another set of elements as the four pillars for developing its brand to communicate its marketing message. These elements are the people which reflects the spirit of the city; pride which is built on the history and the way forward; passion which is demonstrated through the daily lives and the various roles played by the people in the city; and promise which assures the experience to be had (Day, 2011).

The development of brand identity calls for strategic actions as demonstrated in Slovenia where various stakeholders were involved in the process which spanned across a three-step approach; a Delphi method, survey questionnaire and a web-based questionnaire. The outcome was a consensus relating to a range of distinguishing elements to describe the natural and cultural attributes of Slovenia (Konecnik Ruzzier, 2011).

Destination brand identity was successfully demonstrated in New York and Glasgow which were once industrial cities and have now been transformed into vibrant leisure and tourism destinations. Likewise, the 1998 Annual and Travel Research conference recognized New York, Tasmania, Australia, Canada, New Orleans, Oregon, Louisiana and Texas as destinations whose development has been very successful from branding (Ward, 1998). Based on this discourse, it is therefore being proposed that destination brand identity being measured by the natural attributes of the destination, the people and the values communicated by the destination brand will positively and significantly influence the potency of a destination brand, hence, the following:

P_2: Brand identity will positively and significantly influence the potency of a destination brand.

Destination brand association

Brand associations can influence an individual's evaluation of the brand (Low & Lamb, 2000; Um & Crompton, 1990). Three such influencers are brand promise, brand reputation and brand quality. A brand is actually a promise to a customer who anticipates receiving that promise based on perceived expectation and trust (Blain, et al., 2005). Delivering that promise can be difficult as tourism businesses are service-oriented and therefore, it is more challenging to control the actions of the service deliverers (Gilmore, 2002) and create a coherent brand (Hall, 2002).

However, the principal requirement is for the destination brand promise to inspire the service deliverers in the same way it does for the visitors, so that they will naturally exhibit their intrinsic strengths. The brand should not fabricate a false promise but should be based on trust and brand values. Trust is the confidence consumers will have in the product and the delivery and brand values should be consistent (Gilmore, 2002).

With regards to brand reputation, Grant (1991) postulates that it depreciates slowly and thus gives the brand longevity. It can also result in differentiation advantage and creates an entry barrier, both of which can lead to profitability. Keller (1993) points out that a strong, favorable and unique brand association can be created through customer-based brand equity where the customer has become familiar with the brand and has subsequently positioned it in their minds. This is identified as a good basis for implementing the right marketing strategies as in the case of Scotland, where as a destination it was perceived through its brand as being unique in terms of its integrity, inventiveness, tenacity and spirit (Hamilton, 2000).

Brand association is related to brand quality in terms of their synergistic contribution to the value of a brand (Aaker & Joachimsthaler, 2000). Brand quality is usually characterized by the people who deliver the service and so the quality of the brand experience totally depends on how well those people execute the service. Therefore, a good destination brand has to create a vision that everybody in the destination will be able to relate to (Gilmore, 2002). Hence, the following proposition:

P_3: There is a significant and positive relationship between brand associations and destination brand potency

Destination brand features and identity

Pike (2005) postulates that having a slogan could be the link between the aspired brand identity and the actual image of the brand perceived by the market. This is a noteworthy statement as although they are distinct, brand identity and brand image function congruently to communicate the ideals of the brand (Kapferer, 1992; de Chernatony and Riley, 1998). Pike (2005) further points out that the use of a slogan is important as a positioning strategy since destinations are increasingly becoming substitutable and more difficult to differentiate. In fact, it is believed that consequent to the brand identity of Slovenia, the slogan, 'I feel Slovenia' and the accompanying logo are developed to further communicate the brand and emphasize its emotional and experiential experiences (Konecnik Ruzzier, 2011).

A homogenous logo is important for brand identity. In support of this claim, Morgan & Pritchard, (2002) indicate that in the mid-1990s Morocco had several logos to appeal to its different markets and this created confusion and negatively impacted brand identity. As a solution, the Tourist Board has created a new logo with several different visuals which can be individually used for each market. This standardized logo is successful in creating consistency and eliminating the confusion of brand identity. Hence, it appears that the brand features of a destination can make it more identifiable and so the following is being proposed:

P_4: There is a significant and positive relationship between brand features and brand identity.

Destination brand identity and brand association

The constant interaction among brand identity elements can presumably fulfill brand promises (Keller, 1993). Additionally, Pride (2002) in an evaluation of Brand Wales explains how brand reputation can improve the identity of a brand. It is pointed out that for many years Wales suffered from an identity problem because of its link to neighboring England. From its destination branding mission, Wales is able to create a reputation for leisure tourism base on traditional Welsh values and unique personality.

The association between brand identity and brand association can also be linked through the residents. It is postulated that the success of a brand identity highly depends on the residents who should believe in the brand and the message that is being communicated; and consistently demonstrate it through their daily lives (Konecnik Ruzzier, 2011). This is consistent with Gilmore's (2002) claim that everybody in the destination should be able to relate to the vision, an important element of brand identity, so as to achieve a successful branding endeavor. Thus, it is being proposed that:

P_5: There is a significant and positive relationship between brand identity and brand association.

Destination brand potency and destination value

From a resource-based view (RBV) brands have been categorized as relational market-based asset. This suggests that the relationships formed with customers can influence market-place performance and financial return and in that way create higher market share and higher margins (Srivastava, Fahey & Christensen, 2001). Similarly, Aaker, Forurnier and Brasel (2004) refer to brand as a relational factor in the context of consumers' brand relational level where they explain its importance in building a relationship with customers. Market performance is measured by customer satisfaction and customer loyalty and they have been noted to positively influence financial returns (Anderson & Sullivan, 1993; Fornell 1992; Rust & Zahorik 1993). Therefore, a brand should be able to generate market-place performance as well as financial performance.

Furthermore, Homburg and Pflesser (2000) state that market performance is an indicator of financial performance. These findings though realized from a firm's perspective can be applied to a service industry especially as it relates to brand being a market-based asset. As a customer - value element, it can also provide experiential benefits to customers (Srivastava et al., 2001). Hence, a brand should be able to influence destination value through its ability to generate market-place performance (via customer satisfaction and customer loyalty) which will result in financial returns. It is, therefore, plausible to operationalize destination performance as destination value which in turn will be measured in terms of higher market share and higher profit margins. Therefore, the following is being proposed:

P_6: There is a significant and positive relationship between destination brand potency and destination value.

Destination value and competitive advantage

From a RBV perspective, the marketing of brands is an important means of gaining and sustaining competitive advantage. Those brands that have been positively experienced will gain competitive advantage over those that have not. Likewise, the more intangible the customer value elements,

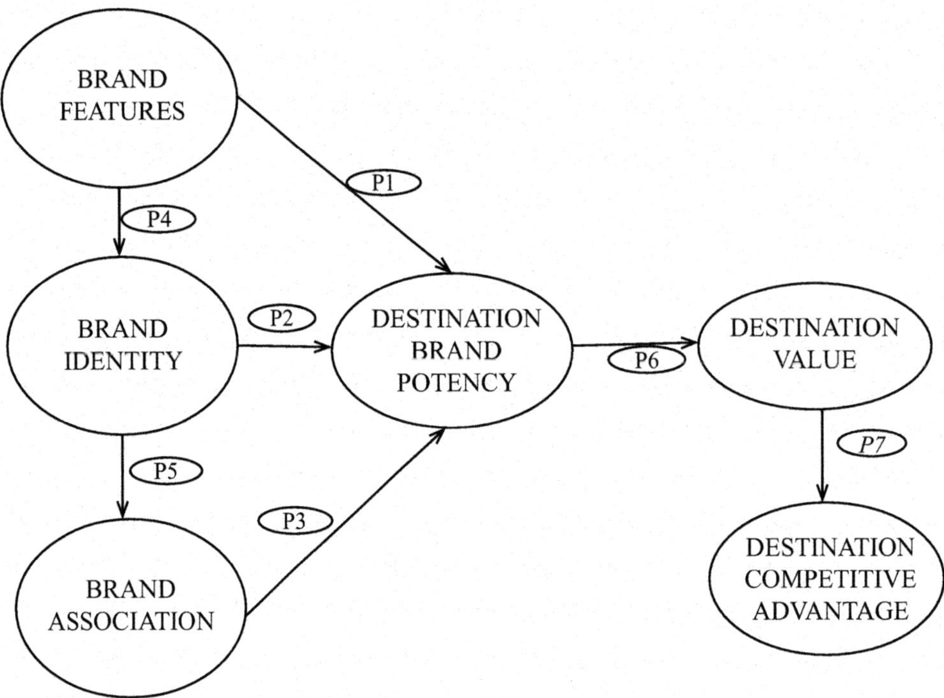

Figure 15.2 Proposed relationship among the brand constructs, brand potency, destination value and the outcome of destination competitive advantage

the harder it becomes for competitors to imitate them. It is, therefore, harder to replicate a brand as it is intangible in nature. Accordingly, being a relational market-based asset, a brand can contribute to generating and sustaining customer value (Srivastava et al., 2001).

It is also argued that many destinations have the same attributes (Blain, et al., 2005) and facilities are no longer differentiating factors (Morgan & Pritchard, 2002), and so, effective destination branding should be unique, thereby making it different from other destinations, so that it will be able to gain and maintain competitive advantage (Blain, et al., 2005). Wood (2000) contends that a brand is perceived as a means of achieving competitive advantage predominantly through its differentiating attributes. This author also points out that competitive advantage can possibly be established in terms of revenue, profit and added value or market share, because customers will be willing to pay for a brand that gives them the satisfaction and the benefits they are looking for. Thus, as shown in Figure 15.2:

> P_7: There is a significant and positive relationship between destination value and destination competitive advantage.

Potential moderators

The literature points to some factors that can possibly moderate the impact of destination brand on destination value and consequently destination value on the destination's competitive advantage.

According to Morgan & Pritchard (2002), destinations are vulnerable to factors of the external environment such as politics, natural disaster, economics, terrorism and international trade. Other factors include communication strategies (Hall, 2002); nation branding (Anholt, 2002) and mega-events (Brown, Chalip, Jargo and Mules, 2002). These are illustrated in Figure 15.3.

Political Issues

Government has a role to play in the sustainable development of a destination's resources (Sinclair-Maragh, 2014) as well as in the marketing of the destination (Mill & Morrison, 2002). Nonetheless, some economies are challenged by budgetary constraints and though they have to be competing globally with other destinations, it is difficult for them to allocate financial resources towards branding as a marketing strategy. Morgan & Pritchard (2002) point out that the World Tourism Organization (UNWTO) is concerned about the limited marketing expenditure by tourism destinations. The UNWTO indicates that even though governments worldwide are spending on annual advertisement, this amount remains inadequate; neither can it be compared to the amount expended by marketers of consumer goods and services. Consequently, many destinations are faced with limited budgets which impact effective marketing of the brand (Morgan & Pritchard, 2002).

With regards to the influence of politics on a destination, Ryan (2002) in examining the politics of branding cities and regions in New Zealand purports that politics is about the use of power and the role of power structures. The conclusion is that tourism has little or no part to play when it comes to policy making and decisions that even impact the industry, though it is economically significant to New Zealand. It is believed that tourism is politically weak in this country and so it has been getting little marketing attention, which has negatively impacted any improvement to the destination's brand. Pike (2005) is of a similar conviction; the view is that DMOs have little influence or control over government's decisions and policies and this can negatively affect the development of a destination's brand. With this review it seems rational that:

P_{8a}: The relationship between destination brand and destination value is moderated by political issues.

P_{9a}: The relationship between destination value and competitive advantage is moderated by political issues.

Communication strategies

Brand advantage is achieved through communication strategies which highlight the specificity of the product in the mind of the consumer, thereby, creating an image about the product and achieving the positioning strategy intended by the marketer (Morgan & Pritchard, 2002). Although destinations should produce this consistent and focused communication strategy (Morgan & Pritchard, 2002), it is impacted by inadequate financial support which consequently affects the destination branding and the corresponding positioning strategy as in the case of Central and Eastern Europe (Hall, 2002).

From another perspective Keller and Lehmann (2006) noted that the branding elements (name, logo and symbol) could be integrated through the use of communication channels involving the use of audio and visual strategies among other means. In this light, communication is believed to be a very important strategy for brand development. Hence, it is being proposed that:

P_{8b}: The relationship between destination brand and destination value is moderated by communication strategies.

P_{9b}: The relationship between destination value and competitive advantage is moderated by communication strategies.

Nation branding

Anholt (2002), in explaining the concept of nation branding, posits that real successful global brands come from countries with a strong brand and, therefore, the product is linked with the country's image. A nation's culture is an important part of how its brand is perceived and is vital in creating sustained prosperity. Nation brand provides certain values and qualifications which arouse the mind of the consumer and as such the brand conveys trust and guarantees quality. The way nation brand is positioned in the global marketplace could stimulate tourism. Reference is made to Brazil as one of the world's most strongly branded destination. Despite the negativity linked with pollution, overpopulation, poverty, crime and corruption, 'Brand Brazil' continues to denote exotic rainforests, beaches, sports, adventure and samba dancing during carnival and therefore tourism has more grounding in nation branding than any other industry (Anholt, 2002). Hence, it seems plausible that:

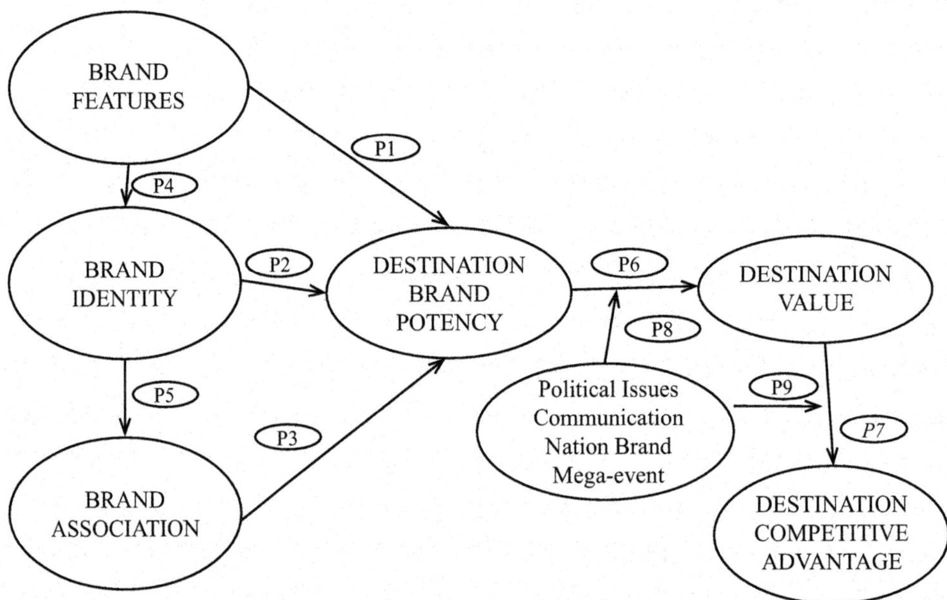

Figure 15.3 Proposed model showing relationship among the brand constructs, brand potency, destination value, destination competitive advantage and possible moderators

P_{8c}: The relationship between destination brand and destination value is moderated by nation branding.
P_{9c}: The relationship between destination value and competitive advantage is moderated by nation branding.

Mega events

A destination's economic growth and development can be positively impacted by the economic activities of mega sporting events, for example, the Olympics in Sydney, Australia and Atlanta, Georgia influenced the macro-economic development of those countries and created opportunities for business development, trade and investment (JAMPRO, 2006 cited in Sinclair-Maragh, 2010). This is confirmed by Brown, et al. (2002) who note that the Sydney Olympics has tremendously improved Brand Australia, thereby having a significant impact on the destination.

Holder (2003) in Sinclair-Maragh (2010) likewise points out that the Cricket World Cup (CWC) held in the Caribbean is a means of further promoting the region as a tourism destination and that the economic gains from the event can improve the destination's value. Thus:

P_{8d}: The relationship between destination brand and destination value is moderated by mega-events.
P_{9d}: The relationship between destination value and competitive advantage is moderated by mega-events.

Implications

The theoretical framework of this proposal can be used to better inform DMOs, destination marketers and tourism planners about the importance of branding. Their understanding of the relationship between destination brand and destination value will be enhanced. Placing emphasis on brand features or elements such as the name, slogan and logo; positioning the brand in terms of its identity as it relates to the natural and cultural attributes of the destination and the values of the brand; and building brand associations in terms of brand promise, brand reputation and brand quality are influential in branding a destination. It therefore, means that destination planners need to allocate the necessary resources required to implement all of these brand marketing strategies.

The result of value creation for the destination is the ideal outcome and this can be realized through improved market share and financial growth due to the use of branding strategies. The literature was very profound in linking this achievement to gaining and maintaining competitive advantage for the destination. Therefore, DMOs, destination marketers and destination planners need to consider the benefits of branding a destination as being more than achieving destination value but achieving sustained competitive advantage. It is also important for them to incorporate branding and its components into their strategic marketing plan, use branding strategies to build potential visitors' perceptions and as a means of mitigating negative opinions of the destination.

From a theoretical perspective, the study also assesses the potential moderating effects of variables such as political factors, communication strategies, nation branding and the role of mega-events and these provide additional insights into the topic. They can further inform DMOs, destination marketers and destination planners of the importance of considering broader environmental issues that are likely to impact destination value and its sustained competitive advantage.

This proposal positions destination branding as an important resource and intangible asset to achieve both market and firm performance, and to gain and sustain competitive advantage. This proposition can be advanced through empirical or statistical analysis to test the proposed assumptions and derive the respective statistical and practical significances. The study was unable to infer the cost associated with branding a destination which could be both quantitative as well as qualitative in nature as it relates to social and cultural factors. Future studies can, therefore, analyze the cost and benefit of branding a tourism destination. The research did not empirically show that a destination brand has influence on travel decisions to any tourism locale; neither did it address the influence of brand loyalty. These, therefore, present other areas for future research. Another research opportunity can be a comparative analysis of two or more tourism destinations, to assess the potency of their brands to the value of the destinations and their realization of competitive advantage.

Conclusion

Destination branding is as important as the branding of tangible goods and firms. The literature indicates that the use of brand features, brand identity and brand association are instrumental in branding a destination for the purpose of creating value as well as generating and maintaining competitive advantage. However, one limitation to the research is that it was reviewed from a theoretical perspective and, therefore, presents the opportunity for scholars to empirically or statistically measure the relationships between the proposed variables.

References

Aaker, D. (1991). *Managing brand equity: Capitalizing on the value of a brand name*. Free Press: New York, NY.

Aaker, D., & Joachimsthaler, E. (2000). *Brand leadership*. Simon & Schuster UK Ltd: London.

Aaker, J., Forurnier, S., & Brasel, S.A. (2004). When good brands do bad. *Journal of Consumer Research*. 31(1), 1–16.

Ambler, T. (1992). *Need-to-know-marketing*. Century Business, London. In L. Wood (2000). Brands and brand equity: Definition and management. *Management Decision*, 38(9), 662–669.

American Marketing Association (1960), *Marketing Definitions: A Glossary of Marketing Terms*, AMA, Chicago, IL. In L. Wood (2000). Brands and brand equity: Definition and management. *Management Decision*, 38(9), 662–669.

Anderson, E.W., & Sullivan, M.W. (1993). The Antecedents and Consequences of Customer Satisfaction for Firms. *Marketing Science*, 12(2), 125–143.

Anholt, S. (2002). Nation-brand for the twenty-first century. *Journal of Brand Management*, 5(6), 395–404.

Baloglu, S., & Mangaloglu, M. (2001). Tourism destination images of Turkey, Egypt, Greece and Italy as perceived by US based tour operators and travel agents. *Tourism Management*, 22(1), 1–9.

Baloglu, S., & McCleary, K.W. (1999). A model of destination image formation. *Annals of Tourism Research*, 26 (4), 868–897.

Baker, B. (2007). *Destination Branding for small cities: The essentials for successful place branding*. Creative Leap Books, Portland.

Bennett, P.D. (1988), *Dictionary of Marketing Terms*, The American Marketing Association, Chicago, IL.

Beritelli, P., Bieger, T., & Laesser, C. (2007). Destination governance: Using corporate governance theories as a foundation for effective destination management. *Journal of Travel Research*, 46(1), 96–107.

Bianchi, R. (2004). Tourism restructuring and the politics of sustainability: A critical view from the European periphery (The Canary Islands). *Journal of Sustainable Tourism*, 12(6), 495–529.
Blain, C., Levy, S.E., & Ritchie, J.R.B. (2005). Destination branding: Insights and practices from destination management organization. *Journal of Travel Research*, 43(May 2005), 328–338.
Bramwell, B. (2011). Governance, the state and sustainable tourism: A political economy approach. *Journal of Sustainable Tourism*, 19(4–5), 459–477.
Brown, G., Chalip, L., Jargo, L., & Mules, T. (2002). *The Sydney Olympics and Brand Australia,* In N. Morgan, A. Pritchard, & R. Pride (2002) *Destination branding: Creating the unique destination proposition*, pp.163–185. Butterworth-Heinemann: Oxford.
Coshall, J.T. (2000). Measurement of tourist's images: The repertory grid approach. *Journal of Travel Research*, 39(1), 85–89.
de Chernatony, L., & Dall'Olmo Riley, F. (1998). Modeling the components of a brand. *European Journal of Marketing*, 32 (11–12), 1074–1090.
de Chernatony, L., & Segal-Horn, S. (2001). Building on services characteristics to develop successful services brands. *Journal of Marketing Management*, 17(7–8), 645–70.
Day, J. (2011). Branding, destination image and positioning: San Antonio. In N. Morgan, A. Pritchard, & R. Pride (2011). *Destination brands, managing place reputation* (3rd ed), pp. 269–290. Elsevier Ltd.
Echtner, C.M., & Ritchie, J.R.B. (1993). The measurement of destination image: an empirical assessment. *Journal of Travel Research*, 31(4), 3–13.
Fornell, C. (1992). A national customer satisfaction barometer: The Swedish experience. *Journal of Marketing*, 56(January), 6–21.
Gallarza, M.G., Saura, I.G., & Garcia, H.C. (2002). Destination image. Towards a conceptual framework. *Annals of Tourism Research*, 29(1), 56–78.
Gilmore, F. (2002). Branding for success. In N. Morgan, A. Pritchard, & R. Pride (2002) *Destination branding: Creating the unique destination proposition.* Butterworth-Heinemann. Oxford.
Grant, R.M. (1991). The resource-based theory of competitive advantage: Implications for strategy. *California Management Review, 22,* 114–135.
Hall, D. (2002). Branding and national identity: The case of Central and Eastern Europe. In N. Morgan, A. Pritchard and R. Pride (2002) *Destination branding: Creating the unique destination proposition*, pp. 90–105. Butterworth-Heinemann: Oxford.
Hamilton, K. (2000). Project galore: Qualitative research and leveraging Scotland's brand equity. *Journal of Advertising Research (Research Currents)*, 40, 107–111.
Hankinson, G. (2004). Relational network brands: Towards a conceptual model of place brands. *Journal of Vacation Marketing*, 10(2), 109–121.
Hankinson, G. (2005). Destination brand images: A business tourism perspective. *Journal of Services Marketing*, 19(1), 24–32.
Hem, L.E., & Iverson, N.M. (2004). How to develop a destination brand logo: A qualitative and quantitative approach. *Scandinavian Journal of Hospitality and Tourism,* 4(2), 83–106.
Hoeffler, S., & Keller, K.L. (2002). Building brand equity through corporate societal marketing. *Journal of Public Policy and Marketing*, 21(1), 78–89.
Holder, J. (2003). What is at stake for the Caribbean in hosting the Cricket World Cup 2007 Event. In G. Sinclair-Maragh, (2010). A socio-economic assessment of the ICC World Cup Cricket on hosting Caribbean territories, *Sports Event Management: The Caribbean Experience*, Ashgate.
Homberg, C., & Pflesser, C. (2000). A multiple-layer model of market-oriented organizational culture: Measurement issues and performance outcomes. *American Marketing Association*, 37(4), 449–462.
Hosany, S., Ekinci, Y., & Uysal, M. (2006). Destination image and destination personality: An application of branding theories to tourism places. *Journal of Business Research*, 59, 638–642.
Hsu, T., Tsai, Y., & Wu, H. (2009). The preference analysis for tourist choice of destination: A case study of Taiwan. *Tourism Management,* 30, 288–297.
JAMPRO (2006), Caribbean Businesses Drive New Mechanism to Strengthen Relations. In G. Sinclair-Maragh, (2010). A socio-economic assessment of the ICC World Cup Cricket on hosting Caribbean territories. *Sports Event Management: The Caribbean Experience*, Ashgate. ISB
Kapferer, J.-N. (1997). *Strategic brand management: creating and sustaining brand equity long term.* Auflage: London.
Keller, K.L. (1993). Conceptualizing, measuring, and managing customer-based brand equity. *Journal of Marketing* 57(January) 1–22.
Keller, K.L., & Lehmann, D.R. (2006). Brands and branding: Research findings and future priorities. *Marketing Science*, 25(6), 70–79.

Kerr, G. (2006). From destination brand to location brand. *Journal of Brand Management*, 13(4–5), 276–283.
Knapp, D., & Sherwin, G. (2005). Image formation, information sources and an iconic Australian tourist destination. *Journal of Vacation Marketing*, 11(2), 163–177.
Konecnik, M. (2004). Evaluating Slovenia's image as a tourism destination: A self-analysis process towards building destination brand. *Brand Management*, 11(4), 307–316.
Konecnik, M., & Gartner, W.C. (2007). Customer-based brand equity for a destination. *Annals of Tourism Research*, 34(2), 400–421.
Konecnik Ruzzier, M (2011). Country brands and identity: Slovenia. In N. Morgan, A. Pritchard, & R. Pride (2011). *Destination brands, managing place reputation* (3rd edn), pp. 291–302. Elsevier Ltd.
Louro, M.J., & Cunha, P.V. (2001). Brand management paradigms. *Journal of Marketing* Management, 17(7–8), 849–876.
Lawson, R., & Thyne, M. (2001). Destination avoidance and inept destination sets. *Journal of Vacation Marketing*, 7(3), 199–208.
Lepp, A., & Gibson, H. (2008). Sensation seeking and tourism: Tourist role, perception of risk and destination choice. *Tourism Management*, 29(4), 740–750.
Low, G.S., & Lamb, C.W. (2000). The measurement and dimensionality of brand associations. *Journal of Product and Brand Management*, 9(6), 350–368.
Mill, R., & Morrison A. (2002). *The tourism system*. Kendall / Hunt Publishing Company, Iowa.
Morgan, N.J., & Pritchard, A. (2002). *Contextualizing destination branding*. In N. Morgan, A. Pritchard, & R. Pride (2002) *Destination branding: Creating the unique destination proposition*, pp. 10–41. Butterworth-Heinemann: Oxford.
Morgan, N., Pritchard, A., & Pigott, R. (2002). New Zealand, 100% pure: The creation of a powerful niche destination brand. *Journal of Brand Management*, 9(4), 335–354.
Morgan, N.J., Pritchard, A., & Pride, R. (2002). *Destination branding: Creating the unique destination proposition*. Butterworth-Heinemann. Oxford.
Pike, S. (2005). Tourism branding complexity. *Journal of Product and Brand Management*, 14(4), 258–259.
Pride, R. (2002). *Brand Wales: 'Natural revival'*. In N. Morgan, A. Pritchard, & R. Pride (2002) *Destination branding: Creating the unique destination proposition*. Butterworth-Heinemann: Oxford.
Qu, H., Kim, L.H., & Im, H.H. (2011). A model of destination branding: Integrating the concepts of the branding and destination image. *Tourism Management*, 32, 465–476.
Ritchie, J.R.B., & Ritchie, R.J.B. (1998). *The branding of tourism destinations: Past achievements and future challenges*. Proceedings of the 1998 Annual Congress of the International Association of Scientific Experts in Tourism Destination Marketing: Scopes and Limitations, edited by Peter Keller, Marrakech, Morocco: International Association of Scientific Experts in Tourism, 89–116.
Ryan, C. (2002). *The politics of branding cities and regions: The case of New Zealand*. In N. Morgan, A. Pritchard, & R. Pride (2002) *Destination branding: Creating the unique destination proposition*, pp. 66–86. Butterworth-Heinemann: Oxford.
Rust, R.T., & Zahorik, A.J. (1993). Customer satisfaction, culture retention and market share. *Journal of Retailing*, 69(2), 193–215.
Sinclair-Maragh, G.M., (2014). Resort-based or resource-based tourism? A case study of Jamaica. *Emerald Emerging Markets Case Studies*, 4(2), 1–12.
Srivastava, R.K., Fahey, L., & Christensen, H.K. (2001). The resource-based view marketing: The role of market-based assets in gaining competitive advantage. *Journal of Marketing*, 27, 777–802.
Tapachai, N., & Waryszak, R. (2000). An examination of the role of beneficial image in tourist destination selection. *Journal of Travel Research*, 39(1), 37–44.
Um, S., & Crompton J.L. (1990). Attitude determinants in tourism destination choice. *Annals of Tourism Research*, 17(3), 432–448.
Ward, S.V. (1998). *Selling places: The marketing of towns and cities*. Routledge: London.
Wood, L. (2000). Brands and brand equity: Definition and management. *Management Decision*, 38(9), 662–669.

16

Communication strategies for building a strong destination brand[1]

Maja Šerić and Maria Vernuccio

Introduction

The current dominant theoretical underpinning of communication strategy is a desire to create a strong brand through the Integrated Marketing Communications (IMC) approach. As with all the other brands, destination brands are not exempt from the need of this integration in marketing communications (Skinner, 2005). In recent years, there has been an increasing interest in IMC and a number of different definitions have been proposed in order to encourage its theoretical foundation. Among the most recent conceptualizations of IMC, Šerić *et al.* (2015, p. 960) defined it as

> a tactical and strategic consumer-centric business process, boosted by advances in Information and Communication Technology (ICT) which, on the basis of information obtained from customers databases, delivers a clear and consistent message through the coordination and synergies of different communications tools and channels, in order to nourish long-lasting profitable relationships with customers and other stakeholders and create and maintain brand equity.

The integration of marketing communications needs to be accomplished both online and offline, meaning that traditional mass communication paradigm has to be integrated with new interactive and social models (Vernuccio and Ceccotti, 2015), where consumers are no longer passive receivers of the messages, but are actively involved in the communication (Schultz and Patti, 2009) and branding process (Gensler *et al.*, 2013).

As suggested by a number of different authors, the ultimate goal of IMC is to create strong brands through reinforcement of their brand equity (e.g. McGrath, 2005; Reid, 2005; Keller, 2009; Šerić, 2017). In fact, brand equity has been frequently considered as an outcome of marketing communication practices. Accordingly, strong brands are highly associated with an outstanding marketing communication strategy and competitive advantage (Keller, 2009). In the tourism context, destination brand equity is about creating an extra value of a brand (Gartner and Konečnik, 2011). This additional value has been assessed through many different ways, leading to a certain disagreement on how destination brand equity should be conceptualized and measured. The goal of this work is to shed light on the role of Integrated Marketing Communications strategy in the development of strong destination brands, more specifically, destination brand equity.

To accomplish this goal, the paper is structured in the following way. After the Introduction section, implementation of IMC strategy and its repercussions for destination brands are discussed in the second section. Destination brand equity is approached in the third section, while the relationships between IMC and destination brand equity are argued in the fourth section. In the final part, conclusions of the work are gathered and future research directions are proposed.

Integrated Marketing Communications (IMC) strategy: implementation and repercussion in tourism destinations

The implementation of an Integrated Marketing Communications strategy depends on a number of circumstantial elements such as cultural and governmental environment (Kim *et al.*, 2004), market factors, media segmentation, ICT availability (Schultz and Kitchen, 2000), and the overall strategic destination management, among others. This suggests that there is no one single pattern for a successful integration of marketing communications. However, while it is true that each destination will undertake the challenges and opportunities of the IMC in a different way, it is possible to observe some common principles of a successful IMC strategy.

In this vein, Schultz and Kitchen (2000) developed a four-level model of IMC development, which advocates for a progress from tactical to strategic integration of marketing communications. According to these authors, the implementation of IMC programs goes through the following levels: 1) tactical coordination of marketing communications; 2) redefining the scope of marketing communications; 3) application of information technology; and 4) financial and strategic integration. Schultz and Kitchen (2000) indicated that these levels do not have to follow the suggested order necessarily. Kliatchko (2008) has criticized the four-step model for being too rigid and proposed a more flexible model composed of four pillars of IMC, namely: 1) stakeholders, 2) content, 3) channels, and 4) results. He suggested that these pillars can be considered as both antecedents and consequences in the process of the development of an IMC strategy and that they are present during each stage of the model proposed by Schultz and Kitchen (2000). In addition, he emphasized that each pillar assumes a particular importance within one stage. Thus, the "content" pillar plays a crucial role in the first stage of the Schultz and Kitchen's (2000) model, while the "channels" pillar is critical during the second stage. The "stakeholders" and the "results" pillars are more associated with the third and the fourth stage, respectively (see Figure 16.1).

These two major proposals of IMC implementation and their implications for tourism destinations are discussed in the following subsections.

Tactical coordination of marketing communications – content

Tactical coordination of marketing communications is a basic aspect of Integrated Marketing Communications, which advocates for "one-voice, one-sound" principle (Schultz and Kitchen, 2000). This means that a central theme needs to be delivered through different logos, slogans, and messages. Accordingly, visual and linguistic communication implemented through different marketing communications tools (i.e. advertising, public relations, sponsorship, events, etc.) and channels (i.e. television, magazines, Internet, social media, mobile, etc.) are considered as a basic principle of the Integrated Marketing Communications paradigm (Šerić *et al.*, 2015).

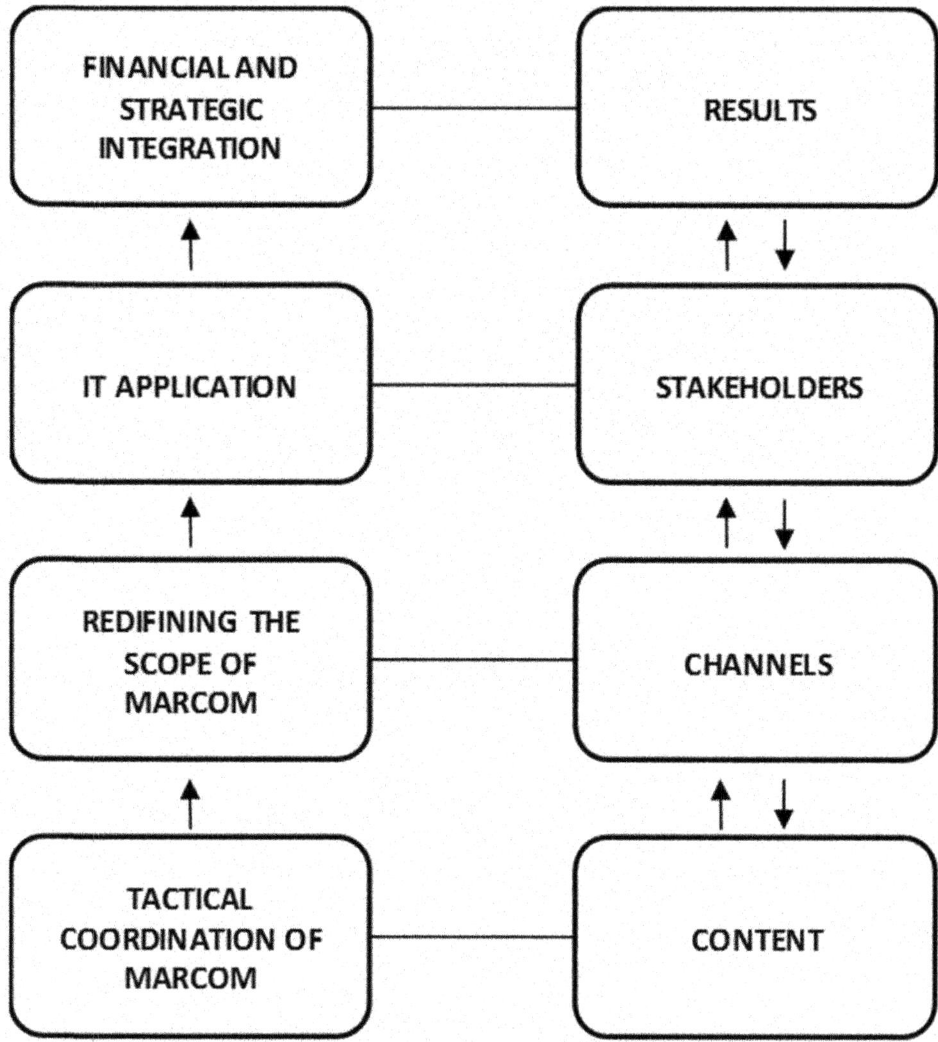

Figure 16.1 Implementation of integrated marketing communications
Source: own illustration based on Schultz and Kitchen (2000) and Kliatchko (2008).
Marcom = Marketing communications

Kliatchko (2008) associates this first stage in IMC development with his "content" pillar. Content consists of messages related to brand concept, ideas or associations and all the other values that are intended to be delivered to customers. It also embraces short-term incentives, such as offers and rewards to consumers (Schultz and Schultz, 2004). Both models agree on the fact that the first goal of IMC is to provide the public with a clear and consistent message.

When promoting destinations, this message consistency needs to be accomplished through several ways. Firstly, the message that a destination wants to promote needs to be consistent with the destination identity (Govers *et al.*, 2007). Secondly, the consistency needs to be pursued among different organizations involved in the promotion of the country (Skinner, 2005).

Thereby, the use of colors, logos, and slogans in promotional material needs to follow the same pattern. Thirdly, consistency should be accomplished even when the campaign is directed to different tourism markets. If tourism marketers use different communication campaigns in different markets, they create a rather confused image of the country (Pike and Page, 2014), thus violating the "one-voice" principle of IMC. This doesn't mean that the message delivered to different audiences needs to be identical, but complementary and non-contradictory (Torp, 2009).

Redefining the scope of marketing communications – channels

Under the IMC paradigm, the objective of marketing communications needs to be redefined, meaning that the outside-in approach needs to be adopted (Schultz and Kitchen, 2000; Šerić *et al.*, 2014). The outside-in approach implies that consumers participate actively in marketing communication campaigns. As suggested by Laurie and Mortimer (2011), this should not be accomplished through consumer-focused practices only, which imply gathering information about consumers' habits and spending patterns, but through a consumer-centric approach, which requires active listening to consumers' needs and continuous efforts to satisfy them (Schultz, 2006). This is actually the reality that destination marketers are facing today through social media sites such as TripAdvisor or Expedia, where consumers share their experiences and opinions about destination brands, thus participating actively in their promotion.

Kliatchko (2008) connects this outside-in approach with the "channels" pillar, since channels are approached from the customer point of view. Put differently, those channels that consumers prefer and consider more relevant are identified as critical for IMC strategy (Vernuccio and Ceccotti, 2015). Channels need to be considered not only from a traditional media perspective, but ought to include all other possible contact points where consumers can get in touch with a brand. In this phase, tourism service providers need to focus all their attention on consumers and try to establish and improve the relationship with them through a quick response to their needs and doing their best in not only meeting their expectations, but through exceeding them, thus generating satisfaction. If managed properly, this might be accomplished through multiple service touchpoints between customers and service providers, which customers perceive prior, during, and after their experience with a destination brand (Stickdorn and Zehrer, 2009). Pre-service touch points embrace both marketing communication messages delivered by tourisms service providers and consumer-generated reviews on social media. During the service, customers experience the tourism product with all their senses and compare them, even subconsciously, with the previously generated expectations towards them. After their experience with the destination brand, they may use the same touchpoints they employed in the pre-service period to share and exchange their opinions and perceptions, thus influencing other consumers and prospects (Stickdorn and Zehrer, 2009). Technology applications are critical in this process, as described below.

Application of information technology – stakeholders

The digital revolution has boosted the integration of marketing communications (Vernuccio and Vescovi, 2016) in the tourism sector (Šerić *et al.*, 2014). Database management supported by ICT enabled maintenance of accessible data sources and development of globally segmented databases. The gathered data need to be incorporated into communication strategy, thus turning customer data into customer knowledge and thereby fully exploiting its potential (Schultz and Kitchen, 2000). According to Kliatchko (2008), stakeholders are all the relevant publics or multiple markets who play a critical role in the third stage of the IMC model proposed by Schultz and Kitchen

(2000). This is because the technological applications of databases provide a greater capacity for stakeholders to identify and understand their most profitable customers.

In the context of destination, there are multiple stakeholders that are involved in the process of marketing communication policies and branding, either directly or indirectly. These are: destination marketing organizations (DMOs), national tourism organizations (NTOs), state tourism organizations (STOs), regional tourism organizations (RTOs), local tourism organizations (LTOs), government departments and ministries, communities, conservation groups, developers, marketing consultants, private sector umbrella lobbying organizations, convention and visitors bureaus, export promotion organizations (EPOs), investment agencies, embassies, hotel and airline companies, travel intermediaries, airports, restaurants, citizens, and, finally, tourist themselves (Dinnie *et al.*, 2010; Cox *et al.*, 2014; Pike and Page, 2014).

Dinnie *et al.* (2010) examined the level of IMC coordination among key organizations (EPOs, NTOs, investment agencies, and embassies) involved in nation branding activities in Southeast Asia. The results suggested seven dimensions of inter-organizational coordination that need to be considered when branding destinations, namely: 1) sector (collaboration between public and private); 2) organization domicile (engagement with organizations operating in both own and host countries); 3) mode (distinction between formal and informal coordination practices); 4) strategy formulation (centralized *vs.* decentralized, i.e. finding balance between a global approach to destination branding and host-specific policies of the examined key organizations); 5) nature of coordination (symbolic and short-term *vs.* substantive and long-term); 6) frequency of meetings (on a time basis *vs.* on an issue basis); and 7) target audience (B2B *vs.* B2C).

All the stakeholders involved in destination branding are affected by ICT applications. Those that provide the tourism services use them to reach their customers and prospects and establish meaningful relationships with them while the actual experience with the destination is taking place (Tussyadiah, 2016). Consumers, who receive the tourism service, not only use ICT to receive information from providers, but to create it and share it with other consumers in the nowadays digital environment (Stickdorn and Zehrer, 2009). In particular, interactions through mobile touchpoints (Tussyadiah, 2016; Wang *et al.*, 2016; Inversini *et al.*, 2017) highly influence travelers' experience with a destination (Neuhofer *et al.*, 2013; Wang and Fesenmaier, 2013) and connection with tourism stakeholders (Stickdorn and Zehrer, 2009).

Financial and strategic integration – results

Integrated Marketing Communications programs need to be strategically oriented, meaning that marketing communications have to be constantly monitored from a return on investment (ROI) perspective. Measurement of results is thereby placed at the last level of the IMC process. It is assumed that organizations that reach this level are those that have fully understood all the requirements of integration, as well as the benefits of its implementation (Schultz and Schultz, 1998). Kliatchko (2008) pointed out that complying with this stage also implies that IMC managers have been able to correctly define and understand the most relevant publics for the organization (the "stakeholder" pillar), identify the most important touchpoints for contacting stakeholders (the "channel" pillar) and that have successfully achieved interaction, dialogue and a certain degree of relationship through an efficient and effective exchange of brand messages (the "content" pillar).

Although it is almost impossible to know which part of revenues are attributable to the implementation of IMC (Kliatchko, 2005), the IMC literature suggests that its results can be measured through brand performance (Reid, 2005). In particular, brand awareness and salience, brand image and identity, brand trust and brand loyalty are some of the final goals of the IMC strategy (Batra and Keller, 2016). Since these brand outcomes have an effect on the financial results, the net result of this chain of impacts will be reflected in the significant increase of market value (Reid *et al.*, 2005) of the destination.

The most recent studies of the IMC literature (e.g. Adetunji *et al.*, 2014; Šerić *et al.*, 2014; Kuang *et al.*, 2015; Luxton *et al.*, 2015; Mongkol, 2015; Šerić, 2017) have centered on corroborating the impact of IMC on brand equity, the latest understood as the incremental utility or value added to a product by its brand in the consumers' minds (Pappu *et al.*, 2006). Only a few of them approached this issue in a tourism-related context, more specifically in upscale hotels in Italy (Šerić *et al.*, 2014) and Croatia (Šerić, 2017). Thus, Šerić *et al.* (2014) found that IMC has a positive and significant impact on three critical dimensions of customer-based brand equity, i.e. brand image, perceived quality, and brand loyalty. In addition, Šerić (2017) has recently concluded that consumers' perception of message consistency delivered through different communication tools and channels by hotel companies influences positively and significantly their overall brand equity, considered as "consumers' different response between a focal brand and an unbranded product when both have the same level of marketing stimuli and product attributes" (Yoo and Donthu, 2001, p. 1). In the following section we will discuss which aspects of brand equity are highly relevant in the context of tourism destinations.

Destination brand equity

One of the most popular topics to arise in the marketing literature has been the concept of brand equity (Aaker, 1991; Yoo and Donthu, 2001; Keller, 2009). As suggested by Keller (2009, p. 140) "brand equity relates to the fact that different outcomes result in the marketing of a product or service because of its brand, as compared to if that same product or service was not identified by that brand." Brand equity can also be considered as "a set of brand assets and liabilities linked to a brand, its name and symbol that adds to or subtracts from the value provided by a product or service to a firm and/or to that firm's customers" (Aaker, 1991, p. 15). Aaker (1991) and Keller (1993) approached the concept from the consumer perspective and are established as the most significant brand equity conceptualizations in the marketing literature.

Consumer-based brand equity for tourism destination was introduced by Konečnik (2006) and since then it has been attracting a lot of interest (e.g. Konečnik and Gartner, 2007; Boo *et al.*, 2009; Pike *et al.*, 2010; Gartner and Konečnik, 2011; Dioko and So, 2012; Gómez and Molina, 2012; Im *et al.*, 2012; Kashif *et al.*, 2015; Yang *et al.*, 2015; Kim *et al.*, 2016). Still, there has been little agreement on dimensionality of the concept (Gartner and Konečnik, 2011), as described below.

Researchers seem to agree on the fact that destination branding can no longer be considered in terms of destination brand image only (Boo *et al.*, 2009; Gartner and Konečnik, 2011), as traditionally suggested by a number of authors (e.g. Papadopoulos and Heslop, 2002; Tasci *et al.*, 2007). Accordingly, most of the authors examining destination brand equity adopted Aaker's (1991) proposal of its measurement (e.g. Konečnik and Gartner, 2007; Pike and Scott, 2009; Pike *et al.*, 2010; Gartner and Konečnik, 2011; Yang *et al.*, 2015; Kim *et al.*, 2016), which in addition to brand image established another three brand equity dimensions, i.e. brand awareness, perceived quality, and brand loyalty.

Some authors slightly changed Aaker's (1991) conceptualization of brand equity by adding or removing some variables. On the one hand, Boo *et al.* (2009) considered brand value as an additional component of destination brand equity and measured the concept through five dimensions. Subsequently, Gómez and Molina (2012) adopted this scale in their study on a wine destination. On the other hand, Kim *et al.* (2016) removed brand awareness from destination brand equity measurement and operationalized the construct through destination image attributes, perceived quality, and loyalty.

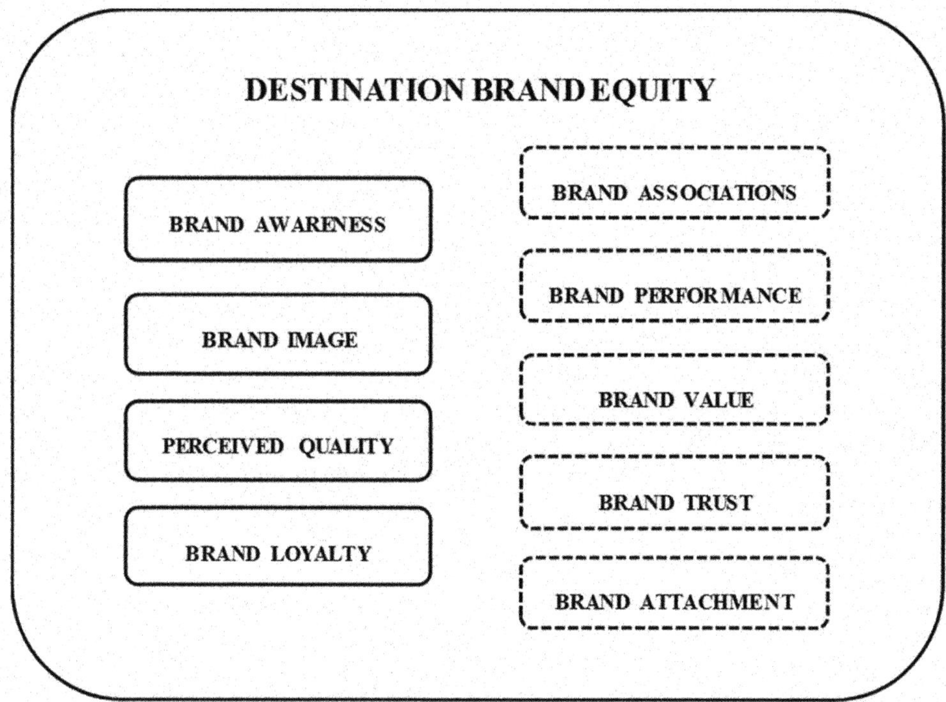

Figure 16.2 Destination brand equity dimensions

Source: own illustration based on previous literature

The solid line frame is for the most frequently employed variables in conceptualization of destination brand equity, while the dashed line frame is for occasionally employed variables.

Furthermore, Dioko and So (2012) proposed a different destination brand equity measure, which consisted of the following five dimensions: image, performance, trust, attachment, and value. The authors employed some items related to perceived quality to measure performance, and following Lassar *et al.* (1995) embraced two components that are critical to the relationship marketing paradigm, i.e. trust and attachment. Im *et al.* (2012) eliminated perceived quality from their destination brand equity model and considered brand associations and brand image separately instead. Kashif *et al.* (2015) adopted this scale in their recent studies on destination brand equity of a UNESCO World Heritage site.

We can therefore conclude that there is still no general agreement about measurement of brand equity for tourism destinations. The most frequently employed variables seem to be those proposed by Aaker (1991), i.e. brand awareness, brand image, perceived quality, and brand loyalty. In addition, brand associations, brand performance, brand value, brand trust, and brand attachment were considered by some academics in their proposals of destination brand equity measurement (see Figure 16.2).

How to create a strong destination brand through IMC

Marketing communications can affect brand equity as a form of accumulated investment in the brand (Liao and Cheng, 2014). Tourism literature suggests that if consumers perceive marketing communication consistency delivered by companies, their overall brand equity will be encouraged (Šerić, 2017). Communication consistency needs to be accomplished as brand with a consistent set of stimuli has more possibilities to deliver a single, unified message to the consumer than brands attempting to deliver different message stimuli (McGrath, 2005). This way consumers and prospect will be less likely to find themselves with confusing images of a tourism destination (Hudson, 2008).

When examining IMC perception from the consumer point of view, it is important to embrace the holistic view of marketing communications and consider different tools and channels that consumers used as information sources. In fact, Yang *et al.* (2015) have failed to prove the impact of marketing communications on customer-based brand equity of a tourism destination as their research was limited to the effects of one single marketing communication tool, i.e. advertising, thus suggesting that other forms of external communication need to be considered.

IMC can influence destination brand equity by affecting the variables that have been previously identified as its relevant dimensions. Thus, IMC can encourage destination brand awareness. Marketers can spread information and knowledge about their tourism products and services within their IMC programs. Through advertising campaigns (Yang *et al.,* 2015) and other marketing communication tools, such as public relations, events, direct marketing and promotions, customers can perceive branded destination's physical appearance before their actual experience with the brand, which leads to a higher brand awareness. This is in line with the findings of So and King's study (2010), which showed that advertising, promotions, and external brand communications influence positively brand awareness in a tourism context, as suggested in Berry's (2000) model for service brand equity.

Further, IMC managed by the local tourism industry have to reflect a true destination identity. In failing to do so, a tourism development strategy gap can be created (Govers *et al.*, 2007). IMC can create brand meaning in the minds of consumers by strategically linking tangible and intangible brand associations with certain properties (Keller, 2009). The strength of brand associations from communication effects will depend on the integration of different forms of brand identities, such as brand name, logo, and symbol (Keller, 1993). Thereby, each experienced service with a destination in general (Stickdorn and Zehrer, 2009) and perception of brand messages in particular can affect the image of a tourism destination and, subsequently, its perceived quality. Accordingly, Yang *et al.* (2015) suggested that consumers tend to rely more on communications from DMOs to shape their image about a destination brand.

Finally, satisfaction, brand loyalty, brand trust, and brand commitment have been identified as some of the outputs of an efficient IMC campaign (Šerić *et al.*, 2015). Marketing literature suggest that communication represents the first step in attracting new customers, as well as maintaining the existing ones, and as such, is positively related with trust and commitment (Morgan and Hunt, 1994). Thereby, companies that are able to communicate their message effectively are considered as highly reliable (Brownell and Reynolds, 2002). Some recent studies conducted in hotel companies (e.g. Leeman and Reynolds, 2012; Šerić *et al.*, 2015) have showed that communication is fundamental to building trust and loyalty, suggesting that it needs to be considered as one of the key elements in developing and maintaining relationships within the hospitality industry. However, the relationship between IMC and brand relationship outcomes in the context of tourism destinations still needs to be empirically tested and corroborated.

Conclusion

This chapter has argued that tourism promotion strategy needs to embrace the Integrated Marketing Communications approach. This approach consists of a number of implementation modalities which can be summarized as follows: 1) planning of communication activities in an integrated manner (Schultz and Schulz, 2004); 2) integration and coordination of marketing communication tools and channels (Keller, 2009), both online and offline (Vernuccio and Ceccotti, 2015); 3) content consistency across different media (Kliatchko, 2008); 4) support of new Information and Communication Technologies (Kim *et al.*, 2004; Keller, 2009) and social media (Šerić, 2017); 5) strong orientation on consumers (Schultz, 2006; Keller, 2009); 6) top management commitment to IMC and cross-functional coordination (Duncan and Moriarty, 1998); 7) coordination of the external communication partners (Smith, 2012); 8) integration of communications directed towards different stakeholders (Kliatchko, 2008); and 9) performance measurement of integrated communication activities (Kliatchko, 2008). Future contributions should provide empirical evidence regarding how tourism destinations implement these modalities in their IMC programs for destination brands.

The literature on marketing communications and branding has highlighted that IMC is a process of creating and maintaining profitable relationships with customers and other stakeholders and providing an extra added value to the brand (Duncan and Moriarty, 1998). This incremental utility or value that consumers attach to a product or service through its brand is considered as brand equity. In the context of tourism destinations, brand equity has been mainly examined in terms of awareness, image, perceived quality, and loyalty. However, to the best of the authors' knowledge, to date, there has been no empirical evidence on the impact of IMC on destination brand equity and its dimensions. Future studies should address this issue in order to corroborate the real potential of IMC in the process of tourism destinations branding.

To conclude, communicating brand values through an integrated marketing approach encourages development of common values and behaviors among stakeholders involved in destination branding (Harris and de Chernatony, 2001). However, diversity of stakeholders operating in tourism destinations and their respective interests might represent an important barrier to implementation of IMC strategy (Dinnie *et al.*, 2010). In fact, it still remains unclear who should be in charge of this continuous exchange of values. On one hand, as pointed out by Cox *et al.* (2014), it is the responsibility of DMOs to promote coordination among other stakeholders in a rather centralized network structure (Scott *et al.*, 2008) and to ensure an effective promotion of brand through promotional material (UNWTO, 2009). On the other hand, Pike and Page (2014) highlighted that DMOs "have little if any control over the quality of the actual visitor experience relative to the promise made in marketing communications" (p. 204) and "have no control over stakeholders' product development, pricing or marketing communications apart from when joint promotions are undertaken (p. 205). Maybe the key is in inviting other stakeholders to actually become members of the DMOs, thus encouraging a stronger participation and share of responsibilities (Hsu *et al.*, 2008).

Note

1 Acknowledgments: This work has been funded by Sapienza University of Rome, Visiting Professor Programme 2016, Resolutions S.A.n.213/16 and C.d.A.278/16.

References

Aaker, D.A., 1991. *Managing brand equity*. Free Press, New York.

Adetunji, R.R., Nordin, S.M. and Noor, S.M., 2014. The effectiveness of integrated advertisement message strategy in developing audience-based brand equity. *Global Business and Management Research*, 6 (4), 308–318.

Batra, R. and Keller, K.L., 2016. integrating marketing communications: new findings, new lessons, and new ideas. *Journal of Marketing*, 80 (6), 122–145.

Berry, L.L, 2000. Cultivating service brand equity. *Journal of the Academy of Marketing Science*, 28 (1), 128–137.
Boo, S.Y., Busser, J.A. and Baloglu, S., 2009. A model of customer-based brand equity and its application to multiple destinations. *Tourism Management*, 30 (2), 219–231.
Brownell, J. and Reynolds, D., 2002. Strengthening the food and beverage purchaser–supplier partnership: Behaviors that make a difference. *Cornell Hotel and Restaurant Administration Quarterly*, 43 (6), 49–61.
Cox, N., Gyrd-Jones, R. and Gardiner, S., 2014. Internal brand management of destination brands: Exploring the roles of destination management organisations and operators. *Journal of Destination Marketing & Management*, 3, 85–95.
Dinnie, K., Melewar, T.C., Seidenfuss, K.U. and Musa, G., 2010. Nation branding and integrated marketing communications: An ASEAN perspective. *International Marketing Review*, 27 (4), 388–403.
Dioko, L. and So, S.I.A., 2012. Branding destinations versus branding hotels in a gaming destination – Examining the nature and significance of co-branding effects in the case study of Macao. *International Journal of Hospitality Management*, 31 (2), 554–563.
Duncan, T. and Moriarty S.E., 1998. A communication-based marketing model for managing relationship, *Journal of Marketing*, 62 (2), 1–13.
Gartner, W.C. and Konečnik Ruzzier, M.J., 2011. Tourism destination brand equity dimensions: Renewal versus repeat market. *Journal of Travel Research*, 50 (5), 471–478.
Gensler, S., Völckner, F., Liu-Thompkins, Y. and Wiertz, C., 2013. Managing brands in the social media environment. *Journal of Interactive Marketing*, 27, 242–256.
Gómez, M. and Molina, A., 2012. Wine tourism in Spain: Denomination of origin effects on brand equity. *International Journal of Tourism Research*, 14 (4), 353–368.
Govers, R., Go, F.M. and Kumar, K., 2007. Promoting tourism destination image. *Journal of Travel Research*, 46 (1), 15–23.
Harris, F. and de Chernatony, L., 2001. Corporate branding and corporate brand performance. *European Journal of Marketing*, 35 (3/4), 441–456.
Hudson, S., 2008. *Marketing for tourism and hospitality. A global perspective* (2nd ed.). Sage: London.
Hsu, C., Killion, L., Brown, G., Gross, M.J. and Huang, S., 2008. *Tourism marketing: An Asia–Pacific perspective.* Milton, QLD: Wiley Australia.
Im, H.H., Kim, S.S., Elliot, S. and Han, H., 2012. Conceptualizing destination brand equity dimensions from a consumer-based brand equity perspective. *Journal of Travel & Tourism Marketing*, 29 (4), 385–403.
Inversini, A., 2017. Managing passengers' experience through mobile moments. *Journal of Air Transport Management*, 62, 78–81.
Kashif, M., Samsi, S.M. and Sarifuddin, S., 2015. Brand equity of Lahore Fort as a tourism destination brand. *Administração de empresas em revista*, 55 (4), 432–443.
Keller, K.L., 2009. Building strong brands in a modern marketing communications environment. *Journal of Marketing Communications*, 15 (2/3), 139–155.
Keller, K.L., 1993. Conceptualizing, measuring, and managing customer-based brand equity. *Journal of Marketing*, 57 (1), 1–22.
Kim, I., Han, D. and Schultz, D.E., 2004. Understanding the diffusion of integrated marketing communication. *Journal of Advertising Research*, 44 (1), 31–45.
Kim, S., Moon, J. and Choe, J., 2016. Comparison of destination brand equity models of competitive convention cities in East Asia. *Journal of Convention & Event Tourism*, 17 (4), 318–342.
Kliatchko, J., 2005. Towards a new definition of integrated marketing communications (IMC). *International Journal of Advertising*, 24 (1), 7–34.
Kliatchko, J., 2008. Revisiting the IMC construct: A revised definition and four pillars. *International Journal of Advertising*, 27 (1), 133–160.
Konečnik, M., 2006. Croatian-based brand equity for Slovenia as a tourism destination. *Economic and Business Review for Central and South-Eastern Europe*, 8 (1), 83–108.
Konečnik, M. and Gartner, W.C. 2007. Customer-based brand equity for a tourism destination. *Annals of Tourism Research*, 34 (2), 400–421.
Kuang-Jung, C., Mei-Liang, C., Chu-Mei, L. and Chien-Jung, H., 2015. Integrated marketing communication, collaborative marketing, and global brand building in Taiwan. *International Journal of Organizational Innovation*, 7 (4), 99–107.
Lassar, W., Mittal, B. and Sharma, A., 1995. Measuring consumer-based brand equity. *Journal of Consumer Marketing*, 12 (4), 4–11.
Laurie, S. and Mortimer, K., 2011. IMC is dead. Long live IMC: Academics' versus practitioners' views. *Journal of Marketing Management*, 27 (13/14), 1464–1478.

Leeman, D. and Reynolds, D., 2012. Trust and outsourcing: Do perceptions of trust influence the retention of outsourcing providers in the hospitality industry? *International Journal of Hospitality Management*, 31 (2), 601–608.

Liao, S. and Cheng, C.C.J., 2014. Brand equity and the exacerbating factors of product innovation failure evaluations: A communication effect perspective. *Journal of Business Research*, 67, 2919–2925.

Luxton, S., Reid, M. and Mavondo, F. 2015. Integrated marketing communication capability and brand performance. *Journal of Advertising*, 44 (1), 37–46.

McGrath, J.M, 2005. A pilot study testing aspects of the integrated marketing communications concept. *Journal of Marketing Communications*, 11 (3), 191–214.

Mongkol, K., 2015. Integrated marketing communication to increase brand equity: the case of a Thai beverage company. *International Journal of Trade, Economics and Finance*, 5 (5), 445–448.

Morgan, R.M. and Hunt, S.D., 1994. The commitment-trust theory of relationship marketing. *Journal of Marketing*, 58 (3), 20–38.

Neuhofer, B., Buhalis, D. and Ladkin, A., 2013. Co-creation through technology: dimensions of social connectedness. In Xiang, Z., Tussyadiah, I. (Eds), *Information and Communication Technologies in Tourism 2014*, pp. 339–352. Springer International Publishing.

Papadopoulos, N. and Heslop, L., 2002. Country equity & country branding: Problems & prospects. *Brand Management*, 9 (4/5), 294–314.

Pappu, R., Quester, P.G. and Cooksey, R.W., 2006. Consumer-based brand equity and country-of-origin relationships. *European Journal of Marketing*, 40 (5/6), 696–717.

Pike, S. and Page, J.S., 2014. Destination marketing organizations and destination marketing: A narrative analysis of the literature. *Tourism Management*, 41, 202–227.

Pike, S. and Scott, N., 2009. Destination brand equity among the host community – A potential source of competitive advantage for DMOs: The case of Brisbane, Australia. *Acta turistica*, 21 (2), 123–250.

Pike, S., Bianchi, C., Kerr, G. and Patti, C., 2010. Consumer-based brand equity for Australia as a long-haul tourism destination in an emerging market. *International Marketing Review*, 27 (4), 434–449.

Reid, M., 2005. Performance auditing of integrated marketing communications (IMC) actions and outcomes. *Journal of Advertising*, 34 (4), 41–54.

Reid, M., Luxton, S. and Mavondo, F., 2005. The relationship between integrated marketing communication, market orientation, and brand orientation. *Journal of Advertising*, 34 (4), 11–23.

Schultz, D.E., 2006. Don Schultz describes new integration. Available online at: www.imediaconnection.com (accessed April 24, 2010).

Schultz, D.E. and Kitchen, P.J., 2000. *Communicating globally. An integrated marketing approach*. NTC Publishing Group: Chicago, IL.

Schultz, D.E. and Patti, C.H., 2009. The evolution of IMC: IMC in a customer driven marketplace. *Journal of Marketing Communications*, 15 (2–3), 75–84.

Schultz, D.E. and Schultz, H., 1998. Transitioning marketing communication into the twenty-first century. *Journal of Marketing Communications*, 4 (1), 9–26.

Schultz, D.E. and Schultz, H.F., 2004. *IMC: The next generation*. McGraw-Hill: New York, NY.

Scott, N., Cooper, C. and Baggio, R., 2008. Destination networks: Four Australian cases. *Annals of Tourism Research*, 35 (1), 169–188.

Skinner, H., 2005. Wish you were here? Some problems associated with integrating marketing communications when promoting place brands. *Place Branding*, 1 (3), 299–315.

Smith, B.G., 2012. Communication integration: An analysis of context and conditions. *Public Relations Review*, 38 (4), 600–608.

So, K.K.G and King, C., 2010. When experience matters: building and measuring hotel brand equity. The customers' perspective. *International Journal of Contemporary Hospitality Management*, 22 (5), 589–608.

Stickdorn, M. and Zehrer, A., 2009. *Service design in tourism: Customer experience driven destination management*. First Nordic Conference on Service Design and Service Innovation, Oslo, November 24–26, 2009, 1–16.

Šerić, M., 2017. Relationships between social Web, IMC and overall brand equity: An empirical examination from the cross-cultural perspective. *European Journal of Marketing*, 51 (3), 646–667.

Šerić, M., Gil-Saura, I. and Ozretić-Došen, Đ. 2015. Insights on integrated marketing communications: Implementation and impact in hotel companies. *International Journal of Contemporary Hospitality Management*, 27 (5), 958–979.

Šerić, M., Gil-Saura, I. and Ruiz-Molina, M.E., 2014. How can integrated marketing communications and advanced technology influence the creation of customer-based brand equity? Evidence from the hospitality industry. *International Journal of Hospitality Management*, 39 (May), 144–156.

Tasci, A.D.A., Gartner, W.C. and Cavusgil, S.T. 2007. Measurement of destination brand bias using a quasi-experimental design. *Tourism Management*, 28 (6), 1529–1540.
Torp, S., 2009. Integrated communications: From one look to normative consistency. *Corporate Communications: An International Journal,* 14 (2), 190–206.
Tussyadiah, I.P., 2016. The influence of innovativeness on on-site smartphone use among American travelers: Implications for context-based push marketing. *Journal of Travel & Tourism Marketing,* 33 (6), 806–823.
United Nations World Tourism Organization – UNWTO, 2009. *Handbook on tourism destination branding.* Madrid: World Tourism Organisation and European Travel Commission.
Vernuccio, M. and Ceccotti, F., 2015. Strategic and organisational challenges in the integrated marketing communication paradigm shift: A holistic vision. *European Management Journal,* 33 (6), 438–449.
Vernuccio, M. and Vescovi, T., 2016. Branding in the digital era. *Mercati e Competitività,* The Journal of the Italian Marketing Association, 4, 15–22.
Wang, D. and Fesenmaier, D.R., 2013. Transforming the travel experience: the use of smartphones for travel. In Cantoni, L., Xiang, Z. (Eds), *Information and Communication Technologies in Tourism 2013,* pp. 58–69.
Wang, D., Xiang, Z. and Fesenmaier, D.R., 2016. Smartphone use in everyday Life and travel. *Journal of Travel Research,* 55 (1), 52–63.
Yang, Y., Liu, X. and Li, J, 2015. How customer experience affects the customer-based brand equity for tourism destinations. *Journal of Travel & Tourism Marketing,* 32 (1), 97–113.
Yoo, B. and Donthu, N., 2001. Developing and validating a multidimensional consumer-based brand equity scale. *Journal of Business Research,* 52 (1), 1–14.

Further reading

Denizci, B., Tasci, A.D.A., 2010. Modeling the commonly-assumed relationship between human capital and brand equity in tourism. *Journal of Hospitality Marketing & Management,* 19 (6), 610–628.
Keller, K.L, 2016. Unlocking the power of integrated marketing communications: How integrated is your IMC program? *Journal of Advertising,* 45 (3), 286–301.
Marcoz, E.M., Mauri, C., Maggioni, I. and Cantù, C., 2016. Benefits from service bundling in destination branding: the role of trust in enhancing cooperation among operators in the hospitality industry. *International Journal of Tourism Research,* 18 (3), 260–268.
Valos, M.J., Haji Habibi, F., Casidy, R., Driesener, C.B. and Maplestone, V.L., 2016. Exploring the integration of social media within integrated marketing communication frameworks: Perspectives of services marketers. *Marketing Intelligence & Planning,* 34 (1), 19–40.
Vernuccio, M., Ceccotti, F. and Pastore, A., 2012. Innovation in Integrated Marketing Communication according to the network actors: A reading with cognitive Mapping. *Sinergie Italian Management Journal,* 88, 93–113.
Xu, J.B. and Chan, A., 2010. A conceptual framework of hotel experience and customer-based brand equity. Some research questions and implications. *International Journal of Contemporary Hospitality Management,* 22 (2), 174–93.

17

Brand personality and destination marketing

Kostas Alexandris

Introduction

Aaker (1997) defined brand personality as "the set of human characteristics associated with a brand" (p. 347), while Azoulay and Kapferer (2003), in a similar definition, viewed brand personality as "the set of human personality traits that are both applicable and relevant for brands" (p. 151). It has been proposed that consumers tend to relate product brands (e.g., KFC, Starbucks, etc.) and product categories (e.g., casual dining, quick food service category etc.) with human personality traits, such as "friendly", "modern", "reliable", "cool", "smart", "conservative", "open" etc. (Aaker, 1997). This process leads to the development of brand personality profiles. Keller (2008) argued that brand personality has a more symbolic or self-expressive meaning and less a utilitarian one. In this line, consumers build brand personality perceptions mainly based on symbolic meanings that brands have for them, and less on evaluating product-related attributes. However, there are studies in the hospitality and tourism field, which provided evidence that service quality evaluations, which involve a utilitarian process, influence the development of brand personality perceptions (Nikolaidis, Chrisikou, & Alexandris, 2016; Tran, Dauchez, & Szemik, 2013). In this line, service quality has been proposed as one of the sources for the development of brand personality.

Symbolic meanings are developed when customers view brands as extensions of their self. This happens when brands are perceived to have similar images with an individual's image and personality. Considering that human personalities are determined by personality traits (e.g., as the traits defined by the Big Five Personality Model – extroversion, agreeableness, conscientiousness, emotional stability and openness to experience), it is then expected that customers associate their human personality traits with their favorite brands (Geuens, Weijters, & De Wulf, 2009). When consumers see a brand as extensions of their self, they develop a psychological attachment with this brand which will lead to identification with it (Alexandris, 2016). An individual, for example, high in innovativeness is more likely to identify himself /herself with a modern hotel that provides opportunities for active and explorative holidays. On the other hand, an introverted individual is more likely to be associated with a hotel, which emphasizes on quietness, privacy and relaxation. Since human personality traits are considered as relatively stable and enduring characteristics, the image of brands with established personality profiles can also be considered as relatively stable and lasting (Aaker, 1997), which provides an argument for the value of building brand personality.

Brand personality is considered today an important topic in marketing, because it can be used by marketers as one of the strategies to achieve brand and/or product differentiation in competitive markets. Brands with distinct and strong personality profiles can be differentiated from the competition, and appeal to specific target groups. Subsequently, brand personality can be used as a tool for guiding brand market positioning and finally developing brand equity (Tran, Dauchez, & Szemik, 2013). Since hospitality and tourism is a mature industry (Angelo & Vladimir, 2011) and the functional characteristics of hospitality and tourism organizations are not substantially differentiated (Tran et al., 2013), the brand personality perceptions, which as discussed above have a symbolic meaning, play an even more important role for brand / product positioning.

The measurement of brand personality

One of the key, but also controversial, issues in the literature has been the measurement of brand personality. Aaker (1997) developed the five-factor brand personality measurement model, which has been extensively used in the marketing literature across different products and services (for a detailed review see Eisend & Stokburger-Sauer, 2013). This scale was developed by Aaker (1997) based on human personality traits that were judged to be applicable to brands. Through empirical testing with several validation statistical techniques, Aaker (1997) proposed five brand personality dimensions, each of which consists of different facets, as follows: (a) sincerity, which includes the facets of down to earth, honest, wholesome, and cheerful; (b) excitement, which includes the facets of daring, spirited, imaginative, up-to-date; (c) competence, which includes the facets of reliable, intelligent, successful; (d) sophistication, which includes the facets of upper-class and charming; (e) ruggedness, which includes the facets of outdoorsy and masculinity.

Although this model has been widely applied, it has also received criticism. Geuens et al. (2009) started their discussion by criticizing the definition of brand personality. They argued that the brand personality definition given by Aaker is vague because she used the term "characteristics" instead of "traits". Subsequently, some of the facets used in the scale to measure brand personality include demographic and psychographic characteristics (e.g., "upper class" brand, "feminine" brand, "young" brand, etc.) and not traits (Azoulay & Kapferer, 2003). Such characteristics might reflect an image of a brand (e.g., "an upper class hotel"), but they do not really correspond to human personality traits (as, for example, the ones defined by the Big-Five Personality Model). Azoulay and Kapferer (2003) argued that, in fact, only three out of the five factors correspond to elements of the Big-Five personality model. The Competence dimension, for example, which is defined as "the know-how" of a company or the ability of someone to carry out a task properly, has nothing to do with personality, since it refers to cognitive abilities (Azoulay & Kapferer, 2003). Subsequently, it is questionable if Aaker's model measures personality of brands or at least if it measures only brand personality. As Geuens et al. (2009) discussed, this conceptual issue creates measurement problems in terms of confusing the sender aspect (perceived brand personality) with the receiver aspect (perceived user characteristic). In this line, Geuens et al. (2009) proposed that a brand personality scale should exclude all non-personality items and include only those that measure personality traits, as defined in the psychology literature and specifically by the Big-Five personality model. So, they proposed and empirically tested a scale with the following dimensions: Responsibility, Activity, Aggressiveness, Simplicity, and Emotionality. This scale has not been tested in the hospitality and tourism context.

A second criticism of Aaker's scale relates to the category confusion problem. There are concerns whether the model can measure perceptions about a product category, a specific brand or both (Avis, 2012; Avis, Forbes, & Ferguson, 2013). In the hospitality and tourism field, the majority of studies measured brand personality of specific brands (e.g., Starbucks, KFC, etc.). A third criticism relates to the issue of applicability of the five dimensions of the model (Sincerity, Excitement, Competence, Sophistication, Ruggedness) and the facets of the model (e.g., daring, spirited, imaginative, up-to-date are proposed to define excitement) across different contexts, segments and products. Even the adjectives that are used to measure its facets might have different meanings when associated with different product categories across different contexts (Avis, 2012). This measurement problem was revealed in the studies conducted in the hospitality and tourism field. So, in the context of luxurious hotels, Lee and Back (2010) used only two of the five dimensions of the model (Competence and Sophistication), while Tran et al., (2013) and Nikolaidis et al. (2016) used four of the five dimensions of the model (Sincerity, Excitement, Competence, and Sophistication). They both agreed that the "ruggedness" dimension is not applicable in this context. There were also several adjustments in the number and nature of the adjectives used to measure each one of the four facets, in relation to the original model.

Studies conducted in restaurants and coffee shop chains reported also variations, in comparison with the original model. Kim, Magnini and Singal (2010), who conducted a study in two restaurants (Olive Garden and Chili's restaurants) is one of the few that empirically supported the original Aaker's model. On the other hand, Lee, Back and Kim (2009) reported that while the five dimensions of brand personality in a sample of restaurants were the same as in the original Aaker's model, the individual facets within the dimensions were different. So, the Sincerity dimension in their study consisted of the facets of Sincere, Honest, Real, and Wholesome, and the Excitement dimension consisted of three facets: Independent, Unique, and Young. Musante, Bojanic and Zhang (2008), who measured the personality profile of quick service and casual restaurants (McDonalds, Wendy's, KFC, and Applee's, Chili's, Friday's, respectively) verified only the four dimensions of brand personality (Competence, Sincerity, Excitement, and Sophistication), while the ruggedness dimension was not found to be applicable in this context.

Variations in the model were also reported by Lin and Huang (2012) in a study of two coffee chains (Starbucks and 85 Degrees) in Taiwan. These authors conducted the analysis separately for each one of the chains. For Starbucks, the dimensions revealed were Excitement, Sophistication, Naivety, Sincerity, and Resolution. For 85 Degrees, the dimensions were Excitement, Sophistication, Naivety, Mildness, and Resolution. Several differences were also reported in terms of the individual facets used to describe each of the dimensions of the brand personality model in comparison to the original Aaker's model.

A last criticism of the model that Geuens et al. (2009) discussed relates to the degree to which the scale is applicable across cultures. This problem was not discussed in hospitality and tourism studies conducted in different countries (e.g., USA, Japan, Korea, etc.). Cultural differences, however, were revealed when brand personality perceptions were compared among consumers of different countries in the few studies that made cross-cultural comparisons. Murase and Bojanic (2004) compared brand personality perceptions among Japanese and American customers of KFC, McDonald's and Wendy's. Their findings showed little cultural differences in the perception of brand personalities of the three brands, but significant differences across brands. KFC has a weaker brand personality in US than McDonald's and Wendy's, because of its lack of clear identity. Furthermore, the brand personalities of KFC and McDonald's were viewed more positive in Japan, and Wendy's was viewed more positive in the U.S. McDonald's was the restaurant with the most consistent image in both the countries. However, it is not clear if these differences reflect cultural differences or if they are due to the business and marketing strategy of each organization in the countries. KFC for example was reported as aiming to provide a more upscale image in Japan (Murase & Bojanic, 2004). Considering the globalization of the hospitality and tourism organizations and the international profile of travelers, it could be argued that the issue of cross-cultural comparison of brand personality perceptions is important; further research is required in this direction.

Antecedents of brand personality

Aaker (1997) proposed that brand personality perceptions are developed when consumers have direct and indirect contacts with a brand. There are several factors that influence the development of brand personality, such as the brand-user imagery, advertising complexity and consistency, the product characteristics and design, consumer demographics and psychographics (Eisend & Stokburger-Sauer, 2013). The first factor that influences brand personality is the brand-user imagery (Lee & Back, 2010), which is defined as "the set of human characteristics associated with the typical user of a brand" (Aaker, 1996, p. 17). Consumers tend to personalize products based on the generalized image of a typical brand user (Lee & Back, 2010). Brand user imagery is the most important antecedent of brand personality, because the personality traits of the users of a brand are transferred directly to the brand and they develop its image (Lee & Back, 2010). User imagery is influenced by direct consumption experience but also indirect interactions. Direct consumption experience in the service industry is affected not only by the core product, but also the augmented product and the interaction with other customers and employees (Zeithaml & Bitner, 2000). In the case of restaurants, for example, it was found that the music in a restaurant influences the development of brand personality perceptions (Magnini & Thelen, 2008). Indirect interactions include non-product related attributes and actions related to the marketing mix of the brand, such as media and sales communication strategies, store location, distribution channels, price, the physical environment (in the case of services), the logo and the brand architecture (Maehle & Supphellen, 2011).

Empirical research on the identification of the sources of brand personality in the hospitality and tourism field is still limited (Tran et al., 2013). Brand user imagery, service quality and perceived price are the three main antecedents of brand personality that have been tested. Lee and Back (2010) who conducted a study in the context of luxurious hotels provided evidence that brand user imagery is one of the main factors that influence the Competence and Sophistication dimensions of hotel brand personality; these two dimensions are the main ones that characterize upper-scale hotel brands. The strong influence of user imagery on brand personality was explained by the theory of self-image congruence (Hosany & Martin, 2012; Sirgy & Su, 2000), according to which consumers tend to consume brands (e.g., stay in an expensive hotel) that correspond to their individual personality traits in order to express and/or enhance their self-concept (image, status, luxury, pride, etc.).

Studies in luxurious hotels provided some evidence that service quality influences the development of brand personality perceptions (Nikolaidis et al., 2016; Tran et al., 2013). The relationship between service quality evaluations and brand personality is not entirely supported by the definition of the construct of brand personality, because service quality evaluations represent a cognitive process (Gremler, Bitner & Zeithaml, 2012). As previously discussed Aaker (1997) argued that brand personality is based more on symbolic than utilitarian (cognitive) processes. On trying to theoretically justify this relationship Lee and Back (2010) argued that cognitive knowledge can lead to affective responses, which lead to the development of symbolic meanings. While Lee and Back (2010) did not empirically support the relationship between service quality and brand personality (measuring only two dimensions: Competence and Sophistication), in the studies of Tran et al. (2013) and Nikolaidis et al. (2016), significant relationships between all the five dimensions of service quality and brand personality dimensions were reported.

Price is a third variable that was reported to influence brand personality in the hospitality and tourism field. According to Lee and Back (2010), it is categorized into objective and perceived price. Objective price is the actual price, while perceived price is a consumer's subjective impression about it. Perceived price perceptions are formed based on consumers' judgments in comparison with a reference price, which is formed based on comparing prices among competitive brands. In the lodging industry the price of a hotel is used as a positioning strategy and as a way to define hotel classes (Lee & Back, 2010). It is well recognized that hotel classes are associated with certain brand personality traits (e.g., reliable, upper class, honest etc.). In this line, the price influences the development of a hotel brand personality (Lee & Back, 2010).

Consequences of brand personality

Brand personality perceptions can influence consumer decision-making. It is well recognized today that brand personality perceptions are associated with multiple positive consumer behavioral outcomes (e.g., consumer loyalty, preferences, emotions and trust). While these positive consequences have been widely studied in the general marketing literature, research in the context of hospitality and tourism field is still developing. A brief review of these positive consumer behavioral outcomes will follow, emphasizing the findings that have been reported in the hospitality and tourism field.

Consumer emotions

Lee, Back and Kim (2009), who conducted a study among customers of restaurants, provided evidence that brand positive personality perceptions can create positive customer emotions and can reduce the negative ones. When customers perceive a restaurant brand as being honest, real, and wholesome, positive emotions can be created, while when customers perceive a restaurant as hard-working and confident, the negative emotions can be reduced (Leung & Tanford, 2016). The link between brand personality and customer emotions was proposed earlier by Aaker (1997), who linked brand personality perceptions not only with functional but also with emotional benefits that consumers expect when buying a product brand. Examples of such benefits for a traveler can be excitement and enjoyment (e.g., a resort hotel), relaxation (e.g., a restaurant or a hotel), exploration (e.g., mountain resort) etc. Research, for example, conducted in the car industry showed that consumers associate certain car brands with specific benefits. So, consumers associate safety with Volvo, excitement with BMW, luxury with BMW, reliability with Toyota, etc. (Aaker, 1996).

Brand preference

Kim, Magnini and Singal (2011), who conducted a study in the context of restaurants, reported that brand personality perceptions facilitate a consumer's decision-making process, because of the development of established brand preferences. The positive link between brand personality and brand preferences was explained based on the notion of the functional benefit representation (Aaker, 1997), according to which brand personality perceptions help consumers organize and build their knowledge about a brand (e.g., Starbucks) and its attributes (e.g., clean facilities, great variety of coffees). Increased brand knowledge is usually associated with improved brand recall, which facilitates consumer decision-making (established preference for a specific brand). Brand recall is defined as the ability of a consumer to remember a specific brand and its characteristics.

Brand loyalty and purchase intentions

Brand loyalty is defined in terms of its behavioral (frequency and quantity of buying) and attitudinal (cognitive, affective and conative) elements (Funk, Alexandris, McDonald, 2016). Brand loyalty can lead to the development of commitment to a particular brand (Alexandris, 2016; Bloemer & Kasper, 1995). The benefits of customer loyalty are multiple for an organization. First of all, it is cheaper to keep an existing customer than to attract a new one, due to reduced marketing and sales costs; these lead to reduced communication costs (Jin, Line & Merkebu, 2016). Furthermore, loyal customers usually spend more money (e.g., buy more frequently and/or higher quantity) than the moderately low customers (Suh, Moon, Han & Ham, 2015).

Research has shown that brands with strong and distinctive personalities are more likely to have loyal consumers (Alexandris, 2016; Karjaluoto, Mattila, & Pento, 2002, Lee & Back, 2010). This is because of the strong identification that consumers frequently develop with such brands (Stokburger-Sauer, 2011). The link between brand personality perceptions and consumer loyalty can be explained based on the construct of self-image congruence (Hosany & Martin, 2012; Sirgy & Su, 2000). Brands have symbolic meanings for consumers; these meanings construct the brand-user image, meaning how would a typical user of this brand look and behave. To decide if they like the brand, individuals try to match their own perceived image with that of the typical user. Consumers tend to consume brands with images (brand and user image) that fit with their self-concept, which is defined as the cognitive beliefs that an individual holds about himself/herself (Stokburger-Sauer, 2011). In simple words, consumers buy products whose image fits with their perceived self-image. Sometimes they even consume such brands in order to boost their self-esteem (Karjaluoto et al., 2015). Research has also shown that consumers are more likely to develop emotional attachment with a brand, in which the link between their self-image and brand personality is strong (Karjaluoto et al., 2015). The development of emotional attachment with a brand is associated with the development of behavioral and attitudinal consumer loyalty (Funk et al., 2016).

A good example of the influence of brand personality perceptions on consumer loyalty was provided in the study of Lee et al. (2009). In the context of family restaurants, they provided empirical evidence for the positive relationship between brand personality and consumer loyalty. These authors explained this relationship based on the expectations that customers develop for brands with established and favorable personality profiles. Satisfaction (or unsatisfaction) of these expectations leads to positive (or negative) emotional responses, influencing the level of loyalty.

Consumer trust

Aaker (1997) proposed that positive brand personality perceptions enhance the development of trust between the consumer and the brand. In this line, brands with favorite brand personality profiles are seen by consumers as partners who are reliable, dependable and trustworthy (Fournier, 1998). Since trust and reliability are mainly developed based on cognitive consumer processes, it is expected that positive consumer evaluations about a brand (e.g., perceived service quality), which are made based on personal experience and brand user imagery are important for the development of consumer trust (Lee & Back, 2010). Since, however, brand personality perceptions are not developed only based on direct experience but also on indirect ones, through external communication, it is clear that communication strategies also play a role in the development of consumer trust (Aaker, 1997; Fournier, 1998). The positive relationship between brand personality and trust was confirmed by a study conducted by Lee and Back (2010) in upper class hotels.

Practical implications of brand personality research

As previously discussed, brand personality perceptions can help managers to position their brands in the market and differentiate them from competition. The study of brand personality obviously requires the collection of primary data, which usually is not the first priority of hospitality and tourism managers; it is, therefore, necessary for practitioners to cooperate with academics in order to design brand personality studies and make full use of primary data. A review of the brand personality studies which was conducted in the hospitality and tourism field shows that researchers developed some good arguments for applying brand personality theory in practice.

The study of Lin and Huang (2012) is a good example for supporting the value of brand personality research on profiling the images of branded coffee places. By comparing the brand personality of Starbucks and 85 Degrees coffee places the authors identified some clear differences and similarities between the two services. So, Starbucks was perceived as being exciting, sophisticated, and sincere. This is in line with the company' strategy to offer customers high quality coffee, serviced in comfortable, distinctive and social environment. On the other hand, excitement was the only main dimension of brand personality that predicted loyalty in the 85 Degrees coffee place, which confirms the common perception that this place is a good location for social activities. Using brand personality research, managers can therefore test the success of their strategies to develop a distinctive image for their brands.

Considering that brand personality perceptions are continuously developing and changing (although personality traits can be considered as a relatively stable characteristic), Lee et al. (2009) proposed that restaurant marketers should design and perform regular brand personality surveys aiming to continuously monitor restaurant customers' brand image perceptions. Such research could show if brand personality perceptions are aligned with the firm's mission, vision, and objectives. Lee et al. (2009) also emphasized the need to build consistent restaurant images that reflect the prime target groups' expected image. Building a consistent image in the hospitality and tourism industry is a challenging activity, because of the intangibility of the service product. The authors provided the upscale market segment as an example; the image is built not only based on the core product (menu) but also on the symbols of luxury, pride, and status, which are influenced by the augmented products. This involves the décor, architecture, and appearance of personnel, all of which should contribute to the development of the restaurant's image.

In the same segment (casual dining restaurants) Kim et al. (2011) made similar suggestions. They proposed that managers should promote not only the functional but also the symbolic attributes of their brands. In order to promote the symbolic attributes, peripheral aspects of their core service (menu) should be developed. Examples of such aspects are the overall ambience, the décor and the atmosphere in the restaurant, the dress code of employees and other customers, and even the kind of music played. The development and promotion of these experiential attributes should be incorporated within the company's marketing strategy in order for the managers to be able to differentiate their brands from competition through the development of distinct personality profiles. Kim et al. (2011) further proposed that the sincerity dimension is a key one for building a distinct and positive brand personality profile; this is also the most important dimension to influence customers' brand preferences.

In the segment of luxurious hotels, Lee and Back (2010) emphasized the need to build brand user imagery as a key construct that influences the development of hotel personality perceptions. So, hotel managers should position their brands in a way to target brand user imagery. In this line, it was proposed (Jamal & Goode, 2001) that gaps between the current brand user imagery and the desired brand user imagery should be identified, in order to develop marketing and communication strategies to close these gaps. Lee and Back (2010) used the luxurious hotel segment in order to justify this argument; customers choose such hotels not only for the quality of their services, but also for the symbols of luxury, pride, and status associated with user imagery.

Finally, Tran et al. (2013) and Nikolaidis et al. (2016), on discussing the brand personality perceptions in the luxurious hotel segment, provided some suggestions on how to build the five dimensions of brand personality. So, a competent hotel is the one which is reliable and successful. Tran et al. (2013) provided the example of Springhill Suites by Marriott in which guests are served by professionals in order to develop its personalized loyalty programs. Perceptions about these dimensions are influenced by the knowledge and expertise of the human aspect of the organisation. Perceptions related to the sophistication dimension of brand personality are influenced by the reliability of the hotel and its ability to be positioned as upper class and charming. Tran et al. (2013) provided the example of Hilton Pensacola Beach Gulf Front and Margaritaville Pensacola Beach Hotel (created by Intercontinental), which have targeted the upper-class consumer based on their personalized consumer programs. An exciting hotel is one which provides opportunities for experiential benefits for customers; these experiential benefits are applicable both in business type hotels and holiday resorts. Tran et al. (2013) provided the example of Holiday Inn Resort Pensacola Beach, which is perceived as exciting because of the Mermaid kid activities developed in the swimming pool. Finally, perceptions about sincerity are influenced by the ability of the organisation and its management to inspire trust, in terms of keeping promises and ensuring safe financial transactions. Relationship marketing programs play an important role for the development of these perceptions. Tran et al. (2013) provided the example of Hampton Inn Pensacola beach created be Hilton, which emphasized hiring motivated employees to serve with the guests' best interests at heart.

Conclusion and suggestions for future research

While brand personality research in the hospitality and tourism field is not extensive, research so far has provided evidence for its value in hospitality and tourism marketing. In the mature and highly competitive hospitality and tourism market, brand personality can be used by marketers to build a distinctive image for their organisations; this can help them differentiate their organisations from the competition and appeal to specific target groups. It provides therefore an opportunity for marketers to test if the perceived image of their organisations is aligned with their marketing strategy and if it fits with what is promoted through formal and informal communication strategies. In terms of consumer decision-making, there has been empirical evidence that positive brand personality perceptions are associated with positive consumer behavioral outcomes. The issue, however, of the measurement of brand personality and the use of a valid, reliable and universally applicable measurement scale is still a controversial one in the literature. While the majority of the published studies in hospitality and tourism field used Aaker's (1997) scale as a basis for their research, they ended up with different factor structures than the original one, which confirms the critique of the model. More research is also required towards identifying the factors that influence brand personality development in the hospitality and tourism field; testing factors such as product characteristics, advertising and communication, consumer demographics and psychographics can help towards this direction (Eisend & Stokburger-Sauer, 2013). Finally, testing the measurement of brand personality, its antecedents and consequences among different cultures, is an area in which further research is needed.

References

Aaker, D.A. (1996) *Building Strong Brands*, New York: The Free Press – A division of Simon & Schuster Inc.

Aaker, J.L. (1997) "Dimensions of brand personality", *Journal of Marketing Research*, 34(3), 347–356.

Alexandris, K. (2016) "Testing the role of sport event personality on the development of event involvement and loyalty: The case of mountain running races", *International Journal of Event and Festival Management*, 7(1), 16, 2–20.

Angelo, R., & Vladimir, A. (2011) *Hospitality today, 7th ed.*, MI: American Hotel and Lodging Educational Institute.

Avis, M. (2012) "Brand personality factor based models: A critical review". *Australasian Marketing Journal*, 20(1), 89–96.

Avis, M., Forbes, S., & Ferguson, S. (2013) "The brand personality of rocks: A critical evaluation of a brand personality scale", *Marketing Theory*, 1–25.

Azoulay, A., & Kapferer, J.N. (2003) "Do brand personality scales really measure brand personality?", *The Journal of Brand Management*, 11(2), 143–155.

Bloemer, J.M.M., & Kasper, H.D.P. (1995) "The complex relationship between consumer satisfaction and brand loyalty", *Journal of Economic Psychology*, 16, 311–329.

Eisend, M., & Stokburger-Sauer, N.E. (2013) "Brand personality: A meta-analytic review of antecedents and consequences", *Marketing Letters*, 24(3), 205–216.

Fournier, S. (1998) "Consumers and their brands: Developing relationship theory in consumer research", *The Journal of Consumer Research*, 24(4), 343–373.

Funk, D., Alexandris, K., & McDonald, H. (2016) "Sport consumer behaviour: Marketing strategies", London: Routledge.

Geuens, M., Weijters, B., & De Wulf, K. (2009) "A new measure of brand personality", *Intern. J. of Research in Marketing*, 26, 97–107.

Gremler, D., Bitner, M., & Zeithaml, V. (2012) *Services marketing: Integrating customer focus across the firm*. New York: McGraw-Hill.

Hosany, S., & Martin, D. (2012) "Self-image congruence in consumer behavior", *Journal of Business Research*, 65, 685–691.

Jamal, A., & Goode, M. (2001) "Consumers and brands: a study of the impact of self-image congruence on brand preference and satisfaction", *Marketing Intelligence & Planning*, 19(7), 482–492.

Jin, N., Line, N.D. and Merkebu, J. (2015) "The impact of brand prestige on trust, perceived risk, satisfaction, and loyalty in upscale restaurants", *Journal of Hospitality Marketing & Management*, 25 (5), 523–546.

Karjaluoto, H., Mattila, M., and Pento, T. (2002) "Factors Underlying Attitude Formation towards Online Banking in Finland", *International Journal of Bank Marketing*, 20(6), 261–272.

Keller, K.L. (2008) *Strategic Brand Management: Building, Measuring and Managing Brand Equity*, Upper Saddle River: Pearson-Prentice Hall.

Kim, D., Magnini, V., & Singal M. (2011) The effects of customers' perceptions of brand personality in casual theme restaurants, *International Journal of Hospitality Management*, 30, 448–458.

Lee, J.S., & Back, K.J. (2010) "Examining antecedents and consequences of brand personality in the upper-upscale business hotel segment", *Journal of Travel and Tourism Marketing*, 27, 132–145.

Lee, Y., & Back, K.J, & Kim, J. (2009) "Family Restaurant Brand Personality and Its Impact on Customer's Emotion, Satisfaction, and Brand Loyalty", *Journal of Hospitality & Tourism Research*, 33(3), 305–328.

Leung, X.Y. and Tanford, S. (2016) "What drives Facebook fans to "like" hotel pages: A comparison of three competing models", *Journal of Hospitality Marketing & Management*, 25(3), 314–345.

Lin, Y, & Huang, W. (2012) "Effects of the Big Five Brand Personality Dimensions on Repurchase Intentions: Using Branded Coffee Chains as Examples", *Journal of Foodservice Business Research*, 15, 1–18.
Maehle, N., & Supphellen, M. (2011) In search of the sources of brand personality, *International Journal of Market Research*, 53(1), 95–114.
Magnini, V., & Thelen, S. (2008) "The Influence of Music on Perceptions of Brand Personality, Décor, and Service Quality: The Case of Classical Music in a Fine-Dining Restaurant", *Journal of Hospitality & Leisure Marketing*, 16(3), 286–300.
Murase, H., & Bojanic, D. (2004) "An Examination of the Differences in Restaurant Brand Personality Across Cultures", *Journal of Hospitality & Leisure Marketing*, 11(2), 97–113.
Musante, M., Bojanic, D., & Zhang, J. (2008) "A Modified Brand Personality Scale for the Restaurant Industry", *Journal of Hospitality & Leisure Marketing*, 16(4), 303–323.
Nikolaidis, D., Chrysikou, C., Alexandris, K. (2016, in press) "Testing the Relationship between Hotel Service Quality and Hotel Brand Personality", *International Journal of Hospitality and Event Management.*
Sirgy, M.J., & Su, C. (2000) "Destination image, self-congruity, and travel behaviour: toward an integrative model", *Journal of Travel Research*, 38(4), 340–352.
Stokburger-Sauer, N. (2011) "The relevance of visitors' nation brand embeddedness and personality congruence for nation brand identification, visit intentions and advocacy", *Tourism Management*, 32, 1282–1289.
Suh, M., Moon, H., Han, H. and Ham, S. (2015) "Invisible and intangible, but undeniable: Role of ambient conditions in building hotel guests' loyalty", *Journal of Hospitality Marketing & Management*, 24(7), 727–753.
Tran, X., Dauchez, C., & Szemik, A. (2013) "Hotel brand personality and brand quality", *Journal of Vacation Marketing*, 19(4), 329–341.
Zeithaml, V.A., & Bitner, M.J. (2000) *Services Marketing: Integrating Customer Focus across the Firm,* New York: McGraw-Hill.

Further reading

Austin, J., Siguaw, J., Mattila, A., (2003) "A re-examination of the generalizability of the Aaker brand personality measurement framework", *Journal of Strategic Marketing*, 11, 77–92 (June).
Brakus, J.J., Schmitt, B.H. and Zarantonello, L. (2009), "Brand Experience: What Is It? How Is It Measured? Does it affect Loyalty"? *Journal of Marketing,* 73(May), 52–68.
Ekinci, Y., & Riley, M. (2000) "Validating quality dimensions", *Annals of Tourism Research, 28*, 202–223.
Freling, T., & Forbes, L. (2005) "An examination of brand personality through methodological triangulation", *Brand Management*, 13(2), 148–162 (a study using a multi-method qualitative approach to triangulate brand personality).
Hultman, M., Skarmeas, D., Oghazi, P., & Behesti, H. (2015) "Achieving tourist loyalty through destination personality, satisfaction, and identification", *Journal of Business Research*, 68(11), 2227–2231 (a study exploring the interrelationships among destination personality, tourist satisfaction, and tourist–destination identification).
Ivens, B., & Valta, K. (2012) "Customer brand personality perception: A taxonomic analysis", *Journal of Marketing Management*, 28(9–10), 1062–1093 (a study aiming to investigate if consumer brand personality perceptions are homogeneous).
Karjaluoto, H., Munnukka, H., & Salmi, M. (2016) "How do brand personality, identification, and relationship length drive loyalty in sports?" *Journal of Service Theory and Practice,* 26(1), 50–71 (a study extending brand identification theory to the sports team context).
Keller, K.L. (2016) "Reflections on customer-based brand equity: perspectives, progress, and priorities" 6 (1), *AMS Review*, 1–16 (a critical literature review).
Klink, R., & Athaide, G. (2012) "Creating brand personality with brand names" *Mark Lett,* 23, 109–117 (a study that investigates how brand names can be formed to create brand personality based on theory and research from sound symbolism).
Lombart, C., & Louis, D. (2016) "Sources of retailer personality: Private brand perceptions", *Journal of Retailing and Consumer Services*, 28, 117–125 (a study investigating the antecedents of retailer personality on trust and attitude toward a retailer brand).
Pan, L., Zhang, M., Gursoy, D., & Lu, L. (2017) "Development and validation of a destination personality scale for mainland Chinese travelers", *Tourism Management,* 59, 338–348 (a study that develops a destination personality scale using a two-step mixed method approach).

Smith, A., Graetz, B., & Westerbeek, H. (2006) "Brand personality in a membership-based organization", *Int J. Nonprofit Volunt Sect Mark*, 11, 251–266 (a study that uses Aaker's model to assess characteristics of a membership based sport organization).

Sung, Y., Choi, S. Ahn, H., & Song, Y. (2014) "Dimensions of Luxury Brand Personality: Scale Development and Validation", *Psychology and Marketing*, 32(1), 121–132 (a study which develops a reliable and valid scale that measures the dimensions of luxury brand personality).

Tsaur, S., Chiu, Y., & Huang, C. (2002) "Determinants of guest loyalty to international tourists' hotels: a neuronal network approach", *Tourism Management*, 23, 397–405.

van Rekom, J., Jacobs, G., Verlegh, P. (2006), "Measuring and managing the essence of a brand personality", *Market Lett*, 17, 181–192.

Venable, B., Rose, G., Bush, V., & Gilbert, F. (2005) "The Role of Brand Personality in Charitable Giving: An Assessment and Validation", *Journal of the Academy of Marketing Science*, 33(3), 295–312.

18

Gastronomy tourism as a marketing strategy for place branding

Albert Barreda

Introduction

This chapter aims to present key information that gastronomy tourism marketers and destination management officials might consider when formulating place branding strategies and effective marketing differentiation. Although gastronomy tourism is accepted as an important and emerging sector of cultural tourism, research of gastronomy tourism as a marketing instrument to build place brand equity is scarce. The author covers a brand value-driven approach to explain how gastronomy is a critical marketing tool to create memorable experience and place brand equity dimensions. The author presents a discussion of the current research in gastronomy tourism, the role of gastronomy tourism on place branding, the relationship between gastronomy and tourism experiences, gastronomy tourism place brand equity and the role of destination management organizations (DMOs).

Leaning on the current literature of gastronomy tourism and place brand equity, the author presents an interesting discussion of how gastronomy tourism is a fundamental instrument to develop place brand value dimensions including place brand awareness, place brand image, place brand quality, and place brand loyalty. The author also presents a discussion about the importance of creating memorable gastro-experiences before developing place branding elements. To conclude, this chapter provides a SWOT analysis of gastronomy tourism in Peru.

This chapter is written to present useful information for tourism marketers, gastronomy organizations, DMOs, and place branding experts to have a clear understanding of the elements to consider including gastronomy offerings, gastro-experiences, branding elements, marketing strategies, and the behavior of international tourists before formulating marketing strategies to differentiate themselves from competitors and effectively position the place.

Literature review

Current research

Conducting a comprehensive review of the literature of destination branding, the author has noticed an opportunity to extend the body of knowledge. As today, there are few scholarly works on utilizing gastronomy tourism as a strategic marketing instrument for developing place branding. However, some researchers have studied similar areas in gastronomy tourism, economic experience, sensory branding, and competitiveness.

The review of the literature has shown scholarly work on experiential value in branding food tourism. Tsai and Wang (2017) examine the impact of experiential value as a precursor of branding in food tourism. Tainan, a historical city in Taiwan, was considered as the research scene. Their findings suggest that one dimension of experiential value namely consumer return on investment impacts a destination's food image that in turn impacts a traveler's positive perceptions towards food tourism. Richards (2015) notes that gastronomy has changed from being a complementary marketing activity for promoting a destination to being one of the key strategies and activities for most tourists to travel and experience in a particular destination. Richards has studied the reasons for this change, in relation to the moving social standing of gastronomy and to the impact of gastronomy as a key promising experience economy. Horng and Tsai (2012) examine the main elements in gastronomy tourism based on resource-based theory in different destinations in order to establish the organization of marketing strategic plans in gastronomy tourism. The authors suggest that marketing strategies in tourism must not only focus on market-based activities but also on product-based activities. These activities may assist the creation of the promotion of sustainable tourism.

Studies on culture heritage and local gastronomy culture study how gastronomy marketers decode local gastronomy and culture in marketing food offerings to satisfy consumer's new trends (Tellström *et al.* 2006). In a more current study, Hillel *et al.* (2013) suggest that not every destination has the capability to offer a genuine gastronomic experience. Their findings show that the failure of the local community to deliver authentic culinary offerings and influential food culture is an impediment to the development of an appealing destination food identity. In another study, Horng and Tsai (2010) study the elements of gastronomy related websites of major Asian countries (Hong Kong, Japan, Korea, Singapore, Taiwan and Thailand). Their study examines the common marketing and branding practices to promote and brand these gastronomic destinations and unique food cultures.

Most of the past and current research is conducted to explain the ongoing evolution of gastronomy tourism and culture tourism as marketing instruments for branding destinations. These studies could be categorized into three groups. The first group includes studies on gastronomic experiences and the relation to destinations. Such works conducted research examining tourists' perceptions of gastronomic experiences and how the creation of memorable experiences through gastronomy influences the development of the community. For instance, Björk and Kauppinen-Räisänen (2014) examine the components that influence tourists' dining experiences with an emphasis on regional food markets.

The next group embraces research works in gastronomy tourism and its role to develop sustainable competitiveness. Mascarenhas and Gândara (2015) examine the impact of gastronomy tourism in the superiority and competitiveness in touristic destinations. However, most of the studies in this group do not propose a comprehensive framework for considering gastronomy tourism as an instrument for place branding. Du Rand and Heath (2006) propose a conceptual model based on the case of a South African analysis.

The third group shows an emerging trend of considering gastronomy tourism to differentiate and promote places. For instance, Pearson and Pearson (2015) study the co-branding effect between the United Nations and cities that are prosperous in becoming UNESCO Creative Cities of Gastronomy. Their study suggests that to obtain this recognition a substantial involvement of different stakeholders (e.g. government, food suppliers, restaurants, hotels, food markets, and the community) is necessary. In addition, a continuous investment is necessary to build brand awareness and positive identity among travelers, investors, and residents. It is evident there is scarce research in the gastronomy field (Beltrán *et al.* 2016). The literature review conducted in this chapter suggests that theory development in gastronomy tourism as a branding tool is at an early stage. Scholars and destination management organizations are recognizing the power of using gastronomy as an asset to differentiate places, develop economies, to build brands, and to develop a prosperous cultural tourism market.

Place branding

Braun and Zenker (2010) define place branding as "a network of associations in the consumers' mind based on the visual, verbal, and behavioral expression of a place, which is embodied through the aims, communication, values, and the general culture of the place's stakeholders and the overall place design." Place branding is a concept that has gained recognition recently as a strategic mechanism to differentiate places worldwide (Govers and Go 2016: 3). The study of place branding is needed to make a country's identity, awareness, equity, and loyalty work on behalf of the development of a prosperous economy and its residents (Falkheimer 2016). Even though several places try to differentiate using the same product (e.g. gastronomy tourism, cultural tourism, adventure tourism, eco-tourism, etc.), they compete among themselves to have an effective positioning and a strong place brand equity (Zenker and Martin 2011; Chacko 1996).

As places and destinations are fiercely competing among each other to generate sustainable competitive advantage and effective branding positioning in the minds of travelers with the goal to increase tourist visits and spending, branding techniques and procedures are necessary at the destination and place level (Herstein *et al.* 2014). Che-Ha et al. (2016) state that places have the ability to develop brand elements in similar manners as organizations. The procedures might appear similar but the process is more complex (Hankinson 2015). According to different scholars, places are able to develop place branding elements such as place brand equity and its elements (e.g. place brand image, place brand awareness, place brand quality, and place brand loyalty) with the use of gastronomy as a critical marketing instrument for effective positioning and branding competitive advantage (Tsai and Wang 2017; Sahin 2015; Williams *et al.* 2014).

To sum up, places may use gastronomy tourism to develop place branding elements that might help these places to create an effective positioning and sustainable competitive advantage by creating memorable experiences with the gastronomic offers they present to travelers in the extremely competitive tourism world. However, places need to adapt original dimensions of branding in order to brand places (countries, cities, and similar geographical entities) due to their complicated character (Lin *et al.* 2011). The following sections discuss the role of gastronomy tourism as a critical marketing and branding instrument together with the development of gastro-experiences, and place brand equity components.

Gastronomy tourism

To begin with, gastronomy tourism falls under the market of cultural tourism (Jovicic 2016) which suggests tourism movement of travelers for uniquely cultural activities. To specify, gastronomy tourism is a form of cultural tourism that fosters the interest of travel looking for the delight of prepared food, drinks and other related food events that may generate remarkable gastronomic experiences (Jalis *et al.* 2009). A traveler who is genuinely interested in gastronomy is regularly engaged in savoring, cooking, testing, exploring, and commenting about gastronomy

(Sidali *et al.* 2015). In this respect, gastronomy tourism does not only center on gastronomic offers but also centers on similar efforts that may reflect local cultural values and local traditions to international travelers (Medina 2015). The concept of gastronomy tourism is viewed as an innovative marketing instrument to build experiences, branding, and loyal travelers. Therefore, gastronomy tourism is being distinguished as significant in branding and marketing assets for place differentiation rather than merely as a strategy to produce economic prosperity (Martins 2016).

Gastronomy tourism is a unique mechanism in the branding process for places, cities, and destinations as it is a type of cultural tourism that does not have restrictions of seasonality and might be promoted all year long. It is a sustainable alternative for some places that do not benefit from natural and historical resources (e.g. sun, sea, and sand) (Kivela and Crotts 2006). This suggests that gastronomy tourism is a needed strategic instrument for sustainable and effective positioning (Dogan and Petkovic 2016).

The role of gastronomy tourism on place branding

The literature suggests the development of place branding through events and meetings (Richards and Richards 2017). A new emerging stream of literature suggests the development of place branding elements through gastronomy tourism (Gordin *et al.* 2016; Beltrán *et al.* 2016). Such opportunity to add to the body of knowledge is taken in the development of the present chapter. Therefore, firstly this section discusses the relationship between place branding and gastronomy tourism and afterwards discusses how gastronomy tourism helps to create memorable experiences and to develop place branding elements.

Gastronomy tourism functions as a destination trigger, meaning that tourists select a specific place because of the expected gastronomic offers and projected experiences (Björk and Kauppinen-Räisänen 2014). The place (city, region, country) might augment the attractiveness of its gastronomic offerings and benefits by promoting them properly. This involves presenting unique gastronomic offerings, providing gastronomic tours, and promoting multicultural perspectives of gastronomy (Björk and Kauppinen-Räisänen 2014). Gastronomic events and festivals have also received important consideration in gastronomy tourism. This is in line with elevating positive perceptions and influencing behaviors as this is an effective way of displaying the authentic gastronomy offerings of a destination and presenting travelers a distinctive cultural experience (Silkes *et al.* 2013). Travelers with high and moderate motivation for gastronomy tourism may decide to attend gastronomic-related events to comprehend the unique traditions and culture of the place. By participating in these events, travelers acquire a realistic and authentic understanding of the culture and heritage (López-Guzmán *et al.* 2017). As the key factor of the gastronomy tourism plan is to showcase food offerings to travelers, marketing and promotional strategies (gastronomic events and festivals) discussed above play a relevant function on how places and destinations are perceived and experienced, which is the foundation for building place branding (Lee and Arcodia 2011).

Gastronomy and tourism experiences

In general, gastronomy tourism is a collection of food offerings, traditions, resources, services, cultural values, heritage, perceptions, and place distinctiveness (Du Rand *et al.* 2016). It has the ability to develop a positive and memorable experience of the place as it is the only component in cultural tourism that might be experienced utilizing all the human senses (taste, sight, smell, hearing and touch), thus intensifying the experience in a deeper manner. Through gastronomy tourism, travelers with high interest in gastronomy have the unique opportunity to have authentic experiences of the place (Williams *et al.* 2014). With gastronomy, places have the competence to communicate a sense of tradition, cultural values of the place therefore the genuineness of the experience, and the capacity to communicate history and status. In addition, gastronomy has the ability to increase value to the traveler experience and is related to a unique type of tourism for tourists in pursuit of new products and experiences that produce a high level of engagement and positive perceptions towards the place (Kivela and Crotts 2006).

Gastronomy tourism includes the participation of tourists in food-related events and gastronomy-related activities during their visit to a place, including participating in gastronomic festivals, buying local foods, consuming local gastronomy, experiencing gastronomy-related practices, and attending gastronomy classes (Shenoy 2005). Participating in these gastronomy-related activities, tourists develop authentic and memorable experiences (Tsai and Wang 2017). Brakus *et al.* (2009) define tourism experiences as subjective reactions and identified four dimensions of an experience (sensory experience, affective experience, intellectual experience, and behavioral experience). As Beerli and Martin (2004) suggest not only the experience is necessary to influence behaviors and perceptions but also the strength of the experience should be considered when developing brand elements. Therefore, the literature suggests that it is critical to influence the intensity of the experience instead of just creating an experience (Alderighi *et al.* 2016). Places that are not able to create memorable experiences by offering unique food offerings, services, festivals, infrastructure, and multicultural experiences will not be able to build perceptions of image, awareness, loyalty, quality, and value (Gómez *et al.* 2015). The next section explains how a gastro-experience has the power to function as a value builder.

Gastronomy experience as a value builder

Another noteworthy relationship is related to the role of gastro-experiences on developing brand value and its intrinsic theoretical dimensions. A gastro-experience is a genuine, unforgettable, gastronomy-related endeavor that includes first-hand reflections supplemented with cultural expressions of a place (Williams *et al.* 2014). Certainly, gastronomy plays a pivotal role on how travelers experience a particular place and most of them form branding perceptions of the place (Khoo and Badarulzaman 2014). Well positioned and differentiated place brands have the capacity to maximize the right selection of a destination and minimize the time and energy travelers invest in assessing alternative places to visit. Through the enhancement of gastro-experiences, places have the capacity to form brand value including place knowledge, behaviors, and place brand quality (Pearson and Pearson 2015). Kivela and Crotts (2005) conclude that gastronomy experiences are powerful instruments for branding and marketing a place.

Gastro experiences are valuable because brand equity expresses the value, the image, the quality and the knowledge of the place, as well as influences travelers to show loyal behaviors. Therefore, the richness of gastronomy and the creation of memorable gastro-experiences are recognized as valuable marketing tools for places to distinctively differentiate and position the place in a globally competitive market (Gordin *et al.* 2016). This affirmation is supported by Dogan and Petkovic (2016) that currently suggest that gastronomy and gastro-experiences of a place are notable assets in branding places. Similar studies examine how gastronomic offerings influence travelers' perceptions of their experience and place image that are formed after being exposed to the cultural elements of the place.

In brief, gastronomy offerings and their afterward gastro-experiences generate different valuable impacts on branding places, including key opportunities for places to develop their brand equity, brand image, brand awareness, brand loyalty, and brand quality. Therefore, places must gradually consider gastronomy tourism and the creation of gastro-experiences to position and differentiate themselves among other touristic places.

Gastronomy tourism place brand equity

Gastronomy and gastro experiences are considered important factors in building gastronomy brand equity (Gómez *et al.* 2015), because gastronomy and the experiences generated through gastronomy tourism are frequently linked with social norms, cultural values, lifestyles, and natural resources of a place, and thus convey a strong perception of value (Jiang *et al.* 2017). It is critically important to develop a strong place brand equity into travelers' memories. Gastronomy tourism not only communicates a perception of the legacy and cultural values of a place but also provides unforgettable experiences that display the genuineness of place and the capacity to communicate reputation and effective positioning (Okumus *et al.* 2013). Gastronomy tourism brand equity is an emerging area of destination branding research that appeals to travelers with memorable gastronomic experiences. The opportunity for destination managers to build place brand equity does not only assist places to develop awareness and positive brand associations of the place but also to emphasize gastronomy offerings and gastro-experiences that may increase loyal behaviors and perceptions of quality (Liu 2016).

Brand equity applied at the place level suggests to travelers about the social and cultural values, characters, identity, and quality of the place. Gómez et al. (2015) suggest that it is pivotal to comprehend destination brand equity through food and wine and also to understand how destination of origin and destination image are critical antecedents of destination brand equity. Liu (2016) also indicates that gastronomy brand equity has the capacity to influence travelers' behavioral intentions and satisfaction in numerous manners through quality and uniqueness of Taiwanese gastronomy. Alderighi *et al.* (2016) suggest that a perception of value will be enhanced after visiting the place/destination. Travelers gain the perception of value after finishing a visit to a particular place. Therefore, the creation and sustainability of gastronomy place brand equity might stimulate a connection among individual personalities, place symbols, place brand association, brand awareness, brand loyalty and may reassure the gastronomy brand quality (Jiang *et al.* 2017).

Effective place brands are considered key assets that generate incremental value for places (Pike and Bianchi 2016). The incremental value generated by the place brand is considered to be the place brand equity (Zenker 2014). Additionally, this added value that a gastronomic place possesses influences tourists to visit the place again, to have the willingness to pay higher prices, to experience regularly the local gastronomy, and to recommend the place to other travelers. Researchers in the area of place branding such as Lim and Weaver (2014) and Bianchi *et al.* (2014) define place brand equity via a tourist based emphasis. Konecnik and Gartner (2007) indicate that place brand equity includes perceptual components (awareness, image, and quality) and a behavioral component (behavioral loyalty).

In this chapter, the author considers that gastronomy tourism place brand awareness refers to the tourist's ability to recall and recognize a gastronomy place under different circumstances (Horng *et al.* 2012) and the intensity of a place in the tourist's mind. Place brand awareness implies that a perception of the place exists in the memories of travelers (Zenker and Beckmann 2013). Gastronomy place brand awareness is critical to motivate tourists to have knowledge about the place and to visit the place, consequently develop their positive brand image perceptions, brand loyalty, and assessment of quality. When places have effective positioning and marketing strategies, they comprehend that travelers' place awareness must be achieved before attempting to develop a positive and strong place brand image. Gastronomy tourism place brand image refers to travelers' functional, social, and sensory elements of gastronomy tourism (Horng and Tsai 2012).

Cai (2002) defines place brand image as "perceptions about the place as reflected by the associations held in tourists' memory" (Cai 2002: 723). Positive, resilient, and genuine place associations are important for building gastronomy branding places (Hanna and Rowley 2011). Similarly, gastronomy place brand quality refers to the expectancies and evaluations of gastronomy tourism products and gastronomic experiences. The role of gastronomy place brand quality considers tourists' assessments of the overall experience of the visit because tourists' evaluations regarding the quality of food offerings, experience, and service quality at the place are fundamental for building place brand equity (Jiang *et al.* 2017). Lastly, the behavioral component of gastronomy place brand loyalty suggests that memorable gastronomic tourist's experiences affect positively attributes of showing loyal behaviors towards the place. Lu *et al.* (2015) state that gastronomy tourism in addition to providing genuine experiences that affect positive brand associations, and the overall knowledge about the place, it has the capacity to augment tourist loyal behaviors to visit and to recommend the place. After tourists have a genuine and authentic gastronomic experience, they start forming individual preferences for the place and feel an increased desire to repeat the experience and to recommend the place to others (Sotiriadis 2015).

Gastronomy tourism and gastronomy offerings are elements that represent the cultural values and idiosyncrasy of a place. Places are able to use gastronomic offerings and unique experiences to differentiate and effectively position the brand place as leading destinations that offer value. For gastronomy place branding, Pearson and Pearson (2015) suggest that to brand a place first we need to ensure the quality of gastronomic offerings and authentic gastronomic experiences, second to build place awareness and image, and third to provide uniformity of service and product quality. In other words, providing memorable gastro-experiences not only influences positively the elements of brand value but also assists gastronomy places to build a consistent and sustainable place brand equity (Liu 2016).

The role of Destination Management Organizations (DMOs)

DMOs worldwide work on the promotion, management, and development of tourism components of a place including the management of gastronomy tourism, business tourism, leisure tourism, events, food festivals, services, attractions, and tourism facilities, just to name a few (Presenza *et al.* 2005). Places have the strategic plan to effectively position and differentiate the place from other global competitors. As the review of the literature suggests, using gastronomy offerings and ensuring memorable gastro-experiences, place marketers can achieve effectively these goals. It is essential that destination marketers consider some marketing strategies for gastronomy tourism and the development of gastronomic experiences and place brand development. Research indicates the following activities for consideration:

- The development of food networks between local food producers, hospitality and tour operators (Richards 2015)
- The promotion of gastronomy tourism through DMOs' websites and published materials (e.g. books, gastronomy-related souvenirs, brochures, booklets, and webpages) (Okumus *et al.* 2013)

- The planning of gastronomy festivals and the promotion of organic farming and agri-tourism (Okumus *et al.* 2013)
- The development of an effective digital marketing campaign (social media, blogs, the internet, mobile applications) promoting traditional and modern gastronomy cultures (national, regional, and ethnic cuisine) (Richards 2015; Horng and Tsai 2010)
- The promotion of specialty restaurants and related gastronomy places (night markets, food events, food demonstrations) (Horng and Tsai 2010)
- The participation in gastronomy-related competitions, events and international awards to increase global awareness (Pearson and Pearson 2015)
- The creation of gastronomic experiences through farmer markets, gastronomy fairs, gastronomy trails, gastronomy tours, and culinary training (Andersson *et al.* 2017)
- The use of high-level promotional materials (digital and paper formats) (Okumus *et al.* 2007)

All these activities suggested in the body of knowledge show that DMOs can use gastronomy-related activities to market and promote places. There are other gastronomy-related activities that have not been covered in this chapter. The following section describes how Peru uses gastronomy tourism as a marketing tool. This section develops a case of Peru and provides a SWOT analysis of the country from a Gastronomy Tourism perspective.

The case of Peru: the world's leading gastronomy place

Peru is situated in South America and is home to a segment of the Amazon rainforest and the ancient citadel, Machu Picchu, situated in the Andes mountains. The tourist attractions in Peru involve mainly sightseeing, ethnic, gastronomy, adventure, and ecotourism (Desforges 2000). Peru is the leading gastronomy destination country in Latin America with more than four million worldwide tourists who are interested in the culture, history, gastronomy, ecotourism, geography, and adventure. A planned tourist tour starts in Lima, considered the gastronomic capital of Latin America (Gilchrist 2016). Lima, the capital of Peru, has developed in the last five years to be considered a world gastronomy center.

Other regions of the tourist circuit include wildlife reserves in Madre de Dios and Paucartambo, Cusco, the enigmatic Nazca lines, a succession of enormous ancient geoglyphs, the colonial town of Arequipa situated in the Andean foothills and surrounded by a diverse series of volcanoes of which the most famous are the Misti volcano that reaches a height of 19,095 feet approximately, Chachani volcano that reaches a height of 19,931 feet approximately, Pichu Pichu volcano that reaches a height of 18,583 feet approximately, Sabancaya volcano that reaches a height of 19,606 feet approximately, Ampato volcano that reaches a height of 20,629 feet approximately, Hualca Hualca volcano that reaches a height of 19,767 feet approximately, and Coropuna volcano that reaches a height of 21,079 feet approximately. The journey of other important tourist attractions continues to Lake Titicaca and the floating reed islands of the Uros Indians both situated in Puno. Though the most visited region in Peru is Machu Picchu, the ancient capital of the Inca's Empire situated in Cusco (Desforges 2000).

Since being recognized in 2016 for the fifth consecutive year as the World's Leading Gastronomy Destination by The World Travel Awards (WTA), Peru is being promoted and branded as the best place in the world for gastronomy. Peruvian gastronomy competes with other gastronomy giants including China, France, India, Italy, Mexico, Spain, Thailand and the United States. The flavors of Peru (ceviche, Pisco sour, Anticuchos, Causa Limeña, Adobo

Arequipeño, Escabeche, and others) are an amalgamation of other cultures including Japanese, Chinese (chifa), Spanish, West African, Creole in addition to organic and regional delightful styles such as Arequipa's cuisine, from the Pacific coast to the highlands, and the Amazons (Gilchrist 2016).

> For Peru, gastronomy tourism is an important branding and marketing strategy to position our country as a global gastronomic place. This has been a joined effort between restaurant operators, local farmers, Prom Peru, residents, chefs, tourism leaders, and hospitality and tourism academic programs.
>
> *(Sandra Zubieta, Universidad San Ignacio de Loyola, Peru, personal communication, May 08, 2017)*

Peruvian gastronomy is a valuable marketing instrument to introduce and market Peruvian organic products. This is applicable not only to agrarian products but also the fishery sector and others (Nakayo 2010). Better place brand awareness of Peruvian gastronomy, organic products, and high-end cuisine help to motivate travelers to visit Peru. On the other hand, Peru has the need to continue understanding consumers' expectations in detail by conducting more market and scientific studies that help tourism marketers to design effective digital and traditional marketing campaigns. In this way, the messages sent to motivate international tourists and foodies (gastronomic experts) to visit Peru will be targeting specific expectations. Another area for improvement is the need to improve innovation and technological practices to improve productivity, quality, and effective business models (Tromme *et al.* 2017). In their article, Tromme *et al.* (2017) suggest that Peru will need to improve on government policies, gastronomy practices in different sectors, reinforce the gastronomy value chain that guarantees quality of products, strict policies to protect biodiversity to ensure the sustainability of these natural resources, and to promote technological innovation to improve production and quality of services. Table 18.1 describes some strengths, weaknesses, opportunities, and threats of the Peruvian gastronomy:

Much of the information in the presented SWOT analysis regarding gastronomy tourism of Peru are elements that different stakeholders in Peru are working to improve. Peru has advanced in the last ten years regarding the effective manner the government, the community, marketing organizations, universities, restaurants, food ambassadors, chefs, farmers, fishermen, entrepreneurs, financial institutions, and others utilize gastronomy as an instrument to brand and position Peru as a gastronomy leader in America and as a unique destination to visit for gastronomy, ecotourism, adventure, business, culture, arts, history, and geography.

Concluding remarks

Regardless of the limited literature and scientific studies in gastronomy tourism as a branding tool for place and destinations, there is an extensive agreement that gastronomy must be utilized as a means to market and brand a country, region, or city. The literature review suggests that most considerations have been focused on promoting and stimulating visits rather than using gastronomy offerings as a trigger of creating memorable experiences that influence the development of gastronomy place brand equity. This chapter could be used to assist destination management managers seeking direction regarding what components to consider in terms of creating place brand value through gastronomy tourism. This chapter suggests that gastronomic offerings

Table 18.1 SWOT analysis of gastronomy tourism in Peru

Strengths	*Weaknesses*
• 5th consecutive year as the World's Leading Gastronomy Destination • Organic products • Market Peruvian gastronomy all year around • Recognized chefs with access to expand Peruvian gastronomy to international markets (Europe, Asia, Oceania, North America) • Gastronomy and Tourism academic programs with international perspective • Gastronomy and Machu Picchu Citadel are well known internationally and tourists have a positive association with Peru • Unique natural resources	• The absence of a solid gastronomy system infrastructure (supply chain of activity including production, process, distribution, trading and financial capital) • The lack of an extensive lodging and restaurant infrastructure • The absence of the promotion and packages of gastronomy circuits that involve main regions and cities (Lima, Arequipa, Cusco, Puno, Tacna, Madre de Dios, La Libertad, etc.) • The lack of technological innovation to advance production and quality of services • The lack of formality in the gastronomy and related sectors • The lack of a continuous scientific research agenda and marketing studies to understand new trends and consumers' expectations regarding service, hospitality, tourism, and gastronomy
Opportunities	*Threats*
• International awareness that Peru is a key gastronomy place/destination • Social and cultural Peruvian values may be expressed through gastronomy • Promote agricultural products through gastronomy in festivals, restaurants, and competitions • Ongoing development of Peru as a destination for business, sporting events, gastronomy festivals, and eco-tourism • Exporting opportunities of organic products to international markets (North America, Asia, and Europe) • Opportunities to promote Cross-border tourism (gastronomy circuits to Peru, Brazil, Chile, Argentina, and Uruguay) • Develop a sustainable gastronomy value chain that includes small businesses (farm, fishery and community garden products, etc.) to produce high-quality organic products • Continue improving gastronomy education for national and international students • The creation and expansion of a Franchising Global Restaurant of Peruvian Gastronomy	• Unstable financial capital for entrepreneurs to develop new business ideas in gastronomy and hospitality • Government policies that do not support tourist to its fullest potential • Natural disasters that damage current infrastructure, businesses, harvests, and stop tourists visiting Peru • Insecurity in some regions of the country is a major concern for international visitors

help to create unforgettable experiences that in turn build brand value dimensions including gastronomy place brand awareness, image, quality, and loyalty.

References

Alderighi, M., Bianchi, C. and Lorenzini, E. (2016) "The impact of local food specialities on the decision to (re) visit a tourist destination: Market-expanding or business-stealing?" *Tourism Management* 57, 323–333.

Andersson, T. D., Mossberg, L. and Therkelsen, A. (2017) "Food and tourism synergies: perspectives on consumption, production and destination development," *Scandinavian Journal of Hospitality and Tourism*, 17(1), 1–8.

Beerli, A. and Martin, J. D. (2004) "Factors influencing destination image," *Annals of Tourism Research* 31(3), 657–681.

Beltrán, F. J. J., Cruz, F. G. S. and López-Guzmán, T. (2016) "Gastronomy as a Factor of Tourism Development: Case Study of the City of Córdoba in Spain," *Journal of Gastronomy and Tourism* 2(1), 1–14.

Bianchi, C., Pike, S. and Lings I. (2014) "Investigating attitudes towards three South American destinations in an emerging long haul market using a model of consumer-based brand equity (CBBE)," *Tourism Management* 42, 215–223.

Björk, P. and Kauppinen-Räisänen H. (2014) "Culinary-gastronomic tourism–a search for local food experiences," *Nutrition & Food Science* 44(4), 294–309.

Brakus, J. J., Schmitt, B. H. and Zarantonello, L. (2009) "Brand experience: what is it? How is it measured? Does it affect loyalty?" *Journal of Marketing*, 73(3), 52–68.

Braun, E. and Zenker, Sebastian (2010) "Towards an integrated approach for place brand management," 50th Congress of the European Regional Science Association: "Sustainable Regional Growth and Development in the Creative Knowledge Economy", 19–23 August 2010, Jönköping, Sweden.

Cai, L. A. (2002) "Cooperative branding for rural destinations," *Annals of Tourism Research*, 29(3), 720–742.

Chacko, H. E. (1996) "Positioning a tourism destination to gain a competitive edge," *Asia Pacific Journal of Tourism Research*, 1(2), 69–75.

Che-Ha, N., Nguyen, B., Yahya, W. K., Melewar, T. C. and Chen, Y. P. (2016) "Country branding emerging from citizens' emotions and the perceptions of competitive advantage. The case of Malaysia," *Journal of Vacation Marketing* 22(1), 13–28.

Collin Post (2016) "Peru wins fifth consecutive tourism award for best food. Peru Reports," available online at: http://perureports.com/2016/12/06/peru-wins-fifth-consecutive-tourism-award-best-food/ (accessed May 12, 2017).

Desforges, L. (2000) "State tourism institutions and neo-liberal development: a case study of Peru," *Tourism Geographies* 2(2), 177–192.

Dogan, E. and Petkovic, G. (2016) "Nation Branding in A Transnational Marketing Context: Serbia's Brand Positioning Through Food and Wine," *Transnational Marketing Journal* 4(2), 84–99.

Du Rand, G. E. and Heath, E. (2006) "Towards a framework for food tourism as an element of destination marketing," *Current Issues in Tourism* 9(3), 206–234.

Falkheimer, J. (2016) "Place branding in the Øresund region: From a transnational region to a bi-national city-region," *Place Branding and Public Diplomacy* 12(2–3), 160–171.

Gilchrist, A. (2016) "Lima, still a World Culinary Capital. Lost World Adventures," available online at: http://www.lostworld.com/travel-blog/lima-a-world-culinary-capital/ (accessed May 12, 2017).

Gómez, M., Lopez, C. and Molina, A. (2015) "A model of tourism destination brand equity: The case of wine tourism destinations in Spain," *Tourism Management* 51, 210–222.

Gordin, V., Trabskaya, J. and Zelenskaya, E. (2016) "The role of hotel restaurants in gastronomic place branding," *International Journal of Culture, Tourism and Hospitality Research* 10(1), 81–90.

Govers, R. and Go, F. (2016) "Place branding: Global, virtual and physical identities, constructed, imagined and experienced," Springer.

Hankinson, G. (2015) "Rethinking the place branding construct. In Rethinking Place Branding," *Springer International Publishing*, 13–31.

Hanna, S. and Rowley, J. (2011) "Towards a strategic place brand-management model," *Journal of Marketing Management* 27(5–6) 458–476.

Herstein, R., Berger, R. and Jaffe, E. (2014) "How companies from developing and emerging countries can leverage their brand equity in terms of place branding," Compe*titiveness Review* 24(4), 293–305.

Hillel, D., Belhassen, Y. and Shani, A. (2013) "What makes a gastronomic destination attractive? Evidence from the Israeli Negev," *Tourism Management* 36, 200–209.

Horng, J. S. and Tsai, C. T. S. (2010) "Government websites for promoting East Asian culinary tourism: A cross-national analysis," Tourism management 31(1), 74–85.

Horng, J. S. and Tsai, C. T. S. (2012) "Culinary tourism strategic development: an Asia-Pacific perspective," *International Journal of Tourism Research* 14(1), 40–55.

Horng, J. S., Liu, C. H., Chou, H. Y. and Tsai, C. Y. (2012) "Understanding the impact of culinary brand equity and destination familiarity on travel intentions," *Tourism Management* 33(4), 815–824.

Jalis, M. H., Zahari, M. S., Zulkifly, M. I. and Othman, Z. (2009) "Malaysian gastronomic tourism products: Assessing the level of their acceptance among the western tourists," *South Asian Journal of Tourism and Heritage* 2(1), 31–44.

Jiang, W. H., Li, Y. Q., Liu, C. H. and Chang, Y. P. (2017) "Validating a multidimensional perspective of brand equity on motivation, expectation, and behavioral intention: a practical examination of culinary tourism," *Asia Pacific Journal of Tourism Research* 22(5), 524–539.

Jovicic, D. (2016) "Cultural tourism in the context of relations between mass and alternative tourism," *Current Issues in Tourism* 19(6), 605–612.

Khoo, S. L. and Badarulzaman, N. (2014) "Factors determining George Town as a city of gastronomy," *Tourism Planning & Development* 11(4), 371–386.

Kivela, J. and Crotts, J. C. (2006) "Tourism and gastronomy: Gastronomy's influence on how tourists experience a destination," *Journal of Hospitality & Tourism Research* 30(3), 354–377.

Konecnik, M. and Gartner, W. C. (2007) "Customer-based brand equity for a destination," *Annals of Tourism Research* 34(2), 400–421.

Lee, I. and Arcodia, C. (2011) "The role of regional food festivals for destination branding," *International Journal of Tourism Research* 13(4), 355–367.

Lim, Y. and Weaver, P. A. (2014) "Customer-based Brand Equity for a Destination: The Effect of Destination Image on Preference for Products Associated with a Destination Brand," *International Journal of Tourism Research* 16(3), 223–231.

Lin, Y. C., Pearson, T. E. and Cai, L. A. (2011) "Food as a form of destination identity: A tourism destination brand perspective," *Tourism and Hospitality Research* 11(1), 30–48.

Liu, C. H. S. (2016) "The Relationships Among Brand Equity, Culinary Attraction, and Foreign Tourist Satisfaction," *Journal of Travel & Tourism Marketing* 33(8), 1143–1161.

López-Guzmán, T., Uribe Lotero, C. P., Pérez Gálvez, J. C. and Ríos Rivera, I. (2017) "Gastronomic festivals: attitude, motivation and satisfaction of the tourist," *British Food Journal* 119(2).

Lu, A. C. C., Gursoy, D. and Lu, C. Y. (2015) "Authenticity perceptions, brand equity and brand choice intention: The case of ethnic restaurants," *International Journal of Hospitality Management* 50, 36–45.

Mascarenhas, R. G. T. and Gândara, J. M. G. (2015) "The role of gastronomy in the quality and competitiveness on touristic destinations," *Cultur: Revista de Cultura e Turismo* 9(1), 60–83.

Martins, M. (2016) "Gastronomic tourism and the creative economy," *Journal of Tourism, Heritage & Services Marketing* 2(2), 33–37.

Medina, F. X. (2015). Tourism and Culture In Names Food And Wine Origin: The Case Of The Region Tokaj (Hungary), *International Journal of Scientific Management and Tourism* 1(3), 167–177.

Nakayo, J. L. J. (2010) "Peru: Country Report," *Training Manuals for Organic Agriculture*, 173.

Okumus, F., Kock, G. Scantlebury, M. M. and Okumus, B. (2013) "Using local cuisines when promoting small Caribbean island destinations," *Journal of Travel & Tourism Marketing* 30(4), 410–429.

Pearson, D. and Pearson, T. (2015) "Branding Food Culture: UNESCO Creative Cities of Gastronomy," *Journal of Food Products Marketing* 1–14.

Pike, S. and Bianchi, C. (2016) "Destination brand equity for Australia: testing a model of CBBE in short-haul and long-haul markets," *Journal of Hospitality & Tourism Research* 40(1), 114–134.

Presenza, A., Sheehan, L. and Ritchie, J. B. (2005) "Towards a model of the roles and activities of destination management organizations," *Journal of Hospitality, Tourism and Leisure Science* 3(1), 1–16.

Richards, G. (2015) "Evolving gastronomic experiences: From food to foodies to foodscapes," *Journal of Gastronomy and Tourism* 1(1), 5–17.

Richards, G. and Richards, G. (2017) "From place branding to placemaking: the role of events," *International Journal of Event and Festival Management* 8(1), 8–23.

Sahin, G. G. (2015) "Gastronomy Tourism as an Alternative Tourism: An Assessment on the Gastronomy Tourism Potential of Turkey," *International Journal of Academic Research in Business and Social Sciences* 5(9), 79–105.

Shenoy, S. S. (2005) "Food tourism and the culinary tourist." Unpublished doctoral dissertation, Clemson University, Clemson, SC.

Sidali, K. L., Kastenholz, E. and Bianchi, R. (2015) "Food tourism, niche markets and products in rural tourism: combining the intimacy model and the experience economy as a rural development strategy," *Journal of Sustainable Tourism* 23(8–9), 1179–1197.

Silkes, C. A., Cai, L. A. and Lehto, X. Y. (2013) "Marketing to the culinary tourist," *Journal of Travel & Tourism Marketing* 30(4), 335–349.

Sotiriadis, M. D. (2015) "Culinary tourism assets and events: Suggesting a strategic planning tool," *International Journal of Contemporary Hospitality Management* 27(6), 1214–1232.

Tellström, R., Gustafsson, I. B. and Mossberg, L. (2006) "Consuming heritage: The use of local food culture in branding," *Place Branding* 2(2), 130–143.

Tromme, J. E., Rivera, D., Gonzales, D., Villagarcia, A., Tostes, M. and Graglia, G. (2017) "Sociedad Peruana de Gastronomia," available online at: http://www.apega.pe/publicaciones/documentos-de-trabajo/agenda-de-innovacion-tecnologica-de-la-gastronomia-peruana.html (accessed May 12, 2017).

Tsai, C. T. S. and Wang, Y. C. (2017) "Experiential value in branding food tourism," *Journal of Destination Marketing & Management*, 6(1), 56–65.

Williams, H. A., Williams Jr, R. L. and Omar, M. (2014) "Gastro-tourism as destination branding in emerging markets," *International Journal of Leisure and Tourism Marketing* 4(1), 1–18.

Zenker, S. and Martin, N. (2011) "Measuring success in place marketing and branding," *Place Branding and Public Diplomacy* 7(1), 32–41.

Zenker, S. (2014) "Measuring place brand equity with the advanced Brand Concept Map (aBCM) method," Place Branding and Public Diplomacy 10(2), 158–166.

Zenker, S. and Beckmann, S. C. (2013) "My place is not your place–different place brand knowledge by different target groups," Journal of Place Management and Development 6(1), 6–17.

Further Reading

Chua-Eoan, H. (2017) "Bloomberg Pursuits: Why Lima Is the World's Best Food City, by the Numbers," available online at: www.bloomberg.com/news/articles/2017-03-02/why-lima-is-the-world-s-best-food-city-by-the-numbers (accessed May 12, 2017).

19

Understanding the destination branding strategies for hospitality and tourism engagement in an intelligent rural community

Samuel Adeyinka-Ojo and Vikneswaran Nair

Introduction

Branding of tourism destinations gained attention in the academic research in 1998 during the annual Travel and Tourism Research Association (TTRA)'s conference (Blain, Levy and Ritchie 2005). The first journal that focused on destination branding was published in 1999 and the subject began to be featured in literature ever since then (Pike 2009). Increase in international competitiveness and globalization has led tourism destinations in recent times to differentiate themselves. The application and adaptation of the traditional marketing strategy to destinations have become well known (Baker and Cameron 2008). Despite extant destination branding research that deals with the importance of tourism destination branding most of these studies are focused on: (a) urban tourist destinations – for example, countries, nations and city-states branding (Ryan and Simmons 1999; Crockett and Wood 1999; Hudson and Ritchie 2009; Fan 2010); (b) regions branding (Cai 2002); (c) states branding (Lee, Cai and O'Leary 2006); and (d) cities branding (Balakrishnan 2008; Stole 2011). In addition to that, branding has been adapted to events in tourism destinations (Brown, Chalip, Jago and Mules 2004; Kalkstein-Silkes 2007; Esu and Arrey 2009). However, destination branding strategies for hospitality and tourism engagement in rural community has received few or no empirical studies. This study is positioned to fill the existing gaps in the destination branding research. Therefore, the aim of this chapter is to develop an understanding of destination branding strategies (DBS) for hospitality and tourism engagement (HTE) in an intelligent rural community. Hence, the main research question that is being investigated for this is: What are the destination branding strategies for hospitality and tourism engagement in an intelligent rural community?

Literature review

This section describes destination branding concepts, destination branding strategies such as strategic stages for hospitality and tourism destination brand building, challenges of hospitality and tourism destination branding, and critical success factors (CSFs) of developing DBS. According to Baker and Cameron (2008), due to increased competitiveness in the global environment, destinations such as nations, states, regions, cities, towns and districts need to differentiate themselves from competitors if they are to attract investment and visitors. A key strategy to achieve this success may be referred to as destination branding strategies (Baker and Cameron 2008) that are applicable to hospitality and tourism in rural destination.

Destination branding concepts and strategies

Morrison and Anderson (2002) describe destination branding as a way of disseminating the uniqueness of a destination's identity through differentiable features from other competing locations. According to Cai (2002), destination branding is selecting a consistent mix of brand elements to identify and distinguish a destination through positive image building. However, this study adopted the definition of destination branding as defined by Blain et al. (2005: 337), where it is stated that: destination branding is a set of marketing activities that: (1) support the creation of a name, symbol, logo, word, mark or other graphics that readily identifies and differentiates a destination; (2) consistently conveys the expectations of a memorable travel experience that is uniquely associated with the destination; (3) serves to consolidate and reinforce the emotional connection between the tourist and the destination; and (4) reduces consumers' search costs and perceived risk. This definition appears to be holistic by taking into consideration the basic elements of tourism destination and the benefits of destination branding. All these characteristics outlined in the definition will create a destination image and branding process that impacts positively on the visitor's decision in choosing a destination to visit. Although there are ample amount of literature sources from the academic stand point as well as practitioners' perspective that destination branding is still a relatively new field (Tasci 2011).

Meanwhile, destination branding is used to promote a specific tourism destination or location. This tourism destination could be a city, town, village or iconic center. For example, destination branding is a term commonly used by scholars in tourism literature to explain how to develop a unique identity for a tourism destination that helps the actual and potential tourists to differentiate a given tourism location from another destination (Greaves and Skinner 2010). Destination branding strategies are presented systematically in the following sections starting with the strategic stages of destination brand building.

Stages in destination branding strategies for hospitality and tourism engagement

This section reviews different stages involved in hospitality and tourism destination brand building. This is important in order to provide an appropriate platform to uncover research gaps in terms of strategic stages of developing DBS for HTE in an intelligent rural community. In this sense, Morgan and Pritchard (2004) have developed five stages involved in destination brand building namely: (a) market investigation, analysis and strategic recommendations; (b) brand identity developments; (c) brand launch and introduction: communicating the vision; (d) brand implementation; and (e) monitoring, evaluation and review.

According to Morgan and Pritchard (2010: 68), the first step in destination brand building is to identify or "establish the core values of the destination" that would attract or "hold saliency for potential tourists". This is followed by market investigation. Subsequently, the next phase is to build the brand identity, communicating the brand vision, launching and implementation. Unlike regular products and services which have life cycles, the destination brand needs monitoring, evaluation and review from time to time. For these stages to be achieved successfully, shareholders should work together (Baker and Cameron 2008; Tasci 2011; Hankinson 2009, 2010; Hanna and Rowley 2011). Further to the existing studies, Anholt (2010) identifies nine main stages involved in developing a destination brand. These stages are: (1) identify your main segments in core markets; (2) involve your destination's key stakeholders from the outset; (3) undertake a destination audit through consultation with stakeholders; (4) undertake qualitative consumer research to identify what visitors in your core segments, and potential segments, think of your destination; (5) undertake a SWOT analysis and a competitor analysis for each main segment; (6) choose a brand-building model to build the destination brand (e.g. rational attributes, emotional benefits, brand personality, brand essence and values); (7) establish a steering group to support in developing the destination brand and in maintaining and driving it forward; (8) appoint a branding agency, or expert to help develop the destination brand; and (9) implement the destination brand (execution and launching).

Challenges in branding strategies for hospitality and tourism destinations

In view of the steps involved in destination branding building outlined from the literature, there are challenges which could inhibit the successful implementation of these different stages. In this regard, Baker and Cameron (2008) observe that despite the benefits of destination branding, there are different challenges faced by destination marketers in developing a destination brand for hospitality and tourism destination. These issues are classified into three namely, financial, political and environmental challenges (Morgan and Pritchard 2010). In most cases, destination management and marketing organizations (DMMOs) have very limited financial resources coupled with political strife or instability in some destinations, economic downsizing, terrorism, wars, outbreak of diseases, negative media coverage and other environmental disasters which affect destination image and brand building efforts (Morgan and Pritchard 2010).

In addition, another constraint to tourism destination branding is the lack of sole control over product and marketing programs unlike regular products and services where a single organization can handle or provide direction for its marketing activities (Morgan and Pritchard, 2004). Furthermore, destination politics is also identified as one of the challenges of destination brand building. According to Baker and Cameron (2008), destination politics is concerned with the complexity of the tourism offerings as well as the issue of multiple stakeholders and the complex relationship among the stakeholders which poses an obstacle for an effective tourism destination branding process. Other factors include difficulty of communicating brand benefits, and brand promise (Baker and Cameron 2008).

Anholt (2010) summarizes eight key challenges in developing a destination brand. These challenges are: (1) understanding visitors and non-visitors; (2) achieving stakeholder buy-in to the destination brand; (3) destination brand architecture (relationship between national and regions brands); (4) stretching the brand through partnership (seeking suitable brand partners for example, airlines, non-governmental organisations (NGOs), government ministries, development agencies); (5) user-generated content and social networking (consider the threat and opportunity); (6) brand coherence: image and cliché (distinguish between stereotypes and icons); (7) branding on a budget (no budget is too small for a destination brand); and (8) brand lifespan and rebrand (otherwise known as destination brand fashion curve to illustrate destination brand life cycle which consists of fashionable, famous, familiar, fatigued and refreshment unlike the phases of product life cycle such as introduction, growth, maturity, saturation and decline). Braun, Kavaratis and Zenker (2010) also mention that in developing destination brand, one of the constraints include the local residents' characteristics and reputation.

Critical success factors in developing a destination brand

This section reviews critical success factors (CSFs) and sub-components of CSFs. These CSFs are key elements in branding strategies for destination brand building. Critical success factors explain why destination marketing practices may achieve the target goals and why these may not be achieved due to the failure of a tourism destination to apply or utilize resources at its disposal to build a successful destination brand (Rainisto 2003). In this sense, the adoption of branding from the marketing paradigm to tourism destination presents a serious challenge to tourism destination stakeholders on what should be a standard for CSFs in developing a destination brand (Hankinson 2009). Due to these challenges, there are limited tourism studies that focus on the best options or managerial concepts to be applied (Hankinson 2009).

However, there are few studies which appear to have unanimously accepted the following factors as being critical in destination branding. For example, Baker and Cameron (2008: 93) identify 33 success factors which are categorized into four main categories. These categories include: strategic orientation; destination identity and image; stakeholder involvement; and brand implementation, monitoring and review (Baker and Cameron, 2008). Hankinson (2001, 2009, 2010) developed antecedents of successful destination branding such as stakeholder partnerships, brand leadership, departmental coordination, brand communication, and brand culture; in addition, brand reality (experience) and brand architecture are identified as mediating factors. Furthermore, Hanna and Rowley (2011) have come up with a multi-level conceptual framework of strategic place brand developed to assist destination managers in applying a comprehensive approach on how a place brand should be managed. It must be stated that, the identified factors in Hanna and Rowley's framework were designed mainly for place management. The factors identified in the framework include the following: brand architecture, brand evaluation, stakeholder engagement, brand communications, brand experience, brand identity and brand leadership these are crucial in determining the CSFs.

Rainisto (2003) develops nine attributes of success factors for place branding which were applied to cities in Northern Europe such as Helsinki, Stockholm, Copenhagen and Chicago, in North America. These success factors are planning group, vision and strategic analysis, place identity and place image, public-private partnerships, and leadership which represent the core destination brand building process. Other factors are, local development, political unity, and global market place. These are required to meet the challenges of the macro-environment where destination brand practices are performed (Rainisto 2003). Other authors include Stole (2011) who identifies factors such as stakeholder engagement, stakeholder partnership, brand leadership, destination identity, destination image and brand reality. To sum up, in building a rural tourism destination brand it is imperative to identify CSFs that are specific to the destination because successful brands involve the application of dynamic marketing strategies which is not always easy to achieve (Morgan and Pritchard 2004). Besides all these arguments, it is essential to also consider and elaborate on the methodology adopted in conducting this research and the study context.

Case study: Bario as an intelligent rural community[1]

Methodology

Bario is a rural Kelabit community located in the heart of Borneo, Sarawak in Malaysia. The occupational identity of Bario is the traditional paddy rice farming which has brought international awards to this local community of 1,200 people (Malaysian Government 2011). Bario is situated 3,200 feet or at an altitude of 1,100m above sea-level (Jiwan, Paul, Teo and Jiwan 2006; Adeyinka-Ojo and Khoo-Lattimore 2013). This rural community is accessible with an 18-seater Twin Otter aircraft twice a day, depending on the weather conditions because the flying route to Bario is always cloudy. Bario can also be reached by four-wheel drive on a logging road for between 12–14 hours from the nearest major city of Miri (Jiwan, Paul, Teo and Jiwan 2006). Bario lacks modern infrastructure and superstructures such as good roads, drinkable water, electricity, hotels, modern houses, banks, a post office, and a senior high school. There are few infrastructures which include a police post, an immigration office, an airport, a community clinic, a forestry department, and a telecommunication facility, an integrated modern rice milling factory, a primary school and a junior high school equipped with computers.

On August 10, 2001, in New York, the World Teleport Association (WTA) announced Bario as one of the top seven intelligent communities in the world (Bulan and Bulan-Dorai 2004: 207). The WTA is the world's only international trade association for teleports and their development partners (Bulan and Bulan-Dorai 2004: 207). In other words, WTA focuses on the business of satellite communications from the grassroots. A review of the press release on the WTA website indicates that the top seven communities are Bario (Malaysia); Ennis (Ireland); LaGrange, Georgia, Nevada, Missouri, and New York City, New York (United States of America); Singapore; and Sunderland (England). Interestingly, Bario is the only rural community from a developing and developed country among the seven destinations. The remaining awardees were from developed countries and they are either a city or a country.

The press release from the WTA website also indicates that the WTA Intelligent Community Forum described the context in which the Bario community was chosen for the award. Bario is viewed as a community that has employed the best application of broadband technology for the common goal of not only creating prosperity, but ensuring that it is shared by all levels of society. One of the major highlights in Bario is that this village was the first rural destination in Malaysia to pioneer the use of internet (eBario in 2001) and also established the first community radio station, called Bario Community Radio, in Malaysia. These projects were sponsored by the Canadian and Malaysian governments (Bulan and Bulan-Dorai 2004). Major institutions in Bario were installed with Very Small Aperture Terminal (VSAT); such places include the public secondary school, community clinic, telecentre, airport and police station. In addition, on March 6, 2002 the Bario community reached another milestone for being given the Industry Innovators Award in New York. The award was given by the Society of Satellite Professionals International (SSPI). This award was received on behalf of the community by the then Principal of Bario's government-run secondary school, and a university don who represented the vice chancellor of a federal-owned institution of higher learning, University Malaysia Sarawak (UNIMAS) in New York. The award was in recognition of UNIMAS' contribution to the success of the Bario project (Bulan and Bulan-Dorai 2004).

The adoption of ICT and internet or telecentre in Bario is important to this study because potential visitors and repeat tourists on a visit find Bario to be well connected to the outside world. This is one of the branding strategies that has been promoted in Bario over the years in the global hospitality and tourism market. These views are consistent with recent studies in Bario and elsewhere that the telecasters have had a positive economic, social and environmental impact on tourism development in Bario (Lo, Cheuk and Atang 2014). Likewise, rural tourism destinations can be reached easily as tourists are able to make personalized bookings for their accommodation and tourism activities at the rural destinations (Reino, Frew and Albacete-Saez 2010). Based on the extant literature, there are no such rural destinations to date like Bario that have received numerous recognitions. Bario has received approximately ten awards as of 2013.

Data collection

A qualitative approach was adopted because of the exploratory nature of this study and as it was the most appropriate in answering the research question (Guba and Lincoln 1994). The purpose is to uncover detailed data that can be used in the data analysis (Lofland and Lofland 1995). More importantly, the researchers are interested in multiple realities of the phenomenon, rather than one specific answer. This study involved in-depth interviews as the method of data collection covered a period of six months from April to September 2014 by visiting Bario, the tourism ministry and DMMO responsible for the destination marketing of hospitality and tourism engagement in this local community. The researchers interviewed 32 respondents that focused on DBS for HTE in an intelligent rural community to the point where theoretical saturation was achieved, when additional data provided no new variables to the study's themes (Strauss and Corbin 2008; Jennings 2010). The in-depth interviews lasted an average of 75 minutes and were digitally recorded (Rasmussen, Ostergaard and Beckmann 2006), and transcribed immediately (Gubrium and Holsten 2001) to ensure the currency of the content of the interview by the researchers (Prayag and Ryan 2011).

Documentary evidence was also used to supplement the in-depth interviews. The use of documentary evidence is very common in a qualitative study (Bailey 2007; Creswell 2007; Yin 2012). For example, in destination branding studies, documents and records may include government reports, published international research, books, journal articles, newspapers and press releases (Balakrishnan 2008).

Data analysis

The six stages of thematic analysis were used to analyze the in-depth interviews as suggested by Braun and Clarke (2006). These stages of thematic analysis allow the researcher to familiarize with the data, develop initial codes, search for the relevant themes, review themes that have emerged, define, label the codes, and finally produce a credible report of the findings (Braun and Clarke 2006). Thematic analysis was used because it is a qualitative analytic method that allows themes to be identified by systematically reading and re-reading the data several times (Fereday and Muir-Cochrane 2006). Likewise, content analysis was adopted to analyze the documentary evidence. Content analysis is found to be a useful technique that can be used to analyse any kind of text (Esterberg 2002; Berg 2004: 286; Puvenesvary et al. 2011). The four criteria suggested by Scott (1990: 7–35) for the selection of documentary evidence were used. These criteria are authenticity, credibility, representativeness and meaning.

Findings and discussion

Findings from this study are aligned with the research question. First, the 32 respondents consisted of ten tourists, two destination branding experts, one academic researcher, six key informants from government agencies involved with tourism and rural development, a key informant from an airline operator, a mechanized rice farming investor in Bario, and 11 local residents. Findings are presented in the following five sections.

Rationales for rural hospitality and tourism destination branding

Findings show that there are various reasons for branding in rural hospitality and tourism destination, and in particular, Bario. A key informant from the Miri tourism task force (MTTF) group in charge of Bario at the Miri residence office, the regional administrative headquarter for Bario in Sarawak, Malaysia commented:

> So it is good that Bario is branded to differentiate the place from other rural destinations in Malaysia because Bario offers a unique experience in terms of accessibility which is mostly by air – that alone is a unique experience for the visitors . . . different archaeological sites to see the megaliths and stones monument . . . which are very rare to find in other parts of Malaysia.

Findings indicate that it is important that Bario should be branded because branding would distinguish Bario from competing rural tourism destinations. The respondents have provided several rationales for the branding strategies of rural destinations, particularly in Bario. These rationales include to promote longhouses/homestays, create a destination awareness, distinguish from competitors, improve local economy and job creation, maintain authenticity, create a niche market, segmentation of rural tourists, build high-end hospitality and tourism destination, geographic location and unique destination accessibility experience.

Roles of attractions in rural hospitality and tourism destination branding

This section seeks to explain the roles of tourism attractions in DBS for HTE in rural destinations. The importance of tourism attractions in tourism destination branding cannot be overemphasized because without these attractions in the first place, there would be nothing to brand. A key informant from the Ministry of Tourism in Sarawak shared these views:

> In Sarawak, our slogan is culture, adventure and nature – those are the attractions we are selling. Bario is very remote and located in the highland and these attractions are important in the branding of Bario. There are tourists' attractions in Bario that are not available in other places . . . like the cool weather. In promoting Bario as a brand, whatever differentiates the place and makes it a unique tourism destination should be used as important factors to brand Bario.

Bario is a highland and fundamentally its major tourist attraction is its remote destination, recreation forest and the Pulong Tau National Park. Findings on the roles of tourism attractions in destination branding from the respondents' opinions include value added activities, increasing tourist arrivals and receipts, unique selling propositions, promoting jungle and pristine forest experience, and potential premium destination where less is more, and there is no mass tourism. According to Leask (2010), these tourism attractions are the main motivators for tourists to choose such a place as a destination of choice to visit and these attractions serve as economic resources for the host community to benefit from.

Strategic stages of hospitality and tourism destination branding

There are few studies that have attempted to outline and explain stages involved in developing a destination branding (Stole 2011; Morgan, Pritchard and Piggott 2002). A volunteer from England who is currently in Bario commented:

> I think the first step is to find out what a destination . . . like Bario has got to offer through marketing investigation, or research of a kind to determine the type of tourist who would like to visit Bario; and these people are the people who would like to visit the community

> for holiday, to attend an event and to know the culture more rather than hearing from other people without experiencing the place.

Findings revealed that the following constructs are stages involved in destination branding strategies: marketing research and analysis, identifying destination core tourism offerings, destination brand planning, destination brand communication benefits and brand promise, destination brand launch, destination brand monitoring, destination logo and slogans, host community, other stakeholders, and non-stakeholders involvement, and brand development committee, strong local leadership, provision of infrastructures and superstructures, destination brand management and sustainability.

Challenges of hospitality and tourism destination branding

Based on the analyses of the views expressed by respondents, findings on the challenges of DBS for HTE from the context of a rural community are numerous. When asked about the challenges of destination brand building, a tourist from Germany stated:

> Accessibility and transportation could be one of the challenges of destination brand. Another challenge is that . . . the destination is not well known, where the image is known to very few people. For example, many people may not know about Bario until they get to Malaysia. Branding is a big project as it requires good funding and political will, I mean, government support.

Findings indicate that the first challenge is the issue of multiple stakeholders and lack of commitment, lack of financial resource, political and environmental issues, host community behaviors, difficulty of communicating brand benefits and failure to fulfill brand promise. Other challenges include destination image and awareness, identifying unique tourism offerings, lack of destination branding experts and manpower, lack of local leadership to drive the brand vision, geographic location and accessibility. These findings are consistent with literature sources on the challenges of building a destination brand. For example, the issues of funding, politics and environment have been reported in previous studies (Baker and Cameron 2008; Morgan and Pritchard 2010).

Critical Success Factors (CSFs) for hospitality and tourism destination branding

The CSFs are basically strategies responsible for the success or failure of hospitality and tourism destination branding strategies development. Extracts from the respondents' opinions on the CSFs of DBS for HTE in rural community are presented in the following statements. A tourist from the United States commented:

> It has to start with the relationship among the . . . Bario people . . . they should work with the local authority and the state to promote . . . and ensure that the destination image of Bario and its attractions are well communicated . . . the community has to build a kind of relationship that will draw support of the government and tourism board in Sarawak or in Malaysia . . . to preserve the culture and the environment . . . preserve the attractions in the area . . . so build relationship with the government and other businesses.

The views expressed by the respondents suggested different CSFs, in particular Bario. These findings include: (a) tourism and visitor information center; (b) innovation and creativity;

(c) value added activities and experience; (d) local destination logo and slogan; (e) host community participation and stakeholders; (f) unique destination accessibility; (g) provision of quality tourism services; (h) develop destination brochures; (i) cultural attractions strategy; (j) funding and infrastructures development; (k) eBario website, social media; (l) human capital development of tourism operators; (m) word-of-mouth; (n) heart of Borneo project BIMP-EAGA; (o) occupational identity, food, farming and forest (FFF) strategy; (p) develop a destination protocol; (q) stakeholders' relationship building; and (r) leadership of Rurum Kelabits Sarawak (RKS). This section has presented findings that seek to answer the study's main research question. The objective was to identify the destination branding strategies for hospitality and tourism engagement in an intelligent rural community.

Conclusion and implications

This study has found that DBS is crucial in the development of hospitality and tourism in rural destinations. This is because the challenge of HTE in a rural community is its limited drawing power and "individual rural destinations are often too small to form a critical mass required of a primary destination" (Cai 2002: 738). Therefore, a rural community that provides hospitality and tourism experience can brand itself by developing DBS to increase its economic competition and gain a share of the hospitality and tourist market (Tasci 2011). Based on the findings, the theoretical contribution from this study is that it has developed a model for DBS for HTE in a rural destination, and in particular Bario. This model has five main constructs and different sub-factors as depicted in Figure 19.1.

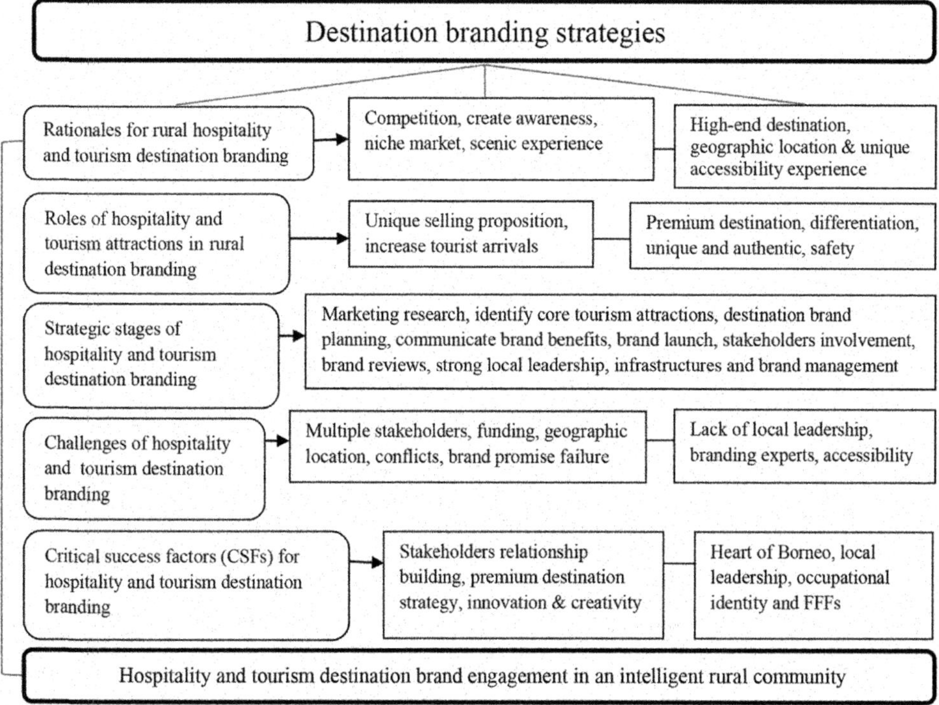

Figure 19.1 A model for the destination branding strategies for rural hospitality and tourism engagement

Implications for the practice suggest that destination management and marketing organizations, practitioners, policy makers, and destination branding experts in rural places should have a good understanding of the five constructs uncovered in this study. This is essential so that DBS for the branding of a rural destination can be successfully implemented in creating a favorable image for the destination, provision of memorable experience to trigger repeat visits, and increase the tourist arrivals and receipts. From the host community point of view as one of the main stakeholders, they should be involved in the destination branding strategy activities. For example, as illustrated on the model the host community should be educated on the rationales, roles of attractions and benefits of branding for hospitality and tourism in rural destination. The involvement of the local community would lead to the sustainability of the DBS, economic benefits and community well-being. In conclusion, this study has contributed to the scholarship of DBS for HTE specifically in Bario, an intelligent rural community.

Note

1 Acknowledgment: The funding for this project was made possible through the research grant obtained from the Malaysian Ministry of Education Long Term Research Grant Scheme (LRGS) Programme [Reference No.: JPT.S (BPKI)2000/09/01/015Jld.4(67)].

References

Adeyinka-Ojo, S.F. and Khoo-Lattimore, C. (2013) "Slow food events as a high yield strategy for rural tourism destinations: the case of Bario, Sarawak," *Worldwide Hospitality and Tourism Themes* 5(4), 353–364. doi: 10.1108/WHATT-03-2013-0012.

Anholt, S. (2010) *Handbook on Tourism Destination Branding*, Madrid: ETC/UNWTO.

Bailey, C.A. (2007) *A Guide to Qualitative Field Research* (2nd ed.), Thousand Oaks, California: Pine Forge Press.

Baker, M.J. and Cameron, E. (2008) "Critical success factors in destination marketing," *Tourism and Hospitality Research* 8(2), 79–97.

Balakrishnan, M.S. (2008) "Dubai – a star in the east," *Journal of Place Management and Development* 1(1), 62–91.

Berg, L.B. (2004) *Qualitative research methods for social sciences* (5th ed.), Boston: Pearson.

Blain, C., Levy, S. and Ritchie, J.R.B. (2005) "Destination branding: insight and practices from destination management organisations," *Journal of Travel Research* 43 (4), 328–338.

Braun, E., Kavaratzis, M. and Zenker, S. (2010) "My city – my brand: the role of residents in place branding," *50th European Regional Science Association Congress*, Jonkoping, Sweden, 19–23 August, 2010.

Brown, G., Chalip, L., Jago, L. and Mules, T. (2010) "Developing brand Australia: examining the role of events," in N. Morgan, A. Pritchard and R. Pride (eds) *Destination branding: Creating the unique destination Proposition* (rev. 2nd ed.), 279–305. Oxford, England: Butterworth Heinemann.

Bulan, S. and Bulan-Dorai, L. (2004) *The Bario Revival*, Kuala Lumpur: Home Matters Network.

Cai, L.A. (2002) "Cooperative branding for rural destination," *Annals of Tourism Research* 29(3), 720–742.

Cresswell, J.W. (2007) *Qualitative Inquiry and Research Design Choosing among Five Approaches* (2nd ed.). Thousand Oaks, CA; Sage.

Esterberg, K.G. (2002) *Qualitative Research Methods in Social Research*. Boston: McGraw-Hill Inc.

Esu, B.B. and Arrey, V.M.E. (2009) "Branding cultural festival as a destination attraction: a case study of Calabar carnival festival," *International Business Research* 2(3), 182–192.

Fan, Y. (2010). "Branding the nation: towards a better understanding," *Place Branding and Public Diplomacy* 6(2), 97–103.

Fereday, J., & Muir-Cochrane, E. (2006) "Demonstrating rigor using thematic analysis: a hybrid approach of inductive and deductive coding and theme development," *International Journal of Qualitative Methods* 5(1), 1–11.

Greaves, N. and Skinner, H. (2010) "The importance of destination image analysis to UK rural tourism," *Marketing Intelligence and Planning* 28(4), 486–507.

Guba, E.G. and Lincoln, Y.S. (1994) "Competing paradigms in qualitative research," in N.K. Denzin and Y.S. Lincoln (eds) *Handbook of Qualitative Research.* Thousand Oaks, California: Sage Publications Inc.

Gubrium, J.A. and Holsten, J.A. (2001) *Handbook of Interview Research: Context and Method*, Thousand Oaks, California: Sage.

Hankinson, G. (2001) "Location branding: a study of the branding practices of 12 English cities," *Journal of Brand Management* 9(2), 127–142.

Hankinson, G. (2009) "Managing destination brands: establishing a theoretical foundation," *Journal of Marketing Management* 25(1–2), 97–115.

Hankinson, G. (2010) "Place branding research: a cross disciplinary agenda and the views of practitioners," *Place Branding and Public Diplomacy* 6(4), 300–315.

Hanna, S. and Rowley, G. (2011) "Towards a strategic place brand-management model," *Journal of Marketing Management* 27(5–6), 458–476.

Hudson, S. and Ritchie, J.R.B. (2009) "Branding a memorable destination experience – the case of 'brand Canada'," *International Journal of Tourism Research* 11, 217–228. doi: 10.1002/jtr.720.

Jennings, G. (2010) *Tourism Research* (2nd ed.) Milton, Australia: Wiley and Sons Australia Limited.

Jiwan, D., Paul, C.P.K., Teo, G.K. and Jiwan, M. (2006) "Integrated highland development in Bario, Sarawak, Malaysia: an overview," *International Symposium Towards Sustainable Livelihoods and Ecosystems in Mountainous Regions.* Chiang Mai, Thailand. 7–9 March.

Kalkstein-Silkes, C.A. (2007) "Food and food related festivals in rural destination branding," Doctoral Thesis Purdue University, Indiana, USA.

Leask, A. (2010) "Progress in visitor attraction research: Towards more effective management," *Tourism Management*, 155–166.

Lee, G., Cai, L.A. and O' Leary, J.T. (2006) "WWW.Branding.State.US: an analysis of brand-building elements in the US State Tourism Websites," *Tourism Management* 27(5), 815–828.

Lofland, J. and Lofland, L.H. (1995) *Analysing Social Settings: A Guide to Qualitative Observation and Analysis* (3rd ed.) Belmont, CA: Wadsworth.

Lo, M-C., Cheuk, S. and Atang, A. (2014) "Telecentre, tourism and their impacts on Bario, Malaysia," *Middle-East Journal of Scientific Research* 21 (6), 950–961.

Malaysian Government (2011) "Population and housing census of Malaysia: preliminary count Report 2010," Malaysia.

Moilanen, T. and Rainisto, S. (2009) *How to Brand Nations, Cities and Destinations – A Planning Book for Place Branding*, Hampshire, UK: Palgrave Macmillan.

Morgan, N., Pritchard, A. and Piggott, R. (2002) "New Zealand, 100% pure. The creation of a powerful niche destination brand," *Journal of Brand Management* 9(4–5), 335–354.

Morgan, N., & Pritchard, A. (2004, 2010) "Meeting the destination branding challenge," in N. Morgan, A. Pritchard and R. Pride (eds) *Destination Branding: Creating the unique destination proposition* (rev.2nd ed.) Oxford: Elsevier Butterworth-Heinemann, 59–78.

Morrison, A., and Anderson, D. (2002) "Destination branding" available online at: www.macvb.org/intranet/presentation/DestinationBranding Pike, S. (2009) "Destination brand positions of a competitive set of near-home destinations," *Tourism Management* 30(6), 857–866.

Pike, S. (2009) "Destination brand positions of a competitive set of near-home destinations," *Tourism Management*, 30(6), 857–866.

Prayag, G. and Ryan, C. (2011) "The relationship between the 'push' and 'pull' factors of a tourist destination: the role of nationality – an analytical qualitative research approach," *Current Issues in Tourism* 14(2), 121–143.

Prideaux, B. and Cooper, C. (2002) "Marketing and destination growth: a symbiotic relationship or simple coincidence," *Journal of Vacation Marketing* 9(1), 35–51.

Puvenesvary, M., Rahim, R.A., Naidu, R.S., Badis, M. Nayan, N.F.M. and Aziz, N.H.A. (2011) *Qualitative Research: Data Collection and Data Analysis Techniques.* Sintok Universiti Utara Malaysia Press.

Rainisto, S. (2003) "Success factors of place marketing: a study of place marketing practices In Northern Europe and the United States," *Doctoral dissertation* Helsinki University of Technology, Institute of Strategy and International Business. Available online at: http://lib.tkk.fi/Diss/2003/isbn9512266849/

Rasmussen, S.E., Ostergaard, P. and Beckmann, C.S. (2006) *Essentials of social Science Research Methodology*, Southern Denmark: University Press.

Reino, S., Frew, A.J. and Albacete-Saez, C. (2010) "ICT adoption and development: issues in rural accommodation," *Journal of Hospitality and Tourism Technology* 2(1), 66–80.

Ryan, C. and Simmons, D. (1999) "Towards a tourism research strategy for New Zealand," *Tourism Management* 20, 305–312.
Scott, J. (1990) *A Matter of Record: Documentary Sources in Social Research*, Cambridge: Polity Press.
Stole, E. (2011) "The road to successful green destination branding," Master Thesis, Copenhagen Business School, Denmark.
Strauss, A.L. and Corbin, J.M. (2008) *Basics of Qualitative Research: Techniques and Procedures for Developing Grounded Theory*, London: Sage Publications Limited.
Tasci, A.D.A. (2011) "Destination branding and positioning," in Y. Wang and A. Pizam (eds) *Destination Marketing and Management Theories and Applications*. Oxfordshire: CABI.
Yin, R.K. (2012) *Case Study Research: Design and Methods* (5th ed.) Thousand Oaks California: Sage Publications, Inc.

Further reading

Berlin, A. and Martin, J.D. (2004) "Factors influencing destination image," *Annals of Tourism Research* 31(3), 657–681.
Braun, V. and Clarke, V. (2006) "Using thematic analysis in psychology," *Qualitative Research in Psychology* 3, 77–101.
Crockett, S.R. and Wood, L.J. (1999) "Brand western Australia: a totally integrated approach to destination branding," *Journal Of Vacation Marketing*, 5: 276–289.
Foley, A. and Fahey, J. (2004) "Incongruity between expression and experience: the role of imagery in supporting the positioning of a tourism destination brand," *Journal of Brand Management* 11(3), 209–217.

Part IV

Tourist behaviour

20

A critical review of tourists' behavior

Uğur Çalişkan

Introduction

In any economic activity, the aim is to meet the needs, expectations or demands of the target group, beneficiaries or customers. Destinations/enterprises may supply new services, but if the reasons why and how tourists make their consumption decisions are not well understood, these initiatives will result in failure (Decrop, 2006). That's why it is crucial to understand what customers demand and how they make decisions (Hudson, 1999; Pearce, 2005; Page, 2007; Swarbrooke & Horner, 2007; Chen and Phou, 2013; Cohen et al., 2014).

People have travelled for vacation purposes for centuries. Today, vacations are a very important aspect of modern life (Walker & Walker, 2011) and understanding consumer behavior and analyzing the factors affecting it represent the very nucleus of the study of tourism (Decrop, 2006; Demir et al., 2014). Since they have much more experience and information, contemporary tourists have higher expectations (Michalkó et al., 2015) and as one of the most researched topics, consumer behavior (CB) is very dynamic and it is a vital issue in tourism, because destinations are in very tough competition with each other and in order to increase or even to defend their market share, they always have to satisfy their guests.

The American Marketing Association defines consumer behavior as 'the dynamic interaction of affect, cognition, behavior and the environment by which human beings conduct the exchange aspect of their lives' (cited in Mattila, 2004, p.449) and consumers are involved before, during and after consumption (Mattila, 2004; Dolnicar, 2004; Beesley, 2005; Swarbrooke & Horner, 2007; Cohen et al., 2014).

In tourism, as in other service sectors, production and consumption happen mostly contemporaneously. The result is not a product; the customer generally can't see, touch, or smell the result before purchasing or after purchasing. The consumers don't own anything tangible, but they will have 'experiences' and 'memories'.

Unlike consumer goods, tourism products do not offer routine consumption and have different behavior patterns from other products and services (Morrison, 2013). This is especially true with regards to the travel component (both to and from destinations), which constitutes the biggest individual difference in tourism consumption (Swarbrooke & Horner, 2007). Clawson and Knetsch identified consumer behavior stages in tourism as:

- an anticipation or pre-purchase,
- a travel to the site segment,
- an on-site experience,
- a return travel component,
- extended recall and recollection

(cited in Pearce 2005, p. 57).

In order to understand what, how, and why tourist demand and purchases may lead a destination (or individual firms) to prepare effective plans and strategies (Hudson, 1999; Cohen et al., 2014) so as to conform with new trends (Swarbrooke & Horner, 2007), tourist behavior studies identify segments to reach and how to reach them effectively.

Concepts in tourism consumer behavior

Consumer behavior studies first focused on manufacturing industries; services came into consideration later. Researchers started to examine consumer behavior in tourism in the 1970s. Studies indicate that tourist behavior is a combination of many factors and in this section we will look into the most important concepts used in the tourist behavior field.

Decision-making

Decision-making is one of the most important and complex parts of consumer behavior. The biggest complexity in tourism stems from the fact that some decisions are taken when the tourist is away from the destination (Dolnicar, 2004), while tourists also need to make decisions while they are at the destination; for example, about daily excursions, meals, etc. (Choi et al., 2012). Moreover, tourism literature emphasizes that traditional (friends, relatives) (Xiang and Gretzel, 2010; Neuhofer et al., 2012) or cyber (travel sites, blogs . . .) (Volo, 2010) word-of-mouth recommendations, descriptions in the novels or travel guides (Herbert, 2001) have great impacts on decision making.

In consumer behavior, the decision process is composed of stages (these stages are addressed in the consumer behavior models section) and there are three approaches to decision-making strategies (Laesser & Dolnicar, 2012):

- *Economic decision-making* dwells on the fact that people behave rationally and choose the most satisfying choice among the alternatives. In tourism, emotionally-driven decisions and behaviors are abundant. Therefore, the application of this approach in tourism may be problematic.
- *Informative decision-making* emphasizes the influences of the internal (personal characteristics, feelings, age, lifestyle, occupation, education, beliefs, perceptions, past experiences, budget, etc.) and external factors (attractions, family, social status/roles, culture, subculture, etc.) on decision-making.
- *Simple decision-making* indicates that to save money and time and to avoid risks, tourists may choose the destinations that they are already familiar with.

Destination

Tourists take their decisions based mainly on travel purpose, knowledge or the perceptions about the destination (Michalkó et al., 2015). Tourism destination can be defined as the geographical space where touristic attractions and activities take place and it is amalgam of different components (Barnes et al., 2014).

Destinations act like 'brands' and are in very tough competition to attract tourists on a sustainable basis. Kozak and Baloglu (2011) define the destination competitiveness as ability to satisfy tourists on a regular basis and to offer different and better services than others. To have a continuous competitive edge, it is very crucial to maintain the satisfaction because in the cyber era, the positive (or negative) experiences can easily be spread all over the world within seconds and it will have incremental impacts (in positive or negative way depending on the comments) (Michalkó et al., 2015).

The branded destinations may differentiate themselves easier (Chen and Phou, 2013) and to create a brand, destinations should fulfill tourists' utilitarian needs and expectations and should touch their emotions and feelings (Michalkó et al., 2015). This will help destinations to build a 'sentimental' bridge towards tourists' minds.

In marketing literature many models were suggested to reveal the characteristics of brands and tourism literature permutes these models to understand the tourist behavior towards destinations (Barnes et al., 2014). These permuted models generally include following very closely related but also different concepts;

- *Destination image* includes personal interpretation of the information and knowledge of a destination (safe, calm, authentic, amusing, expensive, wild, rural/urban) (Baloglu and McCleary, 1999, Ekinci, 2003). The image of destination is one of the basic elements in the decision making process, and image creates a cognizance which will foster (if the image is positive) travel to the destination (Page, 2007).
- *Brand (destination) equity* is a very new concept in marketing and tourism literature and evaluates awareness level of the market about the destination by using the loyalty, image, perceived quality and value issues (Gartner and Ruzzier, 2011; Chen and Phou, 2013)
- *Destination brand identity and personality* tries to identify what type of human characteristics are linked to the destination in tourists' minds (for example, friendly, exciting, sophisticated, sincere, competent, rugged) (Aaker, 1997; Barnes et al., 2014).

Destination brand is still a 'crawling' concept and more studies are required to examine linkages between different components of brand and impacts of the destination brand in competition should be revealed.

Values

Value refers to the given importance of any tangible or intangible thing or action and it is used to decide what is 'good' or 'bad'. Values may be based on moral, ideological (political, religious), social (cultural/subcultural), and aesthetic norms (Rokeach, 1973), and they are stable, predictable and very influential on decisions and behavior (Cohen et al., 2014). Based on the value scales of Rokeach (1973), tourist behavior literature focuses on two basic values:

- Internal values (terminal), which are based on knowledge and some characteristics such as a sense of belonging, self-fulfillment, a sense of accomplishment, self-sufficiency, rationality, and self-respect.

- External values (instrumental), which are based on apparent elements such as a comfortable life, social recognition, family, freedom, health, national security, and culture.

Cultural values gain importance in tourism studies, and in these studies Hofstede's (2001) value dimensions are mostly accepted and used. These dimensions are:

- power distance (strength of social classes, hierarchy),
- individualism or collectivism (acting as 'I' or 'we'),
- uncertainty avoidance (tolerance/resistance towards ambiguity in society),
- masculinity vs. femininity (social gender differences and roles),
- long-term orientation (adaptation to new situations by using past experiences),
- indulgence vs. restraint (social control over the gratification of needs and desires).

Existing studies deal with Western societies and have difficulties in explaining values in a rapidly changing world (Matzler et al., 2016); further studies should focus on these changes and differences between different (European, Asian, African, etc.) societies, whether they are developed, developing, or underdeveloped societies.

Motivations

Any decisions or actions need a motivation. Motivation refers to 'psychological/biological needs and wants, including integral forces that arouse, direct, and integrate a person's behavior and activity' (Yoon & Uysal, 2005, p. 46). The motivations concept attracts a lot of attention in tourism studies because it influences expectations and satisfaction (Demir et al., 2014). Motivations are very personal; even in group travel, every individual has their own motivations (Walker & Walker, 2011). There is not any 'proper' motivator for everyone and no one is always influenced by one particular motivator.

The push-pull model suggested by Dann (1977) is mostly used to explain motivation and suggests that people are pushed by physical and psychological needs and desires, while the features of a destination pull them. In other words, 'push factors determine whether to go, while pull factors determine where to go' (Morrison, 2013). The push factors include escape from a routine physical and social environment, relaxation, exploration and self-development, improvement of family relations and social contacts, and having status/prestige. Pull factors include such things as historical/cultural/natural features, entertainment opportunities, and weather.

In 1982, Philip Pearce proposed a 'travel career ladder' (TCL) approach, similar to Maslow's Hierarchy of Needs (1943). Like Maslow's proposition which assumes once a person satisfies his/her basic needs (physiological needs, safety, etc.), then (s)he moves up to the next levels (psychological and self-fulfillment needs), the TCL emphasizes that when tourists become more experienced, their motivations change. Security and prestige are supposed to be motivators for less experienced tourists, while intellectual purposes and learning are motivators for experienced tourists. According to Pearce, escape, relaxation, achievement, and relationship enhancement are the common motivators for all tourists. Swarbrooke and Horner (2007) added that it is not only the acquisition of experience, but also changes in personal situations – like getting married, having a child, a reduction or increase in income, or an altered state of health – which change motivations.

Many academics have also attempted to create typologies of motivations by integrating theories. The typologies of Iso-Ahola (1982), Beard and Ragheb (1983), Swarbrooke and Horner

(2007), and Mill and Morrison (2012) are instrumental. The models attempt to categorize motivations into the following categories (Table 20.1):

- cultural and intellectual development (learning, discovering new things, skills, cultures),
- physical wellness and challenge (physical challenges in nature, relaxation, sunbathing, sexual affairs),
- socialization and social acceptance (visiting family and/or friends, or to make new friends; self-esteem/love from others),
- physical and psychological relaxation/escape (getting away from a mundane environment, to be in mystic, isolated places; spiritual fulfillment; romance; adventure),
- Mill and Morrison added 'security' as a motivation category, emphasizing that some people's perceptions have changed due to wars, terrorist attacks, and diseases.

Assuming that the motivations of leisure travel have mostly been fully researched, motivations of travel types such as backpacking, gastronomy and wine tourism, faith tourism, health tourism, rural and eco-tourism, dark tourism, and adventure tourism come into prominence (White & Thompson, 2009; Buckley, 2012).

Attitudes

Attitudes are an important aspect in marketing because they direct marketing activities and affect consumption patterns (Cohen et al., 2014). Attitudes are (positive or negative) expressions about objects or persons (Ajzen & Fishbein, 2000) and are not instantaneous feelings or actions (Cohen et al., 2014).

The attitude concept has cognitive, affective and behavioral components. The first element is bound up with beliefs, ideas, thoughts and attitudes towards an object. Affective components are linked with feelings and emotions. For example, if you like to lie on beaches instead of by indoor pools, a positive affective response may lead you to smile when you have sunny weather during a vacation. Behavioral components refer to past behaviors and experiences concerning an object.

Theories used to predict how attitudes impact behaviors are the 'theory of reasoned action', the 'theory of planned behavior', and the 'reasoned action approach'. These theories are sequential and are based on the studies of Ajzen and Fishbein. The theories assume that behaviors are caused by attitudes or subjective norms (how other people evaluate behavior and whether their judgements are important to individuals); if people have a positive evaluation and if they think other people want them to perform, the result will be a higher motivation (intention) and most probably action (Ajzen & Fishbein, 2000).

Perceptions

A perception is 'the process, by which an individual selects, organizes and interprets stimuli in a meaningful and coherent way' (Moutinho, 1987, p. 9). In other words, our perceptions are how we interpret visual, taste, olfactory, tactile and auditory stimuli and thereby understand the real world. People may perceive the same stimuli differently because of differences in lifestyle, past experiences, education or culture (Hansen, 2005). The perception concept in tourism generally focuses on perceptions of service quality, security and risks (crime, diseases, etc.), and sensation seeking; this is an important concept in tourism to help frame service quality and destination image, and also tourist satisfaction, loyalty, and involvement (Meleddu et al., 2015; Lin & Kuo, 2016).

Table 20.1 Motivation categories

<table>
<tr><th></th><th colspan="2">Cultural/intellectual development</th><th>Physical wellness and challenge</th><th colspan="2">Socialization and social acceptance</th><th colspan="2">Physical and psychological relaxation</th><th>Safety</th></tr>
<tr><td>Iso-Ahola (1982)</td><td colspan="2">Personal seeking</td><td colspan="3">Interpersonal seeking</td><td>Personal Escape</td><td>Interpersonal escape</td><td></td></tr>
<tr><td>Beard & Ragheb (1983)</td><td colspan="2">Intellectual</td><td>Competence-mastery</td><td colspan="2">Social</td><td colspan="2">Stimulus-avoidance</td><td></td></tr>
<tr><td>Swarbrooke & Horner (2007)</td><td>Cultural</td><td>Personal development</td><td>Physical</td><td>Personal</td><td>Status</td><td colspan="2">Emotional</td><td></td></tr>
<tr><td>Mill & Morrison (2012)</td><td colspan="2">Self-actualization</td><td>Survival</td><td>Belonging and love</td><td>Esteem</td><td></td><td></td><td>Safety</td></tr>
</table>

Certainly, perceptions will remain of importance and future studies will examine perceptions in the dramatically changing social, physical and technological environment of the tourism sector.

Satisfaction

Satisfied customers are the principal cause of sustaining activities, because satisfaction is a very conducive promoter for re-purchase, to advise others, or to create loyalty (Meleddu et al., 2015). By examining tourist satisfaction, destinations/enterprises may understand strengths and weaknesses and they may create effective plans and market segmentation (Herjanto et al., 2017).

Satisfaction is based on the judgments of pre-consumption perceptions (expectations) and post-consumption evaluations. Evaluations may result in *satisfaction* when the perceived performance exceeds (positive disconfirmation) or meets (confirmation) the expectations, or they result in *dissatisfaction* if they think the service/product should have been better (negative disconfirmation) (Oliver, 1980).

Perceived value, service quality disconfirmation of expectations, and performance are the focus of satisfaction studies and satisfactory features of products/services can be grouped into three categories:

- *Basic factors*, which customers assess as being essential; their presence has no effect on satisfaction, but their absence creates extreme dissatisfaction.
- *Performance factors*; these may increase satisfaction, but deficiencies in performance cause dissatisfaction.
- *Excitement factors*; these increase satisfaction, but absence doesn't result in dissatisfaction.

In tourism, 'cognitive' and 'emotional' approaches are mainly used to explain how tourists make their evaluations (Oliver, 1994; Bigné et al., 2005; Barnes et al., 2014). Cognitive approaches suppose tourists behave rationally and use experiences to evaluate a service/product, while emotional approaches consider feelings as an important constituent of the experience. These approaches generally take the environment, atmosphere or experiences of other people as basic stimuli. For example, people tend to enjoy services in an environment they would like to be in, but if they think their experiences are not as good as other people's experiences in a similar environment, they will not be satisfied.

Trust and loyalty

In order to build a strong relationship with customers, trust is very helpful and necessary. Loyalty is conjoint with two main elements; revisit intention and recommendation intention to others (Barnes et al., 2014). Consumers' intention to (re)purchase the service/product is closely related with how they trust the supplier. Repeated satisfaction will create trust and enduring trust will determine loyalty (Baker & Crompton, 2000; Maier & Prusty, 2016; Sparks & Browning, 2011).

Loyalty is not just an interest; it is commitment and allegiance to a person, group, or destination/enterprise (Kleinig, 2013). In contemporary tourism literature, loyalty is gaining importance and is considered to have vertical, horizontal, and experiential dimensions (Cohen et al., 2014).

- Vertical loyalty occurs when tourists feel loyalty to suppliers in different supply chains; for example, to an accommodation facility and a tour operator.

- When tourists feel loyalty to two or more brands in the same tourism chain (for example, to more than one hotel or travel agency), horizontal loyalty occurs.
- When tourists are loyal to a specific tourism type, particular destination, or accommodation facility, experiential loyalty occurs.

Segmentation

Since all tourists are not aroused by the same motivators and don't seek the same pleasures, it is necessary to identify the market segments. Segmentation can be defined as roughly homogenous customer groups with similar expectations and purchasing behaviors (Swarbrooke & Horner, 2007). Classical market segmentation is based on four criteria:

- Demographic
    - Age
    - Gender
    - Religion
    - Family status (size and life cycle)
    - Education level
    - Income/occupation
    - Education
    - Ethnicity/nationality
    - Generation (Baby-boomers, Generation X, etc.)
- Behavioristic (based on the customers' behavior towards a product/service)
    - Benefits sought (i.e. purpose of travel – business, vacation, health, religion, education, enjoys sports, events, visiting friends or relatives, etc.)
    - Usage rate
    - User status (regular, potential, first-time, etc.)
    - Buyer readiness stage
    - Loyalty to brands
    - Intention to purchase
    - Occasional buyers (Mother's Day, St. Valentine's Day, sports events, etc.)
    - Method of travel (by plane, car, ship, private or public vehicles)
    - Length of journey
- Psychographical
    - Personality
    - Social class
    - Lifestyle
    - Activities, interests and opinions
    - Values
    - Attitudes
- Geographical
    - Region (continent, region, country, provinces, state, neighborhood)
    - Size of metropolitan area
    - Population density (urban, suburban, rural)
    - Climate

Tourist typologies

Many researchers have attempted to classify tourists into comprehensive groups. These typologies may be grouped as traditionalists, constrained, and adventurous tourists. Traditionalists want to avoid risks and to be around familiar spaces, and can be sub-divided into resters, experienced, and contact-seekers. Constrained tourists may have some troubles with income or health, which determine what type of vacation they will have. Adventurous tourists are generally well-educated and they are willing to have venturesome vacations instead of relaxing travels.

Resters are generally not experienced, are cautious about vacations, and familiarity and security are essential for them. They enjoy relaxing vacations; they want to have tanned skin and go to parties. Package vacations are very popular with resters and they prefer to visit the same destination every year or well-known destinations. Even though they don't spend much time on planning where to go, they like talking about vacations very much. New friends and especially 'romantic' or 'sexual' affairs are important for contact-seekers and they prefer to go where they can have 'intimacy'. Experienced traditional tourists prefer generally well-developed destinations and require quality or luxury; additionally, they are looking for intellectual satisfaction. They care about cultural and environmental assets. They like having different vacation types in different destinations.

Constrained tourists may have trouble with their budget (for example, students, young people) or health (especially disabled and sick people). Budget-constrained tourists generally seek low-cost vacations and like using social/financial opportunities. People with health concerns prefer destinations with services available for them.

Adventurous tourists are energetic and search for new, different experiences and destinations. Environmental and cultural assets are *sine qua non* for them. They like to be away from the crowd of tourists. This type of tourist likes to meet local people in a 'non-commercialized' way, to experience the local culture in depth, and to vacation in the way that the local people live.

Table 20.2 shows the typologies of selected authors, which are tabled into traditional, constrained, and adventurous classifications.

Consumer behavior models in tourism

Researchers always try to comprehensively understand how consumers make purchasing decisions and they have proposed some models. The first models of consumer behavior were in the field of marketing and they tried to determine the relations between various factors influencing the customers' decisions. The majority of the CB models in tourism are permutated from marketing theories. The models generally consider decision-making as a linear but perpetual process. They consider decision-making in stages. The stages can be divided into three main phases, as Solomon (1996) does: the actions/decisions before purchasing, the purchasing process, and the evaluations after purchasing.

The models give particular importance to the pre-purchasing phase and consider this stage as 'need recognition', 'information gathering' and 'evaluation of information/alternatives'. Recognition occurs when consumers feel/notice any deficiencies or imbalances between actual states and their desires. Stimuli from commercial and non-commercial environments and increasing the capacity of products/services are considered as the initiators of recognition. After recognizing the needs, consumers start to search for information to decrease the risks and choose the best option (Quintal et al., 2010). Consumers search for information internally, externally or both. Internal searches utilize the memory and past experiences (Abdallat & El-Emam, 2007).

Table 20.2 Tourist typologies of selected researchers

	Traditionalists			*Constrained*	*Adventurous*
	Resters	*Contact-seekers*	*Experienced*		
Cohen, 1972	Institutionalized tourists (Individual or mass tourists)				Non-institutionalized tourists (Explorer tourists, drifters)
Cohen, 1979	Recreational tourists		Diversionaries		Experientialists Experimentalists Existentialists
Plog,1974	Psychocentrics				Allocentrics
Perreault, Darden & Darden,1977	Homebodies Moderates			Budget travelers Vacationers	Adventurers
Westvlaams Ekonomisch Studiebureau, (cited in Swarbrooke & Horner, 2007)	Traditionalists Rest-seekers Active sea lovers Family-oriented sea lovers Nature viewers	Contact-minded vacationers			Discoverers
American Express, 1989	Traditionalists Worriers		Dreamers	Economizers	Adventurers Indulgers
Dalen, 1989	Modern materialists		Traditional idealists Modern idealists	Traditional materialists	
Smith, 1989	Mass tourists Charter tourists		Elites Unusual tourists Incipient mass tourists		Explorers Off-beats
Urry 1990			Post-tourists		
Wood & House, 1992			Good tourists		

Steward, (cited in Hudson, 1999)	The bubble travelers		Idealized experience seekers Wide-horizon travelers		Total Immersers
Wickens, 2002	Heliolatrous (sea lovers)	Ravers Shirley Valentines	Cultural heritage tourists Lord Byrons		
Sung, 2004	Soft moderates Family vacationers			Budget youngsters	Enthusiasts Upper high naturalists Active soloists
Decrop & Snelders, 2005	Habitual tourists Rational tourists Hedonistic tourists Adaptable tourists			Opportunistic tourists Constrained tourists	

When internal information is not sufficient, consumers use external information sources, including non-marketing-controlled sources: personal sources (friends, relatives, colleagues) and public sources (reports and articles in newspapers or magazines about the product/service), as well as marketing-controlled sources, which are promotional and marketing material about the product/service (radio, TV, newspapers, magazines, social media, tour/travel agencies).

When they feel they have adequate information, they evaluate the information, alternatives and other suitable products/services. The consumers also evaluate whether to have a vacation at all, because tourism expenditures compete with other types of expenditures such as housing, education, and health. Destination image, brand name, symbolic values, price, and distance are the most cited criteria used by tourists to select the best alternative.

After evaluation of the alternatives, tourists may decide what type of vacation to have and where to go, or not to have a vacation. Even though some models ignore; religion, perceptions, values, culture, personality, family, social classes and (sub)culture, destination/product image are accepted as influencing factors on decision-making.

In the post-purchase phase, they evaluate their experiences about consumption and they create feedback according to how well their expectations have been fulfilled (Drinkert & Singh, 2017). Expectations can be delineated as what consumers desire to get and this is linked with 'what service providers should offer rather than what they offer' (Cohen et al., 2014). In tourism, the evaluation process starts when the tourists are on vacation and after the vacation they make an overall evaluation. Consumers use these evaluations to make decisions in the future on whether to recommend a vacation to their friends/relatives or discourage them from participation.

Apart from the models mentioned in Table 20.3 (which groups the models' assumptions into 3 basic phases; pre-purchasing, purchasing and post- purchasing), we can mention some other conceptual models. Andreasen (1965) proposed one of the earliest consumer behavior models focusing on information processing, while Zaltam and Burger's model (1975) suggests basic factors (beliefs, attitudes, situational factors) and relations between them affect the decision. Schmoll's (1977) and Mayo and Jarvis' models (1981), Gilbert's model (1991), and the Sheth-Newman-Gross' Model of Consumption Values (1991) propose that psychological (personality, attitudes and values, income, etc.) and social factors (family, social class, culture) influence decisions. Additionally, Sheth, Newman and Gross supposed that some conditional factors – such as St. Valentine's Day, Mother's Day, and wedding anniversaries – affect the intentions of consumers.

Jonathan Gutman (1981) introduced a 'means-end chain model', which assumes that consumers are aware of both negative and positive experiences and that they make a choice from among the alternatives in order to maximize the positive outcomes, satisfaction, and value achievement. The model makes a connection between attributes of product/service but mainly considers that consumers focus on the consequences, not on the attributes (Olson & Reynolds, 2001). Additionally, Sirgy offered a model proposing that 'consumer behavior is determined by the congruence resulting from a psychological comparison involving the product-user image and the consumer's self-concept' (Sirgy et al., 1997). The model is based on self-consistency and self-esteem motives. Briefly, the model proposes that if the self-image (actual or ideal) matches with the product/service image, the consumer will be motivated to consume (Gazley & Watling, 2015). In the case where one of the self-images (actual/ideal) matches with a service/product but the other doesn't, the consumer is moderately motivated, but consumption will not exist when none of the images match the product/service image.

Table 20.3 Selected consumer/tourist behaviour models

<table>
<tr><th rowspan="2"></th><th colspan="7">Pre-purchasing</th><th colspan="2" rowspan="2">Decision/Purchasing</th><th rowspan="2">Post-Purchasing</th></tr>
<tr><th colspan="2">Need recognition</th><th colspan="4">Information gathering</th><th>Evaluation of information/ alternatives</th></tr>
<tr><td>Francesco M. Nicosia, 1966</td><td colspan="2">Organizational communication efforts</td><td colspan="5">Information gathering and evaluations</td><td colspan="2">Purchase</td><td>Post-purchase evaluations and feedback</td></tr>
<tr><td>Howard and Sheth model, 1969</td><td colspan="2"></td><td colspan="4">Extensive problem solving (information gathering)</td><td>Limited problem solving (Alternative evaluation)</td><td colspan="2">Decision process</td><td></td></tr>
<tr><td>Wahab, Crompton & Rothfield, 1976</td><td>Initial framework</td><td>Conceptual alternatives</td><td>Fact gathering</td><td>Definition of assumptions</td><td>Design of stimulus</td><td>Forecast of consequences</td><td>Alternative evaluation</td><td colspan="2">Decision</td><td>Outcome</td></tr>
<tr><td>Engel, Kollat & Blackwell, 1968</td><td colspan="2">Problem recognition</td><td colspan="2">Information input</td><td colspan="2">Search for alternatives</td><td>Alternative evaluation</td><td colspan="2">Purchase</td><td>Outcomes (Satisfaction/ dissatisfaction)</td></tr>
<tr><td>Bettman's Information Processing Model of Consumer Choice (1979)</td><td>Processing capacity</td><td>Attention and perceptual encoding</td><td colspan="5">Information acquisition and evaluation</td><td colspan="2">Decision process</td><td>Consumption and learning process</td></tr>
<tr><td>Mathieson & Wall, 1982</td><td colspan="2">Need or desire for travel</td><td colspan="5">Information collection and evaluation</td><td>Travel decisions</td><td>Travel preparations and travel experience</td><td>Satisfaction evaluation</td></tr>
</table>

(*Continued*)

Table 20.3 (Continued)

<table>
<tr><th></th><th colspan="3">Pre-purchasing</th><th rowspan="2">Decision/Purchasing</th><th rowspan="2" colspan="2">Post-Purchasing</th></tr>
<tr><th></th><th>Need recognition</th><th>Information gathering</th><th>Evaluation of information/ alternatives</th></tr>
<tr><td>Moutinho,1987</td><td>Stimulus filtration</td><td>Search</td><td>Evaluation</td><td>Decision/purchase</td><td>Evaluation after purchasing</td><td>Decision-making for future</td></tr>
<tr><td>Foxall & Goldsmith, 1994</td><td>Forming desire or need</td><td colspan="2">Planning and decision-making processes</td><td>Purchasing</td><td colspan="2">Post-purchase evaluation</td></tr>
<tr><td>Middleton 'Stimulus-Response Model', 1994</td><td>Stimulus input</td><td>Communication channels</td><td>Buyer characteristics and decision process</td><td>Purchase outputs</td><td colspan="2">Post-purchase evaluations and feelings</td></tr>
<tr><td>Solomon 'Comparison Process', 1996</td><td colspan="3">Pre-purchase</td><td>Purchase</td><td colspan="2">Post-purchase</td></tr>
</table>

The models that we have mentioned here have been generally criticized (Swarbrooke & Horner, 2007), because:

- They are based on limited empirical research studies.
- They are simplistic in explaining the complex nature of the purchasing process in tourism.
- They consider decision-making as a process for individuals; they generally do not reflect group decision-making processes.
- They are generally based on the assumption that human beings act rationally. However, emotions, pre-judgments, political issues, etc. (and some models take these factors into consideration) may direct people to decide irrationally.
- They are getting 'old' because they are at least ten years old. This is a remarkable weakness because tourism and tourists are in a continuous state of change.
- Many of the models are linked to studies carried out in North America, Western Europe, or Australia. Therefore, they can't reflect new markets such as South Asia, China, Eastern Europe, Africa, the Arabic world, etc.

Fields for future research

Over time, many general aspects of CB in marketing have been studied and particularly in the field of tourism; some under-researched or newly-emerging fields in tourism exist, such as group or joint decision-making, cultural differences (i.e., emerging markets), responsible behavior patterns, minority segments, family and gender issues, security, Internet and technology, differences between generations and consumer misbehavior, and non-users.

- As the main branch of CB studies focuses on individual decision-making processes, group or joint decision-making is an under-researched field. Families, couples or single parents, friends or colleagues should be studied to reveal the differences between individual and group decision-making processes.
- The majority of consumer behavior studies give insights into Western (especially Anglo-Western) culture. Even though some studies make the point that cultural differences influence consumer behavior (Yu & Ko, 2012; Matzler et al., 2016), more applications from other parts of the world (for example, Eastern Europe, the Middle East, Africa, South Asia, the Far East, South America) are needed to give a comprehensive understanding of CB and to understand how cultural differences affect consumer behavior. It is worthy to keep in mind that the Chinese outbound tourism market is increasing sharply and the managers who want to attract them need to understand their priorities. Also, ethnicity requires deeper studies, since many countries have multi-ethnic populations. Thus, instead of universalizing customers, a deeper knowledge of their differences should be generated.
- Even though, studies on destination marketing are accruing, they focus on product/service features but destination branding literature, especially, destination brand experience, is still lacking. Destination brand studies should be broadened into the tourist–destination relation in different destinations and different types of tourism. Moreover, destination branding requires experimental studies linking the dimensions of image, brand equity, personality and the performance of the destination and the role of the Destination Management Organizations (DMOs) in branding.
- Besides being the consumers of future, the children are effective in families' current consumption decisions. The increasing impacts of children (the nag factor) on families' holiday

decision making process and on planning, management and marketing of tourism destinations need to be revealed.

- Ethical consumption and local cuisine experiences are raising trends and are linked to minimizing negative impacts of tourism on local people and the environment and embedding the local culture and new tastes. Better education and more experience have caused tourists to be more aware of environmentally friendly services/products, human rights, labor exploitation (especially child labor and the mistreatment of women/children). These and other issues related to ethics need to be studied deeply in the field of tourist behavior.
- Gender issues and minority groups such as disabled people, LGBT people and migrant workers have gained importance in tourism CB studies. It is likely that more researchers will deal with minorities. For example, migrant workers were traditionally considered to be a part of production not consumption (Cohen et al., 2014), but their travels to their homelands for vacations and health reasons have created a huge market. Moreover, disabled people are an important focus of accessible tourism. Also, gender orientations are already accepted as a valuable factor in vacation decision-making and the preferences of gays and lesbians for destination management need to be determined.
- Security has become a great interest, because of global terrorist attacks and natural disasters. As safety is one of the basic human needs, crimes against tourists are always important in decision-making, but terrorism has resulted in a shift of security concepts. Terrorist attacks (by Al-Qaeda, Daesh, PKK, neo-Nazis, etc.), Islamophobia, racist behavior all over the world, epidemic diseases (SARS, Mad Cow, AIDS, Pig Flu, Asian Flu, Zika) or natural disasters (tsunamis, hurricanes, earthquakes) have massively affected tourist behavior. Therefore, changes in tourist perceptions about security are vital for destination management.
- Tourism has been influenced considerably by technological improvements since the computerization of reservation systems in the 1960s. Since the new millennium and the increasing use of the Internet, technology has dramatically affected the tourism industry and tourist behavior (Mkono, 2016; Tussyadiah & Wang, 2016). These developments have created not only opportunities but also challenges (Xiang et al., 2015). While the number of Internet users and familiarity with the Internet are increasing – and around 47% of the world's population now has Internet access (International Telecommunication Union, 2016) – the Internet, social media and mobile technologies have made finding and accessing information, sharing knowledge, finding the best deals, and booking easier.
- Researchers should go on to examine relationships between tourist behavior and technology: for example, how tourists integrate online information channels and how these online networks transform tourist behavior, how online communication channels impact advertising/direct marketing activities, or what the new roles of travel agents will be.
- The demographic cohort of generation refers to the aggregation of people born in a certain time span and who share some common behavioral patterns (Li et al., 2013). Even though based on USA and Western societies, Baby Boomers (the generation post-World War II), Generation X (also known as Baby Busters, born between 1965 and 1979), Generation Y (born between 1980 and 2002) and generation Z (born after 2002) are the main generation classifications. All these generations have different characteristics. For example, Baby Boomers are in the Third age and they are generally supposed to desire relaxing but also adventurous experiences, while Generation Ys are more familiar with international travel (Morrison, 2013). Further studies should conceive differences between generations and determine which factors influence behavioral patterns in each generation. This notion of generation should also be examined not only in North American and Western European countries; researchers should study other societies too.

- The consumer behavior concept deals with the 'user', but for many services/products and destinations non-visitors form a significant market (Hudson, 1999) and tourism literature falls behind in explaining why people don't travel. Exploring the non-users' reasons not to purchase is crucial for tourism destinations; therefore, the non-user field is a 'new' area for future tourism studies.
- CB studies assume that people behave properly, but dissatisfaction, negative emotions, motivations, and pre-judgments may lead to improper behavior. Future studies should fill the gap of 'the dark, negative side of the consumer' (Cohen et al., 2014) and the subject of consumer misbehavior should be explored (Torres et al., 2017).

References

Aaker, J.L. (1997) Dimensions of brand personality. *Journal of Marketing Research*, 34; 347–356.

Abdallat, M.M.A. and El-Emam, H.S. (2007) *Consumer Behavior Models in Tourism Analysis Study*. Riyadh, King Saud University. Available online at: http://faculty.ksu.edu.sa/73944/Pages/ConsumerBehavior ModelsinTourism.aspx [Accessed 6th June 2016].

Ajzen, I. and Fishbein, M. (2000) Attitudes and the attitude–behavior relation: reasoned and automatic processes. *European Review of Social Psychology*, 11 (1), 1–33.

American Express (1989) *Unique four National Travel Student Reveals Travelers Types*. London, American Express.

Andreasen, A.R. (1965) Attitudes and Customer Behavior: A Decision Model. In Preston, L.E. (ed) *New Research in Marketing*, Berkeley, Institute of Business and Economic Research, University of California, pp. 1–16.

Baker, D.A. and Crompton, J.L. (2000) Quality, satisfaction and behavioural intentions. *Annals of Tourism Research*, 27 (3),785–804.

Baloglu, S. and McCleary, K.W. (1999) A model of destination image formation. *Annals of Tourism Research*, 26, 868–897.

Barnes, S.J., Mattsson, J. and Sørensen, F. (2014) Destination brand experience and visitor behavior: Testing a scale in the tourism context. *Annals of Tourism Research* 48, 121–139.

Beard, J.G. and Ragheb, M.G. (1983) Measuring leisure motivation. *Journal of Leisure Research*, 15 (3), 219–228.

Beesley, L. (2005) The management of emotion in collaborative tourism research settings. *Tourism Management*, 26, 261–275.

Bettman, J.R. (1979) Issues in research on consumer choice. In Wilkie W.L. and Abor A. (Eds), *NA – Advances in Consumer Research Volume 06*. MI, Association for Consumer Research, pp. 214–217.

Bigné, J.E., Andreu, L. and Gnoth, J. (2005) The theme park experience: An analysis of pleasure, arousal and satisfaction. *Tourism Management*, 26 (6), 833–844.

Buckley, R. (2012) Rush as a key motivation in skilled adventure tourism: resolving the risk recreation paradox. *Tourism Management*, 33, 961–970.

Chen, C.F. and Phou, S. (2013) A closer look at destination: Image, personality, relationship and loyalty. *Tourism Management* 36, 269–278.

Choi, S., Lehto, X.Y., Morrison, A.M. and Jang, S.S. (2012) Structure of travel planning processes and information use patterns. *Journal of Travel Research*, 51 (1), 26–40.

Cohen, E. (1972) Toward a Sociology of International Tourism. *Social Research*, 39 (1), 164–182.

Cohen, E. (1979) Rethinking the sociology of tourism. Annals of Tourism Research, 6 (1), 18–35.

Cohen, S.A., Prayag, G. and Moital, M. (2014) Consumer behavior in tourism: concepts, influences and opportunities. *Current Issues in Tourism*. 17 (10), 872–909.

Dalen, E. (1989) Research into values and consumer trends in Norway. *Tourism Management*, 10 (3), 183–186.

Dann, G. (1977) Anomie, ego-enhancement and tourism. *Annals of Tourism Research*, 4 (4), 184–194.

Decrop, A. and Snelders, D. (2005) A grounded typology of vacation decision-making. *Tourism Management*, 26, 121–132.

Decrop, A. (2006) *Vacation Decision Making*. Oxon, CABI.

Demir S.S., Kozak, M. and Correia, A. (2014) Modelling consumer behavior: an essay with domestic tourists in Turkey. *Journal of Travel and Tourism Marketing*, 31 (3), 303–312.

Dolnicar, S. (2004) Profiling the One- and Two-star Hotel Guest for Targeted Segmentation Action: a Descriptive Investigation of Risk Perceptions, Expectations, Disappointments and Information Processing Tendencies. In Crouch, G.I., Perdue, R.R., Timmermans, H.J.P. and Uysal, M. (Eds), *Consumer Psychology of Tourism, Hospitality, and Leisure*, New York, CAB International, pp. 11–20.
Drinkert, A., and Singh, N. (2017). An Investigation of American Medical Tourists' Posttravel Experience. *Journal of Hospitality Marketing & Management*, 26 (3), 335–346.
Ekinci, Y. (2003) From destination image to destination branding: an emerging area of research. *e-Review of Tourism Research*, 1, 21–24.
Engel, J.F., Kollat, D.T. and Blackwell, R.D. (1968) *Consumer Behavior*. New York, Holt, Rinehart, and Winston.
Foxall, G.R. and Goldsmith, R. (1994) *Consumer Psychology for Marketing*. London: Routledge.
Gartner, W.C. and Ruzzier, M.K. (2011) Tourism Destination Brand Equity Dimensions: Renewal versus Repeat Market. *Journal of Travel Research*, 50 (5), 471–481.
Gazley, A. and Watling, L. (2015) Me, my tourist-self, and I: the symbolic consumption of travel. *Journal of Travel and Tourism Marketing*, 32 (6), 639–655.
Gilbert, D.C. (1991) An Examination of The Consumer Behaviour Process Related to Tourism. In Cooper, C.P. (ed.), *Progress in Tourism, Recreation and Hospitality Management*, London, Belhaven, pp. 78–105.
Gutman J. (1981) A Means-End Model for Facilitating Analyses of Product Markets Based on Consumer Judgement. In Monroe, K.B. and Arbor, A. (Eds), *NA – Advances in Consumer Research Volume 08*, MI: Association for Consumer Research, pp. 116–121.
Hansen, T. (2005) Perspectives on consumer decision making: an integrated approach. *Journal of Consumer Behaviour*, 4 (6), 420–437.
Herbert, D. (2001) Literary places, tourism and the heritage experience. *Annals of Tourism Research*, 28 (2), 312–333.
Herjanto, H., Erickson, E. and Calleja, N.F. (2017). Antecedents of Business Travelers' Satisfaction. *Journal of Hospitality Marketing & Management*, 26 (3), 259–275.
Hofstede, G. (2001) *Culture's Consequences: comparing values, behaviors, institutions, and organizations across nations*. 2nd edn. Thousand Oaks, CA: SAGE Publications.
Howard J.A. and Sheth J.N. (1969) *The Theory of Buyer Behaviour*. New York, John Wiley and Sons.
Hudson, S. (1999) Consumer behavior related to tourism. In: Pizam A. and Mansfeld Y. (Eds), *Consumer Behavior in Travel and Tourism*. New York, Routledge, pp. 7–32.
International Telecommunication Union (2016). *ICT Facts And Figures 2016*. Geneva, ITU. Available online at: http://www.itu.int/en/ITU-D/Statistics/Pages/facts/default.aspx. [Accessed 22 July 2016].
Iso-Ahola, S.E. (1982) Toward a social psychological theory of tourism motivation: a rejoinder. *Annals of Tourism Research*, 9 (2), 256–262.
Kleinig, J. (2013) *Loyalty*. In: Zalta, E.N. (ed.) *The Stanford Encyclopedia of Philosophy*. Available online at: http://plato.stanford.edu/archives/fall2013/entries/loyalty/ [Accessed 3 July 2016]
Kozak, M. and Baloglu, S. (2011) *Managing and marketing Tourist Destinations, Strategies to Gain a Competitive Edge*. New York; Routledge.
Laesser, C. and Dolnicar, S. (2012) Impulse purchasing in tourism – learnings from a study in a matured market. *Anatolia*, 23 (2), 268–286.
Li, X., Li, X.R. and Hudson, S. (2013) The application of generational theory to tourism consumer behavior: an American perspective. *Tourism Management*, 37, 147–164.
Lin, C.H and Kuo, B.Z.L. (2016) The behavioral consequences of tourist experience. *Tourism Management Perspectives*, 18, 84–91.
Maier, T.A. and Prusty, S. (2016). Managing Customer Retention in Private Clubs Using Churn Analysis: Some Empirical Findings. *Journal of Hospitality Marketing & Management*, 25 (7), 797–819.
Maslow, A.H. (1943) A theory of human motivation. *Psychological Review*, 50 (4), 370–396.
Mathieson, A. and Wall, G. (1982) *Tourism: Economic, Physical and Social Impacts*. London, Longman.
Mattila, A.S. (2004) Consumer behavior research in hospitality and tourism journals. *International Journal of Hospitality Management*, 23, 449–457.
Matzler, K., Strobl, A., Stokburger-Sauer, N., Bobovnicky, A. and Bauer, F. (2016) Brand personality and culture: the role of cultural differences on the impact of brand personality perceptions on tourists' visit intentions. *Tourism Management*, 52, 507–520.
Mayo, E. and Jarvis, L. (1981) *The Psychology of Leisure Travel*. Boston: CBI Publishing.
Meleddu, M., Paci, P. and Pulina, M. (2015) Repeated behaviour and destination loyalty. *Tourism Management*, 50, 159–171.

Michalkó, G., Irimiás, A. and Timothy, D.J. (2015) Disappointment in tourism: Perspectives on tourism destination management. *Tourism Management Perspectives* 16, 85–91.
Middleton, V.T.C (1994) *Marketing for Travel and Tourism.* 2nd edn. London, Butterworth-Heinemann.
Mill, R. and Morrison, A. (2012) *The Tourist System.* 4th edn. Dubuque, Kendall/Hunt.
Mkono, M. (2016) The reflexive tourist. *Annals of Tourism Research*, 57, 206–219.
Morrison, A.M. (2013) *Marketing and Managing Tourism Destinations.* New York, Routledge.
Moutinho, L. (1987) Consumer behavior in tourism. *European Journal of Marketing*, 21 (10), 5–44.
Neuhofer, B., Buhalis, D. and Ladkin, A. (2012) Conceptualising technology enhanced destination experiences. *Journal of Destination Marketing and Management*, 1, 36–46.
Nicosia, F.M. (1966) *Consumer Decision Process: Marketing and Advertising Implications*, New Jersey, Prentice Hall.
Oliver, R.L. (1980) A cognitive model of the antecedents and consequences of satisfaction decisions. *Journal of Marketing Research*, 17, 460–469.
Oliver, R.L. (1994) Conceptual issues in the structural analysis of consumption emotion, satisfaction and quality: Evidence in a service setting. *Advances in Consumer Research*, 21, 16–22.
Olson, J.C. and Reynolds, T.J. (2001) The means–end approach to understanding consumer decision making. In: Reynolds, T.J. and Olson, J.C. (Eds), *Understanding Consumer Decision Making: The Means–End Approach to Marketing and Advertising Strategy.* New Jersey, Taylor and Francis, 3–19.
Page, S.J. (2007). *Tourism Management, Managing for Change.* Oxford, Butterworth-Heinemann.
Pearce, P.L. (1982) *The Social Psychology of Tourist Behaviour.* Oxford: Pergamon.
Pearce, P.L. (2005). *Tourist Behavior: Themes and Conceptual Schemes.* Clevedon, Channel View Publications.
Perreault, W.D., Darden, D.K. and Darden, W.R. (1977). A Psychological Classification of Vacation Life Styles. *Journal of Leisure Research*, 9, 208–224.
Plog, S.C. (1974). Why destination areas rise and fall in popularity. *The Cornell Hotel and Restaurant Administration Quarterly*, 4, 55–58.
Quintal, V.A., Lee, J.A. and Soutar, G.N. (2010) Tourists' information search: the differential impact of risk and uncertainty avoidance. *International Journal of Tourism Research*, 12, 321–333.
Rokeach, M. (1973) *The Nature of Human Values.* New York, The Free Press.
Schmoll, G.A. (1977) *Tourism Promotion.* London, Tourism International Press.
Sheth, J.N., Newman, B.I. and Gross, B.L. (1991) Why we buy what we buy: a theory of consumption values. *Journal of Business Research*, 22, 159–170.
Sirgy, M.J., Grewal, D., Mangleburg, T.F., Park, J.-O., Chon, K.-S., Claiborne, C.B., Johar, J.S. and Berkman, H. (1997) Assessing the predictive validity of two methods of measuring self–image congruence. *Academy of Marketing Science Journal*, 25 (3), 229–241.
Smith, V. (1989) *Hosts and Guests: The Anthropology of Tourism.* 2nd edn. Philadelphia, University of Pennsylvania Press.
Solomon, M.R. (1996) *Consumer Behavior.* 3rd edn. New Jersey, Prentice-Hall.
Sparks, B.A. and Browning, V. (2011) The impact of online reviews on hotel booking intentions and perception of trust. *Tourism Management*, 32, 1310–1323.
Sung, H.H. (2004) Classification of adventure travelers: behavior, decision making, and target markets. *Journal of Travel Research*, 42 (4), 343–356.
Swarbrooke, J. and Horner, S. (2007) *Consumer Behavior in Tourism.* 2nd edn. Netherlands, Elsevier Ltd.
Torres, E.N., van Niekerk, M. and Orlowski, M. (2017). Customer and employee incivility and its causal effects in the hospitality industry. *Journal of Hospitality Marketing & Management*, 26 (1), 48–66.
Tussyadiah, I.P. and Wang, D. (2016) Tourists' attitudes toward proactive smartphone systems. *Journal of Travel Research*, 55 (4): 493–508.
Urry, J. (1990) *The Tourist Gaze: Leisure and Travel in Contemporary Society.* London, Sage Publications.
Volo, S. (2010) Bloggers' reported tourist experiences: Their utility as a tourism data source and their effect on prospective tourists. *Journal of Vacation Marketing*, 16 (4), 297–311.
Wahab, S., Crampon, L.J. and Rothfield, L.M. (1976) *Tourism Marketing*, Tourism International Press.
Walker, J.R. and Walker, J.T. (2011) *Tourism: Concepts and Practices.* New Jersey, Pearson Education.
White, C.J. and Thompson, M. (2009) Self-determination theory and the wine club attribute formation process. *Annals of Tourism Research*, 36 (4), 561–586.
Wickens, E. (2002) The sacred and the profane: a tourist typology. *Annals of Tourism Research*, 29 (3), 834–851.
Wood, K. and House, S. (1992) *The Good Tourist: A Worldwide Guide for the Green Traveller.* 2nd edn. London, Mandarin.

Xiang, Z. and Gretzel, U. (2010) Role of social media in online travel information search. *Tourism Management*, 31 (2), 179–188.
Xiang, Z., Magnini, V.P. and Fesenmaier, D.R. (2015) Information technology and consumer behavior in travel and tourism: insights from travel planning using the internet. *Journal of Retailing and Consumer Services*, 23, 244–249.
Yoon, Y. and Uysal, M. (2005) An examination of the effects of motivation and satisfaction on destination loyalty: a structural model, *Tourism Management*, 26, 45–56.
Yu, J.Y. and Ko, T.G. (2012) A cross-cultural study of perceptions of medical tourism among Chinese, Japanese and Korean tourists in Korea. *Tourism Management*, 33 (1), 80–88.
Zaltam, G. and Burger, P.C. (1975) *Marketing Research – Fundamentals and Dynamics*. Hinsdale, IL: The Dryden Press.

Further reading

Arnould, E., Price, L. and Zinkhan, G. (2002) *Consumers*. 1st edn. New York, McGraw Hill. (Broader consumer behavior in a multidisciplinary approach.)
McColl, K.J.R. et al. (1994) *Marketing: Concepts and Strategies*. Singapore, Acumen Overseas Pte. Ltd. (Comprehensive understanding of consumer decision making process.)
Smallman, C. and Moore, K. (2010) Process studies of tourists' decision-making. *Annals of Tourism Research*, 37 (2), 397–422. (An overall review of decision-making models.)
Woodside, A.G. and Dubelaar, C. (2002) A general theory of tourism consumption systems: a conceptual framework and an empirical exploration. *Journal of Travel Research*, 41, 120–132. (Suggestions to managers to increase effectiveness of their strategies.)

21

Destination decision making and selection process

Kurtulus Karamustafa and Kenan Gullu

Introduction

The aim of this chapter is to understand tourists' decision making and selection process regarding tourist destinations. Marketers of tourist destinations are implicitly interested in how and why tourists make decisions. As for the term "decision", we will refer to a commitment, to a course of action that is intended to serve the interests and values of particular people (Yates and Potworowski, 2012). Decision making constitutes a complex process and occurs in our everyday life; people have to decide to do or not to do an action and make choices among the alternatives. The most common definition of consumer decision making is as follows: "[Consumer decision making] is the study of the processes involved when individuals or groups select, purchase, use or dispose of products, services, ideas or experiences to satisfy needs and desires" (Solomon, Bamossy, Askegaard and Hogg 2006: 6). In fact, consumer decision making studies are related with the fields of psychology, sociology, social psychology, cultural anthropology and economics. In this context, marketing academics studying in the field of consumer behavior have developed consumer buying behavior models which try to explain consumer decision making process. As these models indicate, there are both external and internal influences affecting decision making. Here is the attempt to detail those influences in the context of tourists' destination decision making and selection processes. Through this chapter we expect to broaden our understanding on tourists' destination decision making and selection processes, since it evaluates the consumer decision making models holistically based on the current literature.

Classical decision making approaches

Classical decision making can be studied in various approaches (Foxall 1990); (a) economic approach, (b) psychological approach, (c) sociological approach and (d) cognitive approach. No approach is superior to others, each approach attempts to pinpoint complex issues involved in decision making. In fact, each of these approaches to decision making is interwoven and interrelated with each other.

Economic approach

There are economic theories to explain how people make decisions by choosing among desirable alternatives. These theories center on the notion of the subjective value, or utility, of the alternatives among which the decision maker must choose. They point out that people behave rationally, that is, they have transitive preferences, and they choose in such a way as to maximize utility or expected utility. Economic approach to decision making can be understood better if evaluated under the following four theoretical perspectives: (a) the theory of riskless choices; (b) the theory of risky choices; (c) the transitivity of choices; and (d) the theory of games and of decision functions.

The traditional theory of riskless choices, a straightforward theory of utility maximization, is related to the paradigm of rationality. The consumer is considered as a rational decision maker or *homo oeconomicus* (economic man) who wants to maximize his or her personal utility or satisfaction within the limits of his or her budget. In fact, an economic man has three main characteristics of being (Edwards, 1954: 381): (a) completely informed, (b) infinitely sensitive and (c) rational. As indicated in Marshall's Economic Model, decision making is based on rationality; hence, decisions are taken in the context of cost-benefit analysis. In other words, at the end of a decision making, it is expected to provide maximum benefits with minimum costs.

The notion that lies behind the theory of risky choices is to introduce risks or uncertainties related to the consequences of a decision making; hence, any alternative in decision making is required to be evaluated on the basis of both its expected value and its level of risk. Economists assert that choices are transitive. Intransitivity may occur when there is a conflicting stimulus dimension along which to judge. In other words, there are some experimental studies showing intransitive patterns of choice. Finally, the theory of games presents an elaborate mathematical analysis of the problem of choosing among alternative strategies in the games of strategy.

Economic theories to classical decision making put emphasis mostly on the rational dimension of decision making despite taking into account the risks and uncertainties, the transitivity of choices and other structural factors affecting decision making process. The task of the marketer is to understand how and why consumers' behavior deviates from rational decision models. They should also realize that decision making is a complex issue and cannot always be straightforward, and that most of the decisions are likely to be made under stressful, confusing and even frightening conditions. In this context, utility theory and prospect theory are two decision making process models that can help us to understand the reasons of decision making and the methods used in decision making. Utility theory assumes that decision making is dependent on the utility of the outcome of the decision making process, and that the context of the decision making process is not expected to have any influence on the outcome. On the other hand, prospect theory explains that decision making involves uncertainty and irrationality in the context of psychology and economics (Kahneman and Tversky, 1979). Prospect theory has wide-ranging marketing implications. These include but are not limited to (Cochran, 2001): (a) how an advertising message is framed; (b) how a new product is positioned; (c) how a product is priced relative to the competition and consumer expectations; (d) how a product is priced and the premium a consumer is willing to pay; and (e) what markets will respond to what types of offer.

In tourism, economic approaches to decision making have been developed by authors such as Rugg (1973), Morley (1992), Papatheodorou (2001), and Seddighi and Theocharous (2002). Rugg (1973) was the first to apply economic principles to tourism. He introduced three dimensions: time constraint, transportation costs and time costs. Morley (1992) suggested a travel decision process that integrates the following three elements in one utility function along with non-tourism products: (a) the decision to travel or not; (b) the allocation of time and budget; and (c) the choice of the tour. Papatheodorou (2001) developed a model of discrete choice which indicates that the vacationer travels only to the destination that is associated with the highest utility, thereby excluding multidestination tourism. Based on two dimensions (attractions and facilities), he makes a comparative exercise that focuses on the effects related to: (a) expenditure and time impediments, (b) prices, (c) consumer preferences, (d) quality, information and advertising, (e) agglomeration, (f) the emergence of new destinations.

Seddighi and Theocharous (2002) proposed a model of tourist behavior and destination choice which is a fourstep process: (a) travel decision making is induced by a number of socio-economic and demographic indicators to travel or not to travel; (b) people, who wish to travel, have to make a choice between a domestic and a foreign holiday, which is mainly determined by their purchasing power, then they develop perceptions and feelings (attitudes) towards alternative destinations (either domestic, foreign or a combination of both) on the basis of their characteristics; these perceptions and feelings are assumed to serve as decision criteria through an abstraction process from the system characteristics; (c) perceptions and feelings are aggregated into a preference ordering of destination alternatives that is expected to lead to choice (this process is moderated by situational constraints such as holiday availability); and (d) their travel experiences act as a feedback loop to modify the perceptions and feelings towards the visited destinations. Thirteen characteristics were used as variables in the Seddighi and Theocharous's model, such as age, gender, marital status, income, education, previous experience, the cost of living in the destination, the price of the tourist package, facilities, cost of transportation, quality of promotion and advertising, quality of services and political instability.

Psychological approach

According to psychological approaches to decision making, consumers can be motivated towards consuming a product to satisfy their needs with the emphasising of personal characteristics such as needs, motives, learning processes, perceptions, attitudes and beliefs. Freud's psychoanalysis model can be an example of these kinds of approaches to decision making (Freud, 1960). This view posits that behavior is subject to biological influence through "instinctive forces" or "drives" which act outside of conscious thought (Arnold, Silvester, Patterson, Robertson, Cooper and Burnes, 2005). While Freud (1923) identified three facets of the psyche, namely the id, the ego and the superego, Jung (1933) identified sensing, intuition, feeling and thinking as the other ways of experiencing the world.

Sociological approaches

Sociological approaches to decision making, similar to psychological approaches, take into account motivations in consumer buying behavior. However, while internal (personal) factors are influential in psychological approaches, external factors are influential in sociological approaches. In this context, factors surrounding the consumers, such as family, reference groups, social class and cultural values, are effective in determining personal needs and purchasing decisions. The challenge to the destination marketers is to determine which of these social levels is the most important in influencing the demand for their destination. Veblen's socio-psychological model can be an example to this kind of approach to decision making.

Cognitive approach

Consumers do not make consumption coincidently; in fact, buying decision process occurs within the frame of a systematic learning process. However, a rational consumer decision making occurs within the limits of consumer learning and cognitive capacity. Pavlov's learning model can be an example of these kinds of approaches to decision making which studies the relation between learning and behavior. Contemporary cognitive psychology has identified and developed a wide range of factors which are considered to be fundamental to decision making processes including: perception, learning, memory, thinking, emotion and motivation (Sternberg, 1996). In this context, it has been argued that image of a destination is an important element in understanding tourists' decision making and selection process. There is a considerable number of studies emphasizing the relationship between destination image and consumer behavior (Ahmed, 1994; Milman and Pizam, 1995; Pike, 2002; Andrades-Caldito, Sánchez-Rivero and Pulido-Fernández, 2013; Chi and Qu, 2008). Destination image represents a consumer's overall perception or impression of a destination after experiencing it (Fakeye and Crompton, 1991; Baloglu and McCleary, 1999; Karamustafa, Fuchs and Reichel, 2012); in other words, the psychological representation of a place (Alhemoud and Armstrong, 1996) will have an impact on consumers' behaviors when they shop for a tourist destination.

Descriptive (modern) consumer decision making approaches

Classical decision making approaches are inadequate in explaining consumer behaviors; hence, the development of consumer behavior approaches has gained importance. In today's modern world, destination marketers seek to understand how consumers make decisions, and descriptive (modern) consumer decision making approaches are used to understand what types of factors, how and why they influence consumers' decision making process. Widely known consumer decision making models are as follows in chronological order; Howard and Sheth Model (1960 and 1969), Kotler's Behavioral Choice Model (1965), Nicosia Model (1966), Engel, Kollat and Blackwell (EKB) Model (1968), and Hawkins, Best and Coney (HBC) Model (1998). In fact, a consumer behavior model is simply anything used to represent all or a part of the variables of consumer behavior. Essentially, consumer behavior models are indispensable instruments for managerial decision making in marketing practice, and have two main characteristics in common; they perceive (a) consumer decision making as a problem solving process, and (b) consumer as a problem solver. All consumer decision making models indicate that consumers make their decisions step by step under the influence of external (environmental) and internal (personal) factors surrounding them.

According to the famous model developed by Howard and Sheth (1969), the decision making process of consumers (consumers' problem solving) is divided into three stages: (a) extensive problem solving; (b) limited problem solving; and (c) routinized response behavior. To get a better understanding of the stages of consumer decision making in the case of destination decision making, service classification from customers' point of view is useful to destination marketers. Stell and Donoho (1996) classified services into *convenience services*, *preference services*, *shopping services* and *specialty services*. *Convenience services* are relatively inexpensive and frequently purchased with the lowest risk and low involvement. *Preference services* differentiated through branding; and hence brand loyalty is high and require medium risk and involvement. *Shopping services* are high risk and high involvement services. *Specialty services* require very high risks and involvement with ultimate differentiation and brand loyalty. Destinations can offer tourism services which can be in those four categories and vary depending on the level of consumer experience.

In the case of destination decision making, *extensive problem solving* occurs when a traveler discovers a new destination or wants to buy a tourism product he or she does not know well and/or is particularly expensive and/or which may present a significant risk financially, socially, psychologically and physically for him/her. Lack of "experience" in the matter leads to lack of decision criteria to make choice. Since travelling to an unfamiliar, unknown and insecure place may involve risks (Karamustafa *et al.*, 2012), the level of consumer involvement in travel decision making and choice of a destination is relatively high. Travelers may seek to spend a lot of time looking for information and benchmarks to make their choices. The level of uncertainty and confusion about the choice of a tourist product can be high. The purchase process can be usually quite long. This can be the case, as mentioned above, to buy a holiday or a tour to an unfamiliar, unknown, insecure and risky destination.

Limited problem solving, in the case of destination decision making, means that a traveler has a clear vision of travel expectations and decision criteria. He/she has already had an experience with the destination offered, and had information about it, in the case of repeat visitors. However, he/she is still undecided about the brand or a particular tourist product to choose and which one will be the best alternative to meet his/her needs. The level of consumer involvement is moderate, so information seeking is more limited. He/she will compare available products and try to determine especially which one is best for him/her. The purchasing process will be shorter. For instance, on the Mediterranean basin of Turkey, there are quite a lot of destinations offering "sun-sea-sand" type tourist products with some cultural blended features, such as Bodrum, Marmaris and Kusadasi. A traveler may have an experience with Turkey and Turkish Culture, but may not have specific knowledge about these destinations. Therefore, this traveler may have limited problem solving to decide which destination to choose.

Routinized response behavior may occur during the travel in a destination. This is about the everyday purchases with a low level of involvement from the traveler. These are common products that are known well by the traveler. He/she knows what brand to choose and which product suits him. He/she does not need specific information or a specific research time to make his/her choice. The purchase decision is simple and is quickly taken. Usually, the more a product has become a "routine buying behavior" for a traveler, the less he/she will be responsive to stimulus or initiatives, such as advertising and discounting.

Tourists' decision making and destination choice

Tourists' decision making processes are complex, involving many sub-decisions, occurring continuously from prior to deciding "where to go" through to "what are we going to do now that we're here" and beyond (Smallman and Moore, 2010). In order to understand this complex process, various models of consumer behavior have been developed. In his review of models of vacation decision making, Decrop (2006a) makes a distinction between: (a) microeconomic; (b) cognitive; and (c) interpretive models. Microeconomic models try to explain tourism behavior by using traditional demand models with a normative focus on how the consumer should behave. How and why tourists behave as they do is not integrated in these models. Cognitive models constitute the variables of awareness, perceptions and motivation that urge the decision making process. And, finally, interpretive models combine the microeconomic and cognitive models that visualize the decision making process as a multistage process with notions like consideration sets and a rational information search. It can be stated that a number of theories seek to explain why people travel and why they go on holiday and in this context, there has also been a significantly growing number of studies on destination selection and decision making since 1960s; some of them proposed independent models (Clawson and Knetsch, 1966; Wahab, Crampon and Rothfield, 1976; Schmoll, 1977; Mathieson and Wall, 1982; Moutinho, 1982; van Raaij and Francken, 1984; Moutinho, 1987; Gunn, 1989; Woodside and Lysonski, 1989; Um and Crompton, 1990; Goodall, 1991; Mansfeld, 1992; Middleton, 1994; Teare, 1994; Woodside and MacDonald, 1994; Middleton and Clarke, 2001), while others reviewed empirically and tested those proposed models sometimes with proposed alterations (Decrop 1999; Decrop and Snelders, 2004; March and Woodside, 2005; Decrop and Kozak, 2009; Decrop, 2010; Sirakaya and Woodside 2005; Nicolau and Mas, 2005; Oh and Hsu, 2001; Smalman and Moore, 2010; Bargeman and van der Poel, 2006; Bronner and de Hoog, 2008; Dolnicar, Crouch, Devinney, Huybers, Louviere, and Oppewal, 2008; Kang and Hsu, 2005; Quintal, Lee and Soutar, 2010; Sirakaya and Woodside, 2005; Barros, Butler and Correia, 2008; Choi, Lehto, Morrison and Jang, 2012; Hyde and Lawson, 2003; Litvin, Xu and Kang, 2004; Woodside, Caldwell and Spurr, 2006).

Clawson and Knetch (1966) identified a five-phased process in their recreational behavior model: (a) anticipation (planning and thinking about the trip); (b) travel to the site (getting to the destination); (c) on-site behavior (behavior at the site or destination region); (d) return travel (travelling home); and (e) recollection (recall, reflection and memory of the trip). Later, Wahab et al. (1976) elaborated a sequential vacation destination decision making model involving the following eight steps: (a) initial stimulus; (b) conceptual framework; (c) fact gathering; (d) definitions of assumptions; (e) design of alternatives; (f) forecast of consequences; (g) cost–benefit of alternatives; and (h) decision and outcome. The subsequent model of Schmoll's (1977) consists of the following four stages: (a) external stimulus such as trade publications; (b) travel needs and desires determined by personality, social-economic factors, attitude and values; (c) external variables such as confidence in the travel agent, destination image, previous experience, and cost and time constraints; and (d) service characteristics offered by the tourism enterprises in particular and destination in general.

Mathieson and Wall's (1982) tourist decision making process indicates that travel desire is a function of the tourist's profile and his or her awareness of the destination resources and characteristics. It is followed by information collection, assessment of alternatives, actual decisions, travel experience and evaluation. A number of "trip features" (including structural, personal and interpersonal aspects) influences these different aspects of decision making process. Moutinho (1982) proposed the model of tourist decision making process which consists of *pre-decision, post-evaluation* and *future decision making*. The pre-decision stage includes three fields: preference structure, decision, and purchase. The preference structure for a particular destination is based on a set of factors, including internalized environmental influences (cultural norms and values, reference groups, social class), individual determinants (personality, lifestyle, perceived role set and motives), attitude and family, and confidence generation and inhibitors. These factors, then, lead to a decision meaning purchasing or not purchasing. The post-purchase evaluation is important as a reference for future purchase intentions. In the model, the field is labeled as "satisfaction or dissatisfaction" which could either be positive (acceptance), negative (rejection) or neutral (non-commitment). The last part of Moutinho's model is future decision making which can be seen as the practical interface with marketing decision planning concerning the study of the subsequent behavior of the tourist by analyzing repeat-buying probabilities of the tourist products and services (Decrop, 2006a). Moutinho (1987) suggested a more expanded conceptual framework of tourism decisions. In his model, destination choice is a compulsory decision among a group of other sub decisions (travel mode, timing, budget, intermediaries) that comes after tourism need has been aroused, information has been gathered, and deliberated on before travel preparation. Marketing stimulus, social factors, characteristics of the destination and other external factors are listed as influences on the choice of travel destination. However, because of its extreme complexity and comprehensiveness, it has been argued that it is not possible to test Moutinho's model empirically (Decrop, 1999; Sirakaya and Woodside, 2005).

Based on Engel and Blackwell (1982), van Raaij and Francken (1984) and van Raaij (1986) proposed a travel decision making model consisting of five stages as a sequence of subdecisions: (a) the generic decision to spend on a vacation; (b) information acquisition; (c) joint decision making by husband and wife; (d) experience of the vacation; and (e) subsequent levels of satisfaction. Gunn (1989) identified a seven-stage process in the leisure travel experience: (a) accumulation of mental images about vacation experiences; (b) modification of those images by further information; (c) decision to take a vacation trip; (d) travel to the destination; (e) participation at the destination; (f) return travel; and (g) new accumulation of images based on the experience. Based on Howard and Sheth's theory (1969) of buyer behavior, Woodside and Lysonski (1989) designed perhaps the most popular conceptualized model of traveler leisure destination awareness and choice, which depicts eight variables and nine relationships. Two exogenous variables, traveler characteristics and marketing variables are supposed to influence destination awareness. Destination awareness includes four categories: (a) *consideration set* is the subset of brands that a consumer considers buying in a given product class; (b) *inert set* consists of those destinations of which the consumer is aware but has an ambivalent attitude toward, neither negative nor positive. This is often because the consumer does not have enough information about the destination to make a meaningful evaluation; (c) *unavailable/aware set* are those destinations about which the consumer is aware but is unable to purchase due to any number of constraints such as financial, geographic, legal or other limitations; and (d) *the inept or the reject set*, are those destinations of which the consumer is aware but will not consider buying because they create a negative perception based on past experience or negative information. They argue that all destinations of which a consumer is aware will fall into one of these categories.

Crompton (1977) presents a systematic model of the tourist destination choice which occurs in two stages: (a) the first is the generic decision of taking a holiday or not, if a holiday decision is taken; (b) then the second stage of decision follows, this is the place of vacation or destination choice decision which should be conceptualized as the result of the interaction of perceived constraints (such as time, money, and skill) and destination images. Further to that systematic model, in 1990, Um and Crompton developed a more complete framework based on Crompton's above mentioned model of tourist destination choice. Their model is based on three sets of variables: (a) external inputs representing influences from both the social and marketing environment, such as significative (destination attributes), symbolic (promotional messages), and social stimulus; (b) internal inputs deriving from the vacationer's socio-psychological characteristics (personal characteristics, motives, values, and attitudes); and (c) cognitive constructing representing "an integration of the internal and external inputs, into the awareness set of destinations and the evoked set of destinations" (Um and Crompton, 1990: 436). This framework asserts that destination selection is a three-stage process with the composition of *awareness set*, *evoked set*, and *final destination set* (travel destination). In fact, a holistic view of their model of travel destination choice acts as a five-step process: (a) step one includes the formation of beliefs about destination attributes (through passive information catching or incidental learning); (b) step two is the initiation of the destination choice process after the generic decision to go on holiday has been made; (c) step three consists of the evolution of an evoked set from the awareness set of destinations; (d) step four is the formation of beliefs about evoked destinations attributes (through active information search); and (e) step five results in the selection of a specific travel destination from the evoked set.

Goodall (1988) makes a distinction between the holiday selection process and the choice of the resort. Holiday selection is described as

> a process which is systematic and sequential. [This] conceptualization, however, acknowledges the importance of a behavioral perspective in understanding how people make holiday decisions. At best the tourist is a satisficer acting within implicit and explicit constraints of an uncertain environment.
>
> *(Goodall, 1988: 2)*

According to Goodall (1988), the tourist's holiday decision is a process stimulated by holiday needs and desires, which form holiday motivation, and continue with the evaluation of alternative vacations, which is made possible through the formation of mental images, and ends with the final decision of taking or not taking the vacation. In this respect, Goodall introduces three different types of images: preferential (representing the ideal vacation); evaluative (expectation level to which actual vacation opportunities are compared); and naive or factual (pertaining to the perception of each vacation destination). As to the resort choice (for instance, a package involving travel, accommodation and excursions), once the generic holiday decision is reached, sub-decisions (vacation requirements) have to be made and as a result, a search process starts to find the vacation that best matches those requirements, within time and money limits. This search process may be more or less extensive depending on the vacationer type (such as, impulse buyer vs. meticulous planner). The holidaymaker then evaluates the different alternatives following a satisficing rather than an optimizing rule, which leads to the final decision and purchase.

Woodside and MacDonald (1993) used qualitative data in their model to validate a general systems framework of how leisure travelers make their choices. They identified the following eight leisure traveler choice subsystems: (a) destination choices; (b) accommodation choices; (c) activity choices; (d) attractions choices; (e) travel modes and route choices; (f) eating choices; (g) destination areas choices and routes; and (h) self-gifts and other durable purchases. It was proposed that these choices may be activated by four principal start nodes related to the information acquisition and processing sequence. Hyde (2000) extended the framework presented by Woodside and MacDonald (1994) by adding three new aspects. First, he identified a sequence in which travel subdecisions are made (for instance, choice of secondary destinations was made before departure, then choice of travel route, and lastly choice of attractions and activities). Second, he introduced a distinction between the processes that occur before a vacationer's arrival (for instance, information search and planning, leading to a "researched before" set of sub-destinations) and those that occur during the stay at the destination (for instance, again, an active search of information leading to the formation of a "researched after" set, accompanied by the possibility of opportunistic considerations leading to final choices). Third, he explicitly stated the most influential information sources before departure and while on vacation. This can be seen as a first empirical test of the relationship among vacation choices suggested by Woodside and MacDonald (1994). In addition, Middleton (1994) presented a model of travel decision making process based on five components: stimulus input, communication channels, buyer characteristics and decision process, and purchase output. In his study, Middleton indicated motivation as a dynamic variable in travel behavior, bridging the gap between the felt need and the decision to act or purchase.

McCabe, Li and Chen (2015) proposed a new general model based on dual system theory to account for different types of choice strategies, the constructive nature of preferences and to recognize the individual and contextual factors that influence choice processes. They argued that a general tourist choice model should integrate the psychological processes that determine choice strategies, or heuristics, and consider choice context including individual differences, task-related factors, and principles determining system engagement.

A descriptive model of consumer decision making developed by Hawkins, Best and Coney (1989) is a commonly used decision making model in explaining consumer decision making process. Therefore, in this chapter, we will try to explain destination decision making in the context of the model developed by Hawkins et al. (1998). The model of HBC describes consumer decision making as a process to satisfy various consumer needs arising from consumer value styles. The current attempt is to make a holistic approach to tourists' decision making based on the previously developed decision making models.

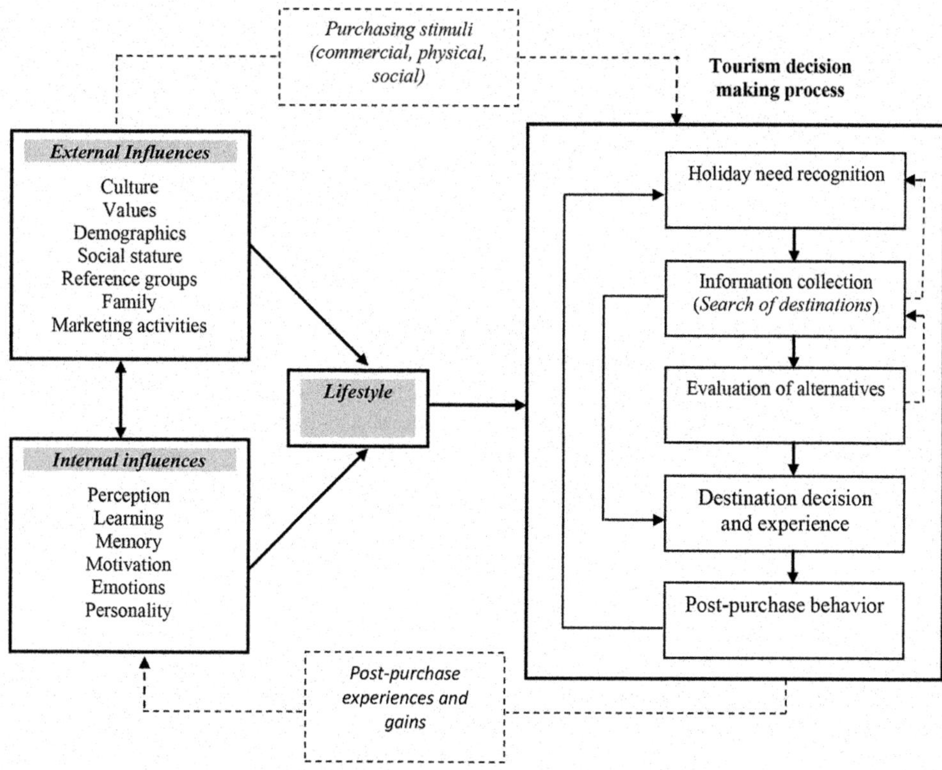

Figure 21.1 Tourists' decision making model

Lifestyle

The term "lifestyle" stems from the fields of psychology and sociology, referring to a person's particular way of living, and has been used primarily for examining the living patterns and mobility of the various social classes (Bei, 2000). It plays a central role in forming consumer needs and buying attitudes, and, hence, the process of consumer purchasing decision. Lifestyle can be simply defined as how a person lives, it is also related to how one perceives the products he/she bought and also himself or herself. Lifestyle also means "personal image" which is formed by culture including individuals' daily life experiences and their personal situations. Each individual, family and society may have different lifestyles.

Lifestyle affects our consciously and unconsciously made decisions. In fact, there are mutual relations between lifestyle and decision making (Lin and Shih, 2012). In other words, a person's decision making is affected by his/her lifestyle which, in turn, affects his/her decision making. Sustainability in a consumption style means sustainability in a lifestyle; if lifestyle changes, consumption style may change. Therefore, destination marketing managers should take into account the point which indicates the relation between consumption style and lifestyle in their destinational marketing planning efforts.

In other words, destination marketing managers should know and understand target markets' lifestyle and factors affecting lifestyle which, in turn, affects travel decision making. For instance, since the lifestyles of a housewife and a working woman, a married person and a single person, a person living in the country and a metropolis are different, their needs and purchasing stimulus will differentiate from each other.

Lifestyle is able to affect every stage of consumer decision making process, such as extensive problem solving, limited problem solving and routinized response behavior. As mentioned above, during the purchase of low involvement products, while price is influential in one lifestyle, brand and prestige can be influential in another lifestyle.

External influences

Destination decision making is often affected by the factors outside travelers' control but which have direct and indirect impacts on making a travel decision to a specific destination. External influences are also recognized as social influences and include cultures, values, demographics, social status, reference groups, family and marketing efforts.

Culture

Researchers frequently use nationality as a proxy for culture, but other factors such as religion and social class can divide people into distinctly identifiable "cultures" as well (Cohen, 2009). Hofstede (1980) provided a more succinct definition of culture. He considered that culture is a kind of "program" that controls behavior. Hofstede (1980; 1991) studied data from 53 countries, and identified four dimensions of cultural variations through studying over 117,000 questionnaires completed by respondents at different time periods, and matching the responses by occupation, age and gender. His research showed that people would have different intentions, give different attributions, and behave differently due to their cultural group. Culture reflects the personality of a society and affects everything done by individuals within that society, and the way people think. It can be learned and even slowly changes in a period of time; in other words, it is not static, it has a dynamic structure. However, culture should not be perceived as a standardized recipe to define all human behavior; it should be seen as a platform on which thinking style and activities of most of the people occur. From the point of our study subject, culture is important since it directs people's thinking and behaviors, and, in this context, it constitutes a considerable degree of effects on consumption style and purchasing decisions of consumers. Hofstede (1980) classifies the human behaviors into four: (a) power distance, (b) the uncertainty avoidance, (c) individualism/collectivism and (d) femininity/masculinity. Subsequently, Hofstede and Bond (1988) conducted another study on the Chinese employees and managers, hence added a new dimension to the cultural values model. They defined this new dimension as the "long term orientation" and explained it as the thinking capability of the society being either long-term or short-term.

Correia, Kozak and Ferradeira (2011) argue that the national culture directly influences the pattern of vacation decisions in various ways. First, power distance is one of the most influential cultural factors in decision making style about tourism destinations, where quality and brands drive the decisions. However, collectivistic cultures are more likely to decide based on brands, prices and the number of alternatives, whereas individualistic cultures tend to decide based on their own criteria. Furthermore, long-term oriented societies are more likely to decide based on brands and a number of information sources that may lead to confusion. They conclude that Western visitors arriving in Lisbon during the New Year events decide mostly based on destination brands, after some sense of uncertainty derived from the number of alternatives evaluated (Correia et al., 2011).

Values

A person's values will determine how they perceive any particular situation. Therefore, values are considered to be important and influential determinants of the human behavior. In its simplest form, values are known as the components, which are learned from family, school, religion and environment in which individuals live, constituting the culture. Cultural values are the beliefs that determine what is right and what should be done. Values are formed by personal, social and environmental elements. In this respect, as Schwartz (1992) argues, *individual values* represent broad and relatively stable personal goals that can be categorized into ten basic types: self-direction, stimulation, hedonism, achievement, power, security, conformity, tradition, benevolence, and universalism. A person's position and transition in his or her life is perceived as a major determinant of the holiday decision (Decrop, 2006a). *Societal values* are related to social tendencies and individuals' relations with the society. In fact, societal values themselves are also determinants of individual values. *Environmental values* consist of the elements representing the viewpoint of a society on the economic environment and ecology. Destination marketers should be aware of the role of these values and their implications on tourists' decision making and choice of destination.

Demographics

Age, gender, education, income, occupation and geographical distribution of population and intensity constitute demographic structure of a society. All parts of these demographic patterns, particularly in generation or in general regions or countries, are important for the destination marketers as they provide an opportunity of objective evaluation. On the other hand, demographic patterns of a society determine the consumption parameters and behaviors. For instance, tourists' decision making, choice of vacation and, hence, choice of destination will be influenced by demographics, particularly age and income (Marcussen, 2011).

Social stature

Social stature is the position of an individual in the society depending on demographics such as education, occupation and income. Social categories formed and lived by individuals, families and organizations in a society is called social class. Values, lifestyles, choices and decision making of consumers living in the same society are close to each other. Knowing and understanding the differences among social classes will help meeting the consumer choices, which change in different social classes, by the service firms through service differentiation. For instance, hotels can offer various services to the people from various income levels in different social classes; differentiating hotel rooms as standard and suite or offering relatively expensive food and beverages in *à la carte restaurants*, and food and beverages at reasonable prices in *table d'hôte*, fast food and cafeteria type food and beverage units.

Reference groups

A group can be defined as a collection of individuals who have regular contact and frequent interaction, mutual influence, common feeling of camaraderie, and who work together to achieve a common set of goals. Groups emerge as a result of the willingness of people to work together or do a job for the purpose of reaching similar goals and exchange knowledge, establish relations among those who have similar interests, objectives, values and beliefs. Many people can be either a part of a small group which constitute few people or a large group constituting a large number of people. Groups affecting consumer decision making are known as consumer reference groups. Family, friend groups, official social groups (like clubs) and working groups can be given as being examples of reference groups. In order to show that the norms and values of a specific club are consistent with theirs, service firms can send a message indicating that their activities are unique to and prestigious for the members of that specific club. For instance, "*Members of Club A*" fly with "*Airlines A*" and stay in "*Hotel A*".

Family

Family, as a reference group, is a small group of society consisting of two or more people, and depends on the relations among relatives. Family plays an important role in forming habits, choices and lifestyles of individuals. In this context, family is an influential element on consumer behaviors. Family plays an important role in deciding what type of services to choose and purchase (Bronner and de Hoog, 2008). For example, family members can be influential on the decisions of independent travel and package tour choices, types of holiday they wish to purchase, types of holiday they will purchase and types of services offered by the hotels they choose. According to Decrop (2006b), the holiday decision making process of families is influenced by determinants such as occupation and economic status.

Marketing efforts

In today's global world, competition is gaining more and more importance in a global perspective with the emergence of demanding consumers whose needs and desires are changing and sophisticated. Therefore, like many other businesses, tourism enterprises, as service offering centers, are in the efforts of forming purchasing stimuli. In this respect, they have many marketing efforts like marketing research and formation of elements of marketing mix. Although traditional marketing mix elements include *product, price, place* and *promotion*, there are an additional three elements for service firms including *people, physical evidences* and *processes*. These seven elements are known as *7Ps* of service mix. Particularly with the applications of promotional activities, services firms are able to enrich by means of bringing intangibility features to tangibility features to some extent. Therefore, while all marketing efforts mentioned above are equally important, the importance of promotional activities, like advertising, public relations, sales promotion and direct marketing, are increasing and they have become important elements in encouraging consumers to buy and consume.

As services businesses, tourism enterprises are advised to take into account service quality dimensions (Figure 21.2) in order to audit changes in the tourist markets and provide customer satisfaction (Parasuraman *et al.*, 1985; 1988), and, of course, this is not exceptional to tourism destinations on the whole. Tangibles refers to the appearance of the physical facilities, equipment, personnel and communication materials. Reliability is the ability to perform the promised service dependably and accurately. Responsiveness is the willingness to help customers and provide prompt service. Assurance is defined as employees' knowledge and courtesy of employees and their ability to inspire trust and confidence. Empathy means to provide individualized attention to its customers.

Tourist destinations are expected to be within marketing efforts which lead them to offer qualified services to satisfy their visitors, and hence to be globally competitive in international tourist markets. It is worth noting that marketing strategies and efforts of tourist destinations and tourism firms should be carried out by taking account the external factors which are known

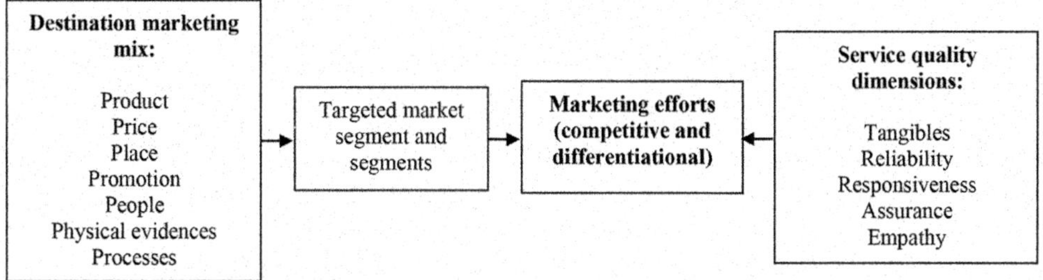

Figure 21.2 Destination marketing efforts

to be influential in determining the tourist decision making as well as internal factors which also have significant influences on tourist behavior. Intangibility nature of services increases the importance given to the internal factors by tourist destinations whose offerings to visitors are mainly service based.

Internal influences

Internal influences emerge from biogenic needs that refer to physiological states of tension such as thirst, hunger; and psychogenic needs that refer to psychological states of tension such as the need for recognition and esteem. In this respect, tourist behavior is not exceptional to this and influenced by a number of internal or psychological factors. These influences are also known as personal influences, and it includes perceptions, learning and memory, motivation, emotions, and personality. These internal influences affect tourists' destination decision making and choice.

Perception

It is the process by which people select, organize and interpret information to produce a meaningful experience of the world (Sirgy, 1982). In other words, it is the process of selecting and understanding the external stimulus based on the five senses to be aware of the environment around the consumer. Basically, the process goes from what people will see, smell, hear, touch and taste, namely from sensation, to perception. In fact, perception is subjective and personal; it may differ from one person to another. For instance, the same stimulus may cause different perceptions for different people; two people can see the exact same thing but give it a different importance. As argued by Kotler, Bowen and Makens (2002), this is because of three perceptual processes: *selective attention, selective distortion*, and *selective retention.* Perception for marketing is about managing the crisis of selective attention, distortion, and retention by making marketing essentially about knowledge – weighing costs and benefits after processing information.

Selective attention is the process of selecting some inputs to attend to while ignoring others; tourists will practice selective retention, holding on only to the information that supports their beliefs and attitudes. Therefore, marketers of tourist destinations have to work hard to attract the notice of consumers who seek a destination for holiday and other travel purposes. It is generally known that people are more likely to notice stimuli that relate to a current need; therefore, Mediterranean destinations emphasize the sun and clear weather for the holidaymakers in Northern European countries that lack in sun and hot weather. Additionally, people are more likely to notice stimuli they anticipate, such as flight tickets sold in a travel agency. Moreover, people are more likely to notice stimuli whose deviations are large in relationship to the normal size of the stimulus; vacationers are more likely to notice an ad offering US$100 off than one offering US$5 off a holiday's price.

Selective distortion is an individual's changing or distortion of information when it is inconsistent with personal feelings or beliefs. Tourists will often distort information to be consistent with prior knowledge, beliefs and expectations. Selective distortion can work to the advantage of marketers in tourist destinations with a strong brand when holiday seekers distort neutral or ambiguous information to make it more positive. In other words, coffee may seem to taste better and the wait in a queuing line may seem shorter, depending on the brand of a destination being visited.

Selective retention is remembering information that supports personal feelings and beliefs and forgetting inputs that do not. Tourists are likely to remember good points about a travel destination they like and forget good points about competing holiday destinations or products. Selective retention once more works to the advantage of strong brands in tourist destinations. It also explains why destination marketers need to use repetition – to make sure their message is not overlooked.

People can reach a decision whether to go to or not go to a tourist destination based on the perception created by the destination marketers and/or the suppliers of tourism services in the destination through marketing communication. Therefore, marketers of tourist destinations are recommended to create positive perceptions in tourist markets through appropriate marketing communication tools (Lumsdon, 1999).

Learning and memory

People learn many things to survive and fulfill their functions within society. Learning, basically, can be defined as being the process of information gathering by people. Learning is not all knowledge based. For example, one may experience the attitudes of indigenous people in one destination being more friendly and helpful to the foreigners than those in another. Tourists thus may develop a preference for one destination over the other; however, if pressed, one may not be able to give a conscious explanation as to the reason for their preferences. In fact, learning involves "a change in the content or organization of long term memory and/or behavior". Learning causes changes in people's long term memory which refers to retention of information over the long term from days to years. When information is stored in the long term memory, learning becomes completed. A lot of values, attitudes, choices, enjoyments and behaviors in people's daily life occur through learning. Information on tourist destinations necessary to satisfy tourists' needs is to be gained and learnt. Therefore, before reaching any purchase decision and choice, tourists have to be aware of *attractions*, *amenities*, *accessibility*, *activities*, *ancillary services* and *available packages* in the destination. Prices, service qualities and images are also to be known by those people who wish to travel to a certain destination. In today's information era, there are many sources of information on tourist destinations and their offerings, such as family, friend groups, mass communication tools, mobile technologies, social media, advertising, commercial and noncommercial organizations and institutions, and personal experiences which can be gained through taking holidays, by listening to others and through a variety of other sources (Lumsdon, 1999).

Motivation

The inner power which pushes an individual to a goal oriented behavior is known as motivation. This inner power generally emerges from an unsatisfied need. In fact, it is the driving force within individuals that impels them to action: (a) which is produced by a state of tension due to an unfulfilled need; and (b) which leads to conscious/subconscious attempts to reduce the tension. The arousal of any particular set of needs at a specific moment in time may be caused by internal stimulus found in the individual's physiological condition (hunger, thirst), by emotional (daydreaming) or cognitive processes (random thoughts) or by stimuli in external environment (cues in the environment; e.g., smell of food). There are basically four types of motives: (a) rational motives refer to goals chosen according to objective criteria (e.g., price); (b) emotional motives means goals chosen according to personal or subjective criteria (e.g., desire for social status); (c) latent motives are the motives that the consumer is unaware of or unwilling to recognize, harder to identify and require projective techniques to identify; and (d) manifest motives are those motives that the consumer is aware of and willing to express. Motivations can be either positive or negative; the former refers to a driving force toward some object or condition while the latter means a driving force away from some object or condition.

Destination marketers can benefit from motivation in order to determine the marketing strategies for their destinations. For this reason, following strategies can be suggested: (a) identify the needs and goals of the target tourist markets by taking into account latent and manifest motives; (b) use knowledge of needs to segment the tourist markets and to position their tourism offerings; (c) use knowledge of needs to develop promotional strategies; and (d) reduce motivational conflict.

What we gather from the above given explanation on motivation is that it is essential for destination marketers to know and understand the motivation of various market segments which is behind the purchasing stimulus of each market segment. By doing this, they will be able to correctly serve customers at the correct time and meet their needs, resulting in tourist satisfaction and loyalty.

Emotions

Individuals' emotions are generally formed by the incidents that occur uncontrollably within the external environment. Basic emotions are those emotions that anybody may have on some occasions (Plutchik, 1980). Physiological changes such as rapid heart rate, sudden sweating and blushing, enlarged pupils and rapid breathing can be biological indicators of individuals' emotions in general. Consumers tend to choose the products that may cause positive emotions for them (Sherman, Mathur and Smith, 1997). However, while a movie or a book may cause sadness, this should not be interpreted as being a bad experience. Services related to entertainment activities such as participating in adventure tours, watching movies, reading books, and listening to music may cause some emotions in consumers. Therefore, destination marketers can benefit from these kinds of activities to create positive emotions on tourist markets to induce demand for their offerings and attractions.

Personality

Personality is the dynamic organization of psycho physiological systems that creates a person's characteristic pattern of behavior, thoughts, and feeling (Allport, 1961). In fact, it is the psychological traits that distinguish one person from another, and these traits constitute personality which is unique to each individual. It is argued that personality plays an important role on consumers' purchasing behavior, particularly in their responses to messages that are sent through advertising (Brody and Cunningham, 1968). It is advocated that influences of personality on consumers' purchasing decisions are much more on unbranded products rather than branded products (Brody and Cunningham, 1968; Carman, 1970). Therefore, it is suggested that tourism destinations should understand the personalities of the targeted tourist markets and develop branded services in line with the personalities of the targeted tourist markets. Personality analysis and differentiation is a difficult task, and hence it can be suggested that branding of destination services can be influential on tourist choices and decision making in the targeted markets.

Purchasing stimuli (*commercial, physical, social*)

External and internal factors explained above are influential on determining consumers' purchasing decisions. In fact, those factors can be classified into three as being *commercial*, *physical* and *social* (Hoffman and Bateson, 2008). Marketing efforts are the purchasing stimuli that are amongst the commercial purchasing stimuli. Tourism destinations can induce purchasing stimuli for the services they offer through promotional activities such as intensive adverting, public relations, sales promotion, personal selling and direct marketing. For instance, a person who never considers taking a holiday can be induced to travel even to a particular destination through a newspaper or internet advertisment that indicates a price advantage to that particular destination.

Biological stimuli are those purchasing stimuli which are amongst the physical purchasing stimuli. For example, an individual working in a stressful environment can feel tired and broken down, therefore he or she may wish to purchase a holiday package which will let him or her to get away from that kind of stressful job environment and feel biologically and mentally relaxed. On the other hand, an individual suffering from rheumatism pains may prefer to go on a holiday to a thermal tourist destination, and hence wishes to purchase a thermal holiday package. In this respect, a holiday need is induced by a physical stimulus.

Culture, values, family, reference groups, demographics and social stature are those purchasing stimuli that are amongst the biological stimuli. For instance, an individual who is not willing to take a holiday may decide to take a holiday with the social influences created by his or her family members or friends. In that case, social environment and position of the person within this social environment can determine the type of the holiday purchased.

As seen, commercial, physical and social stimuli emerge as a result of external and internal influences. Therefore, external and internal influences have to be taken into account holistically as tourists' purchasing stimuli. As explained before, those influences or stimuli affect lifestyle, and, in turn, lifestyle affects tourist decision making.

Tourists' decision making process

Tourists' decision making process consists of five basic stages as indicated in Figure 21.1 – holiday need recognition, information collection (search of destinations), evaluation of alternatives, destination decision and experience and post purchase behavior – which are detailed below. However, as Decrop (2006b) argues, holiday decision making is a rational process consisting of high involvement, high risk perception, extensive problem solving and information search, and a sequential evolution of plans which starts from the generic decision to take a holiday. He examined the holiday decision making process of 27 Belgian households (single, couples, families and groups of friends) by carrying out in-depth interviews four times: three times before their summer holiday and once after it. Many interesting findings emerged which challenged traditional ways of understanding consumer decision making. He indicates that holiday decision-making is an ongoing process which is very difficult to be characterized by fixed sequential stages, and which does not stop once a decision is made. As Decrop (2006b) indicates: (a) the generic decision about whether or not to go on holiday is not always the starting point: and sometimes this generic decision is irrelevant (for instance, in the case of regular holidaymakers); (b) there is seldom a linear (for example, sequential and hierarchical) evolution of holiday plans, situational factors as well as levels of involvement are responsible for many deviations and changes of mind (daydreaming, nostalgia and anticipation are other important influences; (c) final decisions and bookings are often made very late, there are a number of reasons for this, such as risk reduction, expectancy (situational variables), availability (opportunism), loyalty and personality; and (d) informants often express cognitive dissonance or post-decision regret, which they strive to reduce.

Holiday need recognition

Holiday need recognition is the first stage in the tourist purchasing decision process in which a person recognizes a physical and/or mental problem, which can mainly be caused by a stressful working environment and only be overcome through taking a holiday or travelling to other places, or a need of travelling for any purpose of tourism activities. In fact, holiday need recognition is when a person has identified a holiday need perhaps emerging from, as mentioned above, stressful working environment, a curiosity to understand various cultures and visit exotic places, health related problems or willingness to participate in sport or other leisure time activities. This need may be triggered by internal stimuli such as being burnt out in the daily working environment or routines and/or by external stimuli such as exposure to a new destination or advertising message. The chill of the winter might persuade a family to look for a holiday in the sun, or a special offer from a car dealer might convince them to forgo the holiday this year for a new car.

Two different styles of need and problem recognition exist amongst tourists, holidaymakers or travelers. The categories of tourists are those who opt for tourism offerings or a tourist destination as the present tourism product that they are visiting fails to function efficiently. These consumers are referred to as "actual state type vacationers". The second type is the desired state types, who need a tourism service or a destination to visit just because of a desire to take a holiday or travel for the activities of tourism. In this case, the desire becomes the trigger in prospective tourist decision process. Altogether, a holiday maker or a tourist at this stage can be referred to as an aroused consumer who is vulnerable to any stimuli of the marketers' appeal.

Information collection (search of destinations)

Traditionally, touristic information has been studied as a means of making destination choices. In fact, information collection is an important stage in destination decision making and choice. At this stage, tourists improve their knowledge regarding the offered attributes of the geographical regions such as attractions, accessibility, amenities, activities and ancillary services as well as availability of tour packages to the particular destinations they may consider visiting. In today's dynamic and competitive global business environment, understanding how tourists gather information is important for marketing management decisions, designing effective communication campaigns, and service delivery (Srinivasan, 1990; Wilkie and Dickson, 1985). Destination marketers can influence tourists' purchasing decisions during the initial search of information (Schmidt and Spreng, 1996).

Many tourists wisely combine various available information sources (Fodness and Murray, 1998), such as guidebooks and other specific materials of destination, news media, travel companies, knowledge passed on directly from acquaintances/family and own experience, information from electronic social networks and blogs. In this context, for instance, Xiang and Gretzel (2010) argue that social media are playing an increasingly important role as information sources for travelers and the results of their research also confirm the growing importance of social media in the online tourism domain. However, studies have shown that not everyone who collects information actually intends to travel (Messmer and Johnson, 1993; Woodside, 1990; Urry, 1990). Vogt and Fesenmaier (1998) used a decision-making and information search model as a framework for explaining the factors which influence the use of communications as they relate to recreation and tourism experiences. Their expanded approach to information research such as information for social, entertainment, visual, and creativity purposes is taken where many of the leisure and recreation-based motivations are considered. Fodness and Murray (1999) argue that tourist information search strategies are found to be the result of a dynamic process in which travelers use various types and amounts of information sources to respond to internal and external contingencies in vacation planning.

Gursoy and McCleary (2004) develop a comprehensive theoretical model that integrates the psychological/motivational, economics, and processing approaches into a cohesive whole to understand tourists' information seeking behavior. Their model proposes that for immediate pre-purchase information needs, a consumer is likely to utilize either internal or external sources, or both. The search is likely influenced directly by the perceived internal and external costs, and the level of involvement required. Familiarity and expertise, learning and previous visits indirectly influence the search. Jacobsen and Munar (2012) provide empirical evidence of self-reported impacts of selected electronic and other information sources on international tourists' destination choices regarding a popular, mature and mainstream summer holiday location. As they point out, traditional information provisions such as direct word-of-mouth, Web 1.0 sources and own experience are highly resilient and influential when tourists decide to spend their summer holiday in a well-known destination area. Moreover, their results indicate a complementary nature of Web 1.0 and Web 2.0. In this context of destination decision-making, utilitarian information values seem more relevant than socialization opportunities. Moreover, Gursoy and Umbreit (2004) investigated the influence of national-cultures on the external information search behavior of travelers from the European Union (EU) member states. Their findings suggest that national culture significantly influences a traveler's external information search behavior.

Knowledge acquired through past or current experiences which are coded in the memory for future reference is said to be significant in determining tourists' decision making (Teare, 1991; Hemmington, 1994). The consumer is most likely to use this knowledge as a selection tool mechanism for differentiating, valuing and reviewing the tourist offering before reaching a final decision. In conclusion, it is important to note that destination marketers should understand the sources from which customers draw their information if they are to influence the decision process (Gartner, 1993).

Evaluation of alternatives

Once sufficient information is gathered from both the external and the internal sources, potential tourists move into the evaluation of alternatives phase where they evaluate alternative destinations or holiday types in accordance with their needs. They may evaluate the alternatives through systematic (*formal*) or unsystematic (*informal*) techniques.

Alternatives can be evaluated through the application of systematic techniques which require statistical evaluations based on the multi feature models. These types of models require formal stages in tourists' decision making through the evaluation of alternative services. More specifically, these types of models assess some features and basic criteria which are taken into account by the consumers in evaluating alternative services. Potential tourists, before deciding a destination, will evaluate the alternatives on a scale of attributes which have the ability to deliver the benefit that they are seeking. In this respect, they will evaluate the alternative destinations based on the attractions, amenities, accessibility, activities, prices, services qualities, image, and of course prices. To make a quantitative evaluation of alternatives, potential tourists attribute a value to each attribution that destinations offer, and then sum up these values and tend to make their final destination decision and choice considering the highest score of attribution. Unsystematic evaluations are mostly through the intuitional, emotional or subjective criteria. For instance, previous personal experiences and impressions gained through word-of-mouth, movies, news, documentaries, novels, history, myths and other similar sources will affect the evaluation of alternatives in final destination decision making and choice.

In order for destination marketing organizations (DMOs) to increase the likelihood that their destinations are part of the evoked set for many potential tourists, they need to understand what benefits potential tourists are seeking and specifically, which attributes will be the most influential to their decision making process. It is important to note that potential tourists evaluate alternatives in terms of the functional and psychological benefits that they offer. Destination marketers also need to check the potential tourists' consideration set of other destinations to prepare the right plan for their own destinations and their tourist offerings. It is also important to note that when evaluating the alternative tourism services consumers can consider whether they can produce these services by themselves or not. For instance, self-catering enterprises can be chosen and any other possible self-service opportunities can be alternatives for the tourism services offered by the destination which may be under consideration for taking an holiday there. Therefore, the evaluation process of destination tourism services is a complex process which varies depending on the purchasing situation.

Destination decision and experience

After evaluation of alternatives, tourists make the decision whether to travel to a particular destination or take a holiday in a particular destination or not. In fact, tourists' destination decision making and choice is generally to buy the preferred tourism services and take a holiday in a particular tourist destination. However, there are basically two factors which influence whether a purchase intention results in a purchase decision or not. The first factor is the attitude of other people who influence the purchase decision, for example family members. Destination marketers must therefore be aware of those who influence purchasing decision and may use targeted communication to influence their attitudes, as well as those of the purchaser. The second factor is unexpected situational factors such as overbooking and being short of capacity, or finding some element of the marketing mix which does not meet their expectation, such as discovering a price increase or finding the service unsatisfactory in a destination (Kotler, 2002).

Purchasing and consumption of physical products are generally independent from each other and constitute the following three successive stages: (a) physical products are bought, (b) they can be used after a time span (consumed) and (c) having been used or after completing their life cycle, they are either thrown away or they run out. However, for services, it is very difficult and in most cases impossible to separate these three stages from each other. Since ownership right cannot be transferred wholly, it is very difficult to distinguish service purchase from service use with strict lines. In services, long term relations between a service provider and service users are generally developed, therefore production, purchasing and using stages of services are very complex and interwoven with each other, as a result, they are mostly perceived as being one stage. Especially, because of intangible and experiential features of services it is impossible for services to be thrown away.

During the purchasing and consumption processes of services, there occurs direct interaction between particularly the frontline employees and the consumers. This interaction and other factors (i.e., just in time service production, service quality and meeting the consumer expectations) constitute the service experience.

Post purchase behavior

As seen tourists' decision making consists of several independents elements and it is a complicated process. This is because there are many factors affecting the destination decision making process and selection, some of them internal while others are external, some of them are perhaps controllable to some extent while most of them uncontrollable to larger extent. Similarly, post purchase behavior of service customers such as, tourists, is a very complicated process. This process starts with selection stage and continues with consumption (using) stage and afterwards. In fact, this whole process in general and after consumption stage in particular is inevitably under the influence of social, psychological and situational variables. A destination refers to the supply side of tourism that can be regarded as the raison d'être for tourism, providing an amalgam of tourism products such as, attractions, accessibility, amenities and activities which respond to the needs and wants of the demand side of tourism (tourist) (Buhalis and Cooper, 1998). Given this, the supply side of tourism generally consists of three elements (Jafari, 1983). The first is tourism-oriented products which include accommodation services, restaurant and bar facilities, transportation, travel agencies and tour operators, recreation and entertainment facilities, and other tourism and travel services (souvenir stores, camera and film stands, etc.). The second is resident-oriented products which consist of hospitals, bookstores, barbershops, and so on. The third is background tourism elements which include natural, sociocultural and manmade attractions. All three supply elements are equally important in the development and the sustainment of international tourism in a region since these elements draw tourists to that particular region. All these elements represent the tangible sides of what a tourist destination can offer to its visitors, but there are of course intangible sides, which consist of the service side of tourism offerings of a particular tourist destination. In that respect, tourist or visitor satisfaction to a greater extent depends on service providers, other visitors (third parties in the process of service production) and service presentation systems as well as the quality of the place where services are produced. Of course, coordination and harmony among all these independent aspects should not be neglected.

Success or failure of services offered in tourist destinations is directly related to the professional abilities of managers in service enterprises, such as their managerial abilities in the following areas: (a) *interpersonal relations* (customers versus customers and customers versus service employee); and (b) *human-environment interactions* (service employee versus working environment and supporting elements, customers versus working environment and supporting elements). In this way, they may be able to control the tourists' experiences which occur as post purchase behavior.

Expectation disconfirmation

Tourist satisfaction is one of the most frequently examined topics in the literature of tourism marketing as it plays an important role in the survival and future of any tourism offering of a tourist destination. Tourism satisfaction significantly influences the choice of destination, the consumption of tourism services and also the decision to return to the same tourist destination. Tourist satisfaction is defined as a person's feelings of pleasure and disappointment that result from comparing a tourist product's perceived performance to his or her expectations; it is a function of tourist perception. In this context, the expectation disconfirmation model suggests that consumers have prior expectations from a product before actually purchasing (Oliver, 1980). After product consumption they have a positive disconfirmation if the actual performance is better than their expectations. This model further suggests that if tourists are highly satisfied, there is a high likelihood of repeat visit, however if actual performance is not up to expectations they are likely to have a negative disconfirmation. This indicates a dissatisfied visitor. Such visitors are likely to look for other tourist products or destination alternatives.

What is important here for the marketers of tourist destinations is the management of tourist expectations. It is more important than making any specific change in the quality of tourism services. In other words, managing tourist expectations can help the marketers of tourist services to manage tourist satisfaction.

Perceived-control perspective

In evaluating tourists' post purchase behavior, perceived-control model emerges as another model. Psychologists discuss the human need to control situations surrounding our everyday of life. The need to control one's environment is an important driving force for human beings (Bateson 2000). The need to have control over every situation emerges again from another need of humans to establish power, dominance and authority (White, 1959). In this context, three main types of personal control may be distinguished (Averill, 1973): (a) behavioral (direct action on the environment); (b) cognitive (the interpretation of events); and (c) decisional (having a choice among alternative courses of action). More specifically, behavioral control means consumer's perception of what he or she can do to influence the situation or event, exemplified by control over procedure; cognitive control refers to consumers' interpretation of the situation, which is exemplified when consumers obtain information; and decisional control means whether a customer decides to enter a situation or evaluates alternatives (Averill 1973). In perceived control perspective, by directing, consumers may wish to control a service process and direct this process as a result of the confirmation and disconfirmation process.

To understand how the perception of control influences the satisfaction process is of interest because satisfaction has huge importance in predicting a consumer's future choices (Gregory, Severt and Hahm, 2016; Woodruff, Cadotte and Jenkins, 1983). Within this perspective, understanding whether and how co-production may contribute to enhance customers' perceived control and consequently satisfaction appears also relevant.

For destination marketers what can be suggested is establishing well equipped customers relations management schemes which enable visitors express their views depending on their individual needs and wishes independently.

The script perspective

During the service consumption, because of the inseparability feature of services, service providers and consumers act in face-to-face interactions. These interactions are expected to create mutual benefits which can be gained through performing the expected role play of each side during the face to face interaction which is known as "a moment of truth" – an aspect of service production. In other words, on one hand service providers should play their expected role while presenting their role in line with the general expectation of consumers based on social values, norms and manners. On the other hand, consumers are also expected to play their role in line with the general expectations of the service providers which are also based on social values, norms and manners (Hoffman and Bateson, 2008). If a visitor of a destination behaves in line with the expected manners, he or she can be served with respect. On the contrary, if a visitor of a destination does not behave in line with the expected manners, he or she should not expect to receive service with respect.

Conclusion

The aim of this chapter is to evaluate tourists' destination decision making and selection processes based on the current literature. As has been pointed out, tourists' destination decision making is a complex process which requires multidimensional relations among various external and internal factors. However, destination decision making and selection processes, to some extent, vary from traditional consumer decision making. More specifically, right from the beginning stage of holiday need recognition till the post purchase behavior stage, the disparities are evident and noticeable. This is mainly because of the consumption characteristics of physical products and services such as tourism. The focus of traditional consumer decision making is mainly on physical products of which consumption characteristics are not continuous while consumption of tourism services is continuous and mostly experiential. To reach successful results in their marketing efforts, destination marketers should consider every aspect of tourists' destination decision making and selection process from a wider angle.

Acknowledgement

We appreciate the significant proof reading contribution of both Ms. Zeynep Tasdemir and Ayse Yildiz who work as English instructors at the Faculty of Tourism, Erciyes University, Kayseri, Turkey.

References

Ahmed, Z. U. (1994) "Determinants of The Components of A State's Image and Their Marketing Implications", *Journal of Hospitality and Leisure Marketing* 2, 55–69.

Alhemoud, A.M. and Armstrong, E. G. (1996) "Image of Tourism Attractions in Kuwait", *Journal of Travel Research* 34, 76–80.

Allport, G. W. (1961) *Pattern and Growth in Personality*, New York, NY: Holt, Rinehart and Winston.

Andrades-Caldito, L., Sánchez-Rivero, M. and Pulido-Fernández, J. I. (2013) "Differentiating Competitiveness through Tourism Image Assessment: An Application to Andalusia (Spain)", *Journal of Travel Research* 52, 68–81.

Arnold, J., Silvester, J., Patterson, F., Robertson, I., Cooper, C. and Burnes, B., (2005), "Work Psychology: Understanding Human Behaviour in the Workplace", Spain: Prentice Hall.

Averill, J. R. (1973), "Personal Control over Aversive Stimuli and Its Relationship to Stress", *Psychological Bulletin* 4, 286–303.

Baloglu, S. and McCleary, K. W. (1999) "Model of Destination Image Formation", *Annals of Tourism Research* 26, 868–897.

Bargeman, B. and van der Poel, H. (2006) "The Role of Routines in The Vacation Decision-Making Process of Dutch Vacationers", *Tourism Management* 27, 707–720.

Barros, C. P., Butler, R. and Correia, A. (2008) "Heterogeneity in Destination Choice: Tourism in Africa", *Journal of Travel Research* 47, 235–246.

Bateson, J. E. G. (2000) "Perceived Control and The Service Experience" in T. A. Swartz and D. Iacobucci (eds) *Handbook of Services Marketing and Management*, Thousand Oaks: Sage Publications, pp. 127–44.

Bei, Lien-Ti (2000) *The Whitepaper on Lifestyle: A Report of the 2000 Survey on Taiwanese Consumption Habits*, Taipei City: Business Weekly Publications.

Brody, R. P. and Cunningham, C. M. (1968) "Personality Variables and the Consumer Decision Process," *Journal of Marketing Research* V, 50–57.

Bronner, F. and de Hoog, F. (2008). "Agreement and Disagreement in Family Vacation Decision-Making", *Tourism Management* 29, 967–979.

Buhalis, D. and Cooper, C. (1998) "Competition or Co-operation? Small and Medium-Sized Tourism Enterprises at the Destination" in E. Laws, B. Faulkner, and G. Moscardo (eds) *Embracing and Managing Change in Tourism: International Case Studies*, London: Routledge, pp. 324–346.

Carman, J. M. (1970) "Correlates of Brand Loyalty: Some Positive Results," *Journal of Marketing Research*, VII, 67–76.

Chi, C. G. Q. and Qu, H. (2008) "Examining the Structural Relationships of Destination Image, Tourist Satisfaction and Destination Loyalty: An Integrated Approach", *Tourism Management* 29, 624–636.

Choi, S., Lehto, C., Morrison, A.M. and Jang, S. (2012) "Structure of Travel Planning Processes and Information Use Patterns", *Journal of Travel Research* 51, 26–40.

Clawson, M. and Knetsch, J. L. (1966) *Economics of Outdoor Recreation*, Baltimore: The John Hopkins Press.

Cochran, A. (2001) *Prospect Theory and Customer Choice. Retrieved on November 11, 2016 from*, http://alexcochran.com.au/wp-content/uploads/2008/04/propect-theory-customer-choice.pdf.

Cohen, A. B. (2009) "Many forms of culture", *American Psychologist* 64, 194–204.

Correia, A., Kozak, M. and Ferradeira, J. (2011) "Impact of Culture on Tourist Decision-making Styles", *International Journal of Tourism Research* 13, 433–446.

Crompton, J. L. (1977) *A Systems Model of the Tourist's Destination Selection Decision Process with Particular Reference to the Role of Image and Perceived Constraints*, Unpublished Doctoral Dissertation, Texas A&M University.

Decrop, A. (1999) "Tourists' Decision-Making and Behavior Processes" in A. Pizam and Y. Mansfeld (eds) *Consumer Behavior in Travel and Tourism*, pp. 103–133.

Decrop, A. (2006a) *Vacation Decision Making*, Wallingford: CABI Publishing.

Decrop, A. (2006b), "Holiday Decision-Making: an Adaptable and Opportunistic Ongoing Process" in M. Solomon, G. Bamossy, S. Askegaard and M. K. Hogg (eds), *Consumer Behaviour A European Perspective*, Essex: FT Prentice Hall, pp. 3910–3920.

Decrop, A. (2010). Destination choice set: An inductive longitudinal approach. Annals of Tourism Research, 37(1), 93–115.

Decrop, A. and Kozak M. (2009). "Decision Strategies in Tourism Evaluation" in M. Kozak and A. Decrop, *Handbook of Tourist Behavior Theory & Practice*, New York: Routledge, pp. 67–82.

Decrop, A. and Snelders, D. (2004) "Planning the summer vacation: An adaptable process" *Annals of Tourism Research* 3, 1008–1030.

Dolnicar, S., Crouch, G. I., Devinney, T., Huybers, T., Louviere, J. J. and Opperwal, H. (2008) "Tourism and Discretionary Income Allocation – Heterogeneity Among Households", *Tourism Management* 29, 44–52.

Edwards, W (1954), "The Theory Of Decision Making", *Psychological Bulletin* 51, 380–417.

Engel, J. F. and Blackwell, R. D. (1982) *Consumer Behavior*, New York: Rinehart and Winston.

Engel, J. F., Kollat, D. T. and Blackwell, R. D. (1968) *Consumer Behavior*, New York: Holt, Rinehart and Winston.

Fakeye, P. C. and Crompton, J. L. (1991) "Images Differences between Prospective, First-Time and Repeat Visitors to The Lower Rio Grande valley", *Journal of Travel Research* 30, 10–16.

Fodness, D. and Murray, B. (1998), "A Typology of Tourist Information Search Strategies", *Journal of Travel Research* 37, 108–119.

Fodness, D. and Murray, B. (1999) "A Model of Tourist Information Search Behavior", *Journal of Travel Research* 37, 220–230.

Foxall, G. (1990) *Consumer Psychology in Behavioural Perspective*, London: Routledge.

Freud, S. (1923), "The Ego and Id" in J. Strachey (1961), *The Standard Edition of the Complete Psychological Works of Sigmund Freud*, Volume XIX (1923–1925): The Ego and the Id and Other Works, 1–308. London: The Hogarth Press and the Institute of Psychoanalysis, pp. 12–68.

Freud, S. (1960) *The Psychopathology of Everyday Life*, London: Hogarth.

Gartner, W. (1993) "Image Formation Process", *Journal of Travel and Tourism Marketing* 2, 191–215.

Goodall, B. (1988) "How Tourists Chose Their Holidays: An Analytical Framework" in B. Goodall and G. Ashworth (eds), *Marketing in The Tourism Industry; Promotional Destination Regions*, London: Croom Helm, pp. 1–10.

Goodall, B. (1991) "Understanding Holiday Choice" in C. Cooper (ed.) *Progress in Tourism, Recreation and Hospitality Management* 3, London: Belhaven Press, pp. 59–77.

Gregory, A.M., Severt, D.E. and Hahm, J. (2016) "An Attribution Approach and the Subsequent Satisfaction, Value, and Loyalty of Service Delivery in Private Residence Clubs", *Journal of Hospitality Marketing & Management*, 25(1), 91–112.

Gunn, C. (1989) *Vacationscape: Designing Tourist Regions*, New York: Van Nostrand Reinhold Publishers.

Gursoy, D. and McCleary, K.W. (2004) "An Integrative Model of Tourists' Information Search Behavior", *Annals of Tourism Research* 31, 353–373.

Gursoy, D. and Umbreit, W.T. (2004) "Tourist Information Search Behavior: Crosscultural Comparison of European Union Member States", *International Journal of Hospitality Management*, 23, 55–70.

Hawkins, I., Best, R.J. and Coney, K.A. (1989) *Consumer Behavior: Building Marketing Strategy*, New York: Irwin/McGraw-Hill.

Hemmington, N. (1994) "Market Research and Concept Development: Models of Consumer Behaviour" in P. Jones and P. Merricks, (eds), *The Management of Foodservice Operations*, London: Cassell, pp. 18–44.

Hoffman, K. D and Bateson, J.E.G. (2008), *Services Marketing, Concepts, Strategies and Cases*, Mason: South-Western Cengage Learning.

Hofstede, G. (1980) *Culture's Consequences: International Differences in Work-Related Values*, Newbury Park, CA: Sage Publications.

Hofstede, G. (1991) *Cultures and Organizations: Software of the Mind*, London: McGraw-Hill.

Hofstede, G. and Bond, M.H. (1988) "The Confucius Connection: From Cultural Roots to Economic Growth", *Organizational Dynamics* 16, 4–22.

Howard, J.A. and Sheth, J.N. (1960) *The Theory of Buyer Behavior*, New York: John Wiley and Sons.

Howard, J.A. and Sheth, J.N. (1969) *The Theory of Buyer Behavior*, New York: John Wiley and Sons.

Hyde, K. and Lawson, R. (2003) "The Nature of Independent Travel", *Journal of Travel Research* 42, 13–23.

Hyde, K.F. (2000) "A Hedonic Perspective on Independent Vacation Planning, Decision Making and Behavior" in A.G. Woodside, G.I. Crouch, J.A. Mazanec, M. Oppermann and M.Y. Sakai (eds), *Consumer Psychology of Tourism, Hospitality and Leisure*, Wallingford: CABI, pp. 177–192.

Jacobsen, J.K.S. and Munar, A.M. (2012) "Tourist Information Search and Destination Choice in A Digital Age", *Tourism Management Perspectives* 1, 39–47.

Jafari, J. (1983) "Anatomy of the Travel Industry", *The Cornell Hotel and Restaurant Administration Quarterly* 23, 71–77.

Jung, C.G. (1933) *Psychological Types*, New York: Harcourt, Brace and World.

Kahneman, D. and Tversky, A. (1979) "Prospect Theory: An Analysis of Decision under Risk", *Econometrica* 47, 263–292.

Kang, S.K. and Hsu, H. C. (2005) "Dyadic Consensus on Family Vacation Destination Selection", *Tourism Management* 26, 571–582.

Karamustafa, K., Fuchs, G. and Reichel, A. (2012) "Risk Perceptions of a Mixed Image Destination: The Case of Turkey's First Time vs. Repeat Visitors", *Journal of Hospitality Marketing and Management* 22, 243–268.

Kotler, P. (1965) "Behavioural Model for Analyzing Buyers", *Journal of Marketing* 20, 35–45.

Kotler, P. (2002) *Market Management*, Englewood Cliffs, NJ: Prentice Hall.

Kotler, P., Bowen, J. and Makens, J. (2002) *Marketing for Hospitality and Tourism*, New Jersey: Prentice Hall.

Lin, L. and Shih, H. (2012) "The Relationship of University Students' Lifestyle, Money Attitude, Personal Value and Their Purchase Decision", *International journal of Research in Management* 1, 19–37.

Litvin, S., Xu, G. and Kang, S. (2004) "Spousal Vacation-Buying Decision Making Revisited Across Time and Place", *Journal of Travel Research* 43, 193–198.

Lumsdon, L. (1999) *Tourism Marketing*, London: International Thomson Business Press.

Mansfeld, Y. (1992) "From Motivation to Actual Travel", *Annals of Tourism Research* 19, 399–419.

March, R. and Woodside, A. (2005) "Testing Theory of Planned Versus Realized Behavior", *Annals of Tourism Research* 32, 905–924.

Marcussen, C.H. (2011) "Understanding Destination Choices of German Travelers", *Tourism Analysis* 16, 649–662.

Mathieson, A. and Wall, G. (1982) *Tourism: Economic, Physical and Social Impacts*, London: Longman.

McCabe, S., Li, C. and Chen, Z. (2015) "Time for a Radical Reappraisal of Tourist Decision Making? Toward a New Conceptual Model", *Journal of Travel Research* 55, 1–12.

Messmer, D.J. and Johnson, R.R. (1993) "Inquiry Conversion and Travel Advertising Effectiveness", *Journal of Travel Research* 31, 14–21.

Middleton, V.T.C. (1994) *Marketing in Travel and Tourism*, Oxford: Butterworth-Heinemann.

Middleton, V. T. C. and Clarke, J. R. (2001) *Marketing in Travel and Tourism*, London: Butterworth-Heinemann.

Milman, A. and Pizam, A. (1995) "The Role of Awareness and Familiarity with A Destination: The Central Florida Case", *Journal of Travel Research* 33, 21–27.

Moutinho, L. (1982) *An Investigation of Vacation Tourist Behaviour*, Unpublished PhD Dissertation, University of Sheffield.

Moutinho, L. (1987) "Consumer Behavior in Tourism", *European Journal of Marketing* 2, 3–44.

Morley, C. L. (1992) "A Microeconomic Theory of International Tourism Demand", *Annals of Tourism Research* 19, 250–267.

Nicolau, J. and Mas, F. (2005) "Stochastic Modelling: A Three-Stage Tourist Choice Process", *Annals of Tourism Research* 32, 49–69.

Nicosia, F. M. (1966) *Consumer Decision Processes: Marketing and Advertising Implications.* New Jersey: Prentice-Hall.

Oh, H. and Hsu, C. (2001) "Volitional and Nonvolitional Aspects of Gambling Behavior", *Annals of Tourism Research* 28, 618–637.

Oliver, R. L. (1980) "A Cognitive Model of the Antecedents and Consequences of Satisfaction Decisions," *Journal of Marketing Research* 17, 46–49.

Papatheodorou, A. (2001) "Why People Travel to Different Places", *Annals of Tourism Research* 28, 164–179.

Parasuraman, A., Zeithaml, V. A. and Berry, L. L. (1985) "A Conceptual Model of Service Quality and Its Implications for Future Research", *Journal of Marketing* 49, 41–50.

Parasuraman, A., Zeithaml, V. A. and Berry, L. L. (1988) "SERVQUAL: A Multiple Item Scale for Measuring Customer Perceptions of Service Quality", *Journal of Retailing* 64, 12–40.

Pike, S. D. (2002) "Destination Image Analysis – A Review of 142 Papers from 1973 to 2000", *Tourism Management* 23, 541–549.

Plutchik, R. (1980) *A. Psychoevolutionary Synthesis*, New York: Harper and Row.

Quintal, V., Lee, J. and Soutar, G. (2010) "Risk, Uncertainty and The Theory of Planned Behavior: A Tourism Example", *Tourism Management* 31, 797–805.

Rugg, D. (1973) "The Choice of Journey Destination: A Theoretical and Empirical Analysis", *Review of Economics and Statistics* 55, 64–72.

Schmidt, J. and Spreng, R. (1996) "A Proposed Model of External Consumer Information Search", *Journal of the Academy of Marketing Science* 24, 246–256.

Schmoll, G. A. (1977) *Tourism Promotion*, London: Tourism International Press.

Schwartz, S. H. (1992) "Universals in The Content and Structure of Values: Theoretical Advances and Empirical Tests in 20 Countries" in M. P. Zanna (ed.), *Advances in Experimental Social Psychology*, New York: Academic Press, pp. 1–65.

Seddighi, H. and Theocharous, A. (2002) "A Model of Tourism Destination Choice: A Theoretical and Empirical Analysis", *Tourism Management* 23, 475–487.

Sherman, E., Mathur, A. and Smith, R. B. (1997) "Store Environment and Consumer Purchase Behavior: Mediating Role of Consumer Emotions", *Psychology and Marketing* 14, 361–378.

Sirakaya, E. and Woodside, A. (2005) "Building and Testing Theories of Decision Making by Travelers", *Tourism Management* 26, 815–832.

Sirgy, M. J. (1982) "Self-Concept in Consumer Behavior: A Critical Review", *Journal of Consumer Research* 9, 287–300.

Smallman, C. and Moore, K. (2010) "Process Studies of Tourists Decision-Making", *Annals of Tourism Research*, 37, 397–422.

Solomon, M, Bamossy, G. J., Askegaard, S. and Hogg, M. K. (2006) *Consumer Behaviour: A European Perspective*, Harlow: Prentice Hall.

Srinivasan, N. (1990) "Pre-Purchase External Search for Information" in V. A. Ziethaml (ed.), *Review of Marketing 1990*, Chicago: American Marketing Association, 153–189.

Stell, R. and Donoho, C. L. (1996) "Classifying services from a consumer perspective", *Journal of Services Marketing* 10, 33–44.

Sternberg, R. J. (1996) *Cognitive Psychology*, Orlando: Harcourt.

Teare, R. (1991) "Consumer Strategies for Assessing and Evaluating Hotels" in R. Teare and A. Boer (eds), *Strategic Hospitality Management: Theory and Practice for The 1990s*, London: Cassell, pp. 120–143.

Teare, R. (1994) "Consumer Decision-Making" in R. Teare, J. A. Mazanec, S. Crawford-Welch and S. Calver (eds), *Marketing in Hospitality and Tourism: A Consumer Focus*, London: Cassell, pp. 1–96.

Um, S. and Crompton, J. L. (1990) "Attitude Determinants in Tourism Destination Choice", *Annals of Tourism Research* 17, 432–448.

Urry, J. (1990) *The Tourist Gaze: Leisure and Travel in Contemporary Societies*, London: Sage Publications.
van Raaij, W. F. (1986) "Consumer Research on Tourism Mental and Behavioral Constructs", *Annals of Tourism Research* 13, 1–9.
van Raaij, W. F. and Francken, D. A. (1984) "Vacation Destinations, Activities and Satisfactions", *Annals of Tourism Research* 11, 101–112.
Vogt, C. A. and Fesenmaier, D. R. (1998) "Expanding the Functional Information Search Model", *Annals of Tourism Research* 25, 551–578.
Wahab, S., Crampon, L. J. and Rothfield, L. M. (1976) *Tourism Marketing*, London: Tourism International Press.
White, R. W. (1959) "Motivation Reconsidered: The Concept of Competence", *Psychological Review*, 66, 297–323.
Wilkie, W. and P. Dickson (1985) *Shopping for Appliances: Consumers' Strategies and Patterns of Information Search*, Cambridge MA: Marketing Science Institute.
Woodruff, R. B. and Jenkins, R. L. (1983). "Modeling Consumer Satisfaction Processes Using Experience-Based Norms", *Journal of Marketing Research* 20, 305–314.
Woodside, A. and MacDonald (1993) "General System Framework of Customer Choice Processes of Tourism Services" in R. V. Gasser and K. Weiermair (eds), *Spoilt for Choice – Decision Making Processes and Preference Changes of Tourists: Proceedings of the Institute of Tourism and Service Economics International Conference*, University of Innsbruck, 30–59.
Woodside, A., Caldwell, M. and Spurr, R. (2006) "Advancing Ecological Systems Theory in Lifestyle, Leisure, and Travel Research?", *Journal of Travel Research* 44, 259–272.
Woodside, A. G. (1990) "Measuring Advertising Effectiveness in Destination Marketing Strategies", *Journal of Travel Research*, 29, 3–8.
Woodside, A. G. and Lysonski, S. (1989) "A General Model of Traveler Destination Choice", *Journal of Travel Research* 27, 8–14.
Woodside, A. G. and MacDonald, R. (1994) "General System Framework of Customer Choice Processes of Tourism Services" in R. V. Gasser and K. Weiermair (eds), *Spoilt for Choice – Decision Making Processes and Preference Change of Tourists: Intertemporal and Intercountry Perspectives*, Thaur: Kulturverlag.
Xiang, Z. and Gretzel, U. (2010) "Role of Social Media in Online Travel Information Search", *Tourism Management* 31, 179–188.
Yates, J. F. and Potworowski, G. A. (2012) "Evidence-Based Decision Management" in D. M. Rousseau (ed.), *The Oxford Handbook of Evidence-Based Management*, Oxford: Oxford University Press, pp. 716–790.

22

A critical review of consumer trends in tourism and destination marketing

Christine A. Vogt and Jada Lindblom

Introduction

Travel and tourism exist today in a world blighted by crime, war, and natural disaster. Despite negative events that have directly involved the airlines and iconic tourist districts, such as the September 11, 2001 attack and destruction of the World Trade Center in New York City, travel and tourism continues to grow. With this growth, residents in destination areas may encounter new economic opportunities but may also be "priced out" of their homes, or find that their communities have lost their special character or desirable "small town feel." Climate change is a phenomenon that threatens the integrity of coastlines as rising sea levels caused by glacier melting and threatening storms advance upon destination communities. The warmer temperatures in many destination regions are attributed to climate change. The tourism industry is having to adapt to these environmental changes to still meet the expectations of consumers. Warming climates have shortened the length of ski seasons and forced many ski resorts to increasingly rely upon artificial snowmaking (Amelung, Nicholls, and Viner 2007). The tourism industry has actively taken part in the wide assumption that technology and innovations will make up for changed environmental conditions. Hotels, shops and restaurants in the U.S. have collectively contributed to a new societal standard of air conditioning, to an extent so exhaustive that people expect to feel chilly air indoors even on the hottest days in the hottest of places.

Clearly, the globe is changing politically, socially, economically and environmentally. This is the contemporary state we find ourselves in. So what is a tourist to think? Or do? Does a tourist remain a consumer of travel and tourism products by traveling to places near and far from their home? Or do they find substitute experiences closer to home, perhaps even using virtual reality technology, reducing costs and environmental impacts? Today, the tourism industry appears to be more sensitive to the challenges that trends place on consumers and the industry. Tourism businesses and destinations appear to be becoming more responsible and more sustainable in their practices (McMahon 2015). New policies, new collaborations, and a growth in upstart non-profits and travel companies are beginning to show their leadership and impact on the tourism industry, in turn providing more options to the consumer. Marketing campaigns are designed to highlight these new offerings, further persuading travelers to embrace "trends" of sustainability, social equity, and emphases on local, artisanal, and "boutique" products. Individuals are becoming involved as smarter, more mindful, and more empowered consumers as they travel domestically and internationally.

The chapter reviews some of the macro influences in today's tourism industry that are impacting how individuals travel to and tour destinations and how their needs and demands are reflected in marketing approaches. Broadly, the chapter aims to examine the implications that consumers' behavior has to tourism marketing, and more specifically to destination marketing. The chapter begins with an overview of the level of global travel by tourists. The second part presents demographic changes in the U.S. as they impact who travels and how travel is marketed. The third part will discuss the impacts of over 50 years of environmental mindfulness and the expanded use of sustainability in marketing. Parks have played a longstanding role in promoting environmental awareness and activism, while many parks have also been key players in travel and hospitality services. The fourth part will review the impact of technology on how destinations are marketed and how travelers plan trips and make purchases. The chapter will conclude with a look at the recent growth of the sharing economy and the role that individuals have on both the provider and the consumer side of the less formal economic transaction. The sharing economy combines the possibilities of creating markets online and a product experience that is more local and human infused. The chapter considers ways in which individuals play an active role in product innovations that create positive experiences for themselves and lead to fewer negative consequences for the places they visit.

Globalization and destination marketing

Global travel has grown significantly in the past 60 years (World Tourism Organization, 2016). Europe and North America continue to be favorites but other continents are growing at twice the rate of mature destinations. For 2015, WTO reported that Europe garnered over half of the world's tourist arrivals (51%), followed by Asia and the Pacific (24%), the Americas (16%), Africa (5%), and the Middle East (4%). In addition to international travel, WTO estimates that five to six billion tourists travel within their own country. Over the next 15 years, WTO estimates that tourist arrivals in developing countries will increase by 4.4% a year, compared to half that rate in developed countries including those in North America and Western Europe. For outbound travel, four countries dominate. China holds the number one outbound market position with 128 million departures spending $292 billion in other countries. The U.S. is second on spending at $113 billion for 74 million departures. Germany and the United Kingdom are the two other top outbound markets. Despite economic slowing in Chinese economies, Chinese outbound travelers are poised to visit nearby Asian destinations and beyond, including famous U.S. and European destinations. Chinese travelers are becoming known for visiting iconic destinations like Paris, Las Vegas, and U.S. National Parks, frequenting entertainment and gambling venues, spending on luxury goods and other shopping experiences, and eating in restaurants ranging from buffets to signature chefs. Destination marketing organizations (DMOs) and tourism businesses around the globe are in a hunt to customize their product to delight the Chinese consumer.

As global expansion accelerates, countries must be invested in travel services to receive inbound tourists and prepare their own residents for outbound travel. Services are hosted in national tourism offices (NTOs), consulates, chambers, and DMOs. Besides the preparation of necessary travel documents, NTOs may offer programs that assist people from diverse cultures to host and visit new countries and new cultures. Before the internet, these offices were the primary marketing locations for countries to launch travel campaigns for their countries. For example, the British Tourist Authority or VisitBritain has offices in several U.S. cities. In the world's largest cities, it is very common for countries to have an office or consulate that assists with travel planning to their country, including the process of visa applications. DMOs have become the marketer for cities, suburbs and rural areas (Pike and Page 2014). DMOs typically receive their funding to promote an area from accommodation tax revenues paid by guests, or membership fees paid by businesses. The aim of DMOs is to make the destination more competitive to leisure, business and group markets and use pooled funds to create destination image campaigns, collateral, and digital marketing.

Another trend contributing to global travel is transportation and access to destinations. The last half century has truly advanced travel for most global citizens. With the invention of jet airliners in the 1950s, global travel became a possibility for many. Earlier travel across continents was primarily limited to exploration or migration. Travel via boat or ship across any of the oceans was often risky and took a long time. Today, there are over dozens of international airlines, with the largest airlines operating from the U.S. (Southwest, Delta, American, and United). There has been tremendous growth in budget airlines across Europe and Asia, making quick and spontaneous trips to exotic locales a new possibility. Airlines like Emirates have increased exposure of the Middle East as a travel hub and destination. In the 1950s, the World Tourism Organization (WTO) reported there were 25 million international tourist arrivals across the globe. Today, 1.2 billion arrivals are reported for a much larger set of possible destinations (WTO 2016). In developing countries, citizens may have not yet traveled on an airline or to another country because of cost or travel restrictions of the origin or destination countries. Experts see these barriers and boundaries coming down over the long-run even though there will be shock events like wars, closed countries, and diplomatic challenges along the way.

With the increased ease of travel for many of the world's citizens, hotels and other lodging operators have an increased ability to market their offerings to a wider audience, or potentially shift to a new target audience, whether strategically or unintentionally. For example, a destination previously known regionally for family vacations might become a national or international business travel or conference destination as airports and convention centers are developed and improved. Remote islands might become more connected and accessible if regular ferry service is added, or if an airport landing strip is expanded to allow larger passenger planes to land and take off. A community that was formerly only accessible seasonally due to adverse weather conditions or only via 4-wheel drive vehicle might become subject to much larger developments upon the installation of an all-season, high-capacity, paved road. This type of scenario is common in dramatic mountain environments – settings that naturally entice tourists for activities such as hiking, climbing, skiing, and photography, and thus also attracts hotel developers.

Along with the increase and expansion of tourism development, globalization has increased the demands on travel and destination marketing offices as well. However, the responsibilities and mechanisms of these organizations is shifting. Trip planning and visa applications have moved to the internet for efficiencies to the offices and consumers. Australia is one country that allows some travelers to apply for and receive a visa online. Travelers may no longer be requesting printed travel brochures or maps and instead download travel information online and use their phone to navigate once arriving to their destination. Shifting travel advising and visa applications to computerized systems provides some other advantages. With growing demand to travel, individuals can more efficiently process travel arrangements. With globalization and greater mobility, new security threats are prominent. Computer applications are allowing countries to detect issues with certain individuals traveling across borders and continents. Facial recognition software can be used in visa applications and in identifying individuals arriving into a country.

Similarly, advanced technology is used on the marketing side. New software applications are digitally tagging individuals who search for travel information on national or state tourism office websites and then identifying them once they arrive into the country. A traveler's electronic route to a place is allowing travel researchers to more efficiently understand the linkages between travel planning and actuation. These are some of the innovations that the travel industry has seen in recent years that provide intelligence for both security and marketing purposes. As travel across the globe continues to grow, computerized tools will enable international travel to be better monitored at an individual level. In tourism, just as in other areas of technology application, the internet-using consumer is continually confronted with the terms that they must accept a lower degree of personal privacy in return for greater online travel planning convenience and greater assurance of increased travel safety. Some consumers may be perfectly comfortable with this degree of monitoring, while others may view it as an invasion of privacy. Marketers should recognize that people of different generations and cultural backgrounds and identities may have different levels of comfort regarding the information they share and seek online.

Demographic shifts and implications for destination marketing

Just as travel volumes have increased globally, the demographic composition of the travel market has shifted by country of origin, ethnicity, age, and work status, as examples of a few consumer behavior factors impacting tourism marketing. As marketers continue to try to reach potential markets of new travelers or remind past visitors to return, the channels to reach individuals have exploded. The last half century has shown a growth in media channels targeted to racial or ethnic groups. In the earlier days of U.S. television, there were four to six national networks; radio was controlled locally; magazine titles were mostly along the topics of home, sports, leisure interests, or news; and newspapers were mostly metropolitan based. Local radio and newspapers have merged into national media companies that provide national coverage with some local customization. During this time of growth and consolidation of media, more racially and ethnically diverse media companies began to emerge. Univision, started in 1962, has since become a global leader in Spanish-language media and marketing to Latino Americans. Black Entertainment Television (BET) was started in 1983 and has paved the way for other media outlets to consider the possibilities for targeting certain demographics. Media visionaries such as Oprah Winfrey, through her OWN cable TV network and O magazine, have found ways to target certain audiences while also maintaining the feel of a particular brand and lifestyle. Digital media is ripe for greater ethnic, generational, and other demography-based targeting of travelers that has less geographic dependence than broadcast television or print media. For example, a destination advertising campaign created for Indians could be placed on YouTube and accessed anywhere in the world by Indians or other ethnicities. Before digital media existed, media channels lacked this level of customization to consumers and were bound by geographic placements. As global migration increases and greater ethnic diversity within countries exists, more marketers are placing promotions online to target their desired markets.

Across developed countries, people are living longer today than they used to. Currently in the U.S., there is a particularly large cohort of retired seniors from the years after World War II when record numbers of babies were born. These two demographic trends have created a consumer market of older travelers. These trends, along with globalization and the ability to travel to most places in the world, have provided a major thrust in growing travel demand. Another influence of globalization is that many people have lived in multiple places within their own country or internationally. Seniors who wish to visit friends or relatives have many possibilities compared to earlier times when families stayed in one area, unless they migrated or moved for work reasons. Travel businesses have aimed to cultivate a relationship with seniors and the blend of marketing approaches reflects this target market. Magazine advertisements feature active seniors enjoying the outdoors, vacation packages are promoted with pricing that balances luxury and affordability to match pensioner income, and simplified transportation options are provided for easy access to airports and cruise ports. In the U.S., sunny weather communities in Florida, Texas and Arizona, among other states, are designed to offer retirees vacation-like living every day, providing amenities like golf courses, swimming pools, and planned social activities. Retirees have the advantage of greater vacation scheduling flexibility. To fulfill longer-term lodging needs, they may seek second home ownership, timeshare opportunities, or weekly/monthly vacation rentals-by-owner, rather than looking at more traditional accommodation options at hotels or resorts. Other seniors may seek out "grand tour" opportunities that they never had when they were younger (or did have, but wish to repeat now that they once again have the time) by participating in fully-catered international group tours, or taking a cross-country road trip by live-in recreational vehicle, as is popular in the U.S. and Canada.

Another demographic group of interest currently is Millennials, those who were born in the early 1980s to mid-1990s. This demographic cohort is sizable and influential, garnering great interest from marketers. Millennials are perceived as being creative, explorative, experience-driven, and desiring of a unique lifestyle that includes travel. This is also the first cohort to have grown up with technology, particularly the internet, and more recently social media. Marketers see digital marketing as the most effective way to reach these individuals and their social networks. The Arizona Office of Tourism, for example, has created a new online advertising campaign called "The Arizona Experience." The promotions feature videos and photos of landscapes and the human experience; interests such as food and outdoor recreation are integrated, and the actors featured are social media influencers. The goal is for the influencers to share (or distribute) the State of Arizona's campaign on their own media/marketing platforms. Facebook and Instagram are two of the leading platforms for social marketing that have proven to be very useful in the hospitality context. Social media has given individuals their own publicity tools to share their interests, lifestyles, and travels with others, using some of the same media forums as celebrity personalities and top companies. Within the open access framework of social media, destination marketers seek out celebrities, influencers, and average individuals to positively feature their hotel, resort, restaurant or amenities to gain appeal, often to market segments that might otherwise be difficult to reach. In the past, individuals were relatively silent in their relationship with marketers. Social media sites such as TripAdvisor and Yelp have turned the public into critics, local experts, and influencers. Destination and hospitality marketers now use social media to create a socially-infused message and promote the perception that their followers are creative, hip, and cutting-edge consumers.

The challenge to destination managers and marketers is keeping tourism businesses and the community appearing up-to-date and fresh in an environment that is constantly in flux. Consumers can be fickle in their loyalties, and the popular hotel, restaurant or nightclub of today may be considered obsolete the next year. Hotel décor that is designed to be highly on-trend may seem particularly outdated going forward in reflection of its [overly-]enthusiastic embrace of one specific style moment. Businesses must decide whether renovations are going to be regularly incorporated into their budget and planning or whether they will try to stay "fresh" via other means. A restaurant, for example, has the ability to update its menu with newly popular dishes and cocktails, or offer special events or promotions that reflect current culture and demand. Other establishments may find that offering a product or setting that is truly unique (rather than trend-driven) and of high quality will better withstand the tests of time. Between the scrutiny of online reviews and the fast-paced nature of social media, the tourism and hospitality industry must be customer-oriented and highly responsive to keep up with the tech-savvy and experience-driven millennial consumer.

Environmental mindfulness and destination marketing

Travel and tourism is largely dependent on development, like most other industrial sectors. Around the world in developed or developing countries, economies generate financial gains for investors, wages for workers, and taxes for governments. Tourism and hospitality play a significant role in localized, domestic and international economies. As tourism has grown over the past century, greater attention is being directed to the associated environmental costs and degradation of the environment. Johnson and Tyrrell (2005) suggest mathematic models to estimate appropriate levels of tourism volume according to environmental values. However, they conclude that there is no single common optimum that would satisfy both environmental and economic expectations. So, the challenge is finding an appropriate balance going forward to meet the needs of a changing and threatened planet, while continuing the legacy of a unique hospitality experience that is often consumed in fragile natural environments. Many of the places we think of in terms of environmentalism, such as national parks or the U.S. western lands, actually had their roots in hospitality. Even in a national park where the expectation is protection of natural and cultural resources, there are development pressures that produce negative environmental and cultural impacts (Hyslop and Eagles 2007).

In the U.S., as early as the 19th century, individuals like John Muir and Henry David Thoreau and organizations like the Sierra Club called attention to the beauty of nature and how development and increased visitation could alter that beauty. A major thrust of these individuals and others in later years was to create a following of environmentalists and policies that would protect nature from the harm of people. Starting in the 1960s, pressure from citizens persuaded the U.S. government to create policies that enforced greater protections for natural resources but also encouraged the growth of outdoor recreation. Modern-day Americans are citizens who grew up in these decades of conservation achievements, affording them the mindsets to become more environmentally conscious consumers and, perhaps, more reverent to unadulterated outdoor environments. Today, travel and outdoor merchandise brands such as Patagonia and The North Face create marketing narratives that express their shared interests with consumers of nature, adventuring, and sustainably and ethically sourced gear. In some cases, a portion of profits may be re-invested in outdoor destinations, recreational organizations, or environmental causes. These strategies portray the message that innovative, consumer-oriented businesses can find many ways to contribute positively to the creation of a global community.

Visiting parks or other wild areas and participating in outdoor recreation activities is a popular type of vacation in the U.S. and abroad. The paradox is that as nature is protected it has also become a sought-after object of consumption. This leads to several problems. For instance, many travelers wish to view wild or protected animals up close, and sometimes even touch or "ride" them. U.S. National Parks discourage close encounters with wildlife, although issues with this regularly arise, sometimes from a lack of understanding or from cultural differences, and other times from egocentric visitor attitudes. SeaWorld is a well-known U.S. tourism company with many popular, family-oriented attractions that feature spectator and participatory sea animal encounters. Davis (1997) critically examines SeaWorld and reports that the attraction brings some environmental awareness about the negative impacts of people on nature. Yet, she concludes that in the end, SeaWorld is placing captured animals on display. She asks whether this is an endeavor with which people really want to be associated. This question was more broadly asked in 2010 when a SeaWorld Orlando trainer was killed by a featured orca who had a troubled past and history of violence. The subsequent release of the widely-acclaimed documentary film "Blackfish" in 2013 continued this dialogue regarding the ethics of human interaction with (or interruption to) nature. Some twenty years after Davis's book, SeaWorld has changed their mission and visitor experiences to better reflect contemporary values toward nature. SeaWorld is phasing out featuring orcas in shows and breeding them in captivity, and instead is directing their programming towards more of an educational, natural experience (Howard 2016), while still striving to offer an entertaining and engaging tourism product. With a new mission and product experience, consumers will ultimately decide whether SeaWorld has re-created their attractions enough to satisfy growing environmental values that lean away from the captivity and questionable treatment of animals.

National parks in Canada and the U.S. provide case studies on the balancing act of protecting a landscape, generating local jobs, contributing to local economies, and retaining authentic culture of native people and early settlers who played a role in park development. Parks Canada is considered to be the first park agency with a service quality goal oriented to visitor satisfaction (Jamal and Stronza 2009). Parks like Banff National Park were created to protect special features for the enjoyment of tourists who arrived by rail to stay at well-appointed hotels. Around the turn of the 20th century, new U.S. national parks like Yellowstone and Grand Canyon were originally opened for tourism more than for resource management. Today, both Parks Canada and U.S. National Park Service continue to manage parks for tourism and recreation, but greater attention is placed on biodiversity (Phillips 2003).

A recent example of environmental mindfulness and marketing is evident in a recent joint advertising campaign for U.S. National Parks and Subaru. The advertisement draws attention to the 100 tons of garbage that park visitors leave at national parks each year. These are real impacts and costs associated with tourists visiting national parks, particularly overnight visitors, whether they are campers or hotel guests. In this campaign, Subaru, a National Park sponsor for the Centennial of the agency, is positioning themselves in the tourism, recreation and sustainability arenas, using this issue to draw attention to environmental concerns and to associate their brand with sustainability practices. Another initiative in U.S. National Parks is to eliminate water bottles from being sold by food service operations and request park visitors to bring their own reusable containers. These National Park campaigns reflect a shift in commercialism and consumerism in the U.S. and around the world to be more mindful of environmental conditions.

The U.S. National Park Service, along with other federal public land agencies, has increased their focus on urban parks, as a majority of U.S. residents live in cities and international tourists are drawn to metropolitan areas. Unlike western U.S. National Parks, urban parks often are a reuse of land resources, so the focus is initially less about the protection of virgin resources. Urban parks make good environmental sense because they are placed in an existing tourism system that already has infrastructure and visitor services. An urban park also provides a prominent draw for destination marketers to promote. The Presidio in San Francisco, a former military base, is an example of the National Park Service redeveloping an existing site. This location had high "place" value as it is set on the waterfront near the Golden Gate Bridge and is close to downtown San Francisco. The Presidio is featured as an attraction by San Francisco Convention and Visitors Bureau in their marketing materials. The environmental benefit is that the park repurposed many of the buildings rather than building new facilities and infrastructure. Had the decommissioned military base been subdivided and redeveloped or left abandoned, nearby businesses would not have had the same opportunity to economically benefit. City residents and visitors would have had fewer enjoyable open spaces available to escape the bustle of the city. This example showcases contemporary destination development as being more mindful of existing sites and assets and considerate of transportation, accessibility concerns, and human well-being.

Digital marketing for the traveler

Another trend in consumer behavior that has probably had the greatest impact on destination marketing is the creation of the internet. The tourism and hospitality industries have utilized digital marketing to reach travelers beyond the reach of traditional marketing of print collateral and television advertisements (Xiang et al. 2015). Government tourism offices, small entrepreneurs, large branded hospitality businesses, and nonprofits in tourism and hospitality have turn-keyed their marketing efforts to the internet to provide information to clients/consumers and offer automated reservation systems. PhocusWright (2016), a tourism marketing research firm, estimates that 45% of reservations in the U.S. occur with online channels. The online marketplace replaced many traditional travel intermediaries like travel agencies with online travel agencies like Expedia, Kayak, Travelocity, and recently Google Trips. Online travel agencies (OTAs) account for $533 billion in travel spending (Statista 2016). Airlines and hotels are currently trying to invite customers back to their own business websites and reservation systems to reduce commission costs, just as they had attempted to do in the pre-internet days as they competed with in-person travel agents.

The internet has brought further reach for marketers and has also leveraged the use of consumer databases by eliciting and saving email addresses. Personal contact information can be obtained with information search activities by asking internet users to register for newsletters or enter a contest to win prizes. Consumer databases are a significant asset to marketers. Hospitality businesses and destination marketers in turn create regular email messages that further sell their services and experiences to consumers. In some cases, lists might be sold or shared between companies. Entering one online travel contest could result in being added to five different tourism mailing lists. The cost of email marketing is low to the advertiser compared to costs of direct marketing or advertising. Tracking consumer response can be easier with email marketing particularly if a business is offering an incentive or a customized web link.

Technology has also allowed the hotel industry to better understand and predict their inventory minute to minute. Third party distributors such as online travel agents can auction off surplus rooms or advertise last-minute deals at rock-bottom rates. They might directly target their mailing list with limited-time promotions, or pay Google to boost their order in search results or offer targeted sidebar advertisements to internet users who have visited their site before. An even newer innovation is travel services that are offered in smaller bites using idle inventory. A new online firm called Recharge is selling unused hotel rooms priced by the minute for business or leisure travelers who need a hotel room for a short time period. The consumer can spontaneously book a room at any time based on real-time rates determined by hotel inventory. Destination and hospitality marketers must expect and respond to new technology solutions that will shape consumer decision-making, purchasing methods, and products, as well as consumer experiences and satisfaction associated with the product, price, and promotions.

The continually growing trend of social media provides numerous platforms for marketers to team with online search and reservation systems, as well as email marketing. Facebook, Twitter, Instagram and Yelp are popular social media platforms where consumers can share travel stories and pictures and influence brand and destination popularity. Social media is increasingly an information source in travel decision-making (Chung and Koo 2015) and social representation of one's self as a traveler (Lyu 2016). Current marketing strategies are directed at mobile applications for smart phones so that marketers can be constantly available to consumers whether they are at home, at work, or traveling. Marketers are working closely with information technology developers to further integrate digital marketing platforms with fun and useful applications that people will want to download and utilize. Currently, most marketers have multiple consumer lists or followers across platforms and are not clear on how many unique individuals or households are represented.

The sharing economy

If the internet changed the trajectory of tourism and hospitality marketing in the 1990s and 2000s, the sharing economy is currently changing that same industry in the 2010s. Silicon Valley innovators created a new secondary economy for the tourism and hospitality industry by inventing an online marketplace in which individuals with rooms, apartments, houses, cars, or nearly any unused item or capacity can make their resources available to others at reasonable costs. The sharing economy is also called collaborative consumption. Airbnb, VRBO, Lyft, Uber, and others are reshaping the travel experience for people searching for a more local experience and lower costs. Reducing the effort and skills required by the owner/offerer, the company provides a branded, standardized, internet storefront to promote the individual's offerings. The provisions of online payment systems and mobile applications add ease, simplicity and trustworthiness to the user experience. Phocuswright (2016) reports that private accommodations increased from an 8% market share of paid accommodations in 2010 to 25% in 2014, largely from Airbnb. In addition to their widening availability and ease of use, these types of offerings provide a different experience to consumers who want a change from the commercialized, generic, big corporation style of hospitality and transportation from the past half century. Other websites, such as Couchsurfing.com, have created a shared hospitality economy based on social capital rather than actual monetary exchange. Members who are traveling can connect with locals who enjoy socializing with people from around the world and have a couch or bed to spare – at no cost to the traveler. For travel accommodations, the sharing economy offers options from $0 a night for a mat on someone's floor, to complete mansions for $2,000+ a night. Skift, an online travel news firm, suggests that the travel industry is the sector most influenced by the growth of the sharing and collaborative consumption market, and the reach is global (Trivett 2013). Social media serves as a primary promotional engine and framework for this new collaborative consumption.

The host-guest relationship that Valene Smith (1989) wrote about is having a comeback. In this new context, rather than Native Americans or South Pacific Islanders being the center of discussion, cultural commoditization now applies to locals who are involved in their community and willing to share with others, creating a livelihood based on social entrepreneurship and sustainability. Consumers are asking for local, more authentic, and less staged travel experiences during their leisure and business trips. They may seek out farm-to-table cuisine featuring produce from local growers, along with a cocktail spotlighting whiskey from a small-batch local distillery. They may buy gift items from a craftsmen's market rather than a commercial souvenir shop. Pricing of localized travel and hospitality services can be high in order to cover fair living wages and locally grown ingredients, a value proposition embedded in many local businesses. A great emphasis lies on place-making to provide local flavor and personality, and perhaps a more home-like hospitality feel.

In response to the pressures from the sharing economy, the hospitality industry has rebounded by creating new boutique brands that have a social purpose within and around properties. New brands like Marriott's AC, Aloft, and Moxy hotels and Hilton's Canopy and Tru hotels offer guests a large shared space where they can intermingle with friends or meet other fellow travelers. Highlighting human-created products like artwork, live music, barista espresso, and craft beers gives the message that a hotel or restaurant can be considered a place where creativity can be promoted and individualism celebrated, even within a corporate context.

Closing thoughts

Travel is a human activity that has existed for as long as humans have been on earth. Human needs are fairly basic, but the experience around those needs is dynamic. This chapter highlights five themes that currently are influencing or changing the nature of travel. Globalization and the ability of an increasing number of Earth's six billion residents to travel will have profound economic and environmental impacts on the visited countries. Demographic changes in travelers and hospitality guests will change the nature of vacations, particularly in regards to accommodations and food choices. The encompassing reach of globalization also creates a counter effect in driving consumers to seek travel and hospitality experiences that maintain a local, place-based, and personality-rich feel. Consumers are becoming more mindful of the consequences of their travels and marketers are beginning to promote more active sustainability in business practices to appeal to growing consumer concerns. Technology and its applications to tourism are limitless and will continue to shape experiences and create tools that aid in information searching, decision-making, and payment for services. Finally, the sharing economy is creating a technology-savvy new type of host/provider to sell experience inventory and idle resources in a way that was formerly not possible. The topic of consumer behavior in tourism and hospitality marketing is one of excitement. There are so many places to innovate as a business or consumer. The themes featured in this chapter suggest dynamic and responsive ways to encourage travel and promote tourism and hospitality businesses across the globe for a more sustainable future.

References

Amelung, B., Nicholls, S. and Viner, D., 2007. Implications of global climate change for tourism flows and seasonality. *Journal of Travel Research*, 45(3), pp. 285–296.

Chung, N. and Koo, C. 2015. The use of social media in travel information search. *Telematics and Informatics*, 32(2), pp. 215–229.

Davis, S. G. 1997. *Spectacular Nature: Corporate Culture and the Sea World Experience*. Berkeley: University of California Press.

Howard, B.C. 2016. SeaWorld to end controversial orca shows and breeding. National Geographic (Mar 17, 2016). Available online at: http://news.nationalgeographic.com/2016/03/160317-seaworld-orcas-killer-whales-captivity-breeding-shamu-tilikum/

Hyslop, K. E. and Eagles, P. F. J. 2007. Visitor management policy of national parks, national wildlife areas and refuges in Canada and the United States: A policy analysis of public documents. *Leisure/loisir*, 31(2), pp. 475–499. doi:10.1080/14927713.2007.9651392

Feiyue, Y. and Nilsson, E. 2015. US expected to see increase in Chinese tourists next year. China Daily (Dec 7, 2015). Available online at: http://english.gov.cn/news/international_exchanges/2015/12/07/content_281475249688845.htm

Jamal, T., and Stronza, A. 2009. Collaboration theory and tourism practice in protected areas: Stakeholders, structuring and sustainability. *Journal of Sustainable Tourism*, 17(2), pp. 169–189.

Johnson, R.J. and Tyrrell, T.J. 2005. A dynamic model of sustainable tourism. *Journal of Travel Research*, 44, pp. 124–134.

Lyu, S.O. 2016. Travel selfies on social media as objectified self-presentation. *Tourism Management*, 54, pp. 185–195.

McMahon, E. 2015. Ten principles for responsible tourism. *Urban Land*, Sept/Oct, pp. 160–164.

Phillips, A. 2003. Turning ideas on their head. *George Wright Forum*, 20(2), pp. 8–32.

Phocuswright. 2016. *Parsing Shop and Book 2016: How Airlines, Hotels and OTAs Compete on the Desktop and Mobile Web.*

Phocuswright. 2016. *From Hotels to Homes: Opening the Door to the Airbnb Traveler.*

Pike, S. and Page, S. 2014. Destination Marketing Organizations and destination marketing: A narrow analysis of the literature. *Tourism Management*, 41, pp. 202–227.

Smith, V. L. 1989. *Hosts and Guests: The Anthropology of Tourism* (2nd edition). Philadelphia: University of Pennsylvania Press.

Statista Research & Analysis. 2016. Available online at: www.statista.com/topics/2704/online-travel-market/ (accessed October 25, 2016).
Trivett, V. 2013. What the Sharing Economy Means to the Future of Travel. SKIFT. Available online at: http://skift.com/wp-content/uploads/2014/07/skift-what-the-sharing-economy-means-to-the-future-of-travel.pdf
United Nations World Tourism Organization. (2016). *Tourism Highlights.*
Xiang, Z., Wang, D., O'Leary, J. T., and Fesenmaier, D. R. 2015. Adapting to the Internet: Trends in travelers' use of the web for trip planning. *Journal of Travel Research*, 54(4), pp. 511–527.

Further reading

Bowen, D. and Clarke, J. 2009. *Contemporary Tourist Behavior: Yourself and Others and Tourists.* Oxon: CABI. (A modern view of tourists that goes beyond motivation and decision making models.)
Buhalis, D. and Costa, C. 2006. *Tourism Business Frontiers: Consumers, Products and Industry.* Oxford: Elsevier Butterworth-Heinemann. (A compilation of papers with an emphasis on emerging technology.)
Jennings, G. and Nickerson, N.P. 2006. *Quality Tourism Experiences.* Amsterdam: Elsevier Butterworth Heinemann. (An edited book of marketing concepts applied to tourism and destination examples and case studies.)
Pizam, A. and Mansfeld, Y. 1999. *Consumer Behavior in Travel and Tourism.* Binghamton, NY: The Haworth Press. (An edited book of travel behavior concepts.)
Sharpley, R. and Stone, P. 2012. *Contemporary Tourist Experience: Concepts and Consequences.* Routledge. Oxon, England. (A modern view of tourism with a focus on the direction and impacts of tourism.)
Xiang, Z., Magnini, V. P., and Fesenmaier, D. R. 2015. Information technology and consumer behavior in travel and tourism: Insights from travel planning using the internet. *Journal of Retailing and Consumer Services*, 22, pp. 244–249. (An empirical study of consumers' planning trips.)

23

Online travel information and searching behavior

Jie Kong and Gang Li

Introduction

As an information sensitive industry, the tourism and hospitality industry is connected to travel information closely. From the perspective of tourists, travel information plays an important part in the decision making process of travel mode, travel destination, travel route, accommodation, etc. On the other hand, from practitioners' view, travel information is the source to understand tourists' preferences and to develop effective marketing strategy. Therefore, the interest for travel information searching has been high and tourism researchers have spent a lot of attention on this topic. Hitherto, lots of studies have been published in the area of travel information searching (Fodness & Murray, 1997).

Before the Internet, the tasks of travel distribution were carried out by traditional tourism organizations, such as various travel agencies (Buhalis & Licata, 2002). In this case, the travel information is disseminated and accessed through traditional travel information channels such as printed media, telephone, radio broadcasting, television, etc. Even in the early twenty-first century, when searching for information, traditional travel information channels still played an important role, while the Internet was only a supplementary approach (Özturan & Roney, 2004).

However, with the rapid development and popularization of Internet in the first ten years of the twenty-first century, people are increasingly dependent on the Internet to obtain information. According to the Pew Report on Internet growth and distribution in America, the number of Internet users has increased from 52% of all adults in 2000 to 88% in 2016 (Pew Research Center, 2017). In this background, traditional tourism intermediaries have been gradually replaced by new tourism eMediaries based on the Internet (Whitehead, 2012) and people are used to searching for travel information through the Internet. As early as 2003, the Internet was adopted by 73% of American people to search for travel information (Madden & Rainie, 2003). Nowadays, online travel information searching has become a hot issue in tourism research. The research covers tourists' search behavior (Lehto, Kim, & Morrison, 2006; Luo, Feng, & Cai, 2008; Jordan, Norman, & Vogt, 2013), search approach and technique (Beldona, 2008; Wei, Peng, & Lee, 2013; Chung & Koo, 2015), the motivation to search (Kim, Choi, & Kim, 2013; Luo & Zhong, 2010), the factors affecting the search (Okazaki & Hirose, 2009), etc. These studies provided an important opportunity to advance the understanding of the issues related to online travel information searching.

On the other hand, the popularity of mobile Internet and social networks enable tourists to share their experiences, thoughts and opinions much easier than before through online travel community or social network (Yoo & Gretzel, 2008; Lee, Law, & Murphy, 2011). Nowadays in the online travel community (such as TripAdvisor, Yahoo! Travel, Expedia), the online reviews posted by customers with positive or negative altitudes, namely electronic word-of-mouth (eWOM), have become a major information source for travel information searching (Hennig-Thurau et al., 2004). For example, TripAdvisor, which is a famous online travel community, provides 500 million reviews posted by millions of customers. These online reviews cover 7 million attractions, hotels and restaurants and could offer useful advice for travelers (TripAdvisor, 2017). Through the mass of online reviews, the potential customers could conveniently access travel information such as the location of a hotel, quality of service, price, travel route and so on, even if they do not have any experience about the travel destination. Therefore, online review has significantly attracted the attention from the academia of tourism in recent years – for example, the impact of eWOM on the tourism and hospitality industry (Cantallops & Salvi, 2014) and information search (Banerjee & Chua, 2016), consumers' attitude to online review (Vermeulen & Seegers, 2009; Xie et al., 2011), the consumer's motivation for using online social network (Kim, Choi, & Kim, 2013). These works enhance our understanding of the significance of online review or eWOM in travel information search.

In consideration of the widespread application of Internet-based travel information and its significant influence on the way of travel information generation and acquisition, this chapter reviews and analyzes the published articles of the online travel information and information search behavior. The objective of this chapter is to identify the research trend and future research opportunities in Internet-based travel information and searching behavior.

Travel information

The emergence of the Internet as an efficient communication approach, has, therefore, changed consumer's behavior and attitude to obtaining travel information. As a result, it has also changed the way the travel products are distributed and brought a profound impact on the tourism industry (Buhalis & Licata, 2002). Some researchers analyzed the impact and discussed the marketing strategy of applying the Internet-based travel information, as well as the future trends. For instance, the published articles are collected and analyzed to demonstrate the influence of eWOM information for the hotel industry (Litvin, Goldsmith, & Pan, 2008; Cantallops & Salvi, 2014). Schmallegger and Carson (2008) examined how the information influenced the research and practice in tourism industry. Whitehead (2012) forecast the research trends and opportunities in the area of online travel reviews. In this section, the literature of travel information could be reviewed from two perspectives: the generation, as well as the usage of travel information.

The perspective of travel information generation

With the fast rise of the Internet and social networks, online travel information has become a major source of information in tourism practice and research. Travelers can generate and share their knowledge, experiences, emotions, and so on through the Internet, which is an easier and more wide-reaching way than in the past (Buhalis & Law, 2008; Munar & Jacobsen, 2014). What drives users to generate online travel information? How is the online travel information generated? In this section, we try to review the answers to these questions from the perspective of travel information generation.

Users' motivation to generate online travel reviews

Understanding users' motivation to generate online travel reviews has only recently received significant attention in tourism studies (Cheung & Lee, 2012). In recent years, researchers have made lots of different studies on this issue. The results of these studies indicate the reasons which make people generate online travels reviews. These are categorized and listed below.

(1) Personal interests. With this motivation, people generate online reviews to increase their personal welfare. For instance, reputation is often referred to as a reason people share information online. People share information with the purpose of being famous in the online community (Henning-Thurau et al., 2004; Cheung & Lee, 2012). Economic factors (Henning-Thurau et al., 2004) is another motivation in this category. People generate online reviews to gain profit such as remuneration, discount coupons, etc. However, the motivation of economic incentives has not been well investigated in tourism research.
(2) Hedonism. Some people generate and share online travel information in the online community simply to make them feel happy (Wang & Fesenmaier, 2004; Chung & Buhalis, 2008) or successful (Yoo & Gretzel, 2008).
(3) Social need. Social network or online community is a place for people to socialize with each other over the Internet. Some people post travel information in online travel community for social reasons, for example, sense of belonging (Cheung & Lee, 2012; Chung & Buhalis, 2008) which refers to the emotional involvement with the online group; keeping relationships or getting involved with members (Chung & Buhalis, 2008); (Munar & Jacobsen, 2014); social interaction (Hennig-Thurau et al., 2004)
(4) Altruism. There are some other people who write and share online travel information just for helping other travelers. In this process, they also get happiness. Specific motivations in this category include: enjoyment of helping others (Cheung & Lee, 2012); helping other people (Hennig-Thurau et al., 2004; Yoo & Gretzel, 2008); helping the travel service provider (Yoo & Gretzel, 2008); preventing people from using bad products (Munar & Jacobsen, 2014).

Furthermore, there are some features that cannot be ignored. Hennig-Thurau et al. (2004) mention that the reasons to write online travel reviews could be manifold, e.g. some people are motivated by several factors. Yoo and Gretzel (2008) report that releasing frustration through the online review is clearly not a primary motive; gender and income level are related to the difference of motivation (Yoo & Gretzel, 2008).

The creation of the online travel review

Most hotel review websites collect ratings from travelers. The content of the reviews directly affects the eWOM of these hotels, therefore the factors that influence the creation of online travel reviews have attracted some tourism researchers' interests.

Liu and Park (2015) propose that the qualitative features of a review, for instance the readability, are more important than quantitative factors (e.g. the length of reviews, scores of rating) to generate a useful online travel review. Yoo and Gretzel (2011) investigate what reason drives some people to create online travel reviews while some other people only access these reviews (namely lurkers). The result indicates that people's personality is the key factor for the motivation and barrier to creating online travel reviews. Lee, Law, and Murphy (2011) depict the user portrait which creates helpful online travel reviews. The findings show that the creators of helpful online reviews travel a lot, post review frequently, give lower hotel ratings and belong to any gender and age groups.

The perspective of travel information application

The Internet-based travel information has been widely employed in travel planning, hotel booking, transportation arrangement, customer preference analysis, service and competitiveness improvement, etc. In view of this, the perspective of travel information employment concentrates on how the Internet-based travel information is applied in the tourism industry and what influence the information has on tourism practitioners and customers. In this perspective, studies could be divided into following categories.

The influence of tourism product booking

The products of tourism, such as accommodation, catering, service in a scenic spot, are experience goods, which means that the quality of these products could be known only if they have been consumed. The emergence of the Internet-based travel information provides a new approach to understanding the quality. Now, consumers could infer the quality of these products through the access of online reviews. As a result, the reviews have significantly influenced the sales of tourism products (Duan, Gu, & Whinston, 2008).

To understand the influence of Internet-based travel information in the tourism industry, research has been developed to investigate the impact of online reviews in hotel booking (Ye, Gu, & Chen, 2011). Customers' reviews in CTrip, a leading online travel agency in China, have been analyzed through a log-linear regression model. The results of this paper indicate that online reviews could cut down the costs when potential customers are obtaining and processing tourism information, and then increase their perception of hotels, as a result, improve the sales of rooms. Specifically, if the review ratings are increased by 10%, the online room bookings will be increased by 5%. Due to the close relationship between online reviews and sales, managers of tourism industry should seriously consider online reviews about their business (Ye, Law, & Gu, 2009).

Since the customer's impression of a tourism product could be established through online reviews, a question is raised: how do online reviews affect customers' booking decision? Many studies have made their answers for this question. For example:

(1) Ku and Fan (2009) survey the customers who had booked hotel rooms online. Nine most fundamental factors for online shopping are analyzed to understand customers' booking behavior. Privacy, safety, and product quality are found to be the most influential factors for customers' online hotel booking.
(2) Four independent key factors related to online reviews are proposed to explore the effect on customers' hotel booking. The practical implication shows that consumers are probably to be influenced by negative information when they are searching online reviews to book a hotel, especially when the overall evaluation is negative. Consumers' booking intention and trust could be improved by positive reviews with numerical rating scores. When evaluating a hotel through online reviews, customers tend to accept information which is easy to understand (Sparks & Browning, 2011).
(3) Ladhari & Michaud (2013) also investigate whether the positive and negative comments generated on social network influence customers' hotel booking. The result of this research

shows that the level of trust for the online review is a key factor for customers' booking. Low trust level makes booking intention not change obviously regardless of whether the online review is positive. When the level of trust is high, the online review significantly influences booking intention.

The Internet-based travel information can also be used to predict the travel booking. A model which is used to forecast the probability of booking travel products online was developed and tested (Morrison et al., 2001). The model took several factors into account, such as customers' demographic characteristics, travelers' behavior, customers' patterns when using Internet, factors related to the perception of Internet, and factors about travelers' last trip, etc. Implications of this study indicated that:

1. the education level is closely related to online travel booking;
2. the more often a customer visits the online travel agency, the more likely that he or she books travel products on that website;
3. financial benefits was a key factor to the booking;
4. if a customer realized that the other customers are doing likewise, he or she would probably book online too;
5. the booking of some types of the travel products may influence customers' behavior. For example, customers who purchased rental cars or vacation packages would probably book online again.

Impact on customer's decision making

In the era of e-commerce, many of the customers reference online reviews before they make a decision of a travel plan or tourism product. On the other hand, some tourism marketers try to attract customers to tourism products through the Internet-based information (Loda, 2011). How does online travel information influence customer's decision-making? Customers' decision-making process could be divided into four stages: consideration; evaluation; purchasing; enjoyment, advocation, and stickiness. Online social media makes the stages of "evaluation" and "advocation" become more and more relevant (Hudson & Thal, 2013). In the evaluation stage, customers evaluate the tourism product and generate their ensuing decision from online travel information, without tourism marketer's persuasion. Besides, social networks enable the customer to share their opinion, geographical location or purchased tourism product; this information will affect the evaluation stage of other customers. Some studies related to travel decision making through online information are listed below.

Online travel information, such as eWOM, plays an important in travel destination choice. Jalilvand and Samiei (2012) examined the impact of eWOM on travelers' decision of visiting Isfahan, Iran. This study tried to explain the process of travel destination decision making through the theory of planned behavior. Findings of this study indicated that eWOM had a significant, positive, and direct influence on travel destination decision. Customers' attitude for visiting a destination, subjective norm, as well as perceived behavioral control are key factors in the selection of a travel destination. Tham, Croy, and Mair (2013) suggested that different perspectives of a travel destination could be offered online, which improved the visibility of travel destination to the potential travelers, thus affecting travelers' choice of destination.

With the rising of smartphones, travelers commonly use smartphones in their trips, e.g. searching information, making travel plan, booking hotel and air ticket, etc. No and Kim (2014) explored the determinants which influenced traveler's decision of employing smartphones to process travel-related information. The findings of this research suggested that the satisfaction of travel information acquired from the smartphone's usage had distinctly influenced travelers' intention of using smartphones.

Online information can be used not only in the purchase of tourism products but also for an emergency situation during the travel. Schroeder and Pennington-Gray (2015) explored the decision making of using social media to search online information while there is a crisis during travel. The internal, travel-related, and demographic determinants are investigated in this study.

Understanding customers' satisfaction and preference

With the intensification of competition in the tourism industry, tourism managers need to improve the quality of service and competitiveness of their organization, so as to stay ahead in the fierce competition. Customers' satisfaction significantly influences the sales of tourism products. Customers' satisfaction enhances their positive attitudes to the tourism brands. Consequently, the possibility of customers' purchase will also be improved. On the contrary, dissatisfaction would be likely to generate negative attitudes to the brand and reduce the likelihood of repurchase in the same brand (Berezina et al., 2016). Therefore, tourism organizations try to improve customers' satisfaction by understanding customers' preference.

At present, online travel information is often used to understand customers' preference. The analysis of eWOMs of some hotels show that the most common negative reviews are connected to reception services, the cleanliness, the noise, and the bathroom facilities (Levy, Duan, & Boo, 2013). Customers usually pay more attention to the decoration and size of the room, front desk services and bed, unfortunately, they are often dissatisfied (Li, Ye, & Law, 2013). Customers may have multiple criteria when they select a hotel. How to describe their preference according to these criteria is a barrier. To tackle this multi-criteria decision-making (MCDM) problem, Choquet Integral (CI) is introduced to find travellers' preferences, which influence their decision making, through online reviews (Li et al., 2013a). With the progress of the times, customers' preferences change, which influences the performance of hotel business. To tackle this problem, emergent hotel preference features are identified from online reviews through Emerging Pattern Mining technique (Li et al., 2015).

Not only hotels, customers' preferences in other travel services can also be analyzed by online travel information. Liu et al. (2013) investigate the contrast of customers' profiles by their trip mode. The findings of this study show a traveler's expectation and satisfaction when he or she travels with diverse travel modes. The quality of websites is another factor affecting customers' satisfaction. The research of Bai, Law, and Wen (2008) shows that travelers' decision making and satisfaction are influenced by the quality of hotel websites. Rong, Li and Law (2009) analyze the opinions of different user groups for specific hotel websites and suggest a set of properties which plays an important role in developing favorable hotel websites.

Travel information search behavior

The combination of the tourism industry and the Information technology (especially the Internet) significantly changes the way people search for, find, and read travel information. Nowadays, the Internet, by which travelers search and obtain useful travel information, has become a popular approach to access travel information (Law, Leung, & Buhalis, 2009; Chung & Koo, 2015). It is significant for tourism practitioners to understand customers' information search behavior in marketing management, and important for tourism managers to develop effective marketing strategies due to its significant influence in travelers' purchase decision process.

Traditional research of information search behavior

Considering the importance of information search behavior, it had attracted researchers' interests for a long time. Some viewpoints have been proposed in traditional information search behavior research. According to Stinger (1961), customers will continually spend resources (such as time, money, effort, and so on) to search until the earnings obtained from the search cannot cover the search cost. From Hofstede's (1980) view, the behavior of information searching is affected by the purpose of avoiding uncertainty, which means to avoid risks such as losing money, being unable to meet the search need, etc. "Internal and external search behavior" is another widely adopted theory (Beatty & Smith, 1987). The internal search means the search behavior which searches for information from people's long-term memory. On the contrary, the external search refers to retrieval of information which does not exist in people's memory. People usually search for information through internal search. If the internal search cannot provide enough information, the external search will be applied (Jang, 2004).

However, with the development of the Internet, the perspectives of traditional information search behavior are not completely applicable in the Internet Age. As experience goods, tourism products can only be evaluated before experience. The advent of the Internet leads to a more convenient approach to search and compare tourism product information before travelers make the purchase decision. Consequently, the tourism industry is significantly influenced by the Internet and it is significant to identify the features of online travel information search behavior.

Online travel information search behavior

Overview of online travel information search

As the information sources for travelers, online travel information is playing a crucial role nowadays. There is a huge amount of travel information on the Internet, which makes online search the mainstream approach for tourists to get tourism information (Xiang & Gretzel, 2010). For instance, it is reported that search engines (e.g. Google) are used by 76.6% of online travelers for travel planning (U.S. Travel Association, 2010).

Due to its importance, a few studies try to overview the online travel information search to provide an in-depth understanding. Jang (2004) briefly reviews the history and current situation of online travel information search, analyzes its distinct features and benefits for travelers and marketers. Beldona (2005) investigates the differences of travel information search behavior in particular demographic groups from 1995 to 2000. The result of this study validates the notion that the adoption of the Internet in baby boomer cohorts is earlier than traditionally assumed. Law, Leung, and Buhalis (2009) review the research articles corresponding to information search between 2005 and 2007. Xiang and Gretzel (2010) investigate the extent to which online travel information appears in search engine results. On the basis of this study (Xiang & Gretzel, 2010), Walden, Carlsson, & Papageorgiou (2011) identify how social media affect the search of travel information from the perspective of hotel brand search. Chung and Koo (2015) investigate the influential factors involved in travelers' information search from the online social media.

In this section, published articles about online travel information search behavior will be reviewed from three issues: the features of travel information search behavior; the influence of culture or demographic features to the search behavior; the influence of travelers' knowledge on the search behavior.

The influence of culture or demographic features on the search behavior

People with different cultural backgrounds or demographic features have differences in their travel information search behavior characteristics. Before the 1990s, American travelers are the main research object in the study of travel information search behavior and there were only a few researches about information search behaviors which take into account the travelers in different countries (Gursoy & Chen, 2000). Since the twenty-first century, economic globalization has promoted the flow of people worldwide, which made transnational travel more and more popular. Therefore, the information search behavior based on travelers' culture features from different nations has attracted the attention of the research community.

Gursoy and Chen (2000) investigate the information search behavior among English, French, and German travelers. However, the information sources applied in this study are still traditional travel information, such as government tourist office, travel guides, paper media, etc. In 2004, on the basis of Gursoy and Chen's research (2000), the information search behavior of travelers from European Union countries is investigated (Gursoy & Umbreit, 2004). It is worth noting that online information has become a major source in travel information searches with the raising of the Internet. Jordan, Norman, and Vogt (2013) examine the Belgian and American travelers' information search behavior when they are making their travel plan. In this study, Belgians and Americans are considered to be representatives of two cultural backgrounds: high uncertainty avoidance and low uncertainty avoidance. The result indicates the differences in the information search styles when Belgians and Americans are making their travel plan. Lu and Chen (2014) investigate the information search behavior of travelers who come from America, Japan and China, and go to Taiwan. The results of this study indicate that compared to the traditional information source such as paper media, TV, etc., the Internet has become a major source in the travel information search.

The online information search behavior may vary greatly among different traveler groups. For instance, as a major market, college students are a crowd that cannot be ignored. It is reported that social network is one of the major information sources in college students' researching of trip information (Kim & Kim, 2011). Interacting with others on online social networks has a mediating role in their information search behavior (Kim, Choi, & Kim, 2013). A large portion of the existing researches in this area are from the perspective of a single one, Bronner and de Hoog (2010), who investigate the search behavior in the context of family's vacation decision making.

Gender is another feature affecting travelers' information search behaviors. Okazaki and Hirose (2009) investigate the relationship between gender and the media which is chosen by travelers to search for travel information in Japan. The result of this study indicates that the attitude, satisfaction, and habit of using mobile Internet to search travel information are more strongly perceived in males. Kim, Lehto, and Morrison (2007) examine the differences between male and female in travel information search. It is reported there are notable differences between male's and female's attitudes to information channels and their preferences for the functionality of travel websites.

The characteristics and preferences of the search behavior

The analysis and understanding of the characteristics and preferences of online travel information search behavior could help tourism managers better understand travelers' needs and develop competitive tourism products. Some researchers try to identify the differences of travelers' online and offline information search behavior. Luo, Feng, and Cai (2004) examine the relationships and characteristics of travelers' online and offline information search behavior. Some factors significantly related to travelers' preferences of an information source are identified. The findings of this study indicate that the selection of the online or offline information source depend on customers' demographic features. Jun, Vogt, and Mackay (2007) studied the influence of travel information search behaviors on the purchase of tourism product. The findings show that travelers search for online information more than offline for all the products mentioned in this study. The hotel bookings, car rentals and flight ticket purchases are implemented through online approaches more than offline. Travelers' experiences are related to the information search behavior and the purchase of some travel products in the stage of travel planning. Ho, Lin, and Chen (2012) describe the detailed information search process in the online and offline environments.

Some studies try to reveal the characteristics of search behavior itself. Beldona (2008) tries to extract the potential online travel information search modes. Four information search modes are suggested in this study, namely deliberative goal-oriented search, deterministic goal-oriented search, effective experiential search, and innovative experiential search. Jansen, Ciamacca, and Spink (2008) investigate the issues related to online information search in the context of tourism, for example, the advantages, the constitution, and the terms to describe the travel topic of online travel information search,

The influence of travelers' knowledge or experience to the search behavior

Travelers' prior knowledge or experience about the tourism products is another key factor that influences the information search behavior. Prior knowledge or experience enables travelers to evaluate a tourism product and assist their decision-making process in the travel planning stage. Gursoy (2003) suggests that experienced travelers tend to search for travel information through different information sources. Expert travelers have sufficient knowledge about the tourism product, therefore they do not use external information frequently. On the contrary, the familiar travelers may spend more time and money to access the external information in order to reduce the risks of purchasing tourism products. Gursoy and McCleary (2004) investigate the connection between prior experience of travelers and the information source. The findings show expertise and familiarity have the opposite effect in online information search. The influence of familiarity on the external information search is negative while expertise is positive. On internal information search, familiarity has a positive influence while expertise is negative.

Since the Internet has been widely used to obtain travel information, some studies about the effect of knowledge on the travelers' search behavior on the Internet are proposed. Kerstetter and Cho (2004) assess the relationship among the prior knowledge of travelers, the information search behavior, and the credibility of information sources. Consistent with Gursoy's work (2003), the results of this study also indicate that the more prior knowledge travelers have, the less they will use and trust the Internet in information search. Lehto, Kim, and Morrison suggest that the extent and content of information search for travel planning are affected by traveler' prior knowledge of the travel destination. The implications of this study show that the travelers who frequently use offline source to search travel information will be more likely to accept Internet as information source. Travelers who have the experience of using the Internet for a long time or often use the Internet tend to search for travel information on the Internet when planning their vacations (Kah, Vogt, & MacKay, 2008). Jensen (2012) investigates the relationship between information search for purchasing tourism products and the travel experience. Results indicate that travel experience would positively affect the online search and purchase of tourism products. Besides, the relationships between travelers' preference, such as time-saving, price-saving, store-enjoyment, etc., and online information search are analyzed.

New approaches for online travel information research

Since the twenty-first century, IT techniques – e.g. the Internet, social network, mobile Internet, smart phone, GPS, etc. – have been extensively used in the practice and research of tourism industry, thus significantly changing this industry. In this section, new techniques and approaches are adopted in two important issues of online travel information research are introduced.

Data source and collection

As an important issue, data source and data collection are the basis of successful online travel information research. The traditional sources of information used in tourism research include paper media, tourist office, travel guides, television, radio, and so on (Lu & Chen, 2014). Correspondingly, the traditional data collection in tourism research include interviews (Luo, Feng, & Cai, 2004; Wang, Xiang, & Fesenmaier, 2016), surveys (Bronner & De Hoog, 2013; Morrison, et al., 2001) questionnaires (Fodness & Murray, 1997; No & Kim, 2014; Luo & Zhong, 2010), etc. However, the above-mentioned data sources and data collection methods take a lot of manpower and material resources during the practice of data collection and have obvious disadvantages of high cost, low efficiency and low representative level and short representative range of the sample.

The advent of the Internet and the development of information techniques have made the online travel information, such as social network, became a new source of information for tourism research. Based on the online travel information, some new data collection methods, which facilitate the tourism practice and research, have been proposed.

Online survey or questionnaire are common in online travel information collection. The questions in traditional survey or questionnaire are presented in e-mails or websites to collect customers' opinion or attitude. For instance, it is used to understand views of Japanese customers on the use of the Internet to search for travel information (Okazaki & Hirose, 2009) and to collect customers' demographic information related to online travel community (Chung & Buhalis, 2008).

Using Web search engine is another approach to collect online travel information. A Web search engine, such as Google or Bing, is a network software that is used to search for information on the World Wide Web. Walden, Carlsson, & Papageorgiou (2011) query Google by the hotel name and analyze the search result to understand how the information in the social network affects the results of searching by search engine. Cormany and Baloglu (2011) search for online medical tourism facilitators. The medical tourism facilitator websites obtained from a Web search engine are used to analyze their contents and services.

Web crawler is an Internet software that automatically browses the World Wide Web. It could be used to obtain information from the Internet. For instance, a Web crawler is used to obtain web pages on which consumers' reviews and hotel information are posted from the travel website. The obtained information could be applied to investigate the influence of travelers' reviews on the hotel sales (Ye, Law, & Gu, 2009). The textual contents of online travel blogs for a targeted city are collected by Web crawler to identify the city's popular travel locations (Yuan, et al., 2016).

Data mining methods

Data mining is another important issue in tourism research. The collected tourism data need to be analyzed through some methods in order to gain valuable knowledge. Statistical methods are the main approaches to traditional analysis in travel information research. The typical methods include T-Test (Yoo & Gretzel, 2008), ANOVA (Fodness & Murray, 1997; Sparks & Browning,

2011; Xie et al., 2011), Chi-square (Luo, Feng, & Cai, 2004; Bronner & De Hoog, 2013), regression (Morrison et al., 2001; Schroeder & Pennington-Gray, 2015), structural equation (Okazaki & Hirose, 2009; No & Kim, 2014).

In recent years, data mining, as a data analysis method, has begun to emerge in tourism research. According to Fayyad, Piatetsky-Shapiro and Smyth (1996), data mining is the application of specific algorithms for extracting patterns from data, and it combines the principles of mathematics, statistics, machine learning, and database systems. The commonly used data mining methods in travel information research are as follows:

Clustering is used to group a collection of objects into several classes which consist of similar objects. This method is often applied to study the segmentation of travelers or market. Rong, Li, & Law (2009) investigate the segmentation of hotel users through a clustering technique named self-organizing map (SOM), which can transform high-dimensional data into 2D or 3D plots. They also provide an intuitive graphical clustering result to help tourism managers understand the features of multiple customer groups. Bloom (2015) segments the international tourist market to Cape Town through SOM. SOM is also applied to investigate the segmentation of international travelers whose travel destination is Hong Kong (Li, Law, & Wang, 2010). The Gen Y health and wellness travelers' segment is analyzed by means of a K-means clustering algorithm (Hritz, Sidman, & D'Abundo, 2014).

The *association rule* is an approach to find the interdependent relationship between data objects in large scale databases. In tourism research, it could be applied to investigate the connections between customers' demographical features and their travel behaviors (Li et al., 2010). The eWOM of outbound domestic tourism in Hong Kong is analyzed by association rule (Rong et al., 2012). The result of this study shows the relationship of travelers who share and browse the information on the travel websites. Relationships between the customers' satisfaction to restaurants and the attributes which influence the satisfaction are investigated by association rule (Chen, 2015).

Classification is a data mining approach which assigns a new object to predefined categories (Tan, Steinbach, & Kumar, 2006). It is often applied in tourism demand modeling. For instance, tourism demand for shopping (Law & Au, 2000), dining (Au & Law, 2002) and visiting (Au & Law, 2000) are analyzed by rough set, a classification method which could classify the objects with fuzzy and imprecise knowledge. In addition, the common classification methods used in tourism demand modeling include Bayesian model (Wong, Song, & Chon, 2006), decision tree (Kim, Timothy, & Hwang, 2011), etc.

Other new techniques

In addition to the aforementioned information collection and analysis methods, there are still some new technologies which cannot be ignored.

The application of geographic information in tourism research is a new research area in recent years. The popularity of intelligent devices makes it easy for tourists to record their geographical information during their visit. The geographical information can be used in providing references for tourism managers (Vu et al., 2015), understanding travelers' preference (Chang & Caneday, 2011), travel recommendation (Memon et al., 2015). However, most of the geographic information related tourism studies are done by scholars from the information industry.

The usage of smart phones in tourism is another attractive research area. The smart phone is used in various issues of travel practice (Wang, Xiang, & Fesenmaier, 2016), acquiring knowledge about an unfamiliar urban environment through Augmented Reality browsers (Wang, Xiang, & Fesenmaier, 2014), searching for travel information (No & Kim, 2014), pushing recommendation to tourists (Tussyadiah & Wang, 2016).

Moreover, there are some emerging technologies in recent years, such as artificial intelligence, which will likely change the tourism industry profoundly in the near future.

Conclusions

The objective of this chapter is to provide the current state and progress of online travel information research. In this chapter, the generation and the employment of travel information in tourism are introduced first to give readers a comprehensive knowledge of travel information online. The information search behavior in tourism is investigated second to show the features and influencing factors of online information searching. At the end, some new approaches for travel information research are discussed.

Due to space limitations, only a brief introduction of issues related to online travel information is provided in this chapter. For further study, a list of literature is recommended for readers in the further reading section.

References

Au, N., & Law, R. (2000). The application of rough sets to sightseeing expenditures. *Journal of Travel Research*, 39, 70–77.

Au, N., & Law, R. (2002). Categorical classification of tourism dining. *Annals of Tourism Research*, 29, 819–833.

Bai, B., Law, R., & Wen, I. (2008). The impact of website quality on customer satisfaction and purchase intentions: Evidence from Chinese online visitors. *International Journal of Hospitality Management*, 27(3), 391–402.

Banerjee, S., & Chua, A.Y.K. (2016). In search of patterns among travellers' hotel ratings in TripAdvisor. *Tourism Management*, 53, 125–131.

Beatty, S. E., & Smith, S. (1987). External information search: An investigation across several product categories. *Journal of Consumer Research*, 14, 83–95.

Beldona, S. (2005). Cohort analysis of online travel information search behavior: 1995–2000. Journal of Travel Research, 44(2), 135–142.

Beldona, S. (2008). Online travel information search modes: an exploratory study. *Information Technology in Hospitality*, 5(1), 25–33.

Berezina, K., Bilgihan, A., Cobanoglu, C., & Okumus, F. (2016). Understanding Satisfied and Dissatisfied Hotel Customers: Text Mining of Online Hotel Reviews. *Journal of Hospitality Marketing & Management*, 25(1), 1–24.

Bloom, J. Z. (2005). Market Segmentation. *Annals of Tourism Research*, 32(1), 93–111.

Bronner, F., & De Hoog, R. (2013). A new perspective on tourist information search: discussion in couples as the context. *International Journal of Culture, Tourism and Hospitality Research*, 5(2), 128–143.

Buhalis, D., & Law, R. (2008). Progress in information technology and tourism management: 20 years on and 10 years after the Internet – the state of eTourism research. *Tourism Management*, 29(4), 609–623.

Buhalis, D., & Licata, M. C. (2002). The future eTourism intermediaries. *Tourism Management*, 23(3), 207–220.

Cantallops, A. S., & Salvi, F. (2014). New consumer behavior: a review of research on eWOM and hotels. *International Journal of Hospitality Management*, 36(1), 41–51.

Chang, G., & Caneday, L. (2011). Web-based GIS in tourism information search: Perceptions, tasks, and trip attributes. *Tourism Management*, 32(6), 1435–1437.

Chen, L.-F. (2015). Exploring asymmetric effects of attribute performance on customer satisfaction using association rule method. *International Journal of Hospitality Management*, 47, 54–64.

Cheung, C. M. K., & Lee, M. K. O. (2012). What drives consumers to spread electronic word of mouth in online consumer-opinion platforms. *Decision Support Systems*, 53(1), 218–225.

Chung, J. Y., & Buhalis, D. (2008). Information needs in online social networks. *Information Technology & Tourism*, 10(4), 267–281.

Chung, N., & Koo, C. (2015). The use of social media in travel information search. *Telematics and Informatics*, 32(2), 215–229.

Cormany, D., & Baloglu, S. (2011). Medical travel facilitator websites: An exploratory study of web page contents and services offered to the prospective medical tourist. *Tourism Management*, 32(4), 709–716.

Duan, W., Gu, B., & Whinston, A. B. (2008). Do online reviews matter? – An empirical investigation of panel data. *Decision Support Systems*, 45(4), 1007–1016.

Fayyad, U., Piatetsky-Shapiro, G., & Smyth, P. (1996). From data mining to knowledge discovery in databases. *AI Magazine*, 17(3), 37–54.

Fodness, D., & Murray, B. (1997). Tourist information search. *Annals of Tourism Research*, 24(3), 503–523.

Gursoy, D. (2003). Prior Product Knowledge and Its Influence on the Traveler's Information Search Behavior. *Journal of Hospitality & Leisure Marketing*, 10(3–4), 113–131.

Gursoy, D., & Chen, J. S. (2000). Competitive analysis of cross cultural information search behavior. *Tourism Management*, 21(6), 583–590.

Gursoy, D., & McCleary, K. W. (2004). Travelers' Prior Knowledge and its Impact on their Information Search Behavior. *Journal of Hospitality and Tourism Research*, 28(1), 66–94.

Gursoy, D., & Umbreit, W. T. (2004). Tourist information search behavior: cross-cultural comparison of European union member states. *International Journal of Hospitality Management*, 23(1), 55–70.

Hennig-Thurau, T., Gwinner, K. P., Walsh, G., & Gremler, D. D. (2004). Electronic word-of-mouth via consumer-opinion platforms: what motivates consumers to articulate themselves on the internet. *Journal of Interactive Marketing*, 18(1), 38–52.

Hofstede, G. (1980). *Culture's consequences*. Beverly Hills, CA: Sage Publications.

Ho, C.-I., Lin, M.-H., & Chen, H.-M. (2012). Web users' behavioural patterns of tourism information search: From online to offline. *Tourism Management*, 33(6), 1468–1482.

Hritz, N. M., Sidman, C. L., & D'Abundo, M. (2014). Segmenting the college educated generation y health and wellness traveler. *Journal of Travel & Tourism Marketing*, 31(1), 132–145.

Hudson, S., & Thal, K. (2013). The Impact of Social Media on the Consumer Decision Process: Implications for Tourism Marketing. *Journal of Travel & Tourism Marketing*, 30(1–2, SI), 156–160.

Jalilvand, M. R., & Samiei, N. (2012). The impact of electronic word of mouth on a tourism destination choice: Testing the theory of planned behavior (TPB). *Internet Research*, 22(5), 591–612.

Jang, S. (Shawn). (2004). The Past, Present, and Future Research of Online Information Search. *Journal of Travel & Tourism Marketing*, 17(2–3), 41–47.

Jansen, B. J., Ciamacca, C. C., & Spink, A. (2008). An analysis of travel information searching on the web. *Information Technology & Tourism*, 10(2), 101–118.

Jensen, J. M. (2012). Shopping orientation and online travel shopping: The role of travel experience. *International Journal of Tourism Research*, 14(1), 56–70.

Jordan, E. J., Norman, W. C., & Vogt, C. A. (2013). A cross-cultural comparison of online travel information search behaviors. *Tourism Management Perspectives*, 6(6), 15–22.

Jun, S. H., Vogt, C. A., & Mackay, K. J. (2007). Relationships between travel information search and travel product purchase in pretrip contexts. *Journal of Travel Research*, 45(3), 266–274.

Kah, J. A., Vogt, C., & MacKay, K. (2008). Online travel information search and purchasing by Internet use experiences. *Information Technology & Tourism*, 10(3), 227–243.

Kerstetter, D., & Cho, M.-H. (2004). Prior knowledge, credibility and information search. *Annals of Tourism Research*, 31(4), 961–985.

Kim, D.-Y., Lehto, X. Y., & Morrison, A.M. (2007). Gender differences in online travel information search: Implications for marketing communications on the internet. *Tourism Management*, 28(2), 423–433.

Kim, S.-B., & Kim, D.-Y. (2011). Travel Information Search Behavior and Social Networking. *Experimental Brain Research*, 29(3), 419–428.

Kim, S.-B., Choi, K. W., & Kim, D.-Y. (2013). The Motivations Of College Students' Use Of Social Networking Sites In Travel Information Search Behavior: The Mediating Effect Of Interacting With Other Users. *Journal of Travel & Tourism Marketing*, 30(3), 238–252.

Kim, S. S., Timothy, D. J., & Hwang, J. (2011). Understanding Japanese tourists' shopping preferences using the Decision Tree Analysis method. *Tourism Management*, 32(3), 544–554.

Ku, E. C. S., & Fan, Y. W. (2009). The decision making in selecting online travel agencies: an application of analytic hierarchy process. *Journal of Travel & Tourism Marketing*, 26(5–6), 482–493.

Ladhari, R., & Michaud, M. (2015). eWOM effects on hotel booking intentions, attitudes, trust, and website perceptions. *International Journal of Hospitality Management*, 46, 36–45.

Law, R., & Au, N. (2000). Relationship modeling in tourism shopping: A decision rules induction approach. *Tourism Management*, 21, 241–249.

Law, R., Leung, R., & Buhalis, D. (2009). Information technology applications in hospitality and tourism: a review of publications from 2005 to 2007. *Journal of Travel & Tourism Marketing*, 26(5–6), 599–623.

Lee, H. A., Law, R., & Murphy, J. (2011). Helpful reviewers in tripadvisor, an online travel community. *Journal of Travel & Tourism Marketing*, 28(7), 675–688.

Lehto, X.Y., Kim, D.Y., & Morrison, A.M. (2006). The effect of prior destination experience on online information search behaviour. Tourism & Hospitality Research, 6(2), 160–178.

Levy, S. E., Duan, W., & Boo, S. (2013). An Analysis of One-Star Online Reviews and Responses in the Washington, D.C., Lodging Market. *Cornell Hospitality Quarterly*, 54(1), 49–63.

Li, G., Law, R., & Rong, J., Vu, H.Q. (2010). Incorporating both positive and negative asso- ciation rules into the analysis of outbound tourism in Hong Kong. *Journal of Travel & Tourism Marketing*, 27 (8), 812–828.

Li, G., Law, R., & Wang, J. (2010). Analyzing international travelers' profile with self-organizing maps. *Journal of Travel & Tourism Marketing*, 27(2), 113–131.

Li, G., Law, R., Vu, H. Q., & Rong, J. (2013a). Discovering the hotel selection preferences of Hong Kong inbound travelers using the Choquet Integral. *Tourism Management*, 36, 321–330.

Li, G., Law, R., Vu, H. Q., Rong, J., & Zhao, X. (Roy). (2015). Identifying emerging hotel preferences using Emerging Pattern Mining technique. *Tourism Management*, 46, 311–321.

Li, H., Ye, Q., & Law, R. (2013). Determinants of Customer Satisfaction in the Hotel Industry: An Application of Online Review Analysis. *Asia Pacific Journal of Tourism Research*, 18(7), 784–802.

Litvin, S. W., Goldsmith, R. E., & Pan, B. (2008). Electronic word-of-mouth in hospitality and tourism management. *Tourism Management*, 29(3), 458–468.

Liu, S., Law, R., Rong, J., Li, G., & Hall, J. (2013). Analyzing changes in hotel customers' expectations by trip mode. *International Journal of Hospitality Management*, 34, 359–371.

Liu, Z., & Park, S. (2015). What makes a useful online review? Implication for travel product websites. *Tourism Management*, 47, 140–151.

Loda, M. (2011). Comparing Web sites: An Experiment in Online Tourism Marketing. *International Journal of Business and Social Science*, 2(22), 70–78.

Lu, A. C. C., & Chen, B. T. (2014). Information Search Behavior of Independent Travelers: A Cross-Cultural Comparison between Chinese, Japanese, and American Travelers. *Journal of Hospitality Marketing & Management*, 23(8), 865–884.

Luo, F., & Zhong, Y. (2010). Tourist Internet information search motivation: An empirical study of backpackers of university students. In *International Conference on Networking and Digital Society* (pp. 314–317).

Luo, M., Feng, R., & Cai, L. A. (2004). Information Search Behavior and Tourist Characteristics. *Journal of Travel & Tourism Marketing*, 17(2–3), 15–25.

Madden, M., & Rainie, L. (2003, December 23). America's online pursuits: The changing picture of who's online and what they do. Available online at: www.pewinternet.org/reports/toc.asp?Report=106 (accessed 5 May 2017).

Memon, I., Chen, L., Majid, A., Lv, M., Hussain, I., & Chen, G. (2015). Travel recommendation using geotagged photos in social media for tourist. *Wireless Personal Communications*, 80(4), 1347–1362.

Morrison, A.M., Jing, S., O'Leary, J. T., & Cai, L. A. (2001). Predicting usage of the Internet for travel bookings: an exploratory study. *Information Technology & Tourism*, 4(1), 15–30.

Munar, A.M., & Jacobsen, J. K.S. (2014). Motivations for sharing tourism experiences through social media. *Tourism Management*, 43, 46–54.

No, E., & Kim, J. (2014). Determinants of the adoption for travel information on smartphone. *International Journal of Tourism Research*, 16(6), 534–545.

Okazaki, S., & Hirose, M. (2009). Does gender affect media choice in travel information search? On the use of mobile Internet. *Tourism Management*, 30(6), 794–804.

Özturan, M., & Roney, S. A. (2004). Internet use among travel agencies in Turkey: an exploratory study. *Tourism Management*, 25(2), 259–266.

Pew Research Center. (2017). Internet/Broadband Fact Sheet. Available online at: www.pewinternet.org/fact-sheet/internet-broadband/ (accessed 5 May 2017).

Rong, J., Li, G., & Law, R. (2009). A contrast analysis of online hotel web service purchasers and browsers. *International Journal of Hospitality Management*, 28(3), 466–478.

Rong, J., Vu, H. Q., Law, R., & Li, G. (2012). A behavioral analysis of web sharers and browsers in Hong Kong using targeted association rule mining. *Tourism Management*, 33(4), 731–740.

Schmallegger, D., & Carson, D. (2008). Blogs in tourism: Changing approaches to information exchange. *Journal of Vacation Marketing*, 14(2), 99–110.

Schroeder, A., & Pennington-Gray, L. (2015). The Role of Social Media in International Tourist's Decision Making. *Journal of Travel Research*, 54(5), 584–595.

Sparks, B., & Browning, V. (2011). The impact of online reviews on hotel booking intentions and perception of trust. *Tourism Management*, 32(6), 1310–1323.

Stinger, G. J. (1961). The economics of information. *Journal of Political Economy*, 69, 213–225.
Tan, P.-N., Steinbach, M., & Kumar, V. (2006). *Introduction to data mining*. Addison Wesley.
Tham, A., Croy, G., & Mair, J. (2013). Social Media in Destination Choice: Distinctive Electronic Word-of-Mouth Dimensions. *Journal of Travel & Tourism Marketing*, 30(1–2, SI), 144–155.
Tussyadiah, I. P., & Wang, D. (2016). Tourists' attitudes toward proactive smartphone systems. *Journal of Travel Research*, 55(4), 493–508.
U.S. Travel Association. (2010). Travelers' use of the Internet 2010 edition. Available online at: www.dcvb-nc.com/comm/enews/Vol9Issue48/2010_Travelers_Use_of_the_Internet.pdf (accessed 22 May 2017).
Vermeulen, I., & Seegers, D. (2009). Tried and tested: The impact of online hotel reviews on consumer consideration. *Tourism Management*, 30(1), 123–127.
Vu, H. Q., Li, G., Law, R., & Ye, B. H. (2015). Exploring the travel behaviors of inbound tourists to Hong Kong using geotagged photos. *Tourism Management*, 46, 222–232.
Walden, P., Carlsson, C., & Papageorgiou, A. (2011). Travel Information Search – The Presence of Social Media. In *Proceedings of the 44th Hawaii International Conference on System Science* (pp. 1 10).
Wang, D., Xiang, Z., & Fesenmaier, D. R. (2014). Adapting to the mobile world: A model of smartphone use. *Annals of Tourism Research*, 48, 11–26.
Wang, D., Xiang, Z., & Fesenmaier, D. R. (2016). Smartphone use in everyday life and travel. *Journal of Travel Research*, 55(1), 52–63.
Wang, Y., Yu, Q., & Fesenmaier, D. R. (2002). Defining the virtual tourist community: Implications for tourism marketing. *Tourism Management*, 23(4), 407–417.
Wang, Y. C., & Fesenmaier, D. R. (2004). Towards understanding members' general participation in and active contribution to an online travel community. *Tourism Management*, 25(6), 709–722.
Wei, L., Peng, W., & Lee, W. (2013). Exploring pattern-aware travel routes for trajectory search. *ACM Transactions on Intelligent Systems and Technology*, 4(3), 48.
Whitehead, L. (2012). Identifying future research opportunities in online consumer reviews: the case study of 'TripAdvisor'. *International Journal of Technology Marketing*, 6(4), 341–354.
Wong, K. K. F., Song, H., & Chon, K. S. (2006). Bayesian models for tourism demand forecasting. *Tourism Management*, 27(5), 773–780.
Xiang, Z., & Gretzel, U. (2010). Role of social media in online travel information search. *Tourism Management*, 31(2), 179–188.
Xie, H., Miao, L., Kuo, P. J., & Lee, B. Y. (2011). Consumers' responses to ambivalent online hotel reviews: the role of perceived source credibility and pre-decisional disposition. *International Journal of Hospitality Management*, 30(1), 178–183.
Ye, Q., Gu, B., & Chen, W. X. (2011). The influence of user-generated content on traveler behavior: An empirical investigation on the effects of e-word-of-mouth to hotel online bookings. *Computers in Human Behavior*, 27(2), 634–639.
Ye, Q., Law, R., & Gu, B. (2009). The impact of online user reviews on hotel room sales. *International Journal of Hospitality Management*, 28(1), 180–182.
Yoo, K. H., & Gretzel, U. (2008). What motivates consumers to write online travel reviews. *Information Technology & Tourism*, 10(4), 283–295.
Yoo, K.-H., & Gretzel, U. (2011). Influence of personality on travel-related consumer-generated media creation. *Computers in Human Behavior*, 27(2), 609–621.
Yuan, H., Xu, H., Qian, Y., & Li, Y. (2016). Make your travel smarter: Summarizing urban tourism information from massive blog data. *International Journal of Information Management*, 36(6), 1306–1319.

Further reading

Jang, S. (2004). The Past, Present, and Future Research of Online Information Search. *Journal of Travel & Tourism Marketing*, 17(2–3), 41–47. (A survey of traditional tourism information search approach.)
Law, R., Leung, R., & Buhalis, D. (2009). Information technology applications in hospitality and tourism: a review of publications from 2005 to 2007. *Journal of Travel & Tourism Marketing*, 26(5–6), 599–623. (An extensive survey of information technology in tourism.)
Munar, A.M., & Jacobsen, J. K. S. (2014). Motivations for sharing tourism experiences through social media. *Tourism Management*, 43, 46–54. (The generation of online travel information.)

Sparks, B., & Browning, V. (2011). The impact of online reviews on hotel booking intentions and perception of trust. *Tourism Management*, 32(6), 1310–1323. (Explaining the impact of online travel information in travel product sales.)

Tan, P.-N., Steinbach, M., & Kumar, V. (2006). *Introduction to data mining*. Addison Wesley. (An introductory book of data mining.)

Vermeulen, I., & Seegers, D. (2009). Tried and tested: The impact of online hotel reviews on consumer consideration. Tourism Management, 30(1), 123–127. (Understanding travelers' preference)

Vu, H. Q., Li, G., Law, R., & Ye, B. H. (2015). Exploring the travel behaviors of inbound tourists to Hong Kong using geotagged photos. *Tourism Management*, 46, 222–232. (Introducing how to use geographical information in tourism research.)

24

Revisiting destination loyalty

An examination of its antecedents

Christina G. Chi

Introduction

Never before have we seen so much emphasis being placed on consumer loyalty. Businesses are bending over backwards to retain customers. The mushrooming of various loyalty programs offered by different companies is an example of such effort. It is widely acknowledged that loyal customers represent significant present and future value for business profits and continuity. But what make customers loyal? This is a question that draws enormous interests from marketing/management scholars, reflected by the fact that loyalty studies have grown considerably over the past few decades. The unique nature of tourism has made loyalty an elusive goal for destinations and destination organizations. Various factors such as the variety of opportunities, infrequent purchase, the democratic nature of the travel experience, little difference between vast selection of providers, and others have all diminished tourism loyalty (McKercher, Denizci-Guillet & Ng, 2012). Nevertheless, such situation has not discouraged tourism researchers from studying what prompts tourists to return to the same destination and make positive referrals for their favorite destination(s). The purpose of this paper is to conduct a comprehensive review of destination loyalty studies, focusing on factors that lead to tourist loyalty. Table 24.1 provides a summary of recent destination loyalty studies from 2001–2016.

Tourism destination

As Seaton and Bennett (1996) claim, destination is a complex and peculiar animal. In order to understand destinations, consideration has to be given to the differing environmental, social and economic contexts around the world within which tourism destinations exist. Cooper, Fletcher, Gilbert and Wanhill (1998) view a destination as the focus of facilities and services designed to meet the needs of the tourist. The travel destination, however defined geographically, provides a convenient focus for the examination of the tourist movement and its impact and significance. Indeed, the destination brings together all aspects of tourism – demand, transportation, supply, and marketing – in a useful framework. It represents the most important element of the tourism system because destinations and their images attract tourists, motivate the visits and therefore energize the whole tourism system. A destination is the catalyst link that precipitates all the industries in

Table 24.1 Summary of "destination loyalty/behavioral intentions" literature

Authors/Year/ Journal	*Survey procedure/ Location/Sample size*	*Statistical methods*	*Operationalization of destination loyalty / behavioral intentions*	*Antecedents of loyalty/ Intention*	*Study findings*
Bigne, Sanchez and Sanchez, 2001 *Tourism Management*	On site survey of two Spanish tourist resorts; convenience sampling; 251 surveys in Peniscola and 263 in Torrevieja	Path analysis	Intention to return Intention to recommend	Image, quality, satisfaction	Image → Quality; Quality → Satisfaction; Image → Satisfaction; Quality → Return; Image → Recommendation; Image → Return; Satisfaction → Recommendation
Chen and Gursoy, 2001 *International Journal of Contemporary Hospitality Management*	On-site survey of Korean outbound travelers in Seoul International Airport; 265 useful questionnaires	Multiple regression, path analysis, Chi-square	Measured by a single item – "it is a recommendable place" (5-point Likert scale)	Destination safety, cultural differences, Past experience (indirect effect)	**Regression:** cultural difference ($\beta = 0.18$), safety ($\beta = -0.161$), convenience ($\beta = 0.145$) relate to DL; **Path analysis**: Safety ($\beta = -0.11$) and cultural difference ($\beta = 0.235$) directly affect DL; safety mediates between past experience and DL; Past experience affects safety ($\beta = -0.125$)
Lehto, O'Leary and Morrison, 2004 *Annals of Tourism Research*	Survey on flights of over 55 US and foreign airline carriers; two-stage stratified sampling, sample size 2,284 – all are repeat visitors	EFA, SEM			Prior visit influences activity involvement & economic involvement. Most frequent tourists have the narrowest activity choices; expenditure of repeat tourists is more than first time visitors
Yoon and Uysal, 2005 *Tourism Management*	500 self-administered questionnaires to tourists staying in well-known hotels nearby Mediterranean Sea	EFA, CFA, SEM	1) How likely you will revisit xxx? 2) describe your overall feelings about your visit; 3) will you suggest xxx to friends or relatives?	Push & pull motivation, travel satisfaction	Destination loyalty (DL) is positively affected by tourist satisfaction ($\beta = 0.79$) and push motivation ($\beta = 0.41$); Satisfaction is negatively affected by pull motivation ($\beta = -0.54$)

(Continued)

Table 24.1 (Continued)

Authors/Year/ Journal	*Survey procedure/ Location/Sample size*	*Statistical methods*	*Operationalization of destination loyalty / behavioral intentions*	*Antecedents of loyalty/ Intention*	*Study findings*
Alegre and Cladera, 2006 *Journal of Travel Research*	Tourist Expenditure Survey conducted by the Balearic Island (Spain) Regional Government for the year 2002–2003; sample size: 7,564	Ordinal regression (ordered logit model), logarithm of the probability ratio	Whether you intend to spend another holiday in xxx (Yes/no)	Numbers of visits, overall satisfaction, tourist characteristics	Repeat visitors are more likely to return than first time visitors; The major determinant of intention to return is high satisfaction levels; numbers of visits has a small effect on overall satisfaction; for repeat visitors, dissatisfaction has smaller negative effect on return intention than first time visitors
Gallarza and Gil-Saura, 2006 *Tourism Management*	Survey students from private universities in Valencia & Madrid (Spain) who travel in groups; 274 useful responses	SEM	1) Whether to visit the same destination; 2) Positive word of mouth	Value dimensions (positive & negative); Satisfaction	Value dimensions (service quality, play, aesthetics, social value, time and effort spent) and satisfaction directly and positively affect DL; Confirm the "quality → value → satisfaction → loyalty" chain
Oom do Valle, Silva, Mendes and Guerreiro, 2006 *International Journal of Business Science and Applied Management*	486 personal interviews; structured questionnaire; Portuguese & foreign tourists to Arade (Portugal); quota sampling,	SEM, Categorical principal components analysis (CATPCA), cluster analysis	1) Intention to return; 2) Willingness to recommend	Tourist satisfaction	Satisfaction → DL(0.79) → revisit (0.53) / willing to recommend (0.84); Two clusters (1: satisfied & 2: unsatisfied); High satisfaction affects willingness to recommend more than return intention; Two clusters are not socio-demographically different; Cluster 1: more foreigners vs. Cluster 2: more native Portuguese

Um, Chon and Ro, 2006 *Annals of Tourism Research*	Multistage cluster sampling design with stratification, 812 useful interviews in the departure lounge area of the Hong Kong International airport; Omnibus survey delivered: longitudinal data – 740 samples in 2001, 681 in 2002, 450 in 2003	Path analysis, conventional linear regression	How likely would you return to Hong Kong for pleasure travel? (7-point scale)	Perceived attractiveness, satisfaction, service quality & perceived value for money	Perceived attractiveness, satisfaction and perceived value for money all have directly and positively affect revisit intention; Satisfaction is positively affected by perceived attractiveness, quality of service, & value for money; Perceived attractiveness is the most important indicator of DL
Chen and Tsai, 2007 *Tourism Management*	Convenience sampling in Kengtin, Taiwan; 393 usable surveys obtained	EFA, SEM	Likeliness to revisit Willingness to recommend	Destination image, trip quality, perceived value, satisfaction	Destination image → trip quality (0.91); trip quality → perceived value (0.83); perceived value → satisfaction (0.75); Satisfaction → behavioral intention (0.54)
Hui, Wan, and Ho, 2007 *Tourism Management*	Tourists departing Singapore Changi airport, systematic sampling, 424 useable responses (including European, Asian, Oceania & North American tourists)	Multivariate technique - Hotelling T^2, stepwise approach, simple regression	Likelihood of recommendation/ revisiting	Expectation, perceptions, experiences, disconfirmation, overall satisfaction	Likelihood of recommendation/ revisiting is affected by overall satisfaction; tourists' expectation/ perceptions are different in groups (geographically); for all groups: overall convenience & commodities are important to satisfaction; "price" is non-significant in shaping satisfaction, "accommodations and food" is significant for North Americans; "Attractions" is significant for European and Asian tourists, "Culture" is important for Oceania tourists

(Continued)

Table 24.1 (Continued)

Authors/Year/ Journal	*Survey procedure/ Location/Sample size*	*Statistical methods*	*Operationalization of destination loyalty / behavioral intentions*	*Antecedents of loyalty/ Intention*	*Study findings*
Jang and Feng, 2007 *Tourism Management*	Data from the Pleasure Travel Markets Survey in France, total of 1,221 personal interviews, subsample of 163 respondents was drawn from the dataset	SEM	Intention to revisit within the next 12 months (short-term revisit intention); mid-term: revisit within the next three years, long-term: revisit within the next five years	Destination satisfaction, novelty seeking	Satisfaction is a direct antecedent of short-term revisit intention (0.26); novelty seeking is a significant antecedent of mid-term revisit intention (0.12); short-term → mid-term → long-term revisit intention
Lee, Graefe and Burns, 2007 *Leisure Science*	Survey data collected from Umpqua National Forest (USA), stratified sampling, 359 useful responses	SEM, CFA	Attitudinal loyalty; behavior loyalty, conative loyalty	Activity involvement, satisfaction, service quality	**Direct:** Service quality positively affects activity involvement and satisfaction; Activity involvement positively affects attitudinal DL ($\beta = 0.5$) and behavioral DL ($\beta = 0.4$); Satisfaction positively affects attitudinal DL ($\beta = 0.29$) and conative DL ($\beta = 0.53$); **Indirect**: Service quality indirectly affects attitudinal DL & behavioral DL through activity involvement and affects attitudinal DL & conative DL through satisfaction; attitudinal DL → conative DL (0.42) → behavioral DL (0.74)
Chi and Qu, 2008 *Tourism Management*	Cross-sectional survey conducted at Southern USA; Two-stage sampling approach; 345 questionnaires returned	EFA, CFA, SEM	Repeat purchase intentions and WOM recommendations	Overall satisfaction, attribute satisfaction Destination image	Attribute satisfaction ($\beta = 0.12$) and overall satisfaction ($\beta = 0.67$) positively affect DL; Destination image positively affects attribute satisfaction ($\beta = 0.71$) and overall satisfaction ($\beta = 0.29$); Attribute satisfaction positively affects overall satisfaction ($\beta = 0.20$)

Faullant, Matzler and Füller, 2008 *Managing Service Quality*	Data from "TQC" study (annual online survey), 6,172 customers completed survey	SEM, Image-satisfaction-grid; Multiple-group analysis	revisiting intention and word-of-mouth (WOM)	Satisfaction, image	Highest DL: highest image and satisfaction score; Image is more important than satisfaction for repeat visitors; Image is less likely to change and more pronounced for repeat visitors;
Kim, 2008 *Journal of Travel & Tourism Marketing*	Web-based questionnaire sent to college students at Michigan State University (USA), 1st survey 2,437 useful responses, 2nd survey 591 useful responses	SEM; CFA	a) In the next 2 years, how likely you will revisit xxx? b) how likely you will pay more if you revisit; c) describe your overall feelings about your most recent trip (never visit to revisit); (d) Will you suggest xxx to your friends or relatives?	Push and pull motivations, satisfaction, cognitive involvement, affective involvement	Push motivations → Pull motivations (0.57); Pull motivations → Cognitive involvement (0.13); Cognitive involvement → affective involvement (0.62); Cognitive involvement → satisfaction (0.27) → DL; Affective involvement → satisfaction (0.67) → DL
Li and Petrick, 2008 *Journal of Travel Research*	Online panel survey, Useful sample 554, active cruisers	SEM, Multiple regression, correlation analysis	Attitudinal loyalty, behavioral loyalty	Satisfaction, quality of alternatives, & investment size	Among 3 variables: satisfaction mostly predict attitudinal DL; satisfaction (0.55) & investment size (0.34) positively affect attitudinal DL; quality of alternatives (-0.22) negatively affects attitudinal DL; attitudinal DL → behavioral DL
Sandra María Correia Loureiro and Francisco Javier Miranda González, 2008 *Journal of Travel & Tourism Marketing*	Face-to-face interviews in Extremadura (Spain) & Alentejo (Portugal), and online questionnaire (total sample size = 500)	Factor analysis, ANOVA, SEM	Behavior and attitude loyalty	Satisfaction, perceived quality, image, trust	Satisfaction, perceived quality, image, & trust all positively affect DL; Image is a direct antecedent of all other constructs; quality positively affects satisfaction & DL; satisfaction positively affects trust.

(Continued)

Table 24.1 (Continued)

Authors/Year/ Journal	*Survey procedure/ Location/Sample size*	*Statistical methods*	*Operationalization of destination loyalty / behavioral intentions*	*Antecedents of loyalty/ Intention*	*Study findings*
Alegre and Cladera, 2009 *European Journal of Marketing*	Data from survey on Tourist Expenditure in the Balearic Islands (Spain), by regional government and University of Balearic Islands, 6,848 observations	SEM	Ask visitors whether they plan to revisit	Overall satisfaction, number of prior visits	Overall satisfaction is a major determinant of DL, stronger than number of past visits; Past visits positively affect overall satisfaction; satisfaction with basic components of the sun and sand product is crucial to overall satisfaction
Lee, 2009 *Leisure Sciences*	On-site survey in three wetlands in Taiwan (Sihcao, Cigu,& Haomeiliao), systematic sampling among tourists departing via the exit area, 1,244 usable responses	EFA, SEM, path analysis	Willingness to revisit, willingness to recommend, and positive WOM	Destination image, tourist attitude, & motivation (all indirect effect); satisfaction (direct)	Destination image, tourist attitude, & motivation indirectly affect future behavior; They are all directly related to satisfaction ($\Upsilon = 0.27$, 0.41, & 0.33); Satisfaction directly affects future behavior ($\beta = 0.67$) and mediates the relation between the three variables and future behavior
Mechinda, Serirat and Gulid, 2009 *Journal of Vacation Marketing*	Survey distributed to international and domestic repeat tourists in Chiangmai, Thailand; sample size 400, quota sampling	EFA, Chi-square	Attitudinal and behavioral loyalty	attachment, familiarity, perceived value, pull & push motivation, gender, have children or not	Attitudinal DL: mainly driven by attachment, familiarity, and perceived value, pull motivation positively affects both international/domestic tourists; Behavioral DL: negatively affected by push motivation; Gender positively affects attitudinal and behavioral DL among international/ domestic tourists

Campo-Martínez, Garau-Vadell and Martínez-Ruiz, 2010 *Tourism Management*	A survey based on personal interviews with tourists leaving Palma Airport (Mallorca, Spain); Useful responses: 676	Means, Kruskal–Wallis one-way ANOVA, logistic regression analysis	Revisit intention	Satisfaction, global image, prior experience	For total sample: all 3 variables positively affect revisit intention (Satisfaction > Prior experience > Global image); For those with partner/ friends: satisfaction/positive image/ prior experience positively affect revisit intention; For those with family & children: satisfaction/prior experience positively affect revisit intention. For those travel alone: all hypotheses were rejected
Yuksel, Yuksel and Bilim, 2010 *Tourism Management*	Survey conducted at Didim hotels (Turkey), 224 useful responses	Outlier analysis, SEM	Cognitive, affective and conative loyalty	Place attachment operationalized as place dependence (PD), affective attachment (AA), place identity(PI), and satisfaction	**Direct:** PD/AA/PI → cognitive / affective DL; PD/AA/PI → satisfaction; Satisfaction → cognitive DL/conative DL/affective DL; Cognitive DL → Affective/conative DL; Affective DL → conative DL; **Indirect:** Place attachment (PD/AA/PI) → satisfaction → DL
Bosnjak, Sirgy, Hellriegel and Maurer, 2011 *Journal of Travel Research*	Online survey, 973 German tourists were recruited with the aid of nonprobability methods	SEM	Satisfaction, revisiting intentions, and positive word of mouth	Self-congruity, functional congruity, hedonic congruity, economic congruity, safety congruity, moral congruity, & leisure congruity	All 7 types of congruity positively affect postvisit loyalty (top 3: self, functional, & hedonic congruity; bottom 2: economic & moral congruity)

(Continued)

Table 24.1 (Continued)

Authors/Year/ Journal	*Survey procedure/ Location/Sample size*	*Statistical methods*	*Operationalization of destination loyalty / behavioral intentions*	*Antecedents of loyalty/ Intention*	*Study findings*
Chi, 2011 *Journal of Hospitality & Tourism Research*	Data collected at Arkansas (USA), 345 useful responses	Multi-sample structural equations analyses, cross-group comparisons (using SEM), equality / invariance measurement, structural model comparisons, latent mean comparisons	Tourists' intention to revisit xxx and their willingness to recommend xxx	Tourists' demographic characteristics such as age, gender, income, education	Tourists with different age and income have no sig difference in destination image perception, levels of satisfaction, or loyalty; Tourists in different gender and education perceive image differently but have similar satisfaction and loyalty; Holistic loyalty formation process is the same across different demographic groups
Lee, Jeon and Kim, 2011 *Tourism Management*	Survey distributed to Chinese outbound tourists flying between the Beijing International Airport and Incheon Airport (Seoul, Korea); 513 completed surveys	Principal component factor analysis, CFA, SEM	Positive WOM, revisit intention, recommend intention	Tourist expectations, motivations, tour quality, tourist satisfaction, tourist complaints	Tourist expectation ($\Upsilon = -0.084$) & motivation ($\Upsilon = 0.122$) →tour quality; tour quality →tourist satisfaction ($\beta = 0.266$); tourist satisfaction → tourist complaint ($\beta = -0.279$); tourist complaint → tourist loyalty ($\beta = -0.320$)
Velazquez, Gil-Saura and Molina, 2011 *Journal of Vacation Marketing*	Literature review			Commitment, satisfaction, variety seeking trait, demographic variables, service quality, perceived value	Commitment & satisfaction → DL (attitudinal / behavioral), relation between satisfaction and DL is moderated by consumer variety seeking trait & demographic variables; Service quality & perceived value → satisfaction

Chi, 2012 *Journal of Hospitality and Tourism Research*	Data collected from visitors who stopped by the Eureka Springs (USA) Welcome Center, hotels, & motels, art galleries, etc. Proportionate stratified sampling & systematic random sampling, 345 useful responses	Multiple group analysis in SEM	Revisit and referral intention	Previous visits	Destination image leads to overall/ attribute satisfaction, this relation is similar between first-time & repeat visitors; satisfaction leads to DL – this relation is stronger for first-time visitors; repeat visitors have higher revisit intention than first-time visitors.
Forgas-Coll et al., 2012 *Tourism Management*	Personal interviews; 927 questionnaires collected from adult tourists in Barcelona airport (Spain)	SEM (Multi-group analysis), CFA	Affective loyalty and conative loyalty	Satisfaction, perceived value	1. Perceived value →affective loyalty (0.39) 2. Perceived value →satisfaction (0.89) 3. Satisfaction →affective loyalty (0.49) 4. Affective loyalty →conative loyalty (0.84) The nationality of the tourists moderates all the above relations.
Prayag & Ryan, 2012 *Journal of Travel Research*	Quota sampling, self-completed questionnaire with the presence of the interviewers using hotel guests (adults) in Mauritius, effective sample size: 705	CFA; SEM	Revisit and recommend intention	Destination image, personal involvement, place attachment, overall satisfaction	1. Personal involvement → Destination image (0.614); 2. Destination image → Place attachment (0.166); 3. Destination image → Overall satisfaction (0.514); 4. Place attachment → Overall satisfaction (0.148); 5. Personal involvement → Place attachment (0.790); 6. Overall satisfaction → Revisit intentions (0.124); 7. Overall satisfaction→ Recommendation intentions (0.119); 8. Place attachment → Revisit intentions (0.353); 9. Place attachment → Recommendation Intentions (0.273)

(Continued)

Table 24.1 (Continued)

Authors/Year/ Journal	*Survey procedure/ Location/Sample size*	*Statistical methods*	*Operationalization of destination loyalty / behavioral intentions*	*Antecedents of loyalty/ Intention*	*Study findings*
McKercher, Denizci-Guillet and Ng, 2012 *Annals of Tourism Research*	In-depth interviews with a purposive sample of frequent tourists. A total of 20 individuals were interviewed.	Qualitative research	No clear definition was provided	Vertical loyalty, experiential loyalty, and horizontal loyalty	Vertical and experiential loyalty were supported, while less evidence of horizontal loyalty was noted
Sun, Chi & Xu, 2013 *Annals of Tourism Research*	Personal interviews; 498 questionnaires collected from adult tourists in Haikou and Sanya city (China)	EFA, CFA, SEM	Revisit and recommendation intention	Destination familiarity, destination image, perceived value, tourist satisfaction	1. Destination familiarity → destination image (0.49); 2. Destination image → perceived value (0.81); 3. Destination image → tourist satisfaction (0.34); 4. Tourist satisfaction → destination loyalty (0.86); 5. Perceived value → destination loyalty (0.65).
Polo Peña, Frías Jamilena and Rodríguez Molina, 2013 *International Journal of Hospitality Management*	Quota sampling, self-completed questionnaire with the presence of the interviewers using hotel guests (adults) in Mauritius, effective sample size: 572, with 304 (53.15%) categorized as first-timers and 268 (48.85%) as repeaters.	CFA, SEM	Revisit and recommendation intention	Company reputation, satisfaction, previous experience, Affective perceived value (PV), functional perceived value (PV)	Company reputation → loyalty; Customer satisfaction → loyalty; Both functional PV and affective PV → customer satisfaction; The interaction effects between previous experience x functional PV → customer satisfaction; The interaction effects between previous experience x affective PV → customer satisfaction

Chen & Phou 2013 *Tourism Management*	Self-administrated survey, convenience sampling, Sample: 428 foreign tourists visiting the Angkor temple area of Cambodia	SEM	Revisit and recommendation intention	Destination image (cognitive image), Destination personality, Destination relationship (satisfaction, trust, attachment)	Destination image → destination personality (Supported) Destination image → destination satisfaction (Supported) Destination image → destination trust (Supported) Destination personality → destination satisfaction (Supported) Destination personality → destination trust (Supported) Destination satisfaction → destination trust (Supported) Destination satisfaction → destination attachment (Rejected) Destination trust → destination attachment (Supported) Destination satisfaction → destination loyalty (Supported) Destination trust → destination loyalty (Supported) Destination attachment → destination loyalty (Supported)
Zhang, Fu, Cai & Lu, 2014 *Tourism Management*	Meta-analysis	Meta-analysis	Composite loyalty (revisit and recommend Intention)	Affective image Cognitive image Overall image	1. Affective image → loyalty; 2. Cognitive image → loyalty; 3. Overall image → loyalty; 4. Overall image has the greatest impact on tourists' loyalty.

(Continued)

Table 24.1 (Continued)

Authors/Year/ Journal	*Survey procedure/ Location/Sample size*	*Statistical methods*	*Operationalization of destination loyalty / behavioral intentions*	*Antecedents of loyalty/ Intention*	*Study findings*
Gursoy, Chen & Chi, 2014 *International Journal of Contemporary Hospitality Management*	Conceptual paper		Attitudinal and behavioral conceptualization	Satisfaction, perceived quality, perceived value, destination image, involvement, previous experience; place attachment	Satisfaction → destination loyalty; perceived quality→ satisfaction → destination loyalty; value → perceived quality; value → satisfaction; value → destination loyalty; image → satisfaction; image → perceived quality; image → destination loyalty; travel motivation → satisfaction; involvement → perceived quality; involvement → destination image; involvement → destination loyalty; previous experience → destination image; previous experience → involvement; previous experience → satisfaction; previous experience → destination loyalty; place attachment → travel motivation; place attachment → destination image; place attachment → satisfaction; place attachment → destination loyalty

Vigolo, 2014, *International Journal of Tourism research*	self-administered survey, internet sampling targeted at Italian tourists to South Africa (Long-haul destinations) Visitor: 86, Non-visitor: 114	t-test, multiple-regression	Revisit intention, recommendation intention	Tourists attraction, Facilities, Atmosphere, Perceived risk, overall destination attractiveness	Tourists attraction → overall destination attractiveness (yes) Facilities → overall destination attractiveness (yes) Atmosphere → overall destination attractiveness (No: visitor, Yes: non-visitor) Perceived risk → (-) overall destination attractiveness (No) Attractiveness → destination loyalty (yes) Previous experience with destination moderates the attractiveness and loyalty relationship (yes) Previous experience with other long-haul destination moderate the attractiveness and loyalty relationship (yes)
Meleddu, Raci & Pulina 2015, *Tourism Management*	Stratified survey, a total of 1461 questionnaires were collected at the end of a trip at the main ports and airports on the island of Sardinia during the low and high seasons of 2012	Logit specification model, cross-classification	Attitudinal loyalty (intention to recommend), behavioral loyalty (intention to revisit), stated loyalty (composite)	Repeated behavior (past behavior), motivation, overall satisfaction, satisfaction with destination sub-choice, vacation characteristics (Control), individual characteristics (Control)	Satisfaction with services, cultural resources and oeno-gastronomy, along with vacation and some individual characteristics are important determinants that influence stated loyalty. Repeat tourists become increasingly attached to the destination both in the high and low seasons.

(Continued)

Table 24.1 (Continued)

Authors/Year/ Journal	*Survey procedure/ Location/Sample size*	*Statistical methods*	*Operationalization of destination loyalty / behavioral intentions*	*Antecedents of loyalty/ Intention*	*Study findings*
Sirakaya-Turk, Ekinci, Martin 2015, *Journal of Business Research*	Semi-structured, face-to-face interviews and a short survey instrument. Respondents (N = 345) were tourists visiting the Mediterranean resort city of Antalya, Turkey	SEM	Destination re-patronage intention, destination WOM	Hedonic shopping value, Utilitarian shopping value, overall shopping satisfaction	1. Hedonic shopping value → overall shopping satisfaction 2. Utilitarian shopping value → overall shopping satisfaction 3. Overall shopping satisfaction → destination repatronage intention 4. Overall shopping satisfaction → destination WOM 5. Destination repatronage → destination WOM 6. Overall shopping satisfaction mediates hedonic shopping value's effect on destination repatronage intentions and destination word-of-mouth. 7. Overall shopping satisfaction mediates utilitarian shopping value's effect on destination repatronage intentions and destination word-of-mouth (Rejected).

Wong, 2015, *Current Issues in Tourism*	8 experts (from 6 academic researchers and 2 industry practitioners) for Delphi study. A self-administered questionnaire, distributed to international tourists with the assistance of tour operators, hoteliers, and tourist information centres located in Kuala Lumpur, Penang, Melaka, Kota Kinabalu, and Kuching from January 2013 – April 2013 (N = 1093)	Delphi technique, CFA, SEM	Revisit and recommendation intention	Destination competitiveness (functional and abstract attributes), CBBE	This study argues that the construct of destination competitiveness can be classified into the components of: (1) "functional attributes" being the antecedent of customer-based brand equity (CBBE) and (2) "abstract attributes" that are actually influenced by CBBE. 1. Destination competitiveness (functional attributes) → CBBE (yes) 2. CBBE → abstract attributes of destination competitiveness (yes) 3. CBBE → destination loyalty (yes) 4. Functional attributes → abstract attributes (yes) 5. Functional attributes → CBBE → abstract attributes of destination competitiveness (yes) 6. CBBE → abstract attributes of destination competitiveness → destination loyalty (yes)
N. L. Jamaludin, D. L. Sam, G. M. Sandal & A. A. Adam, 2016, *Current Issues in Tourism*	Short-term (n = 174) and long-term, and (n = 315) international students completed an online survey between January and June 2014 (Education tourism)	SEM	Revisit and recommendation intention	Perceived discrimination, orientation to mainstream culture, life satisfaction	1. Perceived discrimination → (-) destination loyalty intention (no) 2. Orientations to mainstream culture → destination loyalty intention (yes) 3. Life satisfaction → destination loyalty intention (no) 4. Orientations to mainstream culture mediates the perceived discrimination and destination loyalty intention relationship (yes) 5. Life satisfaction mediates the perceived discrimination and destination loyalty intention relationship (no)

(Continued)

Table 24.1 (Continued)

Authors/Year/ Journal	*Survey procedure/ Location/Sample size*	*Statistical methods*	*Operationalization of destination loyalty / behavioral intentions*	*Antecedents of loyalty/ Intention*	*Study findings*
Kuo, Chang, Cheng and Lin, 2016, *Journal of Travel & Tourism Marketing*	With the help of travel agencies, questionnaires were handed to groups who visit the Kinmen battlefield over four months (N = 453)	EFA, SEM	Revisit and recommendation intention	Tour guide interpretation, tourist satisfaction (mediator), perceived playfulness, perceived flow (moderators)	Tour guide interpretation has an influence on tourist satisfaction, and that tourist satisfaction in turn influences destination loyalty. Destination loyalty is also indirectly influenced by tour guide interpretation through tourist satisfaction. Correlations between tour guide interpretation and tourist satisfaction as well as tourist satisfaction and destination loyalty are stronger for tourists who perceive a high degree of playfulness and flow in their tourism experience
Nam, Kim and Hwang, 2016, *Journal of Travel & Tourism Marketing*	Self-administrated survey, tourists who visited Japan in the past three months (N = 280). These tourists were located at Gimhae International Airport and Busan Port International Cruise Terminal, Busan, South Korea	SEM	Positive WOM intention	Physical attractiveness of local people, displayed positive emotions of local people, the helpfulness of local people, personal connection to local people, destination distinctiveness	Physical attractiveness of local people → personal connection to those people Displayed positive emotions of local people → personal connection to those people The helpfulness of local people → personal connection to those people Personal connection to local people → destination distinctiveness Personal connection to local people → positive WOM Destination distinctiveness → positive WOM

Yi, Lin, Jin and Luo 2016, *Journal of Travel Research*	The Kaiping watchtower site is located in Kaiping city, Guangdong province, China. Pretest: N = 124, during July 4 to July 6, 2014 Main survey: N = 404, between October 2 and October 6, 2014 (peak visiting season)	CFA, SEM	Revisit and recommendation intention	Perceived authenticity (i.e. architectural heritage (AH), traditional customs (TC), folk culture (FC)); Existential authenticity (i.e. intrapersonal authenticity, interpersonal authenticity)	1. The perceived authenticity of AH→ intrapersonal authenticity of tourists (yes) 2. The perceived authenticity of TC → intrapersonal authenticity of tourists (no) 3. The perceived authenticity of FC → intrapersonal authenticity of tourists (yes) 4. The perceived authenticity of AH→ interpersonal authenticity of tourists (no) 5. The perceived authenticity of TC → interpersonal authenticity of tourists (no) 6. The perceived authenticity of FC → interpersonal authenticity of tourists (no) 7. intrapersonal authenticity of tourists → destination loyalty (yes) 8. interpersonal authenticity of tourists → destination loyalty (no)
Wu, 2016, *Journal of Business Research*	Personal interview questionnaire, 475 valid survey received in Taiwan Tourism Welcome Center from March 1 to April 30, 2015	Fuzzy-set Qualitative Comparative Analysis (fsQCA), structural equation modeling (SEM)	Revisit and recommendation intention, positive WOM, first choice among future destination	Destination image, consumer experience, satisfaction	1. destination image → destination loyalty 2. destination satisfaction → destination loyalty 3. destination image → destination satisfaction 4. consumer experience → destination satisfaction 5. consumer experience → destination loyalty

(Continued)

Table 24.1 (Continued)

Authors/Year/ Journal	*Survey procedure/ Location/Sample size*	*Statistical methods*	*Operationalization of destination loyalty / behavioral intentions*	*Antecedents of loyalty/ Intention*	*Study findings*
Sato, Kim, Buning & Harada, 2016, *Journal of Destination Marketing & Management*	Self-administrated survey, Data were collected from Japanese rafting tourists (N = 597) in Niseko (adventure sport destination)	CFA, multi-group SEM	Revisit and recommendation intention	Satisfaction, motivation (push and pull), decision makers vs. non-decision makers	Decision makers (DMs) and Non-DMs are differently motivated to travel to adventure sport tourism destinations; DMs are more likely to pursue excitement while Non-DMs are more motivated by family-related needs. DMs' destination loyalty is predicted by rafting services and cultural aspects of the destination, as well as satisfaction. Non-DM's destination loyalty is indirectly predicted by these factors through tourist satisfaction.
Breitsohl, and Garrod 2016, *Tourism Management*	Context: Unethical destination incident. An online survey containing a fictional scenario of an unethical destination incident (N = 1350)	SEM	Revisit intentions	Perceived severity, responsibility attributions, destination image, hostility emotions, negative WOM, avoidance	1. Perceived severity → hostility emotions 2. Responsibility attributions → hostility emotions 3. destination image → (-) hostility emotions 4. hostility emotions → negative WOM 5. hostility emotions → avoidance 6. negative WOM → (-) hostility emotions 7. avoidance → hostility emotions

Lee, and Hyun 2016, *Journal of Travel & Tourism Marketing*	Context: Post-disaster tourism destinations A self-report survey of representative loyal Korean visitors to Japan as a destination country was conducted (N = 417) An on-site survey using a non-probability convenience sampling method was conducted for the period from September to December 2014	CFA, SEM	Switching resistance loyalty: revisit intentions Behavioral: Number of visit to Japan	Perceived destination ability, three dimensions of brand love (passionate love, emotional attachment, and self-brand integration)	1. Perceived destination ability→ passionate love 2. Perceived destination ability → emotional attachment 3. Perceived destination ability → self-brand integration 4. Passionate love → switching resistance loyalty in Japan's post-disaster context 5. Emotional attachment → switching resistance loyalty 6. Self-brand integration → switching resistance loyalty 7. Switching resistance loyalty → behavioral loyalty
Su, Hsu, and Swanson, 2017, *Journal of Hospitality & Tourism Research*	Data were obtained from Chinese tourists visiting the Wuyi Mountain National Park, a mixed cultural and natural World Heritage Site located on the Eastern coast of China (inbound tourists, N = 314)	SEM	Positive word-of-mouth referrals and revisit intentions	Relationship perceptions (i.e. Service fairness, destination image, service quality); Relationship quality moderators (i.e. overall destination satisfaction, trust toward destination service provider)	1. Service fairness → overall destination satisfaction 2. Service fairness → trust toward destination service provider 3. Destination image → overall satisfaction 4. Destination image → trust 5. Service quality → overall satisfaction 6. Service quality → trust 7. Overall satisfaction → revisit intention 8. Overall satisfaction → positive WOM 9. Trust → revisit intention 10. Trust → positive WOM

(Continued)

Table 24.1 (Continued)

Authors/Year/ Journal	*Survey procedure/ Location/Sample size*	*Statistical methods*	*Operationalization of destination loyalty / behavioral intentions*	*Antecedents of loyalty/ Intention*	*Study findings*
Agapito, Pinto, Mendes, 2017, *Tourism Management*	A two-phase data collection process having as a target population, tourists visiting Southwest Portugal and staying overnight at rural lodgings in the area, a self-administered survey was conducted from 15 July to 15 December 2011 (N = 181) six months after the visit, completing a second survey online (N = 31)	Content analysis for open-ended questions, Wilcoxon matched-pair signed-rank test, Z-test, Chi-square test	Recommendation intention, positive WOM intention, revisit intention Actual recommendation behavior, positive WOM, and revisit in plan	Sensory tourist experience, long-term memory	Suggests that diversified sensory impressions as perceived by tourists impact the long-term memory. Diversified sensory impressions recalled in the post-visit phase enhance favorable tourist behavior towards destinations. Reveals a link between richer sensory tourist experiences and destination loyalty.
Kim, and Park 2017, *Journal of Travel & Tourism Marketing*	a self-administered questionnaire, Data were collected from 254 visitors of six Community-based ecotourism (CBE) villages in Korea	CFA, SEM	Revisit and recommendation intention, Positive WOM	Economic value of CBE visitors, functional value, social value, emotional value, overall value, tourists satisfaction	1. Economic value of CBE visitors → overall value (no) 2. Functional value of CBE visitors → overall value (yes) 3. Social value of CBE visitors → overall value (yes) 4. Emotional value of CBE visitors → overall value (yes) 5. Overall value of CBE visitors → tourist satisfaction (yes) 6. The satisfaction of CBE tourists → Destination loyalty (yes)

"→" indicates "lead to", in the last column all numbers in parenthesis are "β"s, DL indicates "destination loyalty"

Source: This table is adapted from Sun, Chi & Xu's (2013) study and expanded to include more recent studies.

the tourism sector. Unless people want to go somewhere, provision for transporting them, housing them, feeding them and amusing them will be in vain (Seaton and Bennett, 1996). Similarly, Murphy, Pritchard and Smith (2000) think of a destination as an amalgam of individual products and experience opportunities that combine to form a total experience of the area visited. Hu and Ritchie (1993) consider the tourism destination as "a package of tourism facilities and services, which like any other consumer product, is composed of a number of multi-dimensional attributes."

Consumer loyalty

Consumer loyalty has generally been defined in behavioral terms as repeat purchasing frequency or relative volume of same-brand purchasing (e.g., Tellis 1988). Newman and Werbel (1973) define loyal customers as those who re-buy a brand, consider only that brand, and do no brand-related information seeking. Hawkins, Best and Coney (1995) define loyalty as consumers' intentions or actual behavior to repeatedly purchase certain products or services. Oliver's (1997, p. 392) definition of loyalty emphasizes the two different aspects of loyalty – the behavioral and attitudinal concept: "a deeply held commitment to re-buy or re-patronize a preferred product/service consistently in the future, thereby causing repetitive same-brand or same brand-set purchasing, despite situational influences and marketing efforts having the potential to cause switching behavior." Oliver (1997, p. 392) then defines loyalty at a higher level, which he terms 'ultimate loyalty', as those consumers who "fervently desires to re-buy a product/service, will have no other, and will pursue this quest against all odds and at all costs."

Oliver (1997) proposes three phases of loyalty – cognitive, affective and conative – that culminates in action loyalty, or 'action inertia' (operationalized as repeat usage). Cognitive loyalty focuses on the brand's performance aspects, and loyalty at this phase is based on brand belief only, thus is of a shallow nature. Affective loyalty is directed toward the brand's likeableness – consumers have developed a liking or attitude toward the brand. Conative (behavioral intention) loyalty is developed after consumers experience series of positive affect toward the brand, so they want to repurchase the brand. Action loyalty is where the motivated intentions in the conative loyalty state are transformed into readiness to act. At this phase, consumers are committed to the act of repurchasing, ignoring or deflecting obstacles that might prevent the act.

It has been argued that customer loyalty is a multidimensional concept including both behavioral element (repeat purchases) and attitudinal element (commitment); thus the use of composite measure increases the predictive power of the construct, as each variable cross-validates the nature of truly loyal relationship (Baloglu, 2002; Bowen & Chen, 2001; Dimitriades, 2006). However, this approach has limitations in that not all the weighting or quantified scores may apply to both the behavioral and attitudinal components, which may have different measurements. Parasuraman, Zeithmal and Berry (1994) develop a loyalty scale including dimensions such as loyalty to company, propensity to switch, willingness to pay more, external and internal response to problem. Some researchers (e.g., Taylor, 1998; Yoon & Uysal, 2005) measure consumer loyalty with three indicators: 1) likelihood to recommend a product or service to other; 2) likelihood to purchase a product or service again; and 3) overall satisfaction/feeling. Hepworth and Mateus (1994) adopt similar indices to assess loyalty, including intention to buy same product, intention to buy more product, and willingness to recommend the product to other consumers.

Destination loyalty and its antecedents

Many attractions and tourist destinations rely heavily on the repeat visitor segment. Various studies have examined antecedents to destination loyalty, including destination image, tourist satisfaction, service quality, perceived value, involvement, among others.

Destination image

Three decades of research in travel and tourism has shown the significant role destination image plays in the destination selection process, and the great contribution it makes to the understanding of tourist behavior. Researchers generally concur that destination image represents a global impression. Baloglu and McCleary (1999a, 1999b) consider image as being formed by two closely related components: perceptive/cognitive evaluations and affective appraisals. Perceptual/cognitive evaluations refer to an individual's knowledge and beliefs about an object (an evaluation of the perceived attributes of an object). Affective evaluations correspond to an individual's feelings towards an object. There is a general agreement that the cognitive component is an antecedent of the affective component, i.e., tourists form their feelings as a function of beliefs and opinions. In addition, the combination of these two components forms an overall or composite image of a product/brand. Baloglu and McCleary (1999a, 1999b) showed empirically that perceptual/cognitive evaluations influence the overall image directly as well as indirectly through affective evaluations.

Still other researchers (Gartner, 1996; Dann, 1996) suggest that destination image is made up of three distinct but hierarchically interrelated components: cognitive, evaluative and conative. Derived from fact, the cognitive component is viewed as the sum of beliefs and attitudes of an object leading to some internally accepted picture of its attributes (external forces, pull attributes). The affective component of image is related to motives in the sense that it is how a person feels about the object under consideration (internal forces, push attributes). It is believed that people travel because they are pushed into making travel decisions by internal forces and pulled by external forces of the destination attributes (Crompton, 1979; Dann, 1977). After processing external and internal stimuli of a destination, a decision is made whether or not to travel to the area. This act is the conative component, which is the action component of image, equivalent to behavior. The three components together form the travel decision process.

Satisfaction

Satisfaction is a complex construct that has received broad attention in the marketing literature. Companies are using customer satisfaction data to determine service/product quality and increase customer retention. Many empirical studies have documented that customer satisfaction caps in higher customer loyalty, positive WOM recommendations, increased market share and profitability (e.g., Fornell & Wernerfelt, 1987; Rust & Zahorik, 1993). Therefore, consumer satisfaction is essential to corporate survival due to its substantial bottom-line financial implications as well as quality and service considerations.

After thoroughly reviewing the existing literature, Giese and Cote (2000) identify three general components shared by the definitions of satisfaction in the literature: (1) consumer satisfaction is some type of response, an emotional, cognitive and/or conative judgment; (2) the response is based on an evaluation of a specific focus (expectations, product, consumption experience, etc.); (3) the response occurs at a particular time (prior to purchase, after purchase, after consumption, after extended experience, etc.).

Different approaches have been applied to investigating Customer Satisfaction/Dissatisfaction (CS/D) within hospitality and tourism, such as expectation-perception gap model (Duke & Persia, 1996), expectancy-disconfirmation theory (Pizam & Milman, 1993), congruity model (Chon & Olsen, 1991), and performance-only model (Pizam, Neumann & Reichel, 1978). Yuksel and Rimmington (1998) conduct an empirical study to examine the relative validity and reliability of six alternative measurements of customer satisfaction: 1) performance only, 2) performance weighted by importance, 3) importance minus performance, 4) subjective/direct disconfirmation, 5) subjective disconfirmation weighted by importance, and 6) subtractive/inferred disconfirmation. They conclude that performance-only model is superior to the other five alternatives in predicting customer satisfaction.

It has been proposed that affect is a component of satisfaction apart from cognition (e.g., Mano & Oliver, 1993; Westbrook, 1987; Westbrook & Oliver, 1991). These researchers identify affect as two-dimensional (positive–negative affects) and find that overall affect has a significant impact on satisfaction levels in addition to expectancy-disconfirmation effects. Affect is also proposed to have an influence on consumer behavior (Bagozzi, Gopinath & Nyer, 1999; Liljander & Strandvik, 1997). Specifically, positive affects lead to consumers' decision to stay or continue involvement, and/or share positive experience with others; whereas negative affects will result in consumers' decisions to leave or discontinue involvement, and/or complaining behavior.

Service quality

Service quality has received considerable attention in the literature due to the key role it plays in differentiating service products and building competitive edge. It is defined as customers' overall impression of the relative inferiority/superiority of an organization and its services (Bitner & Hubbert, 1994). The most well-known service quality measurement is developed by Parasuraman, Zeithaml and Berry (1985, 1988), named SERVQUAL, which proposes service quality as a comparison between the expectations consumers hold for a class of service providers and the relative performance of the firm on specific attributes related to quality assessments. The service quality construct is consisting of five different dimensions: tangibles, reliability, responsiveness, assurance, and empathy.

Albeit some overlaps between the conceptualization of satisfaction and service quality, most researchers agree that the two are different constructs. There are, however, different opinions as to the nature of their relationship. Tian-Cole and Crompton (2003) attempt to reconcile six divergent views on the relationship between satisfaction and service quality. They conclude that at the global level, both service quality and satisfaction are attitudes including cognitive and affective components. Service quality is an overall evaluation of the destination while satisfaction is an overall evaluation of the tourist experience at the destination. At the transaction level, satisfaction is affective in nature while service quality is derived from cognitive beliefs. They also find that both overall service quality and overall satisfaction directly influence future destination selection intention.

The link between destination image, service quality, satisfaction and behavioral intentions has been well established (Chi, 2011; Cronin, Brady & Hult, 2000; Lee, Graefe & Burns, 2007; Sun, Chi & Xu, 2013; Um, Chon & Ro, 2006). Baker and Crompton (2000) find that quality has a direct effect on behavioral intentions and an indirect effect on them via satisfaction. In addition, quality has a stronger total effect on behavioral intentions than satisfaction. Bloemer and Ruyter (1998) conclude that image and loyalty have an indirect relationship via perceived quality; and loyalty and service quality has both a direct relationship and indirect relationship via satisfaction. Bigne, Sanchez, and Sanchez (2001) confirm the following sequence established by previous researchers: image → quality → satisfaction → post-purchase behavior. Chi and Qu (2008) test a destination loyalty model in which image and satisfaction are found to have positive impacts on destination loyalty.

Trust and commitment

Trust exists when customers have confidence in a company's integrity and are willing to rely on the company to provide long-term interests for them (Crosby, Evans & Cowles, 1990; Morgan &

Hunt, 1994). Commitment refers to customers' enduring desire to maintain a long-term relationship with a company (Moorman, Zaltman & Deshpande, 1992). Commitment can be treated as a unidimensional construct or be separated into two dimensions: affective commitment and calculative commitment (Gilliland & Bello, 2002; Hennig-Thurau, 2000). Affective commitment reflects a customer's emotional attachment to a company and is based on feelings of identification, affiliation and loyalty (Gundlach, Achrol & Mentzer, 1995; Mattila, 2006); while calculative commitment is the obligation a customer feels to maintain a relationship due to significant social and economic costs (Venetis & Ghauri, 2004). Trust can also be deconstructed into two: trust in benevolence and trust in integrity (Kumar, Scheer & Steenkamp, 1995; Roberts, Varki & Brodie, 2003). The former refers to one's belief that another party will act in their best interests; while the latter refers to one's belief that another party is sincere and will stand by its words. The relationship literature has treated satisfaction, trust and commitment (three core variables of relationship quality) as interrelated and established a causal chain in which satisfaction influences trust which in turn influences commitment (Garbarino & Johnson, 1999; Morgan & Hunt, 1994). Asides from satisfaction, trust and commitment have also been found to be important antecedents to customer loyalty (Hyun 2010; Papassapa & Miller 2007; Pritchard, Havitz & Howard, 1999; Wen & Chi, 2013). Satisfied customers are more inclined to behave in a way that's beneficial to the company. Customer trust and commitment also lead to cooperative and positive behaviors that are conductive to company success.

Perceived value

Both the marketing and tourism/hospitality literature has recognized the critical role that perceived value (PV) plays in influencing consumer behavior, including product choice, purchase intention and repeat purchase (Gallarza & Gil-Saura, 2006; McDougall & Levesque, 2000; Oliver, 1999a; Polo Peña, Frías Jamilena & Rodríguez Molina, 2013; Sun, Chi & Xu, 2013). Perceived value is defined as consumers' global evaluation of the utility of a product based on their perception of what they receive and what they give (Zeithaml, 1988). Early researchers distinguish between acquisition and transaction value difference (Monroe, 1979; Monroe & Chapman, 1987), hedonic and utilitarian value difference (Holbrook & Corfman, 1985; Holbrook & Hirschman, 1982). Holbrook (1999) further refines the conceptualization of perceived value according to a three-dimensional paradigm: extrinsic vs. intrinsic, active vs. reactive, self-oriented vs. other-oriented. Sweeney and Soutar (2001) identify perceived value with four dimensions: emotional value, social value, and functional values (price/value for money and performance/quality. Petrick (2002, 2003) develops a value framework for the service industry, which consists of five dimensions: behavioral price, monetary price, emotional response, quality and reputation. Built on prior works on perceived value, Gallarza and Gil-Saura (2006) propose a value structure in tourism service with two dimensions: positive (service quality, play, aesthetics, and social value) and negative dimension (time and effort spent). More recently, Polo Pena et al.'s (2013) conceptualization of perceived value in rural hospitality enterprises context entails both the functional (staff attention, facilities, and convenience) and affective elements (emotional, social and epistemic).

Perceived value has been shown to exert positive effects on customer satisfaction and loyalty-driven behavior. Gallarza and Gil-Saura (2006) confirm the quality → value → satisfaction → loyalty chain. Polo Pena et al. (2013) indicate that both functional and affective aspects of perceived value contribute to tourist satisfaction, which further leads to their recommendation and repurchase intentions. Sun et al. (2013) also find that perceived value significantly influences tourist satisfaction, which acts as an antecedent to destination loyalty.

Involvement

The construct of involvement has been studied quite extensively in leisure/recreation and tourism field, due to its positive impacts on individuals' attitudes and behaviors. Involvement indicates the degree to which one devotes themselves to an activity, associated product, or experience (Gross & Brown, 2008). It is also defined as an unobservable state of motivation, arousal or interest toward an activity or associated product (Gursoy & Gavcar, 2003). Involvement is either measured using unidimensional scale 'Personal Involvement Inventory' (Zaichkowsky, 1985) or multidimensional scale 'Consumer Involvement Profile' (Laurent and Kapferer, 1985). The 'Consumer Involvement Profile' scale comprises five dimensions: importance, pleasure, sign, risk probability, and risk consequence. Within the leisure/recreation setting, involvement has been measured with three dimensions: attraction, centrality and self-expression (Chen, Li & Chen, 2013; Havitz & Dimanche, 1997; Kyle & Mowen, 2005; Wiley, Shaw & Havitz, 2000). Attraction refers to the perceived importance of a (leisure) activity and the pleasure derived from the activity. Centrality indicates the degree to which one's life is centered on an activity. Self-expression refers to the self-representation or impression one wishes to convey to others via an activity.

Previous research has shown that the degree of an individual's involvement can help predict his/her behavior. For example, Park's (1996) study confirms a significant relationship between consumer involvement and attitudinal loyalty. Lee and Beeler (2009) demonstrate involvement as a good predictor of satisfaction and future intention. Prayag and Ryan (2012) indicate that personal involvement indirectly influences overall satisfaction and loyalty via place attachment and destination image. Chen et al (2013) find leisure involvement as a strong determinant of leisure satisfaction.

Moderator variables

Past experience

Most studies on tourism destination choice stress the importance of previous experience on the destination choice process. Familiarity with a destination may produce a tendency for tourists to quickly select or reject it. They may not even look for information on other destinations for their next destination choice. Therefore, the majority of destination choice models, posited and empirically tested, includes previous experience as one of the factors affecting destination awareness as well as traveler destination preferences (e. g., Mayo & Jarvis 1981; Um & Crompton 1990; Woodside & Lysonski 1989). Past visits/experience with a destination are also shown to be influencing destination image, satisfaction and loyalty (Baloglu & Mangaloglu, 2001; Beerli & Martin, 2004; Kozak & Rimmington, 2000; Oppermann, 2000). Higher familiarity with a destination results in more positive image, higher satisfaction and higher loyalty behavior. Chi (2012) finds that previous experience moderates the relationship between tourist satisfaction and destination loyalty. Satisfaction is more influential in leading to loyalty for first time visitors than for repeat visitors. Polo Pena et al. (2013) find significant moderation effects of previous experience on the relationship between perceived value and customer satisfaction.

Variety/novelty seeking

Both variety seeking theory and novelty seeking theory have been used to explain consumer switching behavior because they are based on the same conceptual foundation that consumers seek optimal levels of stimulation in their choice of behavior (Hebb & Thompson, 1954). The concept of variety/novelty seeking is especially relevant for the tourism industry because travel/tourism is a voluntary activity detached from the daily mundane and surrounded by a certain amount of uncertainty (Godley & Graefe, 1991), which helps satisfy travelers' innate desires for variety/novelty (Cohen, 1979). Previous research finds that tourists' need for variety seeking moderates the relationship between satisfaction and loyalty behavior (Castro, Armario & Ruiz, 2007; Velazquez, Gil-Saura & Molina, 2011). Tourists with high level of variety seeking need show low return intention in spite of high satisfaction level; while tourists with low variety seeking need exhibit higher loyalty to a destination. Feng and Jang (2004) find that travelers with lower novelty-seeking need tend to be continuous repeaters while those with higher novelty seeking need tend to be continuous switchers. Jang and Feng (2007) reveal that higher novelty seeking leads to a lower intent to revisit in the mid-term and long-term, but does not affect immediate revisits. On the contrary, Assaker, Vinzi and O'Connor (2011) demonstrate that tourists with high novelty seeking propensity express lower immediate intent to return, but a greater intent to revisit in the future.

Conclusion

This conceptual paper provides an extensive review of destination loyalty literature and pinpoints some most important antecedents to tourist loyalty, including destination image, service quality, satisfaction, trust, commitment, perceived value, and involvement. Two variables that may moderate the destination loyalty model are also discussed. A conceptual framework for building destination loyalty is developed (Figure 24.1) based on the discussion above. In this model, destination image, perceived quality, perceived value and involvement are direct antecedents to tourist satisfaction. Tourist satisfaction further leads to trust and commitment and all three culminate in destination loyalty. Both variety seeking and previous experience moderate the relationship between satisfaction and loyalty.

When tourists develop a positive image of a destination and enjoy high level of involvement with the destination, when the destination offers them service/product with high quality and good value, tourists will experience high satisfaction. Not all satisfied tourists will exhibit repeat behavior because of their intrinsic desires to seek variety. Satisfied tourists with high variety-seeking need may switch to a different destination for their next visit, but they can help promote the destination they have visited by spreading positive word-of-mouth (WOM) and encouraging others to visit the destination. The multiplicity of virtual media, such as travel website, social networking website and blogs, has made WOM recommendation so much easier and so much more powerful in influencing tourists' travel decisions. Satisfied tourists with low variety-seeking need may return to the same destination and gradually develop trust and commitment with a destination. These tourists may cultivate what Oliver (1997) called 'ultimate loyalty' whereby tourists are so passionate about the destination that they will try to return to the same destination against all odds and at all costs. For tourists with no/little previous experience with a destination, their satisfaction is a determinant factor for them to display loyalty behavior; whereas for tourists with multiple visits to a destination, satisfaction is no longer the primary driver to loyalty but other factors such as trust and commitment take precedence. For example, these tourists may encounter unsatisfactory incidents at a destination, but they may still decide to revisit the destination because they trust that the destination will make things right and act in their best interests; and they have gotten attached to the destination due to previous visits.

This model is not meant to be exhaustive in terms of accounting for the antecedents leading to destination loyalty. There are likely other factors directly or indirectly affecting destination loyalty. Future researchers can build on this model and add/subtract variables to further improve it.

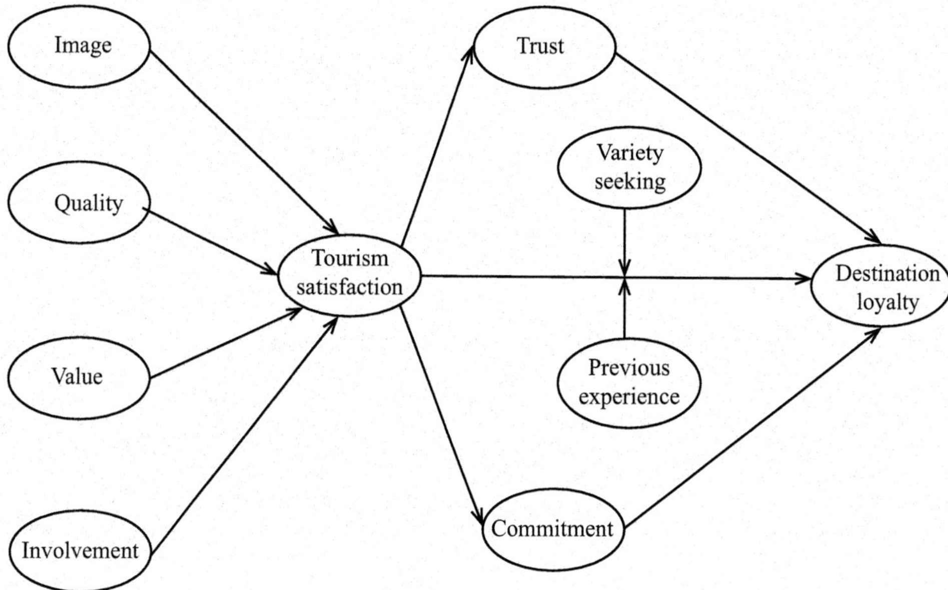

Figure 24.1 Destination loyalty

References

Assaker, G., Vinzi, V. E. & O'Connor, P. (2011). Examining the effect of novelty seeking, satisfaction, and destination image on tourists' return pattern: A two factor, non-linear latent growth model. *Tourism Management*, 32 (4), 890–901.

Bagozzi, R.P., Gopinath, M. and Nyer, P.U. (1999). The role of emotions in marketing. *Journal of the Academy of Marketing Science*, 27 (2), 184–206.

Baker, D. A. and Crompton, J. L. (2000). Quality, satisfaction, and behavioral intentions. *Annals of Tourism Research*, 27 (3), 785–804.

Baloglu, S. (2002). Dimensions of customer loyalty: Separating friends from well-wishers. *Cornell Hotel and Restaurant Administration Quarterly*, 43 (1), 47–59.

Baloglu, S. & Mangaloglu, M. (2001). Tourism destination images of Turkey, Egypt, Greece, and Italy as perceived by US-based tour operators and travel agents. *Tourism Management*, 22 (1), 1–9.

Baloglu, S. and McCleary, K. W. (1999a). A model of destination image formation. *Annals of Tourism Research*, 26 (4), 868–897.

Baloglu, S. and McCleary, K. W. (1999b). U.S. international pleasure travelers' images of four Mediterranean destinations: A comparison of visitors and non-visitors. *Journal of Travel Research*, 38, 144–152.

Beerli, A. & Martin, J. D. (2004). Factors influencing destination image. *Annals of Tourism Research*, 31 (3), 657–681.

Bigne, J. E., Sanchez, M. I., and Sanchez, J. (2001). Tourism image, evaluation variables and after-purchase behavior: Inter-relationship. *Tourism Management*, 22 (6), 607–616.

Bitner, M.J. & Hubbert, A.R. (1994). Encounter satisfaction versus overall satisfaction versus quality. In Rust, R.T., and R.L. Oliver (Eds). *Service Quality: New Directions in Theory and Practice*. Thousand Oaks, CA: Sage Publications, 72–94.

Bloemer, J. & Ruyter, K. (1998). On the relationship between store image, store satisfaction and store loyalty. *European Journal of Marketing*, 32 (5/6), 499–513.

Bowen, J. T. & Chen S.-L. (2001). The relationship between customer loyalty and customer satisfaction. *International Journal of Contemporary Hospitality Management*, 13 (5), 213–217.

Castro, C. B., Armario, M. E. & Ruiz, M. D. (2007). The influence of market heterogeneity on the relationship between a destination's image and tourists' future behavior. *Tourism Management*, 28 (1), 175–187.

Chen, Y. C., Li, R. H. & Chen, S. H. (2013). Relationships among adolescents' leisure motivation, leisure involvement, and leisure satisfaction: A structural equation model. *Social Indicators Research*, 110 (3), 1187–1199.

Chi, C. G.-Q. (2011). Destination loyalty formation and travelers' demographic characteristics: A multiple group analysis approach. *Journal of Hospitality and Tourism Research*, 35 (2), 191–212.

Chi, C. G.-Q. (2012). An examination of destination loyalty: Differences between first time and repeat visitors. *Journal of Hospitality and Tourism Research*, 36 (1), 3–24.

Chi, C. G.-Q. & Qu, H. (2008). Examining the structural relationships of destination image, tourist satisfaction and destination loyalty: An integrated approach. *Tourism Management*, 29 (4), 624–636.

Chon, K. S. & Olsen, M. (1991). Functional and symbolic congruity approaches to consumer satisfaction/dissatisfaction in tourism. *Journal of the International Academy of Hospitality Research*, 3, 2–20.

Cohen, E. (1979). Rethinking the sociology of tourism. *Annals of Tourism Research*, 6 (1), 18–35.

Cooper, C., Fletcher, J., Gilbert, D., and Wanhill S. (1998). *Tourism: Principles and practice*. Longman: New York.

Crompton, J. L. (1979). An assessment of the image of Mexico as a vacation destination and the influence of geographical location upon the image. *Journal of Travel Research*, 18 (4), 18–23.

Cronin, J. J. Jr, Brady, M. K. & Hult, G. T. M. (2000). Assessing the effects of quality, value and customer satisfaction on consumer behavioral intentions in service environments. *Journal of Retailing*, 76 (2), 193–218.

Crosby, L.A., Evans, K.R. & Cowles, D. (1990). Relationship quality in services selling: an interpersonal influence perspective. *Journal of Marketing*, 54 (3), 68–81.

Dann, G. M. (1977). Anomie, ego-enhancement, and tourism. *Annals of Tourism Research*, 4, 184–194.

Dann, G. M. S. (1996). Tourists' images of a destination: An alternative analysis. *Journal of Travel and Tourism Marketing*, 5 (1/2), 41–55.

Dimitriades, Z. S. (2006). Customer satisfaction, loyalty and commitment in service organizations: Some evidence from Greece. *Management Research News*, 29 (12), 782–800.

Duke, C.R. & Persia, M.A. (1996). Performance-importance analysis of escorted tour evaluations. *Journal of Travel and Tourism Marketing*, 5 (3), 207–23.

Feng, R. & Jang, S. (2004). Temporal destination loyalty: A structural initiation. *Advances in Hospitality and Tourism Research*, 9, 207–221.

Fornell, C. & Wernerfelt, B. (1987). Defensive Marketing Strategy by Customer Complaint Management. *Journal of Marketing Research*, 24 (November), 337–46.

Gallarza, M. & Gil Saura, I. (2006). Value dimensions, perceived value, satisfaction and loyalty: an investigation of university students' travel behavior. *Tourism Management*, 27(3), 437–452.

Garbarino, E. & Johnson, M.S. (1999). The different roles of satisfaction, trust, and commitment in customer relationships. *Journal of Marketing*, 63 (2), 70–87.

Gartner, W. C. (1996). *Tourism Development: Principles, Processes, and Policies*. New York: Van Nostram Reinhold.

Giese, J. L. & Cote, J. A. (2000). Defining consumer satisfaction. *Academy of Marketing Science Review*, 2000 (1), 1–24.

Gilliland, D. I. & Bello, D.C. (2002). Two sides to attitudinal commitment: The effect of calculative and loyalty commitment on enforcement mechanisms in distribution channels. *Journal of the Academy of Marketing Science*, 30 (1), 24–43.

Godbey, G. & Graefe, A. (1991). Repeat tourism, play and monetary spending. *Annals of Tourism Research*, 18, 213–225.

Gross, M. J. & Brown, G. (2008). An empirical structure model of tourists and places: progressing involvement and place attachment into tourism. *Tourism Management*, 29 (6), 1141–1151.

Gundlach, G., Achrol, R. and Mentzer, J. (1995). The structure of commitment in exchange. *Journal of Marketing*, 59 (1), 78–92.

Gursoy, D. & Gavcar, E. (2003). International leisure tourists' involvement profile. *Annals of Tourism Research*, 30 (4), 906–926.

Havitz, M. E. & Dimanche, F. (1997). Leisure involvement revisited: conceptual conundrums and measurement advances. *Journal of Leisure Research*, 29 (3), 245–278.

Hawkins, D. I., Best, R. J. & Coney, K. A. (1995). *Consumer Behavior: Implications for Marketing Strategy* (6th Edn). Boston, MA: Richard D. Irwin.

Hebb, D. O. & Thompson, W. R. (1954). The social significance of animal studies. In G. Lindzey (Ed.), *Handbook of Social Psychology* (pp. 551–552). Reading, Mass: Addison-Wesley.

Hennig-Thurau, T. (2000). Relationship quality and customer retention through strategic communication of customer skills. *Journal of Marketing Management*, 16 (1/3), 55–79.

Hepworth, M. & Mateus, P. (1994). Connecting customer loyalty to the bottom line. *Canadian Business Review*, 21 (4), 40–44.
Holbrook, M. B. (1999). *Consumer value: A framework for analysis and research.* London: Routledge.
Holbrook, M. B. & Corfman, K. P. (1985). Quality and value in the consumption experience: Phaedrus rides again. In J. Jacoby & J. C. Olson (Eds), *Perceived quality: how consumers view stores and merchandise.* D.C. Health and Company: Lexington, MA.
Holbrook, M. B. & Hirschman, E. C. (1982). The experiential aspects of consumption: consumer fantasies, feelings and fun. *Journal of Consumer Research*, 9, 132–140.
Hu, Y. and Ritchie, J. (1993). Measuring destination attractiveness: A contextual approach. *Journal of Travel Research*, 32 (2), 25–34.
Hyun, S. S. (2010). Predictors of relationship quality and loyalty in the chain restaurant industry. *Cornell Hospitality Quarterly*, 51 (2), 251–267.
Jang, S. & Feng, R. (2007). Temporal destination revisit intention: The effects of novelty seeking and satisfaction. *Tourism Management*, 28 (2), 580–590.
Kozak, M. & Rimmington, M. (2000). Tourist satisfaction with Mallorca, Spain, as an off-season holiday destination. *Journal of Travel Research*, 38 (1), 260–269.
Kumar, N., Scheer, L.K. & Steenkamp, J. E. (1995). The effects of supplier fairness on vulnerable resellers. *Journal of Marketing Research*, 32 (1), 54–65.
Kyle, G. T. & Mowen, A. J., (2005). An examination of the leisure involvement-agency commitment relationships. *Journal of Leisure Research*, 37(3), 342–363.
Laurent, G. & Kapferer, J. (1985). Measuring consumer involvement profiles. *Journal of Marketing Research*, 22, 41–53.
Lee, J., Graefe, A. R. & Burns, R. C. (2007). Examining the Antecedents of Destination Loyalty in a Forest Setting. *Leisure Sciences*, 29, 463–481.
Liljander, V. & Strandvik, T. (1997). Emotions in service satisfaction. International Journal of Service Industry Management, 8 (2), 148–169.
Mano, H. & Oliver, R. L. (1993). Assessing the dimensionality and structure of the consumption experience: evaluation, feeling, and satisfaction. *Journal of Consumer Research*, 20 (December), 451–466.
Mattila, A. S. (2006). How affective commitment boosts guest loyalty (and promotes frequent-guest programs). *Cornell Hospitality Quarterly*, 47 (2), 174–181.
Mayo, E. J. & Jarvis, L. P. (1981). *The Psychology of Leisure Travel: Effective Marketing and Selling of Travel Services.* Boston: CBI.
McDougall G. H. & Levesque T. (2000). Customer satisfaction with services: Putting perceived value into the equation. *Journal of Services Marketing*, 14 (5), 392–410.
McKercher, B., Denizci-Guillet, B. & Ng, E (2012). Rethinking loyalty. *Annals of Tourism Research*, 39 (2), 708–734.
Monroe, K. B. (1979). *Pricing: Making profitable decisions.* New York: McGraw-Hill Book Company.
Monroe, K. B. & Chapman, J. (1987). Framing effects on buyers' subjective product evaluations. *Advances in Consumer Research*, 14, 193–197.
Moorman, C., Zaltman, G. & Deshpande, R. (1992). Relationships between providers and users of market research: The dynamics of trust within and between organizations. *Journal of Marketing Research*, 29 (3), 314–328.
Morgan, R. M. & Hunt, S. D. (1994). The commitment-trust theory of relationship marketing. *Journal of Marketing*, 58 (3), 20–38.
Murphy, P., Pritchard, M. P. & Smith, B. (2000). The destination product and its impact on traveler perceptions. *Tourism Management*, 21(1), 43–52.
Newman, J. W. & Werbel, R. A. (1973). Multivariate Analysis of Brand Loyalty for Major Household Appliances. *Journal of Marketing Research*, 10 (November), 404–409.
Oliver, R. L. (1997). *Satisfaction: A behavioral perspective on the consumer.* New York: Irwin/McGraw-Hill.
Oliver, R. L. (1999). Whence consumer loyalty? *Journal of Marketing*, 63, 33–44.
Oppermann, M. (2000). Tourism destination loyalty. Journal of Travel Research, 39 (1), 78–84.
Papassapa, R. & Miller, K.E. (2007). Relationship quality as a predictor of B2B customer loyalty. *Journal of Business Research*, 60 (1), 21–31.
Parasuraman, A., Zeithaml, V. A. & Berry, L. L. (1985). A conceptual model of service quality and its implications for future research. *Journal of Marketing*, 49 (Fall), 41–50.
Parasuraman, A., Zeithaml, V. A. & Berry, L. L. (1988). SERVQUAL: a multiple-item scale for measuring consumer perceptions of service quality. *Journal of Retailing*, 64 (Spring), 12–37.

Parasuraman, A., Zeithaml, V. A. & Berry, L. L. (1994). Moving forward in service quality research: Measuring different customer-expectation levels, comparing alternative scales, and examining the performance-behavioral intentions link. Working Paper 94–114, Marketing Science Institute.
Park, S. (1996). Relationships between involvement and attitudinal loyalty constructs in adult fitness programs. *Journal of Leisure Research*, 28 (4), 233–250.
Petrick, J. F. (2002). Development of a multi-dimensional scale for measuring the perceived value of a service. *Journal of Leisure Research*, 34 (2), 119–134.
Petrick, J. F. (2003). Measuring cruise passengers' perceived value. *Tourism Analysis*, 7, 251–258.
Pizam, A. & Milman, A. (1993). Predicting satisfaction among first time visitors to a destination by using the expectancy disconfirmation theory. *International Journal of Hospitality Management*, 12 (2), 197–209.
Pizam, A., Neumann, Y. & Reichel, A. (1978). Dimensions of tourist satisfaction with a destination area. *Annals of Tourism Research*, 5 (3), 314–322.
Polo Pena, A. I., Frias Jamilena, D. M. & Rodriguez Molina, M. A. (2013). Antecedents of loyalty toward rural hospitality enterprises: The moderating effect of the customer's previous experience. *International Journal of Hospitality Management*, 34, 127–137.
Prayag, G. & Ryan, C. (2012). Antecedents of tourist's loyalty to Mauritius: The role and influence of destination image, place attachment, personal involvement, and satisfaction. *Journal of Travel Research*, 51 (3), 342–356.
Pritchard, M. P., Howard, D. R. & Havitz, M. E. (1992). Loyalty measurement: A critical examination and theoretical extension. *Leisure Sciences*, 14 (2), 155–164.
Roberts, K., Varki, S. & Brodie, R. (2003). Measuring the quality of relationships in consumer services: An empirical study. *European Journal of Marketing*, 37 (1/2), 169–196.
Rust, R. T. and Zahorik, A. J. (1993). Customer loyalty, customer retention and market share. *Journal of Retailing*, 69 (2), 193–215.
Seaton, A.V. and Benett, M.M. (1996). *Marketing tourism products: Concepts, issues, cases.* London: International Thomson Business Press.
Sun, A., Chi, C. G. and Xu, H. (2013). Developing destination Loyalty: The case of Hainan Island, China. *Annals of Tourism Research*, 43, 547–577.
Sweeney, J. & Soutar, G. (2001). Consumer perceived value: The development of a multiple item scale. *Journal of Retailing*, 77, 203–207.
Taylor, T. B. (1998). Better Loyalty Measurement Leads to Business Solutions. *Marketing News*, 32 (22), 41–42.
Tellis, G. J. (1988). Advertising exposure, loyalty, and brand purchase: A two-stage model of choice. *Journal of Marketing Research*, 25 (May), 134–144.
Tian-Cole, S. & Crompton, J. L. (2003). A conceptualization of the relationships between service quality and visitor satisfaction, and their links to destination selection. *Leisure Studies*, 22 (1), 65–80.
Um, S. and Crompton, J. (1990). Attitude determinants in tourism destination choice. *Annals of Tourism Research*, 17 (3), 432–448.
Um, S., Chon, K. & Ro, Y. H. (2006). Antecedents of revisit intention. *Annals of Tourism Research*, 33 (4), 1141–1158.
Velazquez, B. M., Gil-Saura, I. & Molina M. E. R. (2011). Conceptualizing and measuring loyalty: Towards a conceptual model of tourist loyalty antecedents. *Journal of Vacation Marketing*, 17 (1), 65–81.
Venetis, K.A. & Ghauri, P.N. (2004). Service quality and customer retention: Building long-term relationships. *European Journal of Marketing*, 38 (11/12), 1577–1198.
Wen, B. & Chi, C. G.-Q. (2013). Examine the cognitive and affective antecedents to service recovery satisfaction: A field study of delayed airline passengers. *International Journal of Contemporary Hospitality Management*, 25 (3), 306–327.
Westbrook, R. A. (1987). Product/consumption-based affective responses and post-purchase processes. *Journal of Marketing Research*, 24 (August), 258–270.
Westbrook, R. A. & Oliver, R. P. (1991). The dimensionality of consumption emotion patterns and consumer satisfaction. *Journal of Consumer Research*, 18 (June), 84–91.
Wiley, C. G. E., Shaw, S. M. & Havitz, M. E. (2000). Men's and women's involvement in sports: An examination of the gendered aspects of leisure involvement. *Leisure Sciences*, 22, 19–31.
Woodside, A. G. & Lysonski, S. (1989). A general model of traveler destination choice. *Journal of Travel Research*, 27 (4), 8–14.

Yoon, Y. & Uysal, M. (2005). An examination of the effects of motivation and satisfaction on destination loyalty: A structural model. *Tourism Management*, 26 (1), 45–56.

Yuksel, A. & Rimmington, M. (1998). Customer satisfaction measurement. *Cornell Hotel and Restaurant Administration Quarterly*, 39 (6), 60–70.

Zaichkowsky, J. L. (1985). Measuring the involvement construct. *Journal of Consumer Research*, 12 (3), 341–352.

Zeithaml, V. A. (1988). Consumer perceptions of price, quality and value: A means-end model and synthesis of evidence. *Journal of Marketing*, 52 (July), 2–22.

25

Role of tourist emotions and its impact on destination marketing

Soma Sinha Roy

The tourism sector represents one or more facet of service industry. The principles adopted in the manufacturing of products are extended to people, process and physical evidence (Parasuraman et al., 1991, Palmer, 2001). In this perspective, the tourism industry demands strategies and tactics that enhance guest experience as a competitive advantage. The guest-host relationship has a crucial role in tourism sector. Engaging in customer coproduction of service experience adds an emotional dimensions to tourism.

According to Dewey (1963), engaging in an experience involves progression over time, anticipation, emotional involvement, a uniqueness that makes it stand out from the ordinary and reaches some sort of completion. Experiences are considered to be successful if customers find such experiences unique, memorable and sustainable over time (Pine and Gilmore, 1998, 1999). The experiential perspective of the buyer behavior reflects a shift from functional consumption to a hedonic consumption. These experiences tend to provide pleasure, aesthetic enjoyment and emotional responses (Sheth, 1969; Olshavsky and Granbois, 1979). This concept brings into its gamut the 3Fs, namely fun, feeling and fantasies into experiential consumption. In the recent past, these have been extended to the 4 Es i.e. experience, entertainment, exhibitionism and evangelism (Holbrook, 2000). Individuals experience emotions prior to making purchase as well as post-purchase. Considering the complex nature of consumption experience, a wide range of emotions are experienced and in varied magnitude (Ritchin, 1977). Richin (1977) has designed the Consumption Emotion Set (CES). Consumption, being an individual's quest for pleasure (as well as need fulfillment), the hedonic consumption focuses on fantasy, multisensory and emotive aspects of product usage (Hirschman and Holbrook, 1982), in addition to the functional utilities of a product. These experiences are subjective, heterogeneous and experiential in nature with a high degree of personal engagement. According to Addis and Holbrook (2001), consumption patterns should be associated with subjectivities – i.e. the personal nature of consumption experiences is charged, taking into consideration the different contexts in which such experiences occur (Eatough, et al., 2006a). Emotions are context-specific – the consumption contexts arouse specific emotions which linger throughout the consumption experiences. The degree of consumer engagement with the consumption experience determines the intensity of emotion and thereby emotional experience. Highly engaging situations result in stronger emotional responses due to involvement at personal level (Brewar, 1988; Mittal, 1994; Hansen, 2005 and Fischer et al., 2008).

As pointed out by Cohen et al., (2008) "arousal intensity of emotion experiences increases an individual's immediate and long-term memory"; thus leading to more memorable encounters.

According to Arnold et al., (2002), there are four stages to consumption process which unfold over time. These are:

1 Pre-consumption experience, involving search, planning, day-dreaming and imaging experience.
2 Purchasing experience, which involves selecting the item, paymet and packaging as well as service encounter and environment.
3 The core consumption, which involves sensation, satisfaction/dissatisfaction, irritation/flow and transformation.
4 Remembered consumption experience and nostalgia experience with photos being used to re-live the past or narratives with friends etc.

The first stage is associated with the anticipation of pleasure an experience will bring. This is particularly pronounced in tourism context in which the consumers imagine, daydream and fantasize about the forthcoming event, thus giving an emotion-rich experience (Pearce, 2009). The post-purchase stage is emotion-rich in itself.

The most widely acknowledged definition of tourism originates from World Tourism Organization as "travel to and stay in places outside their usual environment for not more than one consecutive year for leisure, business and other purposes not related to the exercise of an activity remunerated from within the place visited". There are two elements of tourism – the act of travel and the motive, or experiential quality of the trip (McCabe, 2009). Due to the complex, dynamic and intangible nature of tourism encounters, there is a lack of insight into consumers' consumption experiences.

In the case of tourism and Arnold's et al. (2002) four stage of consumption process, the trip cannot be culminated or tapered to core consumption stage because "thinking, dreaming, talking about vacations and gathering information is ongoing" (Decrop, 2010). Often the consumption might be through fantasies and dreams. Individuals tend to continue to consume such experiences in the "remembered consumption" stage (Arnold et al., 2002) after the occurrence of the event through recall of memories of the event that they share with peer groups and friends. Page (2009) points out that tourism experiences are difficult to identify and predict. Tourism experiences are emotion rich, hedonic consumption is pivotal to the understanding to the role of emotions in tourism. In the context of mainstream tourism, hedonic drive acts as a prime motivator. The motivation for holiday is mostly pleasure-seeking, "the need to escape". Lee and Crompton (1992) define tourists' motivations as being based on excitement, a change in routine, boredom alleviation and feelings of surprise.

Hirshman and Holbrook (1982) stated that "Hedonic consumption refers to consumers' multisensory images, fantasies and emotional arousal in using products. This configuration of effects may be termed as hedonic responses". Hedonism is ideally associated with pleasure and enjoyment. Pleasure is regarded as a positive experience. It is a short-lived affect that provides satisfaction for instant gratification. Therefore, individuals are in a repetitive mode (in pursuit of pleasure) (Compton, 2005). Exclusive pleasurable experiences do not lead to any personal growth. Pleasure is defined as a pattern of sensations that are generally short-lived, satisfying a habit for instant gratification (Csikszentmihalyi, 1990). The experience of pleasure is dependent on the experience of the object (or consumption experience). Pleasure is essentially an incomplete experience. It exists only as "side" or "property", as an "abstract part" (Husser, 1928) of a more comprehensive experience. Engaging experiences exceed mere pleasure. Enjoyment, on the other hand has a potential long-term impact. Enjoyment inculcates a deeper sense of pleasure. According to Seligman and Csikszentmihalyi (2000), experiences that are enjoyable takes place when individuals break from homoeostatic satisfaction, thereby fulfilling deeper desires. Thus unlike pleasantness, enjoyable experiences have deeper impact thus leading to personal growth and long-term happiness. A pleasurable experience is regarded enjoyable if it "involves intensity of attention, sense of achievement and psychological growth" (O'Shaughnessy and O'Shaughnessy, 2002).

Tourism is an emotionally charged consumption experience. Some theorists mention the Holiday Happiness Curve which is an appraisal tool for tourism. The Holiday Happiness Curve is divided into three phases in terms of tourists' moods. The first phase is the "travel phase" which accounts for 0–10% of the holiday, resulting in relatively low mood scores probably due to travel. The second phase is much longer and ranges from 10–80% of the holiday. This is considered to be the "core phase" and is characterized by high mood level. The third phase, ranging from 80–90% is known as the "decline phase" and the mood drops to the lowest level. The final phase is the 'rejuvenation phase' ranging from 90–100% and accounts for high mood level possibly for the happiness of returning home. The absence of a peak in holiday happiness makes tourists remember the end instead (Fredrickson, 2000) which is the phase when the tourists feel worst. This is the phase that determines future holiday purchases (Wirtz et al., 2003). Vacation memories are predictors of future purchase intensions. To overcome this situation, the tourism industry should try to create a peak in holiday happiness – which is a time of high positive emotions. Carefully designed tourist attractions can enhance positive emotion. Destination marketing organizations can create tourism projects that elicit tourists' involvement. This enhances emotions such as interest, hope and pride. Tourism industry needs to lay emphasis on the first few days of a holiday trip. Mood is particularly low in that phase, so special attention must be paid to alleviate tourists' mood. Holiday trips are mostly enjoyable for the tourists, irrespective of socio-demographic status. People generally feel good during a holiday trip and best during the core phase and at the very end. This pattern is similar across different kinds of holidays and across different kinds of people (Nawijn, 2010).

The role of emotions in a tourism destination is associated with destination loyalty or emotional satisfaction. Emotional responses provide detailed information on the feelings of the tourists during their travel experience and it is of great importance for tourism service providers (Pine and Gilmore, 1999). Tourist emotions are most relevant component of affect to the travel industry (Mitas et al., 2012). Emotions have an insidious influence on tourist experiences. At pre-purchase stage, emotions impact the tourist motivation. At the post-purchase stage, emotions influence satisfaction and loyalty. People elicit emotions towards their immediate physical and social environment (Farber and Hall, 2007). Hosany and Gilbert (2010) have developed the Destination Emotion Scale (DES). DES is a three-dimensional (joy, love and positive surprise), 15-item scale with solid psychometric properties. Four items measure joy: pleasure, joy, enthusiasm and delight. The love dimension includes tenderness, love, caring, warm-hearted and affection. Positive surprise includes amazement, ashtonishment, fascination, inspiration and surprise.

The Destination Emotion Scale captures positive valence emotions. Vacations are characterized as a set of positive experiential processes (Mannell and Iso-Ahola, 1987; Nawijin, 2010), primarily consumed for hedonic purposes (Otto and Richie, 1996). Through vacations, tourists seek pleasurable and measurable experiences.

Research in marketing reveals that the emotion of love develops a sense of belonging with the product or service. A positive emotion projects positive image to the products and services. This concept is extended to destination marketing as well; Destination Marketing Organizations (DMO) are in a constant battle to attract travelers. DMOs portray certain characteristics to establish the identity of the destinations. These elements of identity are translated into destination image. The elements of identity are basically the characteristics of destinations that travelers can correlate with as a part of personality. This concept is broadly the destination personality traits. Destination personality is defined as a set of human characteristics associated with a destination (Aaker, 1997). A set of characteristics get instilled in the minds of the tourists creating favorable or unfavorable associations thereby affecting brand equity. A distinctive and attractive destination personality leverages the perceived image of the destination thus influencing tourists' spot selection. People prefer to select those destinations that match with their own personality traits, thereby reflecting their own self-image. Consumers develop relationships with brands based on their symbolic values. Blackstone (1993) points out that brands and consumers are co-equivalent parts of a single system, which is similar to interpersonal relations. Whereas human personality traits are inferred on the basis of a person's behavior, perceptions of the destination personality traits can be formed and influenced by the direct and/or indirect contact that tourists have with the destination (Plummer, 1985). Through interactions of various forms, tourists receive and interpret the various messages sent by the destinations and develop an idea of the "conduct" of the destination. Personality traits can be associated with a destination in a direct way through citizens of the country, hotel employees, restaurants and tourist attractions or simply through tourist imageries. In an indirect manner, personality traits can be attributed to destinations through marketing programs such as cooperative advertising, value pricing, celebrities of the country and media used by the destination for the purpose of communication. Tourist destinations are loaded with symbolic values, histories, events and feelings.

A tourism destination is viewed as a combination of individual products and experiences that blend together to lend it an identity which is transformed into destination image. Tourist motives are a combination of push and pull factors. Push motivations are related to the emotional aspects of the travelers, whereas pull motivations are associated with destination image attributes. Marketers should take into considerations the motivating factors of the tourists so that their marketing efforts are directed to both cognitive and affective aspects of decision-making. Destination markets should develop effective communication methods to introduce a distinctive and attractive personality of the tourist spots. They should concentrate more on building and enhancing the destination images and personality – being more candid in the imageries, message content, choice of media and communication tools. This will help in establishing a distinct image of the place and differentiate a particular place from that of a similar place.

Destination marketers can improve the positive image by developing a strong destination personality through advertising and destination management tactics. Emphasizing the emotional components of experience in the promotional campaigns will differentiate the destination effectively. Marketing campaigns should not only emphasize on the distinctive characteristics of the destination but also on the emotions that are evoked. Kim, Hwang and Fesenmaier (2005) found a strong association between top-of-mind awareness, advertising awareness, request for destination information and the likelihood of visiting the destination. The study by Min, Martin and Jung (2013) reveals that the emotional content of destination advertising campaigns has an influence on tourists' motivation. The higher the emotional involvement of the consumers with the promotional stimuli (such as a travel magazine), the more likely they will use imagery as information processing. Marketing communication experts should provide brochures, advertisements, commercials and videos that consist both of 'stimulus information' (destination and service attributes) and 'hedonic response information' such as consumers' vision, mental images, feelings, moods, emotional experiences and expressions (Goossens, 1994).

Emotions play a predominant role in creating consumer satisfaction, repeat purchase intensions and recommendations. Unfortunately, the role of emotions in tourism industry is yet to be explored in-depth, measured and put to practice. DMOs should ideally pay candid attention to each and every single phase of a leisure journey and adopt individual strategies to address the issues at each stage, in order to make the entire experience memorable, packed with pleasure and joy.

References

Aaker, J.L. (1997). Dimensions of Brand Personality. *Journal of Marketing Research*, 34, 347–356.

Addis, M. and Holbrook, M. B. (2001). On the conceptual link between mass customisation and experiential consumption: An explosion of subjectivity. *Journal of Consumer Behaviour*, 1. (1), 50–66.

Arnould, E. J., Price, L. and Zinkhan, G. (2002). *Consumers*. Columbus: McGraw Hill.

Blackstone, M. (1993). Beyond Brand Personality: Building Brand Relationships. In D. A. Aaker and A. Biel (eds), *Brand Equity and Advertising*. Hillsdale, NJ: Lawrence Erlbaum, pp. 113–124.

Brewer, M. (1988). A dual-process model of impression formation. In T. K. Srull and R. S. Wyer (eds), *Advances in Social Cognition*. New Jersey: Erlbaum.

Cohen, J. B., Pham, M. T. and Andrade, E. B. (2008). The Nature and Role of Affect in Consumer Behavior. In Haugtvedt, C. P., Herr, P. M. and Kardes, F. R. (eds), *Handbook of Consumer Psychology*. New York: Psychology Press.

Compton, W. C. (2005). *Custom Enrichment Module: Introduction to Positive Psychology*. London: Thomson and Wadsworth.

Csikszentmihalyi, M. (1990). *Flow: The Psychology of Optimal Experience*. New York: Harper Collins.

Decrop, A. (2010). Destination choice sets: An inductive longitudinal approach. *Annals of Tourism Research*, 37(1), 93–115.

Dewey, J. (1963). *Experience and education*. New York: Collier Books.

Duncker, K. (1941/1942). On Pleasure, Emotion and Striving. *Philosophical and Phenomenological Research*, 1, 391–430.

Eatough, V. and Smith, J. A. (2006a). 'I was like a wild wild person': Understanding feelings of anger using Interpretative Phenomenological Analysis. *British Journal of Psychology*, 97, 483–498.

Ekinci, Y. and Hosany, S. (2006). Destination Personality: An Application of Brand Personality to Tourism Destinations. *Journal of Travel Research*, 45.

Farber, M.E. and Hall, T.E. (2007). Emotion and Environment: Visitors' extraordinary experiences Along the Dalton Highway in Alaska. *Journal of Leisure Research*, 39 (2), 248–270.

Fischer, R. H. A. and De Vries, W. P. (2008). Everyday behaviour and everyday risk: An approach to study people's responses to frequently encountered food related health risks. *Health, Risk and Society*, 10 (4), 385–397.

Fredrickson, B. L. (2000). Extracting Meaning from Past Affective Experiences: The Importance of Peaks, Ends, and Specific Emotions. *Cognition & Emotion*, 14 (4), 577–606.

Goossens, C.F. (1994b). External Information Search: Effects of Tour Brochures with Experiential Information. *Journal of Travel and Tourism*, 3(3), 89–107.

Goossens, C.F. (2000). Tourism Information and Pleasure Motivation. *Annals of Tourism Research*, 27 (2), 301–321.

Hansen, T. (2005). Perspectives on Consumer decision making: An integrated Approach. *Journal of Consumer Behaviour*, 4 (6), 420–437.

Hirshman, E., and M.B. Holbrook (1982) Hedonic Consumption: Emerging Concepts, Methods and Propositions. *Journal of Marketing*, 46, 92–101.

Holbrook, M. (2000). The Millennial Consumer in the Texts of Our Times: Experience and Entertainment. *Journal of Macromarketing*, 20 (2).

Hosany, S. and Gilbert, D. (2010). Measuring Tourists' Emotional Experiences Toward Hedonic Holiday Destinations. *Journal of Travel Research*, 49 (4), 513–526.

Howard, A. J. and Sheth, J. N. (1969). *Theory of Buyer Behaviour*. New York: John Wiley & Sons Ltd.

Husserl, Edmund. *Logische Untersuchungen*, 4th ed., Halle, 1928, vol. II, 1, III, "Zur Lehre von den Ganzen und Teilen."

Kim, D.K., Hwang, Y.H. and Fesenmaier, D.R. (2005). Modeling Tourism Advertising Effectiveness. *Journal of Travel Research*, 44 (1), 42–49.

Lee, T. H. and Crompton J. L. (1992). Measuring Novelty Seeking in Tourism. *Annals of Tourism Research*, 19, 732–751.

Mannell, R.C. and Iso-Ahola, S.E. (1987). Psychological Nature of Leisure and Tourism Experience. *Annals of Tourism Research*, 14 (3), 314–331.
McCabe, S. (2009). Who is a Tourist? Conceptual and Theoretical Developments. *Philosophical Issues in Tourism*. Bristol: Channel View Publications.
Min, K.S., Martin, D. and Jung, J.M. (2013). Designing Advertising Campaigns for Destinations with Mixed Images: Using Visitor Campaign Goal Messages to Motivate Visitors. *Journal of Business Research*, 66(6), 759–764.
Mitas, O., Yarnal, C., Adams, R. and Ram, N. (2012). Taking a 'Peak' at Leisure Travelers' Positive Emotions. *Leisure Sciences*, 34 (2): 115–135.
Mittal, B. (1994) A Study of the Concept of 'Affective Choice Mode' for Consumer Decisions. *Advances in Consumer Research*, 21, 256–263.
Nawijn, J. (2010). The Holiday Happiness Curve: A Preliminary Investigation into Mood during a Holiday Abroad. *International Journal of Tourism Research*, 12, 281–290.
Nawijn, J., Mitas, O., Lin, Y. and Kerstetter, D. (2013). How Do We Feel on Vacation? A Closer Look at How Emotions Change over the Course of a Trip. *Journal of Travel Research*, 52.
Olshavsky, R. W. and Granbois, D. H. (1979). Consumer Decision Making: Fact or Fiction. *Journal of Consumer Research*, 6 (September), 93–100.
O'Shaughnessy, J. and O'Shaughnessy, N. J. (2002). Marketing, the consumer society and hedonism. *European Journal of Marketing*, 36 (5/6), 524–547.
Otto, J.E. and Ritchie, B.R. (1996). The Service Experience in Tourism. *Tourism Management*, 17(3), 165–174.
Page, S. (2009). *Tourism Management: managing for change*. 3rd edn. Oxford: Butterworth-Heinemann.
Palmer, A. (2001). *Principles of services marketing*. 3rd edn. UK: McGraw-Hill.
Parasuraman, A., Berry, L.L. and Zeithaml, V.A. (1991). Refinement and reassessment of the SERVQUAL scale. *Journal of Retailing*, 67 (4): 420–450.
Pearce, P. L. (2009). The Relationship between Positive Psychology and Tourist Behaviour Studies. *Tourism Analysis*, 14, 37–48.
Pine, B. . and J.H. Gilmore. (1999). *The Experience Economy: Work Is Theatre & Every Business a Stage*. Boston: Harvard Business School Press.
Plummer, J.T. (1985). How Personality Makes a Difference. *Journal of Advertising Research*, 24 (6), 27–31.
Prayag, G., Hosany, S. and Odeh, K. (2013). The Role of Tourists' Emotional Experiences and Satisfaction in Understanding Behavioral Intensions. *Journal of Destination Marketing and Management*, 2, 118–127.
Pullman, M.E. and Gross, M. A. (2004). Ability of Experience Design Elements to Elicit Emotions and Loyalty Behaviors. *Decision Sciences*, 35 (3).
Richins, M. L. (1997). Measuring Emotions in the Consumption Experience. *Journal of Consumer Research*, 24 (2): 127–46.
Seligman, M.E.P. and Csikszentmihalyi, M. (2000). Positive psychology: An introduction. *American Psychologist*, 55, 14.
Wirtz, D., Kruger, J., Scollon, C.N. and Diener, E. (2003). What to Do on Spring Break? The Role of Predicted, On-line, and Remembered Experience in Future Choice. *Psychological Science*, 14 (5), 520–524.

26

Holiday or no holiday! How much power do children have over their parents in determining travel mode and preferred travel destination?

An explorative study in Medan, Indonesia

Christie Xu and Christian Kahl

Introduction

Family tourism started to become a trend and children are being viewed differently compared to in the past. "What do you call a consumer who wants to buy everything you have, does not care what it costs and is less that five feet tall? A marketer's dream? Nope. You call them kids" (AdRelevance Intelligence Report, 2000). Marketers now begin to set children as a main target market not only because of their purchasing power, but due to their influence on their parents' purchasing decision in any products (Guneri et al., 2009). In addition, children are often viewed as potential future consumers. According to Martino, an advertising executive, "We're relying on the kid to pester the mom to buy the product, rather than going straight to the mom." (MediaSmarts [MS], 2014). This proves how strong children's influence on their parents' purchasing decision-making is (Kaur & Singh, 2006). However, children's influence powers are different based on the category of the goods and decision-making stages. Thus, this triggers marketers conduct research on children due to their different roles in family purchasing decision-making stages (Desai, 2008).

This research will highlight the children's view rather than the parents' in family decision-making, which many researchers did in the past (Shoham et al., 2004). They had investigated from product basics such as clothing or toys to luxury goods such as cars and travel destinations (Tinson et al., 2008). This research will focus on travel destination, as tourism industry has significantly grown in the past years (Yeoman et al., 2012). Children will be interviewed personally regarding their influence on family's decision making in choosing travel destination along with their preferred destination to travel in order to achieve the objectives of this research. Different age groups of children from different family structures will be taken from Medan, Indonesia as representatives to answer the research questions, which analyze children's influence power on each of the family decision-making stages in choosing travel destination.

This explorative research is conducted to investigate the trends of family decision-making in choosing travel destination at Medan, Indonesia. The main aim of conducting this research is to determine the degree of children's influence power in each stage in the family decision-making process that relates to different factors such as age groups and types of the family's structures in Indonesian context.

The objectives of this research are:

1 To investigate the trends of family decision-making in choosing travel destination at Medan, Indonesia.
2 To determine the degree of children's influence power in respect to the stages of decision-making with children's age and types of family structure.
3 To investigate children's traveling pattern and preferred travel destinations in Medan, Indonesia.

Literature review

Definition of tourism

According to Mathieson and Wall (1982) cited by Hammersley (2013), tourism can be defined as "the temporary movement of people to destinations outside their normal places of work and residence, the activities undertaken during their stay in those destinations, and the facilities created to cater to their needs." While according to Macintosh and Goeldner (1986), also cited by Hammersley (2013), tourism is "the sum of the phenomena and relationships arising from the interaction of tourist, business suppliers, host government and host communities in the process of attracting and hosting these tourists and other visitors." Both definitions highlight important aspects of tourism and how it differs according to the people.

According to TripAdvisor [TAD] (2014), study stated that 92% of families with children were planning to have a family vacation once in a year in 2010. The same study has also stated that one third of families were planning to have family vacations within country or outside country. From the interview gained in this study, many parents claimed that the chances to spend family time together are the happiest part in the family vacation, with the number and figures increasing.

Trends of family tourism in the world

Overview of family tourism

Family tourism can be defined as the whole family that joins tourism activity depending on their purposes. It can be a visit to a relative's house and family reunion, or even a visit to a tourist attraction within the country or outside the country (Yeoman et al., 2012).

According to Oxford dictionary (2016), family can be defined as "a group consisting of two parents and their children living together as a unit." But, with the changes of people's way of thinking, families exists in different types of numbers and age groups. According to Tourism & More (2003), they always perceive that family holidays consist of two parents and two or three children from aged 9–12. This can be clearly seen by looking at different travel package offers nowadays for families. But the reality looks different; family holidays may range from a single parent bringing a child; two parents bringing teenage children or small children, grandparents traveling with grandchildren or many other combinations of choices (Tourism & More, 2003).

According to Shaw et al. (2008), family tourism is different to other tourism as there is more focus on bonding and values within the family. Gran (2005) argues that there are different purposes of traveling for family members; such as parents search for relaxation, while children search for entertainment and activities. This combination of purposes will result in an argument and conflict among family. While according to Schanzel (2008), family vacation involves different activities that enable bonding time together among family rather than purposes such as escape or break. Yeoman et al. (2012) came out with a definition, whereby family tourism is "a purposive time spent together as a family group (which may include extended family) doing activities different from normal routines that are fun but that may involve compromise and conflict at times."

Looking at a different aspect of family tourism that can be divided to either visits to relatives or visits for sightseeing, both of these purposes do serve the main purpose as to why family travels (Yeoman et al., 2012). In United States, study found that 34% of adults had a visit to a family reunion in the past three years. It does generate in increasing of revenue. The Philadelphia Convention and Visitors Bureau found out that in the past five years of family reunions, it generated up to $519 million of business in the city. Focusing on the sightseeing and leisure purposes, activities that family tourism involve mostly are shopping with 37%, outdoor activities with 21%, historical places and museums with 14% and theme park with 15% based on a survey conducted from U.S. Travel Association (Miller & Kelli, 2013). The trends of kid's programs are also becoming generally popular and most families do use these services such as baby-sitting or special kids' meal. Even there are some parents that allow children to miss school to travel.

Children's influence in family decision-making

Family decision-making has appealed to many researchers and marketers (Guneri, 2009). Even now, in an efficient tourism marketing department, information on involvement of family member in every step of decision making must be analyzed carefully in order to come out with an attractive brand, packaging and price (Wang et al., 2004).

"Purchase decisions within the family are not always the outcome of individual choice but rather, family members influence each other" (Hamilton & Catterall, 2006). Normally, decision making in family had been revealed that it was always either husband or wife that made the final decision on any purchasing such as clothes, foods, and traveling as they are the sources of income. Although that husband and wife are the head of the family, children do take part in family decision-making (Thomson et al., 2007). It has been tremendously changed with increasing children's involvement on negotiation and decision-making on many things. Sometimes children also assert to their parents to buy the things that they desire, which is very common for young children nowadays (Kaur & Singh, 2006). Also, it had been identified that as children get older from childhood to adulthood, their knowledge widens in the sense of their attitudes and thinking as consumers (John, 1999). The more knowledge the children have, the more influence on purchasing decisions (Thomson et al., 2007).

Based on Nickelodeon (2014), the study stated that relationship between parents and kids today are very different compare to the past. From the result gained, parents had a closer relationship to children than their parents were to them in the past. Parents agree that in the past they were not likely to disobey their parents compared to the children now. With the fewer gaps, parents treat their children as important people and friends, which result in favoring the children's opinion and decision (Consoli, 2012).

Children's involvement in the decision-making process

According to Aslan and Karalar (2011), their research classifies purchasing process into three, which are recognition, information search and actual purchase. They found out that if the teens did not influence parents in the first step, he or she would be unable to influence their parents on second or third step. Also, they conclude teens are great influencers when they like the products, but when they are not they will not be active throughout the purchasing process. According to Shoham and Dalakas (2003), the three common practices of decision-making process are initiation, search and evaluation and final decision rather than the whole five or nine decision stages. According to Darley and Lim (1986), children influence more in the early stages, and research found out that children are able to influence more in making the decision about the product to buy but not on the purchasing process. According to Guneri et al. (2009), children did not influence more in related with monetary issue while influence level varied when in the sub-decision stages; depending on which product chosen.

Degree of children's influence power

Based on age groups

According to Guneri et al. (2009), they stated that demographic variables are the main important factors in influence power. The most influencial variable is age from the results that they had gained. According to McNeal and Yeh (2003), there is a positive relationship between children's power of influence and age. They concluded that the younger children's level of influence power is generally lower compared to the older children. According to Ward and Wackman (1972), as the children grow older, the chances of the things that they wanted more are likely to be given by parents for their decision are more relevant. They also stated that things that children buy are different according to their age groups since their interest and generation are different (Guneri et al., 2009). Younger children influence their parents with just a simple question but as they improve and age, children are capable of giving arguments and valid opinion that affect the parent's decision (John, 1999). As well, the older they are, the greater their influence power (Ward & Wackman, 1972).

Based on type of family

Weber classified families into ten family types, which were based on among the 36 families that were being interviewed by him in Sweden. Half of the families were from modern families while the other half were from traditional families (Marshall, 2010).

Shoham et al. (2004) stated that family communication style does affect the child's influence power. Children's influence power is relatively higher while dealing with consensual parents. Consensual parents usually have a more open communication relationship with the children and value the children's opinion more. This means that it falls under friendship families and it is proven that children from friendship families do have a high influence power (Marshall, 2010). Based on the research done by Guneri et al. (2009), results revealed that based on the purchasing power of the family, the children's influence may only be applicable to products for their own use. Those families with higher purchasing power will take the opinion of the children, as prices are not so important for these families (Guneri et al., 2009).

Society categorized these families into a total of six types of family structures such as nuclear family, single parent family, extended family, childless family, stepfamily and grandparent family.

Table 26.1 Family styles

Basis for identification	*Family types*	
	Modern families	*Traditional families*
1. Decision-making mode, parent-child relations communication structure	Friendship	Authoritarian
2. Innovativeness	Trendy	Conservative
3. Orientation towards purchasing, purchasing power	Heavy spenders	Restricted
4. Degree of planning and organization	Spontaneous	Structured
5. Purchasing roles	Intermingled	Role-specialized

Some families may be considered as only one category while some may fall into two or more categories like, for example, single parent family that stays with large families (Blessing, 2014). These six different family types all have different communication patterns and a life that shapes the children's thinking and consumption pattern.

Family in Indonesia and the tourism industry

Overview of Indonesia and family

Indonesia has been widely famous as having the biggest archipelago in the world with approximately 18,108 islands. Not only that, they are also famous as a country with the most diverse cultures and languages, with approximately 583 languages spoken in Indonesia (Garuda Indonesian Restaurant [GIR], 2014). It is a Muslim majority country and takes Indonesian language as their main language (Index Mundi, 2013). With a tropical climate and unique cultural places, their tourism arrival has steadily increased even until now with the most popular cities to visit being Jakarta (capital city) and Bali (GIR, 2014).

Focusing on the family life of Indonesia, family is a very important aspect for Indonesians. As usual, most of the family in Indonesia is the nuclear family, which consists of husband, wife and children, but grandparents or unmarried siblings can be included in the family as well. Thus, it is a common practice to have extended family structure living in the same house (Skwirk, 2014). According to Everyculture [EC] (2014), Indonesians take pride in being married. They assume by being married, they are considered as full adults.

Indonesia family's culture, way of thinking and perception are much more traditional compared to westernized family (Skwirk, 2014). In western countries, children see their parents as a friend and someone to talk comfortably while in Indonesia, there is a certain barrier existing, separating old people and young people. Thus, young people must take a specific action to respect the elderly and acknowledge their wisdom and experience (EC, 2014). But even though Indonesia's families are still traditional, they always claim that family comes first.

Research methodology

Sampling methods

The population of this research study is children age ranging from 10–18 years old at Medan, Indonesia. Criterion sampling is use by collecting data based on age segments, from primary schools (10–11 years old), secondary schools (12–15 years old) and junior high schools (16–18 years old). Sixteen respondents will be selected randomly depending on whether they are allowed to be interviewed. For the age of 10 to 11 years old, 6 respondents will be separated into two groups consisting of three children to be interviewed together. For the age of 12 to 15 years old, 5 respondents will be selected randomly and interviewed individually. This also applies to 16 to 18 years old, taking 5 respondents to be interviewed.

Research instruments

Structured indepth interview was used to collect data from the chosen sample population. Questions were divided into two sections relative to the research questions. Questions that were included were mostly open-ended questions with simple language for young children to understand. Closed-ended questions were used mostly to obtain the profile of the interviewees. The language was in Bahasa Indonesia and for this research translated into English. Duration of the interview varied depending of the interaction between the researchers and the respondents.

Section A included a warm up question for the children such as their profile and background of traveling, as well as questions related to the preferred destination for children to open up their mind about traveling. Section B included questions to answer the remaining research questions listed – to investigate the children's involvement power in each of the decision-making stages.

Transcription and coding

In this research, the authors transcribed the interviews in the specific ways suggested by Wargo (2013). The format that he suggested is to ensure efficient analysis and avoid confusion of the themes with the questions. During the interview, the authors typed the interview response according to the sections respectively on the side. After the interviews were collected through typing, the author translated the data into English and arranged them accordingly first with labeling it with the code name of the interviewees and date of interview. At the end the sets of interview data were arranged according to the variable chosen to answer the research questions (Wargo, 2013).

Profile of respondents

Table 26.2 Children aged 10–11

	Name	*Gender*	*Age*	*Ethnicity*	*Family income level*	*Birth order*	*Family structure*
Interview session 1	Interviewee 1	Male	11	Indonesian	Middle	Oldest child	Nuclear
	Interviewee 2	Male	10	Chinese	Upper	Only child	Nuclear
	Interviewee 3	Female	10	Indonesian	Upper	Middle child	Stepfamily
Interview session 2	Interviewee 4	Female	11	Chinese	Middle	Youngest child	Nuclear
	Interviewee 5	Female	11	Chinese	Middle	Oldest child	Extended
	Interviewee 6	Female	11	Chinese	Lower	Youngest child	Extended

Table 26.3 Children aged 12–15

	Name	*Gender*	*Age*	*Ethnicity*	*Family income level*	*Birth order*	*Family structure*
Interview session 3	Interviewee 7	Male	14	Chinese	Middle	Middle child	Single parent
Interview session 4	Interviewee 8	Female	12	Indonesian	Upper	Youngest child	Nuclear
Interview session 5	Interviewee 9	Male	15	Indonesian	Middle	Youngest child	Extended
Interview session 6	Interviewee 10	Male	15	Chinese	Middle	Middle child	Nuclear
Interview session 7	Interviewee 11	Female	12	Indonesian	Lower	Oldest child	Extended

Table 26.4 Children aged 16–18

	Name	*Gender*	*Age*	*Ethnicity*	*Family income level*	*Birth order*	*Family structure*
Interview session 8	Interviewee 12	Female	16	Indian	Upper	Only child	Extended
Interview session 9	Interviewee 13	Female	16	Indonesian	Lower	Middle child	Extended
Interview session 10	Interviewee 14	Male	18	Chinese	Middle	Youngest child	Nuclear
Interview session 11	Interviewee 15	Female	16	Chinese	Middle	Oldest child	Nuclear
Interview session 12	Interviewee 16	Male	17	Indonesian	Lower	Oldest child	Extended

Findings and analysis

Children's traveling pattern and preferred destinations

From the data collected, several theories are provided regarding children's traveling patterns. Based on their frequencies of traveling, children from families with higher income levels travel more than children from families with a lower income level. Furthermore, children with a better financial background are found to be travelling more internationally while children with a lower financial background are found to be travelling more to places that are reachable by car.

Interviewee 8 (12 years old) – "Yes, I always travel overseas and around Indonesia as well. I had been to many places but I can't recall much."

Interviewee 12 (16 years old) – "My parents always bring me to travel and during some of the holiday, we always go back India to meet our family there."

Children's preferred destinations

When children are able to travel more, some children develop a liking towards traveling. Some of the interviewees stated that they love traveling and it has developed into an interest for them. During the interview, children from different age groups were asked which was their best vacation in their entire life. After data analysis, children's best vacations did not depend on the age group but rather on their family income. The higher their family income is, the further the places that they state while the lower their family income is, the nearer the places that they state. Despite the different ethnicity that the children had, it made no difference in the places that they travel to.

> *Interviewee 3 (10 years old)* – "The best vacation that I have been to is going to Europe playing skis. I also cannot recall which city because I was still young but we stay at my dad's friend house. The reason it was the best because it was my first time playing ski and I love cold places, building snowman. It was the best vacation ever."
>
> *Interviewee 6 (11 years old)* – "The best vacation that I had been to was when we are going to place called Lake Toba [Indonesia], the view there is really amazing and I was amazed."

Children's influence power on decision making in choosing travel destinations

Children's influence powers are believed to be different in each of them, some able to influence their parents in decision-making while some are not able to. The reason why children's influence power is different is due to many reasons such as different types of age groups, family structures, birth order, gender and many more. However, in this research, the author will be focusing on more important variables, which are age and family structures.

According to Guneri et al. (2009), the most influencial variable is age. Different types of age groups give different influence power. Looking overall at the decision-making process, the older the children are, the more influence power they have while the younger the children are, the less influence power they have. While looking at each stage of the decision-making process – need recognition, information search and purchase stages – younger children are able to influence more in the need recognition and purchasing stages while older children are able to influence more in the information search and purchasing stages. This is due to younger children not bothering during the information search and focusing more on having vacation while older children develop an interest in traveling which makes them search for information and plus their opinion are more valuable. Parents tend to trust older children, which is another reason the data is affected in this way.

From the data analysis, children from nuclear families have the greatest influence power compared to the extended family due to different styles of parenting and communication which affect children's influence power. Children from single parent families are not able to influence much while children from stepfamilies are able to, but still a clear conclusion cannot be made due to limited data.

> *Interviewee 6 (11 years old)* – "I ever convinced my parents to go overseas because most of the kids around my ages ever went to before. I just want to experience boarding on the plane. My parents just said all right and will consider it. I think my parents are convinced because my mother said in the future we would be able to ride the plane. I'm so happy."
>
> *Interviewee 12 (16 years old)* – "I ever convince my parents to have vacation during holiday and my parents always agree on me and bring me on every holiday that I had."

On the next stage in the decision-making process – information search – children were asked whether they search for information on where to go during their vacation and are their parents convinced by the information being told by the children. This is to check the children's influence power on the information search since most of them are able to surf the Internet everyday.

Interviewee 10 (15 years old) – "Yes, I do search for information especially if we travel far because I want to know which are the famous places to go. Of course, I told my parents about to go here and there. They agree to me and trust me."
Interviewee 14 (18 years old) – "I normally search for the information about the vacation after we purchase air ticket. I tell my parents about where to go and they convinced because they told me to be their tour guide and they will just follow my recommendation places."

On the last stage of the decision-making process – the purchase stages – children were asked whether they ever ask their parents about places to travel during vacation and were the parents convinced. Statements from the children were compiled and analyze according to the different type of age groups.

Interviewee 3 (10 years old) – "As I was saying just, I did convince them to go Disneyland because most of my friend had been to and my dad was convinced. He did bring us there on our last year vacation."
Interviewee 10 (15 years old) – "I did tell them to go to Europe because there are many places to visit for sightseeing, my parents are convinced and we went there."

Since children from nuclear families were able to influence their parents on need recognition, they were also able to influence them on the purchasing stage which can be shown from the data that four out of seven people were able to influence their parents. Based on the statement, it can be seen that parents listen to what their children said and, regardless of age, they will value their opinion and bring them to go to the places that the children want. Compared to children from extended families, below is a statement given on the purchasing stages on choosing travel destination.

Interviewee 11 (12 years old) – "I ever convince them to go to Korea once a while because I love Korea, their culture seems very traditional and cool. Another reason also maybe because I watch too many Korean drama that made me want to go there. My parents was not convinced enough though."

Children from extended families are not fully able to influence their parents during the purchasing stages, which show out of seven respondents, four unable to influence their parents. Even though children started to develop a liking for, and an interest in traveling, parents still do not value their opinion as much as children from nuclear family. Due to getting less attention, some children do not even try to influence their parents to have a vacation.

Conclusion

Vacations are important for families not just to have a getaway and free themselves from their daily life, but also to increase their family bonding (Yeoman et al., 2012). With the involvement of children's influence power on decision-making (Kaur & Singh, 2006) and family vacation increase (Yeoman et al., 2012), it is the reason why this research was conducted which is to investigate the children's traveling pattern, preferred destination and influence power on decision-making in choosing travel destinations at Medan, Indonesia. Based on the results, there is a positive association between the frequency of children traveling and family income levels. Respondents from upper income families said that they travel quite often while respondents from lower income families said that they seldom travel. From the response obtained, it can be concluded that the most traveled are the children from nuclear families, extended families or stepfamilies, except for single parent families.

Next, children were interviewed regarding their last vacation, and the results compared according to their family income level – the authors came out with one conclusion on this theme. This is that the period from their last vacation and the interview dates are varied according to their family income level. Regardless of age groups, children from upper income family and a few from middle-income family had their last vacation not a long time ago such as during Chinese New Year or last year Christmas or New Year period. Compared to children from lower income families, most of them stated that they had their last vacation last year, which is different from the children from upper income families.

In section B of the interview, children were asked regarding their influence power in family's decision making in choosing travel destinations. Respondents' influence power was assessed at each stage of the decision-making – need recognition, information search and purchasing. The information was compared based on the age groups and family structure, conclusions then being drawn.

First, comparing the results with age groups – three different age groups, which are primary, secondary and junior high school – younger children are able to influence their parents more in the need recognition and purchasing stages while older children are able to influence their parents more in the information search and purchasing stages. This is proven to be true by comparing with the past literature stated that as the children age, they are capable to give valid arguments that affect parent's decision (John, 1999) which means that the older they are, the greater their influence power (Ward & Wackman, 1972). Also, according to Aslan and Karalar (2011), they stated that teens are great influencers when they like the product, which is also applicable to this research's findings.

Second, comparing results by family structure, there are in total four types of family structures gained in the interview – nuclear family, extended family, stepfamily and single parent family. The authors focused more on nuclear and extended families rather than stepfamily and single parent family because they could not be compared with the previous literature due to an insufficient sample number. Children from nuclear families have the greatest influence power due to difference in parenting style and communication This is confirmed by Shoham et al. (2004), which says pluralistic families – for example nuclear family, stepfamily and single parent families – have a generally higher influence power.

References

AdRelevance Intelligence Report, (2000). Available online at: http://www.adrelevance.com/about/release 11sep00.jsp

Aslan, E. and Karalar, R. (2011). *The Effects of Turkish Teens over Family Purchase of Various Products*, Dumlupinar University.

Blessing, M. (2014) *Types of Family Structures* [Blog post]. Available online at: http://family.lovetoknow.com/about-family-values/types-family-structures

Consoli, J. (2012, August 22). *Nickelodeon Study Affirms Kids' Strong Influence on Family Purchasing Decisions* [Press release]. Available online at:http://www.broadcastingcable.com/news/news-articles/nickelodeon-study-affirms-kids-strong-influence-family-purchasing-decisions/113500

Darley, W.F. and Lim, J. (1986). 'Family Decision Making in Leisure-Time Activities: An Exploratory Investigation of the Impact of Locus of Control, Child Age Influence Factor and Parental Type of Perceived Child Influence', in *Advances in Consumer Research*, 13, 370–374.

Desai, T. (2008). *Children's influence on family purchase decision in India* (Doctoral dissertation, University of Nottingham).

Ekström, K.M. (1995). *Children's Influence in Family Decision Making: A Study of Yielding, Consumer Learning and Consumer Socialization*. Göteborg: Basek, För.

Everyculture (2014). *Culture of Indonesia* [Blog post]. Available online at: www.everyculture.com/Ge-It/Indonesia.html#b

Garuda Indonesian Restaurant (2014). *Facts about Indonesia* [Blog post]. Available online at: www.garuda-restaurant.co.uk/facts.htm

Gran, M. (2005). Family Holidays. A qualitative analysis of family holiday experiences. *Scandinavian Journal of Hospitality and Tourism*, 5(1), 2–22.

Guneri, B., Yurt, O., Kaplan, M.D. and Delen, M. (2009). The influence of children on family purchasing decisions in Turkey. *Asian Journal of Marketing*, 3(1), 20–32.

Hamilton, K. and Catterall, M. (2006). Consuming love in poor families: children's influence on consumption decision. *Journal of Marketing Management*, 22(9), 1031–1052.

Hammersley, C. (2013). *Introduction – What is Tourism? Online Lesson.* [Lecture notes]. Available online at: http://www.prm.nau.edu/prm300/what-is-tourism-lesson.htmwww.prm.nau.edu/prm300/what-is-tourism-lesson.htm

IndexMundi (2014). Indonesia Demographics Profile 2013. [Government report]. Available online at: www.indexmundi.com/indonesia/demographics_profile.htmlwww.indexmundi.com/indonesia/demographics_profile.html

John, D.R. (1999). Consumer Socialization of Children: A Retrospective Look at Twenty-Five Years of Research. *Journal of Consumer Research*, 26(3), 183–213.

Kaur, P. and Singh, R. (2006). Children in family purchase decision making in India and the West: A review. *Academy of Marketing Science Review*, 10(8), 1–30.

Marshall, D. (2010). *Understanding children as consumers.* London: Sage.

McNeal, J.U. and Yeh, C. (2003). Consumer behavior of Chinese children: 1995–2002, *Journal of Consumer Marketing*, 20, 542–554.

MediaSmarts (2014). *How Marketers Target Kids.* [Press release]. Available online at: http://mediasmarts.ca/marketing-consumerism/how-marketers-target-kids

Medical Tourism & Travel Blog (2013). *What are the different types of tourism?* [Blog post]. Available online at: www.medtiblog.org/2013/05/14/what-are-the-different-types-of-tourism/www.medtiblog.org/2013/05/14/what-are-the-different-types-of-tourism/

Miller, R.K. and Kelli, W. (2013). *The 2013–2014 US Travel & Tourism Market Research Handbook.* United States.

Nickelodeon (2014). Available online at: www.nick.com/games/

Oxford Dictionary (2016). Available online at: www.oxforddictionaries.com/ms/

Schanzel, H.A. (2008). The New Zealand family on holiday: values, realities and fun, in J. Foundation and K Moore (eds), *Proceedings to the New Zealand Tourism and Hospitality Research Conference.* Canterbury, New Zealand: Lincoln University.

Shaw, S.M., Havitz, M.E. and Delemere, F.M. (2008). I decided to invest in my kids' memories: family vacations, memories, and the social construction of the family. *Tourism Culture and Communication*, 8(1), 13–26.

Shoham, A. and Dalakas, V. (2003). Family consumer decision making in Israel: The role of teens and parents. *Journal of Consumer Market*, 4, 25–38.

Shoham, A., Rose, G.M. and Bakir, A. (2004). The Effect of Family Communication Patterns on Mothers' and Fathers' Perceived Influence in Family Decision Making. *Advances in Consumer Research*, 31.

Skwirk (2014). *Indonesia: understanding our nearest neighbors.* [Blog post]. Available online at: www.skwirk.com/p-c_s-75_u-149_t-452_c-1606/VIC/5/Village-structure/Traditional-community-life/Indonesia-understanding-our-nearest-neighbours/Humanities/

Thomson, E.S., Laing, A.W. and McKee, L. (2007). Family purchase decision making: Exploring child influence behavior. *Journal of Consumer Behavior*, 6, 182–202.

Tinson, J., Nancarrow, C. and Brace, I. (2008). Purchase decision making and the increasing significance of family types. *Journal of Consumer Marketing*, 25(1), 45–56.

Tourism & More (2003, May). *The Family Vacation* [Blog post]. Available online at: www.tourismandmore.com/tidbits/the-family-vacation/

TripAdvisor [TAD] (2014). Available online at: www.tripadvisor.com.my

Wang, K.C., Hsieh, A.T., Yeh, Y.C. and Tsai, C.W. (2004). Who is the decision-maker: the parents or the child in group package tours? *Tourism Management*, 25(2), 183–194.

Wargo, W.G. (2013, April 10). *Qualitative Data Analysis (Coding) of Transcripts.* [Review]. Available online at: www.academicinfocenter.com/qualitative-data-analysis-coding-of-transcripts.html

Ward, S. and Wackman, D.B. (1972). Children's Purchase Influence Attempts and Parental Influence Attempts and Parental Yielding, *Journal of Marketing Research*, 9,316–319.

Yeoman, I., Schänzel, H. and Backer, E. (2012). *Family Tourism: Multidisciplinary Perspectives.* Bristol: Channel View Publications.

27

Personal values, quality of the tourism experience and destination attributes

The case of Chinese tourists in Egypt

Omneya Mokhtar Yacout and Lamiaa Hefny

Introduction

China's political and economic transformation has been the subject of research in many disciplines. In the field of tourism, these changes have led to a tremendous increase in the number of Chinese outbound tourists who are expected to be the fourth largest outbound market by 2020 (Zeng and Go 2013). Most of these tourists come from the more affluent areas with younger travelers dominating (Zeng and Go 2013). As a result, the motivation of Chinese students to travel and the related tourist behaviors have been heavily investigated, however, a number of gaps warrant more studies examining the tourism behavior of Chinese students. First, the student segment represents a significant, separate part of the overall tourism industry with a significant contribution to the overall financial success of tourism (Carr 1988) but little is known about its characteristics, behavior, and motives (Chadee and Cutler 1996). Second, most of studies examining Chinese students' behavior were conducted in traditional educational markets such as Australia (Zhang and Peng 2014), New Zealand (Liu 2008), or USA (Liao 2012) and only one study examining push and pull motivations of Chinese tourists visiting Egypt was reported (Ayad and Shujun 2012). Generalizing from these studies to other tourism markets is not acceptable because variables affecting the intention to visit a destination vary from one destination to another (Jang and Cai 2002) and because of the context-dependency of motivations to specific destinations and tourist market (Andreu et al. 2006). A careful analysis of the personal values, importance assigned to various dimensions of the tourism experience and evaluation of the destination attributes is required to increase the share of Egypt in Chinese outbound tourism. Such efforts might compensate the sharp decline in the number of tourists visiting Egypt because of Arab spring.

Thus, the purpose of this research is to examine the various psychographic segments of Chinese students and how these psychographic profiles vary with respect to perceived destination attributes, importance ratings of the quality of the tourism experience, and re-visitation intentions. Thus, it is expected to contribute to the scant literature examining Chinese students' travel behavior in non-traditional tourism markets. It also contributes to the literature related to tourism experience and hedonic consumption. From a practical side, the findings of this research can provide help to the tourism industry in Egypt and in other countries targeting Chinese students in designing better and novel marketing mixes that cater to the changing utilitarian and hedonic needs of this growing segment of tourists. This is particularly true since efforts on the part of the tourism industry to develop and market tourism-related products to international students have often suffered from poor positioning, failed to motivate prospective participants, and commonly delivered inadequate consumer experiences (Gardiner et al. 2013).

This chapter is organized as follows: we begin with the concept of personal values, personal values and tourist behavior, Chinese culture – something old, something new and something borrowed. We next discuss the research methodology. Finally, we will end with a discussion of results and implications.

Literature review

Personal values

Values represent mental representations of needs (Lages and Fernandes 2005), whether biological, interactional or group welfare (Schwartz and Bilsky 1987). They are intrinsic (Lages and Fernandes 2005), stable over time (Lages and Fernandes 2005; Rokeach 1973), and serve as guiding principles in the life of a person or other social entity (Schwartz 1994; Verplanken and Holland 2002).

Different levels of analysis of values have been developed. Cultural values (e.g., Hofstede 1983), personal values (e.g., Rokeach 1973) and consumption values (Sheth et al. 1991) were identified by researchers. The three levels are hierarchal, and interrelated where social institutions and other macro level variables influence the modal importance of individuals' values within societies (Fischer and Schwartz 2011) and represent the choice an individual made from the variety of social values (Tarka and Rutkowski 2015).

Consumption values are as the consumers' perceived attribute importance of the product or service (Sin and Yau 2001; Tse et al. 1989). Vinson et al. (1977) report a logically structured relationship between global values, related values, evaluation of product attributes, and preference for consumer products or services. Empirically, differences in consumption values are associated with differences in cultural (Park and Rabolt 2009) and personal values (Sin and Yau 2001). Sheth et al. (1991) theorize that consumption values include functional, social, emotional, epistemic, and conditional values. While the functional value is merely utilitarian, the social, emotional, and epistemic consumption values lend themselves to experiential aspects of consumption.

Many researchers contemplated that values should be organized into value domains to facilitate understanding the relationships between values and predictor values such as social structural variables and dependent variables such as attitudes and behavior (Schwartz and Bilsky 1987). They help the individual maintain his self-esteem and consistent behavior in situations of value conflicts and reflect the fact that multiple values affect behavior (McCleary and Choi 1999).

Researchers were not consistent in the specific values systems identified, however. Rokeach (1973) classified values into terminal and instrumental values. Later, Homer and Kahle (1988) developed the list of values (LOV) and reported the existence of two value domains: an *external values* domain which includes values such as sense of belonging, being well-respected and security and an *internal values domain* with includes values such as self-fulfillment and a sense of accomplishment. Other researchers reported different dimensions for values (e.g., Erdem et al. 1999; Kamakura and Novak 1992; Priem et al. 2000; Schwartz and Bilsky 1987; Vinson et al. 1977). Inconsistencies in the underlying structure of the factors may be attributed to their contextual nature (Madrigal and Kahle 1994) where factor loadings may vary slightly from one situation to the next (Madrigal and Kahle 1994).

Personal values and tourist behavior

Values may provide a better understanding of market behavior and a better base for developing cross-cultural marketing strategy than other segmenting methods (McCleary and Choi 1999). Pizam and Calantone (1987) note that values, interests, attitudes, beliefs, and opinions can be hierarchically arranged based on their degree of inclusiveness and specificity from values to interests, attitudes, beliefs, and terminating with opinions which are the narrowest and most specific of these predispositions.

Researchers in the field of tourism marketing have examined personal values and their role in shaping tourism behavior from various perspectives. The first perspective examined the relative importance of various values for tourists (e.g., Ruane and Quinn 2012; Unger and Kernan 1983). The second perspective examined how values might be related to specific tourist behaviors. Among these, the set of variables related to tourist personal values, destination attributes, importance ratings of the tourism experience quality, and tourist future intentions remain among the most important behaviors. In examining the relationships between these variables, two methodologies were used. The means-end chain theory examined the destination attributes, the consequences of having these attributes on the tourist, and the underlying values. For example, Jiang et al. (2014) report that the attribute "nature scenery" was related to the value "world of beauty" and hedonic values. Jewell and Crotts (2002) report that the attribute of the natural setting provided a contrast and calming (consequence) experience to their modern lifestyles, and therefore, a satisfying/pleasurable experience (value).

The second methodology was cluster analysis where tourists were classified based on their value ratings and the corresponding destination attribute ratings, experience quality dimensions, and behavioral intentions. Muller (1991) identified three clusters of United States visitors to a Canadian city and the three clusters demonstrated different importance ratings to various city attributes and different intentions to repeated visit. Devesa et al.'s study (2010) also reports having four clusters of tourists visiting a rural destination. They note that there are certain specific satisfactory elements directly linked to the motivation for the trip.

These studies are based on the premise that if tourists have certain unsatisfied needs that they want to satisfy through visiting the destination, they look for the attributes that satisfy those needs. The correspondence between personal values sought and the destination attributes was strongly reported by a number of studies (e.g., Baloglu and Uysal 1996; Muller 1991; Prayag and Hosany 2014; Zhang and Peng 2014).

A shift in marketing thought was made when Holbrook and Hirschman (1982) introduced fantasies, feelings, and fun to consumption. In the case of overseas destinations, consumers attend to symbolic meaning and directly apply their human values, where the application serves an expressive psychological function (e.g., self-consistency and social approval (Allen 2008)). The importance of the experiential facets of tourism was supported by a number of scholars (Pine and Gilmore 1998; Ritchie et al. 2011; Williams 2006). Empirically, Prayag and Hosany (2014) identified three clusters of Emirati tourists visiting Paris. They were different with respect to motivation, evaluation of various city attributes, as well as evaluation of hedonic aspects.

Mehmetoglu et al. (2010) report that Norwegian travelers with different value systems will place different importance on the hedonic consumption dimensions. Materialists (traditional/modern) were more taken up with hedonistic push motives. Traditionalists were, to a greater degree, interested in status through conspicuous consumption.

Daghfous et al. (1999) report that the conservative cluster places very little importance given to hedonism. The dynamics cluster places an average importance on empathy and hedonism. The hedonist cluster considers fun and pleasure, searching for strong sensations, and establishing warm relationships with others as very important. Both Denys and Mendes (2014) and Phau et al. (2014) report that emotional and epistemic value were the most important consumption values reported by tourists visiting Portugal and Mauritius respectively.

Li and Cai (2012) report that the Chinese respondents' motivations for novelty and knowledge and for self-development were found to be directly influenced by internal values such as warm relationships with others and sense of accomplishment. The external values such as emphasizing security, fun, and enjoyment in life influenced motivation for prestigious and luxury experience, self-development, exciting experience, and escape. Babin and Kim (2001) show that for international students, perceived safety, fun, and educational benefits create travel satisfaction via their effect on personal hedonic and utilitarian travel value perceptions.

A number of studies incorporated behavioral intentions into these models. Liu (2008) segmented the Chinese university student travel market based on travel motivation and activity attributes. Travel motivation contributed to overall travel satisfaction directly or indirectly via travel activities, which affected loyalty. Bosnjak et al. (2011) report that congruity between values and destination attributes affected loyalty.

Such increasing interest in experiential aspects was heightened as Otto and Ritchie (1996) developed a measure of the quality of the service experience where respondents are required to rate the importance of hedonics, peace of mind, involvement. and recognition. Chen and Chen (2010) extracted three factors from Otto and Ritchie's (1996) scale: involvement, peace of mind, and educational experience. Similarly, Kim et al. (2010) developed a 24-item memorable tourism experience scale comprised of seven domains: hedonism, refreshment, local culture, meaningfulness, knowledge, involvement, and novelty. In a different study, Kao et al. (2008) conceptualized experiential quality by four factors: immersion, surprise, participation and fun. They report that the experiential quality relates positively to satisfaction and satisfaction influences visitors' behavioral intentions.

The above literature reveals the important role that personal values play in various steps of the tourist decision-making process starting from selection of the tourism destination and ending with evaluation of the tourism experience and intentions to revisit it. Even though early attempts to incorporate values into tourist decision-making focused on the attributes side only (e.g., Muller 1991), yet, tourism researchers have incorporated hedonic aspects of consumption into values research. These studies provided empirical support for the relationship between personal values and experiential aspects of performance (e.g., Daghfous et al. 1999; Mehmetoglu et al. 2010).

Chinese culture – something old, something new, and something borrowed

Starting in the 1980s, China has progressed in economic leaps sustaining a double-digit economic growth, a tremendous increase in political force and an accompanying change in the Chinese culture (Guthrie 2012). A number of researchers attempted to identify the aspects of the Chinese culture, the changes that took place in these aspects, and whether they have an effect on consumption values. For example, protecting *the face* has been identified as a Chinese cultural value with profound impacts on conspicuous consumption (Wang and Lin 2009) and purchasing new products with familiar brand names (Lowe and Corkindale 1998).

Relational orientation and connected self-construal means that one's identity lies in one's familial, cultural, professional, and social relationships (Markus and Kitayama 1991). It affects the way they perceive shopping as an activity that naturally allows consumers to spend time together, and to be affected by peer pressure and opinion leaders (Wang and Lin 2009). Recent studies have shown a major cultural change in this orientation, however. For example, Xiao and Kim (2009) report that middle-class urban Chinese consumers are pursuing individualistic goals such as self-direction, achievement, stimulation, power, and hedonism, as well as collectivist objectives of conformity, benevolence, and tradition. Egri and Ralston (2004) report that the three Chinese generations since the establishment of Communist China were found to be significantly more self-enhancing than Republican Era Chinese.

The hedonistic orientation. Traditionally, Chinese consumers were described as savers (Wang and Lin 2009) with a strong focus on utilitarian appeals in advertising at the time of the study (Tse et al. 1989). Later, some researchers noted that China is moving towards a consumer culture, where consumer preferences are changing, disposable incomes are increasing, and information and product selections are rising (Wang and Lin 2009). Stout et al. (1994), using a content analysis of advertisements from 1979 to 1991, reported a decline in depictions of utilitarian values in print advertisements and a rise in the hedonistic values. Lin and Lu (2010) note that for China's nouveau riche, consumption patterns are moving toward an "enjoy now" and a focus on satisfying experiential needs. Their stable consumerist value orientations were reported by Wei and Pan (1999): conspicuous consumption, aspiration for self-actualization, and worshipping Western lifestyles specifically among younger, better-educated, and affluent Chinese consumers.

A different stream of research examined the application of RVS in China. The most important terminal values reported were *true friendship* (Lau 1988; Lau and Wong 1992; Rudowicz and Kitto 1994), *happiness* (Lau 1988; Lau and Wong 1992), *self-respect* (Lau 1988), *wisdom* (Lau 1998), freedom (Lau and Wong 1992), comfortable life (Lau and Wong 1992), and health and wealth (Rudowicz and Kitto 1994).

Chinese consumers' psychographic and demographic profiles were also examined. Cui and Liu (2001) report the existence of four segments of urban consumers in China. Yuppies have an active lifestyle and they are highly brand conscious and more sophisticated. The little rich are socially active and brand conscious but they are highly insecure. The salary class members are more conservative and satisfied with the status quo and sometimes seek out foreign brands. The working poor constitute the impoverished, the immobile, and the least satisfied. They buy domestic brands.

Wei (1997) reported the existence of five clusters, the traditionalists and the status quo are savers and prefer Chinese products. Transitioners are much younger and poorer but open to change. The modern segment is affluent and well educated, pursing a fashionable and materialistic life. Generation Xers are the highest in terms of education, disrespect routines and tradition, and worry little about money. Both the modern and generation X segments spend freely and favor a Western lifestyle.

Inconsistencies are highly prevalent in studies examining the various aspects of the Chinese culture, particularly the independent versus the interdependent identity of Chinese consumers and their hedonistic orientation. Priem et al. (2000) provided empirical support that the value domains of global harmony, achievement versus happiness and family security versus freedom were all shown to be resistant to change. Conversely, the domain 'Enjoyment versus Risk' were more like western societies in favoring enjoyment. Dissimilarities among the value profiles of the Chinese across cities, provinces, and countries also exist (Ramasamy et al. 2010). In regions with fast-growing economies, cultural change moves towards autonomy and harmony unlike slow-growing economies which tend to have stable cultures endorsing submissiveness (Ng et al. 1982). Furthermore, Chinese cultural values should not be considered to be a homogeneous system, but to contain elements that are contradictory or distinct to each other (Lin and Lu 2010). They cited examples such as self-constraint and thriftiness and self-expression and extravagance, individualism and collectivism, self-restraint and modesty, and self-assertion and excessiveness. They argue that economic reforms have created the climate for these inconsistencies to appear and created a middle class that did not exist before.

Research method

Data collection and sampling

Data was collected from Chinese international students studying Arabic in the universities of Alexandria and Pharos, Egypt. Student samples were used in numerous studies examining personal values (e.g., Pizam and Calantone 1987) and justified because of ease of access. A total of 150 questionnaires were distributed to Chinese students; 12 students refused to participate and three questionnaires were discarded for missing answers. Thus the total response rate was 90%.

Measurement of research variables

Rokeach terminal values were used to measure personal values (Rokeach 1973). The theoretical arguments of all instruments for measuring values are based mainly on Rokeach's work (Yau 1994). Furthermore, terminal and instrumental values can be considered as universal categories of values (Ng et al. 1982). Their validity was reported in Asian cultures (Allen et al. 2007; Lee 1991; Ng et al. 1982) and it is relatively impervious to social desirability (Kristiansen 1985).

Only terminal values were used in the questionnaire as recommended by many researchers (e.g., Erdem et al. 1999; Priem et al. 2000). They were found to be more comprehensive (Priem et al. 2000) and more related to consumer behavior (Mehmetoglu et al. 2010), travel motivation in particular (Gountas and Gountas 2000) and travel experience (Allen et al. 2002).

Respondents were asked to rate the 18 terminal values on a five-point Likert scale that varied from not important (1) to very important (5). Although the original scale used by Rokeach (1973) was a ranking scale, the use of rating scale was recommended by many authors as it forces respondents to indicate differences where none may actually exist and most people cannot adequately evaluate more than a few items (Tarka and Rutkowski 2015). Rating scales have more useful statistical properties (Reynolds and Jelly 1980; Watkins 2006), they are easier to administer (Watkins 2006), no information is lost due to the ordering process (Mehmetoglu et al. 2010), longer lists of values can be used, and respondents are not forced to discriminate among equally important values (Schwartz 1994).

For the destination attributes, 22 items were adapted from the scale used by Baloglu (2001) on a five-point Likert scale. Destination loyalty was measured using four statements that were adapted from Zeithaml et al. (1996) that reflect recommendation of the destination and future intentions to revisit it. Finally, the personal information section included questions related to gender, age, marital status, income, education and employment.

Validity and reliability of research constructs

To examine the convergent validity of research constructs, exploratory factor analysis was used with principal component analysis with Varimax rotation. AVE for the variables quality of the tourism experience, terminal instrumental values, destination attributes, and behavioral intentions exceeded 50%. Four factors were obtained for the quality of the tourism experience and their factor loadings exceeded 0.5. The first factor was *hedonics* and included items related to doing something memorable, doing something I really want, providing a lifetime experience,

Table 27.1 Demographic profiles of respondents

Age		*Education*	
18–34	128	High school or less	3
35–49	4	College	127
Missing	3	Graduate school	2
Total	135	Missing	3
		Total	135
Gender		*Income*	
Male	53	Under $25,000	74
Female	78	$25,000–$34,999	19
Missing	4	$35,000–$49,999	4
Total	135	$50,000–$74, 999	0
		$75,000–$99,999	1
		$100,000 or more	1
		Missing	36
		Total	135
Marital status		*Employment*	
Single	127	Employed	14
Married	4	Self-employed	6
Other	1	Unemployed	5
Missing	3	Retired	0
Total	135	Student	97
		Missing	13
		Total	135

fun and novelty. The second factor, *involvement*, included being involved, element of choice, sense of control, being educated, and importance and being taken seriously. The third factor, *thrill*, included items related to thrill, escape, stirring imagination, and adventure. The fourth factor, *peace of mind*, included comfort, safe property, and feeling relaxed and secure. The Cronbach alpha coefficients for these dimensions exceeded 74% except for the thrill dimension for which the alpha coefficient was 61%.

AVE for terminal personal values was 54% and the iterations resulted in three factors. The first factor, *excitement value*, included two items: excitement and accomplishment. The second factor, *security*, included the items related to comfort, world of peace, world of beauty, freedom, happiness, inner harmony and pleasure. The third item, *relations with self and others*, included items related to equality, family security, maturity, national security, salvation, self-respect, friendship, and wisdom. Alpha coefficients for security and relations with self and others exceeded 80% and that for excitement value was 60%.

AVE for destination attributes was 63.77% and iterations resulted in four factors. Two items, *nightlife* and the *availability of documents* were eliminated because of cross-loadings. *Modern vehicles* had low factor loadings and was also eliminated from the analysis. The first factor, *hygiene factors*, included the items hygiene, infrastructure, personal safety, experienced providers, and service providers keeping promises. The alpha coefficient for this item was 81% and when experienced providers was removed the alpha coefficient became 82%. The second factor, *scenery*, included the items friendly people, cultural attractions, historical attractions, and beautiful scenery. The third item, *food*, included two items related to food and accommodation. The fourth item, *service*, included helping people, prompt response, information about local entertainment, service right the first time, friendly providers, understanding needs, and friendly relations. Alpha coefficients for these four dimensions exceeded 70%.

Finally, AVE for behavioral intentions reached 73%. The items were: having Egypt as the first destination to visit, recommendation to friends, advising others to visit, and future intentions to visit. All factor loadings exceeded 75% and the alpha coefficient reached 87%.

Cluster analysis

The six-stage model-building approach recommended by Hair et al. (1998) was used. The cluster variate was decided to be the personal values. Destination attributes, quality of the tourism experience, and re-visitation intentions were used to compare objects in the cluster analysis. Then, eight univariate outliers were eliminated from the analysis. The Mahalanobis test of distance was used to detect multivariate outliers and one respondent was eliminated. Thus, the number of observations after deleting all outliers is 126.

The distance measure of similarity selected was the squared Euclidean distance. Variance inflation factors (VIF) was used to measure the degree of linear association of the different variables (Meyers et al. 2006). VIFs of the variables included were less than ten, indicating absence of multicollinearity (Norusis 1990).

Given the small sample size, the hierarchical cluster analysis is recommended (Norusis 1990). Ward's method was selected as the clustering algorithm. It measures the distance between two clusters as the sum of squares between the two clusters summed over all variables (Hair et al. 1998). Three clusters were recommended by the SPSS program. Table 27.2 depicts the demographic profiles of the three clusters.

Three types of tests were performed on the resulting cluster data. First, variable means were calculated in each cluster. Second, ANOVA was performed to examine differences among research variables in the three clusters. Third, Scheffe's post hoc test was undertaken to examine significant differences among each pair of clusters. The results of these tests are summarized in Table 28.3.

The table clearly demonstrates significant differences between groups in the three value domains (harmony, security and excite, $p < .000$). In addition, significant differences between groups were reported with respect to hedonics ($p < .001$), involvement ($p < .000$), peace of mind

Table 27.2 Demographic profiles of clusters

Cluster	*Gender*		*Age*		*Education*			*Marital status*			*Employment*				*Income*			
	M	*F*	*1*	*2*	*1*	*2*	*3*	*1*	*2*	*3*	*1*	*2*	*3*	*4*	*Less than 25000*	*25000 to 34999*	*35000 to 49999*	*More than 100000*
1 n = 30	10	19	28	1	1	1	1	1	2		1	2	0	25	16	2	1	0
2 n = 61	28	30	58	1	5	5	5	5	1		5	0	3	45	37	10	1	0
3 n = 35	9	26	33	2	7	7	7	7	1	1	7	2	1	24	17	7	1	1
Total	47	75	119	4	13	13	13	13	3	1	13	4	4	94	70	19	3	1

Table 27.3 Summary of mean values of variable means in the three clusters

Cluster		*Intent*	*Hedonics*	*Involve*	*Thrill*	*Peace of mind*	*Harmony*	*Security*	*Excite value*	*Hygiene*	*Scenery*	*Service*	*Food*
		$F = 2.557$ $p < .082$	$F = .79$ $p < .001$	$F = .923$ $p < .000$	$F = 1.259$ $p < .288$	$F = 6.009$ $p < .003$	$F = 49.885$ $p < .000$	$F = 158.4$ $p < .000$	$F = 158.4$ $p < .000$	$F = .751$ $p < .474$	$F = .844$ $p < .000$	$F = 4.844$ $p < .009$	$F = 7.98$ $p < .001$
1 n = 30	Mean	3.8000	4.5067	3.8944	3.5083	4.375	4.4898	4.6249	3.7192	3.3295	4.4259	3.9376	3.5167
2 n = 61	Mean	3.9508	4.5963	4.1503	3.7263	4.3657	4.5802	4.6776	4.7541*	3.5708	4.4928	4.1450	3.9884
3 n = 35	Mean	3.5571	4.2078**	3.6091***	3.5571	3.966**	3.7426**	3.7955**	3.6736***	3.5734	4.0214****	3.7464***	3.4143
Total n = 126	Mean	3.8056	4.4671	3.9390	3.6274	4.2569	4.3260	4.4200	4.2075	3.5140	4.3459	3.9849	3.7166

*significantly higher than the other two clusters **significantly lower than the other two clusters ***significantly lower than cluster 2 ****significantly lower than cluster 1

($p < .003$), scenery ($p < .000$), and food ($p < .001$). No significant differences were reported in the thrill and hygiene factors.

The first cluster included respondents who had a high rating for security and the highest ratings for peace of mind. The *balanced cluster* (n = 30) can be described as young, single, female-dominant, low-income students. They come next to the second cluster in many aspects such as hedonics, involvement, thrill, relations, security, excite, hygiene, scenery, service, food, and loyalty.

The second cluster included respondents who had the highest ratings for excitement, and such ratings were significantly different from the other two clusters. The *thrill-seeking cluster (n = 61)* included an almost equal proportion of males and females, who are college students below the age of 25. In total, 37 respondents had an income level of lower than $25,000 and 10 of them had an income between $25,000 and $34,999. This group had the highest ratings in excite values, harmony, hedonics, involvement, and thrill. They had higher ratings for the destination attributes of scenery and food. Their loyalty intentions were the highest although only significant at $p < .08$.

Cluster 3 included respondents who rated lowest on all three personal value domains, as well as hedonics, involvement, thrill, security scenery, and intentions. The *no-thrill* cluster (n = 35) was mainly single college graduates below the age of 25, female dominant, seven were employed.

Discussion

The purpose of this research is to examine the various psychographic segments of Chinese students who visit Egypt and to examine inter segment differences in perceived destination attributes, importance ratings of the quality of the tourism experience and re-visitation intentions. A sample was selected from Chinese students studying the Arabic language at two Egyptian universities. Factor analysis revealed the existence of three value domains: harmony, security, and excitement.

The factor analysis for the terminal values reveals a number of important points to discuss. First, the factors obtained from the factor analysis of personal values resemble to some extent those obtained by some researchers. For example, the factor excitement was reported by a number of researchers as a distinct value domain (e.g., Kamakura and Novak 1992; Muller 1991). Security was also a distinct domain reported by many researchers (e.g., Erdem et al. 1999; Muller 1991; Schwartz and Bilsky 1987). Madrigal and Kahle (1994) report enjoyment and achievement as two separate domains. Conversely, Daghfous et al. (1999) report a conceptualization of values including accomplishment on one hand, and a combination of hedonism and empathy on the other. Priem et al. (2000) reported a value domain which they called achievement versus happiness which encompasses excitement. It also contradicts with the findings of Li and Cai (2012) for Chinese tourists who reported one factor which they called external values including security and excitement. The harmony domain includes equality, family security, maturity, national security, salvation, self-respect, friendship, and wisdom. This factor reflects two types of relationships: relationship with the self-reflected in wisdom, salvation, self-respect, and maturity and warm relationship with others reflected in friendship, family security and national security. This conceptualization contradicts with Homer and Kahle (1988) who reported two dimensions of value: an external values dimension which includes sense of belonging, being well-respected, security, and warm relationships with others and an internal dimension with high loadings for self-fulfillment, sense of accomplishment, and self-respect. This means that for Chinese respondents included in the sample, values related to the inner self are highly related to those related to others. These contradictions in research findings reflect the differences between western and eastern cultures in determining identity. The independent construal of the self means that the inner self is most significant in regulating behavior. The interdependent construal of the self means that one's identity lies in one's familial, cultural, professional, and social relationships (Markus and Kitayama 1991). Madrigal and Kahle (1994) also explain inconsistencies in results of factor analysis as a result of contextuality of the underlying structure of the factors (Madrigal and Kahle 1994).

The cluster analysis revealed the existence of three clusters with significant intersegment differences in most research variables. The *balanced* cluster had high ratings for security and the highest ratings for peace of mind. They come next to the second cluster in many aspects such as hedonics, involvement, thrill, relations, excite, hygiene, scenery, service, food, and loyalty.

The *thrill-seeking cluster* had the highest ratings for excitement and such ratings were significantly different from the other two clusters. This group had the highest ratings in harmony, hedonics, involvement, thrill, scenery, and food. This group reflects to some extent the hedonist group reported in many studies (e.g., Daghfous et al. 1999) as they place high importance on excitement, hedonics, involvement and thrill of the tourism experience. It should be noted that although this group reported the highest loyalty ratings, the effect was not significant. This finding contradicts with the findings of Pitts and Woodside (1986) who reported different ratings of loyalty for different value-based segments.

Cluster 3 included respondents who rated lowest on all three personal value domains, as well as hedonics, involvement, thrill, security scenery and intentions. The *no-thrill* (n = 35) cluster was mainly single college graduates below the age of 25 and were mostly females.

The cluster analysis findings mean that the experiential aspects of the tourism experience cannot be treated as one dimension. In other words, distinct value-based tourist segments have different preferences for different aspects of the tourism experience. The balanced cluster places high importance on peace of mind, while the thrill-seekers rate hedonism, involvement, and thrill in their tourism experience. The no-thrill segment seems to underrate the various aspects of the tourism experience. This segment might place more importance on utilitarian aspects of the visit or it might include the thrifty tourists who place less importance on experiential aspects. More research is needed in this area.

Although the thrill-seeking segment had the highest score on loyalty intentions, yet the difference was statistically significant at $p < .08$. Many authors noted loyalty is created when there is congruency between the personal values and the tourist attributes (e.g., Zhang and Peng 2014). Congruity between values and destination attributes was not examined in this research but it provides a good opportunity for future research.

Research implications

This research has many academic and practical implications. Academically, it highlights the importance of some personal values which are highly experiential in nature such as excitement. It thus provides support for Holbrook and Hirschman (1982) that leisure activities greatly lend themselves to experiential consumption. But the findings also support the importance of peace of mind for tourists who place high importance on security. The research also adds to the accumulated research on the student market as a distinct segment which might have different value priorities than other markets.

From a practical view point, the research offers practitioners some guidance in designing marketing strategies. With respect to segmentation and targeting, the findings imply that the use of value-based segmentation is a worthwhile endeavor. Value-based segments do have distinct preferences for various experiential aspects and they also vary in their evaluation of destination attributes and re-visitation intentions.

References

Allen, M. W. (2008) "The Direct And Indirect Influences of Human Values on Consumer Choices," Unpublished Doctoral thesis, Victoria University of Wellington, available online at: http://researcharchive.vuw.ac.nz/xmlui/bitstream/handle/10063/316/thesis.pdf?sequence=2 (accessed June 12, 2016).

Allen, M. W., Hung Ng, S., and Wilson, M. (2002) "A Functional Approach to Instrumental And Terminal Values And The Value-Attitude-Behavior System of Consumer Choice," *European Journal of Marketing* 36(1/2), 111–135.

Allen, M. W., Ng, S. H., Ikeda, K. I., Jawan, J. A., Sufi, A. H., Wilson, M., and Yang, K. S. (2007) "Two Decades of Change in Cultural Values and Economic Development in Eight East Asian And Pacific Island Nations," *Journal of Cross-Cultural Psychology* 38(3), 247–269.

Andreu, L., Kozak, M., Avci, N., and Cifter, N. (2006) "Market Segmentation by Motivations to Travel: British Tourists Visiting Turkey," *Journal of Travel and Tourism Marketing* 19(1), 1–14.

Ayad, T.H., and Shujun, Y. (2012) "Travel Motivations of Chinese Tourists to Egypt," International Conference on Trade, Tourism and Management (ICTTM 2012) December 21–22, Bangkok (Thailand).

Babin, B. J., and Kim, K. (2001) "International Students' Travel Behavior: A Model of The Travel-related Consumer Dissatisfaction Process," *Journal of Travel and Tourism Marketing* 10(1), 93–106.

Baloglu, S. (2001) "Image Variations of Turkey by Familiarity Index: Informational And Experiential Dimensions," *Tourism Management* 22(2), 127–133.

Baloglu, S., and Uysal, M. (1996) "Market Segments of Push And Pull Motivations: A Canonical Correlation Approach," *International Journal of Contemporary Hospitality Management* 8(3), 32–38.

Bosnjak, M., Sirgy, M. J., Hellriegel, S., and Maurer, O. (2011) "Postvisit Destination Loyalty Judgments Developing And Testing a Comprehensive Congruity Model," *Journal of Travel Research* 50(5), 496–508.

Carr, N. (1998) "The Young Tourist: A Case of Neglected Research," *Progress in Tourism and Hospitality Research* 4(4), 307–318.

Chadee, D. D., and Cutler, J. (1996) "Insights into International Travel by Students," *Journal of Travel Research* 35(2), 75–80.

Chen, C. F., and Chen, F. S. (2010) "Experience Quality, Perceived Value, Satisfaction And Behavioral Intentions for Heritage Tourists," *Tourism Management* 31(1), 29–35.

Cui, G., and Liu, Q. (2001) "Executive Insights: Emerging Market Segments in a Transitional Economy: A Study of Urban Consumers in China," *Journal of International Marketing* 9(1), 84–106.

Daghfous, N., Petrof, J. V., and Pons, F. (1999) "Values And Adoption of Innovations: A Cross-Cultural Study," *Journal of Consumer Marketing* 16(4), 314–331.

Denys, V., and Mendes, J. (2014) "Consumption Values And Destination Evaluation in Destination Decision Making," *Journal of Spatial and Organizational Dynamics* 2(1), 4–22.

Devesa, M., Laguna, M., and Palacios, A. (2010) "The Role of Motivation in Visitor Satisfaction: Empirical Evidence in Rural Tourism," *Tourism Management* 31(4), 547–552.

Egri, C. P., and Ralston, D. A. (2004) "Generation Cohorts And Personal Values: A Comparison of China And The United States," *Organization Science* 15(2), 210–220.

Erdem, O., Oumlil, A. B., and Tuncalp, S. (1999) "Consumer Values And Importance of Store Attributes," *International Journal of Retail and Distribution Management* 27(4), 137–144.

Fischer, R., and Schwartz, S. (2011) "Whence Differences in Value Priorities? Individual, Cultural, or Artifactual Sources," *Journal of Cross-Cultural Psychology* 42(7), 1127–1144.

Gardiner, S., King, B., and Wilkins, H. (2013) "The Travel Behaviours of International Students Nationality-based Constraints And Opportunities" *Journal of Vacation Marketing* 19(4), 287–299.

Gountas, J. Y., and Gountas, S. C. (2000). A new psychographic segmentation method using Jungian MBTI variables in the tourism industry. *Tourism Analysis*, 5(2–3), 151–156.

Guthrie, D. (2012). *China And Globalization: The Social, Economic And Political Transformation of The Chinese society*, New York: Routledge.

Hair, J. F., Black, W. C., Babin, B. J., Anderson, R. E., and Tatham, R. L. (2013). *Multivariate Data Analysis* (7th edn). New York: Pearson.

Hofstede, G. (1983) "National Cultures in Four Dimensions: A Research-based Theory of Cultural Differences Among Nations," *International Studies of Management and Organization* 13(1–2), 46–74.

Holbrook, M. B., and Hirschman, E. C. (1982) "The Experiential Aspects of Consumption: Consumer Fantasies, Feelings, And Fun," *Journal of Consumer Research* 9(2), 132–140.
Homer, P.M., and Kahle, L. R. (1988) "A Structural Equation Test Of The Value-attitude-Behavior Hierarchy," *Journal of Personality and Social Psychology* 54(4), 63–646.
Jang, S., and Cai, L. A. (2002) "Travel Motivations and Destination Choice: A Study of British Outbound Market," *Journal of Travel and Tourism Marketing* 13(3), 111–133.
Jewell, B., and Crotts, J. C. (2002) "Adding Psychological Value to Heritage Tourism Experiences," *Journal of Travel and Tourism Marketing* 11(4), 13–28.
Jiang, L., Phillips, P. C., and Yu, J. (2014) "A New Hedonic Regression for Real Estate Prices Applied to the Singapore Residential Market," Working Paper.
Kamakura, W. A., and Novak, T. P. (1992) "Value-system Segmentation: Exploring The Meaning of LOV," *Journal of Consumer Research* 19(1), 119–132.
Kao, Y. F., Huang, L. S., and Wu, C. H. (2008) "Effects of Theatrical Elements on Experiential Quality And Loyalty Intentions for Theme Parks," *Asia Pacific Journal of Tourism Research* 13(2), 163–174.
Kim, J. H., Ritchie, J. B., and McCormick, B. (2010) "Development of a Scale to Measure Memorable Tourism Experiences," *Journal of Travel Research* 51(1), 12–25.
Kitayama, S., and Park, J. (2010) "Cultural Neuroscience of The Self: Understanding The Social Grounding of The Brain", *Social cognitive and affective neuroscience* 5(2-3), 111–129.
Kristiansen, C. M. (1985) "Social Desirability And The Rokeach Value Survey," *The Journal of social psychology* 125(3), 399–400.
Lages, L. F., and Fernandes, J. C. (2005) "The SERPVAL Scale: A Multi-Item Instrument for Measuring Service Personal Values," *Journal of Business Research* 58(11), 1562–1572.
Lau, S. (1988) "The Value Orientations of Chinese University Students in Hong Kong," *International Journal of Psychology* 23(1-6), 583–596.
Lau, S., and Wong, A. K. (1992) "Value and Sex-Role Orientation of Chinese Adolescents," *International Journal of Psychology* 27(1), 3–17.
Lee, K. C. (1991) "The Problem of Appropriateness of The Rokeach Value Survey in Korea," *International Journal of Psychology* 26(3), 299–310.
Lehto, X. Y., Jang, S. S., Achana, F. T., and O'Leary, J. T. (2008) "Exploring Tourism Experience Sought: A Cohort Comparison of Baby Boomers and the Silent Generation," *Journal of Vacation Marketing* 14(3), 237–252.
Li, M., and Cai, L. A. (2012) "The Effects of Personal Values on Travel Motivation and Behavioral Intention," *Journal of Travel Research* 51(4), 473–487.
Liao, D. (2012) "Travel Motivations of Chinese Students in The United States: A Case Study of Chinese Students in Kent University," *Hospitality and Tourism Management* 3(2), 336–445.
Liu, G. (2008). "Travel Behavior and Expenditure Patterns of The Chinese University Student and the Associated Visiting Friends and Relatives (VFRs)Markets in New Zealand" (unpublished doctoral dissertation). Hamilton, New Zealand: The University of Waikato.
Lowe, A. C.-T., and Corkindale, D. R. (1998) "Differences in "Cultural Values" And Their Effects on Responses to Marketing Stimuli: A Cross-cultural Study between Australians and Chinese from The People's Republic of China," *European Journal of Marketing* 32(9/10), 843–867.
Markus, H. R., and Kitayama, S. (1991) "Culture and The Self: Implications for Cognition, Emotion, And Motivation," *Psychological Review* 98(2), 224–253.
Madrigal, R., and Kahle, L. R. (1994) "Predicting Vacation Activity Preferences on The Basis of Value-System Segmentation," *Journal of Travel Research* 32(3), 22–28.
McCleary, K. W., and Choi, B. M. (1999) "Personal Values as a Base for Segmenting International Markets," *Tourism Analysis* 4(1), 1–17.
Mehmetoglu, M., Hines, K., Graumann, C., and Greibrokk, J. (2010) "The Relationship between Personal Values and Tourism Behavior: A Segmentation Approach," *Journal of Vacation Marketing* 16(1), 17–27.
Meyers, L. S., Gamst, G., and Guarino, A. J. (2006) *Applied multivariate research: Design and interpretation*. Sage.
Muller, T. (1991) "Using Personal Values to Define Segments in an International Tourism Market," *International Marketing Review* 8(1), 57–70.
Ng, S. H., Hossain, A. B. M. A., Ball, P., Bond, M. H., Hayashi, K., Lim, S. P., and Yang, K. S. (1982) "Human Values in Nine Countries," *Diversity and Unity in Cross-Cultural Psychology* 17, 169–172.
Norusis, M. J. (1990) *SPSS: Advanced Statistics User's Guide*, Chicago: SPSS.
Otto, J. E., and Ritchie, J. B. (1996) "The Service Experience in Tourism," *Tourism Management* 17(3), 165–174.

Park, H. J., and Rabolt, N. J. (2009) "Cultural Value, Consumption Value, And Global Brand Image: A Cross-national Study," *Psychology and Marketing* 26(8), 714–735.
Phau, I., Quintal, V., and Shanka, T. (2014) "Examining a Consumption Values Theory Approach of Young Tourists toward Destination Choice Intentions," *International Journal of Culture, Tourism and Hospitality Research* 8(2), 125–139.
Pine, B. J., and Gilmore, J. H. (1998) "Welcome to The Experience Economy," *Harvard Business Review* 76, 97–105.
Pitts, R., and Woodside, A. (1986) "Personal Values and Travel Decisions," *Journal of Travel Research* 25, 20–25.
Pizam, A., and Calantone, R. (1987) "Beyond Psychographics – Values as Determinants of Tourist Behavior," *International Journal of Hospitality Management* 6(3), 177–181.
Prayag, G., and Hosany, S. (2014) "When Middle East Meets West: Understanding The Motives and Perceptions of Young Tourists from United Arab Emirates," *Tourism Management* 40, 35–45.
Priem, R. L., Love, L. G., and Shaffer, M. (2000) "Industrialization and Values Evolution: The Case of Hong Kong and Guangzhou, China," *Asia Pacific Journal of Management* 17(3), 473–492.
Ramasamy, B., Au, A., and Yeung, M. (2010) "Managing Chinese Consumers' Value Profiles: A Comparison between Shanghai and Hong Kong," *Cross Cultural Management: An International Journal* 17(3), 257–267.
Reynolds, T. J., and Jolly, J. P. (1980) "Measuring Personal Values: An Evaluation of Alternative Methods," *Journal of Marketing Research* 17, 531–536.
Ritchie, J. R. B., Tung, V. W. S., and Ritchie, R. J. B. (2011) "Tourism Experience Management Research: Emergence, Evolution and Future Directions," *International Journal of Contemporary Hospitality Management* 23(4), 419–438.
Rokeach, M. (1973) *The Nature of Values*. New York: Free Press.
Ruane, S., and Quinn, D. (2012) "The Holiday Experience and Personal Values: An Irish Case Study," THRIC, available online at: http://arrow.dit.ie/tfschmtcon/42/ (accessed June 30, 2016).
Rudowicz, E., and Kitto, J. (1994) "Empirical investigation into the value systems of Hong Kong Chinese students." *Psychological Reports*.
Schwartz, S. H. (1994) "Are There Universal Aspects in The Structure and Contents of Human values?" *Journal of Social Issues* 50(4), 19–45.
Schwartz, S. H., and Bilsky, W. (1987) "Toward A Universal Psychological Structure of Human Values," *Journal of Personality and Social Psychology* 53, 550–556.
Sheth, J. N., Newman, B. I., and Gross, B. L. (1991) "Why We Buy What We Buy: A Theory of Consumption Values," *Journal of Business Research* 22(2), 159–170.
Sin, L. Y. M., and Yau, O. H. M. (2001) "Female Role Orientation and Consumption Values: Some Evidence from Mainland China," *Journal of International Consumer Marketing* 13(2), 49–75.
Stout, D. A., Martin, D. G., and Zhang, L. (1994) "Changes in Consumption Values Reflected in Chinese Newspaper Advertising," *Atlantic Journal of Communication* 2(2), 146–168.
Tarka, P. and Rutkowski, P. I. (2015) "Scale for testing hedonic-consumerism values," in Andreani J.-C., *Proceedings of the International Marketing Trends Conference*, January 23–24.
Tse, D. K., Belk, R. W., and Nan Zhou (1989) "Becoming a Consumer Society: A longitudinal and Cross-cultural Content Analysis of Print Ads from Hong Kong, The People's Republic of China, And Taiwan," *Journal of Consumer Research* 15(4), 457–472.
Unger, L. S., and Kernan, J. B. (1983) "On The Meaning of Leisure: An Investigation of Some Determinants of the Subjective Experience," *Journal of Consumer Research* 9(4), 381–392.
Verplanken, B., and Holland, R. W. (2002) "Motivated Decision Making: Effects of Activation and Self-centrality of Values On Choices and Behavior," *Journal of Personality and Social Psychology* 82(3), 434–447.
Vinson, D., Scott, J., and Lamont, L. (1977) "The Role of Personal Values in Marketing and Consumer Behavior," *Journal of Marketing* 41(2), 44–50.
Wang, C. L., and Lin, X. (2009) "Migration of Chinese Consumption Values: Traditions, Modernization and Cultural Renaissance," *Journal of Business Ethics* 88(3), 399–409.
Watkins, L. (2006). Culture, Values and Japanese Tourism Behavior (Doctoral dissertation, University of Otago).
Wei, R. (1997) "Emerging Lifestyles in China and Consequences for Perception of Advertising, Buying Behavior and Consumption Preferences," *International Journal of Advertising* 16(4), 261–275.
Wei, R., and Pan, Z. (1999) "Mass Media and Consumerist Values in The People's Republic of China," *International Journal of Public Opinion Research* 11(1), 76–97.
Williams, A. (2006) "Tourism and Hospitality Marketing: Fantasy, Feeling and Fun," International Journal of Contemporary Hospitality Management 18(6), 482–495.

Xiao, G., and Kim, J. O. (2009) "The Investigation of Chinese Consumer Values, Consumption Values, Life Satisfaction, And Consumption Behaviors," *Psychology and Marketing* 26(7), 610–624.
Yau, O. H. M. (1994). *Consumer Behavior in China: Customer Satisfaction and Cultural Values*, New York: Routledge.
Zeithaml, V. A., Berry, L. L., and Parasuraman, A. (1996) "The Behavioral Consequences of Service Quality," *The Journal of Marketing*, 60, 31–46.
Zeng, G., and Go, F. (2013). "Evolution of middle-class Chinese outbound travel preferences: an international perspective," *Tourism Economics*, 19(2), 231–243.
Zhang, Y., and Peng, Y. (2014). "Understanding travel motivations of Chinese tourists visiting Cairns, Australia," *Journal of Hospitality and Tourism Management*, 21, 44–53.

Further readings

Arlt, W.G. (2006). *Chinese Outbound Tourism*, New York: Routledge.
Crompton, J. L. (1979) "Motivations for Pleasure Vacations," *Annals of Tourism Research* 4, 408–424.
Hirschman, E. C. (1984) "Experience Seeking: A Subjectivist Perspective of Consumption," *Journal of Business Research* 12(1), 115–136.
Feather, N. T. (1986) "Cross-cultural Studies with The Rokeach Value Survey: Flinders Program of Research on Values," *Australian Journal of Psychology* 38(3), 269–283.
Tai, S. H. (2008) "Relationship Between the Personal Values and Shopping Orientation of Chinese Consumers," *Asia Pacific Journal of Marketing and Logistics* 20(4), 381–395.
Uriely, N. (2005) "The Tourist Experience: Conceptual Developments," *Annals of Tourism Research* 32(1), 199–216.
Vargo, S.L., and Lusch, R.F (2004) "Evolving to a New Dominant Logic for Marketing," Journal of Marketing 68, 1–17.
Verhoef, P. C., Lemon, K. N., Parasuraman, A., Roggeveen, A., Tsiros, M., and Schlesinger, L. A. (2009) "Customer Experience Creation: Determinants, Dynamics and Management Strategies," *Journal of Retailing* 85(1), 31–41.
Watkins, L., and Gnoth, J. (2005) "Methodological Issues in Using Kahle's List of Values Scale for Japanese Tourism Behavior," *Journal of Vacation Marketing* 11(3), 225–233.
Xu, J., and Chan, A. (2010) "Service Experience and Package Tours," *Asia Pacific Journal of Tourism Research* 15(2), 177–194.

Part V
Sustainability and the environment

28

Corporate social responsibility and sustainability in tourism

Huong Ha and Hui Shan Loh

Introduction

Corporate Social Responsibility (CSR) has been an on-going and pressing topic of debates for the past several decades. Many corporations have implemented different CSR initiatives, and many of CSR practices have been incorporated into corporations' business strategies (Pearce and Doh, 2005). Yet, insufficient research studies have been done with regards to the links between CSR and sustainability in the context of the tourism industry.

In his first publication about CSR, Bowen (1953) explained that CSR should be one of the obligations of the business sector to the communities and the society at large. Davis (1960) suggested that the business sector should be responsible for their business decisions and actions which affect the society, and share part of their economic gain to the society. Other scholars have expanded the scope of CSR to include corporations' legal and environmental responsibilities (McGuire, 1963; Davis, 1967; Carroll, 1991, Lantos, 2002; Boeger, Murray and Villiers, 2008; Carroll and Buchholtz, 2009; Benoit-Moreau and Parguel, 2011; Asaf, Josiassen and Cvelbar, 2012; Oberseder et al., 2014; Susnienė and Žostautiene, 2016). Lee and Heo (2009), and Manaktola and Jauhari (2007) studied how CSR initiatives influence customers. Lee and Park (2009) examined the impact of CSR on a corporation's financial performance.

Carroll (1991) classified CSR into four categories: economic, legal, ethical and philanthropic; whereas other authors discussed many CSR domains related to consumers, employees, suppliers, shareholders, the environment, the community and society (Brunk, 2010; Vurro and Perrini, 2011; Oberseder et al., 2014; Ferrell, Ferrell and Sawayda, 2014). However, given the severe impact of climate change and environmental degradation on the hotel industry, this chapter will focus on the environmental domain. In addition, Cheung et al. (2009) and Mazurkiewicz (n.d.) explained that CSR related to environment could provide corporations with both internal drivers, including relevant environmental rules, policies and practices, and external drivers, including environmentally friendly corporate image. Further, the positive effects of environmental CSR on consumers' behaviour have been discussed by many authors, such as Laroche et al. (2001) and Chen (2010). Laroche et al. (2001) found that the purchasing intention of consumers who pursued an ecologically friendly lifestyle was strongly associated with environmentally friendly

CSR activities practised by corporations. Lastly, Chen (2010) also found that the green corporate image had a positive effect on consumers' satisfaction.

The objective of this chapter is to discuss (i) the concepts of CSR and sustainability and their linkages, and (ii) the benefits of and arguments against CSR. This chapter also includes a case study to demonstrate how the hotels, an important sector of the tourism industry, around the world have practised CSR and the outcomes of such CSR practices. Secondary data were gathered from the review of academic and non-academic literature regarding CSR and environmental sustainability.

Given the fact that the tourism industry is one of the most affected industries by the impact of climate change and the challenges regarding environmental sustainability, this chapter is significant as it provides better insights for further research on CSR and sustainability, and the impacts of CSR on the operations of the hotel industry. It also contributes to the body of knowledge of an interdisciplinary topic including CSR, sustainability and consumer behaviour in the context of the tourism industry.

Concepts of corporate social responsibility (CSR)

Various concepts of CSR have been discussed and debated in the past several decades. From the socioeconomic view, CSR refers to the activities executed by corporations which can produce positive socio-cultural impacts and the positive effects on the natural environment (Carroll and Shabana, 2010; Ha, 2012). CSR, or *responsible business conduct* (RBC) (OECD, 2011) refers to corporation's activities and practices which go beyond legal and regulatory requirements, instead of focusing only on profit maximisation, in order to contribute to community and social development (McShane et al., 2015). The business case for CSR focuses on activities to improve employee welfare, environmental management, executive payment (Desrochers, 2009), and voluntary industry self-regulation (Matten and Crane, 2005; Matten and Moon, 2008). CSR also refers to trusteeship (Chakrabarty 2011), and a corporation's duty to allocate resources to improve the benefits of various groups of stakeholders, not only shareholders (Husted, 2014). Overall, corporations should be involved in activities which can improve social welfare and well-being and community development.

Ramasamy and Yeung (2009) commented that CSR is often discussed by business leaders with regard to mitigating environmental problems and building good 'relationships with stakeholders for the common good' (p. 44). Lee et al. (2011) explained that the overall performance of the organisation lies with the implementation of 'good ethics' and the awareness of the involved stakeholders in being 'socially responsible' (p. 97). In other words, corporations would use ethical codes (or code of conduct) to encourage stakeholders to carry out CSR activities (Lee et al., 2011). This, in return, will contribute to developing corporations' competitive advantages and increase employee motivation and morale because the involved stakeholders will receive the message of being socially responsible, and work together to further establish an ethical or socially responsible image of the corporations. There has been an increase in the consciousness towards socially and ethical behaviour, resulting in more organisations implementing CSR (Ramasamy and Yeung, 2009). Slaper and Hall (2011) added that the triple bottom line concept has allowed corporations to accurately evaluate their sustainability performance.

To make it simple, CSR is a set of activities planned and voluntarily implemented by corporations in order to address socio-cultural and environmental issues which can generate benefits for corporations and create positive impacts on the society as a whole (Collings, 2003). According to Carroll (1998, 2008), corporations should demonstrate their CSR on four aspects: economic, legal, ethical and philanthropy. Lee et al. (2011) also concurred that corporations should consider these CSR aspects. However, many corporations view legal responsibility as a compulsory act and not an optional one.

Öberseder et al. (2014) defined a corporation with CSR as a socially responsible company which can integrate social and environmental related activities in 'its core business activities and acts responsibly towards its employees, its customers, the environment, its suppliers, the local community, its shareholders and society' (p. 103). They classified CSR activities into seven domains, namely 'employees, customers, environment, suppliers, the local community, shareholders, and society' (Öberseder et al., 2014, p. 103). The CSR employee domain includes working conditions at the work place, fair treatment, avoiding practising discrimination and/or favouritism, paying fair remuneration, etc. (Gond et al., 2010). The CSR customer domain focuses on issues associated with product quality, fair prices, provision of sufficient information, compliance with product labelling, and product safety (Lee and Heo, 2009; Garcia de Leaniz and Rodriguez, 2015). The CSR environment domain focuses on addressing environmental problems, such as reduction of energy and water consumption, reduction of waste and CO_2 emissions (Laroche, Bergeron and Barbaro-Forleo, 2001). The CSR supplier domain aims to tackle issues of fair trade practices, code of conduct for suppliers, supplier selection and auditing and payment (Cheung et al., 2009). The CSR local community domain stresses the importance of employment creation, as well as contribution to the economy and community development (Öberseder et al., 2014). The CSR shareholder domain requires corporations be responsible for meeting the shareholders' needs, i.e. profits, dividends and share prices (Öberseder et al., 2014). Nevertheless, many hold the view that corporations should focus on business sustainability, long-term financial and non-financial success, and responsible investments. The final CSR domain focuses on the society at large, for example, do charity work for good causes, support social enterprises and social projects, support the disabled, the elderly, the minority, etc. (Öberseder et al., 2014).

The three pillars of sustainable development

Sustainable development is defined as 'development which meets the needs of the present without compromising the ability of future generations to meet their own needs' (World Commission on Environment and Development, 1987, p. 43). In other words, corporations must meet the needs of the current groups of stakeholders, and also the future generations given the current limited resources (Drexhage and Murphy, 2010). The three main pillars of sustainable development are economic, social and environmental pillars (Allen and Craig, 2016). The economic pillar of sustainable development focuses on activities which can help corporations create added values to improve their financial performance. As explained by Zabihollah Rezaee (cited in Thomson, 2016), sustainability is about 'creating the right balance of short- and long-term continuous improvement of both financial ESG (environmental, social and governance) and non-financial ESG sustainability performance' (para. 7). The social pillar incites corporations to take into consideration the impact of their activities on the communities and the society at large. These activities include programs to promote social inclusion, social fairness, community cohesion and development, etc. (Chan and Lee, 2008; Dempsey et al., 2009; Murphy, 2012; Missimer, 2013). The environmental pillar refers to activities which can contribute to protecting the environment and conserving natural resources (Holden and Linnerud, 2007; Allen, 2016).

For the purpose of this chapter, CSR activities aiming to achieve environmental sustainability will be the focus of the discussion. The argument is that environmental problems have posed great challenges to today's society (Shanga, Basil and Wymer, 2009). Consumers have become increasingly aware of the adverse impact of environmental related issues, such as global warming, climate change, insufficient energy and clean water (Barlow, 2008). Thus, corporations should focus

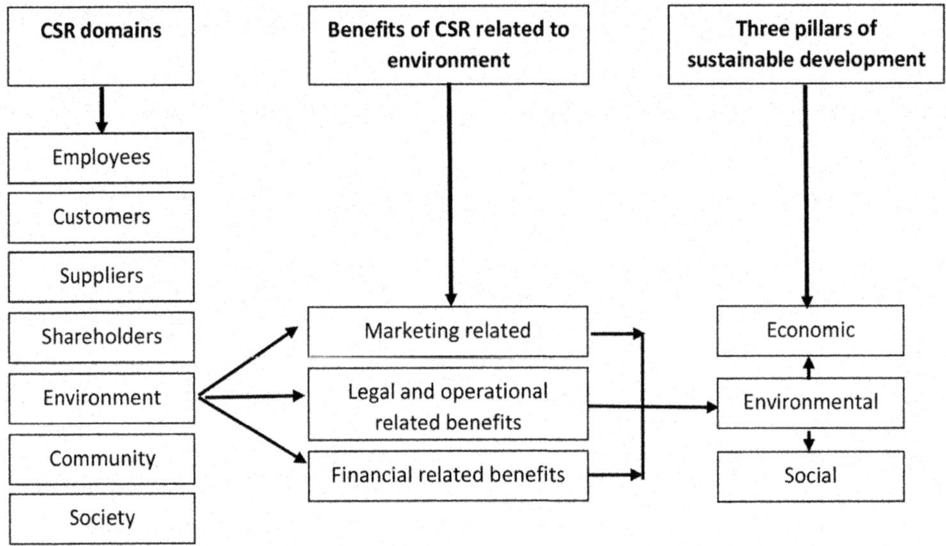

Figure 28.1 CSR domains, CSR benefits and the three pillars of sustainable development

on value creation for different groups of stakeholders, especially the environment (Carroll, 1998). Embarking on green, reuse and recycle projects to achieve environmental sustainability enables corporations, particularly those in the tourism industry, to improve their economic, social and environmental performance. In other words, corporations should go beyond the legal compliance to act ethically to all groups of stakeholders, especially the environment (Carroll and Shabana, 2010). The CSR environment domain discussed by Öberseder et al. (2014) is aligned with the three pillars of sustainability as shown in Figure 28.1.

Overall, corporations should seriously consider values, principles and strategies which go beyond profit maximisation or wealth accumulation for stockholders (Arnold and Valentin, 2013). Corporations should exercise 'broad self-restraint and altruism' in order to achieve both financial and non-financial objectives in a sustainable way (Windsor, 2006, p. 98).

Benefits of CSR

Benefits of implementation of CSR initiatives can be classified into three groups: (i) marketing related benefits, (ii) operational and legal related benefits, and (iii) financial related benefits. Yet, these benefits are related to one another and enable corporations achieve the three pillars of sustainable development.

First, marketing related benefits include better reputation, positive corporate image and public relations, increase in customer loyalty and positive customer perception of corporations. Many studies by Nielsen (2008), Valchos et al. (2009) and Öberseder et al. (2013) revealed that there has been an increase in consumers' interest in CSR. Consumers believe that corporations should engage in various social activities to meet the demands of different groups of stakeholders which would benefit them and the society at large (Nielsen, 2014). In addition, a number of empirical researchers demonstrated that consumers have considered CSR as one of the criteria to evaluate corporations and/or to make purchase decision since some consumers usually equate CSR with provision of better quality products and/or services (Green and Peloza, 2011; Öberseder et al., 2013).

CSR will also help corporations to improve customer satisfaction via better products and services (Galbreath, 2010).

In the context of the tourism industry, CSR can be considered as a competitive advantage which makes hotels with strong CSR focus superior to the competitors (Heikkurinen 2010), and helps to foster their identity and image (Balmer et al. 2007; Bravo et al. 2011). As explained by Heikkurinen (2010) and Martınez, Perez and Rodrıguez del Bosque (2014), tourism related organisations, such as hotels, which practised CSR could be perceived by consumers as responsible corporations (Heikkurinen, 2010). Perez and del Bosque (2014) stated that the implementation of CSR actually boosts 'corporate image' and 'customer loyalty' (p. 571), whereas others would involve 'values' (Ramasamy and Yeung, 2009, p. 44). The study by Park, Lee and Kim (2014) revealed that there was a direct and positive correlation between economic and legal CSR initiatives and corporate reputation. Economic success improves consumer expertise trust; whereas legal and ethical CSR initiatives positively impact integrity trust. In addition, philanthropic CSR activities did affect consumers' social benevolence trust in the corporations (Park et al., 2014). In other words, practice of CSR contributes to nurturing consumers' trust in the products and services of a corporation and the corporations itself (Castaldo et al., 2009). Trust would result in better relationships between consumers and corporations (Sirdeshmukh, Singh and Sabol, 2002; Pivato et al., 2008; Valchos et al., 2009).

Secondly, with regards to operational and legal related benefits, CSR can make corporations become more attractive employers by showing their commitment to improve employees' welfare and well-being (Gond et al., 2010). Such commitment also includes training and development to increase employees' skill level and job effectiveness (Riordan, Gatewood and Bill, 1997; Gond et al., 2010). Tourism related corporations, such as hotels and travel agencies which practise CSR will be able to guard themselves against the costs of non-compliance with legal requirements, i.e. CSR helps corporations 'ward off government regulation' (Carroll and Shabana, 2010, p. 89). If corporations exercise self-regulation by adopting codes of conduct, codes of ethics and self-disciplined standards as well as meet the stakeholders' expectations, government intervention can be minimised.

Also, business has a pool of human and physical resources which could be given opportunities to address social problems (Werner, 2009). Moreover, implementation of CSR can be considered as a proactive approach to plan, initiate and avoid problems which can reduce social and opportunity costs (Carroll and Buchholt, 2009). Given the challenges of climate change and other environmental problems, if corporations proactively implement CSR sustainability-related initiatives, they will be able to avoid the costs of non-compliance with stricter environmental legal requirements and the direct and indirect adverse effects of climate change (Wei and Fang, 2012; Allen and Craig, 2016).

Finally, financial related benefits include cost savings, for example, 'costs of recruitment, worker turnover, penalty payments for non-compliance with environmental and labour laws, labour disputes, accidents, carbon tax payments, etc.' (Deutsche Gesellschaft für Internationale Zusammenarbeit (GIZ) and the Chinese Ministry of Commerce (MofCom, 2012, p. 4). Some CSR initiatives, which can help corporations achieve sustainability via reduction of energy and water consumption and waste of resources, 'reduce emissions, recycle, dispose of waste correctly, invest in research and development regarding environmental protection, corporate environmental protection standards' (Öberseder et al., 2014, p. 107), can contribute to reduce corporations' operational costs (Rangan, Chase and Karim, 2015). In other words, corporations can create environmental impacts, focusing on the following main areas, namely 'water, waste, paper, energy and transport' (Mazurkiewicz, n.d., p. 8). Many corporations in emerging markets have been involved in such areas which led to increase in their revenue and other business benefits (Mazurkiewicz, n.d.).

Also, activities to improve employees' working conditions, health care, or training and education may enhance productivity and quality which will be translated into cost saving (Werner, 2009). Galbreath (2010) found that CSR contributes to the retention of existing customers which, in turn, positively influences corporations' financial performance. The studies by Belu and Manescu (2013) and Rodriguez-Fernandez (2016) also affirmed that corporate social policies can be transformed into higher profits.

Arguments against CSR

Although there are many benefits associated with practising CSR, there are arguments against CSR. One of the advocates against the implementation of CSR initiatives is the late Milton Friedman (1962). Friedman (1962 cited in Carroll and Shabana, 2010) explained that the most important and only responsibility of corporations is to achieve profit maximisation for their owners and/or shareholders, and the second responsibility is to obey the law of the country where they operate. Hotels, travel agencies and airlines, etc. should not be pressurised to address social issues which are supposed to be the public and the third sectors' responsibility. Also, managers working in corporations may not have the expertise and skills or are not trained to make decisions which are socially oriented (Davis 1973; Carroll and Buchholtz, 2009; Carroll and Shabana, 2010). Corporations should not allocate the resources to perform activities with which they are not familiar (Coelho, McClure and Spry, 2003), and may distract from their main business purposes. In addition, since the business sector has been powerful enough, should they be given opportunities to gain more power in other arenas as questioned by Carroll and Shabana (2010)? Yet, evidence proves that the benefits of CSR outweigh the costs of practising CSR.

CSR and environmental sustainability in the tourism industry: a case study

This case study discusses how the hotels around the world have practiced CSR and the benefits associated with such CSR practices because hotels and accommodations are basic components of tourism and they are very important in promoting sustainable tourism.

CSR practices by the hotels

Popular CSR initiatives related to the environment include (i) prevention and reduction of water pollution, (ii) reduction of energy consumption, (iii) recycling, and (iv) reduction of water consumption.

Hotels have also applied cost cutting methods which are listed as follows:

- Use of compact fluorescent lights – saves energy;
- Reuse of linens – saves water, detergent, energy and greenhouse gases;
- Low-flow shower systems – saves water and energy;
- Local products – save transportation costs;
- Installation of green roofs – saves energy;
- Installation of solar heaters or other renewable energy source – saves energy

(Graci and Kuehnel, 2010)

For example, *Shangri-La Hotels and Resorts* has participated in the *Carbon Disclosure Project* which aims to address the issues associated with climate change. Many of its hotels have employed innovative solutions, such as using 'glass water bottling, rainwater harvesting, use of solar energy and the incorporation of composting and herb gardens to manage food waste' to address environmental problems (Shangri-La International Hotel Management Ltd, 2016, para. 3). *Marriott Hotel* group has achieved LEED certification, 'a pre-certified green hotel prototype for the hospitality industry', and have provided electric vehicle (EV) charging stations to customers who park at Marriott hotels (Marriott International, Inc, 2016). This aims to achieve a green environment for hotel guests.

Benefits associated with CSR implementation

CSR and destination marketing

According to UNWTO (2011), and Serra, Font and Ivanova (2016), destination marketing is considered one of the key drivers of the growth and sustainability of tourism destinations given the dynamic and competitive market in the global economy. Gretzel, Fesenmaier, Formica and O'Leary (2006) suggested that all groups of stakeholders should take responsibility for the future development and sustainability of destinations where the local resources have been exploited for the short gain by irresponsible corporations. Responsible destination marketing requires a holistic approach to market destinations in an answerable manner, i.e. marketers should take into account the limited resources of the local communities, the constraints and the risk of environmental degradation when trying to meet unlimited wants of tourists.

Traditionally, CSR with regard to destination marketing refers to improving the corporate image and operations (Serra et al., 2016). However, in contemporary context, responsible destination marketing also focuses on creating shared values for all groups of stakeholders in order to gain competitive advantage in the long term (Serra et al., 2016). Tourism related corporations can achieve these objectives by

1 introducing innovative products and services or modifying current products and markets in order to serve the existing markets and customers better and/or allow access to new markets/destinations (Vaidyanathan and Scott, 2012; Serra et al., 2016);
2 redefining the way the supply chain operates in order to increase the productivity and create added values to stakeholders via better quality, lower cost, more efficient processes, reducing waste and saving scarce resources (Vaidyanathan and Scott, 2012);
3 contributing to the development of supporting industries and local clusters, i.e. developing collaboration and networks in a way in which their operation can be sustainable. At the same time, they can also support the local communities by contributing to improve social infrastructure (e.g. provide employment to local residents, provide training and education to local employees, develop local talents, comply with local practice, provincial and national legal frameworks), and physical infrastructure (e.g. build roads, improve communication systems/networks) (Serra et al., 2016).

Cost savings and gaining competitive advantage

As discussed previously, financial benefit is one of the most important determinants which influence corporations' behaviour towards environmental responsibilities. This is especially obvious to hotels operating in a very competitive market and where the cost of energy, water and waste disposal account for a significant portion of their operational costs (Graci and Kuehnel, 2010). Thus, hotels have tried to be cost efficient via the implementation of CSR in order to create core competencies and gain strategic competitive advantages. Here are some examples of the benefits of CSR. In Singapore, hotels can gain competitive advantage by being recognised for their green business. For instance, *Grand Copthorne Waterfront Hotel Singapore, Hotel Royal Queens Singapore, Goodwood Park Hotel* and *Hotel Boss* were awarded the Singapore BCA Green Mark Award for Buildings in 2016 (Building and Construction Authority, 2016).

Grand Copthorne Waterfront Hotel Singapore has saved about 1,856,762 kWh/yr (energy) and water savings are estimated at 152 m^3/yr. The hotel has used (i) 'energy efficient heat pumps to generate hot water' for customers to save energy, (ii) 'efficient T5 fluorescent and LED light bulbs for common corridors and lobbies', and (iii) 'eco-digester to convert food waste to water' (Building and Construction Authority, 2016, p. 63). Another good example is the *InterContinental Hotels Group* (IHG), comprising *Holiday Inn Express, Holiday Inn, Crowne Plaza* Hotels and *Candlewood Suites*, etc. (Lee, 2016). The group introduced tools, such as the *Green Engage Program*, to measure 'each [member] hotel's energy, carbon, water and waste use and uses actual data to provide customised recommendations', such as 'developing a non-smoking policy on the premises (to benefit air quality), installing low-flow toilets and cutting down energy usage by installing motion detector sensors to switch on lights in areas that aren't used regularly, like stairwells' (Lee, 2016, para. 4).

Employee retention

Employees are identified as one of the main CSR domains by Öberseder et al. (2013, 2014). Per the social identity theory, hotel employees have become more environmentally aware and more sophisticated with regard to identifying themselves with employers whose principles and practices are aligned with their values (Graci and Kuehnel, 2010). Therefore, many hotels have adopted environmental initiatives to achieve cost savings, and at the same time, to motivate employees to work as a team. Many hotels have transferred some financial savings earned from environmental programs to other rewards for employees. The hotel industry is known for high employee turnover rate, and thus an increase in retention rate has contributed to saving operational costs (Faldetta, Fasone and Provenzano, 2013).

A good example is *Holiday Inn Express* in Liverpool which has organised the *Green Week* by the Green Team. This program has involved employees in all departments of the hotel. The organising team held 'quizzes, green training, a treasure hunt and even an up-cycling competition' which created very good impressions to the hotel guests who positively responded to their green initiatives (InterContinental Hotels Group, 2016, para. 4). Their Academy program has produced desirable outcome, i.e. many of their employees participating in the program continue to work at different departments of the hotel. Hotel employees have been engaged in such programs, and their responses have been very positive since they have witnessed success of the participants in terms of skills and confidence improvement (InterContinental Hotels Group, 2016).

Enhancement of corporate image and customer loyalty

Apparently, CSR practices contribute improving corporate image and reputation (Perez and del Bosque, 2014), which, in turn, results in better customer loyalty (Valchos et al., 2009). Consumers' expectations and demands have been shifted towards environmental concerns although many hotel guests choose to stay at a hotel based on price, location, facilities and service (Graci and Kuehnel, 2010). However, empirical studies reveal that CSR has positively influenced customer trust, commitment, and identification with the company (Ramasamy and Yeung, 2009; Garcia de Leaniz and Rodriguez, 2015). Also, customer rating of hotels with environmental certifications is higher (Peiró-Signes et al., 2014). According to Dodds and Joppe (2005), there were about 55 million 'geo-travellers' in America who were socially and environmentally responsible. These travellers had high expectations for 'unique and culturally authentic travel experiences that protect and preserve the ecological and cultural environment' (Dodds and Joppe, 2005, p. 13). In line with this, there has been an increase in the number of hotel guests who are willingness to pay premium prices for hotels' green initiatives (Kang et al., 2011).

Regulatory compliance

Finally, government intervention is one of the forces to be considered when analysing the specific external environment in the strategic analysis process (Hanson et al., 2014). Adopting self-regulation and innovation with regards to environmental protection would help hotels to avoid the costs of non-compliance with legal requirements (Allen and Craig, 2016). This is one of the benefits of CSR discussed in the previous section. In other words, hotels which implement measures to respond to societal and regulatory pressures regarding the environment, will be able to achieve cost savings, including regulatory non-compliance costs and potential new areas of benefits (Graci and Kuehnel, 2010).

A good example is the cost reduction for hotels which comply with the 'Ohio Fire Code-based fire and life safety standards' and 'Ohio Revised Code-based sanitary guidelines' (Young, 2014, para. 4). Hotels, which practice CSR and ensure compliance with such standards, can save the fees for inspection by government officers.

Conclusion

This chapter has discussed different concepts of CSR, and the links between CSR and sustainability in the context of the tourism industry. It has provided the justification of practising CSR activities by corporations. It has also examined what CSR initiatives have been implemented by hotels around the world. The findings suggest that corporations can reap various types of benefits when they implement CSR initiatives. Such benefits include cost savings, gaining competitive advantage, reduction of turnover, improvement of corporate image and customer loyalty, and enhanced compliance with government regulations in order to avoid costs of regulatory non-compliance.

Given the limited studies on CSR in the tourism industry, especially the hotels, any research on CSR will certainly contribute to the development of a theoretical framework and practical approaches to solve on-going problems and future challenges associated with environmental sustainability and business viability faced by the business sector, in general, and by the hotels, in particular. Future research should focus on what CSR initiatives are effective in developing customer purchase intention in the hotels, and how engagement of different groups of stakeholders can facilitate CSR implementation.

References

Allen, M. W. (2016). *Strategic communication for sustainable organizations: theory and practice.* New York: Springer Publishing Company.

Allen, M. W. and Craig, C. A. (2016). Rethinking corporate social responsibility in the age of climate change: a communication perspective. *International Journal of Corporate Social Responsibility*, 1(1). DOI: 10.1186/s40991-016-0002-8.

Arnold, D. G. and Valentin, A. (2013). Corporate social responsibility at the base of the pyramid. *Journal of Business Research*, 66(2013), 1904–1914.

Asaf, A.G. Josiassen, A. and Cvelbar, L.K. (2012) Does Triple Bottom Line Reporting Improve Hotel Performance? *International Journal of Hospitality Management.* 31(1), 596–600.

Balmer, J.M.T., Fukukaw, K. and Gray, E.R. (2007). The nature and management of ethical corporate identity: A commentary on corporate identity, corporate social responsibility and ethics. *Journal of Business Ethics*, 76(7), 7–15.

Barlow M. (2008) Blue Covenant: The Global Water Crisis and the Coming Battle for the Right to Water. New Press.

Belu, C. and Manescu, C. (2013). Strategic corporate social responsibility and economic performance. *Applies Economics*, 45(19), 2751–2764. http://dx.doi.org/10.1080/00036846.2012.676734

Benoit-Moreau, F. and Parguel, B. (2011). Building brand equity with environmental communication: an empirical investigation in France, *EuroMed Journal of Business*, 6(1), 100–116.

Boeger, N. Murray, R. and Villiers, C. (2008). *Perspectives on Corporate Social Responsibility: Corporations, Globalisation and the Law.* Cheltenham: Edward Elgar Publishing Limited.

Bowen, H.R. (1953). *Social Responsibilities of the businessmen.* New York: Harper & Row.

Bravo, R., Matute, J. and Pina, J.M. (2011). Corporate social responsibility as a vehicle to reveal the corporate identity: A study focused on the websites of Spanish financial entities. *Journal of Business Ethics*, 107(2), 129–146.

Building and Construction Authority (BCA) (2016). *BCA Awards 2016: Recognising Excellence in Building Environment.* Singapore: Building and Construction Authority.

Brunk, K.H. (2010). Exploring origins of ethical company/brand perceptions – A consumer perspective of corporate ethics. *Journal of Business Research,* 63(3), 255–262.

Carroll, A.B. (1991). The Pyramid of Corporate Social Responsibility: Toward the Moral Management of Organizational Stakeholders. *Business Horizons,* 34(4), 39–48.

Carroll, A.B. (1998). The Four Faces of Corporate Citizenship. *Business and Society Review*, 100(1), 1–7.

Carroll, A.B. (2008). A history of CSR: concept and practices. In A. Crane, D. Matten, A. McWilliams, J. Moon and D. Siegel (Eds.), *The Oxford handbook of corporate social responsibility* (pp.19–45). Oxford, UK: Oxford University Press.

Carroll, A.B. and Buchholtz, A.K. (2009). *Business and Society: Ethics and Stakeholder Management,* 7th edn. Mason, OH: South-Western Cengage Learning.

Carroll, A.B. and Shabana, K.M. (2010). The Business Case for Corporate Social Responsibility: A Review of Concepts, Research and Practice. *International Journal of Management Reviews*, 10(1), 85–105.

Castaldo, S., Perrini, F., Misani, N. and Tencati, A. (2009). The missing link between corporate social responsibility and consumer trust: The case of fair trade products. *Journal of Business Ethics*, 84(1), 1–15.

Chakrabarty, B. (2011). *Corporate Social Responsibility in India.* London: Routledge.

Chan, E. and Lee, G.K.L. (2008). Critical factors for improving social sustainability of urban: Renewal projects. *Social Indicators Research*, 85, 243–256.

Chen, Y.S. (2010). The drivers of green brand equity: green brand image, green satisfaction, and green trust. *Journal of Business ethics*, 93(2), 307–319.

Cheung, D.K., Welford, R. J. and Hills, P.R. (2009). CSR and the environment: Business supply chain partnerships in Hong Kong and PRDR, China. *Corporate Social Responsibility and Environmental Management,* 16(5), 250–263.

Coelho, P.R.P., McClure, J.E. and Spry, J.A. (2003). The Social Responsibility of Corporate Management: A Classical Critique, *American Journal of Business,* 18(1), 15–24.

Collings, R. (2003). Behind the Brand: Is Business Socially Responsible? *Consumer Policy Review*, 13(5), 159–167.

Davis, K. (1960). Can Business Afford to Ignore Social Responsibilities? *California Management Review,* 2(3), 70–76.

Davis, K. (1967). Understanding the Social Responsibility puzzle: What does the businessman owe to society? *Business Horizons*, 10(4), 45–50.

Davis, K. (1973). The case for and against business assumption of social responsibilities. *Academy of Management Journal*, June, 312–322.

Dempsey, N., Bramley, G., Power, S. and Brown, C. (2009). The Social Dimension of Sustainable Development: Defining Urban Social Sustainability. *Sustainable Development*, *19*(5), 289–300. DOI: 10.1002/sd.417

Desrochers, P. (2009). Victorian Pioneers of Corporate Sustainability. *Business History Review*, 83, 703–729.

Deutsche Gesellschaft für Internationale Zusammenarbeit (GIZ) and the the Chinese Ministry of Commerce (MofCom) (2012). Sino-German Corporate Social Responsibility Project: *Costs and Benefits of*

Corporate Social Responsibility (CSR) – A company level analysis of three sectors: Mining industry, chemical industry and light industry. Beijing: Deutsche Gesellschaft für Internationale Zusammenarbeit (GIZ) and the Chinese Ministry of Commerce (MofCom).

Dodds, R. and Joppe, M. (2005). *CSR in the Tourism Industry? The Status of and Potential for Certification, Codes of Conduct and Guidelines*. Washington D.C.: World Bank.

Drexhage, J. and Murphy, D. (2010). *Sustainable Development: From Brundtland to Rio 2012*. New York: United Nations.

Faldetta, G., Fasone, V. and Provenzano, C. (2013). Turnover in the hospitality industry: can reciprocity solve the problem? *Revista de Turismo y Patrimonio Cultural*, 11(4): 583–595.

Ferrell, O. C., Ferrell, L. and Sawayda, J. (2014). "The Domain of Corporate Social Responsibility and Marketing", *Handbook of Research on Marketing and Corporate Social Responsibility*, USA: Edward Elgar, pp. 43–67.

Galbreath, J. (2010). How does corporate social responsibility benefit firms? Evidence from Australia, *European Business Review*, 22(4), 411–431.

Garcia de Leaniz, P.M. and Rodriguez, I. R. De. Bo. (2015). Exploring the Antecedents of Hotel Customer Loyalty: A Social Identity Perspective. *Journal of Hospitality Marketing and Management*, 24(1), 65–75.

Gond, J-P., El-Akremi, A., Igalens, J. and Swaen, V. (2010). *Corporate Social Responsibility Influence on Employees*. No. 54–2010 ICCSR Research Paper Series. Nottingham: International Centre for Corporate Social Responsibility Nottingham University Business School Nottingham University.

Graci, S. and Kuehnel, J. (2010). *Why Go Green? The Business Case for Sustainability*. Available online at: http://green.hotelscombined.com/Gyh-The-Business-Case-For-Sustainability.php

Green, T. and Peloza, J. (2011). How does corporate social responsibility create value for consumers? *Journal of Consumer Marketing*, 28(1): 48–56.

Gretzel, U., Fesenmaier, D., Formica, S. and O'Leary, J. (2006). Searching for the future: Challenges faced by DMO. *Journal of Travel Research*, 45(2), 116–126.

Ha, H. (2012). Corporate Socially Responsible Practice by Banks in Singapore, Board Directors and Corporate Social Responsibility, Great Britain: MacMillan, pp. 233–251.

Hanson, D., Hitt, M. A., Ireland, R. D. and Hoskisson, R. E. (2014). *Strategic Management: Competitiveness and Globalisation* (5th Asia-Pacific ed.). South Melbourne, Australia: Cengage.

Heikkurinen, P. (2010). Image differentiation with corporate environmental responsibility. *Corporate Social Responsibility and Environmental Management*, 17, 142–152.

Holden, E. and Linnerud, K. (2007). The sustainable development area: satisfying basic needs and safeguarding ecological sustainability. *Sustainable Development*, 15, 174–187.

Husted, B. W. (2014). Corporate Social Responsibility Practice from 1800–1914: Past Initiatives and Current Debates. *Business Ethics Quarterly*, 25(1), 125–141.

InterContinental Hotel Group (2016). *An interview with Helen Roberts, General Manager at Holiday Inn Express Liverpool – Albert Dock*. Retrieved from https://www.ihgplc.com/responsible-business/our-stories/an-interview-with-helen-roberts

Kang, K. H., Stein, L., Heo, C.Y. and Lee, S. (2011). Consumers' willingness to pay for green initiatives of the hotel industry. *International Journal of Hospitality Management*, 31(2), 564–572.

Lantos, G. P. (2002). The ethicality of altruistic corporate social responsibility social responsibility, *Journal of Consumer Marketing*, 19(3), 205–230.

Laroche, M., Bergeron, J. and Barbaro-Forleo, G. (2001). Targeting consumers who are willing to pay more for environmentally friendly products. *Journal of Consumer Marketing*, *18*(6), 503–520.

Lee, J. (2016). InterContinental Hotels Group Sets Gold Standard for Environmental Sustainability. Triple Pundit, 16 Aug 2016. Available online at: www.triple pundit.com/2016/08/intercontinental-hotels-group-sets-gold-standard-environment al-sustainability/

Lee, S. and Heo, C.Y. (2009). Corporate social responsibility and customer satisfaction among US publicly traded hotels and restaurants. *International Journal of Hospitality Management*, 28(4), 635–637.

Lee, S. and Park, S. (2009), "Do socially responsible activities help hotels and casinos achieve their financial goals?" *International Journal of Hospitality Management*, 28(1), 105–112.

Lee, Y-K., Kim, Y. S., Lee, K. H. and Li, D-X. (2012). The impact of CSR on relationship quality and relationship outcomes: A perspective of service employees. *International Journal of Hospitality Management*, 31, 745–756.

Manaktola, K. and Jauhari, V. (2007), "Exploring consumer attitude and behaviour towards green practices in the lodging industry in India", *International Journal of Contemporary Hospitality Management*, 19(5), 364–377.

Marriott International, Inc. (2016). *Environment*. Maryland: Marriott International, Inc.
Martınez, P., Perez, A. and Rodrıguez del Bosque, I. (2014) Exploring the Role of CSR in the Organizational Identity of Hospitality Companies: A Case from the Spanish Tourism Industry. *Journal of Business Ethics*, 124, 47–66.
Matten, D. and Crane, A. (2005). Corporate Citizenship: Toward an Extended Theoretical Conceptualization. *Academy of Management Review*, 30(1), 166–179.
Matten, D. and Moon, J. (2008). 'Implicit' and 'Explicit' CSR: A Conceptual Framework for A Comparative Understanding of Corporate Social Responsibility. *Academy of Management Review*, 33(2), 404–424.
Mazurkiewicz, P. (n.d.). *Corporate Environmental Responsibility: Is a common CSR framework possible?* Washington D.C.: World Bank.
McGuire, J. W. (1963). *Business and Society*, New York: McGraw-Hill.
McShane, S., Olekalns, M., Newman, A. and Travaglione, T. (2015). *Organisational Behaviour: Emerging Knowledge. Global Insights* (5th edition). Australia: McGrawHill.
Missimer, M. (2013). *The Social Dimension of Strategic Sustainable Development*. Karlskrona, Sweden: Blekinge Institute of Technology.
Murphy K. (2012). The social pillar of sustainable development: a literature review and framework for policy analysis. *Sustainability: Science, Practice & Policy*, 8(1),15–29.
Nielsen (2008). *Corporate ethics and fair trading: A Nielsen Global consumer report*. New York: The Nielsen Company.
Nielsen (2014) Global Consumers Are Willing to Put their Money Where their Heart is When it Comes to Goods and Services from Companies Committed to Social Responsibility. New York: The Nielsen Company.
Öberseder, M. and Schlegelmilch, B. B. and Murphy, P. E. (2013) CSR Practices and Consumer Perceptions. *Journal of Business Research*, 66(10), 1839–1851.
Oberseder, M., Schlegelmilch, B. B., Murphy, P. E. & Gruber, V. (2014). Consumers' Perceptions of Corporate Social Responsibility: Scale Development and Validation, *Journal of Business Ethics*, 124(1), 101–115.
Park, J. Lee, H. and Kim, C. (2014) Corporate social responsibilities, consumer trust and corporate reputation: South Korean consumers' perspectives. *Journal of Business Research*, 67, 295–302.
Pearce, J. A. and Doh, J. P. (2005). The high impact of Collaborative Social Initiatives, *Sloan Management Review*, 46(3), 30–39.
Peiró-Signes, A., Segarra-Oña, M., Verma, R., Mondéjar-Jiménez, J. and Vargas-Vargas, M. (2014). The impact of environmental certification on hotel guest ratings [Electronic version]. *Cornell Hospitality Quarterly*, 55(1), 40–51.
Perez, A. & del Bosque, I. R. (2014). Customer CSR Expectations in the Banking Industry, *International Journal of Bank Marketing*, 32(3), 223–244.
Pivato, S., Misani, N. and Tencati, A. (2008). The impact of corporate social responsibility on consumer trust: the case of organic food. *Business Ethics: A European Review*, 17(1), 3–12.
Ramasamy, B. and Yeung, M. (2009). Chinese consumers' perception of corporate social responsibility (CSR). *Journal of Business Ethics*, *88*(1), 119–132.
Rangan, V. K., Chase, L. and Karim, S. (2015). The Truth about CSR. *Harvard Business Review*, 93(1/2), 40–49.
Riordan, C. M., Gatewood, R. D. and Bill, J. B. (1997) Corporate Image: Employee Reactions and Implications for Managing Corporate Social Performance. *Journal of Business Ethics*, 16, 401–412.
Rodriguez-Fernandez, M. (2016). Social responsibility and financial performance: The role of good corporate governance. Business Research Quarterly, 19(2), 137–151.
Shanga, J., Basil, D. Z. and Wymer, W. (2009) Using social marketing to enhance hotel reuse programs. *Journal of Business Research*, 63 (2010) 166–172.
Shangri-La International Hotel Management Ltd (2016). *Focus Areas*. Hong Kong: Shangri-La International Hotel Management Ltd.
Serra, J., Font, X. and Ivanova, M. (2016). Creating shared value in destination management organisations: The case of Turisme de Barcelona. *Journal of Destination Marketing and Management* (2016) available online at: http://dx.doi.org/10.1016/j. jdmm.2016.06.005i
Sirdeshmukh, D., Singh, J. and Sabol, B. (2002). Consumer trust, value, and loyalty in relational exchanges. *Journal of Marketing*, 66(1), 15–37.
Slaper, T. F. and Hall, T. J. (2011). The Triple Bottom Line: What Is It and How Does It Work? *Indiana Business Review*, 86(1), 4–8.

Susnienė, D. and Žostautiene, D. (2016) Synergy of Corporate and Marketing Culture in Fostering Corporate Social Responsibility. *Journal of Promotion Management*, 22(2), 209–223.
Thomson, J. (2016). Why CFOs should embrace sustainability for strategic growth. Bloomberg Finance L.P.
UNWTO (2011). *Policy and practice for global tourism*. Madrid: UNWTO.
Vaidyanathan, L. and Scott, M. (2012). Creating share value in India: The future for inclusive growth. *VIKALPA*, 37(2), 108–113.
Valchos, P. A., Tsamakos, A., Vrechopoulos, Adam, P. and Avramidis, P. K. (2009). Corporate social responsibility: Attributions, loyalty, and the mediating role of trust. Journal of the Academy of Marketing Science, 37(2), 170–180.
Vurro, C. and Perrini, F. (2011). Making the Most of Corporate Social Responsibility Reporting: Disclosure Structure and Its Impact on Performance, *Corporate Governance*, 11(4), 459–474.
Wei, Y. and Fang, Y. (2012). Impacts and adaptation of climate change on urban economic system: a perspective from the urban planning. *Applied Mechanics and Materials, 174–177*, 2270–2277. DOI:10.4028/www.scientific.net/AMM.174–177.22 70.
Werner, W. J. (2009). Corporate Social Responsibility Initiatives Addressing Social Exclusion in Bangladesh. Journal of Health Population and Nutrition, 27(4), 545–562.
Windsor, D. (2006). Corporate social responsibility: Three key approaches. *Journal of Management Studies*, 43, 93–114.
World Commission on Environment and Development (1987). *Our Common Future*. Oxford: Oxford University Press.
Young, L. (2014). Contractors, hotels gain state incentives to comply with Ohio regulations. *The Columbus Dispatch*. Available online at: www.dispatch.com/content/stories/business/2014/09/02/contractors-hotels-gain-incentives-to-comply.html

29

Consumers' environmental attitudes and tourism marketing

Hsiangting Shatina Chen

Introduction

Adopting "green" initiatives or implementing environmentally sustainable practices has become a prevailing phenomenon in the tourism industry. Many tourism businesses have addressed environmental issues, such as reducing the consumption of natural resources and producing less waste (Chan & Hsu, 2016). This emerging "green" movement is driven by companies' financial outcomes (i.e., saving costs), conservational regulations by policy makers, and consumers' environmental awareness. Over decades, consumers have become more conscious about environmental conservation and believe they can make a difference through their consumption (McDonagh & Prothero, 2014). More and more consumers are searching for information about green hotels, environmentally friendly restaurants, and sustainable tourism (Barber, 2014). For tourism practitioners, understanding and incorporating consumers' environmental attitudes into their green marketing strategies is a necessity. Academic researchers have also endeavored to understand how consumers' environmental attitudes and concerns influence their purchasing behavior (Peattie & Charter, 2003). However, since consumers' attitudes consist of various facets and can be assessed in numerous ways, research often indicates inconclusive or contradictory findings in terms of consumers' attitudes and purchasing behavior (Baker, Davis, & Weaver, 2013; Manaktola & Jauhari, 2007, Peattie & Charter, 2003). A consumer's attitude is comprised of personal beliefs, emotions, and their likelihood of responding toward a particular matter. Furthermore, an attitude can be reformed once the person receives new information or embraces environmental changes. This chapter aims to outline current theories applied regarding consumers' environmental attitudes, green marketing applications in tourism marketing, and recommendations for future research into consumers' environmental attitudes.

Current theories related to consumers' environmental attitudes

Research has extensively embraced a definition of "attitude" from the Theory of Planned Actions (TPA) and Theory of Planned Behavior (TPB) by Ajzen (1991) and Fishbein and Ajzen (1975), which states that a consumer's attitude is the measurement of an individual's favorable and unfavorable appraisal of a subject. In the context of ecological behavior, consumers' attitudes are formed by their environmental concerns and beliefs of socially responsible consumption

(Gao, Mattila, & Lee, 2016; Haws, Winterich, & Reczek, 2013; Laroche, Bergeron, & Barbaro-Forleo, 2001). Attitudes are more likely influenced by individuals' internal appraisal; when consumers perceive higher degree of importance about ecological issues and personal altruistic value, they are more willing to engage in eco-friendly behavior. Since TPA and TPB are foundational theories and classical paradigms that state how humans' behavioral beliefs constitute the person's attitudes, this theoretical basis has been extensively used to explain how consumers' environmental attitudes influence their recycling intention, inclination to visit green hotels and restaurants, and their intentions to purchase (Chen & Tung, 2014; Han, Hsu, & Sheu, 2010; Kim, Njite, & Hancer, 2013).

Similarly, the second research stream of acknowledging how individuals' values and beliefs constitute their environmental attitudes is applying the value-belief-norm (VBN) theory of environmentalism to explain the formation of individuals' pro-environmental behavior. Stern (2000) explains the VBN theory as "the theory links value theory, norm-activation theory, and the New Environmental Paradigm (NEP) perspective through a causal chain of five variables leading to behavior." The VBN theory specifies how an individual's intent and personal commitment orient environmental behavior. Personal commitment, also referred to as personal norms or a sense of obligation to alleviate environmental problems, is influenced by an individual's biosphere value, awareness of consequence, and ascription of responsibility (Stern, Dietz, Abel, Guagnano, & Kalof, 1999). Thus, from this perspective, an individual environmental attitude is not only limited to a person's favorable or unfavorable evaluation of the behavior, it is also comprised of various facets, including an ecological worldview, altruism, self-interest, and personal normative beliefs (Stern et al., 1999; Stern, 2000).

In addition to personal norms, belief, and value of ecological issues that form consumers' environmental attitudes, researchers stated that the perceived inconvenience of being environmentally friendly also contributes to the attitudinal factors (Baker et al., 2013; Gao et al., 2016; Laroche et al., 2001). Consumers may consider compelling sustainability practices personally inconvenient, which in turn, offsets their attitudes of engaging in environmentally friendly behavior. Based upon motivational theories, the perception of inconvenience and difficulty serve as a negative fundamental reinforcement, which motivates consumers to retain or change their behaviors (Tabernero & Hernández, 2011). For instance, if consumers think that it takes additional time and effort for them to recycle materials, they may not fully commit to the recycling behavior. Research indicates that the inconvenience of being environmentally friendly also influences their intention to stay in green hotels and willingness to pay more for green products (Baker et al., 2013; Han et al., 2011; Laroche et al., 2001). It is possible that personal inconvenience may diminish consumers' level of comfort, which results in negative attitudes toward consuming tourism products (Weaver, 2008).

Another approach toward understanding consumers' environmental attitudes is determining consumers' attitudes of socially responsible consumption and perceptions of corporate social responsibility (Roberts, 1995; Webb, Mohr, & Harris, 2008). The definition of socially responsible consumption is "those consumer behaviors that take into account the impact on the environment of private consumption decisions or which use purchasing power to express current social concerns" (Roberts, 1995, p. 98). The notion of socially responsible consumption is built upon an individual's belief that his or her behavior can contribute to solving environmental problems. Consumers who are conscious about ecological issues are more inclined to minimize or eliminate any harmful effects on the environment and society while purchasing and using products (Webb et al., 2008). Thus, consumers' attitudes of socially responsible consumption can be an important underlying motivation that compels environmentally friendly behavior, such as choosing green products/services or boycotting those that cause environmental damage (Paek & Nelson, 2009).

Similarly, consumers' attitudes and intent to purchase can be influenced by their perception of a company's corporate social responsibility (CSR), which recognizes environmental and social concerns in business organizations (Mohr, Webb, & Harris, 2001). Environmental corporate social responsibility (ECSR) represents a dimension of CSR and identifies a firm's environmental commitment and ecological responsiveness toward shifting their products, processes, and policies to use sustainable resources (Bansal & Roth, 2000). Research shows that ECSR not only impacts a corporation's strategic communication and marketing, but is also related to consumers' positive attitudes toward brand evaluation, loyalty, and product evaluations (Klein & Dawar, 2004; Rashid, Rahman, & Khalid, 2014). Consumers who are environmentally conscious recognize that the tourism industry consumes substantial quantities of water and energy while generating a large amount of waste from food, beverages, products, and service consumption. Therefore, consumers tend to positively respond to a firm's ECSR practices, such as staying in green hotels, purchasing organic and fair trade products, or using recyclable materials. Because of the expectation that green practices are necessary in a hospitality and tourism firm, consumers' environmental attitudes can be reinforced and supported by their perception of the company's CSR.

Applications in hospitality and tourism marketing research

Marketing is an influential communication technique, which is often used to reinforce messages and change consumers' attitudes. Hospitality and tourism marketing research has extensively investigated how green practices have been adopted by business organizations in a wide spectrum, such as in the lodging industry (Baker et al., 2013; Han et al., 2010; Kang, Stein, Heo, & Lee, 2012; Lee, Hsu, Han, & Kim, 2010; Manaktola & Jauhari, 2007), the restaurant industry (Namkung & Jang, 2014; Schubert, Kandampully, Solnet, & Kralj, 2010), tourism (Bergin-Seers & Mair, 2009; Hassan, 2000; Juvan & Dolnicar, 2016), and events and meetings (Boo & Park, 2013; Tinnish & Mangal, 2012; Wong, Wan, & Qi, 2015). Research has begun to emphasize environmental issues and sustainable practices in hospitality and tourism business operations and has provided insightful implications to hospitality and tourism marketing. Specifically, researchers have underlined how consumers' environmental attitudes determine their decision-making process towards willingness to pay more for products/services, customer satisfaction, positive word-of-mouth, revisit or repurchase intentions, intent to visit green hotels or restaurants, brand loyalty, and positive brand equity and image. In addition to understanding consumers' behavioral outcomes, there has also been research in profiling environmental-conscious consumers and determining their levels of environmental purchase behavior (Barber, 2014). "The shades of green" indicate there are different types of green consumers, who are segmented by demographic, aspirational values, awareness and knowledge of green issues, and lifestyle (Barber, 2014; Bergin-Seers & Mair, 2009). Instead of targeting the general population, hospitality and tourism marketers endeavor to identify specific green consumer segments, understand the green consumers' preferences and behaviors, further establish green marketing strategies to create a green image, and position themselves in the consumers' minds (Barber, 2014). Thus, targeting environmentally-conscious consumers could provide an effective marketing effort by tailoring environmental benefits to customers, engaging customers in the marketing program, and increasing customer loyalty (Tanford & Malek, 2015).

While profiling green consumers can offer hospitality and tourism marketers some insight to understand the relationship between consumers' environmental attitudes and their purchasing behavior, some research indicates that consumers' attitudes will differ and occasionally stand as a dependent exception. This situation-specific exception influences consumers' current beliefs and behaviors. For instance, research has found that consumers show different environmental attitudes in household and hotel settings (Baker et al., 2013; Miao & Wei, 2013, 2016). When consumers stay in a hotel, they expect the hotel will provide comfort and a luxurious experience. However, consumers may perceive that they have to compromise personal comfort and benefits when committing to environmentally friendly behavior (e.g., reuse towels for water conservation or reduce plate portion size to prevent food waste). Therefore, this dissonance and confrontation may offset people's attitudes of green practices when consuming hospitality and tourism products and services. Miao & Wei (2016) indicate consumers' underlying hedonic motivations predominantly influence their environmental behavior, and represent an important attribute when consumers are confronted with environmental concerns, self-interests, costs, and effort. Thus, situational influences may lead consumers to react differently toward hospitality and tourism organizations' green practices. Researchers suggest that hospitality and tourism marketers should carefully develop green communication messages in order to change the perception that personal comfort is sacrificed when engaging in green practices (Baker et al., 2013). In addition, hospitality and tourism marketers could incorporate altruistic motivation in green communication, which encourages consumers to act socially responsible and stay engaged in green behavior (Miao & Wei, 2016). For instance, a message such as "feeling good by doing good," could encourage consumers to respond to business organizations' corporate social responsibility and reinforce environmentally friendly attitudes (Bhattacharya & Sen, 2004).

Recommendations for future research

Over decades, environmental studies in hospitality and tourism research have been escalating and expanding in various subjects. Perhaps the most sustained research attention is in the subject of consumer's' environmental attitudes and their green consumption of hospitality and tourism products and service (Chan & Hsu, 2016). Consumers' attitudes essentially affect their perceptions of green marketing and the effectiveness of sustainable practices from hospitality and tourism firms. Therefore, there is continuing research that investigates how attitudinal factors govern consumers' environmental behavior. While TPB, TPA, and VBN frameworks have been powerful and predictive models to explain consumers' environmental behavior, still, much research shows contradictory results and indications of an enigmatic gap between attitudes and behavior. A consumer's decision-making process often incorporates several motivational and situational attributes, which complicate the understanding of a person's behavioral outcomes. Consumers' involvement, knowledge and experience, and perceived effectiveness may substantially influence the attitude-behavioral intention gap in terms of sustainable product consumption (Vermeir and Verbeke, 2006). Thus, further research could address how different motivational and situational attributes sway and guide consumers' environmental attitudes toward their behaviors.

In addition, many hospitality and tourism marketing research studies have investigated consumers' behavioral intention; however, the research is limited to a self-reported survey method. One criticism of conducting online surveys is that consumer behavior and response to certain situations in an actual setting are not captured. Studies associated with reusing towels in hotels, revisiting green hotels, and willingness to pay a premium in green restaurants, have mainly employed a questionnaire, scenario-based, or quantitative research method to access consumers' opinion based on some assumptions. The survey method is critical to determine how individuals' environmental attitudes genuinely predominate their decision-making toward acting for environmental sustainability. Moreover, consumers may respond to questionnaire items in a socially desirable manner and intend to meet the perception of social expectations about green behavior, which in turn, generates biases and overestimation in environmental behavior research (Juvan & Dolnicar, 2016). For this reason, researchers have argued that examining consumers' attitudes and intentions does not truly reflect or predict their actual behaviors (Chandon, Morwitz, & Reinartz, 2005; Oates & McDonald, 2014). While some may argue that measuring consumers' actual behavior is difficult to conduct in a research setting and it is not always possible (e.g., hard to control variables or unaffordable to conduct research onsite), researchers have suggested developing more valid measures by utilizing different research designs, such as behavioral observation, field experiments, open-end questions, self-generated validity measurement, or semantic analysis, to delve into different aspects of individuals' environmental attitudes and behaviors (Chandon et al., 2005, Juvan & Dolnicar, 2016; Oates & McDonald, 2014). In addition, researchers are encouraged to use a more qualitative research approach to discover and enrich the knowledge of consumer behavior (Chan & Hsu, 2016). Consequently, we need to cautiously develop research designs, as well as cultivate a wide-range of research methods to scrutinize green consumers' attitudes and behaviors.

In regard to examining behavioral outcomes, hospitality and tourism marketing researchers should consider a broader spectrum when studying consumer behavior. Purchasing intention is only one facet of consumer behavior (Hawkins, Mothersbaugh & Best, 2013; also see Pham 2013 for more discussions). Other aspects, such as consumers' wants and needs for environmental sustainability practices, consumers' acquisitions of green products/services, and consumers' consumption and green product disposal, are still available for researchers to investigate and provide meaningful implications to hospitality and tourism firms. Therefore, we need to extend the studies of inspecting consumers' purchase intentions, as well as embrace various aspects of the consumption process, to ascertain consumer pro-environmental behavior.

The topics of green consumptions and consumer behavior reflect that hospitality and tourism firms should take a proactive role to adopt environmental sustainability in their marketing programs. Previous research has primarily focused on consumers' purchasing decisions, specifically as they relate to pricing strategy (i.e., willingness to pay premium in green hotels/foods). Indeed, pricing strategy is a substantial component that determines successful marketing, and it is more relevant from a business standpoint. However, there are other activities associated with green marketing that should be emphasized, such as product development, product distribution, logistics, and promotion strategy (Dief & Font, 2010). Hospitality and tourism firms who claim to be environmentally sustainable should incorporate and embrace sustainable practices in all marketing components, and not only address the impact of pricing. For instance, regarding a restaurant's sustainability practices, from the restaurant's food procurement, product innovation, facilities and operations, employee training, packaging and product delivery, advertising, to the positive environmental impacts on the community, consumers' attitudes may respond differently to each aspect of sustainable practices. As such, more research is needed to explore how consumers' environmental attitudes influence a hospitality and tourism firm's environmental schemes in terms of product development, distribution, communication, and other marketing activities.

Finally, most hospitality and tourism research has addressed consumers' environmental attitudes and behavior in the context of hotels (Chan & Hsu, 2016; Myung, McClaren, & Li, 2012). Perhaps, since the environmental issues considerably impact the bottom line of the hotel industry, researchers and practitioners have focused on consumers' perceptions of hotels' environmental initiatives and the implications to hotels' environmental management. However, more studies in foodservice, tourism, and event management sectors should not be neglected. For instance, several organizations in the meeting and event industry have tried to establish standards and guidelines to address the concerns of environmental sustainability. Yet, questions such as how meeting planners address and adopt green practices, what challenges they have faced while implementing green practices, and how attendees respond to green practices in events, are still under researched. Moreover, in terms of the foodservice sector, issues of sustainable practices have mainly focused on restaurants' sustainable practices, such as recycling and reusing materials, reducing energy usage, or purchase organic foods. However, research into restaurants and food waste management is largely ignored. Restaurants generate a massive amount of food spoilage and waste, both from restaurants' operation and patrons' consumptions, which ends up in landfills and causes a significant impact on the natural environment (Betz, Buchli, Göbel, & Müller, 2015). Researchers are encouraged to conduct more studies related to food waste prevention in the foodservice sector, provide insight for increasing consumers' awareness, reinforce consumers' environmental attitudes, and further encourage their pro-environmental behavior.

References

Ajzen, I. (1991) "The theory of planned behavior". *Organizational Behavior and Human Decision Processes*. 50(2), 179–211. DOI:10.1016/0749-5978(91)90020-T

Baker, M. A., Davis, E. A., & Weaver, P. A. (2013) "Eco-friendly attitudes, barriers to participation, and differences in behavior at green hotels." *Cornell Hospitality Quarterly*, 1938965513504483.

Bansal, P., & Roth, K. (2000) "Why companies go green: A model of ecological responsiveness." *Academy of Management Journal*, 43(4), 717–736.

Barber, N. A. (2014). "Profiling the potential 'green' hotel guest: Who are they and what do they want?" *Journal of Hospitality & Tourism Research*, 38(3), 361–387.

Bergin-Seers, S., & Mair, J. (2009) "Emerging green tourists in Australia: Their behaviours and attitudes." *Tourism and Hospitality Research*, 9(2), 109–119.

Betz, A., Buchli, J., Göbel, C., & Müller, C. (2015) "Food waste in the Swiss food service industry–Magnitude and potential for reduction." *Waste Management*, 35, 218–226.

Bhattacharya, C. B., & Sen, S. (2004) "Doing better at doing good: When, why, and how consumers respond to corporate social initiatives." *California Management Review*, 47(1), 9–24.

Boo, S., & Park, E. (2013) "An examination of green intention: the effect of environmental knowledge and educational experiences on meeting planners' implementation of green meeting practices." *Journal of Sustainable Tourism*, 21(8), 1129–1147.

Chan, E. S., & Hsu, C. H. (2016) "Environmental management research in hospitality." *International Journal of Contemporary Hospitality Management*, 28(5), 886–923.

Chandon, P., Morwitz, V. G., & Reinartz, W. J. (2005) "Do intentions really predict behavior? Self-generated validity effects in survey research." *Journal of Marketing*, 69(2), 1–14.

Chen, M. F., & Tung, P. J. (2014) "Developing an extended Theory of Planned Behavior model to predict consumers' intention to visit green hotels." *International Journal of Hospitality Management*, 36, 221–230.

Chou, C. J., Chen, K. S., & Wang, Y. Y. (2012) "Green practices in the restaurant industry from an innovation adoption perspective: Evidence from Taiwan." *International Journal of Hospitality Management*, 31(3), 703–711.

de Groot, J. M., & Steg, L. (2008) "Value Orientations to Explain Beliefs Related to Environmental Significant Behavior: How to Measure Egoistic, Altruistic, and Biospheric Value Orientations." *Environment & Behavior*, 40(3), 330–354. DOI:10.1177/0013916506297831

Dief, M. E., & Font, X. (2010) "The determinants of hotels' marketing managers' green marketing behaviour." *Journal of Sustainable Tourism*, 18(2), 157–174. DOI:10.1080/09669580903464232

Fishbein, M., & Ajzen, I. (1975). *Belief, attitude, intention, and behavior: An introduction to theory and research*. Reading, MA: Addison-Wesley.

Gao, Y. L., Mattila, A. S., & Lee, S. (2016) "A meta-analysis of behavioral intentions for environment-friendly initiatives in hospitality research." *International Journal of Hospitality Management*, 54, 107–115.

Han, H., Hsu, L. T. J., & Sheu, C. (2010) "Application of the theory of planned behavior to green hotel choice: Testing the effect of environmental friendly activities." *Tourism Management*, 31(3), 325–334.

Han, H., Hsu, L. T. J., Lee, J. S., & Sheu, C. (2011) "Are lodging customers ready to go green? An examination of attitudes, demographics, and eco-friendly intentions." *International Journal of Hospitality Management*, 30(2), 345–355.

Hassan, S. S. (2000) "Determinants of market competitiveness in an environmentally sustainable tourism industry." *Journal of travel research*, 38(3), 239–245.

Hawkins, D. I., Mothersbaugh, D. L., & Best, R. J. (2013) *Consumer behavior: Building marketing strategy*. McGraw-Hill Irwin.

Haws, K., Winterich, K. P., & Reczek, R. W. (2013) "Seeing the world through GREEN-tinted glasses: Green consumption values and responses to environmentally friendly products." *Journal of Consumer Psychology*, 24(3), 336–354.

Juvan, E., & Dolnocar, S. (2016) "Measuring environmentally sustainable tourist behavior." *Annals of Tourism Research*, 59, 30–44.

Kang, K. H., Stein, L., Heo, C. Y., & Lee, S. (2012) "Consumers' willingness to pay for green initiatives of the hotel industry." *International Journal of Hospitality Management*, 31(2), 564–572.

Kim, Y. J., Njite, D., & Hancer, M. (2013) "Anticipated emotion in consumers' intentions to select eco-friendly restaurants: Augmenting the theory of planned behavior." *International Journal of Hospitality Management*, 34, 255–262.

Klein, J., & Dawar, N. (2004) "Corporate social responsibility and consumers' attributions and brand evaluations in a product–harm crisis." *International Journal of research in Marketing*, 21(3), 203–217.

Laroche, M., Bergeron, J., & Barbaro-Forleo, G. (2001) "Targeting consumers who are willing to pay more for environmentally friendly products." *Journal of Consumer Marketing*, 18(6), 503 520.

Lee, J. S., Hsu, L. T., Han, H., & Kim, Y. (2010) "Understanding how consumers view green hotels: how a hotel's green image can influence behavioural intentions." *Journal of Sustainable Tourism*, 18(7), 901–914.

Manaktola, K., & Jauhari, V. (2007) "Exploring consumer attitude and behaviour towards green practices in the lodging industry in India." *International Journal of Contemporary Hospitality Management*, 19(5), 364–377.

McDonagh, P., & Prothero, A. (2014). "Sustainability marketing research: Past, present and future." *Journal of Marketing Management*, 30(11–12), 1186–1219.

Miao, L., & Wei, W. (2013) "Consumers' pro-environmental behavior and the underlying motivations: A comparison between household and hotel settings" *International Journal of Hospitality Management*, 32, 102–112.

Miao, L., & Wei, W. (2016) "Consumers' pro-environmental behavior and its determinants in the lodging segment" *Journal of Hospitality & Tourism Research*, 40(3), 319–338.

Mohr, L. A., Webb, D. J., & Harris, K. E. (2001) "Do consumers expect companies to be socially responsible? The impact of corporate social responsibility on buying behavior." *Journal of Consumer Affairs*, 35(1), 45–72.

Myung, E., McClaren, A., & Li, L. (2012) "Environmentally related research in scholarly hospitality journals: Current status and future opportunities." *International Journal of Hospitality Management*, 31(4), 1264–1275.

Namkung, Y., & Jang, S. S. (2014) "Are consumers willing to pay more for green practices at restaurants?" *Journal of Hospitality & Tourism Research*, 1096348014525632.

Oates, C. J., & McDonald, S. (2014) "The researcher role in the attitude-behaviour gap." *Annals of Tourism Research*, 46, 168–170.

Paek, H. J., & Nelson, M. R. (2009) "To buy or not to buy: Determinants of socially responsible consumer behavior and consumer reactions to cause-related and boycotting ads." *Journal of Current Issues & Research in Advertising* 31(2), 75–90.

Peattie, K., & Charter, M. (2003). "Green marketing." *The Marketing Book 5*, 726–755.

Pham, M. T. (2013). "The seven sins of consumer psychology." *Journal of Consumer Psychology*, 23(4), 411–423.

Rashid, N. R. N. A., Rahman, N. I. A., & Khalid, S. A. (2014) "Environmental Corporate Social Responsibility (ECSR) as a Strategic Marketing Initiatives." *Procedia-Social and Behavioral Sciences* 130, 499–508.

Roberts, J. A. (1995) "Profiling levels of socially responsible consumer behavior: a cluster analytic approach and its implications for marketing." *Journal of marketing Theory and practice* 3(4), 97–117.

Schubert, F., Kandampully, J., Solnet, D., & Kralj, A. (2010). "Exploring consumer perceptions of green restaurants in the US." *Tourism and Hospitality Research*, 10(4), 286–300.

Stern, P. C. (2000). "New environmental theories: toward a coherent theory of environmentally significant behavior." *Journal of Social Issues*, 56(3), 407–424.

Stern, P. C., Dietz, T., Abel, T. D., Guagnano, G. A., & Kalof, L. (1999). A value-belief-norm theory of support for social movements: The case of environmentalism. *Human Ecology Review*, 6(2), 81–97.

Tabernero, C., & Hernández, B. (2011) "Self-efficacy and intrinsic motivation guiding environmental behavior." *Environment and Behavior* 43(5), 658–675.

Tanford, S., & Malek, K. (2015) "Segmentation of reward program members to increase customer loyalty: The role of attitudes towards green hotel practices." *Journal of Hospitality Marketing & Management* 24(3), 314–343.

Tinnish, S. M., & Mangal, S. M. (2012) "Sustainable Event Marketing in the MICE Industry: A Theoretical Framework." *Journal of Convention & Event Tourism*, 13(4), 227–249. DOI:10.1080/15470148.2012.731850

Vermeir, I. and Verbeke, W., (2006) "Sustainable food consumption: Exploring the consumer "attitude–behavioral intention" gap." *Journal of Agricultural and Environmental Ethics* 19(2), 169–194.

Weaver, D. B. (2009) "Reflections on sustainable tourism and paradigm change." *CM Stefan Gössling, Sustainable Tourism Futures*, 33–40.

Webb, D. J., Mohr, L. A., & Harris, K. E. (2008) "A re-examination of socially responsible consumption and its measurement." *Journal of Business Research*, 61(2), 91–98.

Wong, I. A., Wan, Y. K. P., & Qi, S. (2015) "Green events, value perceptions, and the role of consumer involvement in festival design and performance." *Journal of Sustainable Tourism*, 23(2), 294–315.

Further reading

Kollmuss, A. and Agyeman, J., (2002) "Mind the gap: why do people act environmentally and what are the barriers to proenvironmental behavior?" *Environmental Education Research*, 8(3), 239–260.

Pham, M. T. (2013) "The seven sins of consumer psychology." *Journal of Consumer Psychology*, 23(4), 411–423.

30

A review of green experiential quality, green farm image, green equity, green experiential satisfaction and green behavioral intentions

The case of Green World Ecological Farm

Hung-Che Wu

Introduction

The term "ecological farming" is a holistic production management system which promotes and enhances the ecosystem. Ecological farms have been identified as a leading pioneer in direct marketing, nowadays also increasingly practiced by conventional farmers. The purposes of ecological farms are to create globally sustainable land management systems and to encourage review of the importance of maintaining biodiversity in food production and farming end products. The mission of ecological farms is to nurture healthy, just, and ecologically sustainable farms, food systems, and communities by bringing people together for education, alliance building, advocacy and celebration.

Green World Ecological Farm is located in Hsinchu of Taiwan and covers an area of over 70 hectare (170 acres). Green World Ecological Farm includes an educational farm, a house, a zoo, and a botanical garden that occupies about 173 acres (70 ha) and hosts over 2,000 species of plants and animals. It is a large-scale ecological farm combining the natural ecology of animals and plants with leisure, educational and recreational purposes. When entering Green World Ecological Farm, the natural environment with beautiful green plants will make visitors feel very refreshed. This farm is a good place for adults to relax and for children to have a good time. Creating memorable experiences is critical to retaining old visitors and attracting new ones (Yelkur 2000). Therefore, in order to enable visitors to return or revisit the green farm, the issue of green behavioral intentions should attract more attention in the tourism industry.

In general, loyal visitors or those who enjoy positive experiences with services or products are more likely to become a stable base of satisfied visitors (Kim and Lough 2007; Wu and Li 2015). It is because they tend to have better social interactions with service providers. Therefore, it can be safely postulated that the enrichment of service production and delivery can create satisfaction which in turn results in behavioral intentions (Al-alak 2009). Indeed, several studies have shown that both satisfaction and quality perceptions positively impact the behavioral intentions of a visitor (Patterson and Spreng 1997; Rust and Oliver 1994). Interestingly, Cronin and Taylor (1992) suggest that satisfaction has been found to have a stronger and more consistent effect on behavioral intentions than quality. Also, experiential quality has been considered to be an antecedent of image and equity, which in turn result in experiential satisfaction and behavioral intentions respectively (Wu and Ai 2016a; Wu and Li 2017). However, the concepts of green experiential quality, green farm image, green equity, green experiential satisfaction and green behavioral intentions remain scarce for green farms.

Numerous studies (Brady and Cronin 2001; Dabholkar, Thorpe and Rentz 1995; Dagger, Sweeney and Johnson 2007; Wu and Ai 2016a; Wu and Li 2017) point out that a multi-dimensional model can help to address the disadvantages of the traditional SERVQUAL and SERVPERF models. Such a model can be more accurate in assessing visitors' perceptions of green experiential quality. However, little research focuses on assessing visitors' perceptions of green experiential quality using a multi-dimensional model.

There are two objectives in this chapter. The first objective is to explore the characteristics of green behavioral intentions using a multi-dimensional approach and to show that the path formed by the green behavioral intention construct can be used to identify the dimensions of green experiential quality and their relative importance based on green farm visitors' perceptions. The second objective is to examine the relationship between green behavioral intentions of visitors and the other higher order constructs: green experiential quality, green farm image, green equity and green experiential satisfaction as perceived by green farm visitors.

The chapter focuses on those five constructs and their interrelationships. Next, in order to simplify the conceptualization of those five constructs, a proposed conceptual framework is introduced. Finally, there is a summary and discussion of implications.

Concepts and operational definitions

Service quality

Parasuraman, Zeithaml and Berry (1988) define service quality as the ability of the organization to meet or exceed customer expectations. It is the difference between customer expectations of service and perceived service (Zeithaml, Parasuraman and Berry 1990). Perceived service quality results from comparisons of customers' expectations with their perceptions of service delivered by the suppliers (Zeithaml *et al.* 1990).

Buttle (1996) indicates that the SERVQUAL model has been widely used to measure and manage service quality across different service settings and various cultural backgrounds. The SERVQUAL model proposes that customers evaluate the quality of a service on five distinct dimensions: reliability, responsiveness, assurance, empathy, and tangibles. This model consists of 22 statements for assessing customers' perceptions and expectations regarding the quality of a service. Perceived service quality results from comparisons of consumers' expectations with their perceptions of service delivered by the service providers (Zeithaml *et al.* 1990). However, SERVQUAL has been the object of controversies and criticism (Buttle 1996). Teas (1993) argues against the validity of perception-expectation gap with conceptual and operational problem in the definition of the expectation. Brown, Churchill and Peter (1993) raise psychometric concerns regarding the use of difference scores and propose that the gap model would display poor reliability, because expectation and perception can be positively correlated to each other.

Cronin and Taylor's (1992) empirical work controvert the framework of Parasuraman, Zeithaml and Berry (1985) with respect to conceptualization and measurement of service quality, and propose a performance-based measure of service quality called 'SERVPERF', illustrating that service quality is a form of consumers' attitude. Cronin and Taylor (1994) propose that SERVPERF should explain more of the variance in an overall measure of service quality than SERVQUAL. However, Nadiri and Hussain (2005) indicate that SERVPERF cannot form its five assumed dimensions: tangibles, reliability, responsiveness, assurance and empathy in the service industry. The SERVQUAL and SERVPERF scales agree on the five dimensions of service quality, but it is doubtful that the existing scales are sufficient to explain service quality in the hospitality industry. It is therefore important to re-examine the dimensions of experiential quality in the hospitality literature. Several researchers (Chen and Chen 2010; Kao, Huang and Wu 2008; Wu and Li 2017) support the use of a multi-dimensional structure developed by Brady and Cronin (2001) and Dabholkar *et al.* (1995) to appropriately conceptualize and measure perceptions of experiential quality for green farms.

Green experiential quality

Green experiential quality is a fast-emerging multidisciplinary field based on social psychology, cognitive science, economics, and engineering science, focused on understanding overall human quality requirements. It is the blueprint of the visitor's experience of eco-friendly products or services that can contribute to environmental conservation. This chapter proposes a novel concept – green experiential quality – and defines the term as a subjective measure of a visitor experience with an ecological farm. Green experiential quality is applied to measure the extent to which ecological farm management considers the specific needs of the visitors in delivering environmentally-friendly products or services. Therefore, green experiential quality is a subjective measure from ecological farm visitors' perspectives of the overall value of the product or service provided, and thus does not replace, but augments end-to-end green experiential quality by providing the quantitative link to the visitor perception (Xu and Chan 2010). Although green experiential quality is perceived to be subjective, it is the only measure that counts for visitors of an eco-friendly service or product.

Numerous studies have focused on the components of experiential quality. Cole and Scott (2004) indicate that entertainment, education and community form experiential quality. Cole and Chancellor (2009) propose that programs, amenities and entertainment are components of experiential quality. Several studies (Jin, Lee and Lee 2015; Kao *et al.* 2008; Kao, Huang and Yang 2007) argue that the measurement of experiential quality is based on immersion, surprise, participation and fun. Lemke, Clark and Wilson (2011) propose that product category, involvement, product complexity and relationality are components of experiential quality. Several studies (Dagger *et al.* 2007; De Rojas and Camarero 2008; Wu and Ai 2016a; Wu and Li 2017) demonstrate that experiential quality comprises interaction quality, physical environment quality, outcome quality, access quality and administration quality. In order to appropriately measure visitors' perceptions of green experiential quality, a multi-dimensional model of green experiential quality should be applied.

Olorunniwo, Hsu and Udo (2006) believe that quality is an antecedent of satisfaction, arguing that since quality is a cognitive evaluation, a positive service quality perception can result in satisfaction. Jin *et al.* (2015) have found that the quality of visitors' experiences significantly affects satisfaction. Dabholkar (1995) suggests that the antecedent role of quality and satisfaction is situation specific and that if a consumer is cognitively oriented, he or she will perceive the relationship as quality causing satisfaction, whereas if a consumer is affectively oriented he or she will perceive the relationship as satisfaction suggesting quality.

Green farm image

For ecological farms, while visitors are aware of environmental impacts and are willing to address these to some extent, they still want to visit and are not willing to give upon this part of their lifestyle. This opens up an opportunity for ecological farms to focus their marketing communication on environmental credentials and therefore create a green image that could be attractive to visitors. Image is used by customers to differentiate between organizations (Liou and Chuang 2010). This chapter therefore refers to the definitions of Chang and Fong (2010) and Chen (2008), defining green farm image as the perceptions developed from the interaction between the ecological farm and visitors that are linked to environmental commitments and environmental concerns.

Wu, Li and Li (2018) indicate that image precedes satisfaction and that image plays a critical role in increasing satisfaction. Grönroos (1990) shows that customers' perceptions of quality influence image. In a service organization, the perception of image can be derived from the technical and functional components of quality, fueled by any marketing promotion that takes place (Grönroos 1990). If the perception of an organization's image is favorable, minor mistakes would be tolerated, but if the mistakes occur often, then the image of an organization would be tarnished. Image has been considered to be a predictor of behavioral intentions, indicating that image positively influences behavioral intentions (Wu, Lin and Hsu 2011). Indeed, Han and Back (2008) identify that image is a strong predictor of customers' attitudes and behavioral responses to services and products.

Green equity

Equity, the intangible property, is the hidden value inherent in a well-known organizational name (Yasin, Noor and Mohamad 2007). Higher equity can enable customers to be willing to pay more for the same level of quality due to the attractiveness of the name attached to the product or service (Bello and Holbrook 1995). Rust, Lemin and Zeithaml (2004) propose that equity can be measured as "the total of the discounted lifetime values summed over all of the organization's current and potential customers" (p. 110). In order to maximize the long-term performance of an organization, marketing managers require pursuing a more accountable marketing investment by continuous monitoring of perceived equity (Ramaseshan, Rabbanee and Hui 2013). This chapter proposes a novel construct – green equity – and defines the term as the visitor's subjective and intangible assessment of environmentally-friendly products or services provided by a green farm, above and beyond its objectively perceived value (Kayaman and Arasli 2007). This evaluation is shaped by the green farm's services marketing strategy and tactics and is influenced by the visitor through visiting experiences and associations with the green farm.

Quality has been considered to be an important and direct antecedent of perceived equity, as it provides a reason for customers to differentiate an organization from its competitors (Pappu, Quester and Cooksey 2005). Yoo, Donthu and Lee (2000) were the pioneers of empirically exploring a direct relationship between perceived quality and perceived equity, suggesting a significant but weak relationship between perceived quality and perceived equity. Olsen and Johnson (2003) indicate that equity's role as an antecedent or consequence of satisfaction has become unclear. Although equity should drive transaction-specific satisfaction, Olsen and Johnson (2003) argue that equity plays a very different role in influencing perceptions of cumulative satisfaction and subsequent behavioral intentions. Nam, Ekinci and Whyatt (2011) propose that equity entails favorable disposition that may not necessarily result in purchasing behavior. Therefore, behavioral intentions are one of the consequences of equity, rather than its component.

Green experiential satisfaction

In fact, satisfaction is also an important variable in experiences (Oliver 1980; Westbrook and Oliver 1991). Customer satisfaction of a specific transaction is the immediate evaluation after purchase, or the positive feeling towards recent transaction experiences (Oliver 1993). Customers use their personal experiences to form cognitive and effective evaluation of service relationships and therefore form the degree of satisfaction (Storbacka, Strandvik and Grönroos 1994). Experiential satisfaction is conceived of on the basis of the concept of service satisfaction even though it extends beyond service satisfaction in that it focuses on consumers' overall evaluation of their experiences after consumption. Therefore, from an experiential perspective, experiential satisfaction reflects the satisfaction experienced from the service content associated with a specific transaction. Customers compare their experiences with their prior expectations, causing positive or negative disconfirmation (Kao *et al.* 2008). The emotional responses resulting from positive or negative confirmation form the basis for customer satisfaction or dissatisfaction (Bigné, Andreu and Gnoth 2005). Therefore, the concept of experiential satisfaction is proposed based on an experiential perspective and it is defined as the result of consumers' evaluation of the contents presented by service providers (Kao *et al.* 2008).

Ecological farms are currently facing a growing pressure to become responsible and green. Several stakeholders press organizations to reduce their negative impacts on society and the natural environment (Barnett 2007). With the rise of environmentalism, not only are consumers more willing to purchase products that generate minimum impact, but also society is more concerned with the environment. Therefore, this chapter creates a novel concept – green experiential satisfaction, which is defined as visitors' overall evaluation of environmentally-friendly content based on their experience in an ecological farm (Ho and Tsai 2010; Kao *et al.* 2008). Green experiential satisfaction has been found to be the outcome of the consumption where the performance met or exceeded the green needs of visitors, requirements of environmental regulations, and sustainable expectation of ecological farms (Chang and Fong 2010; Ho and Tsai 2010; Wu 2017; Wu and Ai 2016; Wu, Ai and Cheng 2016; Wu and Cheng 2017; Wu, Cheng and Ai 2017a; Wu, Cheng and Hong 2017b, 2017c; Wu and Li 2017; Wu *et al.* 2018).

Past research has revealed that satisfaction contributes to behavioral intentions (Anderson and Srinivasan 2003). Several researchers (Cronin and Taylor 1992; Cronin, Brady and Hult 2000; Patterson and Spreng 1997; Rust and Oliver 1994) propose that both satisfaction and quality perceptions positively impact the behavioral intentions of a customer. Interestingly, Cronin and Taylor (1992) suggest that satisfaction has been found to have a stronger and more consistent effect on behavioral intentions than quality.

Green behavioral intentions

The behavioral intentions are defined as a signal of whether customers will retain or discard the relationship with the service provider (Zeithaml, Berry and Parasuraman 1996). Although there are numerous definitions for behavioral intentions defined by numerous researchers, the underlying interest as recognized in the literature is that of predictor of the profitability of service organizations (Anderson, Fornell and Lehmann 1994). It is remarkable to note that both costs and revenue of organizations are affected by repeat purchases, positive word-of-mouth (WOM) recommendations and customer feedback (Pai and Chary 2014).

In this chapter, green behavioral intentions are conceptualized as three dimensions, including green purchase intentions, word-of-mouth intentions and willingness to pay towards green products (Zeithaml *et al.* 1996). Following Oliver (1999: 34), green loyalty is defined as "a deeply held commitment to rebuy or patronize a preferred environmental friendly product or service consistently in the future. Also, purchase intention is used as an indicator of loyalty" (Zeithaml *et al.* 1996) which refers to "the likelihood that a consumer would rebuy a particular product resulting from his or her environmental needs" (Chen and Chang 2012: 507).

Netemeyer, Krishnan, Pullig, Wang, Yagci, Dean and Wirth (2004: 220) define the willingness to pay a premium for green products or services as "the amount a customer is willing to pay for his/her preferred green product or brands over non-green ones." Following the definitions of Anderson and Gerbing (1988: 6) and Harrison-Walker (2001: 63), green word-of-mouth intentions are referred to as "customers' willingness to communicate about their preferred green products or services with other persons' informal, person-to-person communication between a perceived non-commercial communicator and a receiver regarding a brand, a product, an organization or a service."

Wu and Li (2015, 2017) argue that experiential satisfaction is an antecedent of behavioral intentions, indicating that visitors' experiential satisfaction positively influences their behavioral intentions. Anderson and Sullivan (1993) argue that the more satisfied the visitors, the greater is their favorable behavioral intention. This view is supported by the studies of Wu, Ai, Yang and Li (2015) and Wu and Li (2017), indicating the effects of satisfaction on behavioral intentions have been identified to be significant and positive. Specifically, the levels of satisfaction will influence the level of behavioral intentions and this is supported by past research in a wide variety of studies (Brady and Robertson 2001; Patterson and Spreng 1997; Rust and Zahorik 1993; Taylor and Baker 1994).

A proposed conceptual model

Despite widespread research (Carman 1990), the theories and appropriateness of service quality measures including the SERVQUAL and SERVPERF scales are subject to ongoing debate (Cronin and Taylor 1994; Zeithaml, Berry and Parasuraman 1993). In light of the aforementioned criticisms of SERVQUAL and SERVPERF, the multi-dimensional method is applied to measure green experiential quality. Brady and Cronin (2001) and Wu and Ai (2016a) argue that this method can be applied to explain the complexity of the perception progress better than prior conceptualizations. Therefore, a multi-dimensional structure as a basic framework to develop the conceptual model adapted from several studies (Brady and Cronin 2001; Dabholkar *et al.* 1995; Shonk and Chelladurai 2008; Wu and Ai 2016a; 2016b). The multi-dimensional model reflects the proposition that visitors form their perceptions of each of the dimensions: green interaction quality, green peer-to-peer quality, green physical environment quality, green outcome quality, green management quality and green venue quality, in order to form an overall green experiential quality perception (Figure 30.1).

There are six dimensions used to form green experiential quality. The first dimension of green experiential quality, green interaction quality, explores how the environmentally-friendly service is provided (Brady and Cronin 2001; Czepiel, Solomon and Suprenant 1985). Several studies (Chang and Fong 2010; Wu and Ai 2016a; Wu and Li 2015) indicate that the interaction between employees and visitors is in the green farm and the subjective rating of how the environmentally-friendly service is delivered through the interaction. The second dimension, green peer-to-peer quality, refers to the perceived judgment of the superiority of visitors' eco-friendly interaction with others. According to this notion, a visitor's helpful (distracting) behavior may influence other visitors' visiting experiences positively (negatively) (Choi and Kim 2013). The third dimension of green experiential quality, green physical environment quality, is based on the equipment provided when an environmentally-friendly service is given to a visitor (Bitner 1992). This dimension is considered to be one of the most important aspects in a green experiential quality

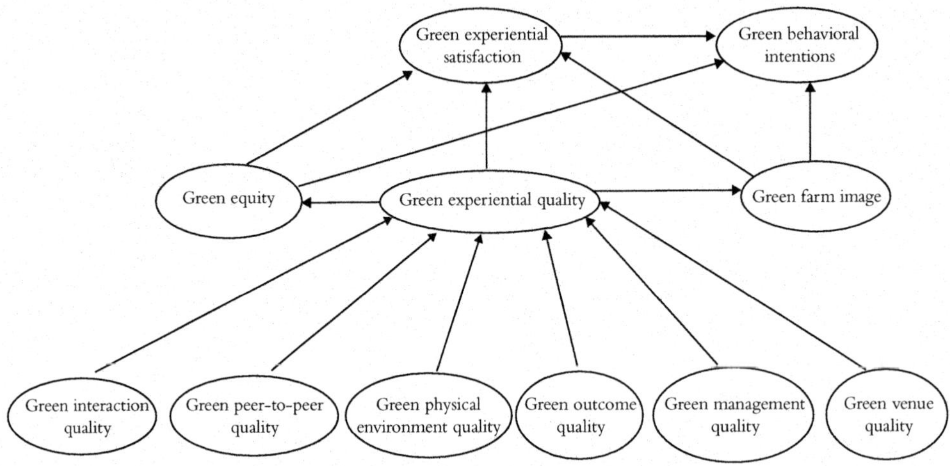

Figure 30.1 A conceptual research model

evaluation (Wu and Li 2017; Wu *et al.* 2018). The fourth dimension of green experiential quality, green outcome quality, places emphasis on the results of the environmentally-friendly service and the concept of quality (Ko and Pastore 2005). Green outcome quality reflects the visitor's perception of the superiority of environmentally-friendly visiting experiences (Brady and Cronin 2001; Grönroos 1984; Wu and Li 2017). The fifth dimension of green experiential quality, green management quality, focuses on the elements in service quality including assurance, employees' environmentally-friendly knowledge and courtesy and their environmentally-friendly ability to inspire trust and confidence in delivering an outcome desired by the visitors (Abdullah, Wasiuzzaman and Musa 2014). The sixth dimension of green experiential quality, green venue quality, refers to the eco-friendly facility where the event is scheduled to take place (Shonk and Chelladurai 2008). This dimension plays a critical role in increasing green experiential quality.

Furthermore, green experiential quality is assumed to influence green equity and green farm image. Green experiential quality, green equity and green farm image are postulated to influence green experiential satisfaction. Green behavioral intentions are expected to be influenced by green equity, green farm image and green experiential satisfaction.

Summary and implications

This chapter contributes to the theoretical advancement of the field of green farm management by empirically testing the relationships among green experiential quality, green farm image, green equity, green experiential satisfaction and green behavioral intentions. In addition, the comprehensive multi-dimensional model developed in this chapter provides a valuable framework for future researchers who might be interested in examining the relationships among the constructs of green farms. Furthermore, the multi-dimensional modeling approach will address some of the weaknesses of traditional measurement methods, such as SERVQUAL (a disconfirmation-based measure of service quality) and SERVPERF (a performance-based measure of service quality) and thus provide a more accurate method for assessing perceived green experiential quality for green farms. From a practical perspective, this chapter provides further insight for green farm management to better understand green behavioral intentions by using the proposed model, providing useful information to services marketing managers who are designing the products and services in green farms. Also, this chapter will provide green farm management with a clear understanding of relevant dimensions of green experiential quality because they derive from the green farm visitors' perspectives so that so that management will know exactly how to make a choice about the best way to allocate scarce resources.

Green farm management can use the multi-dimensional model developed in this chapter in its strategic planning process as a green farm provides a framework for evaluating visitors' perceptions of their overall visiting experiences. Understanding visitors in a green farm setting will help green farm management to better understand what its visitors want. However, as the dimensions of green experiential quality may vary across industries and cultures, green farm management should note that dimensional structures may need to be factored for its own specific situation and cultural setting. This information will enable green farm management to accurately measure its visitors' perceptions of visiting experiences.

References

Abdullah, A.H., Wasiuzzaman, S. and Musa, R. (2014) "The Effects of University Quality on Emotional Attachment: A Case from a Private Higher Education Institution," *Procedia-Social and Behavioral Sciences* 130, 282–92.

Al-Alak, B.A. (2009) "Measuring and Evaluating Business Students Satisfaction Perceptions at Public and Private Universities in Jordan," *Asian Journal of Marketing* 3(2), 33–51.

Anderson, E.W., Fornell, C. and Lehmann, D.R. (1994) "Customer Satisfaction, Market Share, and Profitability: Findings from Sweden," *Journal of Marketing* 58(3), 53–66.

Anderson, J.C. and Gerbing, D.W. (1988) "Structural Equation Modeling in Practice: A Review and Recommended Two-step Approach," *Psychological Bulletin* 103(3), 411–23.

Anderson, E.W. and Sullivan, M. (1993) "The Antecedents and Consequences of Customer Satisfaction for Firms," *Marketing Science* 12(2), 125–43.

Anderson, R.E. and Srinivasan, S.S. (2003) "E-satisfaction and E-loyalty: A Contingency Framework," *Psychology & Marketing* 20(2), 123–38.

Barnett, M.L. (2007) "Stakeholder Influence Capacity and the Variability of Financial Returns to Corporate Social Responsibility," *Academy of Management Review* 32(3), 794–816.

Bello, D.C. and Holbrook, M.B. (1995) "Does an Absence of Brand Equity Generalize Across Produce Classes," *Journal of Business Research* 34(2), 125–31.

Bigné, J.E., Andreu, L. and Gnoth, J. (2005) "The Theme Park Experience: An Analysis of Pleasure, Arousal and Satisfaction," *Tourism Management* 26(6), 833–44.

Bitner, M.J. (1992) "Servicescapes: The Impact of Physical Surroundings on Customers and Employees," *Journal of Marketing* 56(2), 57–71.

Brady, M.K. and Cronin, J.J. (2001) "Some New Thoughts on Conceptualizing Perceived Service Quality: A Hierarchical Approach," *Journal of Marketing* 65(3), 34–49.

Brady, M.K. and Robertson, C.J. (2001) "Searching for a Consensus on the Antecedent Role of Service Quality and Satisfaction: An Exploratory Cross-national Study," *Journal of Business Research* 51(1), 53–60.

Brown, T.J., Churchill, G.A. and Peter, J.P. (1993) "Improving the Measurement of Service Quality," *Journal of Retailing* 69(1), 127–39.

Buttle, F. (1996) "SERVQUAL: Review, Critique, Research Agenda," *European Journal of Marketing* 30(1), 8–35.

Carman, J M. (1990) "Consumer Perceptions of Service Quality: An Assessment of the SERVQUAL Dimensions," *Journal of Retailing* 66(1), 33–55.

Chang, N.J. and Fong, C.M. (2010) "Green Product Quality, Green Corporate Image, Green Customer Satisfaction, and Green Customer Loyalty," *African Journal of Business Management* 4(13), 2836–44.

Chen, C.F. and Chen, F.S. (2010) "Experience Quality, Perceived Value, Satisfaction and Behavioral Intentions for Heritage Tourists," *Tourism Management* 31(1), 29–35.

Chen, Y.S. (2008) "The Driver of Green Innovation and Green Image–Green Core Competence," *Journal of Business Ethics* 81(3), 531–43.

Chen, Y.S. and Chang, C.H. (2012) "Enhance Green Purchase Intentions: The Roles of Green Perceived Value, Green Perceived Risk, and Green Trust," *Management Decision* 50(3), 502–20.

Choi, B.J. and Kim, H.S. (2013) "The Impact of Outcome Quality, Interaction Quality, and Peer-to-Peer Quality on Customer Satisfaction with a Hospital Service," *Journal of Service Theory and Practice* 23(3), 188–204.

Cole, S.T. and Chancellor, H.C. (2009) "Examining the Festival Attributes that Impact Visitor Experience, Satisfaction and Revisit Intention," *Journal of Vacation Marketing* 15(4), 323–33.

Cole, S.T. and Scott, D. (2004) "Examining the Mediating Role of Experience Quality in a Model of Tourist Experiences," *Journal of Travel & Tourism Marketing* 16(1), 79–90.

Cronin, J.J., Brady, M.K. and Hult, G.T.M. (2000) "Assessing the Effects of Quality, Value, and Customer Satisfaction on Consumer Behavioral Intentions in Service Environments," *Journal of Retailing* 76(2), 193–218.

Cronin, J.J. and Taylor, S.A. (1992) "Measuring Service Quality: A Reexamination and Extension," *Journal of Marketing* 56(3), 55–68.

Cronin, J.J. and Taylor, S.A. (1994) "SERVPERF Versus SERVQUAL: Reconciling Performance-based and Perceptions-minus-expectations Measurement of Service Quality," *Journal of Marketing* 58(1), 125–31.

Czepiel, J.A., Solomon, M.R. and Suprenant, C.E. (1985) *The Service Encounter*, Lexington Books, Lexington, MA.

Dabholkar, P.A. (1995) "A Contingency Framework for Predicting Causality between Satisfaction and Service Quality," in F.R. Kardes and M. Sujan (eds) *Advances in Consumer Research*, Vol. 22, Provo, UT: Association for Consumer Research, 101–06.

Dabholkar, P.A., Thorpe, D.I. and Rentz, J.O. (1995) "A Measure of Service Quality for Retail Stores: Scale Development and Validation," *Journal of the Academy of Marketing Science* 24(1), 3–16.

Dagger, T.S., Sweeney, J.C. and Johnson, L.W. (2007) "A Hierarchical Model of Health Service Quality Scale Development and Investigation of an Integrated Model," *Journal of Service Research* 10(2), 123–42.

De Rojas, C. and Camarero, C. (2008) "Visitors' Experience, Mood and Satisfaction in a Heritage Context: Evidence from an Interpretation Center," *Tourism Management* 29(3), 525–37.

Grönroos, C. (1984) A service quality model and its marketing implications," *European Journal of Marketing* 18(4), 36–44.

Grönroos, C. (1990) *Service Management and Marketing: Managing the Moments of Truth in Service Competition*, Lexington, MA: Lexington Books.

Han, H. and Back, K.J. (2008) "Relationships among Image Congruence, Consumption Emotions, and Customer Loyalty in the Lodging Industry," *Journal of Hospitality & Tourism Research* 32(4), 467–90.

Harrison-Walker, L.J. (2001) "The Measurement of Word-of-mouth Communication and an Investigation of Service Quality and Customer Commitment as Potential Antecedents," *Journal of Service Research* 4(1), 60–75.

Ho, P.T. and Tsai, H.Y. (2010) "A Study of Visitors' Recreational Experience Types in Relationship to Customer Retention in Leisure Farm," *Journal of Global Business Management* 6(2), 1–7.

Jin, N.P., Lee, S. and Lee, H. (2015) "The Effect of Experience Quality on Perceived Value, Satisfaction, Image and Behavioral Intention of Water Park Patrons: New Versus Repeat Visitors," *International Journal of Tourism Research* 17(1), 82–95.

Kao, Y.F., Huang, L.S. and Wu, C.H. (2008) "Effects of Theatrical Elements on Experiential Quality and Loyalty Intentions for Theme Parks," *Asia Pacific Journal of Tourism Research* 13(2), 163–74.

Kao, Y.F., Huang, L.S. and Yang, M.H. (2007) "Effects of Experiential Elements on Experiential Satisfaction and Loyalty Intentions: A Case Study of the Super Basketball League in Taiwan," *International Journal of Revenue Management* 1(1), 79–96.

Kayaman, R. and Arasli, H. (2007) "Customer based Brand Equity: Evidence from the Hotel Industry," *Journal of Service Theory and Practice* 17(1), 92–109.

Kim, H.D. and Lough, N. (2007) "An Investigation into Relationships among Constructs of Service Quality, Customer Satisfaction, and Repurchase Intention in Korean Private Golf Courses," *The ICHPER-SD Journal of Research in Health, Physical Education, Recreation, Sport & Dance* 2(1), 14–22.

Ko, Y.J. and Pastore, D.L. (2005) "A Hierarchical Model of Service Quality for the Recreational Sport Industry," *Sport Marketing Quarterly* 14(2), 84–97.

Lemke, F., Clark, M. and Wilson, H. (2011) "Customer Experience Quality: An Exploration in Business and Consumer Contexts Using Repertory Grid Technique," *Journal of the Academy of Marketing Science* 39(6), 846–69.

Liou, J.J. and Chuang, M.L. (2010) "Evaluating Corporate Image and Reputation Using Fuzzy MCDM Approach in Airline Market," *Quality & Quantity* 44(6), 1079–91.

Nadiri, H. and Hussain, K. (2005) "Perceptions of Service Quality in North Cyprus Hotels," *International Journal of Contemporary Hospitality Management* 17(6) 469–80.

Nam, J., Ekinci, Y. and Whyatt, G. (2011) "Brand Equity, Brand Loyalty and Consumer Satisfaction." *Annals of Tourism Research* 38(3), 1009–30.

Netemeyer, R.G., Krishnan, B., Pullig, C., Wang, G., Yagci, M., Dean, D. and Wirth, F. (2004) "Developing and Validating Measures of Facets of Customer-based Brand Equity," *Journal of Business Research* 57(2), 209–24.

Oliver, R.L. (1980) "A Cognitive Model of the Antecedents and Consequences of Satisfaction Decisions," *Journal of Marketing Research*17(4), 460–69.

Oliver, R.L. (1993) "Cognitive, Affective, and Attribute Bases of the Satisfaction Response," *Journal of Consumer Research* 20(3), 418–30.

Oliver, R.L. (1999) "Whence consumer loyalty?" *Journal of Marketing* 63(4), 33–44.

Olorunniwo, F., Hsu, M.K. and Udo, G.J. (2006) "Service Quality, Customer Satisfaction, and Behavioral Intentions in the Service Factory," *Journal of Services Marketing* 20(1), 59–72.

Olsen, L.L. and Johnson, M.D. (2003) "Service Equity, Satisfaction, and Loyalty: from Transaction-specific to Cumulative Evaluations," *Journal of Service Research* 5(3), 184–195.

Pai, Y. and Chary, S.T. (2014) "The Impact of Healthscape on Service Quality and Behavioral Intentions," *International Journal of Conceptions on Management and Social Sciences* 2(2), 18–22.

Pappu, R., Quester, P. and Cooksey, R.W. (2005) "Consumer-based Brand Equity: Improving the Measurement-empirical Evidence," *Journal of Product and Brand Management* 14(3), 143–54.

Parasuraman, A., Zeithaml, V.A. and Berry, L.L. (1985) "A Conceptual Model of Service Quality and Its Implications for Future Research," *Journal of Marketing* 49(4), 41–50.

Parasuraman, A., Zeithaml, V.A. and Berry, L.L. (1988) "SERVQUAL: A Multiple-item Scale for Measuring Consumer Perceptions of Service Quality," *Journal of Retailing* 64(1), 12–40.

Patterson, P.G. and Spreng, R.A. (1997) "Modeling the Relationship between Perceived Value, Satisfaction and Repurchase Intentions in a Business-business, Services Context: An Empirical Examination," *International Journal of Service Industry Management* 8(5), 414–18.

Ramaseshan, B., Rabbanee, F.K. and Hui, L.T.H. (2013) "Effects of Customer Equity Drivers on Customer Loyalty in B2B Context," *Journal of Business & Industrial Marketing* 28(4), 335–46.

Rust, R.T., Lemon, K.N. and Zeithaml, V.A. (2004) "Return on Marketing: Using Customer Equity to Focus Marketing Strategy," *Journal of Marketing* 68(1), 109–127.

Rust, R.T. and Oliver, R.L. (1994) "Service Quality: Insights and Managerial Implications from the Frontier" In R.T. Rust and R.L. Oliver (eds) *Service Quality: New Directions in Theory and Practice*, Thousand Oaks, CA: Sage, 1–19.

Rust, R. and Zahorik, A.J. (1993) "Customer Satisfaction, Customer Retention, and Market Share," *Journal of Retailing* 69(2), 193–215.

Shonk, D.J. and Chelladurai, P. (2008) "Service Quality, Satisfaction, and Intent to Return in Event Sport Tourism," *Journal of Sport Management* 22(5), 587–602.

Storbacka, K., Strandvik, T. and Grönroos, C. (1994) "Managing Customer Relationships for Profit: The Dynamics of Relationship Quality," *International Journal of Service Industry Management* 5(5), 21–38.

Taylor, S.A. and Baker, T.L. (1994) "An Assessment of the Relationship between Service Quality and Customer Satisfaction in the Formation of Consumers' Purchase Intentions," *Journal of Retailing* 70(2), 163–78.

Teas, K.R. (1993) "Expectations, Performance Evaluation and Customer's Perceptions of Quality," *Journal of Marketing* 57(9), 18–34.

Westbrook, R.A. and Oliver, R.L. (1991) "The Dimensionality of Consumption Emotion Patterns and Consumer Satisfaction," *Journal of Consumer Research* 18(1), 84–91.

Wu, H.C. (2017) "What Drives Experiential Loyalty? A Case Study of Starbucks Coffee Chain in Taiwan," *British Food Journal* 119(3), 468–496.

Wu, H.C. and Ai, C.H. (2016a) "Synthesizing the Effects of Experiential Quality, Excitement, Equity, Experiential Satisfaction on Experiential Loyalty for the Golf Industry: The Case of Hainan Island," *Journal of Hospitality and Tourism Management* 29, 41–59.

Wu, H.C. and Ai, C.H. (2016b) "A Study of Festival Switching Intentions, Festival Satisfaction, Festival Image, Festival Affective Impacts and Festival Quality," *Tourism and Hospitality Research* 16(4), 359–384.

Wu, H.C., Ai, C.H., and Cheng, C.C. (2016) "Synthesizing the Effects of Green Experiential Quality, Green Equity, Green Image and Green Experiential Satisfaction on Green Switching Intention," *International Journal of Contemporary Hospitality Management* 28(9), 2080–2107.

Wu, H.C. and Cheng, C.C. (2017) "What Drives Experiential Loyalty towards Smart Restaurants? The Case Study of KFC in Beijing," *Journal of Hospitality Marketing & Management*. DOI: 10.1080/19368623.2017.1344952

Wu, H.C., Cheng, C.C. and Ai, C.H. (2017a) "A Study of Experiential Quality, Equity, Happiness, Rural Image, Experiential Satisfaction and Behavioral Intentions for the Rural Tourism Industry in China," *International Journal of Hospitality & Tourism Administration* 18(4), 393–428.

Wu, H.C., Cheng, C.C. and Hong, W. (2017b) "An Empirical Analysis of Green Convention Attendees' Switching Intentions," *Journal of Convention and Event Tourism* 18(3), 159–190.

Wu, H.C., Cheng, C.C. and Hong, W. (2017c) "An Assessment of Zoo Visitors' Revisit Intentions," *Tourism Analysis* 22(23), 361–375.

Wu, H.C., Ai, C.H., Yang, L.J. and Li, T. (2015) "A Study of Revisit Intentions, Customer Satisfaction, Corporate Image, Emotions and Service Quality in the Hot Spring Industry," *Journal of China Tourism Research* 11(4), 371–401.

Wu, H.C. and Li, T. (2017) "A Study of Experiential Quality, Perceived Value, Heritage Image, Experiential Satisfaction, and Behavioral Intentions for Heritage Tourists," *Journal of Hospitality & Tourism Research* 41(8), 904–944.

Wu, H.C. and Li, T. (2015) "An Empirical Study of the Effects of Service Quality, Visitor Satisfaction, and Emotions on Behavioral Intentions of Visitors to the Museums of Macau," *Journal of Quality Assurance in Hospitality & Tourism* 16(1), 80–102.

Wu, H.C., Li, M.M. and Li, T. (2018) "A Study of Experiential Quality, Experiential Value, Experiential Satisfaction, Theme Park Image and Revisit Intention," *Journal of Hospitality & Tourism Research* 42(1), 26–73.

Wu, J.H.C., Lin, Y.C. and Hsu, F.S. (2011) "An Empirical Analysis of Synthesizing the Effects of Service Quality, Perceived Value, Corporate Image and Customer Satisfaction on Behavioral Intentions in the Transport Industry: A Case of Taiwan High-speed Rail," *Innovative Marketing* 7(3), 83–100.

Xu, J.B. and Chan, A. (2010) "A Conceptual Framework of Hotel Experience and Customer-based Brand Equity: Some Research Questions and Implications," *International Journal of Contemporary Hospitality Management* 22(2), 174–93.

Yasin, N.M., Noor, M.N. and Mohamad, O. (2007) "Does Image of Country-of-Origin Matter to Brand Equity?" *Journal of Product and Brand Management* 16(1), 38–48.

Yelkur, R. (2000) "Customer Satisfaction and the Services Marketing Mix," *Journal of Professional Services Marketing* 21(1), 105–15.

Yoo, B., Donthu, N. and Lee, S. (2000) "An Examination of Selected Marketing Mix Elements and Brand Equity," *Academy of Marketing Science* 28(2), 195–212.

Zeithaml, V.A., Berry, L.L. and Parasuraman, A. (1993) "The Nature and Determinants of Customer Expectations of Service," *Journal of the Academy of Marketing Science* 21(1), 1–12.

Zeithaml, V.A., Berry, L.L. and Parasuraman, A. (1996) "The Behavioral Consequences of Service Quality," *Journal of Marketing* 60(2), 31–46.

Zeithaml, V.A., Parasuraman, A. and Berry, L.L. (1990) *Delivering Quality Service*, The Free Press, New York, NY.

Further reading

Buttle, F. (1996) "SERVQUAL: Review, Critique, Research Agenda," *European Journal of Marketing* 30(1), 8–35. (An extended review and critique of the SERVQUAL scale.)

Dabholkar, P.A., Thorpe, D.I. and Rentz, J.O. (1995) "A Measure of Service Quality for Retail Stores: Scale Development and Validation," *Journal of the Academy of Marketing Science* 24(1), 3–16. (A multi-dimensional and hierarchical model of service quality for the retailing industry.)

Kao, Y.F., Huang, L.S. and Wu, C.H. (2008) "Effects of Theatrical Elements on Experiential Quality and Loyalty Intentions for Theme Parks," *Asia Pacific Journal of Tourism Research* 13(2), 163–74. (The dimensions of experiential quality.)

Parasuraman, A., Zeithaml, V.A. and Berry, L.L. (1988) "SERVQUAL: A Multiple-item Scale for Measuring Consumer Perceptions of Service Quality," *Journal of Retailing* 64(1), 12–40. (The dimensions of the SERVQUAL scale.)

Rust, R.T. and Oliver, R.L. (1994) "Service Quality: Insights and Managerial Implications from the Frontier" In R.T. Rust and R.L. Oliver (eds) *Service Quality: New Directions in Theory and Practice*, Thousand Oaks, CA: Sage, 1–19. (A discussion of the service quality dimensions.)

Wu, H.C. and Li, T. (2017) "A Study of Experiential Quality, Perceived Value, Heritage Image, Experiential Satisfaction, and Behavioral Intentions for Heritage Tourists," *Journal of Hospitality & Tourism Research* 41(8), 904–944. (A multi-dimensional and hierarchical model of experiential quality for heritages.)

Part VI

Innovation in destination marketing

31

Innovations in destination marketing

Evrim Çeltek and İbrahim İlhan

Introduction

Innovation is one of the key issues that affects businesses competitiveness. Today's customers are progressively using social media, mobile phones, and PCs. With these technologies, customers easily realize what they need, compare with alternative items, get recommendations from friends, family, and colleagues, purchase from where they're located, and tell their experiences to others afterward. The balance of power has clearly shifted from suppliers to customers. In today's Internet and mobile-enabled world, customer expectations are being formed by daily interactions with companies across varied industries. However, this transformation would require new ways of thinking about company culture, business processes, and technology investments (Sharma and Sharma, 2014).

Destinations are places that attract visitors for a temporary stay, ranging from continents to countries, to states (Pike, 2004). However, destination promoting and management may be a complicated issue which requires a comprehensive, holistic and systematic approach to knowing it. From the demand side, travelers have a range of selections about destinations; from the supply side, destination marketing organizations are trying their best to compete for attention from a highly competitive marketplace (Wang, 2011).

Tourism destinations are one of the most difficult "products" to promote, involving large numbers of stakeholders and have a brand image destination marketing manager who generally has little control over that. The range and complexity of tourism destinations makes marketing very difficult for national, regional and local tourism organizations. Information and communication technologies (ICTs) revolutionize tourism and create opportunities for promotion and interaction with the tourist (Buhalis, 2003). The target of this chapter is to outline the innovative applications in destination marketing.

Innovative approaches to destination marketing

Creating innovative product and marketing innovative services is presently one of the most frequently studied topics in terms of science and analysis in tourism. The tourism market requires innovative services and products (Maráková and Medved'ová, 2016). Marketers in all industries are currently creating interesting, useful and entertaining stories to interact and interest customers to start long-term relationships. In recent years, the innovation processes in marketing channels have occurred with high intensity and speed, particularly following the changes spurred by technology that allowed the adoption of more efficient organizational solutions (Musso, 2010). In tourism industry, marketers have developed and applied technology based on innovative marketing strategies that are utilized in destinations marketing. This chapter determines virtual reality, advergame, augmented reality and QR codes from the perspective of innovative approaches to destination marketing and their advantages.

Virtual reality in destination marketing

Virtual reality (VR) is defined as the use of a computer-generated 3D environment – called a "virtual environment" (VE) – that one can navigate and possibly interact with, resulting in real-time simulation of one or more of the user's five senses. "Navigate" refers to the ability to move around and explore the VE, and "interact" refers to the ability to select and move objects within the VE. (Guttentag, 2010). Virtual reality application represents three-dimensional, interactive, computer-generated environments. These environments can be models of real or imaginary worlds, and their purpose is to represent information through a synthetic experience. The virtual reality technology was born from the merging of many disciplines, including psychology, cybernetics, computer graphics, data-base design, real-time and distributed systems, electronics, robotics, multimedia, and telepresence (Gurau, 2007). From a marketing perspective, VR has the potential to revolutionize the promotion and selling of tourism (Williams and Hobson, 1995). Just as VR can be used to plan and manage a destination, it also can be used to market a destination (Cheong, 1995).

Many tourism products already use VR or VR-type technologies to attract tourists. For instance, on the Internet one can find many hotels (e.g. www.showhotel.com) and destinations (e.g. www.virtualgettysburg.com) offering "virtual tours." These "virtual tours" often are simply panoramic photographs that do not permit any free navigation, meaning they are not genuine VR, but they importantly still reveal an interest in VR-type technologies (Guttentag, 2010). One VR travel community named "Itchy Feet" (www.itchy-feet.org) is already being developed as an SL-type virtual world in which tourists can seek out travel information, communicate with other tourists, and make travel purchases (Cheong, 1995).

Advantages of virtual reality in destination marketing

Virtual experiences provide more practical advertising than brochures for each theme park and natural park. A "virtual tour" of panoramic photos on a hotel website might provide psychological relief to people feeling travel anxiety. Visiting a museum's website will increase one's interest in visiting the real museum, and serves as indirect evidence that visiting tourism destinations in VR might encourage real visitation (Guttentag, 2010). For instance, someone interested in exploring an island destination would be able to enter virtual island destinations like Hawaii, Virgin Islands, the Seychelles, the Maldives, Jamaica, and others. Having vicariously experienced some of what the islands have to provide, the consumer would be in a better position to make an informed decision and initiate travel arrangements. Even though the alternative destinations haven't been chosen, images from the virtual experience still linger within the consumer's mind and these might create a desire and induce the client to go to those places within the future (Cheong, 1995).

Virtual reality can serve as a marketing instrument for destinations. Virtual reality systems afford tourist the opportunity to experience previews of destinations and their respective attractions and facilities. They would be able to "sample" the delights and have a "feel" of each destination's atmosphere before making their decision as to which tourist spot to visit (Guttentag, 2010). In addition to serving as a tourism marketing tool, VR systems can also be used for direct marketing (Cheong, 1995).

Advergames in destination marketing

Advergames are a strong tool to create brand loyalty and capture crucial information about existing and potential customers. They include distinctive interactive games with a suite of advertising inventively inbuilt. By combining games and ads, it's attainable to boost branding, boost product awareness and collect detailed information about participants. Branding conception is additionally a vital issue for tourist destinations. Advergames are seen as conceptually new and innovative channels of communication particularly likely to succeed in well-defined target markets (Kretchmer, 2003).

In the literature, advergaming has been defined in many ways. Solomon (2003, 166) states "Advergaming, the use of product placement in computer games, is one of the new frontiers in online promotion. Games built around brands enhance realism and further reinforce the connection between brand images and social attributes." In another study, Afshar (2004, 16) defines advergaming as follows: "Advergaming is the use of interactive gaming technology to deliver embedded advertising messages to customers." In addition to these studies, advergaming has been researched in others. "Advergaming is the use of interactive gaming technology to deliver embedded advertising messages to consumers. Advergaming incorporates branding directly into the gaming environment. With an advergame, companies lure the consumer into interaction with their brand" (Mráček and Mucha, 2011). Under the term "advergaming" the brand on-line games can be understood as the promotional tool, where the main objective of the game is handing-over of message of the brand. The games then represent the advertising material, designed to support the product or brand (Wise et al., 2008). Advergaming, which is "delivery of advertising messages through electronic games," has become an accepted strategy among marketers to reach a target audience (Hernandez and Chapa, 2010, 59). In advergaming, the aim is to offer entertainment and to engage web or electronic game users in order to make an emotional connection between the game and the brand featured within it (Dahl, Eagle and Baez, 2006). Advergames are a form of viral marketing in which "Word of mouse" rewards customers when they help with some of the heavy lifting that comes with releasing a new product or promoting an existing brand. At one extreme is a game that simply slaps a logo on the screen or displays a banner ad. At the other extreme is a game that is created from the ground up, specifically to showcase the unique features of the brand and immerse the player in the message (Afshar, 2004, 20).

Advergames are beneficial in many ways for destination marketing. To start with, a well-designed game can generate interaction and involvement with the destination; make the destination more top of mind for consumers (Rodgers, 2001). If the game is intensely playable, it will have a strong pass along rate. By consumers passing along destination's game, which in essence is destination's message, they are endorsing destination's brand (Zodal, 2008).

Advantages of advergames in destination marketing

Games allow different levels of brand promotion, from passive placement of destination, to the destination being an integral part of the game itself. Advergame advantages for destinations are as follows;

- Non-annoying advertising; it is introduced within the content which customers are enjoying. It allows understanding the preferences of the customers; at the same time creates a greater implication with the message and identification with the destination brand name. Personalized; it is interactive and capable of meeting the person after the advertisement; it is possible to adjust publicity to each person and moment of the day (www.unkasoft .com, 2008).
- According to Santos, Gonzalo and Gisbert (2007), advergame advantages are stated as follows: it reinforces brand image; databases created from the advergame can be used for demographics research, targeted markets can be reached by your advertising (when the game link is emailed), and visitors may spend more time on the site.
- It provides a low-cost marketing in comparison with the traditional advertising channels, such as TV and radio, which leads to a captured audience that can transmit valuable personal information about their demographic profile, behavior, needs, attitudes and preferences; customer retention keeping in mind that the average time spent in an advergame is 7 to 30 minutes, which cannot be achieved in the case of a classical TV advertisement; and viral marketing – 81% of the players will email their friends to try a good game (Gurau, 2008).
- Moreover, the advergaming can also be beneficial for the maintaining of long-term good relations with the customers. The long-term good relations then influence the customer satisfaction. The advergame can even be perceived as a sort of supplement to the product or service. So as to strengthen the relationship with the customers, the quality of the advertising game (advergame) itself should be paid attention to (Mráček and Mucha, 2011; Talvar, 2005).

Case study

UK tourist destination

On May 21, 2009 Shakespeare Country launched the game "Romeo wherefore art thou?" to promote Shakespeare Country as a UK tourist destination. Both UK and worldwide audiences were encouraged to interact with the game based on William Shakespeare's birth place of Stratford Upon Avon. The primary objective of Shakespeare Country was to raise brand awareness for the area incorporating some of the attractions that can be found at the location followed by capturing email addresses and drive traffic to the Shakespeare Country website. To encourage players to leave their e-mail address, a competition (running for 12 months) was held for players to win a short break to Shakespeare Country each month along with tickets to Warwick Castle, the Royal Shakespeare Company and the Shakespeare Houses. In the game, there are certain buttons named as *high score competition entry button, challenge/share your score with your friends button* and *visit Shakespeare country web site button.* The following statistics may give an idea of how the game was received: game was played by 7.5 million in 6 weeks, 38 million played after 18 months and 51 million played after 137 weeks. According to memecounter there was a 39% return rate and an average view time of 8.25 minute (first 6 weeks). 1.7 million clicks in the first 6 weeks, 2.5 million clicks in less than 3 months to the website Shakespeare-country.co.uk. Over 24 million plays in less than a year and 180,000 e-mail addresses are added to the database. There are over 500,000 additional unique visitors in its first full month after launch. More than 200,000 additional unique visitors visit the Shakespeare Country web site every month. Over 20,000 comments on game sites about the game; ratings between 76 to 82 on a scale of 100 (Veenendaal, 2014).

VeGame

The Venice Game project explores how mobile gaming can help users enhance their experience of art and history through a pleasant and challenging interaction with an urban environment's heritage and people. VeGame's participants form teams that share a handheld and play along Venice's narrow streets, discovering the city's art and history through engaging microgames (Bellotti et al., 2003). VeGame is a mobile game which has the intention to enhance user's experiences of architecture, art and history. The playground of the game is urban environment of Venice, where students and tourists play along the city's streets, discovering its art and history. The structure of the game resembles a treasure hunt (http://cordis.europa.eu/ictresults/index.cfm/section/news/tpl/article/BrowsingType/Features/ID/57335/highlights/VeGame). VeGame can be played in teams or individually and each participating team uses a pocket PC with VeGame software. It stimulates competition between players by assigning scores for player's activity and a team or a player wins by completing the challenging tasks of the game best, not fastest. VeGame has a messaging and chat system which lets the team exchange comments about their experiences. During the game, participants go through different stages which are associated with different points of interest in Venice – churches, squares, and palaces. Each stage is divided into smaller trials – microgames, which can be of different types: HistoricalQuize, VisualQuize, RightPlace, Couples, Dialect, Casanova, Memory, VideoGame and others. When a stage in VeGame completes, the next destination (the start of the next stage) and the low-detail map that helps the player to reach it are shown to the player. VeGame doesn't use any automatic positioning system. Completing an enrolment situated in the destination area is required in GeographicQuize. The player launches upon reaching the new stage's start (Lopatina, 2005, p. 17).

Rio de Janeiro and Korea

Rio de Janeiro has embedded QR codes into their sidewalks to assist tourists to learn more regarding the city and more easily get to where they are going. The codes have been embedded into the city's traditional mosaic sidewalks in the form of black and white tiles. The codes provide tourists with additional information regarding the most visited spots such as Ipanema beach. In order to activate such codes, users have to take a picture of the code and the data can then be read by an application downloadable to their mobile phones. The scanned code offers links to websites or different interactive content. In Gibraltar, QR codes take users to a Wikipedia page of information regarding the tourist attraction they are visiting. Once the tiles are scanned, a local map and information is provided to the user in English, Spanish, or Portuguese. Brazil plans to embed roughly 30 QR codes at beaches, vistas and numerous historic sites round the city, helping Rio's two million foreign visitors every year get around (www.bbc.com, 2013). Gangnam-gu recently placed QR codes on the sidewalks for the first time in Korea. These QR codes contain tourist information regarding major tourist attractions within the Gangnam area. The QR code is 60cm in width and length and can be found in eight places around Sinsadong Garosu-gil Road and COEX. By simply scanning the QR Code with a smartphone, tourist can notice information on nearby tourist sites. For this, Gangnam-gu transformed printed tourism promotional materials such as tourism brochures of Gangnam-gu, Garosu-gil, and COEX into mobile contents and created mobile pages with them (Younghee, 2013).

Augmented reality in destination marketing

The growing use of smart phones is driving the mobile applications market to be one of the fastest growing media outlets in the history of consumer technology (Eden and Gretzel, 2012).

Many destinations use augmented reality (AR) to attract customers and to increase customer engagement (Höllerer and Feiner, 2004). AR allows smart phone and tablet computer users to point their phone's or tablet's cameras at certain objects (Azuma, 1997; Linaza et al, 2012) – be it a print advertisement or even a coffee cup or brochures /magazines – that trigger a 3D video. AR gives tourism businesses opportunities to unexpectedly integrate the digital world with the real world, which appeals to younger tech-lovers who are usually skeptical of traditional advertising methods (Craig, 2013). However, AR does not only appeal to the young generation, but also the older generation, which explains why ABI Research estimates the market for augmented reality in the US will reach $350 million in 2014, up from only $6 million in 2008 (Russell, 2012).

AR is the process of taking and integrating digital information with a live streaming video or with the user's actual, real time environment. This technology will take a current picture and will blend the new information into the image (Höllerer and Feiner, 2004; Craig, 2013; Berryman, 2012). The source of the AR is the software that was developed. The AR that is utilized by smart phones will utilize GPS technology and allow the users location to be pinpointed in order to determine the device orientation (Taylor, 2013). The basic goal of an AR system is to enhance the user's perception of and interaction with the real world through supplementing the real world with 3D virtual objects that appear to coexist in the same space as the real world (Azuma et al, 2001).

AR applications are characterized as an overlay of computer graphics to the user's actual field of view (Haala and Böhm, 2003). In AR technology, reality and virtual world are enhanced or augmented, which assures the users experience the combination of both worlds (Carmigniani et al, 2011; Russell, 2013). By AR, virtual images are generated by computers and these images could be superimposed onto physical objects in real time. In other words, virtual images are used to interact with the users in a smooth way (Billinghurst, 2002).

AR is utilized to present new products and thus attract prospective customers. AR is used in museums to provide their customers with additional information about an object or current displays. Similar to museums, AR is used in sightseeing to provide information about a destination, a tourist attraction or the reconstructions of ruins in a particular place. Berryman (2012) states that AR is even used to provide "situated documentaries" that "narrate historical events that took place in the user's immediate area by overlaying 3-D graphics and sound on what the user sees and hears" (Kounavis et al, 2012).

Advantages of augmented reality in destination marketing

AR has many advantages for the tourism destinations and customers. These advantages are explained below:

- Their use in marketing is particularly appealing, as not only can additional, detailed content be put within a traditional 2D advert, but also the results are interactive, cool, engaging and, due to the initial novelty, have high viral potential. Consumers react positively to fun, clever marketing, and as a result, brands become memorable (Singh and Pandey, 2014; Dubois, 2011).
- It is possible for the advertiser to personalize the communication as per the user since user is in charge of the navigation. There is no restriction of space or time like the traditional media (Kounavis et al, 2012; Damala, Marchal and Houlier, 2007).
- If done properly, an AR advertisement has the potential of going viral. One satisfied consumer would recommend it to his friends; thus, number of scans increases (Singh and Pandey, 2014). There is the opportunity for customers to share their personalized content with others.

- An AR application can be developed at a much lower cost than those on other traditional media. Also, the advertisers can measure the response to the advertisement in real time (Singh and Pandey, 2014).

AR strengthens tourism destination connection with mobile consumers seeking for more information, entertainment, when and where they want it. Customers can augment any object or image that has a unique visual profile like brand logo, land marks, posters, bill boards, tourism catalogs, magazine cover/page, posters, signage, brochures, retail displays, business cards, and the like (Carmigniani et al, 2011; Berryman, 2012).

QR codes in destination marketing

Quick Response code or QR code is a two-dimensional (2-D) bar code developed in 1994 by Denso Wave Corporation (Zhang, Yao and Zhou, 2012, p. 817; Albăstroiu and Felea, 2015); QR code got this name as a result of it was developed to improve the reading speed of complex-structured second barcodes. This kind of code was at first used for tracking inventory in vehicle components manufacturing; currently it is utilized in a diversity of industries and innovative applications (Briseno et al, 2012, p. 222).

QR codes may be applied on labels or wrappings of product, on flyers, brochures, catalogs, billboards, posters, adverts in newspapers/magazines, transporting tickets, invitations to events, greetings cards, business cards etc. depending on the kind of information recognized and therefore the nature of the application. Various actions can follow the decoding stage, like (Rouillard, 2008): a phone number may be automatically dialed, a brief text message (SMS) may be sent, a web page corresponding to the decoded URL (Uniform Resource locator used for localization and identification of resources on the Internet) may be displayed in a mobile browser, an individual's contact details and indication of a geographical location may be viewed (Lai et al., 2015). Thereby, the two-dimensional barcodes serve as "mobile tags" and therefore the above outlined process is related to the new conception of "mobile tagging," that refers to the possibilities to transfer information from a physical object to the mobile device (Marakos, 2015). Even the reason of the term used to name this code (Quick Response) lies exactly within the fact that it permits fast access to data (Cata, Patel and Sakaguchi, 2013) (such as websites addresses, e-mails, phone numbers, geographical coordinates etc.) through mobile devices. QR codes are described in literature in this manner, as tools that are able to offer adequate, accurate, and customizable data which enable the user to access the data anyplace and anytime (Albăstroiu and Felea, 2015, p. 197).

Countries like Australia, USA, Japan, India, etc. are investing hugely in the use of QR codes on tourist attractions. Using 2-D bar codes in a tourism environment allows them to deliver organized information to each tourist by linking the official website of the tourist center, Wikipedia page or YouTube video to minimize printing costs of visitor's guides, to advertise tourist attractions and share thoughts of visitors on social media with friends and families (Hassen, 2015, p. 22).

Advantages of using QR code in destination marketing

QR code has the following advantages: (1) it contains additional info (Demir, Kaynak & Demir, 2015); (2) it represents not solely English and numeric alphabets, but also Chinese, Japanese and even different forms of multimedia; (3) the scanning of QR code is easier and has better fault tolerance; (4) it's based on open standard, therefore the coding technique may be customized and encrypted (Susono and Shimomura, 2006). According to Burillak (2011) the advantages of

QR codes are: (1) user convenience, (2) environmentally friendly, (3) cost effective, (4) versatile, (5) device independent, (6) measurable and (7) have competitive differentiation. According to Rizal and Sutrisno (2013) QR code advantages are: (1) massive capacity, (2) simple to scan, (3) ability to save kanji letters, (4) may be read from a variety of directions, (5) Small size, (6) resistant to dirt and breakage, (7) may be divided. Explanations of the advantages are provided below:

- QR codes cost nothing to produce; their use is merely limited by your promoting strategy (Burillak, 2011). It is remarkably cheap to get started with QR codes and it's less costly to maintain than different current technologies. The software for making the codes is widely available on the web and mostly free (Medic and Pavlovic, 2014).
- Actions triggered via QR codes can be traced with internet analytics or different tools for promoting campaign measurement. With the QR code, not solely will the customer scan the advertisement and get info; however, the company scans the customer, therefore accessing customer-specific info such as location and previous buying behavior (Gönül, Qui and Zhou, 2015).
- A QR code offers the user a large quantity of data. With print advertisements restricted by space, it shows solely the most vital information and lists the web site for users to induce additional information (Demir, Kaynak and Demir, 2015). QR codes in printed materials can drive additional traffic to a web site.
- QR code allows the creating of direct sales. The reader scanning the code placed below the advertisement within the printed version could buy that product by connecting to the web site of that product (Kuyucu, 2013).

Conclusions

To strengthen the development of marketing communication and branding in destinations the following recommendations may be considered by governments and responsible city/region authorities that wish to turn the destinations and cities into an example of branded and popular destinations:

- Identifying the potential tourist and advergame players.
- Preparing the message to communicate with the tourist who plays the advergame. It must include short words; emphasize the destination brand, using an ideal picture or image of destination targeting the adult customers.
- Creating a themed advergame which underlines the destinations' or cities' touristic information.

Current AR implementations in tourism facilitate the tourists to pinpoint their location and provide information on the immediate surrounding based on sources from the world-wide-web (Höllerer and Feiner, 2004). Other applications of AR have been tested in museums to serve as virtual tourist guide to enhance the way tourists see, experience and interact with the exhibitions and enable the tourist to interpret art pieces in various ways (Damala et al., 2007). Especially for tourist attractions that are linked to a heritage or religious site, regulations for maintaining the site often restrict the use of information boards and signs, which can alter or affect the heritage site negatively. Therefore, AR has been seen as potential method to provide information depth to tourists without affecting the environment by utilizing the virtual space (Jung and Han, 2014). The benefit that AR comprises is widespread and does not only affect the business sector, but increasingly the end-user. With the increasing use of the Internet for tourism purposes, the tourism product has become more transparent empowering the tourist to get in contact with the destination prior to the actual trip. However, a common dilemma with industries such as tourism, that are based on intangible experiences, is that the possibility to interact with the destination has been limited. Through the introduction of mobile AR advertisement applications, tourists are able to interact with a tourism product prior to the trip as well as on site (Lu and Smith, 2008).

Travelers can get detailed information by scanning the QR coded galleries, places, vineyards or monuments and visiting there without using a travel guide. QR code offers opportunities to broaden visitor engagement and supply further information in museums, archeological sites, destinations, hotels. The foremost useful ways in which tourism destinations can use a QR code are (Marakos, 2015, p. 63):

- To link to a website, where guests would have the chance to view additional information regarding the destination,
- To link directly to a video that may explain the story of the artifact or the story of an excavation (storytelling),
- To download a helpful app automatically,
- To link to a tour guide where tourists can listen to audio tracks regarding the artifacts or view a map regarding the interesting spots of a heritage site,
- To inform guests regarding upcoming events,
- To link to a social media page (Facebook, Twitter) so as to take feedback and hear what guests wish,
- To link to coupons and discounts. Customers will show their phones to their server so as to receive their coupons or discounts. A video promoting QR code coupons and discounts is a great way for customers to know to use the QR codes and come back to the business so as to receive further discounts.

References

Advergaming. (2008) Available online at: www.unkasoft.com/en/advergaming_en

Afshar, R. (2004) Advergaming Developer's Guide: Using Macromedia Flash MX 2004 and Director MX. Hingham, MA, USA: Charles River Media.

Albăstroiu, I., & Felea, M. (2015) "Exploring The Potential of QR Codes in Higher Education Considering the Attitudes and Interests among Romanian Students," The 11th International Scientific Conference eLearning and Software for Education Bucharest, April 23–24.

Azuma, R., Baillot, Y., Behringer, R., Feiner, S., Julier, S., & MacIntyre, B. (2001) "Recent advances in augmented reality," *IEEE Computer Graphics and Applications*, 21 (6), 34–47.

Azuma, R.T. (1997) "A survey of augmented reality," *Teleoperators and Virtual Environment*, 6 (4), 355–385.

Bellotti, F., Berta, R., De Gloria, A., Ferretti, E., & Margarone, M. (2003). "VeGame: Field Exploration of Art and History in Venice," *IEEE Computer*, 36 (9), 48–55.

Berryman, D.R., (2012) "Augmented reality: a review," *Medical Reference Services Quarterly*, 31 (2), 212–218.

Billinghurst, M. (2002) "Augmented reality in education, New horizons for learning." Available online at: www.it.civil.aau.dk/it/education/reports/ar_edu.pdf.2002

Briseno, M.Z., Hirata, F.I., Lopez J. de D.S., Garcia, E.J., Cota, C.N., & Hipolito, J.I.N. (2012) "Using RFID/NFC and QR-Code in Mobile Phones to Link the Physical and the Digital World." In I. Deliyannis (ed.) *Interactive Multimedia*. Rijeka, Croatia: InTech Janeza.

Buhalis, D., & Law, R. (2008) "Progress in information technology and tourism management: 20 years on and 10 years after the Internet – The state of eTourism research," *Tourism Management*, 29 (4), 609–623.

Buhalis, D. (2003) *eTourism: information technology for strategic tourism management*. London: Pearson.

Burillák, C. (2011) *Stunning QR codes – the really easy way to earn big cash fast*. Kindle Edition.

Carmigniani, J., Furht, B., Anisetti, M., Ceravolo, P., Damiani, E., & Ivkovic, M. (2011) "Augmented reality technologies, systems and applications," *Multimedia Tools and Applications*, 51 (1), 341–477.

Cata, T., Patel, P.S., & Sakaguchi, T. (2013) "QR Code: A New Opportunity for Effective Mobile Marketing," *Journal of Mobile Technologies, Knowledge and Society*.

Cheong, R. (1995) "The virtual threat to travel and tourism," *Tourism Management*, 16 (6), 417–422.

Craig, A.B. (2013) *Understanding Augmented Reality, Concepts and Applications*, 1st edn. Imprint: Morgan Kaufmann.

Dahl, S. Eagle, L.C., & Baez, C. (2006) "Analyzing Advergames: Active Diversions or Actually Deception." Available online at: http://ssrn.com/abstract=907841

Damala, A., Marchal, I., & Houlier, P. (2007) "Merging Augmented Reality Based Features In Mobile Multimedia Museum Guides. Anticipating the Future of the Cultural Past," CIPA Conference 2007, Athens, Greece.

Demir, S., Kaynak, R., & Demir, K.A. (2015) "Usage Level and Future Intent of Use of Quick Response (QR) Codes for Mobile Marketing among College Students in Turkey." Proceedings of the 3rd International Conference On Leadership, Technology And Innovation Management, Procedia. *Social and Behavioral Sciences*, 181 (2015), 405–413.

Dubois, L. (2011) "How to use augmented reality in advertising." Available online at: www.inc. com/guides/201104/how-to-use-augmented-reality-in-advertising.html

Eden, H.K., & Gretzel, U. (2012) "A taxonomy of mobile applications in tourism," *E-Review of Tourism Research* (eRTR), 10 (2).

Gönül, F.F., Qiu, C., & Zhou, E. (2015) "Whether or Not to Use a Quick Response (QR) Code in the Ad." Available online at: http://ssrn.com/abstract=2487939

Gurau, C. (2007) "Virtual Reality Applications in Tourism," *Information and Communication Technologies in Support of the Tourism Industry, IGI Global*, 180–197.

Gurau, C. (2008) "The Influence of Advergames on Players' Behaviour: An Experimental Study," *Electronic Markets*, 18 (2), 106–116.

Guttentag, D.A. (2010). "Virtual reality: Applications and implications for tourism," *Tourism Management* 31, 637–651.

Haala, N., & Böhm, J. (2003) "A multi-sensor system for positioning in urban environments," *ISPRS Journal of Photogrammetry & Remote Sensing* 58, 31–42.

Hassen, I. (2015) "Context Aware Tourist Information and Recommendation System using iQR Code." Unpublished master's thesis, Addis Ababa University.

Hernandez, M., & Chapa, S. (2010) "Adolescents, advergames and snack foods: effects of positive affect and experience on memory and choice," *Marketing Communications in the Food Sector*, 12 (1–2), 59–68.

Höllerer, T.H., & Feiner, S.K. (2004) "Mobile augmented reality," in H. Karimi and A. Hammad (eds) *Telegeoinformatics: Location-Based Computing and Services*. Taylor & Francis Books Ltd., http://www.grtagtour.org (2016) "About the Project." Available online at: www.grtagtour.org/about.php

Jung, T., & Han, D. (2014). "Augmented reality (AR) in urban heritage tourism." Conference on Information and Communication Technologies in Tourism ENTER. Volume 5 Research Notes. (Usage of AR at heritage sites.)

Kounavis, C.D., Kasimati, A.E., & Zamani, E.D. (2012) "Enhancing the tourism experience through mobile augmented reality: challenges and prospects," *International Journal of Engineering Business Management*, 4.

Kretchmer, S.B. (2003) "The Emergent Advergames Industry: Developments, Impact, and Direction." Digital Games Industries: Developments, Impact and Direction Conference. 19th–20th September 2003. ESRC Centre for Research on Innovation and Competition. University of Manchester, England.

Kuyucu, M. (2013) "The Transformation of Traditional Newspaper to New Global Media with the QR Code." Athens: ATINER'S Conference Paper Series, No: CBC2013–0894.

Lai, K.Y., Cheng, L.S., Yee, L.S., Leng, L.W., & Ling, T.P. (2015) "Weelicious Cuisine Quick Response (QR)." International Conference on E-Commerce (ICoEC), 20–22 October Malaysia. Edited by Aidi Ahmi, Akilah Abdullah, Norhaiza Khairudin.

Lopatina, I. (2005) "Context-aware Mobile Gaming." Unpublished Master Dissertation, University of Troms.

Lu, Y., & Smith, S. (2008). "Augmented reality e-commerce: how the technology benefits people's lives." Human-computer interaction. (Usage of AR in commerce.)

Marakos, P. (2015) "Implementing QR code in museums and archaeological sites." International Workshop on Virtual Archaeology: Museums & Cultural Tourism 23–26 September 2015, Delphi, Greece.

Maráková, V., & Medved'ová, M. (2016) "Innovatıon In Tourısm Destınatıons," *Forum Scientiae Oeconomia* 4 (1), 34–43.

Medic, S., & Pavlovic, N. (2014) "Mobile Technologies in Museum Exhibitions," TURIZAM, 18 (4), 166–174.

Mráček, P., & Mucha, M. (2011). "Advergaming: Application of Knowledge in the Process of the Competitive Advantage Improvement," *Trends Economics and Management*, 5 (8), 139–147.

Musso, F. (2010) "Innovation in Marketing Channels," *Symphonya Emerging Issues in Management* (www.unimib.it/symphonya), 1, 23–42.
Pike, S. (2004) *Destination marketing organisations, Advances in Tourism Research*, Elsevier.
Rizal, U., & Sutrisno, W.S. (2013) "The Analysis of History Collection System Based on Android Smartphone With QR Code Using QR Code Case Study." Museum Lampung. 2nd International Conference on Engineering and Technology Development, ISSN 2301–6590.
Rodgers, A.L. (2001) "Game Theory." Available online at: www.fastcompany. com/articles/2002/01/yaya.html.
Rouillard, J., (2008) "Contextual QR Codes." In Proceedings of the Third International Multi-Conference on Computing in the Global Information Technology – ICCGI, 50–55, Conference Publishing Services of IEEE Computer Society, Los Alamitos, p. 51.
Russell, M. (2012) "11 Amazing Augmented Reality Ads." Available online at: www.businessinsider.com/11-amazing-augmented-reality-ads-2012-1?op=1
Santos, E., Gonzalo, R., & Gisbert, F. (2007) "Advergames: Overview," *International Journal Information Technologies and Knowledge*, 1, 203–208.
Sharma, S., & Sharma, V. (2014) "Innovations in marketing – with special reference to innovative services," *International Journal of Business Management*, 1 (2), 50–54.
Singh, P., & Pandey, M. (2014) "Augmented Reality Advertising: An Impactful Platform for New Age Consumer Engagement," *IOSR Journal of Business and Management* (IOSR-JBM), 16 (2), 24–28.
Solomon, M.R. (2003) "Conquering Consumer space: Marketing Strategies for a Branded World." Saranac Lake. Amacom, NY, USA.
Susono, H., & Shimomura, T. (2006) "Using mobile phone and QR codes for formative class assessment." In A. Mendez-Vils, A. Solano Martin, J.A. Mesa Gonzalez (eds) *Current Developments in Technology-Assisted Education* 2, 1006–1010. Badajoz, Spain: Formatex.
Talvar, S. (2005). "Internet Adverganing: The New Mantra to Deliver Brand Message." Available online at: https://urldefense.proofpoint.com/v2/url?u=http-3A__www.exchange4media.com_e4m_izone1_izone-5Ffullstory.asp-3F&d=DwIFaQ&c=C3yme8gMkxg_ihJNXS06ZyWk4EJm8LdrrvxQb-Je7sw&r=-tBDfNZQV1wmiHRHeJ_dEA&m=sTkw8hfk0I7qr9aS-0P6gfDWuOktUKXuI0LqLfupu0c&s=w7J_1Qcr6NjxfdftRCCqOE_6ZzsSJLbtN2xyM9DQUuk&e=Section_id=4&news_id=16958&tag=11688
Taylor, B. (2013) "Augmented reality applications – from the consumer to the business." Available online at: www.creativeguerrillamarketing.com/augmented-reality/augmented-reality-applications-from the-consumer-to-the-business/
Veenendaal, P.V. (2014) "Case Study: Shakespeare Country." Available online at: www.viralblog.com/research-cases/case-study-shakespeare-country/
VeGame (2008) Available online at: http://cordis.europa.eu/ictresults/index.cfm /section/news/tpl/article/BrowsingType/Features/ID/57335/highlights/VeGame
Wang, Y. (2011) "Destination Marketing and Management: Scope, Definition and Structures." In Y. Wang and A. Pizam (eds) *Destination Marketing and Management*, CAB International.
Williams, A.P., & Hobson, J.S.P. (1995) "Virtual reality and tourism: fact or fantasy?" *Tourism Management*, 16 (6), 423–427.
Wise, K., Bolls, P., Kim, H., Venkataraman, A., & Meyer, R. (2008) "Enjoyment of advergames and brand attitudes: the impact of thematic relevance," *The Journal of Interactive Marketing*, 9 (1), 27–36.
www.bbc.com. (2013). "Mosaic QR codes boost tourism in Rio de Janeiro." Available online at: www.bbc.com/news/technology-21274863
Younghee, S. (2013). "Sidewalk QR Codes in Gangnam-gu Seoul Korea." Available online at: http://alphaguesthouse.blogspot.com.tr/2013/01/sidewalk-qr-codes-in-gangnam-gu-seoul.html
Zhang, M., Yao, D., & Zhou, Q. (2012). "The Application and Design of QR Code in Scenic Spot's eTicketing System – A Case Study of Shenzhen Happy Valley," *International Journal of Science and Technology*, 2 (12), 817–822.
Zodal. (2008). "The lure of the advergame." Available online at: www. zodal.com/pdf/Advergames-Zodal.pdf.

Further reading

Connolly, P., Chambers, C., Eagleson, E., Matthews, D., & Rogers, T. (2010). "Augmented reality effectiveness in advertising." 65th Midyear Conference Engineering Design Graphics Division of ASEE. October 3–6, Houghton, Michigan. (Explanations of AR advantages.)

Finžgar, L., & Trebar, M. (2011). "Use of NFC and QR code identification in an electronic ticket system for public transport, Software." Telecommunications and Computer Networks (SoftCOM), 2011 19th International Conference on, Split, pp.1–6. (Usage of QR codes in transportation.)
Francesco B., Riccardo B., Alessandro De G., Edmondo F., & Massimiliano M. (2003). "VeGame: Exploring art and history in Venice," *Computer*, 36 (9), 48–55. (Explanation of advergame about Venice city of Italy.)
Karabacak, Z.İ. (2014). "Digital marketing with QR code." Digital Communication Impact International Academic Conference, 16–17 October. (Usage of QR codes in marketing.)
Krevelen, D.W.F., & Poelman, R. (2010). "A survey of augmented reality technologies, applications and limitations.," *The International Journal of Virtual Reality*, 2010, 9 (2):1–20. (Types of AR technologies.)
Law, C., & So, S. (2010) "QR codes in education," *Journal of Educational Technology Development and Exchange*, 3 (1), 85–100.
Linaza, M., Marimon, D., Carrasco, P., Alvarez, R., Montesa, J., Aguilar, S.R., & Diez, G. (2012) "Evaluation of mobile augmented reality applications for tourism destinations," in Fuchs, M., Ricci, F., and Cantoni, L. (eds) *Information and Communication Technologies in Tourism*, Springer-Verlag/Wien.
Narang, S., Jain, V., & Roy, S. (2012). "Effect of QR Codes on Consumer Attitudes," *International Journal of Mobile Marketing*, 7 (2), 52–64. (Customer behaviors about using QR code.)
Russell, H. (2013) "How augmented-reality ads could change everything." Available online at: http://news.cnet.com/8301-1023_3-57591998-93/how-augmented-reality-ads-could-change everything/
Strout, A. (2013) "The Death of the QR Code. In Marketing Land." Available online at: http://marketingland.com/the-death-of-the-qr-code-37902
Terlutter, R., & Capella, M.L. (2013). "The Gamification of Advertising: Analysis and Research Directions of In-Game Advertising, Advergames, and Advertising in Social Network Games," *Journal of Advertising*, 42 (2–3), 95–112, DOI:10.1080/00913367.2013.774610 (Game applications in advertising.)
Young, K., & Won, K. (2014). "Implementation of augmented reality system for smartphone advertisements," *International Journal of Multimedia and Ubiquitous Engineering*, 9 (2), 385–392 (Usage of AR as an advertisement application at smartphones.)
Wan, C.-S., Tsaur, S.-H., Chiu, Y.-L., & Chiou, W.-B. (2007) "Is the advertising effect of virtual experience always better or contingent on different travel destinations?" *Information Technology & Tourism*, 9 (1), 45–54.

32

Innovation in product/service development and delivery

Osman Ahmed El-Said Osman

Introduction

New product/service innovations receive increasing attention from marketing practitioners and academics (Ettlie and Rosenthal, 2011). In today's business landscape, service firms must continuously renew their processes and offerings to remain competitive. These innovations serve as the engine for the growth of the service sector (Thakur and Hale, 2013). In reality, the service industry is in urgent need for new approaches of design, development strategies and operation systems to overcome the industry challenges, to achieve market competitiveness, and to secure long-term prosperity (Ho, Wong, Sarwar, and Lau, 2000). Therefore, successful service organizations need to implement successful innovations which are critical for not only survival but also for long-term stability and profitability (Cooper and Edgett, 1999). Goktan (2005) confirmed that service organizations must become more innovative to face the rising turbulence and competitiveness of organizations' environments. Innovation was defined as

> the introduction of a new idea into the marketplace in the form of a new product or service, an improvement in the organization or an improvement in processes within the organization and it ranges from minor changes to existing products, processes or services to breakthrough products, processes or services with unprecedented features or performance.
>
> *(Baumol and Blinder, 2000)*

Background

Product/service innovation evolution models

The review of innovation literature revealed that the evolution of innovation can be categorized into five models. According to Rothwell (1992) the first model for innovation evolution, prevalent during the 1950s and 1960s, was the *research-push* model. This approach assumes that innovation is a linear process, beginning with scientific discovery, passing through invention, engineering, and manufacturing activities, and ending with the marketing of a new product or process. Until the 1970s, many government policy-makers and managers of major industrial companies had accepted the view that a new product or process is the result of discoveries in basic science, brought to the attention of the parent organization by its research staff for possible commercial application. The management challenge in this process is simple: invest more resources in R&D. In this model there are no forms of feedback. The model was rapidly shown to apply only to science-based industries (Rothwell, 1992). He continued his interpretation for innovation evolution and pioneered from the early to mid 1960s a second model of innovation named the *demand-pull* model appeared. In this model, new innovations arise from users' demand for the product or service, which in turn affects the direction and rate of technology development. Kamien and Schwartz (1975) argued that in this model innovations are induced by the departments that deal directly with customers, who indicate problems with a design or suggest possible new areas for investigation. The solutions to any problems raised are provided by research staff. To some extent this approach reflected the corporate practices of that time, which emphasized planning and saw the creation of large centralized planning departments, believed to be able to predict future requirements.

The third model was the *coupling* or third-generation model integrating both research-push and demand-pull (Rothwell and Zegveld, 1985). The emphasis in this model is on the feedback effects between the downstream and upstream phases of the earlier linear models. The stages in the process are seen as separate but interactive. The management challenge of this process involves significant investments in cross-organizational communications and integration. The high level of integration between various elements of the firm in innovation is captured in the fourth-generation, *collaborative, or chain-linked* model of Kline and Rosenberg (1986), which showed the complex iterations, feedback loops, and interrelationships among marketing, R&D, manufacturing, and distribution in the innovation process. This process reflected growing understanding about the way innovation involved more than broad based input from the science base and the market, but close relationships with key customers and suppliers. The fifth-generation innovation model included the growing strategic and technological integration among different organizations. It moves away from functional divisions towards organization according with business processes. This increased strategic and technological integration often aims to improve competitiveness through the timely delivery of goods and services (Dodgson, Gann, and Salter, 2008).

Innovation in product/service development and delivery

Product innovations involve the introduction of new products that the organization produces, sells, or gives away (Knight, 1967). Song and Xie (2000) mentioned that a product's degree of innovativeness can be determined by the product's newness to the firm that develops the product and to the industry within which the firm operates. Product innovation is considered a potentially vital source of competitive advantage and organizational renewal, and in marketing the conventional meaning of the term innovation largely refers to new product-related breakthroughs (Lewis, Welsh, Dehler, and Green, 2002). According to De Jong and Vermeulen (2006) firms need to develop new products, at least on occasion, to gain competitive advantage. The rate at which they are capable of developing these new products has been linked to performance and long-term survival (Banbury and Mitchell, 1995). Tsai and Ghoshal (1998) viewed product innovation as social capital outcomes, the result of social interactions and trustworthiness combining with resource exchanges to produce tangible organizational gain.

Previous research has shown that sectors vary in terms of the sources, paces and rates of product change (Pavitt, 1984). Previous literature has also extensively examined the benefits of product innovation as for example, Dodgson and others (2008) stated that the benefit of product innovation is so great that despite many obstacles and difficulties firms continually seek to develop new offerings. According to a classic study of product innovation conducted by Clark and Wheelwright (1993), the potential benefits of effective new product development are two-fold. First, there is the question of market position as a new product can set industry standards, standards that become a barrier to competitors or open up new markets. Superior products and services are a means to gain a lead on competitors, build on existing advantages by creating stronger competitive barriers, establish a leadership image that translates into dominant designs in the market, extend existing product offerings, and increase market share (Clark and Wheelwright, 1993). Secondly, there are benefits of resource utilization, which can include capitalizing on prior R&D investments, improving the returns on existing assets, applying new technologies for both products and manufacturing processes, and eliminating or overcoming past weaknesses that prevented other products or processes from reaching their full potential (Clark and Wheelwright, 1993).

On the other hand, Verma and others (2008) developed a collective definition for service innovation:

> Service innovation is the introduction of new or novel ideas which focus on services that provide new ways of delivering a benefit, new service concepts, or new service business models through continuous operational improvement, technology, investment in employee performance, or management of the customer experience.

From their point of view, Berry and Lampo (2000) indicated that service firms can be innovative with what exists just as they can be innovative with what does not. They stated that the application of technology unleashes unlimited possibilities for service redesign as for example, "smart cards," represent an application of technology that is transforming many traditional services. Hilton hotels, for example, are experimenting with smart cards to allow arriving guests to bypass lobby lines during check-in. By swiping a smart card at a kiosk, guests can change their reservations, record frequent-stay points, print directions to their rooms, and receive room keys. Similarly, airlines such as Lufthansa are using smart cards for passengers to check in, receive frequent-flyer miles, select seats, obtain boarding passes, and change flights (Berry and Lampo, 2000).

Previous research has identified four groups of new service innovation success factors; product related, market-related, process-related, and organization-related (De Brentani, 2001). Product advantage has been identified as the number-one success factor in product development. In services, however, though the service product is important, it is not considered to be the key success factor. Instead, it is the perceived quality of the interaction with the customer that is of more relevance for new services (De Brentani, 2001). The expertise and enthusiasm of frontline staff is a particularly crucial aspect because it has a direct effect on customers' perceptions of service quality (Hartline, Maxham and McKee, 2000). According to Selden and MacMillan (2006) companies should continually increase their understanding of who their customers are and what specific wants and needs they have. Service innovations, which were targeted at large and high-growth markets, were three times as successful as those aimed at smaller, slower growth segments (Cooper and De Brentani, 1991).

Process-related determinants include market-oriented and proficient development practices (Atuahene-Gima, 1996), employee involvement (De Brentani, 2001), launch preparation (Leiponen, 2006), effective communication (Leiponen, 2006), and process management (Atuahene-Gima, 1996). The use of a formal, complete, and proficient process is strongly linked to new service success. Good communication between all departments during the development process, the support of top management, and the guidance of an experienced new service innovation manager are also important (De Brentani, 2001). A lack of understanding of customers and competitors has been linked to unsuccessful outcomes. Involving employees throughout the new service innovation process is therefore doubly important because of their knowledge of customer demands and their ability to improve service quality (Ottenbacher and Gnoth, 2005). Finally, organization-related determinants include the synergies between new services and the firm's marketing, management, and financial resources (Johne and Storey, 1998), as well as the reputation of the firm (Storey and Easingwood, 1998). In essence, it is the proficiency of the market-oriented development process and the focus on the synergy between the requirements of the new service and the resources of the firm that help determine the success of a new service.

Verma and others (2008) indicated that when service organizations executives pioneered future efforts to encourage service innovation, they outlined many challenges they face. Some of the challenges mentioned included:

> (1) how to measure service innovation's effects on profit, (2) understanding what delights customers, (3) how to predict whether a technological innovation will be accepted by customers and employees, (4) establishing employee reward and motivation systems to encourage innovation, and (5) the fact that innovations can be easily imitated.

They indicated that most executives were using the traditional tools of customer surveys, namely, questionnaires and focus groups to promote innovation. According to participants in the roundtable (Verma et al., 2008), innovative customer survey methods that are designed to help determine customers' preferences include customer choice modeling. Verma (2007) stated that

> In customer choice modeling, potential customers are asked to choose between different sets of hypothetical service options. Some sets have a high level of a particular service, low levels of another service, and omit other services entirely. Other sets have a longer list of services, or a shorter list of services and varying levels of those services. After making several iterations of choices, one can determine the important attributes of a service.

Innovations in product/service delivery are regarded as novel mechanisms of delivery that offer customers greater convenience and improve a firm's competitive position (Chen, Tsou and Huang, 2009). They stated that:

> Service/product delivery refers to the actual delivery of a service/product and the delivery of services and products to the customer. It concerns where, when, and how a service/product is delivered to the customer and whether this is with high, medium, or low contact.

The difference between product and service innovation

Verma and others (2008) have suggested the distinction between service and product innovation. Accordingly, they stated that

> although it is possible to run limited tests of service innovations, the fact remains that services are simultaneously produced and consumed. Furthermore, since the development and delivery of a service innovation coincide, the testing of service innovations tends to occur in the actual marketplace, no matter how limited the test, while product innovations can often be tested in a lab or in tightly controlled focus groups. As a result,

> failures for service innovations are viewed as being extremely costly and considered more risky than product innovations. Compounding that frustration, in most cases, service innovations are easy to imitate. Another key difference between service innovations and product innovations is that a single person can develop a new product, but it takes a team to implement a new service. As the roundtable members put it, service innovation tends to follow a democratic process where a leader needs to create a culture that motivates employees to innovate.

Moreover, the research of Garvin (1992) indicated that new product and service innovations are a risky activity; firms introducing new product and service innovations face: market risks – uncertainty about demand, competitive risks – what will competitors do?, technological risks – will the product or service work?, organizational risks – what organizational changes are needed?, operational risks – can the product be made and the service delivered? and financial risks – large upfront investments are required for uncertain pay-offs. Recently, Dodgson and others (2008) pointed out that failure of new product and service development is common and has demonstrated the reasons for that failure in many ways. For example because products and services: do not meet users' needs, are not sufficiently differentiated from the products and services of competitors, do not meet technical specifications, are too highly priced compared to their perceived value, do not comply with regulatory requirements, compete with the company's other products and services and lack strategic alignment with the company's business portfolio. Despite the fact that new product and service innovations may fail, Maidique and Zirger (1985) argued that past product and service failures may be beneficial as they provide the basis for: new approaches to marketing, new product concepts, new technological alternatives, new information about customers that may lead to major product reorientation, identification of weak links in the organization and inoculation of strong elements of the organization against replication of failure patterns.

Moreover, Dodgson and others (2008) indicated that even the most successful innovative firms do not have a perfect track record in product and service innovations. Failure is part of the cost of being an innovative firm; nothing ventured, nothing gained. Managing technological innovations involves an appreciation of the role of failure and of how great innovators can get it wrong. They indicated that in order to eliminate failure new products and services should be properly designed. Design is the process by which choices are made in the selection and refinement of ideas from a range of possible options arising out of creative and experimental work and it involves imagination and creativity, vision and judgment about alternative options needed to create products or services, and decision-making within the constraints of cost, time, and quality (Dodgson et al., 2008). These decisions can be expressed as three questions; can we afford to make or deliver this idea within our budget and sell it at a price that the market will bear? will the quality we can provide meet customer requirements and market expectations of functionality and durability? Design involves assessing options and risks within an economic framework whilst ensuring elegant and efficient results (Roy and Riedel, 1997). Design is the process by which existing customers' demands, or likely future user preferences, are incorporated into new product and service development. Successful firms add value to their range of products and services through design, by creating and exploiting brand identity and reputations for providing particular aesthetic and functional qualities (Whyte, 2003). Marsili and Salter (2006) found that amongst Dutch manufacturers, investments in design were positively associated with innovative performance, including the ability of the firm to develop products that were new to the world. Investments in design are also associated with productivity growth amongst UK firms (Marsili and Salter, 2006).

Sources of new product/service innovations

Schumpeter (1934) described how the fundamental character of the search for innovation requires firms to find and carry out 'new combinations' among technologies, knowledge, and markets. In this respect, search for innovation can be defined as 'an organization's problem-solving activities that involve the creation and recombination of technological ideas' (Katila and Ahuja, 2002). For Drucker (2002) most innovations result from a conscious, purposeful search for innovation opportunities. Such search processes require managerial capabilities to build relationships with and absorb knowledge from external sources, and to bring together knowledge from inside the firm, combining experiences and ideas from different departments, divisions, and disciplines. As such, the search for innovations requires investment in the formation of networks and social capital inside the firm and with external actors (Powell, Koput, and Doerr, 1996). Managers need to deal with different actors' ways of working, routines, norms, and habits (Brown and Duguid, 2000). According to Dodgson and others (2008) understanding the sources of innovation is one of the most important elements of managing innovation efforts. They argued that if managers know where to find innovations they can dramatically increase their innovation efforts. The importance of different sources of innovation varies by industry and by country. The most recent data from the European Community Innovation Survey (CIS), including responses from 15 EU countries as well as Norway and Iceland, shows how internal resources, clients, and customers are the most important sources for innovation in European firms, followed by suppliers and competitors. In comparison, few European firms indicated that they gain information for innovation from universities or government laboratories (European Commission, 2004). Dodgson and others (2008) concluded that the search for new combinations often requires ways of integrating knowledge from many different parts of the firm and working with various actors outside the firm, including consultants, customers, suppliers, and universities:

Customers and users

For many industries the role of customers and users as a source of innovation is very important especially in production and operational processes (Womack, Jones, and Roos, 1990). For example, in Germany, customers are the major source of technological change in electronic automotive systems; a key factor determining the possibilities for innovation in that industry is therefore the closeness and quality of the links between the car assemblers and customers (Womack, et al., 1990). Firms derive competitive advantage from being expert at satisfying and exceeding customer expectations and needs. This requires firms to develop the capacity to capture and absorb ideas and technologies developed by others, and learn especially from the ideas and insights of their customers and users (Cohen and Levinthal, 1990).

Suppliers

A number of studies have found that process innovators draw particularly on knowledge from suppliers (Reichstein and Salter, 2006). Indeed, capital goods manufacturers' may create process innovations among their customers. Regardless of whether a firm sells its products directly to the retail market, or to other businesses, it is often necessary to work closely with suppliers to understand and utilize the full potential of a new technology (Dodgson et al., 2008).

Individuals

The Cambridge managing technological innovation survey of over 3,600 UK and US firms (Cosh, Hughes, and Lester, 2006) confirmed that most important sources of knowledge for innovation derive internally from within the company. Innovations can come from many different sources within the firm. A study of Canadian firms found that the most common source of innovation within the firm was management and production workers (Baldwin and Da Pont, 1996). This was followed by sales and marketing, and then R&D staff, indicating that the R&D department is not necessarily the main source of innovation inside a firm. The use of financial incentives for innovative ideas needs to be handled with care as they can lead to unanticipated outcomes (Osterloh and Frey, 2000). In some cases, cash prizes were greater than salaries, leading to attention being shifted from working to prize winning (Voelpel, Dous, and Davenport, 2005). Firms are making increasing use of various kinds of networks to generate and commercialize new ideas (Cross and Parker, 2004). Networks provide opportunities for individuals to bring together different pools of knowledge (Burt, 2005).

Universities

Dodgson and others (2008) indicated that universities may not appear to be important as a source of innovation compared to other sources, and there is major debate about how they can best support innovation activities in firms. They are the source of graduate employees and have always been a key source of ideas for radical innovation. Also, the development of scientific instruments, designed to help scientists do their research better, has major consequences for innovation (Rosenberg, 1992). Firms that are connected to the science system are able to gain access to ideas before they are published (Fleming and Sorenson, 2004). Narin, Hamilton and Olivastro (1997) recommended that governments throughout the developed world should demand that in return for public investments in research, universities and their staff should become active in directly supporting innovation and technology transfer. The number of citations to academic research in US patents, for example, increased six fold over the decade of the 1980s, indicating a tighter linkage between academic research and industrial innovation (Narin, et al., 1997). Many universities, with varying degrees of success, have established industrial liaison or research commercialization and technology transfer offices. Mowery and Sampat (2005) put the role of industrially focused research into context: "The research university plays an important role as a source of fundamental knowledge and, occasionally, industrially relevant technology in modern knowledge-based economies." Washburn (2005) cited evidence that industry funding now directly influences 20–25 percent of university research. She showed that 180 US universities own stakes in 886 start-ups, and in 2002 they generated nearly $1 billion in licensing and royalty income. Governments' efforts to push universities closer to industry should also be assessed in the context of what industry actually wants from universities. Research addressing this question shows their requirements to be: (1) well-educated, talented graduates; (2) creative, fundamental research; and (3) distinctive research cultures (Dodgson et al., 2008).

Organizations

Morris (2004) argued that there are many possibilities of innovation efforts in organizations. Morris found that in such an organization there are at least 37 distinctive opportunities for innovation. All aspects of operations, from the design of its organization and the structure of its supply chain, to its marketing, customer support, products, and services could be innovation targets.

Other sources

In the same context, Dodgson and others (2008) indicated that firms also draw on ideas from other sources such as: government technology transfer agencies, trade and academic publications, trade and professional associations, exhibitions, conferences, regulations and standards, various networks and communities and the analysis of patents.

References

Atuahene-Gima, K. (1996) "Differential potency of factors affecting innovation performance in manufacturing and services firms in Australia," *Journal of Product Innovation Management* 13, 35–52.

Baldwin, J. and Da Pont, M. (1996) "Innovation in Canadian Manufacturing Enterprises," in Dodgson, M., Gann, D. and Salter, A. (2008) *The Management of Technological Innovation Strategy and Practice.* Oxford: Oxford University Press.

Banbury C. and Mitchell, W. (1995) "The Effect of Introducing Important Incremental Innovations on Market Share and Business Survival," in De Jong, J. and Vermeulen, A. (2006) "Determinants of product innovation in small firms: A comparison across industries," *International Small Business Journal* 24, 587–609.

Baumol, W. and Blinder, A. (2000) "Macroeconomics: Principles and policy," in Goktan, A. (2005) *The role of strategy in the innovation process: a stage approach*, a published PhD dissertation, University of North Texas.

Berry L. and Lampo, S. (2000) "Teaching an old service new tricks: The promise of service redesign," *Journal of Service Research* 2, 265–275.

Brown, J. and Duguid, P. (2000) *The Social Life of Information.* Boston: Harvard Business School Press.

Burt, R. (2005) *Brokerage and Closure: An Introduction to Social Capital.* Oxford: Oxford University Press.

Chen, J. Tsou, T. and Huang, A. (2009) "Service Delivery Innovation: Antecedents and Impact on Firm Performance," *Journal of Service Research*, 12, 36–55.

Clark, K. and Wheelwright, S. (1993) *Managing New Product and Process Development: Text and Cases.* New York: The Free Press.

Cohen, W. and Levinthal, D. (1990) "Absorptive capacity: A new perspective on learning and innovation," *Administrative Science Quarterly* 35, 128–152.

Cooper, R. and Edgett, S. (1999) "Product development for the service sector," in Ottenbacher, C. (2007) "Innovation Management in the Hospitality Industry: Different Strategies for Achieving Success," *Journal of Hospitality & Tourism Research* 31, 431–454.

Cosh, A., Hughes, A. and Lester, R. (2006) *UK PLC: Just How Innovative Are We?* Cambridge: Cambridge University Press.

Cross, R. and Parker, A. (2004) *The Hidden Power of Social Networks.* Boston: Harvard Business School Press.

De Brentani, U. (2001) "Innovative versus incremental new business services: Different keys for achieving success," *Journal of Product Innovation Management* 18, 169–187.

De Jong, J. and Vermeulen, A. (2006) "Determinants of product innovation in small firms: A comparison across industries," *International Small Business Journal* 24, 587–609.

Dodgson, M., Gann, D. and Salter, A. (2008) *The Management of Technological Innovation Strategy and Practice.* Oxford: Oxford University Press.

Drucker, P.F. (2002). "The discipline of innovation," *Harvard Business Review* 80, 95–104.

Ettlie, J., and Rosenthal, S. (2011) "Service versus manufacturing innovation," *Journal of Product Innovation Management* 28, 285–299.

European Commission (2004) "Innovation in Europe: Results for the EU, Iceland and Norway," in Dodgson, M., Gann, D. and Salter, A. (2008) *The Management of Technological Innovation Strategy and Practice.* Oxford: Oxford University Press.

Fleming, L. and Sorenson, O. (2004) "Science as a Map in Technological Search," *Strategic Management Journal* 25, 909–928.

Garvin, D. (1992) "Operations Strategy, Text and Cases," in Dodgson, M., Gann, D. and Salter, A. (2008) *The Management of Technological Innovation Strategy and Practice.* Oxford: Oxford University Press.

Goktan, A. (2005) "The role of strategy in the innovation process: a stage approach." A published PhD Dissertation, University of North Texas.

Hartline, M., Maxham J. and McKee, D. (2000) "Corridors of influence in the dissemination of customer-oriented strategy to customer contact employees," *Journal of Marketing* 64, 35–50.

Ho, L., Wong, Y., Sarwar, M. and Lau, S. (2000) "An Engineering Research and Development Framework for the Challenges Faced by the Hotel Industry: Hong Kong Case Study," *Journal of Hospitality & Tourism Research* 24, 350–372.

Kamien, M. and Schwartz, N. (1975) "Market Structure and Innovation," in Dodgson, M., Gann, D. and Salter, A. (2008) *The Management of Technological Innovation Strategy and Practice.* Oxford: Oxford University Press.

Katila, R. and Ahuja, G. (2002) "Something Old, Something New: A Longitudinal Study of Search Behavior and New Product Introduction," *Academy of Management Journal* 45: 1183–1194.

Knight, K. (1967) "A descriptive model of the intra-firm innovation process," in Goktan, A. (2005) *The role of strategy in the innovation process: a stage approach.* A published PhD Dissertation, University of North Texas.

Leiponen, A. (2006) "Managing knowledge for innovation: The case of business-to business services," *Journal of Product Innovation Management* 23, 238–258.

Lewis, W., Welsh, A., Dehler, G. and Green, S. (2002) "Product development tensions: Exploring contrasting styles of project management," *Academy of Management Journal* 45, 546–564.

Maidique, M. and Zirger, B. (1985) "The New Product Learning Cycle," in Dodgson, M., Gann, D. and Salter, A. (2008) *The Management of Technological Innovation Strategy and Practice.* Oxford: Oxford University Press.

Marsili, O. and Salter, A. (2006) "The Dark Matter of Innovation: Design and Innovative Performance in Dutch Manufacturing," *Technology Analysis and Strategic Management Review* 18, 515–534.

Morris, L. (2004) "Business Model Warfare: The Strategy of Business Breakthroughs," An Innovation Lab's White Paper, prepared and published jointly with the Ackoff Center of the University of Pennsylvania.

Mowery, D. and Sampat, B. (2005) "Universities in National Innovation Systems," in Fagerberg J. and Nelson, R. (2006) *The Oxford Handbook of Industrial Innovation.* Oxford: Oxford University Press.

Narin, F., Hamilton, K. and Olivastro, D. (1997) "The Increasing Linkage Between US Technology and Public Science," in Dodgson, M., Gann, D. and Salter, A. (2008) *The Management of Technological Innovation Strategy and Practice.* Oxford: Oxford University Press.

Osterloh, M. and Frey, B. (2000) "Motivation, knowledge transfer, and organization forms," *Organization Science Review* 11, 538–550.

Pavitt, K. (1984) "Sectoral Patterns of Technological Change: Towards a Taxonomy and Theory," in De Jong, J. and Vermeulen, A. (2006) "Determinants of product innovation in small firms: A comparison across industries," *International Small Business Journal* 24, 587–609.

Powell, W., Koput, K. and Doerr, L. (1996) "Interorganizational Collaboration and the Locus of Innovation: Networks of Learning in Biotechnology," *Administrative Science Quarterly* 41, 116–145.

Reichstein, T. and Salter, A. (2006) "Investigating the Sources of Process Innovation Among UK Manufacturing Firms," *Industrial and Corporate Change Review* 15, 653–682.

Rosenberg, N. (1992) "Scientific Instrumentation and University Research," *Research Policy Review* 21, 381–390.

Rothwell, R. (1992) "Successful Industrial Innovation: Critical Factors for the 1990s," *R&D Management* 22, 221–39.

Rothwell, R. and Zegveld, W. (1985) "Reindustrialization and Technology," in Dodgson, M., Gann, D. and Salter, A. (2008) *The Management of Technological Innovation Strategy and Practice.* Oxford: Oxford University Press.

Roy, R. and Riedel, J. (1997) "Design and Innovation in Successful Product Competition," in Dodgson, M., Gann, D. and Salter, A. (2008) *The Management of Technological Innovation Strategy and Practice.* Oxford: Oxford University Press.

Schumpeter, J. (1934) "The theory of economic development," in Goktan, A. (2005) *The role of strategy in the innovation process: a stage approach.* A published PhD Dissertation, University of North Texas.

Selden, L. and MacMillan, I. (2006) "Manage customer-centric innovation systematically," *Harvard Business Review* 84, 108–116.

Song, M. and Xie, J. (2000) "Does innovativeness moderate the relationship between cross functional integration and product performance?" *Journal of International Marketing* 8, 61–89.

Storey, C. and Easingwood, C. (1998) "The augmented service offering: A conceptualization and study of its impact on new service success," *Journal of Product Innovation Management* 15, 335–351.

Thakur, R., & Hale, D. (2013) "Service innovation: A comparative study of U.S. and Indian service firms," *Journal of Business Research* 66, 1108–1123.

Tsai, W. and Ghoshal, S. (1998) "Social capital and value creation: The role of intrafirm networks," *Academy of Management Journal* 41, 464–477.

Verma, R. (2007) "Unlocking the Secrets of Customer Choices," *Cornell Hospitality Report* 7, 1–20.

Verma, R., Anderson, C., Dixon, M., Enz, C., Thompson, G. and Victorino L. (2008) "Key Elements in Service Innovation: Insights for the Hospitality Industry," *Cornell Hospitality Roundtable Proceedings.*
Voelpel, S., Dous, M. and Davenport, T. (2005) "Five Steps to Creating a Global Knowledge-Sharing System: Siemens's Sharenet," *Academy of Management Executive* 19, 9–23.
Washburn, J. (2005) *The Corporate Corruption of Higher Education.* New York: Basic Books.
Whyte, J. (2003) "Innovation and Users: Virtual Reality in the Construction Sector," *Construction Management and Economics Review* 21, 565–572.
Womack, J., Jones, D. and Roos, D. (1990) *The Machine that Changed the World: The Story of Lean Production.* New York: Rawton Publishing.

Further reading

Cooper, R. and De Brentani, U. (1991) "New industrial services: What distinguishes the winners," *Journal of Product Innovation Management* 8, 75–90.
Gustafsson, A. and Johnson, M. (2003) *Competing in a service economy: How to create a competitive advantage through service development and innovation.* San Francisco: Jossey-Bass Inc.
Johne, A. and Storey, C. (1998) "New service development: A review of literature and annotated bibliography," *European Journal of Marketing* 32, 184–251.
Kline, S.J. and N. Rosenberg (1986) "An Overview of Innovation," in Berger, M. and Diez, R. (2006) "Technological Capabilities and Innovation in Southeast Asia: Results from Innovation Surveys in Singapore, Penang and Bangkok," *Science, Technology and Society Journal* 11, 108–147.
Ottenbacher, M. and Gnoth, J. (2005) "How to develop successful hospitality innovation," *Cornell Hotel and Restaurant Administration Quarterly* 46, 205–222.

33

The sharing economy and tourism destination marketing

Adam Pawlicz

What is sharing economy?

The renting of empty rooms by locals to tourists is common in resorts and other tourist-attractive places. Before the internet revolution, renters were usually waiting at the railway or bus station approaching potential tourists in the hope of getting some extra money. As many tourists were coming to destinations without prior reservation this, intermediary-free, way of profiting from idle resources was a blessing.

Now things are changed. Renters do not need any more to freeze on the railway station and tourists may reserve an idle space in a way which is similar to booking a hotel room. This process was facilitated by the emergence of dedicated internet platforms that match supply and demand. New technologies allowed transaction costs to become significantly lower which resulted in an enormous increase of P2P (peer to peer) hospitality market while mutual review systems kept the impediments of customers that were afraid of dealing with strangers at bay. Moreover, the spare rooms are rented also outside well-known tourists areas and contribute to the tourist supply of numerous destinations ranging from main metropolis to small villages. What previously was called renting rooms to tourists now is proudly named a "sharing economy".

The emergence of the sharing economy has profoundly changed not only the supply structure of the hospitality market but also impacted the whole destination tourism product and the way it is presented on the market. From a destination's view, it presents on one hand an opportunity, as more accommodation capacity and entirely new marketing channel attracts more tourists while local community members are granted new earning possibilities. On the other hand, the sharing economy development poses numerous challenges such as unresolved legal issues, spatial distribution of accommodation units and changes on long-term rental and real estate markets. Little is also known about the sharing economy's impact on destination marketing. As its proliferation profoundly changes the destination product, other marketing instruments also need corresponding adjustments. Sharing economy platforms constitute a tremendous opportunity that may facilitate reaching completely new target groups of predominantly leisure tourists. Individual providers in the sharing economy, similarly to other accommodation establishments, can be used as an effective information channel between marketers and tourists that already arrived to destination.

Although sharing economy phenomenon is emerging on various markets related to tourism, in this chapter a particular emphasis will be placed on hospitality. They are platforms that facilitate transportation both between destinations (e.g. BlaBlaCar), or within destination (e.g. Uber) and tour guides (e.g. Vayable). Although those are partially used by tourists, their impact on destination marketing is still very limited.

Definitions of the sharing economy

According to Pargman, Eriksson, & Friday (2016) the concept and the term "sharing economy" gained popularity with publication of seminal book of Rachel Botsman and Roo Roger's "What is mine is (y)ours: The rise of collaborative consumption" and few other newspaper articles.

The term sharing economy, similarly to other terms used widely in popular and business environment, seems to have more synonyms than any other expression used in academic dispute in tourism marketing. Collaborative consumption, short term rental market, access-based consumption, the mesh, peer economy, peer-to-peer economy, on-demand economy, gig economy, trust economy are just the most popular terms which cover this area.

There are numerous definitions of the sharing economy. Some of them put forward altruistic origins of this business, some hint at the different aspects of business model such as contract development, trust formation or highlight the importance of market mediation (Cusumano, 2014; Demary, 2015). Although the view of Botsman (2013) that all mentioned above synonyms have a slightly different meaning is shared by few scholars (e.g. Hawlitschek & Teubner, 2016) in this section the academic discussion about the exact meaning of sharing economy is skipped for two reasons. First, as our interest area is limited to hospitality market, the differences are anyway irrelevant. Second, the differences in definitions mentioned in literature will have no impact on the following discussion.

The Oxford Dictionary provides maybe the clearest and most accurate definition of sharing economy which will be accepted across this chapter: An economic system in which assets or services are shared between private individuals, either free or for a fee, typically by means of the Internet. This definition is in line with those provided by Belk (2014) and Miller (2016) and excludes the B2C market which is sometimes also regarded as part of sharing economy (Demary, 2015).

The term sharing economy does not belong to academia, though, but is nonetheless used very freely especially among marketing practitioners. As the sharing economy is rapidly evolving and considered as an elusive concept (Miller, 2016), development of numerous new definitions can be expected in the future rather than emergence of a shared one. The popularity of sharing economy led even to the formation of term "we-washing" which is used in much the same way to "greenwashing". According to Pargman et al. (2016) it refers "to practices that are supposedly environmentally or socially beneficial while in reality referring to nothing much but a strategic use of language that sanitizes deeply problematic practices". In this view the term "sharing economy" will resemble other vague terms from tourism economics that lack commonly accepted definition such as: sustainable development or tourism product etc.

Origins and drivers of P2P hospitality market

The sharing economy emerged in the hospitality market at the end of the first decade of 2000s. It was based on the phenomenon of turning unused or under-used assets owned by individuals into new supply on the hospitality market. The *reason d'etre* of sharing economy development is usually associated with sharing economy platforms or technology-driven change which resulted in tremendous increase of market efficiency. Still the reality seems to be more complex and the rise of sharing economy is usually attributed to the confluence of three different factors:

- Technological development
- Societal development
- Other factors (economic, political etc.)

The technological development is the most obvious catalyst of the rise of sharing economy. Invention and proliferation of internet is regarded as an obvious *sine qua non* for subsequent innovations that enabled massive reduction of transaction costs (Hoffman & Offutt, 2015). Ertz et al. (2017) trace sharing economy origins back to the development of P2P sharing platforms (e.g. iTunes, Rhapsody, Netflix) which enabled consumers open access to desired resources. The next step was marked by development of P2P platforms that facilitated the exchange of tangible goods (e.g. eBay, Amazon). The emergence of sharing economy companies (or platforms) which transforms many durable goods into services is seen as logical consequence of previous developments and other technological innovations which facilitated internet trade such as: usage of mobile devices, electronic payments systems (e.g. PayPal) and two-way reputation systems (Benjaafar, Kong, Li, & Courcoubetis, 2015; Fraiberger & Sundararajan, 2015; PWC, 2015). Still Ert, Fleischer, & Magen (2016) consider the direct interaction between hosts and guests as the main difference between early P2P markets and contemporary sharing economy.

Other factors that facilitated the rise of the sharing economy are of societal nature and cover an increase in population density in metropolitan areas, the rise of anxiety about the environment (sharing economy is viewed as a more sustainable option to conventional modes of consumption and sometimes connected with term "asset light lifestyle"), and increased desire for community and altruism among the young and educated (Benjaafar et al., 2015). Sundararajan (2016) argues that contemporary digital technologies are resembling familiar sharing behaviors from the past such as self-employment and community-based exchange, but thanks to internet connectivity the term "community" has an entirely new meaning and scope (Sundararajan, 2016). Ertz et al. (2017) argues that the first forms of internet collaboration can be seen in IT professionals' cooperation over the development of new software. The emergence of Web 2.0 which enabled the exchange of views and opinions by non-professional internet users led to the social media development which changed the interpersonal communication. Networking activities laid the very important ground for foundation of sharing economy and is sometimes regarded as natural consequence of changing consumer behavior (Ho, 2015; John, 2013).

Other factors consist of economic and political changes that facilitate the sharing economy development. Demary (2015) argues that the advent of the sharing economy coincides with the global financial crisis (2008–2009) (this refers to US market as she still underlines that in European countries like Germany, France, Italy or the United Kingdom the concept started to be used in late 2013 the earliest). Austerity policies, recession and deindustrialization connected with growing unemployment undermined household incomes and their purchasing power. Ertz et al. (2017) argues that sharing economy not only enabled those households to access goods and services they otherwise could not afford, but it can even be seen as a challenge for established intermediaries and make existing marketing system obsolete. Although, according to Google Trends, the term sharing economy starts to gain importance in search engines in the first months of 2013, numerous sharing economy companies were launched before this time. Ertz et al. (2017) sees, moreover, the rise of the sharing economy as a result of consumers' perception of the withering of the state (and religious institutions) from an increasing number of key domains in their life. Sharing economy with its networking activities and building the sense of community addresses this gap. The factors influencing the rise of sharing economy are summarized on the Figure 33.1.

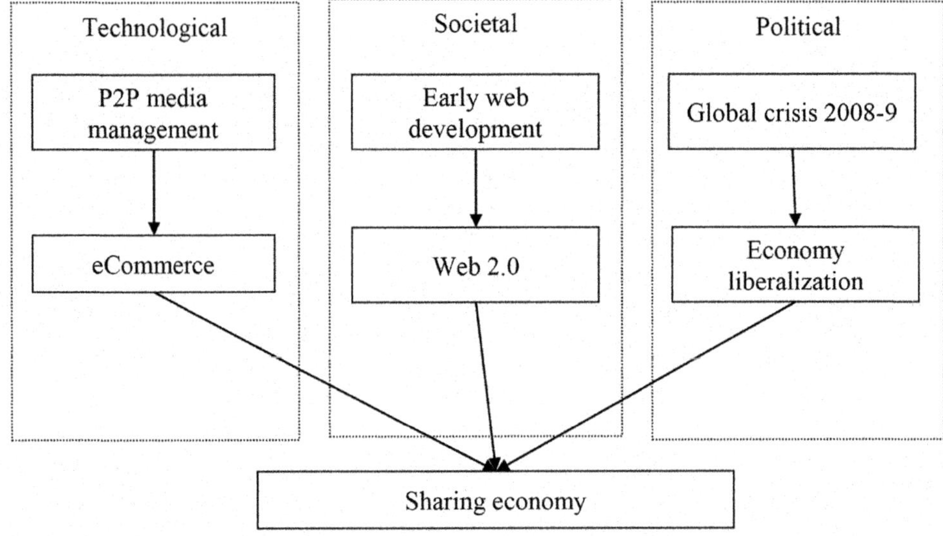

Figure 33.1 Factors influencing the development of the sharing economy

The business model of the sharing economy continues to be applied to new industries from car sharing to peer-to-peer fashion, among many others (Cannon & Summers, 2012). Kessler (2015) even called the sharing economy a "warm and fuzzy inevitability". Tourism and hospitality markets which are natural part of a service economy laid ground for many successful ventures that changed the market nature (Tussyadiah & Pesonen, 2016). The innovation clock is getting faster and faster as consumers become more trusting of relationships tied to social sentiment and communities of users (PWC, 2015).

Actors on a sharing economy hospitality market

Every market consists of supply, demand, intermediaries and rules that actors must follow. The very first impression of an analysis of the sharing economy research results in the conclusion that, similarly to other P2P markets, the distinction between supply and demand is blurred. Individuals that represent both supply and demand are called peers (Figure 33.2), and a majority of the market research in sharing economy refers to peers in general, while other separate investigations about supply and demand representatives are limited.

Peers

Those that rent their idle rooms, flats or houses and thus form the supply side of hospitality sharing economy market are referred as suppliers, hosts or providers (but surprisingly the term "landlord" which is traditionally used for a person or organization that owns and leases apartments to others is not used). Sometimes they are even called (micro-)entrepreneurs (Dillahunt & Malone, 2015) or low-risk microentrepreneurs (Wang, Li, Guo, & Xu, 2016). The demand side on the market is represented by consumers, who sometimes are referred simply as tourists or travelers.

The demographic characteristics of peers engaged in sharing economy are usually matching an attractive marketing target: young, middle income, living in cities, with children and IT-literate.

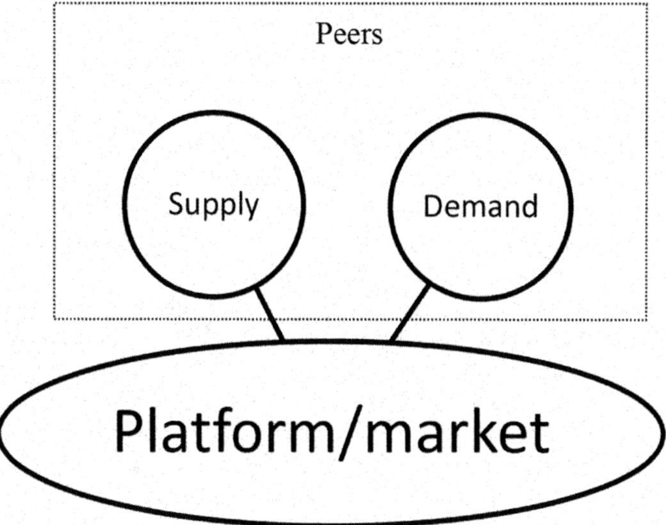

Figure 33.2 Structure of the sharing economy market

According to the PWC (2015) survey conducted in December 2014 among sampled US consumers, 44% of population is familiar with the sharing economy while 19% has been engaged in sharing economy transactions (6% in hospitality and dining services). Providers in the sharing economy are usually young (38% is under 34 and 62% of them is under 44 years old) and 57% with the household income over $50k (PWC, 2015). Given the fact that a median age in United States is ca. 37.6 and median household income $53,657 according to the U.S. Census Bureau, the demographic characteristics of providers are roughly matching those of the population in general.

Individuals engage in the sharing economy for numerous reasons. Sharing economy platforms advertise it as an activity which is highly ecologically sustainable, involves enriching societal experiences and creates additional income for providers or saves money for clients. The study of PWC (2015) showed that among US adults familiar with the sharing economy:

- 86% agree it makes life more affordable
- 83% agree it makes life more convenient and efficient
- 76% agree it's better for the environment
- 78% agree it builds a stronger community
- 63% agree it is more fun than engaging with traditional companies
- 89% agree it is based on trust between providers and users

The very founding idea of sharing economy platforms, which is supported by declarations, can only partially be confirmed by an academic research. A study of Fraiberger & Sundararajan (2015) shows that the most welfare gains from the existence of sharing economy will be enjoyed by below-median customers.

Hamari et al. (2015) showed that participation in sharing economy activities might have multiple motivations as different as sustainability, enjoyment of activity as well as economic gains. Furthermore, they observed that people have a positive attitude towards sharing economy activities but this attitude is not always followed by an action. Also in the study of Balck and Cracau (2015) who applied a constant sum technique in two surveys, the authors identified Cost, Rarity, Environment, Access, and No Ownership as the five main motives (the importance of Cost was a dominating motive especially in accommodation sector). Similar results has been found in Bardhi and Eckhardt's (2012) research among Zipcar users. The authors found that self-interest and utilitarianism (i.e., reducing expenses and increasing convenience) are frequent motives for access-based car sharing and that those motives are weighted even stronger than considerations about collective utility. Members do not want to socialize with other members, as they seemingly operate primarily from selfish, pragmatic, and individualistic motivations rather than out of altruism, concern for the environment, or concern for a collective good. Additionally, in Europe, Neeser (2015) found that Airbnb's "cultural experience" makes it relatively more attractive for foreigners than locals.

Figure 33.3 depicts the typology of customers' motives when using sharing economy. The main one is connected with the price, but transaction costs (convenience, time) also play an important role. On the other hand, the needs of socializing and preserving environment are important particularly to customers using non-profit platforms.

The product in hospitality, regardless whether offered in the sharing economy or not, has all the traits of a service whose main characteristic is inseparability i.e., the production and consumption is simultaneous. Hence, it is difficult to separate the traditional supply side (supplier) and the product itself, so the service provider becomes an integral part of the experience (Ert et al., 2016).

Kaplan & Nadler (2015) cited an independent research which stated that 86% of Airbnb users in San Francisco had only one residence listed, and 98% had three or fewer, suggesting that only a minuscule proportion of users seek to operate on a commercial scale.

Although the existence of the sharing economy seems to be democratic, the patterns of participation in the sharing economy are complicated. Cansoy & Schor (2016) using data from 104 metropolitan statistical areas in the US were able to show that although white people have fewer listings and fewer reviews, these still have better ratings and demand higher prices. They also

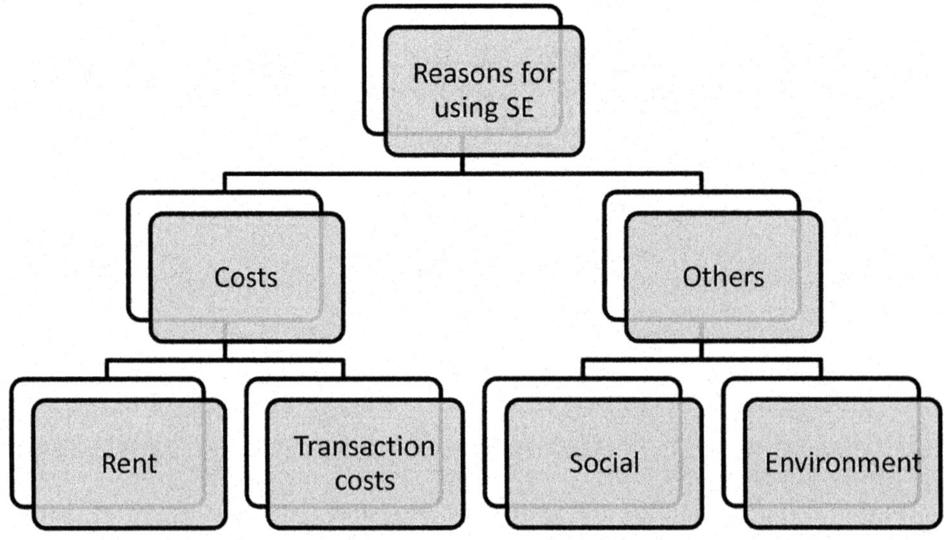

Figure 33.3 Typology of using sharing economy motives

found that education was an important influential factor in these patterns. Digital discrimination over Airbnb was also found in the earlier studies (Edelman & Luca, 2014) and confirmed by an experiment conducted by Edelman, Luca and Svirsky (2017). Ert et al. (2016) were tracking, on the other hand, the relationship between quality of a photo to the price and likelihood of booking which was more important than a host's reputation, communicated by her online review scores.

Although there no specific data about the users' reasons for travelling while using sharing economy, one may assume that a majority are leisure travelers. Still Airbnb and its competitors are gradually entering business market. By 2015, Airbnb reports that just below 10% of its guests are business travelers but this figure grew by 249% around the world in 2015 (Henten & Windekilde, 2016).

Sharing economy companies

Sharing economy companies (platforms, businesses) are usually based on online platforms that match demand and supply. Demary (2015) argues that in this model products are exchanged between individuals and a sharing economy company does not produce either good or service and merely acts as an intermediary. As they have no actual control over the process and its development and do not constitute part of a transaction, the term "information broker" would be more accurate or, as other scholars call them, "economical-technological coordination providers" (Hamari et al., 2015) or "virtual matchmakers" (Kaplan & Nadler, 2015). Both providers and consumers usually pay a fee for using the platform but sometimes its service may be free of charge. Sharing economy platforms are able to lower transaction costs and facilitate arrangements that might otherwise have been too burdensome, which led to the emergence of markets on a previously unimaginable scale.

Cusumano (2014) argues that sharing economy companies are naturally linked with the social media platforms such as Facebook, Pinterist or TripAdvisor. As peer to peer networks may grow exponentially, its power of using network effects may contribute to the success of sharing economy platforms (Wang & Zhang, 2012). Peer networks and connectivity with social media assures trust and cooperation which are indispensable for successful exchanges (Dillahunt & Malone, 2015).

All sharing economy companies offer a wide variety of different services, but have three common traits as found by Kaplan & Nadler (2015):

1 they are based on new IT technological advances
2 they compete with well-established competitors that are fundamentally disrupted by the sharing economy's emergent ability to provide innovative alternatives
3 they operate in interstitial areas of the law because they present new and fundamentally different issues that were not foreseen when the governing statutes and regulations were enacted.

Even though there have been numerous startups that base their business concept on the sharing economy, only few were successful enough to survive. Botsman and Rogers (2010) created a set of characteristics of a successful sharing economy company:

1 trust between strangers
2 idle capacity
3 belief in the commons
4 critical mass.

As sharing economy transactions, by definition, include the usage of private apartments by visitors, creating trust between parties is essential. Trust is built through reputation systems (ratings and comments), personal pictures and connection to social media. Idle capacity simply means that individuals have free resources there is a demand for. Kessler (2015), while analyzing the development of sharing economy platforms, pointed at transactions costs in the system which must not be too high in relation to the product price. In this way she explained the failure of many sharing economy companies for snap goods (which were simply too cheap comparing to transactions costs needed to rent them).

Weber (2014) notes a key impediment to sharing is a lender's concern about damage due to unobservable actions by a renter, usually resulting in a moral hazard. Still according to Katz et al. (2015) what drives the popular demand for the services in the sharing economy is trust. To address this issue, property ratings have been established. Zervas, Proserpio and Byers (2015) show, however, that property ratings on Airbnb are very positive. The average Airbnb rating was 4.7 (with extremely low variance) in 1 to 5 scale, while in TripAdvisor, which does not use bilateral reviewing system, average rating was 3.8. For that reason visual-based trust is most important for consumers' choices (Ertz et al., 2017). The success of sharing economy companies means they manage through their regulation to create trust among peers. According to Katz et al. (2015) 64% of consumers claimed that in the sharing economy, peer regulation was more important than government regulation and 69% said they will not trust sharing economy companies unless they are rated by someone they trust.

Belief in the commons, similarly to critical mass, is connected with networking effects. Every additional member of community adds value to the system by amplifying the demand or supply side. What distinguishes flourishing and failing sharing economy companies is the critical mass. It means that consumers must have enough choices to feel satisfied. Dillahunt & Malone (2015) add that critical mass is needed for social proof and acceptance among others. Sharing economy companies may simply either rise or vanish as economies of scale in this industry are enormous and marginal costs almost do not exist. Demary (2015) points that there are notable sunk costs which must be incurred before and just after launching the platform but there are almost no flexible costs afterwards. Moreover, networks are characterized by high switching costs that create lock-in effects. This results in oligopoly on the market where minor players might not survive unless they find a niche segment. Similar trends were seen on the Global Distribution Systems market in 1980s, tour operator market in 1990s and online travel agencies in 2000s.

Back in 2014, Cusumano (2014) describing the sharing economy platforms called them "internet startups", while today they are highly valued multinational corporations. The major player on the hospitality sharing economy market is undoubtedly Airbnb, who had a higher valuation than the Hyatt hotel chain even back to 2014 and is operating truly globally. Still there are numerous competitors who are struggling on the growing market:

- HomeAway.com (VRBO.com, VacationRentals.com)
- Wimdu.com
- PerfectPlaces.com
- 9flats.com
- FlipKey.com
- CouchSurfing.com
- Tripping.com

All these platforms are either mainstream Airbnb competitors or operate in niche market. Probably Homeaway is the strongest one, as it is a subsidiary of Expedia and between 2005 and 2014 made acquisitions of 14 other sites (among them VBRO and VacationRentals.com). Other direct competitors are Wimdu and 9flats, P2P companies with headquarters in Germany. Perfectplaces.com covers vacation rental property market while Flipkey was founded by TripAdvisor. CouchSurfing.com acts more like a social platform, where no payment is mandatory. Tripping.com is rather a metaengine which covers "properties from the world's top rental sites" out of which are such diverse companies as Homeaway and Booking.com. Overall there are numerous sharing companies on the hospitality market but it is difficult to assess their real presence as there no credible statistics either official or industry-based.

Impact of sharing economy on tourism market

Market size and price level

The emergence of new sharing economy platforms leads to the three aspects of competition:

1 Between suppliers that offer services on the sharing platforms
2 Between various sharing platforms
3 Between platforms, their providers and traditional businesses

Competition between suppliers on the sharing platform is currently a blank area in hospitality research. Heterogeneity of the product, very high (and undifferentiated) ratings render it very difficult to apply, for example, the hedonic price model, which is traditionally used for business tourism destinations (Pawlicz & Napierala, 2017).

Intensity of competition between sharing economy platforms depends on the extent of sunk costs incurred in starting up a platform, economies of scale, customer switching costs, network effects that provide an advantage to platforms with an existing user base and actions by incumbents to deter new entry (Deloitte Access Economics, 2015).

The main interest of mass media and (to lesser extent) academics is associated with the impact of new players on the existing market. Hospitality associations claim that competition is fierce and new incumbents cannibalize existing markets while, on the other hand, studies commissioned by sharing economy companies claim that they create an entirely new demand on hospitality market. Academic evidence is until now scarce and provides mixed results.

A highly cited study of Zervas, Proserpio, & Byers (2016) projected that a 1% increase in Airbnb listings results in only a 0.05% decrease in hotel revenues. They calculated that the impact on the more vulnerable hotels' revenue is about an 8–10% decrease over five years and were able to show that cheaper hotels were impacted the most. Results on this study were not supported by Neeser (2015), who, extending methodology of Zervas et. al. (2016) to Nordic countries (in Europe), did not observed a significant revenue fall. Still they observed a price fall in regions where Airbnb entered the most. On the other hand Choi, Jung, Ryu, & Kim (2015) did not support hypothesis of relationship between the entry of sharing economy companies and a hotel revenue in Korea.

For that reason, it seems unlikely that a new model will eradicate the existing one. As Henten & Windekilde (2016) show, if sharing economy companies were able to gain part of the market, they will be able to tip the market in favor of the new operators as the margins in some industries are already very low.

The competitive position of the hospitality industry versus new sharing economy platforms is rather weak and reminds of the difficult relationships of hospitality industry with Global Distribution Systems and Online Travel Agencies. From one side there is a fragmented hospitality industry with a majority of entities belonging to independent hoteliers and from another a multinational corporation operating as an intermediary on highly concentrated market.

Some studies show that the introduction of new companies on the market results in lower prices (Neeser, 2015) and higher quality. For instance, Wallsten (2015) was able to show that the emergence of Uber in Chicago led to the increase of service quality provided by all taxi companies but there is no similar evidence from the hospitality industry.

Sharing economy impact on tourism destinations

The emergence of the sharing economy not only affected competition on the hospitality market, but also it has a deep influence on the whole destination total tourism product. As the impact is not either unilaterally positive or negative the emergence of the sharing economy poses new challenges for destination marketers.

The founders of Airbnb claimed to share their first beds in San Francisco in 2008 with convention participants who could not either find a free hotel room or afford it. In this way, turning idle private beds into a hospitality product enlarged accommodation base for a destination making it able to meet tourists' expectations especially in peak season. More capacity and a more diversified hospitality product results in more competition with traditional accommodation establishments. This makes the traditional inelastic supply curve not only shift rightwards but also bend forward as price rises.

Few empirical studies that examine the impact of sharing economy on a destination show that it generates additional tourism traffic, increases length of stay or increase travel frequency (Tussyadiah & Pesonen, 2015). Sometimes the emergence of the sharing economy is compared to the introduction of low cost carriers on the air market which positively contributed to the increase of tourism around secondary airports and thus induced new tourists to visit destinations. Whether the sharing economy phenomenon will have a similar power is still a pure conjecture as related studies are scarce. It must be noted, however, that low costs airlines, before opening new routes, usually demand so-called "promotion fees" from destinations, which are, in reality, a hidden subsidy (still, unlike low cost carriers sharing economy companies do not require any fees). New tourists looking for low-cost accommodation might be desirable in major destinations but not in well-known tourism areas (e.g. Amsterdam, Barcelona) where tourism policy is aimed at an increase of tourism spending rather than a rise in tourism arrivals.

Introduction of sharing economy is also changing the geographical structure of hospitality market. Many studies claim that new hospitality services are offered in residential areas where no hotels are available (Cansoy & Schor, 2016; Kaplan & Nadler, 2015; D. Wang et al., 2016). A spatial dispersion of tourists and an increase in negative side effects of tourism, especially on local residents not participating in sharing economy, are a real challenge to city planners. Locals face increased traffic, reduced curbside parking and interference from unfamiliar persons, noises and odors (Widener, 2015). On the other side, assuming that sharing economy providers are a direct substitute for traditional hospitality, its development outside city centers may facilitate steps towards reduction of tourists' ghettos and increase the popularity of lesser known tourist attractions placed outside the core tourists areas.

As sharing economy providers operate very often at least partly illegally, a shift of demand from registered hospitality supply might mean less taxes to the local government. It results moreover in lesser impact of public authorities on the product quality, whose deterioration might eventually decrease the total tourists' satisfaction and affect other players in a destination. Sharing economy platforms judge providers' service quality by the review system. As mentioned, reviews are given mutually (the guest is also reviewed by host), they are high with extremely low variance. Zervas et al. (2015) found that nearly 95% of Airbnb properties boast an average user-generated rating of either 4.5 or 5 stars (the maximum). However, the comparison of quality between private accommodation and professional establishments has still never been a subject of independent scientific research.

The sharing economy also has an indirect impact on destinations which is usually associated mainly with markets for long-term accommodation and real estate. As renting an apartment for a short period to tourists via a sharing platform is a direct substitute for a permanent rental, it is obvious that this increase of supply on the hospitality market is directly connected with a corresponding decrease of supply on the rental market. This naturally results in a new equilibrium on rental market and results in higher price and lower quantity (unless prices are regulated. In that case this results in excess of demand on the market). Neeser (2015) cited a report from the city of San Francisco which claims that Airbnb could be taking about 40% of potential rentals off the market. This phenomenon might lead to depopulation of city centers and loss of their identity.

A rise of sharing economy market impacts also real-estate market. It drives additional demand for new flats which will are bought purposefully for short term rental. This has similar effects on the long-term rental market: less quantity and higher prices.

Another issue is raised by Kessler (2015) who underlines that the sharing economy might resemble "a different spin on the whole 'robots taking over human jobs' issue". The sharing economy might lead to a reduction of demand for housekeeping and other hotel staff especially in the budget segment, which will not be balanced by the rise of working places for those that clean private accommodation and deliver keys. Another vague issue is the quality of jobs in sharing economy. Various issues connected with impact of sharing economy on destination tourism are depicted in Figure 33.4.

At the advent of the sharing economy, Botsman and Rogers (2010) argued that it would disrupt the unsustainable practices of hyperconsumption. However, the contemporary sharing economy is as business-oriented as traditional economy, and has little in common with its socially and environmentally engaged ancestors. The sharing economy while boosting the tourism market in destinations, hardly contributes to the sustainable development of a destination. A bulk of new tourists that are tempted to destinations by low prices does not promise either sustainability nor any reduction in consumption. Providers on the hospitality market are increasingly professionalized. Hospitality organizations even claim that there are, instead of a hotel, entire properties built for sharing economy providers. They operate similarly to traditional hotels with reception, housekeeping, management and new distribution channels but without industry-specific regulation burdens. Hence the issue of sharing economy regulations gains popularity both among scholars and practitioners.

Issues of regulation of the sharing economy in hospitality

A free market might fail to produce an efficient equilibrium which assures best allocation of scarce resources and maximizes social (i.e., both consumers and producers) benefits. It happens because various types of market failures exist, such as: information asymmetry, negative and positive externalities, monopolies and merit goods. Hospitality, similarly to other service markets where a product is intangible experience good, belongs to those markets where government regulation is common. The main rationale for hospitality regulation is based on the information asymmetry. As product quality cannot be verified before purchase, many countries introduce state classification

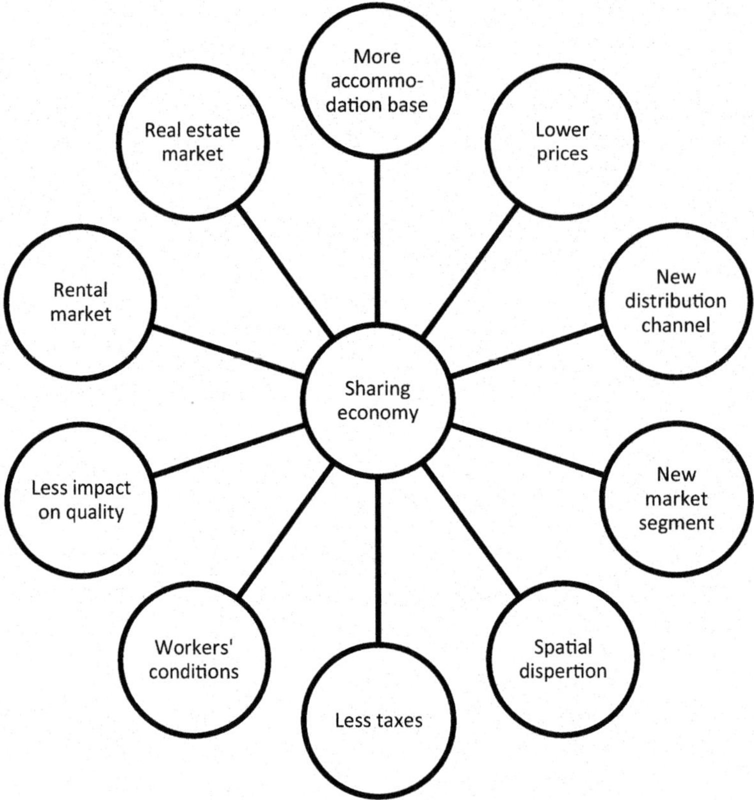

Figure 33.4 Issues of sharing economy impact on a destination

systems and extend customer protection beyond standard civil law. This is supposed to protect customers and lower transaction costs. In most countries, most regulations are imposed by state authorities, but in some countries (especially in US and Northern Europe) hospitality classification schemes are operated by hospitality or tourism organizations.

Both hospitality organizations and many academics advocate that sharing economy is operating in grey areas, as providers do not pay taxes (both tourism and general) and do not need to comply with numerous industry-specific regulations with which every single small accommodation establishment is concerned. In this way competition between sharing economy companies and traditional hospitality sector is unfair. The main problem with highlighting the sharing economy is its completely new form which prevents the application of existing regulations. While accepting that the development of the sharing economy is unavoidable and in general it increases the market and eventually benefits the customer, necessary information is required to protect the diverse stakeholders in the tourism destination. Current regulatory schemes usually fail to ensure safety, regulate anticompetitive behavior, protect workers and monitor finances (Dyal-Chand, 2015). These problems are not easily addressed by regulators, who act, in contrast to rapidly changing technological and societal environment, in a rather conservative way. This results with outdated regulations (Katz et. al. (2015) gives an example of a hospitality act where "almost one-quarter of the regulations pertain to how an inn owner can place a lien on a customer's horse") and a paucity of intergovernmental collaboration between governments.

An important issue for competition is "regulatory neutrality" between sharing economy providers and traditional businesses. It is difficult, however, to expect someone renting a room in his flat or even renting their apartment to follow all regulations a hotelier is expected to. On the other side a certain regulation for both sharing economy providers and sharing economy platforms is required. For providers in order to protect customers, and for platforms to protect competition as they operate on the oligopolistic market and may use its market power in their relations with providers, similarly to famous OTA–hospitality contractual disputes. It is possible that those platforms would gain market power versus individual providers in cities similarly to tour operators versus hotels in Mediterranean or online travel agencies versus business hotels in cities. Finally, although regulation is believed to be the most important hurdle to prospect expansion for sharing economy platforms, major sharing economy platforms may welcome regulation in a hope of building a barrier to prospective competitors. As shown by Cannon and Summers (2012) they explain the concept of sharing economy, are responsive to regulatory concerns by showing their own regulatory schemes, conduct intense public relations campaigns by sharing best practices of regulation and publish destination economic impact studies.

They are three main strategies a (local) government might pursue when dealing with sharing economy platforms. The first strategy, which is still prevalent, is to ignore the phenomenon, the second is an attempt to ban sharing economy all together, while the third one is to adapt existing regulations (Figure 33.5).

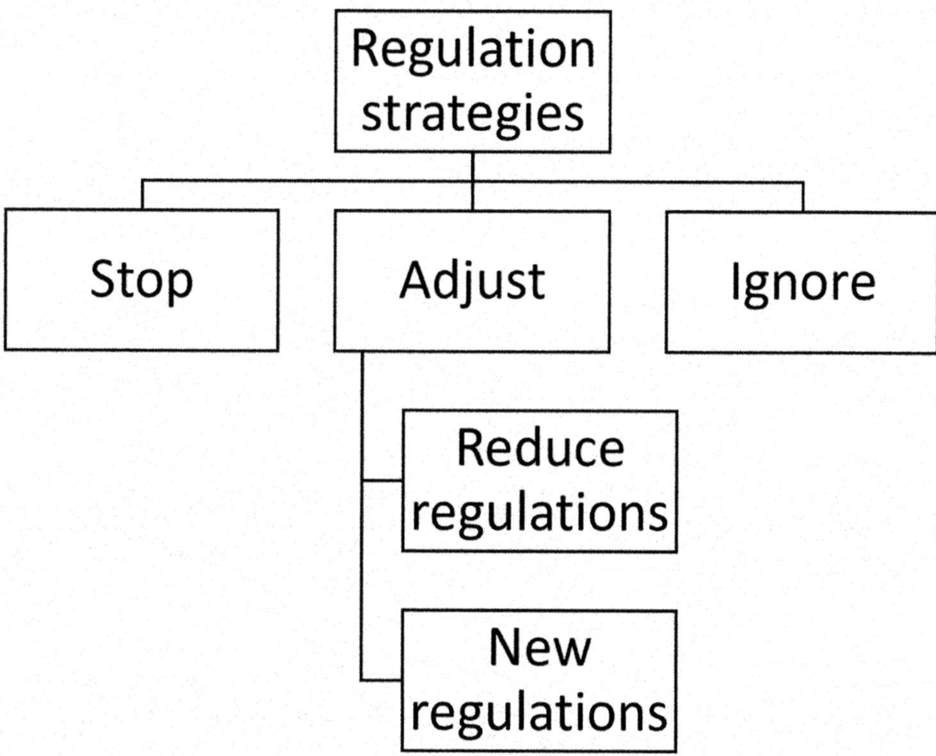

Figure 33.5 Sharing economy regulation strategies

Adapting existing regulations usually leads to the erection of new regulations for individuals that rent their accommodation establishments. A standard dilemma for government is to assess where sharing ends and pure business commences. It is difficult to apply same regulations to one individual that rents a room in his own flat and to the other that rents multiple apartments.

Current regulatory environment differs in various cities but in most countries there is still no regulatory response. In many cities it is possible to rent just a room in a flat where the innkeeper permanently lives while others limit the number of days where an apartment might be the subject of short term rental or limit an income. Airbnb on its website provides six areas of regulations that might apply to potential hosts: business licenses, building and housing standards, zoning rules, special permit, taxes and other rules. Although a variety of regulation approaches towards sharing economy platforms can be found, there is a paucity of best practices, as the nature of city tourism may impact the optimal solution.

Still, the success of sharing economy platforms may render the regulations that are applied to hotels and other traditional accommodation establishments obsolete. If platforms are able to reduce information asymmetry and protect customer rights without state interference then the best solution would be a reduction of overall regulation level rather than imposing new ones. This solution is still not popular, though.

Challenges for destination marketing

There is a consensus among scholars that successful destination marketing requires cooperation between all stakeholders involved in tourism: public authorities, enterprises, local community, non-profit sector and media. The emergence of sharing economy implies a new blended stakeholder: local individuals being micro-entrepreneurs. Moreover, a new powerful intermediary in the leisure market appears – sharing economy platforms. The research into these stakeholders' impact on destination marketing is still in a nascent stage.

The stakeholders' propensity to cooperate with a destination marketing organization has usually negative correlation with the size of the organization. Tourism companies with high turnover are usually more likely to engage in all sort of initiatives aimed at the improvement of public goods (and destination marketing certainly is one of those). From this perspective it is unlikely to expect any financial support for destination marketing from individual providers. Moreover, it has to be underlined that the use of sharing economy phenomenon in destination marketing is only feasible when a regulation "adjust strategy" is adopted, otherwise destination marketers simply do not know their partners. Daylighting the sharing economy is certainly a prerequisite for cooperation with both individual providers and platforms.

Destination product is usually composed of tourism services, infrastructure and attractions. The emergence of sharing economy profoundly changes all its parts, especially in city destinations. First it leads to the growing of accommodation capacity with great variety, second there is still little public control over spatial dispersion of the phenomenon resulting in growing numbers of tourists in non-tourism areas and local population leaving the historic centers. In order to target these issues, public authorities may introduce special taxation or other incentives for development of private accommodation in socially desirable areas.

Sharing economy platforms are still rarely seen as an intermediary between tourists and providers. Similarly to other powerful intermediaries in tourism such as online travel agencies, tour operators or global distribution systems, they possess a power of shifting tourism demand between destinations. Unlike other intermediaries they have limited influence over the price of service but they may place the product on their website or target a desired segment of platform users.

Some platforms are also already experimenting with service packaging which, if proven successful, would eventually give them even more market power. This marketing channel is still not used by marketers, and potential partnerships between platforms and major tourism destinations seem likely to appear in near future.

At the local level providers may be used, similarly to other accommodation establishments, as a communication channel with incoming tourists. Through the distribution of leaflets and other promotional materials destination marketing organization may achieve a selection of goals such as: promoting events, special offers, enhancing tourism in desirable areas, tourism education etc. Furthermore, as sharing economy platforms are a mutation of social platforms they represent an opportunity of additional electronic word of mouth marketing.

Although sharing economy companies are striving to enter business market segment, it seems unlikely that they succeed, at least unless business tourists' needs will radically change. PWC (2015) predicts ongoing bifurcation of consumer types – those who are more prone to look for a unique experience, and those who seek the reassurance of consistency. It is unlikely that heterogeneous sharing economy market may produce standardized product. Moreover, lessons from other parts of tourism sector do not provide similar evidence as even low costs carriers did not manage to attract business customers until now.

Partnerships between destination marketers and sharing economy providers and platforms may open new opportunities and challenges. Providing that the emergence of the sharing economy is desirable for a destination, it may open new communication channels with both potential and *in situ* tourists. As with all previous technological and social business revolutions, marketers need to stay agile and constantly look for a competitive advantage.

References

Balck, B., & Cracau, D. (2015). Empirical analysis of customer motives in the shareconomy: a cross-sectoral comparison. Working Paper Series. Otto von Guericke University Magdeburg.

Bardhi, F., & Eckhardt, G. M. (2012). Access-Based Consumption: The Case of Car Sharing. *Journal of Consumer Research*, 39, 1–19. http://doi.org/10.1086/666376

Belk, R. (2014). You are what you can access: Sharing and collaborative consumption online. *Journal of Business Research*, 67(8), 1595–1600. http://doi.org/10.1016/j.jbusres.2013.10.001

Benjaafar, S., Kong, G., Li, X., & Courcoubetis, C. (2015). *Peer-to-Peer Product Sharing: Implications for Ownership, Usage and Social Welfare in the Sharing Economy*.

Botsman, R. (2013). The Sharing Economy Lacks A Shared Definition | Co.Exist | ideas + impact. Available online at: www.fastcoexist.com/3022028/the-sharing-economy-lacks-a-shared-definition

Botsman, R., & Rogers, R. (2010). What's Mine Is Yours – How Collaborative Consumption is Changing the Way we live. *Business*. http://doi.org/10.1016/S0168-9525(00)00086-X

Cannon, S., & Summers, L. H. (2012). How Uber and the Sharing Economy Can Win Over Regulators. *Journal of Business Venturing*, 27(5), 544–558.

Cansoy, M., & Schor, J. (2016). Who Gets to Share in the "Sharing Economy": Understanding the Patterns of Participation and Exchange in Airbnb. Unpublished Paper, Boston College.

Choi, K., Jung, J., Ryu, S., & Kim, S. Do. (2015). The relationship between Airbnb and the hotel revenue: In the case of Korea. *Indian Journal of Science*, 8(26), 1–8. http://doi.org/10.17485/ijst/2015/v8i26/81013

Cusumano, M. A. (2014). How traditional firms must compete in the sharing economy. *Communications of the ACM*, 58(1), 32–34. http://doi.org/10.1145/2688487

Deloitte Access Economics. (2015). The Sharing Economy and the Competition and Consumer Act. Sydney.

Demary, V. (2015). Competition in the sharing economy. IW Policy Paper, 19.

Dillahunt, T., & Malone, A. (2015). The promise of the sharing economy among disadvantaged communities. In CHI '15 Proceedings of the 33rd Annual ACM Conference on Human Factors in Computing Systems. http://doi.org/http://dx.doi.org/10.1145/2702123.2702189

Dyal-Chand, R. (2015). Regulating Sharing: The Sharing Economy as an Alternative Capitalist System. *Tulane Law Review*, 90(2), 241–309.
Edelman, B., & Luca, M. (2014). Digital discrimination: The case of airbnb. com. . . . Business School NOM Unit Working Paper. http://doi.org/10.2139/ssrn.2377353
Edelman, B., Luca, M., & Svirsky, D. (2017). Racial Discrimination in the Sharing Economy: Evidence from a Field Experiment. *American Economic Journal: Applied Economics*, 9(2), 1–22.
Ert, E., Fleischer, A., & Magen, N. (2016). Trust and reputation in the sharing economy: The role of personal photos in Airbnb. *Tourism Management*, 55, 62–73. http://doi.org/10.1016/j.tourman.2016.01.013
Ertz, M., Durif, F., Arcand, M., Ertz, M., Durif, F., & Arcand, M. (2017). An Analysis of the Origins of Collaborative Consumption and Its Implications for Marketing. *Academy of Marketing Studies Journal*, 21(1), 1–17.
Fraiberger, S. P., & Sundararajan, A. (2015). Peer-to-Peer Rental Markets in the Sharing Economy. *NYU Stern School of Business Research Paper*, 1–44. http://doi.org/10.2139/ssrn.2574337
Hamari, J., Sjöklint, M., & Ukkonen, A. (2015). The Sharing Economy: Why People Participate in Collaborative Consumption. *Journal of the Association for Information Science and Technology*, 67(9), 2047–2059. http://doi.org/10.2139/ssrn.2271971
Hawlitschek, F., & Teubner, T. (2016). Understanding the Sharing Economy – Drivers and Impediments for Participation in Peer-to-Peer Rental. In 2016 49th Hawaii International Conference on System Sciences (HICSS) (pp. 4782–4791). http://doi.org/10.1109/HICSS.2016.593
Henten, A., & Windekilde, I. (2016). Transaction costs and the sharing economy. In 26th European Regional Conference of the International Telecommunications Society (Vol. 18, pp. 1–15). Madrid: ITS. http://doi.org/10.1108/info-09-2015-0044
Ho, J. (2015). An examination on the theories and practices of the sharing economy with special reference to the Hong Kong case. *European Academic Research*, 3(6), 6376–6400.
Hoffman, C., & Offutt, B. (2015). *Travel Innovation and Technology Trends 2015*. New York: Phocuswright Inc.
Kaplan, R., & Nadler, M. (2015). Airbnb: A case study in occupancy regulation and taxation. *The University of Chicago Law Review Dialogue*, 82, 103–116.
Katz, V., Dostmohammad, S., & Long, J. (2015). Regulating the Sharing Economy. *Berkeley Technology Law Journal*, 30(4), 1067–1128.
Kessler, S. (2015). *The Sharing Economy is Dead and We Killed It*. Fast Company.
Miller, S. (2016). First principles for regulating the sharing economy. *Harvard Journal on Legislation*, 53(1), 147–202. http://doi.org/10.2139/ssrn.2568016
Neeser, D. (2015). *Does Airbnb Hurt Hotel Business: Evidence from the Nordic Countries*. Madrid: Universidad Carlos III de Madrid.
Pargman, D., Eriksson, E., & Friday, A. (2016). Limits to the sharing economy. In Proceedings of the Second Workshop on Computing within Limits. http://doi.org/10.1145/2926676.2926683
Pawlicz, A., & Napierala, T. (2017). The determinants of hotel room rates: an analysis of the hotel industry in Warsaw, Poland. *International Journal of Contemporary Hospitality Management*, 29(1), 571–588. http://doi.org/10.1108/IJCHM-12-2015-0694
PWC. (2015). *The sharing economy*. PricewaterhouseCoopers.
Sands, M. (2015). Why Digital Marketing Should Join The Sharing Economy. Available online at: http://marketingland.com/digital-marketing-join-sharing-economy-151191
Sundararajan, A. (2016). *The Sharing Economy: The End of Employment and the Rise of Crowd-Based Capitalism*. London: MIT Press.
Tussyadiah, I. P., & Pesonen, J. (2016). Impacts of Peer-to-Peer Accommodation Use on Travel Patterns. *Journal of Travel Research*, 55(8), 1022–1040. http://doi.org/10.1177/0047287515608505
Wallsten, S. (2015). *The Competitive Effects of the Sharing Economy: How is Uber Changing Taxis ?* Technology Policy Institute. New York.
Wang, C., & Zhang, P. (2012). The evolution of social commerce: The people, management, technology, and information dimensions. *Communications of the Association for Information Systems,* 31(5), 1–23.
Wang, D., Li, M., Guo, P., & Xu, W. (2016). The Impact of Sharing Economy on the Diversification of Tourism Products: Implications for Tourist Experience. In A. Inversini & R. Schegg (eds), *Information and Communication Technologies in Tourism* (pp. 683–694).
Weber, T. (2014). Intermediation in a sharing economy: insurance, moral hazard, and rent extraction. *Journal of Management Information Systems*, 31(3), 35–71.
Widener, M. (2015). *Shared Spatial Regulating in Sharing-Economy Districts*. Seton Hall L. Rev.

Zervas, G., Proserpio, D., & Byers, J. (2015). A First Look at Online Reputation on Airbnb, Where Every Stay is Above Average. Where Every Stay Is Above . . ., New York: ACM Press, 1–22.

Zervas, G., Proserpio, D., & Byers, J. (2016). The rise of the sharing economy: Estimating the impact of Airbnb on the hotel industry. *Boston U. School of Management Research Paper*, 2013–16. http://doi.org/http://dx.doi.org/10.2139/ssrn.2366898

Further reading

Ismail, A. (2015). How The Sharing Economy Will Impact Marketing. Available online at: http://techcrunch.com/2015/01/17/how-the-sharing-economy-will-impact-marketing/

John, N. A. (2013). The social logics of sharing. *The Communication Review*, 16(3), 113–131. http://doi.org/10.1080/10714421.2013.807119

34

Innovative approach to destination marketing

The smoke-free support hotel concept

Marie Chan Sun and Robin Nunkoo

Introduction

Marketing is a social and managerial process by which individuals and groups obtain what they need through creating and exchanging products and value with others (Kotler, Bowen & Makens, 1999). As for destination marketing, the first definition of tourism destination marketing by Wahab, Crampon & Rothfield (1976) was as follows:

> The management process through which the National Tourist Organizations and/or tourist enterprises identify their selected tourists, actual and potential, communicate with them to ascertain and influence their wishes, needs, motivations, likes and dislikes, on local, regional, national and international levels, and to formulate and adapt their tourist products accordingly in view of achieving optimal tourist satisfaction thereby fulfilling their objectives.

Pike & Page (2014) pointed out that this definition has been shown in practice to be idealistic in light of the following:

> Many transformations have occurred within the tourism sector since the destination marketing literature commenced in the early 1970s, which have had wide ranging implications for DMOs. Among these changes were the introduction of jet aircraft, privatisation and the outsourcing of government services, the demise of communism, global recognition of sustainability issues, explosion in media channels, globalisation, disintermediation and online distribution, information communications technologies (ICT) and social media networking, the decline of the traditional passive all-inclusive coach tour and the rise of independent travellers and travel packages, the rise of short breaks and emergence of low cost carriers and last minute discount pricing, and resurgence of cruising, backpackers, adventure travellers and ecotourism, dark tourism and medical tourism; and the rise of terrorism and ensuing security measures, all of which have stimulated research on the implications for destinations.

Traditionally, marketing practice focused on the concept of the 4 Ps, product, price, promotion and place (Borden 1964); but this concept has nowadays been extended to include partnerships, people, programming and packaging (Shoemaker & Shaw 2008). The 8 Ps are the requirement on which specialists in destination marketing need to focus. However, a prerequisite for flourishing tourism industry is the need to offer innovative products to help tourism destinations, as well as the individual providers of services (Maráková & Medveďová 2016). As a matter of fact, the field of destination marketing has huge potential for development of innovation (Maráková & Medveďová 2016).

Innovative approaches

Innovative approaches consist of at least one of the following: (1) the implementation of a new marketing concept, (2) the development of a new customer segment in the market, (3) the development of fresh relationship between visitor and destination, (4) the enhancement of brand perception, (5) the merging of brands where all stakeholders in the region unite to propose a unique marketing brand, (6) the revamping of relationships with the media people, (7) the creation of a framework for integrated management of the destination which involves all stakeholders, (8) the identification of means for sustainable development of the destination (Maráková & Medveďová 2016). The most frequent innovations in tourism destinations are product innovations and management innovations (Maráková & Medveďová 2016).

Innovative approaches to destination marketing

During the past decades, there have been various innovative approaches to destination marketing, two of the main approaches being ecotourism and golf tourism. A more recent innovative approach is wedding tourism which is rapidly growing through a newly developed customer segment in search of exoticism. Medical tourism which is one of the most known innovations has been constantly increasing. Health tourism is also on the rise as more and more people are shifting to healthy lifestyles.

Contemporary issue

Over and above these innovative approaches, there has been a change in the landscape from hotels previously providing rooms for smokers to smoke-free hotels in countries implementing smoking bans in public places. The change in the hospitality landscape has occurred as a consequence of the World Health Organization (WHO) Framework Convention on Tobacco Control (FCTC) which is an international health treaty for global tobacco control (WHO, 2003). As per the FCTC, signatory countries take the commitment to implement smoke-free legislation that bans smoking in indoor workplaces and other public places in order to decrease exposure to tobacco smoke (WHO, 2003).

The issue which is being raised here is the partial implementation of smoking bans whereas the FCTC mandates comprehensive ban for effective protection from second hand smoke. While hotels situated in countries which have ratified the FCTC are implementing smoking bans in hotel rooms, restaurant and reception to variable extent, we witness that smoking has been delocalised from indoors to outdoor premises. The number of smokers seen at hotel entrances, on hotel car park or within the dedicated smoking area for hotel staff and clients who smoke is, in my opinion, not positive for the image of hotel chains! This is a contemporary matter which needs to be addressed by the hotel chain team, including Marketing, Human Resource, Health & Safety and General Managers. However, these managers need to be empowered to take the right decision for the health of clients/employees and for the protection of the environment so that the smoking ban in hospitality venues is profitably turned into an evidence-based innovative approach to destination marketing.

Aim and objectives

There is need to provide tourism stakeholders and policy makers with the latest evidence with respect to the dangers of tobacco use, the harms of Second Hand Smoke (SHS), the importance of 100% smoke-free hotels, and the need to provide support to staff and clients for smoking cessation. The outcomes of 100% smoke-free hotels will be better health of clients and staff but also improved staff productivity and customer satisfaction.

The objectives of this chapter are thus as follows:

(1) To highlight the innovative approach to adopt to become *real* smoke-free hotels,
(2) To discuss the means to become smoke-free *support* hotels,
(3) To identify the criteria to be fulfilled by smoke-free destinations,
(4) To discuss Mauritius as destination for marketing as smoke-free island and
(5) To look into the economic and social impact of smoke-free hotels.

In light of its objectives, this chapter aims at sensitizing tourism stakeholders and policy makers on the need for a paradigm shift from partial smoke-free to comprehensive smoke-free hotels through an innovative approach to smoke-free destination marketing.

Literature review

Dangers of tobacco use

All forms of smoked tobacco products are deadly (WHO 2006). They all cause instant addiction as the drug nicotine is delivered to the brain immediately after smokers inhale; the delivery of the addictive drug to the brain is considered to be as rapid as an intravenous injection (Benowitz, 1996). As these effects of smoked tobacco are brief, lasting only a few minutes; smokers experience withdrawal symptoms if they do not continue to smoke (Hendricks *et al.*, 2006). Moreover, bidis, small hand-rolled cigarettes, produce three times more carbon monoxide and nicotine and five times more tar than regular cigarettes (Gottlieb, 1999). In general, one out of every two long-term smokers will die of smoking related death (Doll *et al.*, 1994; Peto *et al.*, 1996), on average 15 years prematurely (Peto, 1992; Peto *et al.*, 1996; Surgeon General, 2014).

To the already long list of diseases known to have a causal relationship with tobacco use, the Surgeon General (2014) *adds* that smoking is a *cause* of type 2 diabetes mellitus, with smokers having 30–40% higher risk than non-smokers and with the risk increasing as the number of cigarettes smoked increases (Surgeon General, 2014). Colorectal cancer and liver cancer are two *additional* cancers caused by smoking (Surgeon General, 2014). As a matter of fact, it has long been reported that 90% of all lung cancers are caused by smoking (WHO 2002). It has also been known that smoking causes cancers of the oral cavity, nasal cavities/sinuses, pharynx, larynx, oesophagus, stomach, liver, pancreas, kidney, urinary bladder and renal pelvis, uterine cervix and myeloid leukaemia (Surgeon General, 2014). It is important to draw the attention of men and women who aspire to become parents to the fact that erectile dysfunction, facial clefts in infants and ectopic pregnancy are caused by smoking (Surgeon General, 2014). The other diseases which are added in this report are tuberculosis, adverse health outcomes in cancer patients and survivors, age-related macular degeneration, rheumatoid arthritis, inflammation, and impaired immune function (Surgeon General, 2014).

Harms of SHS

Exposure to tobacco smoke is associated with public health harms, such as premature death, lung cancer, coronary heart disease and chronic obstructive pulmonary disease (Fong *et al.*, 2013). Hospitality workers have a significantly increased risk of tobacco-related diseases as they are exposed daily to high doses of tobacco smoke as compared to other workers (Siegel & Skeer, 2003).

It is brought to the attention of tourism stakeholders that lung cancer among non-smokers is classified as a health outcome caused by SHS, which can be both from work exposure and from spousal smoking (Oberg *et al.*, 2011). Several international authorities have established since 1986 a causal relationship between lung cancer among non-smokers and SHS exposure (Surgeon General, 1986). Indeed, Fontham *et al.* (1994) had shown that non-smokers exposed to SHS in the workplace have a 16 to 19% increased risk of developing lung cancer (Fontham *et al.*, 1994). Based on a total of 25 epidemiological studies, the Surgeon General (2006) confirmed the consistent effect of occupational SHS exposure on the risk of lung cancer, after elimination of potential confounding errors, such as lifestyle variables or other occupational exposures (Surgeon General, 2006).

In addition to lung cancer, it is important to note that "exposure to SHS causes significantly more deaths due to cardiovascular disease than due to lung cancer" (Surgeon General, 2014). As a matter of fact, numerous studies in various countries demonstrated that SHS exposure induced a significant increase in risk of Ischaemic Heart Disease (IHD); approximately 30% of IHD are induced by SHS exposure (Surgeon General, 2006). Ameta-analysis by the Surgeon General (2006) confirmed that SHS exposure was associated with an increased risk for IHD mortality, morbidity and symptoms (Oberg *et al.*, 2011).

Importance of comprehensive smoke-free hotel

Comprehensive smoke-free enforcement, that is, total ban on indoor smoking without any exemption or designated smoking room, is the only effective way to ensure full protection of non-smokers from second hand smoke exposure (Surgeon General, 2006). The implementation of a 100% smoke-free environment has a positive impact on the respiratory health of hospitality workers, as shown by various studies in many countries worldwide and as confirmed by Schoj *et al.* (2010). In fact, the evidence regarding the need for a 100% smoke-free environment policy to protect the health of hospitality workers has already been emphasized (Schoj *et al.*, 2010).

As a matter of fact, non-smoking areas of venues that allowed smoking in ventilated designated smoking rooms had nicotine concentration in the air 3.2 times higher than completely smoke-free venues (Erazo *et al.*, 2010). Moreover, well-functioning designated smoking rooms, although functioning properly failed to prevent second hand smoke leakage to the indoor smoke-free areas due to the opening and closing of doors (Lee *et al.*, 2010). The need for comprehensive smoke-free environment is supported by Naiman, Glazier & Moineddin (2011) who demonstrated that comprehensive legislation is more effective in reducing exposure to tobacco smoke pollution than partial legislation. In the same vein, Gleich, Mons & Pötschke-Langer (2011) provide the evidence that comprehensive smoke-free legislation has larger effects on improving indoor air quality than partial smoke-free legislation.

Comprehensive smoke-free law greatly improves air quality in public places, contributing to clean and sustainable societies. For instance, in Cyprus, the median indoor levels of particulate matter (PM2.5) associated with SHS in hospitality venues after the implementation of the law dropped by 98% from 161 $\mu g/m^3$ pre-ban to 3 $\mu g/m^3$ post-ban (Christophi *et al.*, 2013). In a previous study conducted in pubs before and two months after the implementation of Scottish smoke-free law, indoor levels $PM_{2.5}$ reduced significantly from 246 μg/m^3 to 20 μg/m^3, showing a reduction of 86% (Semple *et al.*, 2007). Another important finding which policy-makers in the tourism sector need to be appraised of is the recent and interesting study by Matt *et al.* (2014) who demonstrated that:

> Air nicotine levels in smoking rooms were significantly higher than those in non-smoking rooms of hotels with and without complete smoking bans. Hallway surfaces outside of smoking rooms also showed higher levels of nicotine than those outside of non-smoking rooms. Non-smoking confederates staying in hotels without complete smoking bans showed higher levels of finger nicotine and urine cotinine than those staying in hotels with complete smoking bans.

The authors thus concluded that:

> Partial smoking bans in hotels do not protect non-smoking guests from exposure to tobacco smoke and tobacco-specific carcinogens. Non-smokers are advised to stay in hotels with complete smoking bans. Existing policies exempting hotels from complete smoking bans are ineffective.

Furthermore, third hand smoke was documented as toxins from tobacco smoke remain even after the cigarette has been extinguished; consequently, indoor spaces become contaminated with tobacco toxins even after the visible smoke disappears (Singer *et al.*, 2002). Matt *et al.* (2014) demonstrated that non-smoking rooms fail to protect non-smoking hotel guests from tobacco smoke exposure because of third hand smoke and exposure in California hotels. Moreover, Matt *et al.* (2016) put forward that when smokers quit, exposure to nicotine and carcinogens persists from third hand smoke. As a matter of fact, it was found that residents in the house of a smoker who quit continued to be exposed to carcinogens for up to six months after the smoker stopped smoking.

In addition to air quality, Ferrante *et al.* (2011) showed that comprehensive smoke-free legislation is more effective in reducing acute coronary syndrome admissions than partial smoke-free legislation. Considering smoking cessation behavior, Nagelhout *et al.* (2014) showed that comprehensive smoke-free workplace legislation in England was followed by an increase in quit success. It is pertinent to realize that smoke-free legislation reduces the social acceptability of smoking (Brown, Moodie & Hastings, 2009; Albers *et al.*, 2004), limits smoking opportunities (Longo *et al.* 2001; Levy & Friend, 2003), and leads to less socially cued smoking (Edwards *et al.*, 2008; Trotter, Wakefield & Borland, 2002). A World Bank report on the global tobacco epidemic concluded that smoking restrictions can reduce overall tobacco consumption by 4–10% (Lee *et al.*, 2010).

Importance of support in smoke-free hotels

Smoking is the leading cause in the world of death which can be prevented (Peto *et al.* 1996). Therefore, there is need to provide support to smokers to quit smoking. Many hotels are already contributing to the protection of the environment by encouraging clients to re-use same towels and bed sheets if possible. Hotels which will choose to implement the SFS Hotel Concept will be contributing to prevent death, disability and disease in addition to the protection of the environment. The branding will be very noble.

According to the WHO (2003), there is need to support smokers to empower them to quit. Offering help to quit is one of the components of the MPOWER package (WHO, 2008). The Ottawa Charter of Health Promotion includes the provision of supportive environment as an essential feature in health promotion (WHO, 1984). For the case of smoking cessation, supportive environment, specifically smoke-free environment, which is exempt of temptation and peer-pressure to smoke, facilitates behaviour change. However, smoking cessation is challenging and behavioural interventions have had only minimal success (Law & Tang, 1995). Therefore, the smoke-free supportive hotel concept is an attractive means to offer help to smokers for smoking cessation in a supportive environment.

Studies have shown that the effectiveness of pharmacotherapy varies as follows: The most common smoking cessation drug therapy has been Nicotine Replacement Therapy [NRT] (Silagy *et al.*, 2004). Anti-depressant therapy, specifically the agent bupropion (Hughes, 2004, 2007) and the selective nicotinic acetylcholine receptor partial agonist, namely varenicline (Oncken *et al.*, 2007, 2006) have also been prescribed as smoking cessation therapy. Cahill *et al.* (2014) confirms that these three medications have been proven to help people to quit and thus licensed in Europe and the USA for smoking cessation therapy. Moreover Cahill *et al.* (2014) reported that varenicline (27.6%) and combination NRT (31.5%) (example: patch plus inhaler) were most effective for achieving smoking cessation. Higher rates of smoking cessation were also associated with NRT (17.6%) and bupropion (19.1%) compared with placebo (10.6%). In addition to the efficacy of these agents, their safety has also been demonstrated as none of these therapies was associated with any increased rate of serious adverse events (Cahill & Lancaster, 2014).

Brose *et al.* (2011) concluded as follows:

> Routine clinic data support findings from randomised controlled trials that smokers receiving stop-smoking support from specialist clinics, treatment in groups and varenicline or combination NRT are more likely to succeed than those receiving treatment in primary care, one-to-one and single NRT. All smokers should have access to, and be encouraged to use, the most effective intervention options.

Innovative approach to smoke-free destination marketing

When the importance of smoke-free hotels has been understood, tourism stakeholders will then be able to work towards the implementation of comprehensive smoke-free hotels if they care for staff, clients and the tourism destination itself. Destination Marketing Organizations (DMO) have a leading role to play. According to Zavattaro & Daspit (2016), cities are turning toward marketing strategies to attract economic and social development, considering that innovation is a key component of success for DMO. A grounded theoretical approach by Zavattaro & Daspit (2016) to understanding innovation in destination marketing organizations revealed the need for (1) an innovation-centered organizational culture, (2) the ability to use external stakeholders as knowledge sources, and (3) the ability to use and develop knowledge internally (Zavattaro & Daspit, 2016).

Adopting the innovative approach to become real smoke-free hotels

As external stakeholders, we are proposing to countries, SIDS and cities the possibility to adopt an innovative approach to destination marketing.

Chan Sun & Nunkoo (2016) describe the SFS Hotel Concept as follows:

> Based on Article 8, 12 and 14 of the FCTC, the SFS Hotel Concept is a marketing strategy for the tourism industry and the health sector for the development of health tourism. The Concept is a three-in-one hotel accommodation package to attract both smokers and non-smokers. This concept has three components: (1) comprehensive smoke-free environment in the hotel indoor and outdoor premises for healthy hotel stay and work place, (2) stop smoking service by experts in the field of smoking cessation for smokers who want to quit, and (3) health culture sensitization for the promotion of public health. As a matter of fact, the SFS Hotel Concept relates to a business strategy which also has environmental and financial consequences: It is a business strategy for SIDS to present a competitive advantage over those islands which keep the Sea, Sand, Sun marketing strategy.

Becoming smoke-free support hotels

Through decision-making, by policy makers and/or management board, to implement the SFS Hotel Concept, the implementation team will transform partial smoke-free hotels into smoke-free support hotels by adding the resources required for smoking cessation services. The required resources are human, physical and financial with an overall culture for health for employers, employees and clients. Marketing strategies to brand the hotels implementing the concept as SFS Hotels will need to put in place, as well as communication strategies for the involvement of each and every member of the hotel staff team. Incentives will be given to all employees and clients to adopt healthy lifestyles in view of the development of the health culture within SFS Hotels. More specifically, employees who smoke will be encouraged to quit smoking by benefiting from the same smoking cessation services offered to clients. The smoking cessation services will be provided within a health and environment friendly package to hotel clients. Hotel operators and marketing managers with the support of DMO will have to promote the concept with efficient marketing tools and communication strategies.

Hotels branded as SFS Hotels will have to enforce the smoking bans in all areas of the hotel so as to protect all the clients from second hand smoke. Health professionals will offer help to smokers who want to quit through counselling, pharmacotherapy and rewarding system. Stop smoking services will be maintained through social network after smoker leaves the hotel. Besides, children will benefit from health education about the dangers of smoking. All these measures will contribute to fight on a national and global basis the tobacco epidemic for which the vector of the disease is the tobacco industry.

Choosing destinations for marketing

The SFS Hotel Concept, which is an innovative means for hotel marketing in general, is being recommended as an innovative approach to destination marketing by Small Island Developing States (SIDS). This new concept which can nonetheless be developed in various places in the world is expected to perform well, especially in countries where bans on smoking in public places are being enforced in the context of global tobacco control policies. The destinations which can aspire to this innovative approach are SIDS, which have ratified the FCTC. Developed countries, which have ratified the FCTC have implemented smoking bans in public places and have the required trained health professionals with respect to smoking cessation services, can easily work towards this type of destination marketing. Certain cities in specific countries can decide to use the concept for marketing of the city as a smoke-free city providing support for smoking cessation, with its implementation in hotels with the required physical and human resources.

Discussing Mauritius as a case study

The SFS Hotel Concept is a means to marketing Mauritius as a destination for smoking cessation. What makes Mauritius an optimal destination for the first ever implementation of the SFS Hotel Concept is undoubtedly the tobacco control landscape. As a signatory country to FCTC, Mauritius has passed the Public Health (Restrictions on Tobacco use products) Regulations 2008. Smoke-free regulations revised in 2008 are now applicable to the following places: indoor and outdoor premises of educational and health institutions, indoor and outdoor sporting premises, any public conveyance, bus stands and stations, any indoor workplace (excluding designated smoking areas), any indoor area open to the public, recreational public places like gardens (except beaches), cafés, bars, night clubs, and restaurants, while preparing, serving or selling food for/to the public, and while driving or travelling in a private vehicle carrying passengers. With these regulations, Mauritius aspires to become a smoke-free island and positions itself as the first destination to exploit the innovative SFS Hotel Concept for destination marketing. Health and wellness tourism can be developed through the SFS Hotel Concept.

In light of the SFS Hotel Concept, we propose to market, SIDS, by taking Mauritius as an example:

> Mauritius, a small island in the blue waters of the Indian Ocean, but a leader in tobacco control of the African region, will challenge you. The synergy of smoke-free policies, enforcement and support makes the smoke-free supportive hotel concept so charming that the scene is set for a healthy and peaceful holiday for couples and families. Here, you have the opportunity to experience constant professional support to quit smoking in a tropical holiday destination: a service of quality offering help to smokers for quitting which is beyond the WHO recommendation. Here, you will discover your potential and self-efficacy – a realization that will boost up all your motivations to stop smoking within a supportive tropical environment.

Earning the economic impact of SFS Hotels

Constituting a very innovative marketing strategy for the tourism industry, the SFS Hotel Concept will present economically a competitive advantage by attracting both non-smokers and smokers. It will also contribute to a healthier and cleaner society which will support smokers to quit smoking. It is pertinent to note that a growing number of smokers support smoke-free laws (Nagelhout *et al.*, 2014). Furthermore, Christophi *et al.* (2013) showed a positive impact on hospitality business one year after implementation of the smoking ban in Cyprus, with 4.1% increase in hotel turnover rate and 6.4% increase in restaurant revenue. Smoke free legislations, when enforced, are highly effective in improving the air quality with positive socio-economic impact.

From another perspective, King *et al.* (2011) showed that the implementation of smoke-free homes is greater among individuals with higher socio-economic status. This finding is particularly interesting to stakeholders in the tourism sector as this is the category of tourists which they will appreciate attracting because of their socio-economic status. The smoke-free supportive hotel concept will constitute another concrete step towards global momentum for a smoke-free world. In order to follow its leading trend in connection with tobacco control, Mauritius will have to be the first island in the sun to implement the smoke-free supportive hotel concept.

Conclusion

To sum up, hotels embarking on the SFS Hotel Concept will have to enforce the smoking bans in all areas of the hotel. Smokers will be offered help to quit while children will benefit from health education to prevent uptake of smoking. The SFS Hotel Concept will contribute to fight on a national and global basis the tobacco epidemic for which the vector of the disease is the tobacco industry. In light of the SFS Hotel Concept which is to be considered as health tourism, the health of the tourists will be enhanced beyond enjoying their holidays. Our concept goes beyond the traditional non-smoking rooms which have been enforced by many hotel chains which are basically only providing a smoke free environment with special zones for smokers.

Smoking is being de-normalized in our smoke-free global society: Parents of small children do not wish to let their children see smokers as they are not good examples to follow. Management teams of hotels and especially prestigious hotel chains cannot condone such an undesired situation whereby the smoking has moved from indoors to the outdoor premises of the hotel. The image of the hotel is polluted by the smoke emanating around the hotel: this can be remedied by implementing the SFS Hotel Concept which will result in enhanced employee-customer relationship as an innovative means of marketing.

To conclude readers are invited to critically reflect on the role of each and every one of us with respect to this contemporary issue of smoking on the outdoor premises of prestigious hotels.

References

Albers, A.B., Siegel, M., Cheng, D.M., Biener, L. *et al.* (2004). Relation between local restaurant smoking regulations and attitudes towards the prevalence and social acceptability of smoking: a study of youths and adults who eat out predominantly at restaurants in their town. *Tobacco Control*, 13(4), pp. 347–355.

Been, J.V., Nurmatov, U.B., Cox, B., Nawrot, T.S. *et al.* (2014). Effect of smoke-free legislation on perinatal and child health: a systematic review and meta-analysis. *The Lancet*, 383(9928), pp. 1549–1560.

Benowitz, N.L. (1996). Cotinine as a biomarker of environmental tobacco smoke exposure. *Epidemiologic reviews*, 18(2), pp. 188–204.

Borden, N.H. (1964). The concept of the marketing mix. *Journal of Advertising Research*, 4(2), pp. 2–7.

Brose, L.S., West, R., McDermott, M.S., Fidler, J.A. *et al.* (2011). What makes for an effective stop-smoking service? *Thorax*, 66(10), pp. 924–926.

Brown, A., Moodie, C. and Hastings, G. (2009). A longitudinal study of policy effect (smoke-free legislation) on smoking norms: ITC Scotland/United Kingdom. *Nicotine & Tobacco Research*, doi: 10.1093/ntr/ntp087

Cahill, K., Stevens, S. and Lancaster, T. (2014). Pharmacological treatments for smoking cessation. *JAMA*, 311(2), pp. 193–194.

Cahill, K. and Lancaster, T. (2014). Workplace interventions for smoking cessation. *The Cochrane Library*.

Callinan, J.E., Clarke, A., Doherty, K. and Kelleher, C. (2010). Legislative smoking bans for reducing secondhand smoke exposure, smoking prevalence and tobacco consumption. *Cochrane Database Syst Rev, 4*.

Chan Sun, M & Nunkoo, R. (2016). Perception of international tourism stakeholders on the novel Smoke-Free Support Hotel Concept. In *The 6th Advances Hospitality and Tourism Marketing and Management Conference*. [online] Guangzhou: Publisher of the Proceedings, p. 19. Available online at: www.ahtmm.com/wp-content/uploads/2016/08/2016.pdf [Accessed 13.11.2016].

Christophi, C.A., Paisi, M., Pampaka, D., Kehagias, M., Vardavas, C. *et al.* (2013). The impact of the Cyprus comprehensive smoking ban on air quality and economic business of hospitality venues. *BMC Public Health*, 13(1), p. 1.

Doll, R., Peto, R., Wheatley, K., Gray, R. and Sutherland, I. (1994). Mortality in relation to smoking: 40 years' observations on male British doctors. *BMJ*, 309(6959), pp. 901–911.

Edwards, R., Thomson, G., Wilson, N., Waa, A. *et al.* (2008). After the smoke has cleared: evaluation of the impact of a new national smoke-free law in New Zealand. *Tobacco Control*, 17(1), p. e2.

Erazo, M., Iglesias, V., Droppelmann, A., Acuna, M. *et al.* (2010). Secondhand tobacco smoke in bars and restaurants in santiago, chile: Evaluation of partial smoking ban legislation in public places. *Tobacco Control*, 19(6).

Ferrante, D., Linetzky, B., Virgolini, M., Schoj, V. *et al.* (2012). Reduction in hospital admissions for acute coronary syndrome after the successful implementation of 100% smoke-free legislation in Argentina: a comparison with partial smoking restrictions. *Tobacco Control*, 21(4), pp. 402–406.

Fong, G.T., Craig, L.V., Guignard, R., Nagelhout, G.E.*et al.* (2013). Evaluating the effectiveness of France's indoor smoke-free law 1 year and 5 years after implementation: findings from the ITC France Survey. *PloS one*, 8(6), doi: 10.1093/her/cyt073

Fontham, E.T., Correa, P., Reynolds, P., Wu-Williams, A. *et al.* (1994). Environmental tobacco smoke and lung cancer in nonsmoking women: a multicenter study. *JAMA*, 271(22), pp. 1752–1759.

Gleich, F., Mons, U. and Pötschke-Langer, M. (2011). Air contamination due to smoking in German restaurants, bars, and other venues before and after the implementation of a partial smoking ban. *Nicotine & Tobacco Research*, doi: 10.1093/ntr/ntr099

Gottlieb, N. (1999). Indian cigarettes gain popularity, but don't let the flavor fool you. *Journal of the National Cancer Institute*, 91(21), pp. 1806–1807.

Hendricks, P.S., Ditre, J.W., Drobes, D.J. and Brandon, T.H. (2006). The early time course of smoking withdrawal effects. *Psychopharmacology*, 187(3), pp. 385–396.

Hoh, E., Hovell, M.F. and Winston, C. (2014). Thirdhand smoke and exposure in California hotels: non-smoking rooms fail to protect non-smoking hotel guests from tobacco smoke exposure. *Tobacco Control*, 23(3), pp. 264–272.

Hughes, G. (2004). Tourism, sustainability, and social theory. *A companion to tourism*, p. 498.

Hughes, H. (2007). Rainbow, renaissance, tribes and townships: tourism and heritage in South Africa since 1994. *State of the nation: South Africa*, pp. 266–288.

Kelleher, C.C. and Frazer, K. (2014). An International Smoking Ban – How Many Lives Will Be Saved? *Current atherosclerosis reports*, 16(6), pp. 1–7.

King, D.P., Paciga, S., Pickering, E., Benowitz, N.L. *et al.* (2012). Smoking cessation pharmacogenetics: analysis of varenicline and bupropion in placebo-controlled clinical trials. *Neuropsychopharmacology*, 37(3), pp. 641–650.

Kotler, P., Bowen, J.T. and Makens, J.C. (1999). *Marketing for Hospitality and Tourism, 5/e.* Pearson Education India.

Law, M. & Tang, J.L. (1995). An analysis of the effectiveness of interventions intended to help people stop smoking. *Archives of Internal Medicine*, 155(18), 1933–1941.

Lee, K., Hahn, E.J., Robertson, H.E., Whitten, L. *et al.* (2010) Air quality in and around airport enclosed smoking rooms. *Nicotine & Tobacco Research*, 12(4). Available online at: www.ncbi.nlm.hih.gov/pubmed/20410143http://www.ncbi.nlm.hih.gov/pubmed/20410143 (accessed on 5 April 2012).

Lee, S., Grana, R.A. and Glantz, S.A. (2014). Electronic cigarette use among Korean adolescents: a cross-sectional study of market penetration, dual use, and relationship to quit attempts and former smoking. *Journal of Adolescent Health*, 54(6), pp. 684–690.

Levy, D.T. and Friend, K.B. (2003). The effects of clean indoor air laws: what do we know and what do we need to know? *Health Education Research*, 18(5), pp. 592–609.

Longo, D.R., Johnson, J.C., Kruse, R.L., Brownson, R.C. *et al.* (2001). A prospective investigation of the impact of smoking bans on tobacco cessation and relapse. *Tobacco Control*, 10(3), pp. 267–272.

Maráková, V. and Medved'ová, M. (2016). *Innovation in Tourism Destinations.* In *Forum Scientiae Oeconomia*, 4(1), pp. 33–43.

Matt, G.E., Quintana, P.J., Fortmann, A.L., Zakarian, J.M. *et al.* (2014). Thirdhand smoke and exposure in California hotels: non-smoking rooms fail to protect non-smoking hotel guests from tobacco smoke exposure. *Tobacco Control*, 23(3), pp. 264–272.

Matt, G.E., Quintana, P.J., Zakarian, J.M., Hoh, E. *et al.* (2016). When smokers quit: exposure to nicotine and carcinogens persists from thirdhand smoke pollution. *Tobacco Control*, http://dx.doi.org/10.1136/tobaccocontrol-2016–053119

Nagelhout, G.E., Wolfson, T., Zhuang, Y.L., Gamst, A. *et al.* (2014). Population support before and after the implementation of smoke-free laws in the United States: Trends From 1992 to 2007. *Nicotine & Tobacco Research*, http://dx.doi.org/10.1136/tobaccocontrol-2016–053119

Naiman, A.B., Glazier, R.H. and Moineddin, R. (2011). Is there an impact of public smoking bans on self–reported smoking status and exposure to secondhand smoke?. *BMC Public Health*, 11(1), p. 1.

Öberg, M., Jaakkola, M.S., Woodward, A., Peruga, A. *et al.* (2011). Worldwide burden of disease from exposure to second-hand smoke: a retrospective analysis of data from 192 countries. *The Lancet*, 377(9760), pp. 139–146.

Oncken, C., Gonzales, D., Nides, M., Rennard, S. *et al.* (2006). Efficacy and safety of the novel selective nicotinic acetylcholine receptor partial agonist, varenicline, for smoking cessation. *Archives of Internal Medicine*, 166(15), pp. 1571–1577.

Oncken, C.A., Gonzales, D., Nides, M., Rennard, S. *et al.* (2007). Varenicline: a 42 nicotinic acetylcholine receptor partial agonist as an aid to smoking cessation. *Medication treatments for nicotine dependence. Boca Raton: CRC/Taylor & Francis*, pp. 213–221.

Peto, R., Lopez, A.D., Boreham, J., Thun, M. *et al.* (1996). Mortality from smoking worldwide. *British Medical Bulletin*, 52(1), pp. 12–21.

Peto, R., Boreham, J. and Lopez, A.D. (1996). *Mortality from smoking in developed countries*. Oxford University Press.

Peto, R., Boreham, J., Lopez, A.D., Thun, M. *et al.* (1992). Mortality from tobacco in developed countries: indirect estimation from national vital statistics. *The Lancet*, 339(8804), pp. 1268–1278.

Pike, S., & Page, S. (2014). Destination Marketing Organizations and destination marketing: A narrative analysis of the literature. *Tourism Management*. 41, pp. 1–26.

Schoj, V., Alderete, M., Ruiz, E., Hasdeu, S. *et al.* (2010) The impact of a 100% smoke-free law on the health of hospitality workers from the city of Neuquén, Argentina. *Tobacco Control*, 19, pp. 134–137.

Semple, S., Maccalman, L., Naji, A.A., Dempsey, S. *et al.* (2007). Bar workers' exposure to second-hand smoke: the effect of Scottish smoke-free legislation on occupational exposure. *Annals of Occupational Hygiene*, 51(7), pp. 571–580.

Shoemaker, S. and Shaw, M. (2008). *Marketing essentials in hospitality and tourism*. Upper Saddle River, NJ: Pearson/Prentice Hall.

Siegel, M. and Skeer, M. (2003). Exposure to secondhand smoke and excess lung cancer mortality risk among workers in the "5 B's": bars, bowling alleys, billiard halls, betting establishments, and bingo parlours. *Tobacco Control*, 12(3), pp. 333–338.

Silagy, C., Lancaster, T., Stead, L., Mant, D. *et al.* (2004) Nicotine replacement therapy for smoking cessation. Cochrane Database of Systematic Reviews, Issue 3. Art. No.: CD000146.

Singer, B.C., Hodgson, A.T., Guevarra, K.S., Hawley, E.L. *et al.* (2002) Gas-phase organics in environmental tobacco smoke. 1. Effects of smoking rate, ventilation, and furnishing level on emission factor. *Environ. Sci. Technol.*, 36 (8). Available online at: www.ncbi.nlm.nih.gov/pubmed/11918006 (accessed on 5 April 2012).

Surgeon General. (2006). The Health Consequences of Involuntary Exposure to Tobacco Smoke; Office on Smoking and Health, Centers for Disease Control and Prevention: Atlanta, GA, USA, p. 727.

Surgeon General. (2014). The Health Consequences of Smoking – 50 Years of Progress; Office on Smoking and Health, Centers for Disease Control and Prevention: Atlanta, GA, USA.

Trotter, L., Wakefield, M. and Borland, R. (2002). Socially cued smoking in bars, nightclubs, and gaming venues: a case for introducing smoke-free policies. *Tobacco Control*, 11(4), pp. 300–304.

Wahab, S., Crampon, L.J. and Rothfield, L.M. (1976). Tourism marketing: a destination-orientated programme for the marketing of international tourism. Tourism International Press.

WHO. (1984). The Ottawa Charter for Health Promotion [WWW Document]. WHO. Available online at: www.who.int/healthpromotion/conferences/previous/ottawa/en/index1.html (accessed 4.21.15).

WHO. (2002)

WHO. (2003). *Framework Convention on Tobacco Control*. Geneva. Available online at: www.who.int/fctc/text_download/en/www.who.int/fctc/text_download/en/

WHO. (2006)

WHO. (2008). *Report on the Global Tobacco Epidemic, 2008 – The MPOWER package*. Geneva: World Health Organization. Available online at: www.who.int/tobacco/mpower/2008/en/

WHO. (2009)

WHO. (2011). *Report on the global tobacco epidemic, 2011 Warning about the dangers of tobacco*. Geneva: World Health Organization. Available online at: www.who.int/tobacco/global_report/2011/en/

WHO. (2013). *Report on the global tobacco epidemic 2013*. Geneva: World Health Organization. Available online at: www.who.int/tobacco/global_report/2013/en/

WHO. (2014)

WHO. (2015). 10th Anniversary of the WHO Framework Convention on Tobacco Control – SAVING LIVES FOR A DECADE. Available online at: www.who.int/fctc/FCTC_Anniversary_leaflet_web.pdf?ua=1

Zavattaro, S.M. and Daspit, J.J. (2016). A grounded theoretical approach to understanding innovation in destination marketing organizations. *Journal of Vacation Marketing*, https://doi.org/10.1177/1356766715623826

Part VII
Internet and technology

35

Impact of internet and technology on tourist behavior

Aviad A. Israeli, Swathi Ravichandran and Shweta Singh

Introduction

The internet and technological advancements have changed consumer behavior in general and specifically in tourism. With technology, consumers are more informed and are seeking unique and personalized experiences (Minazzi, 2015). Web 2.0 has given more power and control to consumers through enhanced knowledge and access to information (Murphy, Chen, & Cossutta, 2016; Minazzi, 2015). Overall, these technological developments have been touted as the "social movement" and the driver of "democratization of technology" by scholars (Minazzi, 2015, p. 3). The internet offers a social space where endless social interactions occur generating content in various forms. This content includes weblogs, organization sites, and review websites (Ayeh, Au, & Law, 2013; Stoeckl, Rohrmeier, & Hess, 2007).

The development of social media (SM) has intensified two-way many-to-many communication that consumers can use to share information and experiences (Daugherty & Hoffman, 2014). These drastic developments reconstructed consumer behavior in general and especially the behaviors that pertain to consumers' use of electronic Word of Mouth (eWOM), consumers' purchase intentions, and Consumer Complaint Behavior (CCB). The following paragraphs focus on these issues in the context of the tourism industry. First, we review how technology has transformed consumer behavior. Then we highlight main theories and models of consumer engagement with technology; and finally, we present trending technologies in tourist behavior.

How technology transformed consumer behavior

One of the core assumptions of economic theory is that agents act in their own self-interest (Stigler, 1961). Traditionally, the common business transaction was considered a sequential procedure starting with a well-informed seller who offers goods and services to less-well-informed consumers (Nayyar, 1990). Consumers act in their own self-interest and try to reduce asymmetry by seeking and communicating information. If successful, consumers could make better decisions that would successfully promote their self-interest (Stigler, 1961). The better informed party may exploit its informational advantage at the expense of less informed parties (Makadok, 2011). Historically, information asymmetry has put sellers in a more favorable position. The informational disadvantage of buyers was due to the fact that buyers did not usually know where to collect information about the value of goods or services and Word of Mouth (WOM). This primarily included post-purchase communication by consumers, which was limited.

Internet and technology has dramatically changed the balance of power between businesses and customers (Teece, 2010). This change included the widespread use of eWOM which is faster and has a significantly larger reach compared to WOM. eWOM includes user-generated content (UGC) that may include online comments, reviews, recommendations or opinions and any other informal communication directed at consumers through internet-based technology related to the usage or characteristics of particular goods and services, or their sellers (Litvin, Goldsmith, & Pan, 2008).

eWOM affected the traditional proportion of information asymmetry between buyers and sellers. Technology allows consumers to share these messages over large networks with little or no limitations on the message's potential publicity. eWOM facilitates sharing information between sellers and consumers as well as among consumers themselves. With the growing importance of eWOM, research in tourism has primarily focused on two main research streams: one dedicated to studying the dynamics of *writing* eWOM (review generation and CCB) and the other on the dynamics involved with *reading* eWOM (purchase intensions and decisions).

Relationship between written *eWOM and consumer complaint behavior (CCB)*

Research on the dynamics of *written* eWOM in the context of tourism suggests that customers engage in generating eWOM about hotels, restaurants, and destinations on different SM platforms, ranging from their own private individual SM channels to public SM platforms, to providing reviews of products and services (Zhang, Ye, Law, & Li, 2010). Contributing to eWOM on SM can be triggered by different factors including self-directed motivations (Bronner & de Hoog, 2010), a sense of community belonging and the will to provide information to help other consumers (Casaló, Flavian, & Guinaliu, 2010), and satisfaction and delight with the quality of service (Crotts, Mason, & Davis, 2009). The main motivation to write eWOM is a service failure event (Cantallops & Salvi, 2014; Swanson & Hsu, 2009). In the traditional CCB literature (Day & Landon, 1977) dissatisfied customers could take public action by contacting the vendor, complaining to a third party (such as customer protection agency), or taking legal action. Before the prevalence of SM, these customers were not able to access a widespread, media rich, and public channel to voice complains. The widespread public channel offered by the internet and SM has caused eWOM to become the primary platform for CCB (Casidy & Shin, 2015).

After experiencing a service failure, consumers may turn to SM to share their experience with others, seek a solution to their problems, pursue retribution, or vent frustration (Hennig-Thurau, Gwinner, Walsh, & Gremler, 2004). These eWOM communications escalate from "good" to "bad" and to "ugly" (Grégoire, Salle, & Tripp, 2015). The "good" eWOM category include *directness* which includes a message of seeking a resolution. This message is often communicated via Facebook or Twitter to the company. *Boasting* includes positive eWOM about extraordinary service recovery. Customers will use such messages when their problem was addressed satisfactorily following a service failure. They may then forgive and continue doing business with the firm and even share their positive experiences on SM. The "bad" category include *badmouthing* which is a negative eWOM communicated over SM but without contacting the firm and without allowing an opportunity to fix the issue. This category also includes *tattling* which is eWOM that involves complaining to a third party (as the Better Business Bureau or other consumer agencies) with the goal of seeking assistance. Finally, two types of SM messages are included in the "ugly" category. *Spite* includes spreading negative eWOM to get revenge against a firm by sharing information about their experience in an effort to punish the firm (and not to seek retribution). The ultimate reward for customers who write spite eWOM is when their messages go viral. Lastly, *feeding the vultures* is an example of how competitors take advantage of a customer's unfavorable eWOM. This communication is based on a customer's SM complaint that goes viral and competitors take advantage of the message, resulting in more publicity on SM platforms, thus influencing other customers' purchase and repurchase decisions (Balaji, Jha, & Royne, 2015).

Israeli, Lee, and Karpinski (2017) studied consumer eWOM behavior following service failure in restaurants. Their findings show that when service failures become more severe, customers are more likely to spread negative eWOM. They show that with the escalation of service failures, consumers' eWOM tend to escalate from "good" (directness, boasting) to "bad" (badmouthing). However, the study also showed that consumers limited the aggressiveness of their negative eWOM, thus limiting the use of other "bad" message styles (tattling) and refraining from using "ugly" eWOM (spite, feeding the vultures). This trend implies that customers demonstrate a certain amount of self-control when they engage in negative eWOM on SM.

Relationship between reading *eWOM and purchase intentions*

Research on the dynamics of *reading* eWOM suggests that it reinforces purchase intentions (Erkan & Evans, 2016). Collecting eWOM information about products and services before making a purchase decision is specifically valuable with experience goods (Morrison & Cheong, 2008). Tourism products and services are classic experience goods because their value cannot be fully evaluated before consumption (Zhang et al., 2010). Therefore, consumers try to mitigate the uncertainty about the value of tourism goods and services by acquiring information. In recent years, the primary source for this information has been through eWOM published on review sites on hotels, restaurants, tourism destinations, etc. (Pantelidis, 2010). Among the most popular sites are Yelp, UrbanSpoon, Zagat, TripAdvisor and Dine.com to name a few.

The significance consumers assign to eWOM read on SM is evaluated through a measure of its perceived usefulness (Cheung, Lee, & Rahbjon, 2008). Consumers' evaluations of information usefulness serve as a precursor to information adoption, which ultimately impact purchase decision (Rabjohn, Cheung, & Lee, 2008). Salehi-Esfahani, Ravichandran, Israeli, and Bolden (2016) investigated how consumers read and evaluate eWOM posted in restaurant review sites. Their findings revealed a significant relationship between eWOM negativity and its perceived usefulness suggesting that more negative eWOM is considered more useful. This finding is quite interesting and suggests that customers may not necessarily consider raving reviews and instead, they may pay close attention to negative comments when they make purchase decisions.

The writers of eWOM on SM may not be familiar to readers. Therefore, readers evaluate different factors such as the comprehensiveness and length of the reviews (Mudambi & Schuff, 2010) and their general perceptions about the site quality (Bai, Law &, Wen, 2008). eWOM credibility is a significant factor evaluated by consumers. Credibility is a construct of trustworthiness and expertise which both impact how the eWOM is perceived and judged (Dou, Walden, Lee, & Lee, 2012). Studies of eWOM in tourism (Salehi-Esfahani et al., 2016; Pornpitakpan, 2004) show that credibility assigned by the reader to the restaurant review writer was a significant predictor of perceived eWOM usefulness. Credibility is considered high when there is an indication that the message was written by someone who has a certain level of expertise which makes that reader perceive the eWOM as trustworthy.

Theories and models of consumer engagement with technology

Several theories serve as foundations for research related to the impact of technology and internet on consumer behavior in the tourism and travel industry. The following paragraphs review the theories and highlight empirical studies in tourism.

Technology Acceptance Model (TAM)

TAM is widely regarded as the most influential and widely applied theory for explaining individuals' acceptance and use of information systems (Lee, Kozar, & Larsen, 2003). TAM adapted Fishbein and Ajzen's (1975) theory of reasoned action (TRA) to explain the hypothesized causal relationship where beliefs are the antecedents of attitudes, which could explain variation in behavioral intention in adoption of information systems. TRA suggests that attitude toward a behavior and subjective norm are immediate determinants of intent to perform a behavior (Ajzen & Fishbein, 1980; Fishbein & Ajzen, 1975) and behavioral intentions are posited to be antecedents of actual behavior. The theory of planned behavior, another relevant consumer behavior theory, adds perceived behavioral control as an antecedent to behavioral intention. The more resources and opportunities an individual thinks he or she possesses, the greater is their perceived control over their behavior (Ajzen, 1985).

Davis (1989) proposed two specific scales – perceived usefulness and perceived ease of use – as determinants of user acceptance of information technology. Both were significantly correlated with both self-reported current and future usage of information technology. However, perceived usefulness was found to have a significant greater correlation with usage behavior compared to ease of use.

A number of studies employed TAM to evaluate consumers' intention to use consumer-generated media or SM to make travel decisions. For example, Castaneda, Frias, and Rodriguez (2009) extended TAM and applied it to a broad sample of international tourists who traveled through Malaga airport in the Andalusia region in Spain. Perceived usefulness was found to be the main determinant of both actual and future use of internet by tourists. Using an online survey of travel consumers, Ayeh et al. (2013) studied the intention to use consumer-generated media (CGM) for travel planning by adding new constructs to the conventional TAM. Findings implied that individuals who would normally ignore CGM for travel planning would use it if doing so was useful, fun, and easy. Contrary to what information systems literature suggests, perceived enjoyment and ease of use were found to have influence on use of CGM for travel planning.

Di Pietro, Di Virgilio, and Pantano (2012) investigated how social networks can assist with obtaining fast and detailed information when travelers make choices regarding tourism destinations. Using responses from 1,397 students, employees, and academics from tourism programs in various universities in southern Italy, the research tested an extended TAM adding eWOM communication and enjoyment. Perceived usefulness, perceived ease of use, and eWOM were found to impact attitude toward the use of social networks to obtain information for making travel choices.

Extended Unified Theory

Venkatesh, Morris, Davis and Davis (2003) formulated a unified model of consumer behavior that integrated elements from eight existing models termed Unified Theory of Acceptance and Use of Technology (UTAUT). Using data from employees in six organizations representing a variety of industries and business functions, the authors confirmed the unified model explained significantly more variance in user intentions to use information technology compared to each of the models, when considered individually. Venkatesh, Thong, and Xu (2012) created UTAUT2 by incorporating three additional constructs; hedonic motivation, price value, and habit, to study consumer acceptance and use of technology. UTAUT2 explained a substantially higher variance in consumer behavioral intention and technology use compared to UTAUT.

Escobar-Rodriguez and Carvajal-Trujillo (2013) examined drivers of online consumer airline ticket purchase behavior utilizing the UTAUT2 theoretical framework. Using data from Spanish consumers who had bought tickets through airline company websites, the authors concluded that relevance, habit, price saving, performance expectancy, and facilitating conditions predicted online purchase intentions.

Flow Theory

Csikszentmihalyi (1975) stated that "flow denotes the wholistic sensation present when we act with total involvement" (p. 43). Senecal, Gharbi, and Nantel (2002) found that a website's hedonic and utilitarian features can create a flow experience. McGinnis, Gentry, and Gao (2008) added that service providers need to understand what drives flow for consumers in order to enhance their experience. Bilgihan, Nusair, Okumus, and Cobanoglu (2015) examined the roles of online consumer experiences and flow in influencing customers' loyalty to a hotel booking site. Based on data collected from 20,000 randomly selected individuals in the US who were interested in purchasing travel products, the authors concluded that hedonic features had a stronger effect on flow compared to utilitarian features. Also, if customers experience flow when they book hotel services online, they develop a sense of trust toward the website (Bilgihan et al., 2015). Hotel website quality has also been found to influence customers' perceived flow, which in turn, influences customer satisfaction and purchase intention (Ali, 2016). This conclusion was reached based on a sample of hotel guests who booked rooms via online travel agencies and/or hotel websites.

Integrated models

Given the large number of consumer behavior models, researchers have combined various models to explain variability on consumers' online shopping behavior. Amaro and Duarte (2015) integrated TRA, TPB, TAM, and Innovation Diffusions Theory (IDT) to explore which factors affected travelers' intentions to purchase online. Based on data from internet users, the authors concluded that online travel purchases were mostly influenced by attitude toward online travel, perceived risk, and perceived compatibility. Perceived compatibility, an IDT construct, is defined as "the degree to which an innovation is perceived as being consistent with existing values, past experiences, and needs of potential adopters" (Rogers, 1995, p. 15).

Casalo, Flavian, and Guinaliu (2010) combined TPB, TAM, and Social Identity Theory to determine what motivated customers to participate in firm-hosted online travel communities. The authors gathered data via a web survey that included members of several firm-hosted online travel communities (e.g., TripAdvisor). The model provided a sound theoretical framework to explain customers' intention to participate in these travel communities. In addition, the intention to participate also increased their intention to use the firm's products and services and recommend the host firm. On a similar vein, Nusair, Bilgihan, Okumus, and Cobanoglu (2013) developed a theory-based model to determine Generation Y travelers' commitment to online social networks (OSNs) as OSNs are used extensively to share travel experiences and offer vacation suggestions (Goldberg, 2015). Examples of OSNs include Facebook, Twitter, and LinkedIn. After surveying students from six universities, Nusair et al. (2013) concluded that perceived utility and trust were positively related to both affective and calculative commitment. The theoretical underpinnings for their study included organizational commitment theory, commitment-trust theory of relationship marketing, the perceived risk construct, and the perceived utility construct.

Trending technologies in tourist behavior

Existing consumer-oriented technologies in tourism

The application of Web 2.0 in tourism is referred to as Travel 2.0 and indicates a shift from Travel 1.0 or the shift from offline to online bookings (Wolf, 2006). While search engines provide users with access to information about a product or service, SM has changed the face of online communication (Sigala, Christou, & Gretzel 2012). Google has become a leading source of information about hotels, restaurants, bars, and other attractions. Other online travel agency (OTA) sites such as Hotels.com, Trivago.com and Kayak.com are also popular sources of information. The popularity of these sites can be attributed to their ability to provide information about a variety of tourism attractions and ease of use (Murphy et al., 2016).

Consumers gather and share information on SM platforms in different ways. *Personal SM* allows consumers to post, share, and access content by logging on to their personal pages on SM sites such as Facebook, Twitter, Instagram, Snapchat, and Pinterest. Consumers also share information on *review sites* such as TripAdvisor, Yelp, and Zagat that publish crowdsourced reviews contributed by travelers who share their personal experiences. Sites such as TravelPost and Trivago.com offer reviews and rates and allow side-by-side comparison of rates and services in an effort to assist consumers to make informed decisions.

Independent review sites such as Feefo, Reevoo, and itrust-reviews offer reviews from guests who have stayed at the specific property. These review sites award the property a rating based on these user responses. Trust is the most important aspect of a review and these new review sites have an upper hand since the reviewers are guaranteed to have stayed at the property, unlike TripAdvisor or Google reviews (Keenan & Frary, 2015).

The shift to mobile consumer technologies in tourism

The increased adoption of smartphones proffers a new environment which facilitates and encourages on-the-go travel planning (Wang, Park, & Fesenmaier, 2012). Smartphones and tablets enable superior connectivity, communication, content access, and content creation (Want, 2009). They allow for spontaneity in travel decisions, enabling a last minute hotel booking or restaurant reservation (Lamsfus, Wang, Alzua-Sorzabal, & Xiang, 2015). With mobile consumer technology, users are able to manage unforeseen circumstances with more ease (Wang et al., 2012).

Mobile technology, laced with various applications, is changing the way travelers are using the internet for planning and choosing a service (Wang et al., 2012). Smartphone apps not only offer features available on websites such as property search, information about the property, and the ability to make reservations but also have exclusive smartphone services such as interactive maps and current location identification. The system intelligence searches for a service on the basis of the current location of users and so, tourism businesses with better proximity are given priority (Wang, Xiang, Law, & Ki, 2016). For example, Starbucks allows customers to order coffee via its mobile app before they even arrive at the store. Customers can choose a pickup time and location in advance to save time and to avoid standing in queue. Their mobile app also displays the menu of the closest Starbucks outlet, based on the user location. Many apps incorporate the company's website and even their loyalty programs to provide seamless user experience. These apps also connect the user with popular SM outlets enabling information sharing for decision-making and spreading eWOM (Carlsson, Walden, & Yang, 2008; Wang et. al, 2016).

Future of consumer-oriented technologies in tourism

Online travel planning is increasing the focus on mobile devices as travelers are using multiple devices when searching for hotels and restaurants, while the personal computers are losing their charm (Murphy et al., 2016). According to the latest report from comScore, 65 percent of all digital media time is consumed by mobile technology, with mobile apps accounting for 56 percent of that usage. Desktops not only have slipped down to accounting for only 35 percent of digital media time but the mobile-only use has also surpassed the desktop-only internet use. In the end of 2015, comScore reported a 79 percent smartphone penetration. Of these users, 93 percent were between the ages of 18 and 34 (Sterling, 2016). More and more consumers are choosing smartphones for booking hotels (Murphy et al., 2016), restaurant (Hwang & Park, 2015) and travel (Wang, Xiang & Fesenmaier, 2016).

System intelligence is increasingly being used to gather "position-aware context" and the delivery of "context-aware information" on mobile devices (Wang et. al, 2016, p. 294). One such technology is called "Beacon Technology" which is a small device that can be placed on physical objects at strategic locations in order to communicate with smartphones or tablets. A beacon can push any information or a promotional offer to smart mobile devices in the surrounding area. It can very well be used as a point-of-sale system and, in return, to collect information about consumers. This technology has the potential to change guest-business interaction. The best-known application of Beacon so far is the Apple iBeacon as the company has yet not developed a physical device. Companies like McDonald's, Starwood Hotels & Resorts and Marriott International are already testing this technology at select properties ("Can Your Hotel Survive," 2015).

Advances in modern age technologies are highly customer-focused (Aldebert, Dang, & Longhi, 2011), as consumers are seeking unique experiences and have begun to create their own customized values (Anne Coussement & Teague, 2013). The consumer has evolved as a major actor in co-creation of experience and value, and information and communications technology (ICT) has become the force behind this shift (Ramaswamy & Guillart, 2010). Oyner and Korelina (2016) identified the five forms of co-creation activities as "feedback, co-production, firm-driven service innovation, customer-driven customization and co-creation," (p. 327) and noted that hotels practice customization, service innovation, and co-production more often than co-creation.

As SM continues to shape consumer behavior, its scope is no longer restricted to networking with other users but has extended to the way users communicate, search for information, and even buy a product. SM outlets like Facebook, Instagram, and Pinterest have integrated e-commerce by introducing the *buy button*. Users now can buy the product without having to leave the app.

Live stream and *in-the-moment* sharing of content on SM are becoming popular as users get almost real-time updates. Some of the examples are the *live video* feature of Facebook and *live video broadcast* feature of Twitter along with already existing similar-concept apps like Snapchat and Instagram. This trend will give way to more sophisticated visual technologies, while virtual reality will finally become main stream.

SM will continue to change the way users search for information. Google might be the most popular search engine, but users seek the more trustworthy advice of their peers and other users via platforms like Facebook, Yelp, and Youtube. This explains why Facebook is working on developing a more powerful search engine of its own (Litvin et al., 2008). With such features, users will be able to gather information and buy and share their purchase and review it by logging into a single profile page of their preferred SM site/app.

Implications of trending technologies for tourism service providers

Our review of technology and its influence on consumer behavior suggests that the internet and SM is allowing consumers to conduct most of their communications over online networks (Israeli et al., 2017). Consumer experience that leads to writing online content is mostly triggered by service failures. Consumer motivations that relate to reading eWOM suggests that the content is more useful when the eWOM includes negative content (Salehi-Esfahani et al., 2016). These findings are consistent with a universal trend that highlights the growing popularity of negative events, negative messages, and negative behaviors in cyber space. A potential explanation for this may be that individuals are able to maintain anonymity online. Phillips (2015) offers a historical perspective of social dynamics and suggests that cyber reality evolved in such a way that it allows individuals to abandon social restrictions and inhibitions that would otherwise be present if their identity was known. Huang, Hong, and Burtch (2015) reviewed the consequences of online social anonymity showing that it leads people to exhibit rude behavior. Stein (2016) focused on the growing number of trolls, who use their anonymity to engage in pranks, harassment, and violent threats.

The general trend of progression in internet behavior and specifically in consumer behavior suggests a focus on negativity. In general, more anonymous users and trolls roam the internet with negative motivations. And specifically in consumer behavior, as it pertains to tourism management, a growing proportion of negative eWOMs are written and read (Litvin et al., 2008). The challenges for the future would be to change course and adopt a more productive, less negative tone in tourism consumer behavior. This should be a joint challenge, for both service providers and consumers. Service providers will have to focus on improving their ability to recover service failures, thus minimizing consumer motivation for writing negative eWOM. Consumers should be challenged to avoid resorting to negative messages and adopt a productive, less negative tone to their eWOM.

References

Aldebert, B., Dang, R. J., & Longhi, C. (2011). Innovation in the tourism industry: The case of Tourism@. *Tourism Management, 32*(5), 1204–1213. DOI: http://dx.doi.org/10.1016/j.tourman.2010.08.010

Ali, F. (2016). Hotel website quality, perceived flow, customer satisfaction and purchase intention. *Journal of Hospitality and Tourism Technology*, 7(2), 213–228. DOI: http://dx.doi.org/10.1108/JHTT-02-2016-0010

Amaro, S., & Duarte, P. (2015). An integrative model of consumers' intentions to purchase travel online. *Tourism Management, 46*, 64–79. DOI: http://dx.doi.org/10.1016/j.tourman.2014.06.006

Ayeh, J. K., Au, N., & Law, R. (2013). Predicting the intention to use consumer-generated media for travel planning. *Tourism Management, 35*, 132–143. DOI: http://dx.doi.org/10.1016/j.tourman.2012.06.010

Balaji, M. S., Jha, S., & Royne, M. B. (2015). Customer e-complaining behaviours using social media. *The Service Industries Journal, 35*(11–12), 633–654. DOI: http://dx.doi.org/10.1080/02642069.2015.1062883

Bai, B., Law, R., & Wen, I. (2008). The impact of website quality on customer satisfaction and purchase intentions: Evidence from Chinese online visitors. *International Journal of Hospitality Management, 27*(3), 391–402. DOI: 10.1016/j.ijhm.2007.10.008

Bilgihan, A., Nusair, K., Okumus, F., & Cobanoglu, C. (2015). Applying flow theory to booking experiences: An integrated model in an online service context. *Information & Management, 52*, 668–678. DOI: http://dx.doi.org/10.1016/j.im.2015.05.005

Bronner, F., & de Hoog, R. (2010). Vacationers and eWOM: Who posts, and why, where, and what? *Journal of Travel Research, 50*(1), 15–26. DOI: 10.1177/0047287509355324

Can Your Hotel Survive Without Beacon Technology? [Web log post]. (2015). Retrieved from http://blog.youvisit.com/virtual-tours/blog/beacons-can-your-hotel-survive-without-them/

Cantallops, A. S., & Salvi, F. (2014). New consumer behavior: A review of research on eWOM and hotels. *International Journal of Hospitality Management. 36*, 41–51. DOI: http://dx.doi.org/10.1016/j.ijhm.2013.08.007

Carlsson, C., Walden, P., & Yang, F. (2008, July). Travel MoCo – A mobile community service for tourists. In *2008 7th international conference on mobile business* (pp. 49–58). IEEE. DOI: 10.1109/icmb.2008.40

Casalo, L. V., Flavian, C., & Guinaliu, M. (2010). Determinants of the intention to participate in firm-hosted online travel communities and effects on consumer behavioral intentions. *Tourism Management, 31*, 898–911. DOI: 10.1016/j.tourman.2010.04.007

Casidy, R., & Shin, H. (2015). The effects of harm directions and service recovery strategies on customer forgiveness and negative word-of-mouth intentions. *Journal of Retailing and Consumer Services, 27*, 103–112. DOI: http://dx.doi.org/10.1016/j.jretconser.2015.07.012

Castaneda, J. A., Frías, D. M., & Rodríguez, M. A. (2009). Antecedents of internet acceptance and use as an information source by tourists. *Online Information Review, 33*(3), 548–567. DOI: http://dx.doi.org/10.1108/14684520910969952

Cheung, C. M. K., Lee, M. K. O., & Rahbjon, N. (2008). The impact of electronic word-of-mouth: The adoption of online opinions in online customer communities. *Internet Research, 18*(3), 229–247. DOI: http://dx.doi.org/10.1108/10662240810883290

Crotts, J. C., Mason, P. R., & Davis, B. (2009). Measuring guest satisfaction and competitive position in the hospitality and tourism industry. *Journal of Travel Research, 48*(2), 139–151. DOI: 10.1177/0047287508328795

Csikszentmihalyi, M. (1975). *Beyond boredom and anxiety.* San Francisco, CA: Jossey-Bass.

Daugherty, T., & Hoffman, E. (2014). eWOM and the importance of capturing consumer attention within social media. *Journal of Marketing Communications, 20*(1–2), 82–102. DOI: http://dx.doi.org/10.1080/13527266.2013.797764

Day, R. L., & Landon, E. L. (1977). Toward a theory of consumer complaining behavior. *Consumer and industrial buying behavior, 95*, 425–437.

Di Pietro, L., Di Virgilio, & Pantano, E. (2012). Social network for the choice of tourist destination: Attitude and behavioural intention. *Journal of Hospitality and Tourism Technology, 3*(1), 60–76. DOI: 10.1108/17579881211206543

Dou, X., Walden, J. A., Lee, S., & Lee, J. Y. (2012). Does source matter? Examining source effects in online product reviews. *Computers in Human Behavior*, 28, 1555–1563. DOI: http://dx.doi.org/10.1016/j.chb.2012.03.015

Erkan, I., & Evans, C. (2016). The influence of eWOM in social media on consumers' purchase intentions: An extended approach to information adoption. *Computers in Human Behavior, 61*, 47–55. DOI: http://dx.doi.org/10.1016/j.chb.2016.03.003

Escobar-Rodriguez, T., & Carvajal-Trujillo, E. (2013). Online drivers of consumer purchase of website airline tickets. *Journal of Air Transport Management, 32*, 58–64. DOI: http://dx.doi.org/10.1016/j.jairtraman.2013.06.018

Fishbein, M., & Ajzen, I. (1975). *Belief, attitude, intention, and behavior: An introduction to theory and research.* Reading, MA: Addison-Wesley.

Goldberg, D. (2015, December 17). 3 ways social media has changed the way we travel. *US News & World Report Travel.* Retrieved from: http://travel.usnews.com/features/3-ways-social-media-has-changed-the-way-we-travel/

Grégoire, Y., Salle, A., & Tripp, T. M. (2015). Managing social media crises with your customers: The good, the bad, and the ugly. *Business Horizons, 58*(2), 173–182. DOI: http://dx.doi.org/10.1016/j.bushor.2014.11.001

Hennig-Thurau, T, Gwinner, K., Walsh, G., & Gremler, D. (2004). Electronic word-of-mouth via consumer-opinion platforms: What motivates consumers to articulate themselves on the internet? *Journal of Interactive Marketing, 18*(1), 38–52. DOI: 10.1002/dir.10073

Huang, N., Hong, Y., & Burtch, G. (2015). Anonymity and language usage: A natural experiment of social network integration. In *2015 International Conference on Information Systems: Exploring the Information Frontier* (pp. 1–10). Fort Worth, TX: Association for Information Systems.

Hwang, J., & Park, S. (2015). Social Media on Smartphones for Restaurant Decision-Making Process. In *Information and Communication Technologies in Tourism* 2015 (pp. 269–281). Springer International Publishing.

Israeli, A. A., Lee, S., & Karpinski, A. C. (2017). Investigating the dynamics and the content of social media reporting after a restaurant service failure. *Journal of Hospitality Marketing and Management*, 26(6), 606–626. DOI: https://doi.org/10.1080/19368623.2017.1281193.

Keenan, S., & Frary, M. (2015, March 27). How TripAdvisor took over the travel information market. Retrieved October 04, 2016, from http://news.wtmlondon.com/how-tripadvisor-took-over-the-travel-information-market/

Lamsfus, C., Wang, D., Alzua-Sorzabal, A., & Xiang, Z. (2015). Going mobile defining context for on-the-go travelers. *Journal of Travel Research*, *54*(6), 691–701. DOI: 10.1177/0047287514538839

Litvin, S. W., Goldsmith, R. E., & Pan, B. (2008). Electronic word-of-mouth in hospitality and tourism management. *Tourism Management*, *29*, 458–468. DOI: http://dx.doi.org/10.1016/j.tourman.2007.05.011

Makadok, R. (2011). Invited editorial: The four theories of profit and their joint effects. *Journal of Management*, *37* (5), 1316–1334. DOI: 10.1177/0149206310385697

McGinnis, L. P., Gentry, J. W., & Gao, T. (2008). The impact of flow and communitas on enduring involvement in extended service encounters. *Journal of Service Research*, *11*(1), 74–90. DOI: 10.1177/1094670508319046

Minazzi, R. (2015). *Social media marketing in tourism and hospitality*. Cham, Switzerland: Springer.

Morrison, M. A., & Cheong, H. (2008). Consumers' reliance on product information and recommendations found in UGC. *Journal of Interactive Advertising*, *8*(2), 38–49. DOI: http://dx.doi.org/10.1080/15252019.2008.10722141

Mudambi, S. M., & Schuff, D. (2010). What makes a helpful online review? A study of customer reviews on Amazon.com. *MIS Quarterly*, *34*(1), 185–200.

Murphy, H. C., Chen, M. M., & Cossutta, M. (2016). An investigation of multiple devices and information sources used in the hotel booking process. *Tourism Management*, *52*, 44–51. DOI: http://dx.doi.org/10.1016/j.tourman.2015.06.004

Nayyar, P. R. (1990). Information asymmetries: A source of competitive advantage for diversified service firms. *Strategic Management Journal*, *11*(7), 513–519. DOI: 10.1002/smj.4250110703

Nusair, K., Bilgihan, A., Okumus, F., & Cobanoglu, C. (2013). Generation Y travelers' commitment to online social network websites. *Tourism Management*, *35*, 13–22. DOI: DOI: 10.1016/j.tourman.2012.05.005

Oyner, O., & Korelina, A. (2016). The influence of customer engagement in value co-creation on customer satisfaction: searching for new forms of co-creation in the Russian hotel industry. *Worldwide Hospitality and Tourism Themes*, *8*(3). DOI: http://dx.doi.org/10.1108/WHATT-02-2016-0005

Pantelidis, L. S. (2010). Electronic meal experience: A content analysis of online restaurant comments. *Cornell Hospitality Quarterly*, *51*(4), 483–491. DOI: 10.1177/1938965510378574

Phillips, W. (2015). *This is why we can't have nice things: Mapping the relationship between online trolling and mainstream culture*. Cambridge, MA: MIT Press.

Pornpitakpan, C. (2004). The persuasiveness of source credibility: A critical review of five decades' evidence. *Journal of Applied Social Psychology*, *34*(2), 243–281. DOI: 10.1111/j.1559-1816.2004.tb02547.x

Rabjohn, N., Cheung, C., & Lee, M. K. (2008, January). Examining the perceived credibility of online opinions: Information adoption in the online environment. *Proceedings of the 41st Hawaii International Conference on System Sciences*, 2862–286. DOI: 10.1109/HICSS.2008.156

Ramaswamy, V., & Guillart, F. (2010). *The power of co-creation*. New York, NY: Free Press.

Rogers, E. M. (1995). *Diffusion of innovations* (4th ed.). New York, NY: The Free Press.

Salehi-Esfahani, S., Ravichandran, S., Israeli, A., & Bolden III, E. (2016). Investigating Information Adoption Tendencies Based on Restaurants' User-generated Content Utilizing a Modified Information Adoption Model. *Journal of Hospitality Marketing & Management*, *28*(8), 925–953. DOI: http://dx.doi.org/10.1080/19368623.2016.1171190

Senecal, S., Gharbi, J. E., & Nantel, J. (2002). The influence of flow on hedonic and utilitarian shopping values. *Advances in Consumer Research*, *29*(1), 483–484.

Sigala, M., Christou, E., & Gretzel, U. (Eds). (2012). *Social media in travel, tourism and hospitality: Theory, practice and cases*. Burlington, VT: Ashgate Publishing, Ltd.

Stein, J. (2016, August 18). How Trolls are ruining the internet. *Time Magazine*. Retrieved from: http://time.com/4457110/internet-trolls/

Sterling, G. (2016). All digital growth now coming from mobile usage – comScore. Retrieved from: http://marketingland.com/digital-growth-now-coming-mobile-usage-comscore-171505

Stigler, G. J. (1961). The economics of information. *The journal of political economy*, *69* (3), 213–225.

Stoeckl, R., Rohrmeier, P., & Hess, T. (2007). Motivations to Produce User-Generated Content: Differences Between Webloggers and Videobloggers. Paper presented at the *20th Bled eConference eMergence: Merging and Emerging Technologies*, Processes, and Institutions, Bled, Slovenia, 4–6 June 2007.

Swanson, S. R., & Hsu, M. K. (2009). Critical incidents in tourism: Failure, recovery, customer switching, and word-of-mouth behaviors. *Journal of Travel & Tourism Marketing, 26*(2), 180–194. DOI: http://dx.doi.org/10.1080/10548400902864800

Venkatesh, V., Thong, J. Y., & Xu, X. (2012). Consumer acceptance and use of information technology: Extending the United Theory of Acceptance and Use of Technology. *MIS Quarterly, 35*(1), 157–178.

Wang, D., Park, S., & Fesenmaier, D. R. (2012). The role of smartphones in mediating the touristic experience. *Journal of Travel Research, 51*(4), 371–387. DOI: 10.1177/0047287511426341

Wang, D., Xiang, Z., & Fesenmaier, D. R. (2016). Smartphone use in everyday life and travel. *Journal of Travel Research, 55*(1), 52–63.

Wang, D., Xiang, Z., Law, R., & Ki, T. P. (2016). Assessing hotel-related smartphone apps using online reviews. *Journal of Hospitality Marketing & Management, 25*(3), 291–313. DOI: http://dx.doi.org/10.1080/19368623.2015.1012282

Want, R. (2009). When cell phones become computers. *IEEE Pervasive Computing, 8*(2), 2–5. DOI: 10.1109/MPRV.2009.40

Wolf, P. C. (2006, June). Travel 2.0 Confronts the Establishment: Phocuswright. Retrieved from: http://www.phocuswright.com/Travel-Research/Research-Updates/2006/Travel-2-0-Confronts-the-Establishment

Zhang, Z., Ye, Q., Law, R., & Li, Y. (2010). The impact of e-word-of-mouth on the online popularity of restaurants: A comparison of consumer reviews and editor reviews. *International Journal of Hospitality Management, 29*(4), 694–700. DOI: http://dx.doi.org/10.1016/j.ijhm.2010.02.002

Further reading

Ajzen, I. (1985). From intentions to actions: A theory of planned behavior. In J. Kuhl & J. Beckman (Eds), *Action-control: From cognition to behavior* (pp. 11–39). Heidelberg, Germany: Springer.

Ajzen, I., & Fishbein, M. (1980). *Understanding attitudes and predicting social behavior.* Englewood Cliffs, NJ: Prentice-Hall.

Anne Coussement, M., & J. Teague, T. (2013). The new customer-facing technology: mobile and the constantly-connected consumer. *Journal of Hospitality and Tourism Technology, 4*(2), 177–187. DOI: http://dx.doi.org/10.1108/JHTT-12-2011-0035

Davis, F. D. (1989). Perceived usefulness, perceived ease of use, and user acceptance of information technology. *MIS Quarterly, 13*(3), 319–339. DOI: 10.2307/249008

Lee, Y., Kozar, K. A., & Larsen, K. R. T. (2003). The technology acceptance model: Past, present, and future. *Communications of the Association for Information Systems, 12*, Article 50. Retrieved from: http://aisel.aisnet.org/cais/vol12/iss1/50

Teece, D. J. (2010). Business models, business strategy and innovation. *Long Range Planning, 43*(2), 172–194. DOI: http://dx.doi.org/10.1016/j.lrp.2009.07.003

Venkatesh, V., Morris, M. G., Davis, G. B., & Davis, F. D. (2003). User acceptance of information technology: Toward a unified view. *MIS Quarterly, 27*(3), 425–478.

36

Consumer empowerment in the hospitality industry

Jeynakshi Ladsawut and Robin Nunkoo

Introduction

In this era of change, increased usage of social media points to a power shift in cyberspace. Social media is defined as an internet application system based on Web 2.0 logistics which allows users to create content online (Kaplan and Haenlein 2012). The roots of social media go back to 1980 where two graduates from Duke University created a newsgroup system which was used as a discussion platform (Kaplan and Haenlein 2012). These discussions led to the creation of content by online users which is commonly referred to consumer generated content. In the 1990's consumers mostly used the internet as a search tool until the introduction of blogs in 1995 (Kaplan and Haenlein 2010). The initiation of blogging allowed consumers to post their customised content online and it also involved interactions with other online users. Hence, any customer was able to publish content online through blogs. This transition caused businesses to adopt new distribution strategies such as e-commerce. The launch of online interaction gave birth to corporations such as eBay and Amazon. Looking at online statistics, Forrester Research points that 75% of online users were using social media platforms as part of their internet activity usage in 2008. Gruzd *et al.* (2011) report that with the evolution of technology, a change of behaviour has been observed resulting in increased reliance on emails and social media.

Many hotels are now visible to the world as a result of increased usage of technology. Gone are the days of Web 1.0 where customers only searched information on the internet. The evolution leading to the technical infrastructure of Web 2.0 allowed more engagement between service providers and customers leading to increased interactivity in the hospitality industry. Twenty-first century customers are spanning content online thus engaging on platforms such as social media as these channels portray several advantages. Law, Qi and Buhalis (2010) view the internet as a less costly medium where updated information is conveyed at high speed given the presence of Web 2.0. Web 2.0 Applications allow customers to engage with both businesses and other consumers online. The popularity of social networking sites like Facebook, YouTube, TripAdvisor and Pinterest amongst others motivate adopters of technology to browse through information online. Increasingly, hospitality marketers communicate with potential customers through integration; that is techniques where they are promoting their products through various channels combining both online and offline channels.

In this regard, hospitality industry suppliers are redefining their marketing techniques to be part of the social media ecosystem. The adoption of newfangled technologies is motivating online collaboration of information between hospitality industry suppliers and travelers. Hospitality marketers are increasingly using digital communications as a promotional tool. Adoption of new platforms allows hospitality marketers to be more visible in the marketplace and hence more competitive. Moreover, hospitality marketers need to further understand how to connect their hotel brand to potential customers. A change in consumer behaviour is highly apparent in line with adoption of new technology. Consumers are more user-friendly with social media and empowered to co-create information in the hospitality industry on such sites. Tourists for example use their power to generate content about their experiences on social media platforms which are beyond hospitality marketers' control. On the other hand, marketers use their power to distribute information about their products and services to consumers through online promotional strategies. However, with the shift of power, marketers are losing control as consumers are avoiding their content online. This can be observed through shielding mechanisms which block marketers' communications to potential users. Potential customers can block direct communication messages through emails and other social media platforms. They have the power to unsubscribe themselves to marketers' online community. Some sites such as YouTube are even embedded with options to skip advertising from marketers. An overview of the hospitality literature shows that there is a paucity of research around the loss of control of marketers and tourist empowerment. The purpose of this study is therefore to outline the motivators for tourists to use social media leading to tourist empowerment. Power shift will also be unearthed in line with social media oriented architecture and implications for hotel marketers will be assessed based on their loss of control.

Tourist motivations to the use of social media

Since the expansion of the Web, social media has gained popularity and its frequency of use has increased. Social media are generally known as internet based applications that are supported by Web 2.0 foundations allowing users to create or exchange content (Kaplan and Haenlein 2010). Common examples of social media are Twitter, Facebook, Snapchat, YouTube, Wikipedia, and TripAdvisor amongst others. Usage of social media networking sites has significantly increased in the hospitality industry. Tourists continuously adopt this tool as they derive various benefits from its applications. They can search for information on social networks, browse through updated content created by tourists who recently visited suppliers of the hospitality industry and even book their rooms instantly on these sites instead of using various intermediaries. Once tourists are motivated to travel they are involved in searching for information. This process can be done through online channels where social media is an option for tourists to search for accommodation. Information search is a complex process with high risks (Sirakaya and Woodside 2005). High level of uncertainty is anticipated for tourists especially if it is a first time visit (Kotler, Bowen and Makens 2010) to a hotel. The use of social media can buffer the complexity of search through the content generated and lower risks through the interactivity component. In other words, social media encourages online members to like, share, post or comment on the user generated media. Customers can voice out their opinions on social media platforms which can eventually be used by businesses and other consumers. These Web 2.0 applications provide peer recommendations and online reviews which facilitate decision making processes as opposed to traditional information searches which often results in overload of information (Bellman *et al.* 2006). Therefore, tourists are allowed to participate in discussions on social media and are allowed to seek information by communicating with other tourists who have already visited the chosen hotel or the service providers. The ability of social media to provide two-way communication between potential customers and existing customers online diminishes the risks of purchase of experiences through aggregated data received by similar buyers at low costs (O'Connor 2008). Cox *et al.* (2009) ascertain that interactions on social media sites have the possibility of converting prospects into buyers. In view of the fact that the hospitality product is experiential in nature, customers cannot judge their satisfaction level until they have consumed the product or service. Storytelling of previous visitors' experiences therefore becomes vital to their purchase decision making. Additionally, reviews on social media improve tourists' confidence and reduces risk perception in tourism decision making process (Gretzel *et al.* 2007) thereby easing purchase of travel and tourism experiences. Cox *et al.* (2009) ascertain that the usage of social media is higher before travelling rather than during and after the trip. Saying this, tourists will use social media after their trip with the aim of sharing their experiences with their peers. This constitutes the interactivity element on hotels' social media platforms where visitors share their experiences and provide reviews on the hotel. Lin and Huang (2006) view social media marketing as a powerful tool because social media have the capacity to create interest through information dissemination online, initiate the desire to visit the hotel and plan to purchase. The ability of web technology to induce both qualitative and quantitative sources of feedback on tourism industry suppliers generates scores that reflects the general satisfaction of a particular destination (O'Connor 2008). Additionally, research supports that companies whose services are reviewed on social media are known to have an enhanced business reputation (Cox *et al.* 2009). The infrastructure of social media enlarges the scope of communication between an organisation and its customers (Mangold and Faulds 2009). Social media, being mobile multiple device friendly, can be easily accessed due to its adaptability on various technological devices such as laptops, desktops, mobile phones and tablets. Its convenience promotes high reach towards various audiences and allows marketers to reach through thousands of people (Mangold and Faulds 2009). This platform motivates users to share their company's promotional content through social media practices of sharing, liking, tweeting and commenting. Therefore, it is important to understand the benefits of the use of social media in the tourism ecosystem. Increased usage of social media forced consumers to change and adapt to a new mindset. Traditionally, communication between marketers and consumers happened through controlled channels of the promotional mix such as advertising, public relations, sales promotion and direct marketing. Nowadays, with the expansion of Web activities, there has been a major change in technology adoption. Hospitality marketers consequently need to understand the implication of changes aligned with web technology.

Shift in technology adoption

Research points that there is a paradigm shift from traditional integrated marketing communication where companies communicate to customers through consumer generated media (Mangold and Faulds 2009). This shift is explained in line with a change in consumer behaviour. The shift has caused travelers to look for information online rather than through the traditional use of travel agents. In early 2006, trends point that the frequency of travel information distribution through social media has increased (Jepsen 2006). It can be deduced that customers rely more on online reviews from various web element sources such as social media (Buhalis and Law 2008). Yoo *et al.* (2011) ascertain that the number of travelers engaging with travel suppliers through social media channels has increased which is viewed as a key information source when planning for travels. O'Connor (2008) states that advances in technology have brought new ways to communicate and the distribution and accessibility of information is easier on consumers. Therefore, this becomes an important way to search for information and evaluate the different alternatives available to tourists. Evolution of technology has as well impacted on the tools that tourists use. With advanced technology, applications and platforms are becoming more user-friendly hence motivating tourists to adopt technology instead of traditional methods. This also gave rise to increased online engagement. In view that the Web 2.0 is new, Cox *et al.* (2009) purport that this new way of providing information acts as a catalyst for users to increase their knowledge and interact with companies online. Marketers are having increased pressure to manage their budget nowadays (Pan 2015) and through evolution of the internet, it is more cost effective to use search engine optimization as an advertising medium as opposed to traditional channels of communication. Hanna *et al.* (2011) purport that although marketers of the twenty-first century are aware that their online presence is essential, they do not have knowledge of the right metrics to measure the effectiveness of their online campaigns. Eventually, this extends in a shift of power dynamics resulting in a loss of control of marketers with the advent of technology evolution.

Consumer empowerment

Power emanates from the field of sociology and psychology (Magee and Galinsky 2008) and highly influences behaviour but is rarely discussed in the consumer behavior literature (Rucker *et al.* 2011). This is even less apparent in hospitality research and therefore is viewed as a gap in literature. Whilst significant relationships have been found in the literature between power and marketing, the focus in this research revolves around a shift of power distribution in the hospitality industry with the advent of technology. The stakeholders of power in the hospitality industry is shared between hospitality marketers and users of their services, most precisely tourists. A shift in power dynamics has been observed from hospitality marketers to tourists in line with empowerment of customers. Consumer empowerment is the term coined in this regard. Wathieu *et al.* (2002) define consumer empowerment as allowing consumers to control components which were previously established by the company's marketers. According to Wang, Weaver and Kwek (2015), power can be conveyed individually or as part of an organizational approach. The power given to consumers can be explained through the evolution of the Web where the new element of interactivity prompts consumers to react online and hence consumers participate on various platforms. Hoffman *et al.* (1999) propose that consumer empowerment is the shift of power from service providers to consumers. The rationale for this power shift is firstly due to increased competition amongst various markets and secondly because of augmented transparency where consumers can easily compare different offerings available online (Harrison *et al.* 2006). In short, with the advent of the internet, tourists have more choices and hence are empowered as a whole. Before the twenty-first century, when the Web was still a static medium, power was in the hands of suppliers (Samli 2001) rather than consumers. In that era, hospitality suppliers were to decide which information to reveal to tourists as part of their marketing campaign. Even if information was available online, the Web 1.0 allowed tourists to only search for information that was produced by hospitality suppliers and marketers only. Nowadays, with the evolution of Web 2.0 and the integration of interactivity, the web is more dynamic. Tourists can easily connect with several suppliers and compare information instantly. Online reviews and online word of mouth generated by tourists who previously used hospitality suppliers are readily available for prospects to accumulate information before purchase. Therefore, hospitality marketers can no longer control the content or information available online as there is a mix of input and reviews published by both hospitality marketers and online consumers. Labreque *et al.* (2013) proposes a framework where four sources of consumer power are explained.

These are categorized into first individual-based power sources, that is demand and information based power; and second network-based power sources which are known as network and crowd based power. The framework shows that consumers are more empowered as they can, through internet applications, create their own websites or blogs and share information on any subject matter. The demand-based power shows that tourists can demand goods and services through internet medium instead of using traditional distribution channels such as travel agencies. In the hospitality industry, information-based power is easily recognized as hotel marketers share information about their offerings online. Hoteliers also allow consumers to produce content through their social media platforms and the latter can express their opinions about their consumption. Network based power revolves around the ability of marketers to add value to their offerings online. This is specifically through the usage of social media networks where marketers can add videos and images on their social networking sites, enhancing their image online. If the content is appealing, consumers would react by posting comment or sharing the content on their own platforms hence adding value to the hotel brand. This can also be a form of earned media for the marketer as customers are spreading electronic word of mouth online. Finally, crowd based power revolves around the ability of consumers to act as a community online. Consumers can use their power as a crowd for various purposes. For example, they can pool together and buy hotel deals through sites like Groupon. This is a win-win situation for both the marketer and the consumer as the marketer will be able to increase sales while consumers buying together gets larger rebates and deals online. As can be depicted from Labreque's framework, consumers can be empowered through various means online. In another framework, Denegri-Knott (2006) illustrates that consumer empowerment consists of four key strategies: control, information, aggregation and participation. Following Denegri-Knott's framework, in an online environment, tourists can control which communication or advertising they want to react to as they use their power to shield unwanted communication messages. Tourists can also find information on their own online as there is a pool of information available from various sites hence they are empowered to look for information at their own pace. Tourists can also use their power to collectively react on online environments such as comment on hotels as an online community. Lastly, tourists can use their power to create or curate content online hence participating on service providers platforms through consumer generated content.

Implications for hospitality marketers

Research points that traditional forms of promotion have decreased as consumers rely more on online opinions from their peers (Sethuraman *et al.* 2011: Gligorijevic and Luck 2012). This points that hospitality marketers may lose all their power if they rely wholly on traditional means to promotion. Thus, hospitality marketers should use a more integrated approach in communicating with their consumers through their presence on various social networking sites. Engaging customers online enables companies to provide customised information to online users (Dijkmans *et al.* 2015) as well as encourage users to commit to brands. The evolution of the internet has given rise to consumer empowerment through electronic word of mouth (Hennig-Thurau *et al.* 2004). In parallel, marketers lose control over their content execution once content is created or shared by customers and thus cannot control the frequency that the same content appears online (Mangold and Faulds 2009). Through consumer empowerment, the marketing exchange processes is dictated by the consumer (Hanna *et al.* 2011). O'Connor (2008) views the Web to be evolving continuously hence a shift is observed from business to consumers where content generation is a more peer oriented sharing behaviour. Due to the high interactive nature of the Web, collaboration has given tourists the choice to filter marketing communications targeted to them. Tourists therefore autonomously filter marketing communications from hospitality marketers and display their tourism empowerment by controlling which information is relevant to them.

In the light of loss of control of marketers through paid media, hospitality marketers need to shift their approach by using owned and earned media. In other words, since tourists are filtering marketing communications as they are empowered, hospitality marketers must encourage tourists to record their feedback online through hospitality suppliers' owned assets such as Facebook, Twitter, YouTube, and TripAdvisor amongst others. Since the tourist's feedback is published online and is visible to other users, earned media will be generated through electronic word of mouth. It is important to bear in mind that once users subscribe to a page e.g. liking the page of a tourism provider, information would be continuously provided to the user by the marketer. The updated information and the frequency of information generated to consumers is controlled by the marketer. Wang, Weaver and Kwek (2015) posit that suppliers are motivated to restrict tourist empowerment. This balances the proportion of power between marketers and consumers. It is worth pointing out that this slight shift of power allows marketers to influence consumers by communicating with them. By being part of service provider's community and receiving information through this channel subconsciously causes the subscriber to retain information about the tourism supplier. Mangold and Faulds (2009) also state that since companies cannot control content which is enabled by customers, they can try to influence customer to customer conversations. These conversations are known as electronic word of mouth (eWOM).

In a hospitality context, since everyone is an online publisher, the amount of fake information has increased over online platforms. Thus, the quality of information posted on hotel websites can be questioned. However, this can be debated as tourists are empowered hence most of them will share their own experiences which provides a general overview of the hotel and its proposed services. The loss of control however outlines the need for hospitality marketers to manage their online reputation. Therefore, marketers need to manage consumer generated content. Gössling, Hall and Andersson (2016) recommend that hotel managers need to monitor their online reviews daily and respond to online comments within 24 hours. Online reputation management is key if hospitality marketers want to control information traffic about their company online. To date, there are no metrics in place to measure the quality of a website (Loiacono *et al.* 2007) or social media platforms. Marketers need to devise the adequate metrics to track the quality of consumer generated content. Wang, Weaver and Kwek (2015) highlight that service providers also use their power to encourage tourists to trust them as opposed to voicing out dissatisfaction on their platforms. This can be used to encourage brand advocacy and hence have a pool of loyal customers who can spread the supplier's promotional messages on various social media platforms, hence enhancing the visibility of hospitality suppliers.

References

Bellman, S., Johnson, E.J., Lohse, G.L. and Mandel, N. (2006) "Designing marketplaces of the artificial with consumers in mind: four approaches to understanding consumer behavior in electronic environments," *Journal of Interactive Marketing* 20(1), 21–33.

Buhalis, D. and Law, R. (2008). "Progress in information technology and tourism management: 20 years on and 10 years after the internet – The state of eTourism research," *Tourism Management*, 29(4), 609–623.

Cox, C., Burgess, S., Sellitto, C. and Buultjens, J. (2009) "The role of user-generated content in tourists' travel planning behavior," *Journal of Hospitality Marketing and Management* 18(8), 743–764.

Denegri-Knott, J. (2006) "Consumers behaving badly: deviation or innovation? Power struggles on the web," *Journal of Consumer Behaviour* 5(1), 82–94.

Dijkmans, C., Kerkhof, P. and Beukeboom, C.J. (2015) "A stage to engage: Social media use and corporate reputation," *Tourism Management* 47, 58–67.

Fotis, J., Buhalis, D. and Rossides, N. (2012) "Social media use and impact during the holiday travel planning process". In M. Fuchs, F. Ricci, and L. Cantoni (2012) (eds) *Information and communication technologies in tourism* (pp. 13–24). Vienna, Austria: Springer-Verlag.

Gligorijevic, B. and Luck, E. (2012). "Engaging Social Customers–Influencing New Marketing Strategies for Social Media Information Sources." In *Contemporary research on e-business technology and strategy* (pp. 25–40). Berlin, Heidelberg: Springer.

Gössling, S., Hall, C.M. and Andersson, A.C. (2016) "The manager's dilemma: a conceptualization of online review manipulation strategies," *Current Issues in Tourism,* 1–20.

Gretzel, U., Yoo, K.H. and Purifoy, M. (2007) "Online travel review study: Role and impact of online travel reviews," *Laboratory for Intelligent Systems in Tourism*, Texas: A&M University.

Gruzd, A., Wellman, B. and Takhteyev, Y. (2011) "Imagining Twitter as an imagined community," *American Behavioral Scientist*, 55(10), 1294–1318.

Hanna, R., Rohm, A. and Crittenden, V.L. (2011) "We're all connected: The power of the social media ecosystem," *Business horizons*, 54(3), 265–273.

Harrison, T., Waite, K. and Hunter, G.L. (2006) "The internet, information and empowerment," *European Journal of Marketing*, 40(9/10), 972–993.

Hennig-Thurau, T., Gwinner, K.P., Walsh, G. and Gremler, D.D. (2004) "Electronic word-of-mouth via consumer-opinion platforms: What motivates consumers to articulate themselves on the Internet?" *Journal of Interactive Marketing*, 18(1), 38–52.

Hoffman, D.L., Novak, T.P. and Peralta, M. (1999) "Building consumer trust online," *Communications of the ACM*, 42(4), 80–85.

Jepsen, A.L. (2006). "Information search in virtual communities: is it replacing use of off-line communication?" *Journal of Marketing Communications*, 12(4), 247–261.

Kaplan, A.M. and Haenlein, M. (2010) "Users of the world, unite! The challenges and opportunities of Social Media," *Business Horizons*, 53(1), 59–68.

Kaplan, A.M. and Haenlein, M. (2012) "Social media: back to the roots and back to the future," *Journal of Systems and Information Technology*, 14(2), 101–104.

Kotler, P., Bowen, J. and Makens, J.C (2010) *Marketing for hospitality and tourism* (5th edn). Boston, MA: Pearson Education.

Labrecque, L.I., vor dem Esche, J., Mathwick, C., Novak, T.P. and Hofacker, C.F. (2013) "Consumer power: Evolution in the digital age," *Journal of Interactive Marketing,* 27(4), 257–269.

Law, R., Qi, S. and Buhalis, D. (2010) "Progress in tourism management: A review of website evaluation in tourism research," *Tourism Management*, 31(3), 297–313.

Lin, Y.S. and Huang, J.Y. (2006). "Internet blogs as a tourism marketing medium: A case study," *Journal of Business Research*, 59(10), 1201–1205.

Loiacono, E.T., Watson, R.T. and Goodhue, D.L. (2007) "WebQual: An instrument for consumer evaluation of web sites," *International Journal of Electronic Commerce*, 11(3), 51–87.

Magee, J.C. and Galinsky, A.D. (2008) "8 Social Hierarchy: The Self-Reinforcing Nature of Power and Status," *The Academy of Management Annals*, 2(1), 351–398.

Mangold, W.G. and Faulds, D.J. (2009) "Social media: The new hybrid element of the promotion mix," *Business Horizons,* 52(4), 357–365.

O'Connor, P. (2008) "User-generated content and travel: A case study on TripAdvisor. Com," *Information and Communication Technologies in Tourism*, 47–58.

Pan, B. (2015) "The power of search engine ranking for tourist destinations," *Tourism Management,* 47, 79–87.

Peters, K., Chen, Y., Kaplan, A.M., Ognibeni, B. and Pauwels, K. (2013) "Social media metrics – A framework and guidelines for managing social media," *Journal of Interactive Marketing*, 27(4), 281–298.

Rucker, D.D., Dubois, D. and Galinsky, A.D. (2011) "Generous paupers and stingy princes: power drives consumer spending on self versus others," *Journal of Consumer Research*, 37(6), 1015–1029.

Salehi-Esfahani, S., Ravichandran, S., Israeli, A. and Bolden III, E. (2016) "Investigating Information Adoption Tendencies Based on Restaurants' User-generated Content Utilizing a Modified Information Adoption Model," *Journal of Hospitality Marketing and Management*, 1–29.

Samli, A.C. (2001) *Empowering the American Consumer: Corporate Responsiveness and Market Profitability*, Westport, CT: Quorum Books.

Sethuraman, R., Tellis, G.J. and Briesch, R.A. (2011) "How well does advertising work? Generalizations from meta-analysis of brand advertising elasticities," *Journal of Marketing Research*, 48(3), 457–471.

Sirakaya, E. and Woodside, A.G. (2005) "Building and testing theories of decision making by travelers," *Tourism Management*, 26(6), 815–832.

Wang, Y., Weaver, D.B. and Kwek, A. (2015) "Beyond the Mass Tourism Stereotype Power and Empowerment in Chinese Tour Packages," *Journal of Travel Research*, 55(6), 724–737.

Wathieu, L., Brenner, L., Carmon, Z., Chattopadhyay, A., Wertenbroch, K., Drolet, A., Gourville, J., Muthukrishnan, A.V., Novemsky, N., Ratner, R.K. and Wu, G. (2002) "Consumer control and empowerment: a primer," *Marketing Letters*, 13(3), 297–305.

Yoo, K.H., Gretzel, U. and Zach, F. (2011) "Travel Opinion Leaders and Seekers", in R. Law, M. Fuchs and F. Ricci (eds), *Information and Communication Technologies in Tourism* (pp. 525–535). New York, NY: Springer.

37

Evolving destination and business relationships in online distribution channels

Disintermediation and re-intermediation

Marios Sotiriadis

Introduction

The aim of every distribution strategy is to provide targeted consumers with easy access to the means of obtaining information and making a purchase. A broad definition suggests that "a distribution channel is any organized and serviced system, paid for out of marketing budgets and created or utilized to provide convenient points of sale and/or access to consumers, away from the location of production and consumption" (Middleton et al. 2009: 282). Creating and using distribution channels are normally essential to provide an efficient way to reach a wider market and generate advance sales. For consumers, distribution channels can simplify the purchase decision by offering products in a convenient form from a trusted source at a time and place of their choice.

The distribution in tourism industry is both complex and unique. It is unique because of the influence that intermediaries have on customers' choices. It is complex because of the diversity of organizations involved and their relationships with each other (Buhalis and Laws 2004; Morrison 2013). Literature stresses the growing competition of the online tourism industry, specifically referring to organizations and destinations who contest for the attention of consumers with access to various channels (see, for instance, Dale 2003; Sotiriadis et al. 2015). It is further indicated that these developments pushed tourism providers towards disintermediation, re-intermediation, outsourcing and collaborations (Buhalis & Licata 2002; Dale 2003; Sotiriadis et al. 2015). This phenomenon is especially evident in the tourism-related industries drastically changing distribution channels. The main reason for this restructuration in tourism is the swift increase in online intermediaries or tourism e-mediaries (Dale 2003).

This chapter takes a destination and tourism business perspective and focuses on the supply side with the aim to investigate the evolving business environment and relationships in the field of online tourism distribution. More specifically, it explores the role of tourism e-mediaries as a distribution channel; it outlines and highlights the main trends and the periods of evolution in this field; and it addresses the question whether there is disintermediation and/or re-intermediation. The paper is concluded with a summary of suggestions for the tourism industry.

Electronic travel trade and distribution channels

Since the beginning of the previous decade e-commerce was booming and tourism-related services are one of the most popular items to buy online. The ICTs provided new tools that have changed how distribution is accomplished in tourism industry. A new type of tourism intermediary emerged as a response to the technological developments and opportunities offered by the establishment and wide spread of the Internet. Some call these online tourism intermediaries or e-mediaries.

The term "Tourism e-Mediaries" (TEMs) is often used interchangeably with other terms, such as "online travel agents" (Kracht and Wang 2010), "third-party websites" (Toh et al. 2011) and "e-tourism intermediaries" (Buhalis & Licata 2002). The term TEMs is adopted for the purpose of this chapter. TEMs are not travel agencies, wholesalers or tour operators and for this reason do not fit easily to traditional channels of distribution. They create an additional channel which potentially can be used by other intermediaries and principals that provide internet access to their inventory. The main issues of the online travel trade are outlined below.

Online distribution channels in tourism

The main impact of ICTs is that consumers now have easier, more convenient and faster access to a much wider choice of travel and tourism possibilities. Thus, ICTs and the Internet have transformed tourism markets from a consumer-centric market to a consumer-driven market where consumers have a big part in creating and sharing tourism information through social and review websites (Buhalis and Jun 2011). The tourism marketing is now consumer and technology dominant.

A majority of tourism organizations had to go through a significant business process overhaul in order to successfully take advantage of the emerging technologies to renovate their processes and ability to operate in the global market. This overhaul was necessary as more experienced consumers are empowered by ICTs and use TEMs to improve their personal efficiency and competencies. A number of definitions have been suggested for TEMs. The most comprehensive and adequate was, in our view, proposed by Dale (2003: 110) defining them as "organizations offering services via a network of virtual channels to stakeholders, and which are not constrained by geographical boundaries".

Tourism and travel organizations need to attract consumers through effective technology and by offering the right product and at the right price globally. TEMs conduct business electronically; they engage in electronic commerce (e-commerce). These intermediaries are basically search engines in the form of a website which allows consumers to request information on the availability and pricing of specific tourism services (e.g. transportation, accommodation, tours, attractions and events). The TEM is allowed to search these principals' websites and to access their inventory (Inkson and Minnaert 2012).

It is the role of TEMs to match principals with the consumers demanding their services and products. TEMs represent an established distribution channel for the tourism industry as they promote consumer choice, access, confidence, protection and information in the digital environment (Hill and Cairncross 2011). These intermediaries provide several benefits for customers, the major of which are as follows (Turban et al. 2008): assistance in planning trips/holidays; availability of online pricing comparisons for tourism services; convenience and easy access to tourism information; potential of securing lower prices on tourism services; ability to self-book online; and immediate confirmation of bookings. For these reasons, tourism organizations and destinations realized the potential and benefits of TEMs and are quite involved in working with this distribution channel (Dale 2003; Morrison 2013).

Main tourism e-mediaries: a brief presentation

A vast number of TEMs are being active in the online tourism marketplace. These can be categorized into five big groups of TEMs, which emerged as a result of various mergers, acquisitions and collaborations (Table 37.1).

According to recent statistics (published in August 2016), Booking.com is the leading TEM based on the number of website visits (Alexia 2016), whilst Orbitz provides the best quality service (Lee 2016). The ranking and rating of the top TEMs are presented in Table 37.2.

Table 37.1 Main TEMs

Group	*Tourism e-Mediaries*
Amadeus IT	TravelTainment, Opodo and Vacation.com
Expedia	Expedia.com, Anyway.com (Expedia.fr), Egencia (formerly Expedia Corporate Travel), Hotels.com, Hotwire.com, Travelnow.com, ClassicVacations.com, Venere.com, TripAdvisor, eLong.net, and SeatGuru.com
Orbitz	Orbitz, ebookers, RatesToGo, CheapTickets, HotelClub, Asia hotels, Orbitz for Business and the Away Network
Priceline	Priceline.com, Agoda.com, Booking.com and Active Hotels.com
Sabre Holdings Inc.	Sabre Travel Network, Sabre Hospitality Solutions, Sabre Airline Solutions, Nexion, Travelocity.com*, IgoUgo, Cubeless, Holidayautos.com, GetThere, Trams, Lastminute.com, Travelguru, Moneydirect, Zuji, Travelocity Business and World Choice Travel

* In January 2015 Expedia and Sabre Corporation announced that Expedia, Inc. has acquired Travelocity from Sabre Corporation for $280 million in cash. The acquisition follows the 2013 strategic marketing agreement between Expedia, Inc. and Travelocity.

Table 37.2 Ranking and rating of online tourism intermediaries (August 2016)

*Ranking of TEMs**	*Tourism online intermediary*	*Focus/services*	*Rating of TEMs***
1	www.booking.com	Worldwide accommodation reservations	
2	www.tripadvisor.com	Information on hotels and attractions, reviews from tourists with star ratings	
3	www.expedia.com	Compare prices, shop for a vacation trip or reserve a hotel room or rent a car	7
4	www.hotels.com	Accommodation reservations: best rate on all hotel rooms, reserve rooms online	
5	www.kayak.com	Metasearch engine for flights, hotels, and rental car rates from numerous websites	10

*Ranking of TEMs**	*Tourism online intermediary*	*Focus/services*	*Rating of TEMs***
6	www.agoda.com	Reservations for hotels and resorts in Asia and worldwide	
7	www.priceline.com	Worldwide auctioneer of hotel rooms, flights, and rental cars, model 'Name Your Own Price'	3
8	www.orbitz.com	Prices for flights, hotels, and rental cars	1
9	www.travelocity.com	A variety of travel services, including fare finder, hotel and car rental information	5
10	www.trivago.com	Search and compare hotel prices from multiple booking websites	
12	Yahoovacationstore.com	Trip planning and making reservations at Yahoo!Travel	
13	www.hotwire.com	Online booking of flights, hotels, car rentals, cruises, vacation packages	9
14	www.travelzoo.com	Publishes handpicked sales and specials from hundreds of tourism principals	
15	www.skyscanner.com	Travel search engine providing comparisons for cheap flights, hotels, and car rentals	
16	www.onetravel.com	Online booking for air fares, cruises, and discount hotels	6
17	www.cheaptickets.com	Tourism services, i.e. airline tickets, cruise tickets, car rentals, and hotel reservations	2
18	www.laterooms.com	Late availability rooms worldwide	
19	www.ebookers.com	Travel portal offering vacation packages, hotels, air fares, and car hire	
20	www.hoteltravel.comm	Discount online hotel reservations, with interactive maps, travel forums and tips	

Notes: * Ranking: The most popular in terms of website visits according to the ranking 2016 by Alexia.com. The own brand websites (e.g. Delta United, Marriott, Hilton) and sharing economy platforms (e.g. Uber, Vacation Rentals, Home Away) are not included in this classification (the world's top websites in travel).

** Rating: The best in terms of quality websites (Lee 2016). This is a website providing reviews, evaluations and comparisons of products and services independently. The overall rating of top 10 online travel websites was based on 4 main criteria (Lee, 2016): Booking and search, Ease of use, Additional features, Help and support. In the 4th and 8th places of this rating are CheapOair and AirGorilla respectively, which do not appear in the most popular websites.

The TEMs holding the top three spots as the most popular since 2013 have built vast networks and alliances with a series of tourism organizations (Sotiriadis et al. 2015).

Business models in electronic tourism and travel trade

Traditionally, intermediaries of the tourism industry have been outbound and inbound travel agencies and tour operators (Buhalis and Laws 2004; Egger and Buhalis 2008). However, the Internet restructured the entire tourist value chain, forcing the existing intermediaries to take up the new medium and to develop corresponding business models. The two main categories of business models that are applied to the electronic travel trade are the Global Distribution Systems (GDSs) and the TEMs, briefly presented below.

Global distribution systems

The airline Computer Reservation Systems (CRSs) had developed into GDSs by gradually expanding their geographical coverage as well as by integrating both horizontally with other airline systems, and vertically by incorporating the entire range of principals, such as accommodation, car rentals, train and ferry ticketing, entertainment and other services. They are CRSs that access many databases of hotel providers, airlines, car rental firms, et cetera across the world (Buhalis and Laws 2004; Middleton et al. 2009). In the early 1990s, GDSs emerged as the major driver of ICTs, as well as the backbone of the tourism industry. In essence, GDSs matured to tourism supermarkets (Thakran and Verma 2013).

Amadeus, Galileo, Sabre, and Worldspan are currently the strongest GDSs in the marketplace. The GDSs are among the first e-commerce companies in the world facilitating B2B e-commerce. According to Amadeus, its greatest strength is its knack for forming successful partnerships. Over 70 of the world's leading airlines use the Amadeus e-Travel Airline Suite to power over 250 websites in more than 80 markets (Sotiriadis et al 2015).

It must be noted that GDSs did not provide the end user (consumer) with direct access to its databases. The travel agencies continued to act as intermediary until the Internet revolution shook the foundations of the trade. But, even now, it is these original GDSs that provide the backbone to the Internet-based tourism distribution systems. The major difference between the GDSs and the TEMs is that the latter permits the consumer to access the database unmediated by the travel agency (Buhalis and Laws 2004).

Business models for tourism e-mediaries

Daniele and Frew (2004) summarized five business models for TEMs, namely agency, merchant, distressed inventory, demand collection and comparison shopping. These models are briefly presented below.

Agency: Many TEMs act as an intermediary between the tourism principals (e.g. airlines and hotels) and consumers (i.e. business and leisure tourists). In this model, the TEMs have direct access to and arrange bookings for inventory held by the principal but made available to the TEMs at agreed-on prices, for which they receive an agreed-on commission on each transaction (Tranter et al. 2009). Customers are given a confirmation number that needs to be presented to the hotel upon arrival and they pay the hotels for their stays. TEMs will bill the hotels for their commissions and payment to the TEM occurs on checkout (Toh et al. 2011). Providers have been offering less in commission to intermediaries the past few years; this is why TEMs have started moving away from this business model.

Merchant: Under the merchant model, the TEM purchases hotel rooms or other tourism services at a discounted rate and marks them up for sale at a profit (Tranter et al. 2009). In so doing, the TEM accepts the risk of unsold inventory and earns revenue when a room or other service is booked (Lee et al. 2013). Hotels typically agree to sell their rooms to the TEMs at wholesale rates, and the TEMs will then mark them up at contract-specified margins to sell to tourists. Notice that even under the merchant model, TEMs do not buy the rooms until they are sold. The essential difference is that under the agency model the hotel collects from the guest and remits the commission to the TEM, whereas under the merchant model the TEM collects from the guest and then remits the wholesale price to the hotel (Toh et al. 2011). TEMs operating from a merchant model often have a higher gross profit level than TEMs working from the agency model (Lee et al. 2013).

Distressed inventory: This is a subsection of the merchant model, where TEMs focus entirely on selling distressed inventory which is characteristically available from about two weeks prior to the consumption date. Lastminute.com is an example of a TEM who's business model in predominantly based on selling distressed inventory.

Demand collection (or Opaque): It is also called opaque because the identity of the principal is unknown to the purchaser until the transaction has been completed (Pizam 2011). This model takes advantage of the power of information sharing and communications via the Internet, and allows consumers to dictate what price they are prepared to pay for a particular service and how far they are willing to compromise and accept substitutes. The best known of these intermediaries are Priceline and Hotwire, though other TEMs such as Travelocity.com and CheapTickets.com have introduced their own versions of opaque selling. A TEM using the opaque model has an agreement with a hotel to distribute rooms, subject to the hotel's agreement to the offered price.

When a TEM accepts bids from buyers, the hotel may decline the transaction. If it accepts, the TEM matches buyers' bids with the lowest bid from the seller to maximize TEM's profits through price differentials (Lee et al. 2013). The TEM's business involves having information about the buyer that is unavailable to the seller and information about the seller that the buyer cannot know. This model enables principals to generate revenue without interfering with their existing distribution channels or retail pricing structures (Pizam 2011). It is basically a revenue management technique the purpose of which is to generate more revenue from a fixed inventory.

Comparison shopping (or travel meta-search engines): This model is providing the consumer with the service of comparing flight and accommodation rates sourced from a number of principals or other TEMs. There are some variations within this model, based on how the revenue is gathered and the revenue model (i.e. an advertising, consumer service fee or commission basis). The TEM can gather data either through allowing principals to upload their data directly onto its website, or through the use of sophisticated meta-crawlers which scan GDSs and provider databases for the cheapest rates. The travel meta-search engines (TSEs) appear between principals and consumers to aggregate and filter out relevant and pertinent information from the wealth of material (Egger and Buhalis 2008). TSEs (e.g. Sidestep and Kayak) enable consumers to compare offers and rates by carrying out live queries to principals and TEMs and presenting the results transparently.

Christodoulidou et al. (2010) suggest that in order for TEMs to become more profitable and competitive, they need to adopt and implement one of the above models. Some popular TEMs and their business models are summarized in Table 37.3.

Table 37.3 Popular TEMs and their business models

Popular TEMs	*Group/affiliated Company*	*Business model*
Expedia.com	Expedia, Inc.	Merchant and agency
Hotels.com	Expedia, Inc.	Merchant and agency
Hotwire.com	Expedia, Inc.	Opaque
Booking.com	Priceline.com, Inc.	Agency
Priceline.com	Priceline.com, Inc.	Opaque
Orbitz.com	Orbitz Worldwide, Inc.	Merchant
Cheaptickets.com	Orbitz Worldwide, Inc.	Merchant
Ebookers.com	Orbitz Worldwide, Inc.	Merchant
Travelocity.com	Sabre Holdings	Opaque, merchant and agency
Lastminute.com	Sabre Holdings	Merchant and agency

Source: Lee et al. 2013: 97

Lee et al. (2013) suggest that TEMs use one or more of either the merchant, the agency and opaque model. The agency model accounts for roughly one-third of the arrangements with hotels (Toh et al. 2011). The popularity of TEMs is attributed to their client-centric approach, the convenience they offer, and consumers' growing confidence in online purchasing (Kim et al. 2009; Lee et al. 2013).

The next section deals with the critical issue of the evolution of online distribution channels in the tourism industry and the technological advances affecting the business relationship between tourism industry and TEMs.

The evolving business environment in online tourism trade

As indicated above, the development of the Internet has had a major impact on the intermediaries, not least because it has enabled principals to reach some consumers directly and cut out intermediaries. However, through dynamic packaging, the travel trade industry (travel agencies and wholesalers) have been able to defend their positions (Inkson and Minnaert 2012; Sotiriadis et al. 2015). TEMs are also evolving as consumers become more sophisticated purchasers of tourism products and services; these intermediaries already provide an important tool for them to engage in DIY travel purchasing (Morrison 2013). Further, the relationships of TEMs with tourism businesses are of significant importance and variable over time. The nature of these relationships has evolved during the current decade, from confrontation to collaboration (Lee et al. 2013; Sotiriadis et al. 2015). This section deals with the evolution of online distribution channels and the business relationships between TEMs and the tourism industry.

Evolution of online distribution channels in tourism

The evolving digital arena within the tourism industry is characterised by constant change. On the one hand, advancements in the online arena have opened new ways of effectively communicating with and promoting to the consumers; but on the other hand, these advancements have made tourism distribution a complex management function.

The study by Thakran and Verma (2013) attempted to summarize the four digital eras in the tourism industry, characterized as GDS, Internet, SoLoMo, and Hybrid periods. Table 37.4 depicts the key features of each era with respect to the tourism distribution channels.

Table 37.4 The digital eras in tourism distribution system

Era	*Changes in tourism distribution channels/Key features*
GDS (1960–1995) / Intermediation The rule of GDS and the growth of travel agencies	Heavy dependency on the GDSs and travel agents. Increased reach of individual tourism providers across borders. However, this advancement had the following effects: • Increased competition among tourism organizations and intermediaries within the distribution system. • Dependency on travel agencies and payment of high transaction fees. • The balance of power shifted away from the principals to the intermediaries.
Internet (1995–2000)/ Disintermediation Growth of the Internet changed the online distribution landscape/ Emergence of TEMs	The first cost-effective tool for direct distribution by tourism principals and destinations. Effects: • Global geographical reach and providers investing in brand websites. • Distribution started to move away from intermediation (GDSs) toward disintermediation (brand websites and booking engines). However, the launch of search engines (e.g. Google), brought about a new form of intermediation. As the Internet gained popularity, many TEMs entered the distribution landscape. The growth of TEMs once again kept the principals heavily dependent on the distribution channel intermediaries. • Tourism organizations started experiencing a loss of control over the pricing of their services to TEMs. • Benefits for consumers: obtain the lowest rate within their desired market segment, coupled with the price transparency on the Internet. • Continued growth of online distribution intermediaries: over time, the direct booking websites lost business to the TEMs.
SoLoMo (2000–2012)/ Matured Disintermediation SoLoMo, www.brand.com	With digital advancements, a new category of technology has emerged, known as customer engagement technology (CET), which includes a wide variety of "SoLoMo" applications; that is, social-, location-, and mobile-based applications to simplify the booking process for consumers. The beginning of the SoLoMo era was marked by the growth and popularity of the social and travel community websites such as TripAdvisor and Facebook. Extensive adoption and use of SM and smartphones represent another disruption in online tourism intermediation. Consumers in the SoLoMo era have different expectations from the consumers in the Internet era. Therefore, it essential for providers to keep the customers engaged through social, local, and mobile channels with a view to a long-term sustainable relationship.
Hybrid (2013 and forward)/ Multi-channel and Re-intermediation Year 2013: 'the year of three screens – computers, tablets, and smartphones'	The consumers are increasingly depending on online search. To accomplish that search, they are using multiple screens as they search for the tourism organization information that they want. On the other end, tourism organizations are investing in direct channels and trying to provide customized and high-quality experience to the consumer. In short, the tourism industry is slowly moving to a hybrid distribution system: • Back to the disintermediation phase with multi-channels. • Existing online intermediaries, including GDS-supported travel agents, TEMs, and search engines, remain an important part of the tourism distribution channels.

Source: Adapted from Thakran and Verma (2013).

The online distribution channels will continue to evolve in response to external influences and there will be shifts in the structure of the industry as a whole (Pearce and Schott 2005; Kracht and Wang 2010). Let us look at an example of this trend in the online tourism market.

Example/Micro-Case 1: Uber taps into travel booking services – is this a threat for TEMs?

After completely disrupting the taxi industry, Uber may well become a threat to TEMs. The popular hail-riding platform has patented a travel booking service that seems to signal its entry into the online tourism distribution. In the patent application for Uber Travel, the company says it aims to provide a perfectly timed and seamless end-to-end trip, including the booking of flights, ground transport and accommodation. The system would also monitor flight and vehicle delays, and alert the appropriate airline and hotel systems, re-accommodating the tourist when necessary.

Uber's potential entry into the online distribution channels could well see more TEMs move to address the local transport gap in their itineraries. There is definitely room for innovation and competition in this field, which could start happening via partnerships and acquisitions. TEMs who rely solely on the traditional TEM business models are in danger of thinking that doing the same thing will work year in and year out. Whether or not Uber will disrupt the tourism industry as significantly as they have the taxi industry remains to be seen. Currently the tourism industry is a multifaceted chain affected by many variables and whether or not it is something that can be 'uberized' as easily as one facet of a trip (hailing a taxi) is yet to be seen.

(Source: http://www.tourismupdate.co.za/article/106076/Watch-out-OTAs-Uber-taps-into-travel, 3 Feb 2016 [Accessed 10 August 2016]).

Disintermediation and re-intermediation

The process of cutting out the intermediary is called disintermediation, and tourism organizations clearly favor this approach. This disintermediation means that consumers bypass the travel agencies in the tourism industry when principals take distribution back into their own hands by setting up websites that allow guests to make bookings online (Tse 2003). When the Internet first became widely used, there was a prediction that it would lead to a "disintermediation" of distribution channels, with an increasing number of consumers booking direct with principals and cutting out the intermediaries.

Although direct booking has certainly grown massively, what has actually happened is more complex. First, the market conditions and disintermediation have led to a very new kind of competition: the competition among traditional travel agencies and electronic agencies. Most traditional travel agencies have also embraced the Internet as a tool for communicating with their own customers (Inkson and Minnaert 2012). Second, at the same time, the established companies (mainly Tour operators) have reinvented themselves online, offering the customer additional benefits, including the ability to tailor their own holiday through dynamic packaging and to compare their experiences with others on the review websites (e.g. TripAdvisor). The websites of Thomas Cook and Thomson rival those of Expedia and Lastminute in the top 10 TEMs used in different markets (Morrison 2013).

Third, the Internet has created business opportunities for a range of different TEMs offering essentially the same services online as their traditional rivals did on the high street. There is another reason though why intermediaries continue to hold an important position. Most of these new intermediaries provide what is known as the information overload reduction function

(Christodoulidou et al. 2010). While a consumer can "Google" for products and services online and buy from one of the millions of companies that the search results brings in, the "information overload" upon the consumer caused by this is enormous. The consumers turn to the travel agent for expert help. Many travel agencies have found a business opportunity here and have reincarnated in various degrees as TEMs. For instance, an option for the consumer is to visit a travel search engine like Kayak.com and specify his/her criteria. This TSE significantly simplifies the consumer's task.

Thus, disintermediation is not a one-way trend. In more recent times, new intermediaries have emerged to fill the opportunities created by disintermediation; a trend for re-intermediation (Middleton et al. 2009). This re-intermediation suggests that the principles of distribution still apply in the now dominant online era, in particular: (i) many consumers with busy lives value the convenience of a 'one-stop-shop' for all their travel and tourism purchases – both online and off it; (ii) faced with a bewildering choice, consumers value the reassurance provided by a well-known brand; and (iii) principals value the efficient access to wide consumer markets provided by intermediaries. Re-intermediation by these TEMs is likely to continue as a dominant form of distribution even as social community websites do offer a viable alternative (Thakran and Verma 2013). Therefore, it could be said that we are experiencing a hybrid digital era in tourism distribution, i.e. disintermediation and re-intermediation as well as a variety of channels simultaneously.

Let us look at an example of a TEM representing a typical example of re-intermediation.

Example/Micro-case 2: Kayak, a travel meta-search engine

One of the business models of TEMs is the travel meta-search website (TSE). These intermediaries are Internet search engines that provide a website for consumers to request availability and price information about specific products (e.g. transportation, accommodation, attractions and wholesalers), and other TEMs may allow these search machines access to their inventory.

One example is Kayak.com that was founded in 2005. It does not sell anything; instead it searches the websites of principals and some intermediaries, displays the relevant information, and allows the consumer to click through to the principal to make a booking. It has links to hundreds of airlines, almost 160,000 hotels, and 17 cruise lines, as well as all the major car hire firms, TEMs and wholesalers. It searches hundreds of travel websites from all over the world to provide the information to the consumer in an easy-to-use display and send him/her directly to the source to make the purchase. In addition, its fare alerts and fare history help tourists stay on top of changing prices.

The business model of Kayak is click-based: it earns an amount when tourists click on its advertisements. This business model is different from the model offered by Expedia in that the latter one makes the consumer do the booking and payment with rather than directing consumers to the original source. When a consumer clicks through to a principal's website to make a booking, the search engine receives a fee from the principal. The consumer does not pay to use Kayak.com; its revenue comes from the website that the consumer clicks through to. Another channel of revenue generation is similar to that of Google, when consumers click on the results from tourism principals like airlines, hotels, and rental car companies (Inkson and Minnaert 2012).

The digital arena is evolving, so are the relationships between the providers of tourism services. The next subsection is dealing with the business relationship between tourism industry and TEMs.

Tourism industry and TEMs: evolving business relationships

The subject of relationships between tourism industry and TEMs has been debated over the last years (see, for instance, Lee et al. 2013; Sotiriadis et al. 2015). The reason for this is that tourism organizations are anxious of losing control over their inventory and pricing strategies, should they decide to use the distribution channel of TEMs. Tourism principals further feel pressured to commit to long-term relationships with no exit clauses in the contract and at rates they feel are not sustainable (Lee et al. 2013; Toh et al. 2011).

Christodoulidou et al. (2007b) identified the top five issues and challenges in online distribution for tourism industry, namely: rate control, staff training, customer loyalty, principal's website interface, and control of the corporate image. This chapter argues that four issues are of high importance:

- The value of visibility enjoyed by principals resulting from being listed on a TEM's website. The presence of principals in different distribution channels, including TEMs, has a significant impact on their bookings and resulting revenue (Inversini and Masiero 2014).
- Cutting the booking cost: TEMs have tried to attract consumers by reducing the cost of booking as much as possible (e.g. additional fees). This will undoubtedly put pressure on TEMs to invest in reducing their own transaction costs.
- Commissions charged: the cost of using TEMs is considerable (Lee et al. 2013).
- Desire for rate parity (similar rates) among all distribution channels (Toh et al. 2011).

Tourism organizations and TEMs have often been in competition in recent years. To offset the competition, principals have invested in developing and marketing their own brand websites, with some imitating TEMs and offering flight and car hire booking services online. Tourism organizations often prefer transactions to be completed through their own websites, but some consumers have a number of favorite TEMs whom they trust and would rather use to facilitate a booking (Christodoulidou et al. 2010; Toh et al. 2011).

However, lately we have witnessed the development of a more collaborative approach to achieving common benefits. It has come to light that tourism organizations and travel trade (tour operators, TEMs, etc.) share common strategic aims that would be achieved more effectively by working together through the creation of strategic networks/relationships (Sotiriadis et al. 2015). Tourism organizations need to attract consumers through effective technology and the right products and pricing. Principals and TEMs are both using technology to match supply with demand; they are both trying to entice consumers to buy travel and tourism services. Therefore, principals and destinations can take advantage of large TEMs investment in technology and marketing to achieve common benefits for all, through growing market share, reduction in consumer acquisition costs and sharing promotional costs (Christodoulidou et al. 2010).

Thus, the business relationships between destinations, providers of tourism services and TEMs evolved from confrontation to being more collaborative. Through this approach each party involved recognizes the role of the other and, consequently, the business relationships become mutually beneficial.

Conclusion

The feasibility and sustainability of an intermediary as a business activity depends upon whether it adds any extra value to the original service that is tradable directly between the principal and the consumer. Although the role of travel intermediaries has changed, there will always be a role in the tourism system for them. Tourism organizations need to use a wide range of distribution channels to reach their targeted markets. Online distribution channels and TEMs are providing an additional channel which can be used by principals in improving their exposure, visibility and sales in the online market.

This chapter focused on the supply perspective with the aim to analyze the main trends and features in the field of online tourism distribution. More specifically, the important role of TEMs as a distribution channel was explored and the main digital periods and trends of evolution in this field were presented. The evolving business environment and relationships were also outlined, and the question whether there is disintermediation or re-intermediation in the distribution system was addressed; the answer being that since 2013 we have been witnessing a hybrid online distribution era. This process is continuing to evolve and there is a constant imperative for the tourism industry to manage distribution more effectively.

From the above analysis it is quite clear that there is continuous change and evolution in the online tourism market. Within this context, the tourism industry has to continuously monitor, analyze and cope with the digital developments in the online tourism market. This chapter thus concludes by suggesting a series of strategies and actions for tourism industry practitioners in order to effectively compete with TEMs and improve sales performance:

- Ensure suitable use of all distribution channels available in the online market.
- Facilitate the efficient use of all tools and media available within an approach of integrated marketing communications with potential and current customers.
- Find ways of steering customers to principal's brand website, e.g. invest resources on own websites in enhancing trust and value of online reviews.
- Evaluate the performance of TEMs and other online channels available to them (e.g. GDS and TSEs) in order to select distribution channels carefully.
- Extend their networks to encompass more TEM partners, thereby avoiding overreliance on one TEM.
- Collaborate with TEMs; develop a symbiotic relationship with close- and long-term interactions between them.
- Employ SM as an online distribution tool, a way of interacting with customers and a service recovery tool to develop relationships with customers and build brand loyalty.

At the same time, within the digital arena, DMOs should develop specific capabilities and skills such as: (i) Experience facilitators and brokers: DMOs arrange experiences for tourists within their destinations. They find out what experiences consumers want and work with tourism stakeholders to design these experiences. They stay in touch with tourists to ensure that their experiences go well and meet their expectations. (ii) Digital content masters and facilitators: DMOs are also masters at managing digital content. They encourage local residents, tourism stakeholders and tourists to develop content and to engage in conversations about the destination (Ford and Peeper 2008; Morrison 2013).

It is believed that all the abovementioned strategies should contribute to improving the effectiveness of distribution management of the tourism industry within the hybrid digital era.

References

Alexia (2016). Ranking 2016 by Alexia.com Available online at: http://www.alexa.com/topsites/category/Recreation/Travel [Accessed 12 September 2016].

Buhalis, D. and Jun, S.H. (2011). *E-Tourism*. Oxford: Goodfellow Publishers.

Buhalis, D. and Laws, E. (2004). *Tourism Distribution Channels: Practices, Issues and Transformations*. London: Thomson Learning.

Buhalis, D. and Licata, M.C. (2002) "The Future of eTourism Intermediaries", *Tourism Management*, 23(3), 207–20.

Christodoulidou, N., Brewer, P. and Countryman, C.C. (2007a) "Travel Intermediaries and Meta Sites: Comparing Customer Perception of Value", *Journal of Information Technology & Tourism*, 9(3/4), 227–44.

Christodoulidou, N., Brewer, P., Feinstein, A.H. and Bai, B. (2007b) "Electronic Channels of Distribution: Challenges and Solutions for Hotel Operators", *FIU Hospitality and Tourism Review*, 25(2), 92–100.

Christodoulidou, N., Connolly, D.J. and Brewer, P. (2010) "An Examination of the Transactional Relationship between Online Travel Agencies, Travel Meta Sites, and Suppliers", *International Journal of Contemporary Hospitality Management*, 22(7), 1048–62.

Dale, C. (2003) "The Competitive Networks of Tourism e-Mediaries: New Strategies, New Advantages", *Journal of Vacation Marketing*, 9(20), 109–18.

Daniele, R. and Frew, A. (2004). From Intermediaries to Market-Makers: An analysis of the Evolution of e-Mediaries. Available online at: www.ifitt.org [Accessed 10 July 2016].

Egger, R., and Buhalis, D. (2008). *eTourism Case Studies: Management and Marketing Issues*. Burlington, MA: Elsevier.

Ford, R.C. and Peeper, W.C (2008). *Managing Destination Marketing Organizations*. Orlando, FL: ForPer Publications.

Hill, J.R. and Cairncross, G. (2011) "How Small Regional Accommodation Providers View and Respond to Online Intermediaries", *Journal of Vacation Marketing*, 17(4), 249–62.

Inkson, C. and Minnaert, L. (2012). *Tourism Management: An Introduction*. London: Sage Publications.

Inversini, A. and Masiero, L. (2014) "Selling Rooms Online: The Use of Social Media and Online Travel Agents", *International Journal of Contemporary Hospitality Management*, 26(2), 272–92.

Kim, J., Bojanic, D.C. and Warnick, R.B. (2009) "Price Bundling and Travel Product Pricing Practices used by Online Channels of Distribution", *Journal of Travel Research*, 47(4), 403–12.

Kracht, J. and Wang, Y. (2010) "Examining the Tourism Distribution Channel: Evolution and Transformation", *International Journal of Contemporary Hospitality Management*, 22(5), 736–57.

Lee, B. (2016) "Online Travel Sites Reviews on Top Ten Reviews, 2016". Available online at: www.toptenreviews.com [Accessed 12 September 2016].

Lee, H., Guillet, B.D. and Law, R. (2013) "An Examination of the Relationship between Online Travel Agents and Hotels: A Case Study of Choice Hotels International and Expedia.com", *Cornell Hospitality Quarterly*, 54(1), 95–107.

Middleton, V.T.C., Fyall, A., Morgan, M., with Ranchhod, A. (2009). *Marketing in Travel and Tourism* (4th edn), Oxford: Elsevier.

Morrison, A.M. (2013). *Marketing and Managing Tourism Destinations*, New York: Routledge.

Pearce, D.G. and Schott, C. (2005) "Tourism Distribution Channels: The Visitors' Perspective", *Journal of Travel Research*, 44(1), 50–63.

Pizam, A. (2011) "Editorial – Opaque Selling in the Hotel Industry: Is it Good for Everyone?", *International Journal of Hospitality Management*, 30, 485.

Sotiriadis, M., Loedolff, C. and Sarmaniotis, C. (2015) "Tourism E-mediaries: Business Models and Relationships with Providers of Tourism Services". In: Gursoy, D., Saayman, M. & Sotiriadis, M. eds., *Collaboration in Tourism Businesses and Destinations: A Handbook*, 225–40. Bingley, UK: Emerald Publishing.

Thakran, K. and Verma, R. (2013) "The Emergence of Hybrid Online Distribution Channels in Travel, Tourism and Hospitality", *Cornell Hospitality Quarterly*, 54(3), 240–47.

Toh, R.S., Rven, P. and DeKay, F. (2011) "Selling Rooms: Hotels vs Third-party Websites", *Cornell Hospitality Quarterly*, 52(2), 181–89.

Tranter, A.K, Stuart-Hill, T. and Parker, J. (2009). *An Introduction to Revenue Management for the Hospitality Industry: Principles and Practices for the Real World*. Upper Saddle River, NJ: Prentice Hall.

Tse, A.C.-B. (2003) "Disintermediation of Travel Agents in the Hotel Industry", *International Journal of Hospitality Management*, 22(4), 453–60.

Turban, E., King, D., McKay, J., Marshall, P., Lee, J., and Viehland, D. (2008). *Electronic Commerce 2008: A Managerial Perspective*. Upper Saddle River, NJ: Pearson Education.

Further reading

Christodoulidou, N., Connolly, D.J. and Brewer, P. (2010) "An Examination of the Transactional Relationship between Online Travel Agencies, Travel Meta Sites, and Suppliers", *International Journal of Contemporary Hospitality Management*, 22(7), 1048–62. (The relationship structure between travel intermediaries and tourism suppliers throughout the distribution value chain.)

Kim, J., and Connolly D.J. (2012) "Hospitality in the Age of Customer Empowerment. First Annual Customer Engagement Technology Study, Hospitality Technology". Available online at: http://luiscodo.files.wordpress.com/2012/09/customer-engagement2012.pdf (Changes in tourism consumer behavior within the context of customer engagement technology.)

Kracht, J. and Wang, Y. (2010) "Examining the Tourism Distribution Channel: Evolution and Transformation", *International Journal of Contemporary Hospitality Management*, 22(5), 736–57. (Evolution and progression of tourism distribution channels).

Lee, H.A., Guillet, B.D. and Law, R. (2013) "An Examination of the Relationship between Online Travel Agents and Hotels: A Case Study of Choice Hotels International and Expedia.com", *Cornell Hospitality Quarterly*, 54(1), 95–107. (Ways to make the most effective possible use of available technology and distribution channels.)

Thakran, K. and Verma, R. (2013) "The Emergence of Hybrid Online Distribution Channels in Travel, Tourism and Hospitality", *Cornell Hospitality Quarterly*, 54(3), 240–47 (The four digital eras in the tourism online market since 1960s.)

Xiaolong Guo, X., Ling, L., Dong, Y., and Liang, L. (2013) "Cooperation Contract in Tourism Supply Chains: The Optimal Pricing Strategy of Hotels for Cooperative Third Party Strategic Websites", *Annals of Tourism Research*, 41, 20–41. (Optimal pricing strategy for hotels within online distribution channels.)

38

How to successfully handle online hotel reviews

Practical recommendations

Beykan Çizel and Edina Ajanovic

Introduction

Since its introduction in 1990s, the Internet has changed people's communication and interaction patterns in both virtual and real world. Therefore, it should not be surprising that the effects of Information Communication Technologies and Web evolution became one of the most popular and fruitful research areas of tourism studies (Buhalis & Law, 2008) emphasizing the globalization of tourism industry, which has significant effects on both tourism demand and supply. As the Internet was evolving from a static platform known as Web 1.0, where interaction between content creators and users was at minimum (Rudman, 2010), to a more collaborative Web 2.0 platform, tourist behavior was significantly affected – now they can participate in creating the online content regarding tourism and hospitality companies. With a more information-centric Web 1.0 platform (Murugesan, 2010) information flow was unidirectional and web site administrators had full control of the created content. Accordingly, businesses in tourism and hospitality sector had the opportunity to predict effects of their marketing efforts on tourist perceptions and behavior. However, with Web 2.0 Internet applications started to be distributed as "online software as a service" which gets continuously updated as the number of users increases by combining data from multiple sources and user-generated content or UGC (O'Reilly, 2007). With this new platform, the Internet evolved from a broadcasting media into a participation platform where users have the opportunity to generate their own online content and interact with other participants who are using the same application. Murugesan (2010) called this platform people-centric due to its emphasis on user-generated content and inter-user interaction. The ability to reach the software and resources through cloud computing on multiple devices and platforms, where users have the opportunity to create or share the content, are some of the main features of the Web 2.0 platform (Rudman, 2010) which brought revolutionary changes in all life aspects and industries, with tourism being one of the most affected sectors.

The two "mega trends" that had the main influence on tourism and hospitality industry were search engines and social media (Leung et al. 2013). According to Xiang and Gretzel (2010), social media represents an important element of the tourism domain especially in the trip planning process. These authors especially emphasized the online travel review sites such as

TripAdvisor, VirtualTourist and similar as becoming extremely popular and taking the leadership among online travel information sources (Gretzel, Yoo and Purifoy, 2007). Other most commonly used social media channels are travel blogs and microblogs (e.g. Blogger, Twitter), media sharing (e.g. Flickr, Instagram, YouTube) and knowledge sharing sites (e.g. Wikitravel, Viator).

Considering the significant impact that technological development and especially social media had on the whole tourism industry and tourist behavior, academic research was devoted to building theoretical frameworks which could be used in studying and understanding social media. These theoretical frameworks may be divided on three groups: micro-theories, macro theories and pseudo theories (Pan and Crotts, 2012). There are micro theories studying individual actors in social media communications, their interaction, influence and behavioral patterns. On the other hand, macro theories provide global perspective on structures, dynamics and content shared on social media. The last group of pseudo theories use new frameworks proposed by non-academics in the field of marketing and social media. Most of the pseudo theories make sense intuitively as they are the product of many years of industry experience and testing different scenarios in practical work, but these are still to be tested empirically.

In this chapter the authors will try to provide a short overview of what has been done in the field of online reputational management which is considered to be highly important in new competitive virtual environment. This overview will be based on both empirical evidence derived from academic studies and practical advices coming from hospitality experts found on many non–academic web sites dealing exclusively with the issue of online reputation management.

Contemporary consumer behavior in tourism: the changes brought by Web 2.0

Technology has been regarded as one of the factors with major impact on tourism consumer behavior especially in information search, purchase and sharing opinion and experiences (Cohen et al 2014). With the development of new Web technologies, customers were put in the focus of tourism companies' business activities. As the Web became more participatory oriented it had significant influence on the profile, expectations and decision-making process among travelers while the tourism and hospitality enterprises were forced to adopt new technologies and adapt their business models to the online environment (Sigala 2011). The emergence of online travel-related content caused significant changes in how travelers search for information and make holiday reservations. According to the World Tourism Organization report (WTO 2014) consumers visit on average almost 14 different travel-related sites and conduct nine travel-related searches on search engines before making the actual hotel reservation. In making this decision they use official hotel classifications as a filter mechanism and at the end they consult online guest reviews to make the final choice. Considering the importance of online guest reviews, the WTO has proposed an integrative approach of incorporating guest reviews in the hotel classifications systems considering their qualitative contribution in classification process (WTO 2014).

Taking into consideration the intangible nature of tourism products, the personal experience of other people or word-of-mouth (WOM) has tremendous impact on travel decision making. With the development of new technologies and rise of awareness among users, business properties are being faced with "content democracy" where everyone, whether personally or anonymously, is able to publish their view or share their media content on social media. In this new context, traditional WOM (word of mouth) was transformed into eWOM (electronic word of mouth) defined as "all informal communications directed at consumers through Internet-based technology related to the usage of characteristics of particular goods and services, or their sellers" (Litvin et al 2008: 461). The main characteristics of eWOM are information communicated via the Internet to the multiple individuals/consumers, which remain available over a long time and are mainly anonymous (Hennig-Thurau et al. 2004). In this communication both business to customer and customer to customer aspects can be included.

Sharing opinions online represents a generational shift and revolution in terms of attitudes towards privacy and sharing, which raises special issues for hotels and travel agencies. Stories and narratives presented by consumers provide a reliable information source when making travel purchasing decisions. Customers have the same potential and authority as tourism marketers, by taking control and framing descriptions within their personal experiences (Pan and Fesenmaier 2006). They now have instant online access to information about these properties by reading reviews coming directly from the customers who had the opportunity to experience the product or service. Considering the potential broader impact of eWOM, which may go far beyond the users' life and country borders (Yoo and Gretzel 2011), it is inevitable for tourism business properties to put more attention on published online content, including not only those found on the web platforms which are under their control, but also on all other social media channels. Therefore, constant content monitoring will be of great importance for their future business success and reputation.

Online travel sites: new communication environment and effects of online travel reviews

With the development of new technologies and widespread access to the Internet on different computing devices, people are engaging more in social networking in the virtual world. In this way new virtual or online communities were being shaped, becoming one of the most frequently visited applications in the online space. These social networking sites, like any other social community, have numerous functions with user-generated recommendations and reviews based on experience of others being the major ones (Chung and Buhalis, 2008). People are participating in online travel communities driven by functional, social, psychological and hedonic needs (Wang and Fesenmaier, 2004). In order to fulfill their functional needs, online travel users join online communities to look for and browse information they need in the travel decision-making process. As for social needs, people gather in order to communicate with other members and to build relationships, while in terms of psychological needs community becomes a part of a user's life where he/she actively gets involved in creating content and building new forms of communications and relationships. Finally, people are engaging with online travel communities for enjoyment and fun, in other words for hedonic reasons.

In their work Yoo and Gretzel (2011) provided a detailed review of the literature on what are the factors and reasons for people to generate their own content on online travel communities' web sites. They confirmed the current knowledge of altruistic and hedonic motives to be important motivators for content generation, while lack of interest and time are seen as the barriers. Besides current knowledge that different socio-demographic factors (age, gender, income, education level etc.) and culture affect the UGC creation, these authors contributed by adding traveler's personality traits as important determinants of active production in travel related content.

There are three ways in how people may get engaged with UGC (Yoo and Gretzel, 2011). The first one is consuming or browsing the content by simply watching and reading without any personal contribution. The second one includes mere content production or participation which may include interaction between user-to-user or user-to-content such as commenting on current posts, sharing, liking, voting etc. However, this type of user cannot be considered as a content creator but rather as a content contributor. Finally, people may be dealing with UGC as content producers who are actively involved in content creation by posting their own reviews, text, videos, answering to other users' questions or engaging in online social interaction.

In the context of travel UGC, using and creating travel reviews is being viewed as one of the most popular UGC activities (Gretzel, Yoo and Purifoy, 2007). Travel reviews allow customers to share their own personal experience which is shaped into a unique information source on a wide variety of topics regarding accommodation, destination, restaurants, tour operators, local people – in a word, everything a person may find important or interesting to share. Previous research has shown that user-generated content is being perceived by other customers as highly reliable and trustworthy (Dickinger, 2011). One of the explanations for this may be the belief that customers who have experienced a certain product or service will present and evaluate product more honestly than the producer or service provider, who can potentially hide the negative aspects of product/service (Park, Lee & Han, 2007). Therefore, it is not surprising that many travel-related web sites such as those of online travel agencies, hotels, destination management organization, restaurants etc. are changing their web site structure in order to be more user responsive and appropriate for the generation of customers' online reviews.

Authors of online reviews are likely to express themselves in a good, believable and 'not to blame' way (Sparks and Browning, 2010). Due to the non-commercial nature of online reviews, there is an element of trust occurring after a service failure event (Hart and Blackshaw, 2005). Accordingly, if someone expresses dissatisfaction with the product or service encountered, this will take the form of negative eWOM which may significantly affect a company's reputation and purchasing decisions. Different social media channels provide guests with the opportunity to express their dissatisfaction when there is no opportunity to do that at the service point. This dissatisfaction is being articulated in the form of negative reviews on one of the numerous travel web sites such as TripAdvisor, HolidayCheck, Zoover, TopHotel.ru etc. Sparks and Browning (2010) found in their research that even what one hotel finds as a small and insignificant failure, may result in an online review stating that not only will the writer of the review not consider coming back to the hotel but that they also warn others to not repeat the same mistake.

In their research Spark and Browning (2010) also looked at structure and form of online complaints based on the narrative analysis principles by Labov (in Spark and Browning, 2010). This approach involved drawing upon the analysis of stories which can be constructed around six key elements: abstract, orientation, complicating action, evaluation, resolution and coda. According to Spark and Browning, the online complaints did not contain the abstract since these are relatively short texts. However, an orientation element was found due to the fact that in most of the online reviews there was a contextual statement about the reasons for going on a trip and choosing the specific hotel. The event or situation that caused the complaint was always present as well. As for the evaluative component, most of the complaint writers were giving their own personal opinions about star ratings, expressions with strong emotions etc. There is often an expression of some action done by the review writer or hotel staff concluding with the return to present in terms of whether one thinks of coming back to this hotel or not or warning others about it. This storytelling pattern, which can be observed in online complaints, has the potential to really catch the reader's attention who gets potentially drawn into the story and is able to understand the whole context that brought the complaint in the first place. That is why it is seen as a powerful weapon in projecting negative images of a hotel which can remain in the mind of the reader for a longer period (Spark & Browning, 2010). Therefore, it is necessary for hotels to develop necessary strategies to manage these online reviews in a more proactive manner. Dijkmans, Kerkhof and

Beukeboom (2015) saw social media as "stage to engage" in order to enhance trustworthiness, brand awareness and commitment with customers. These activities are all encompassed in the term online reputation management.

Online reputation management

Reputation has been defined as the "perceptual representation of a company's past actions and future prospects that describe the firm's overall appeal to all its key constituents when compared to other leading rivals" (Fombrun, 1996: 72). According to Lang, Lee and Dai (2011), three dominant dimensions of reputation are: degree of awareness that customer holds, perceived representation of the company and generalized favorability which sees reputation as socially constructed and accepted concept.

Reputation management is a vital strategic issue for those companies that mainly rely on their intangible attributes in building competitiveness such as creativity, innovation, intellectual capital and high levels of services (Kay, 2004). Accordingly, the hotel industry is highly dependent on the positive reputation that may affect customers' purchasing decisions. With the rise of eWOM, a new genre in terms of providing answers to online reviews from the business perspective appeared. These are known as "web care," "customer care," "online reputation management" or "service recovery" in case an online review contains elements of complaint about the provided service (Zhang & Vasquez, 2014). When it comes to the hotel business, reputation management usually addresses the proper use and proactive dealing with the content shared on travel review sites (TripAdvisor, HolidayCheck, Zoover, TopHotels etc.),

The emergence of user-generated content has provided a new perspective for reputation management, which, in the online environment, is being considered as a more dynamic process. Social media has offered a revolution in this area since nowadays reputation is not considered only as an intangible asset related to performance but also a platform for successful management of the reputation. As Baka (2016) states, user-generated content is challenging the current reputation management strategies where TripAdvisor is representing one of the most powerful platforms for the reputation battle. What started as only a numerical rating system on the TripAdvisor platform, with a content generation feature in the form of multimedia (text, photo and video, etc.), has revolutionized the way people share their travel experience, the level of control which hotel property has (or hasn't) over the content being provided as well as the changing tourist pre- and post-purchase behavior (information seeking, sharing opinions, complaining etc.). TripAdvisor is more than an additional marketing channel; it throws hoteliers into a dynamic process of "reputation building and rebuilding" (Baka, 2016: 154) as exposure to online reviews from this web site increases awareness of a given hotel among customers (Vermeulen and Seegers, 2009).

In her research study, Baka (2016) proposed a conceptual model to manage online reputation in the new technology era where hotels systematically redefine their strategies and practices. According to this concept, which represents a combination of theoretical and practical knowledge, reputation is being seen as cyclical process which includes following manageable moments (Baka, 2016: 156–157):

- identification of all the relevant reputation management tools such as Google Analytics, ReviewPro etc. as well as what are the most critical online travel review sites (TripAdvisor, HolidayCheck, TopHotels.ru and similar);
- following changes in terms of ranking and listings over time for better monitoring of online reputation management actions;

- defining the publication reach of user-generated content which is easily visible to both hotel owners and users on travel sites such as TripAdvisor;
- benchmarking from other competitors' performance;
- reviewing ranking methodologies of content generated on travel web sites; and
- increasing reputational scores by providing exceptional service and encouraging people to share their positive experience.

Responses to online reviews posted on TripAdvisor were also in the focus of the work of Zhang and Vasquez (2014) especially their structure when it comes to answering customers complaints. They started from the point that online travel reviews and responses to the same represent genres chains of inter-textually connected computer-mediated communication (Swales, 2004). In this study the authors tried to examine the responses to hotel online reviews left on TripAdvisor from a discourse perspective by conducting top-down analysis of rhetorical moves which are the most common in these types of online communication. A typical sequence of moves that occurs in many hotel responses is shown in Figure 38.1.

The biggest variation between answers to online reviews is the degree to which they refer back to customer's review and the extent to which they are dealing and providing detailed explanations to the issue raised in reviews. The biggest shortage is in terms of repeating the same response patterns showing a lack of management's specific approach to answering customers' reviews. The reason for this may lie in: management's desire for prompt answering, standardization of responses, uncertainty with language use (poor grammar, language proficiency), waiting for more positive online reviews to come so that the negative ones gets pushed down or maybe the management is aware of the problem addressed in review but they are intentionally avoiding to address it in their response.

Creelman (2015) also put emphasis on the great responsibility and challenge placed on people who provide responses to online reviews as their answers will have a wide impact, reciprocal to that of the original online review. This dialogue between review writer and hotel management will include more than just information and perspective exchange, but it will also affect the customer's perception of corporate brand, identity, reputation, loyalty, trust and similar.

Useful tips for getting the most from online review responses

In the following section, short guidelines about how to conceptualize and write the most effective online review responses from a hotel management side is provided. It was derived as a summary

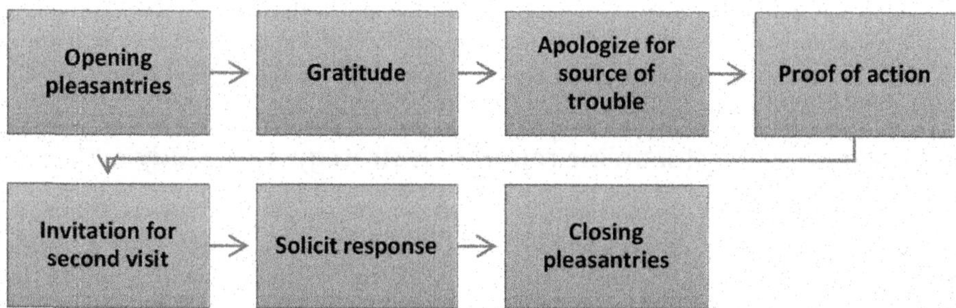

Figure 38.1 Typical sequence of rhetorical moves that occur in hotel responses to negative reviews

of papers found in the academic literature (Ajanovic and Çizel, 2015; Baka, 2016; Zhang and Vasquez, 2014) and advice from experts in the field which may be found on numerous web sites related to successful hotel online marketing (www.ehotelier.com, www.reviewpro.com, www.tripadvisor.com, www.trustyou.com, etc.).

- To be able to write an effective online review response, first the online reputation management practices should become part of the company's business strategy. All the technology developments should be followed with great care, with empowerment and necessary knowledge provided for all hotel staff.
- Before starting involvment in online reputation management the hotel property management should be convinced that the decision of entering into social media marketing and management is the right one. There are numerous examples of hotel and travel agencies that opened accounts on some of the social media channels and then realized they do not have enough time or resources to preserve the presence on these platforms, they do not interact enough with customers and do not keep pace with Web developments and new customer behavioral patterns on social media.
- The best practices should be drafted and documented ensuring that the person who is responsible for handling responses on travel online reviews is the best representative of the hotel, working in its best interest. Marketing messages found in the highlights of the online review response should be conceptualized according to the property's business strategy, it should be brand-aligned and presented in a manner that builds consumer confidence.
- When writing the response to online reviews one must bear in mind that the nature of the online communication excludes non-verbal cues which are often used in offline communication. Therefore, great emphasis should be placed on the selection of appropriate words and expressions in order to avoid potential misunderstandings.
- Responses should be empathy-driven concentrating on the issues in the review. Accordingly, answers which suggest necessary remedies or offer an apology should be provided. The major problem with hotel management responses is that they use common patterns which constantly repeat, regardless of what is written in the original online review. These common patterns show that the hotel does not pay full attention to the original content provided by the customers, that expressions of gratitude and apology are not sincere, which results in the perception of hotel as highly unprofessional.
- It is necessary to encourage people to share their experiences online, even more if these are the positive ones.
- It is not advisable to attack or argue with customers in review responses, no matter the writing style or facts presented in the online review. Instead, a polite answer stating the opposite opinion can potentially leave a much better impression. In the case of a false review, such as a suspicious one on a travel review site such as TripAdvisor, the hotel has the option to report and prove the invalidity of the online reviews posted online by the customers.

What makes a successful online reputation strategy: case study

Ajanovic and Çizel (2015) conducted research in order to find out what are the elements of successful online reputation management. In total, 364 travel reviews followed by management response posted on the TripAdvisor page of one of highly rated hotels in Los Angeles were analyzed and the result showed that the success lies in the presences of the following elements: unique content creation, personalization, emphasis on property values and dealing with negative reviews.

Creating unique content: By referring to the content generated directly from the customer in their response, hotel management will be in possession of unique and organic content about their property. In the online era this is very useful for search engine optimization or SEO efforts which means higher ranking on searching engines such as Google, Yahoo, Yandex etc. In addition, repeating the positive eWOM in management responses allows the use of unique and reliable promotional material. In the case of the renovating hotel, content coming directly from the customers was being used to successfully deal with the transition process by reassuring them there was a continuity of quality service provision across the renovation period.

Personalization: Polite greetings using the TripAdvisor user's name, expressions of gratitude, organizing the response in a way that it contains highlights of the hotel stay mentioned by the guest in the review are some examples of management's efforts to address each customer's review separately. By reading a management response on TripAdvisor it can be easily noted when a review was coming from a loyal guest because the reply was filled with special warmth going beyond a simple reply to a positive review.

Emphasizing property values: Hotel management used every opportunity to refer to the hotel's properties and features wherever it was appropriate. Paying attention to small details in the review and emphasizing them in the response leaves the reader with the promise of providing a supreme service. Additionally, special emphasis was put on the quality of intangible assets such as hotel staff.

Dealing with negative reviews: In the response to one case there was clear encouragement for guest review writers to share their negative experiences with the hotel so that a maximum quality service performance could be obtained. When service failure occurs, a thorough notification of all the responsible departments was being expressed in the management responses with personal assistance offered on future visits by the person who wrote the response.

By analyzing the hotel responses of successful hotels on online travel review sites such as TripAdvisor it can be noticed that these high rankings and ratings are the product of great concern about conducting a successful online reputation strategy which should combine efforts to strengthen brand awareness, increase customer care and satisfaction, deal with complaints and proactively react to new technological developments in order to meet the needs of customers.

Conclusion

In the new generation of Internet evolution we are already talking about Web 3.0 or the Semantic Web which is based on the computer's ability to gather, recognize and generate new information, enabling machine-to-machine interaction (Mistilis and Buhalis, 2012). The basis of Web 3.0 will be the integration of massive data sets into useful information that will be delivered by intelligent agents – software programs which are able to follow users' interaction with the Web, collect the data based on this interaction and perform certain tasks on behalf of the user (Morris, 2011; Rudman & Bruwer, 2016). In the future this will have a tremendous impact on tourism and hospitality businesses and consumer behavioral patterns in tourism especially in terms of information searches. Not only will it save the time and effort of performing repeated searches but these new Semantic Web software agents will present search results meaningful to the user, based on their defined online preferences and previous interactions in the online environment. However, the necessity to present meaningful content in these sophisticated search results will still be of great importance and the level of its persuasiveness can affect the success of the online user-generated content whether it is customer-to-customer or business-to-customer oriented. Thus, special emphasis should be placed on online reviews and management responses left on one of the travel recommendation sites, as these communication tracks will also be in the pool of massive data sets which will be combined and presented to future users according to their preferences.

The main aim of this chapter was to show the importance of online reviews and the necessity for hotel management to provide well conceptualized and meaningful responses to these. Although the importance of user-generated content in the form of online reviews is well understood and accepted in the hospitality sector, a systematic approach towards successful review management is still not fully established. This can be noticed in the lack of academic and empirical research on these concepts followed by diverse and general information on the topic all over the Internet. Hotel management should take a more proactive and systematic approach towards studying and analyzing user-generated content, especially online reviews, since these are potentially significant information sources to be used in future successful marketing management.

First of all, online reviews should not be observed as obstacles but more as valuable data sources. These data may be used to improve the communication with previous and potential customers, strengthen the company's brand and improve guests' loyalty. In addition, by obtaining information about service failure or service excellence, management will be aware of the aspects of service which are functioning well or the gaps in service provision that need improvement.

Second, it is not only about writing responses but it is more about extracting and analyzing the information patterns coming from guests' reviews. By following and using the physical and service-related measures, necessary changes should be generated and this readiness to change should be reflected in the management response.

Finally, most of the hotel staff (except those directly answering hotel reviews) are excluded from the online reputation management process. Appropriate training for hotel staff should be provided as they can be used as powerful tools in building and protecting the hotel's reputation. For instance, in terms of service delivery failure, in most cases hotel staff may understand the guest's problems but do not have the necessary training, empowerment or support from the supervisor. Therefore, the successful online reputation strategy should involve the whole hotel staff and the responses should be broadcasted throughout the whole hotel in order to ensure that employees are aligned toward meeting guests' expectations in the present and in the future.

References

Ajanovic, E. & Çizel, B. (2015) "What makes a successful hotel reputation management strategy: qualitative research on TripAdvisor hotel reviews," *SITCON 2015 – Conference Proceedings*, Singidunum International Tourism Conference, pp. 182–6.

Baka, V. (2016) "The becoming of the user-generated reviews: Looking at the past to understand the future of managing reputation in the travel sector," *Tourism Management* 53, 148–62.

Buhalis, D. & Law, R. (2008) "Progress İn İnformation Technology And Tourism Management: 20 Years On And 10 Years After The Internet – The State Of E-tourism Research," *Tourism Management* 29 (4), 609–23.

Chung, J., Y. & Buhalis, D. (2008) "*Web 2.0: A Study Of Online Travel Community*," in P. O'Connor, W. Höpken & U. Gretzel (eds), *Information and Communication Technologies in Tourism*, Vienna, Austria: Springer-Verlag Wien, 70–81.

Cohen, S., A., Prayag, G. & Moital, M. (2014) "Consumer Behavior In Tourism: Concepts, Influence And Opportunities," *Current Issues in Tourism* 17 (10), 872–909.

Creelman, V. (2015). "Sheer Outrage: Negotiating Customer Dissatisfaction and Interaction in the Blogosphere," in Erica Darics, *Digital Business Discourse,* London, UK: Palgrave-Macmillan, 160–85.

Dickinger, A. (2011) "The Trustworthiness of Online Channels For Experience and Goal- Directed Search Tasks," *Journal of Travel Research* 50 (4), 378–91.

Dijkmans, C., Kerkhof, P. & Beukeboom, C.J. (2015) "A Stage to Engage: Social Media Use and Corporate Reputation," *Tourism Management* 4, 58–67.

Fombrun, C.J. (1996) *Reputation: Realizing Value from The Corporate Image.* Harvard Business School Press.

Gretzel, U., Yoo, K.H. & Purifoy, M. (2007) *Online Travel Review Study: Role and Impact Of Online Travel Reviews.* Laboratory for Intelligent Systems in Tourism, Texas A&M University.

Hart, C. & Blackshaw, P. (2006) "Internet Inferno," *Marketing Management* 15, 18–25.
Hennig-Thurau, T., Gwinner, K.P., Walsh, G. & Gremler, D.D. (2004). "Electronic word of mouth via consumer opinion platforms: What motivates consumers to articulate themselves on the internet?" *Journal of Interactive Marketing* 18 (1), 38–52.
Kay, J. (2004). *The truth about markets: why some nations are rich but most remain poor.* London: Penguin.
Lang, D., Lee, P.M. & Dai, Y. (2011). "Organizational reputation: a review," *Journal of Management* 37, 153–84.
Labov, W. (1997). "Some further steps in narrative analysis," *Journal of Narrative & Life History* 7 (1–4), 395–415.
Leung, D., Law, R., van Hoof, H. & Buhalis, D. (2013). "Social Media in Tourism and Hospitality: A Literature Review," *Journal of Travel & Tourism Marketing* 30, 3–22.
Litvin, S.W., Goldsmith, R.E. & Pan, B. (2008). "Electronic Word-of-Mouth in Hospitality and Tourism Management," *Tourism Management* 29 (3), 458–68.
Mistilis, N. & Buhalis, D. (2012). "Challenges and potential of the Semantic Web for tourism," *e-Review of Tourism Research (eRTR)* 10 (2), 51–5.
Morris, R.D. (2011). "Web 3.0: implications for online learning," *TechTrends* 55 (1), 42–6.
Murugesan, S. (2010). *Web X.O: A Road Map. Handbook of Research on Web 2.0, 3.0and X.O: Technologies, Business and Social Applications,* Information Science Reference.
O'Reilly, T. (2007). "What is Web 2.0: design patterns and business models for the next generation of software," *Communications & Strategies* 1, 17–37.
Pan, B. & Crotts, J. (2012). "Theoretical models of social media, marketing implications, and future research directions," in Sigala, M., Christou, E. & Gretzel, U. (eds). *Social Media in Travel, Tourism and Hospitality: Theory, Practice and Cases* (pp. 73–86). Surrey, UK: Ashgate.
Pan, B. & Fesenmaier, D. (2006). "Online information search, Vacation planning process," *Annals of Tourism Research* 33 (3), 809–32.
Park, D.H., Lee, J. & Han, I. (2007). "*The Effect of On-Line Consumer Reviews on Consumer Purchasing Intention: The Moderating Role of Involvement,*" *International Journal Of Electronic Commerce* 11 (4), 125–48.
Rudman, R.J. (2010). "Incremental negative impacts in Web 2.0 applications," *The Electronic Library* 28 (2), 210–30.
Rudman, R. & Bruwer, R. (2016). "Defining Web 3.0: opportunities and challenges," *The Electronic Library* 34 (1), 132–54.
Sigala, M. (2011). "Preface Special Issue on Web 2.0 in travel and tourism: Empowering and changing the role of travelers," *Computers in Human Behavior 27 (2)*, 607–8.
Sparks, B.A. & Browning, V. (2010). "Complaining in the cyberspace: The motives and forms of hotel guests' complain online," *Journal of Hospitality Marketing and Management* 19 (7), 797–818.
Swales, J. (2004). "Research Genres: Explorations and Applications," in Zhang, Y. & Vasquez, C. (2014). "Hotels' responses to online reviews: Managing consumer dissatisfaction," *Discourse, Context and Media* 6, 54–64.
Vermeulen, I.E. & Seegers, D. (2009). Tried and tested: the impact of online hotel reviews on consumer consideration. *Tourism Management*, 30, 123–127.
Wang, Y.C. & Fesenmaier, D. (2004). "Towards understanding members' general participation in and active contribution to an online travel community," *Tourism Management* 25 (6), 709–22.
World Tourism Organization (2014). *Online Guest Reviews and Hotel Classification Systems – An Integrated Approach*, UNWTO, Madrid.
Xiang, Z. & Gretzel, U. (2010). "Role of social media in online travel information search," *Tourism Management* 31 (2), 179–88.
Yoo, K.H. & Gretzel, U. (2011). "Influence of personality on travel-related consumer-generated media creation," *Computers in Human Behavior* 27 (2), 609–21.
Zhang, Y. & Vasquez, C. (2014). "Hotels' responses to online reviews: Managing consumer dissatisfaction," *Discourse, Context and Media* 6, 54–64.

Internet sources

www.customer-alliance.com/en/articles/hotel-reputation-management/
https://ehotelier.com/insights/2015/11/23/top-tips-for-successful-online-reputation-management-of-independent-hotels/

www.tripadvisor.com
www.trustyou.com/
www.reviewpro.com

Further reading

Ayeh, J.K., Au, N. & Law, R. (2013). "'Do we believe in TripAdvisor?' examining credibility perceptions and online travelers' attitude toward using user-generated content," *Journal of Travel Research* 52 (4), 1–16. (Trust in online travel communities.)

Bergh, D.D., Ketchen, D.J., Boyd, B.K. & Bergh, J. (2010). "New frontiers of the reputation – performance relationship: insights from multiple theories," *Journal of Management* 36, 620–32. (More infromation on reputation management.)

Doh, S.-J. & Hwang, J.S. (2009). "How consumers evaluate eWOM (electronic word-of-mouth) messages," *Cyberpsychology & Behavior* 12 (2), 193–7. (More on eWOM.)

Filieri, R. (2015). "Why do travelers trust TripAdvisor? antecedents of trust towards consumer-generated media and its influence on recommendation adoption and word of mouth," *Tourism Management,* 51, 174–85. (Trust in user-generated content.)

Tsao, W., Hsieh, M., Shih, L. & Lin, T.M.Y. (2015). "Compliance with eWOM: The influence of hotel reviews on booking intention from the perspective of consumer conformity," *International Journal of Hospitality Management* 46, 99–111. (Effects of eWOM.)

39

Destination marketing

Approaches to improve productivity in an era of technology disruption

Yinghua Huang

Introduction

Destination marketers and tourism researchers constantly seek ways to improve marketing productivity in order to gain competitiveness in the global tourism market (Li & Wang, 2010; Soteriades, 2012). The concept of productivity consists of two elements: effectiveness (doing the right things) and efficiency (doing things right) (Sheth & Sisodia, 2002). On the one hand, the effectiveness of a marketing campaign depends on identifying the best strategy among all possible strategies to maximize the long-run profitability (Keh et al., 2006). On the other hand, the question of efficiency focuses on optimizing the allocation of resources across alternative use (Achabal et al., 1984). When both high effectiveness and high efficiency are achieved, a destination marketing campaign is considered productive, which results in a satisfying tourism experience, loyal travelers, and low marketing costs (Soteriades, 2012; Song & Liu, 2017).

In the past twenty years, rapid developments in information and communication technologies (ICTs) have not only dramatically transformed the traveler's behavior, but also changed the landscape of destination marketing (Buhalis & Wagner, 2013; Xiang & Fesenmaier, 2017). The disruptive innovations of social media, smartphones, wearable devices, virtual reality (VR), augmented reality (AR), and the internet of things (IoTs), enable today's travelers to search, generate, and share information and knowledge through all the stages of tourism consumption. Travelers are looking for seamless interactive communication through multiple marketing channels at anytime and anywhere (Buhalis & Foerste, 2014; Buhalis & Amaranggana, 2015). A numerous amount of information about travelers' destination experiences, known as tourism "big data," were generated and captured by various devices, sensors, and systems. Latest studies and practices have indicated that big data is a valuable resource for extracting business insights and gaining market competitiveness (McGuire et al., 2012). In this regard, the widespread adoption of ICTs and changes of traveler behaviors require the destination marketing organizations (DMOs) to adopt new approaches and techniques to improve marketing effectiveness and efficiency.

This chapter synthesizes existing literature and discusses how DMOs can improve their marketing productivity in an era of technology disruption. In particular, the analysis focuses on three innovative approaches – big data analytics (BDA), social-context-mobile (SoCoMo) marketing, and virtual reality/augmented reality marketing – and their advantages. The following sections also present relevant literature and real-world cases to illustrate the application of each approach in destination marketing. The conclusion discusses some open issues and future directions for improving marketing productivity.

Big data analytics and destination marketing productivity

In 2001, Laney outlined three characteristics of big data: volume (massive amount of data), velocity (high speed of data spreading throughout networks), and variety (diverse data types and sources). In 2012, Beyer and Laney updated the previous definition by adding another "V": veracity (sense of truthfulness and accuracy). More recently, additional Vs such as value, virality, visualization, validity, and variability, were also proposed to describe the concept of big data (Owais & Hussein, 2016). After synthesizing the common themes of existing definitions, De Mauro et al. (2015) provided a consensual definition of big data, saying it "represents the information assets characterized by such a high volume, velocity and variety to require specific technology and analytical methods for its transformation into value" (p. 103).

In tourism domain, massive information is generated and collected through the entire process of tourism consumption. Hashem et al. (2015) identified five sources of big data: the web and social media, machine-generated data, sensing devices, transaction data, and IoT. Examples of tourism big data include user-generated content (UGC) from social media websites such as TripAdvisor and Travelocity, tourism website traffic data, mobile location data, databases of tourism-related transactions (e.g., flight purchase, hotel reservation, etc.), and sensing data captured by the IoT network. The structured and unstructured information ranging from terabytes to many exabytes requires advanced technologies to analyze and visualize the data (Scharl et al., 2017; Song & Liu, 2017). Because tourism big data depicts the complex decision-making process of tourism consumption, BDA will help destination marketers to understand consumer behaviors better and improve marketing productivity.

BDA uncovers patterns and correlations in big data using analysis algorithms that demand powerful supporting platforms (Hu et al., 2014). Tourism researchers suggest that big data analytics can enhance our capabilities to "understand the consumer market at unprecedented scale, scope and depth" (Xiang & Fesenmaier, 2017, p. 303). The benefits of BDA include cheaper and faster data processing, supporting a better decision-making process, developing new products and services, and managing real-time customer relationships (Davenport, 2013). Compared to traditional marketing analytics, the BDA approach has advantages in improving marketing productivity for several reasons.

First, BDA ensures higher reliability than traditional marketing research methods. When interconnecting all available information sources together, BDA provides a more comprehensive and holistic view of the decision-making process. The traditional research methods often use survey data and take samples from the population as a whole, which would suffer measurement errors due to recall ability, cognitive overload, or sampling bias. In contrast, BDA gathers and investigates more behavioral data about tourist's real actions rather than stated intention or answers to questionnaires (Song & Liu, 2017). The high volumes of big data increased the sample base for analysis and reduced the risk of information loss (Meeker & Hong, 2014).

Second, BDA enhances "now-casting" with real-time dynamic data, which helps marketers to quickly understand consumers' contemporaneous activities (Song & Liu, 2017; Fuchs et al., 2014). BDA involves sophisticated algorithms dealing with dynamic datasets about traveler's activities so that the marketers can draw useful insights and implement real-time customer relationship management. For example, BDA enables real-time processing of sentiments regarding tourism experiences from social media. This allows destination marketers to become more efficient in grasping travelers' opinions and respond to their needs almost instantly (Scharl et al., 2017).

Third, BDA includes machine learning techniques that enable the business intelligence system to continuously learn and apply the analysis to a higher quality level. Unlike traditional marketing analytics, the power of machine learning thrives with growing datasets. Machine learning is a branch of artificial intelligence with a capability of learning from data automatically (Berger & Doban, 2014). The more data received by a machine learning system, the better insights can be drawn. Therefore, machine learning empowers the destination marketers to process massive data faster and constantly improve the accuracy of data analytics.

Applications of big data analytics in destination marketing

Given the advantages of BDA and the information-intensive nature of tourism, more and more DMOs and hospitality service providers have started to use BDA for the decision-making process. Machine learning and data mining techniques play important roles in the application of BDA (Berger & Doban, 2014; Ducange et al., 2017). In tourism literature, a variety of big data techniques has been applied to investigate destination marketing issues, including text mining, sentiment analysis, natural language processing, user profiling and localization, network analysis, and visual analysis. Table 39.1 lists several recent studies of big data analytics in destination marketing.

The tourism literature indicates that BDA can help to improve destination marketing productivity in many ways (Költringer & Dickinger, 2015; Xiang & Fesenmaier, 2017). For example, the user-generated content on social media is the richest and most diverse online data source for big data analytics (Lu & Stepchenkova, 2015). A number of studies have examined the UGC data for understanding destination images and tourists' behavior (Marine-Roig & Clavé, 2015a, 2015b). Költringer & Dickinger (2015) adopted content mining techniques to examine the UGC data, news media websites, and DMO websites for the city of Vienna, Austria. They found that the destination image revealed in the UGC data does not necessarily match the branding messages communicated by DMO websites. Since the BDA approach integrates multiple data sources together, it enables the destination marketers to identify gaps between their image projection strategies and tourists' actual perceptions. In this regard, DMOs can streamline their communication efforts across different platforms and react to travelers' comments more effectively. Beside review threads, the UGC data also includes other forms like photos, videos, emoticons, images, and so on. BDA can also be used to explore these nonverbal forms of UGC. Paldino et al. (2015) studied more than 90 million photographs available online to investigate how people experience the place. Using content mining techniques, Paldino et al. (2015) characterized touristic activity within a destination, which can help DMOs to improve tourism attractions.

In industry practices, many companies such as IBM, Google, Expedia, TripAdvisor, and Amadeus, have developed BDA tools and platforms for destination marketing. For example, IBM is using Watson's cognitive computing technology to help marketers of destinations and hospitality companies. Cognitive computing is the third era of computing; which involves robust self-learning systems that mimic how the human brain works. The cognitive analytics can learn new knowledge at scale, and interact with people in natural language. The IBM Watson makes it possible to simplify and refine personalized travel recommendations based on a variety of factors including location, budget, traveler profile, web history, and past travel transactions. Destination marketers have benefited from this new computing technology. For instance, Lanzarote, a small island in West Africa, worked closely with IBM to develop a cognitive app to

Table 39.1 Recent studies of big data analytics in destination marketing

Article	*Data sources*	*Analytical methods*	*Subject destination*	*Marketing implications*
Scharl et al. (2017)	Website and online newspapers	Sentiment analysis Visual analytics	Scandinavian capitals	Using visual tools and tourism intelligence system can help DMOs monitor and benchmark destination brands.
Baggio & Scaglione (2017)	Passive mobile positioning data	Network analysis	Fribourg, Switzerland	The study examines the real spatial movement patterns of travelers in a destination.
Költringer & Dickinger(2015)	UGC, news media websites, DMO websites	Content mining, keyword analysis, sentiment analysis	Vienna, Austria	Web content mining offers useful insights into brand identity and image perceptions for destinations.
Sun et al. (2015)	IoT data from personal sensors, open data, and participatory sensing	Generic Enablers, Hadoop	Trento, Italy	Personalized service and promotions can be offered to users through a context-aware recommendation system.
Marine-Roig & Clavé (2015a)	UGC	Content mining	Barcelona	Massive UGC data analytics reveals the image of a destination, and provide insights concerning destination management issues.
Paldino et al. (2015)	Online geotagged photographs	Content mining	Cities around the world	Analyzing massive photographs helps to characterize touristic activity within a destination and informs tourism product development.
Fuchs et al. (2014)	Customer behavior data, customer perception and experience data, and economic performance data	Online analytical processing analysis	Sweden	Using real-time business intelligence such as a destination management information system can help the destination marketers to gain real-time knowledge on tourists' behavior.
Heerschap et al. (2014)	Mobile phone data	Data visualization	Netherlands	The study makes it possible to distinguish flows of tourists within a destination.

provide information for both visitors and marketing agents. The app is trained to diagnose and resolve common questions visitors ask in near real-time so that marketing agents can focus on more complex issues. For a visitor to Lanzarote, the app serves as a personal guide that adapts to individual tastes based on personal profile analysis. The more the app is used, the more Watson can personalize the recommendations to a tourist. In this way, Lanzarote gets to understand the traveler's behavior better, provide customer-centric experience, and therefore improve traveler satisfaction.

Besides big technology companies, many startup firms specialized in tourism big data analytics, including TCI research, Mabrian, InAtlas, Nsight, have been established in recent years. These startup firms focus on analyzing big data in the tourism and hospitality sector and have helped DMOs to improve marketing productivity. For example, TCI research, a Belgium-based company, is the first UNWTO awarded agency fully specializing in data-driven tourism research and destination rating. The company combines the advantages of traditional and big data analysis to help destinations of all sizes to understand travelers' opinions and desires better. The company received UNWTO award for innovation in 2011 and is currently providing services to over 80 DMOs around the world. Another good example is Mabrian, a small Spanish company providing comprehensive analytics service for the travel industry. The Cuban government is currently using Mabrian's BDA platform to monitor the performance of its lodging and tourism facilities, tracking all social media sentiments about the major tourist attractions, collecting all discussions of Cuba and other destination competitors in social networks, and categorizing and segmenting all that information (Valerio, 2015).

SoCoMo marketing for tourism destinations

Thanks to the advances in big data analytics and ICTs, today's marketers can integrate context-aware technologies and social media in smartphones for improving marketing efficiency and effectiveness. The buzzword "SoCoMo marketing" was created to describe the advanced approach of context marketing (Co) on mobile devices (Mo) which "facilitates the creation of social media (So) empowered context-aware offers and information" (Buhalis & Foerste, 2014, p. 176). Context, here, includes any information about users' circumstances that might affect their consumption choices, such as the time of day, date, weather, and location (Lamsfus et al., 2010). Buhalis and Foerste (2014; 2015) proposed a conceptual framework to explain the key characteristics of SoCoMo marketing and its implications for tourism, which the following paragraphs summarize.

SoCoMo marketing is based on in-depth BDA about the consumer. The social media, context-based, and smart mobile devices are used to collect detailed information about travelers. There are three main information sources:

1 Social media platforms such as blogs and social networks. A traveler may reveal his or her likes, personal history, needs, or wishes on social media. Destination marketers can use these data to design personalized tourism products matching individuals' preferences.
2 Sensors embedded in mobile devices can collect information within the context of a traveler's external context. The contextual information may include weather, traffic, location, time, temperature, and so on. For example, smartphones' global positioning systems can help to track a traveler's location, so that marketers may provide relevant information about the nearby environment.
3 The mobile device can document information related to user behavior and personal preferences, including mobile usage, language preference, usage frequency, timing, and so on.

By bringing all these information sources together, SoCoMo marketing enables destination marketers to use BDA to draw a comprehensive picture of the traveler and the person's real-time situation (Buhalis & Foerste, 2015).

Another advantage of SoCoMo marketing is that it is an advanced form of context marketing, which makes it possible to contact a potential customer at the right time with the right marketing message and product through the right channel (Zhao & Balagué, 2017). Understanding the consumer's needs and the current situation is a key to the success of SoCoMo marketing. Previous research has shown that such context can influence consumers' decision-making process (Liu & Fan, 2013; Lamsfus et al., 2015). Buhalis and Foerste (2014) categorized contextual information into internal and external contexts. The former is relevant to human factors such as personal itinerary, tasks, mood, and social relationships, while the latter relates to the physical environment such as location, proximity, weather, sounds, or humility (Prekop & Burnett, 2003).

With the wide adoption of context-aware technologies, marketers are empowered to capture and analyze the contextual information, then monitor the consumer's real-time situation on the move. Location is the most-used contextual component in context-marketing. Therefore, sometimes the term "social-local-mobile" (SoLoMo) is used interchangeably with SoCoMo. Examples of popular SoLoMo applications include Foursquare, Yelp, Groupon, and Google Latitude. The SoLoMo apps allow travelers to share their location with friends within the social networks and rewards people who check in at the location with discounts and exclusive offers. Through location-sharing behavior on social media, travelers help service providers to promote products. By knowing the traveler's location and other internal context information, destination marketers can recommend special offers about the nearby restaurants, hotels, transportation, or points of interests to the traveler through a smartphone. In this regard, DMOs are able to enhance tourists' travel experience by providing more relevant information, and further increase the conversion rate of marketing recommendations.

Because context contains much more complex information besides location, SoCoMo marketing covers a wider scope than SoLoMo and can help marketers to communicate with travelers more effectively based on the internal and external context through mobile applications. The context-aware technologies collect real-time information about weather change, air quality, and traffic accidents or emergencies during the trip so that the marketers can help travelers to cope with the unexpected situation immediately through mobile communications for alternative plans or activity suggestions. For example, the smartphone sensor can detect the speed of the user movement, so that we can know if the user is on foot, cycle, or car. Based on the location and movement mode, a destination app can recommend the best tour route and activities for the traveler. Moreover, if the context-aware technology notices the poor air quality in an outdoor tourism attraction, the DMO app can suggest alternative indoor activities for the traveler. This being said, SoCoMo marketing enables real-time customer relationship management through understanding the traveler's current situation and respond to individuals' needs with personalized products and services. In this regard, SoCoMo marketing opens up unprecedented opportunities for value co-creation between DMOs and tourists (Buhalis & Foerste, 2015).

VR and AR technologies for destination marketing

In this era of technology disruption, the evolution of ICTs technologies offers many innovative applications for destination marketing. Virtual reality and augmented reality are other up-and-coming technologies that have proved particularly valuable for tourism and hospitality industries. Many researchers have acknowledged VR/AR's potential to revolutionize the promotion, selling, and delivery of tourism products (Prideaux, 2002; Huang et al., 2016). While VR is used mainly pre- and post-trip, AR is primarily applied at a destination.

Virtual reality is a computer-generated 3D environment. It allows users to simulate the sensation that they are moving within the created environment and sometimes interact with it; it typically stimulates the visual and auditory senses but may also stimulate others such as olfactory (Guttentag, 2010). The VR technology differs from other similar technologies in its capacity to offer psychological presence and physical immersion for the users (Gutiérrez et al., 2008; Vince, 2004). VR-type technologies emerged in the 1960s, and the latest VR systems are sufficiently sophisticated to enable the users to explore the virtual environment and stimulate different senses effectively (Guttentag, 2010). For example, VR can be used by DMOs to provide a 360 degree live and interactive view of the tourism attractions in order to persuade potential tourists to visit their destinations. Many destinations such as Las Vegas, New York, Amsterdam, and Scotland, have provided virtual tours for travelers to experience the place before they take the actual trip. Table 39.2 lists some examples of VR applications in tourism.

The main benefit of VR for the tourism industry is reducing product intangibility and perceived uncertainty. Because VR allows travelers to see and feel a particular point of interest prior to the trip, the travelers receive more sensory information for their travel decision-making process. VR allows the travelers to conveniently experience things that would otherwise be complex to investigate, making the trip planning process fun and efficient. For a destination with diverse activity options, a VR tour offers travelers a chance to plot out an itinerary that matches their

Table 39.2 Examples of VR and AR apps in the tourism domain

	App Name	*Description*	*Sample destination*
VR Apps	VR Postcards	A VR travelogue that shares popular destinations and real travel stories with Marriott guests.	Chile Rwanda Beijing
	Ascape	A live VR travelogue that provides beautiful 360 VR video of iconic locales and travel destinations.	Hawaii New York
	Wild Within	Interactive, 360° videos developed by Destination B.C. to promote the pristine coastal wilderness of British Columbia, Canada.	British Columbia, Canada
	Scotland VR	3D attraction models and video tours for over 25 iconic Scottish attractions.	Scotland
AR apps	Departures Switzerland	Providing real-time information on Switzerland's public transportation network.	Switzerland
	ViewRanger Skyline	Offering thousands of trail guides to navigate outdoor adventures.	San Francisco
	Tuscany+	Offering travelers in Tuscany an interactive, real-time guide for the local tour.	Tuscany
	Discover Moscow Photo	Motivating travelers to scout the streets in Moscow to visually experience all the iconic persons of the bygone era: writers, poets, musicians, artists, military men, politicians.	Moscow

personality and desires. Previous studies have shown that a potential traveler may form a more realistic tourism expectation after taking a virtual tour, which in turn could lead to a more satisfactory vacation (Guttentag, 2010). According to YouVisit (a company specializing in VR tours), more than 13% of people who experienced a VR tour of a destination were motivated to plan an actual trip.

Augmented reality is another technology related to VR. Compared to the complete virtual environment created by VR, an AR system projects computer-generated information onto a real-world camera view using virtual annotations. AR enables the tourists to view useful information related to an object of interest within the surrounding environment. The virtual annotations may include images, video, audio, symbols, or captions for all kinds of landmarks. The information can be descriptions of tourist attractions, restaurants, monuments, weather, bus station, banks, and parking lots, even geo-coded UGC including tweets, videos, photos, and comments. Therefore, unlike traditional audio commentary systems, the AR systems offers a much more lively and realistic experience for tourists. Table 39.2 provides some examples of AR tourism applications.

When tourists use an AR application in a destination, they access an augmented tourism experience. Augmented tourism provides virtual information about the physical world in real time, thus as Yovcheva et al. (2013) contend it invokes particular feelings as well as knowledge and skills to augment an experience. The AR applications can enhance tourists' awareness of their surroundings, increase their feelings of safety and control, and enable tourists to explore the unfamiliar surroundings better (Yovcheva et al., 2012).

Conclusions

This chapter discussed the important contribution that big data analytics, SoCoMo, and VR/AR marketing are making to the productivity of destination marketing. Through literature review, this chapter examined the specific role of these approaches and their impact on the tourist experience and DMO's marketing strategies. Significantly, big data analytics have become a prerequisite for the success of destination marketing. The BDA approach enables the DMOs to process data faster and generate insights for the better decision-making process. With the development of BDA and ICTs, DMOs can develop personalized products and manage customer relationships in real time. In particular, the SoCoMo marketing approach helps DMOs to understand travelers' current situations through analyzing real-time information collected by context-aware technologies. The mobile social network empowers the DMOs to target the on-the-move travelers with personalized messages corresponding to their context at any time and any place. Using virtual tours, the DMOs can entice the tourists with livelier presentations and increase the effectiveness of customer acquisition. AR technology enables tourists to easily access useful information about unfamiliar surroundings, which enhances the tourists' destination experience to another level. The real-world examples mentioned in this chapter have shown that DMOs' marketing campaigns can operate more efficiently and effectively when using these approaches.

As the technology becomes more sophisticated, the application of BDA and ICTs in tourism marketing will continue to grow quickly. Nevertheless, there are several issues that deserve greater attention from tourism researchers and industry professionals. First, big data analytics is not a panacea, and the effectiveness and efficiency of the BDA approach require people skilled in big data manipulation and considerable investment to integrate various sources of customer information (Davenport, 2013). One of the major obstacles to implementing BDA approaches is that they require personnel with sophisticated analytical skills. Training and education on BDA are therefore essential for DMOs. Recent studies have shown that the top performers in the tourism and hospitality industry are about twice as likely to train their management and frontline staff on analytics and tools for maintaining a competitive advantage as their competitors (Ayisi, 2014).

Second, it is worth stressing that travelers have privacy rights worthy of protection. While the context-aware technologies are extremely useful to travelers, the personal information collected would make the traveler vulnerable in terms of privacy. The BDA approach and SoCoMo marketing raise concerns with respect to information governance and correct use of big data. Previous research has indicated that customers want control over who can access their personal data and the right to provide feedback on the use of their data (Chatfield et al., 2005; Buhalis & Amaranggana, 2015). Therefore, it is important for marketers to clearly inform customers about data collection and use, as well as to provide opt-in procedures for customers. Trust is the key in successful marketing campaigns.

Third, despite the exciting potential of VR/AR technology to enhance tourists' experiences, the effective and usable design of VR/AR apps for travel is still in its infancy. While the development of ICTs is driven from areas outside the tourism discipline, there is very limited research on VR/AR marketing in the tourism domain. Current literature does not adequately address the specific issues associated with VR/AR application for travel. It is not clear how tourists evaluate the various functions of VR/AR apps or their motivations to use a VR/AR application. Further research is needed to investigate how to market tourism destinations effectively to virtual participants around the world.

References

Achabal, D. D., Heineke, J. M., & McIntyre, S. H. (1984). Issues and perspectives on retail productivity. *Journal of Retailing, 60,* 107–127.

Ayisi, S. (2014). Why big data matters to you. *Hospitality Upgrade* (pp. 10–26). Roswell, GA: Siegel Communications, Inc.

Baggio, R., & Scaglione, M. (2017). Strategic visitor flows (SVF) analysis using mobile data. In *Information and Communication Technologies in Tourism 2017* (pp. 145–157). Springer International Publishing.

Berger, M. L., & Doban, V. (2014). Big data, advanced analytics and the future of comparative effectiveness research. *Journal of Comparative Effectiveness Research, 3*(2), 167–176.

Beyer, M. A., & Laney, D. (2012). The importance of 'big data': a definition. Stamford, CT: Gartner.

Buhalis, D., & Amaranggana, A. (2015). Smart tourism destinations enhancing tourism experience through personalisation of services. In *Information and Communication Technologies in Tourism 2015* (pp. 377–389). Springer International Publishing.

Buhalis, D., & Foerste, M. K. (2014). SoCoMo marketing for travel and tourism. In *Information and Communication Technologies in Tourism 2014* (pp. 175–185). Springer International Publishing.

Buhalis, D., & Foerste, M. (2015). SoCoMo marketing for travel and tourism: Empowering co-creation of value. *Journal of Destination Marketing & Management, 4*(3), 151–161.

Buhalis, D., & Wagner, R. (2013). E-destinations: Global best practice in tourism technologies and applications. In *Information and Communication Technologies in Tourism 2013* (pp. 119–130). Berlin Heidelberg: Springer.

Chatfield, C., Carmichael, D., Hexel, R., Kay, J., & Kummerfeld, B. (2005). Personalisation in intelligent environments: managing the information flow. In *Proceedings of the 17th Australia conference on Computer-Human Interaction: Citizens Online: Considerations for Today and the Future* (pp. 1–10). Computer-Human Interaction Special Interest Group (CHISIG) of Australia.

Davenport, T. H. (2013). At the Big Data Crossroads: turning towards a smarter travel eperience. *Amadeus IT Group.* Available online at: http://blogamadeus. com/wp-content/uploads/Amadeus-Big-Data-Report. pdf (accessed April 10, 2017).

De Mauro, A., Greco, M., & Grimaldi, M. (2015, February). What is big data? A consensual definition and a review of key research topics. In G. Giannakopoulos, D. P. Sakas, & D. Kyriaki-Manessi (Eds), *AIP conference proceedings* (Vol. 1644, No. 1, pp. 97–104). AIP.

Ducange, P., Pecori, R., & Mezzina, P. (2017). A glimpse on big data analytics in the framework of marketing strategies. *Soft Computing*, 1–18.
Fuchs, M., Höpken, W., & Lexhagen, M. (2014). Big data analytics for knowledge generation in tourism destinations – A case from Sweden. *Journal of Destination Marketing and Management, 3*(4), 198–209.
Guttentag, D. A. (2010). Virtual reality: Applications and implications for tourism. *Tourism Management, 31*(5), 637–651.
Gutiérrez, M., Vexo, F., & Thalmann, D. (2008). Stepping into virtual reality. London: Springer.
Hashem, I. A. T., Yaqoob, I., Anuar, N. B., Mokhtar, S., Gani, A., & Khan, S. U. (2015). The rise of "big data" on cloud computing: Review and open research issues. *Information Systems, 47*, 98–115.
Heerschap, N., Ortega, S., Priem, A., & Offermans, M. (2014, May). Innovation of tourism statistics through the use of new big data sources. In *12th Global Forum on Tourism Statistics, Prague, CZ.* Available online at: http://tsf2014prague. cz/assets/downloads/Paper (Vol. 201).
Hu, H., Wen, Y., Chua, T. S., & Li, X. (2014). Toward scalable systems for big data analytics: A technology tutorial. *IEEE Access, 2*, 652–687.
Huang, Y. C., Backman, K. F., Backman, S. J., & Chang, L. L. (2016). Exploring the implications of virtual reality technology in tourism marketing: An integrated research framework. *International Journal of Tourism Research, 18*(2), 116–128.
Keh, H. T., Chu, S., & Xu, J. (2006). Efficiency, effectiveness and productivity of marketing in services. *European Journal of Operational Research, 170*(1), 265–276.
Költringer, C., & Dickinger, A. (2015). Analyzing destination branding and image from online sources: A web content mining approach. *Journal of Business Research, 68*(9), 1836–1843.
Lamsfus, C., Alzua-Sorzobal, A., Martin, D., & Salvador, Z. (2010). Semantic-based contextual computing support for human mobility. In U. Gretzel, R. Law, & M. Fuchs (Eds), *Information and Communication Technology in Tourism* (pp. 603–615). Vienna: Springer.
Lamsfus, C., Wang, D., Alzua-Sorzabal, A., & Xiang, Z. (2015). Going mobile: defining context for on- the-go travellers. *Journal of Travel Research, 54*,1–11.
Laney, D. (2001). 3D data management: Controlling data volume, velocity and variety. *META Group Research Note, 6*(70).
Li, X., & Wang, Y. (2010). Evaluating the effectiveness of destination marketing organisations' websites: evidence from China. *International journal of tourism research, 12*(5), 536–549.
Liu, D. S., & Fan, S. J. (2013). Tourist behavior pattern mining model based on context. *Discrete Dynamics in Nature and Society*, 1–12.
Lu, W., & Stepchenkova, S. (2015). User-generated content as a research mode in tourism and hospitality applications: Topics, methods, and software. *Journal of Hospitality Marketing & Management, 24*(2), 119–154.
Marine-Roig, E., & Clavé, S. A. (2015a). Tourism analytics with massive user-generated content: A case study of Barcelona. *Journal of Destination Marketing & Management, 4*(3), 162–172.
Marine-Roig, E., & Clavé, S. A. (2015b). A method for analysing large-scale UGC data for tourism: Application to the case of Catalonia. In *Information and communication technologies in tourism 2015* (pp. 3–17). Springer International Publishing.
McGuire, T., Manyika, J., & Chui, M. (2012). Why big data is the new competitive advantage. *Ivey Business Journal, 76*(4), 1–4.
Meeker, W. Q., & Hong, Y. (2014). Reliability meets big data: Opportunities and challenges. *Quality Engineering, 26*(1), 102–116.
Owais, S. S., & Hussein, N. S. (2016). Extract Five Categories CPIVW from the 9V's Characteristics of the Big Data. *International Journal of Advanced Computer Science & Applications, 1*(7), 254–258.
Paldino, S., Bojic, I., Sobolevsky, S., Ratti, C., & González, M. C. (2015). Urban magnetism through the lens of geo-tagged photography. *EPJ Data Science, 4*(1), 5.
Prekop, P., & Burnett, M. (2003). Activities, context and ubiquitous computing. *Computer Communications, 26*, 1168–1176.
Prideaux, B. (2002). The cybertourist. In G. M. S. Dann (Ed.), *The Tourist as a Metaphor of the Social World* (pp. 317–339). New York: CABI Publishing.
Scharl, A., Lalicic, L., & Önder, I. (2017). Tourism Intelligence and Visual Media Analytics for Destination Management Organizations. In *Analytics in Smart Tourism Design* (pp. 165–178). Springer International Publishing.
Sheth, J. N. & Sisodia, R. S. (2002). Marketing productivity: Issues and analysis. *Journal of Business Research, 55*, 349–362.

Song, H., & Liu, H. (2017). Predicting Tourist Demand Using Big Data. In Z. Xiang & D. R. Fesenmaier (Eds), *Analytics in Smart Tourism Design* (pp. 13–29). Springer International Publishing.
Soteriades, M. (2012). Tourism destination marketing: approaches improving effectiveness and efficiency. *Journal of Hospitality and Tourism Technology, 3*(2), 107–120.
Sun, Y., Song, H., Jara, A. J., & Bie, R. (2016). Internet of things and big data analytics for smart and connected communities. *IEEE Access, 4*, 766–773.
Valerio, P. (2015). Cuba Turns To Analytics, Big Data To Help Tourism. Available online at: http://www.informationweek.com/cuba-turns-to-analytics-big-data-to-help-tourism/a/d-id/1320312 (accessed April 20, 2017).
Vince, J. (2004). *Introduction to virtual reality*. New York: Springer.
Xiang, Z., & Fesenmaier, D. R. (2017). Big Data Analytics, Tourism Design and Smart Tourism. In Z. Xiang & D. R. Fesenmaier (Eds), *Analytics in Smart Tourism Design* (pp. 299–307). Springer International Publishing.
Yovcheva, Z., Buhalis, D., & Gatzidis, C. (2012). Overview of smartphone augmented reality applications for tourism. *e-Review of Tourism Research (eRTR), 10* (2), 63–66.
Yovcheva, Z., Buhalis, D., & Gatzidis, C. (2013). Engineering augmented tourism experiences. In *Information and Communication Technologies in Tourism 2013* (pp. 24–35). Springer Berlin Heidelberg.
Zhao, Z., & Balagué, C. (2017). From Social Networks to Mobile Social Networks: Applications in the Marketing Evolution. In *Apps Management and E-Commerce Transactions in Real-Time* (pp. 26–50). IGI Global.

Further reading

Serna, A., Gerrikagoitia, J. K., & Bernabé, U. (2016). Discovery and classification of the underlying emotions in the user generated content (UGC). In *Information and Communication Technologies in Tourism 2016* (pp. 225–237). Springer International Publishing.
Smith, S. C. I., Matthews, T., LaMarcas, A., Tabert, J., & Powledge, P. (2005). Location disclosure to social relations: Why, when, and what people want to share. *Proceedings CHI, Portland, USA, 24*.

Index

Note: Information in figures is indicated by page numbers in *italics*. Information in tables is indicated by page numbers in **bold.**